To Hell and Back

THE PENGUIN HISTORY OF EUROPE

General Editor: David Cannadine

*already published

IAN KERSHAW

To Hell and Back

Europe, 1914–1949

VIKING

VIKING

An imprint of Penguin Random House LLC
375 Hudson Street
New York, New York 10014
penguin.com

First published in Great Britain by Allen Lane, an imprint of Penguin Random
House UK

ISBN 978-0-670-02458-2

Printed in the United States of America
1   3   5   7   9   10   8   6   4   2

Set in Sabon LT Std

Contents

List of Illustrations

List of Maps

Europe in 1914

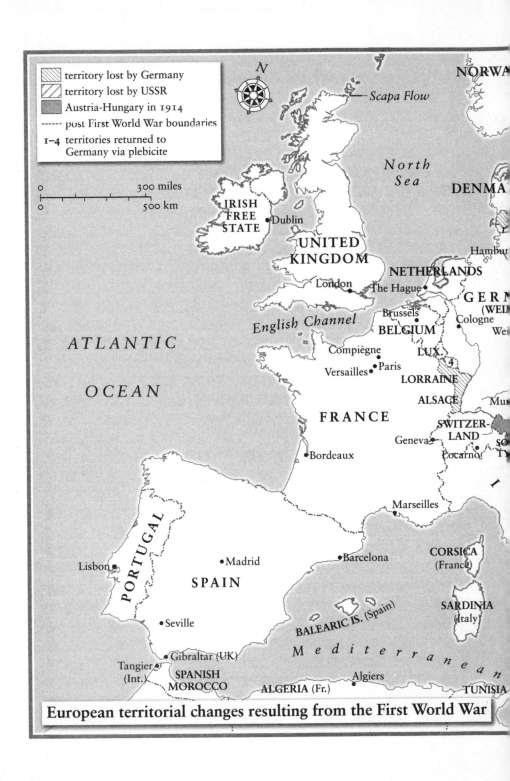

European territorial changes resulting from the First World War

Europe under Nazism, late 1942

N

ICELAND

NORWAY

SWEDEN

Northern Ireland

DENMARK

Danz

Hamburg

Berlin

GREAT BRITAIN

NETH.

EIRE

GREATER GERMANY

BELGIUM

ATLANTIC OCEAN

Prague

REICHSPROTEKTORAT BOHEMIA AND MORAVIA

Vienna

FRANCE

SWITZ.

H

CROA

ITALY

Adriatic Sea

PORTUGAL

Corsica

SPAIN

Sardinia

Mediterranean Sea

Sicily

MOROCCO

ALGERIA

TUNISIA

Malta

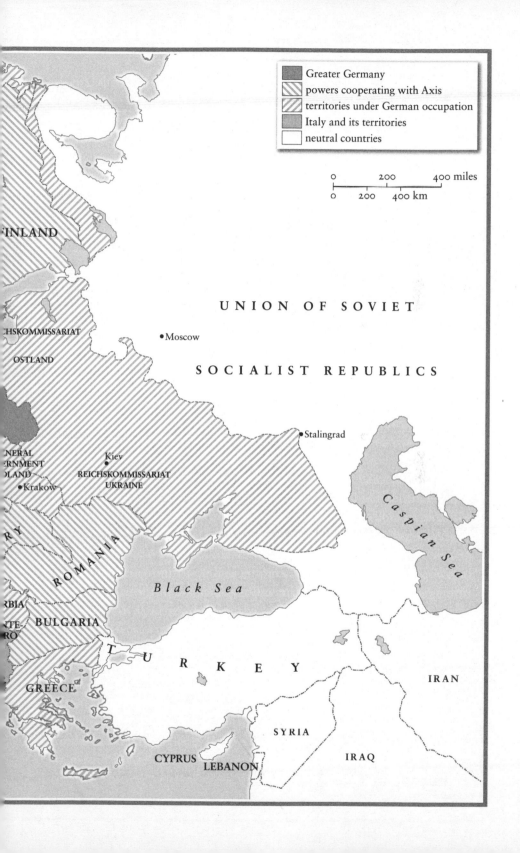

Greater Germany
powers cooperating with Axis
territories under German occupation
Italy and its territories
neutral countries

0   200   400 miles
0   200   400 km

FINLAND

CHSKOMMISSARIAT

OSTLAND

UNION OF SOVIET

• Moscow

SOCIALIST REPUBLICS

• Stalingrad

NERAL
ERNMENT
OLAND

Kiev
•
REICHSKOMMISSARIAT
UKRAINE

• Krakow

Caspian Sea

RY

ROMANIA

Black Sea

RBIA

TE-
RO

BULGARIA

TURKEY

IRAN

GREECE

SYRIA

IRAQ

CYPRUS LEBANON

Europe in 1949

German zones occupied
the Allies (1945–55)

	UK
	USA
	France
	USSR

FINLAND

Helsinki •

• Leningrad

• Stockholm

ESTONIA

*Baltic
Sea*

LATVIA

LITHUANIA

Moscow •

R U S S I A

R

• Kaliningrad

Niemen

S

WHITE RUSSIA

S

Don

O L A N D

• Warsaw

U

Kiev •

Kharkov •

Donets

Vistula

U K R A I N E

Dnieper

CHOSLOVAKIA

• Vienna

• Budapest

Odessa •

CRIMEA

H U N G A R Y

Zagreb •

ROMANIA

Sebastopol •

Black Sea

• Belgrade

Bucharest •

U G O S L A V I A

BULGARIA

• Sofia

ALBANIA

Istanbul •

T U R K E Y

GREECE

*Aegean
Sea*

• Athens

CYPRUS

LIBYA

EGYPT

European territorial changes resulting from the Second World War

Acknowledgements

A book like this depends more than most on the suggestions and encouragement of others – sometimes without them being aware of how they were helping. In a variety of ways I am grateful to: Joe Bergin, Richard Bessel, John Breuilly, Franz Brüggemeier, Chris Clark, Paul Corner, David Dilks, Christopher Duggan, Richard Evans, Detleff Felken, Jürgen Förster, Norbert Frei, Elke Fröhlich, Mary Fulbrook, Dick Geary, Robert Gerwarth, Christian Göschel, Mike Hannah, Joe Harrison, Julia Hoffmann, Dov Kulka, Eberhard Jäckel, Margit Ketterle, Peter Liddle, Klaus A. Maier, Michael Mann, Andy Marrison, members of the Cambridge Modern History Seminar, Hans Mommsen, Bob Moore, Irene Nielsen, Frank O'Gorman, Peter Pulzer, Aron Rodrigue, Mary Vincent, George Wedell, Hans-Ulrich Wehler, Frieder Weitbrecht, Charlotte Woodford, Hans Woller, Jonathan Wright and Benjamin Ziemann.

I am indebted to Gerhard Hirschfeld for sending me the outstanding and authoritative encyclopaedia of the First world War which he co-edited (and which has subsequently appeared in a splendid English edition). Bernt Hagtvet was more than kind in supplying me with two extremely useful and informative volumes which I had not come across and deserve to be better known: the collection of essays edited by Dirk Berg-Schlosser and Jeremy Mitchell on the crises of democracy in inter-war Europe, and that by Stein Ugelvik Larsen on the transition from fascism to democracy after 1945. I'm also grateful to Norman Davies, who pointed me towards a number of first-hand accounts of events in Poland, including the fascinating memoirs of a village mayor, Jan Słoma, and to Andreas Kossert for further references to Polish sources.

I owe special gratitude to a number of people for their critical commentaries on the text. Beverley Eaton erased many typographical errors. Traude Spät made some excellent suggestions (and she and Ulrich provided their usual generous hospitality on my stays in Munich). At an expert level I owe warm thanks for their valuable points of constructive criticism to David Cannadine (general editor of the Penguin History of Europe series), Laurence Rees and Nicholas Stargardt. And when the drafts were complete, Richard Mason proved a splendidly meticulous copy-editor.

As on earlier occasions it was a pleasure to work with the excellent team at Penguin. Simon Winder was as always an exemplary editor. He and Maria Bedford were also a great help in researching and helping to select the pictures, while Richard Duguid oversaw the production with his customary efficiency. My thanks, too, to Auriol Griffith-Jones for her skilful compilation of the index. I am grateful as ever to Andrew Wylie, a literary agent *sans pareil*, and at the Wylie Agency in London to James Pullen and Sarah Chalfant for unfailing help and advice.

Betty, David and Stephen have been throughout an unending source of support and encouragement. Betty raised a number of pertinent queries about points of detail in the text, while discussions of the drafts with David in the Royal Oak in Didsbury were highly enjoyable as well as constructive. Finally, our five grandchildren, Sophie, Joe, Ella, Olivia and Henry, have never ceased to provide wonderful and happy distraction from the dismal tale I have had to tell here. Let us hope that they and others of their generation enjoy a future Europe that can exist without the divisions, rancour and hatreds that have darkened its past.

Ian Kershaw,
Manchester, May 2015

Preface

This is the first of two volumes on the history of Europe from 1914 to our own times. It is by some distance the hardest book I have undertaken. Each book I have written has in some sense been an attempt to gain a better understanding on my part of a problem in the past. In this case, the recent past contains a multiplicity of extremely complex problems. But whatever the difficulties, the temptation to try to understand better the forces that have in the recent past shaped the world of today was irresistible.

There is, of course, no single way to approach a history of the twentieth century in Europe. Some excellent histories with varying interpretations and structures – among them, each with a different slant on the century, the works of Eric Hobsbawm, Mark Mazower, Richard Vinen, Harold James and Bernard Wasserstein – already exist. This volume and the one to follow it necessarily represent a personalized approach to such a momentous century. And like every attempt to cover a vast panorama over a lengthy time span, it has to rely heavily upon the pioneering research of others.

I am more than conscious of the fact that for practically every sentence I wrote a plethora of specialist works, often of great quality, was available. Only for a few aspects, mainly relating to Germany between 1918 and 1945, can I claim to have carried out primary research. Elsewhere, I have had to depend upon the excellent work of other scholars in many different fields. Even with greater linguistic competence than I possess this would have been inevitable. No single scholar could possibly carry out archival work throughout Europe, and, since invariably experts on particular countries and on specific historical themes have already done such work, the attempt would be pointless anyway. Such an overview as I am presenting has, therefore, to rest on the countless achievements of others.

The format of the Penguin History of Europe series precludes references to the many indispensable works of historical scholarship – monographs, editions of contemporary documentation, statistical analyses, and specialized studies of individual countries – on which I have relied. The bibliography reflects some of my more important debts to other scholars. I hope they will forgive the inability to refer to their works in footnotes, and will accept my deep appreciation of their great endeavours. Any originality rests, therefore, solely on structure and interpretation – how the history is written and the underlying nature of the argument.

The introduction, 'Europe's Era of Self-Destruction', lays out the framework of interpretation of this volume as well as indicating the approach to the second volume (yet to be written). As regards the structure, I have organized the chapters that follow chronologically with thematic sub-divisions. This reflects my concern to pay particular attention to precisely how the drama unfolded, and to the specific shaping of events by concentrating on fairly short periods while necessarily dealing separately within those periods with the differing formative forces. So there are no chapters devoted expressly to the economy, society, culture, ideology or politics, though these find their place, if not necessarily with equal weight, within individual chapters.

The first half of the twentieth century, the subject of this volume, was dominated by war. This raises its own problems. How is it possible to deal with the vast and momentous topics of the First and Second World Wars within such a wide-ranging volume as this? Whole libraries of works exist on both conflicts. But readers may justifiably be expected not simply to be referred to other works (though naturally these can be followed up on every theme of the volume). So I thought it worthwhile to begin the chapters relating directly to the two world wars with extremely concise surveys of the developments on the fronts. However tersely described – largely for orientation, and to highlight in the briefest terms the scale of the calamities that determined the immensity of their consequences – it is obvious that these events were crucial. In other instances, too, I pondered whether to take for granted that all readers would be well acquainted with, for example, the background to the rise of fascism in Italy or to the course of the Spanish Civil War, before deciding that, again, brief surveys might prove useful.

Throughout, I have been anxious to blend in personal experiences of contemporaries to give an indication of what it was like to live through this era, so near in time yet so different in nature to present-day Europe. Of course, I recognize that personal experience is just that. It cannot be taken as statistically representative. But it can often be seen as indicative – reflective of wider attitudes and mentalities. In any case, the inclusion of personal experiences provides vivid snap-shots and gives a flavour, detached from abstractions and impersonal analysis, of how people reacted to the mighty forces that were buffeting their lives.

A history of Europe cannot, of course, be a sum of national histo-ries. What is at stake are the driving forces that shaped the continent as a whole in all or at least most of its constituent parts. A general synthesis has naturally to offer a bird's-eye rather than a worm's-eye view. It has to generalize, not concentrate on peculiarities, though unique developments only in fact become visible through a wide lens. I have tried not to ignore any areas of Europe, and often to emphasize the specially tragic history of the eastern half of the continent. But inevitably, some countries played a greater (or more baleful) role than others and correspondingly warrant more attention. Europe in this volume and the next is taken to include Russia (then the Soviet Union); it would be unthinkable to leave out such a crucial player in European history, even if extensive parts of the Russian, then Soviet, Empire lay geographically outside Europe. Similarly, Turkey is included where it was significantly involved in European affairs, though this sharply diminished after 1923 once the Ottoman Empire had broken up and the Turkish nation state had been established.

This volume begins with a brief overview of Europe on the eve of the First World War. Chapters then follow on the war itself, its imme-diate aftermath, the short-lived recovery in the mid-1920s, the searing impact of the Great Depression, the looming threat of another world war, the unleashing of a further great conflagration within a gener-ation, and the devastating collapse of civilization that this Second World War produced. At this point I interrupt the chronological structure with a thematic chapter (Chapter 9), which explores a number of long-term thematic developments that cross the short-term chronological boundaries of earlier chapters – demographic and socio-economic change, the position of the Christian Churches, the stance of intellectuals and the growth of popular entertainment. A concluding chapter returns to a chronological framework.

I had thought of ending this first volume in 1945, when the actual fighting in the Second World War stopped. But, though formal hostilities in Europe ceased in May of that year (continuing until August against Japan), the fateful course of the years 1945–9 was so plainly determined by the war itself, and reactions to it, that I thought it justifiable to look beyond the moment when peace officially returned to the continent. The contours of a new, post-war Europe were scarcely visible in 1945; they only gradually came clearly into view. It seemed to me, therefore, appropriate to add a final chapter dealing with the immediate aftermath of the war, which not only saw a period of continuing violence but also indelibly shaped the divided Europe that had emerged by 1949. So the first volume ends not in 1945, but in 1949.

One of the most beloved clichés of football commentators, when the half-time interval has brought a remarkable change of fortunes, is: 'It's a game of two halves.' It is very tempting to think of Europe's twentieth century as a century of two halves, perhaps with 'extra time' added on after 1990. This volume deals only with the first half of an extraordinary and dramatic century. This was the era in which Europe carried out two world wars, threatened the very foundations of civilization, and seemed hell-bent on self-destruction.

Ian Kershaw, Manchester, November 2014

To Hell and Back

Introduction:
Europe's Era of Self-Destruction

The wars of peoples will be more terrible than those of kings.
Winston Churchill (1901)

Europe's twentieth century was a century of war. Two world wars followed by over forty years of 'cold war' – itself the direct product of the Second World War – defined the age. It was an extraordinarily dramatic, tragic and endlessly fascinating period, its history one of huge upheaval and astounding transformation. During the twentieth century, Europe went to hell and back. The continent, which for nearly one hundred years after the end of the Napoleonic Wars in 1815 had prided itself on being the apogee of civilization, fell between 1914 and 1945 into the pit of barbarism. But a calamitous self-destructive era was followed by previously unimaginable stability and prosperity – though at the heavy price of unbridgeable political division. Thereafter, a reunified Europe, facing huge internal pressures from intensified globalization and serious external challenges, experienced increasing inbuilt tensions even before the financial crash of 2008 plunged the continent into a new, still unresolved, crisis.

A second volume will explore the era after 1950. This first volume, however, looks at Europe's near self-destruction in the first half of the century, during the era of the two world wars. It explores how the dangerous forces emanating from the First World War culminated in scarcely imaginable depths of inhumanity and destruction during the Second. This catastrophe, together with the unprecedented levels of genocide from which the conflict cannot be separated, makes the

Second World War the epicentre and determining episode of Europe's troubled history in the twentieth century.

The chapters that follow explore the reasons for this immeasurable catastrophe. They locate these in four interlocking major elements of comprehensive crisis, unique to these decades: (1) an explosion of ethnic-racist nationalism; (2) bitter and irreconcilable demands for territorial revisionism; (3) acute class conflict – now given concrete focus through the Bolshevik Revolution in Russia; and (4) a protracted crisis of capitalism (which many observers thought was terminal). Bolshevism's triumph was a vital new component after 1917. So was the almost constant state of crisis of capitalism, alleviated for only a brief few years in the mid-1920s. The other elements had been present before 1914, though in far less acute form. None had been a primary cause of the First World War. But the new virulence of each was a crucial outcome of that war. Their lethal interaction now spawned an era of extraordinary violence, leading to a Second World War far more destructive even than the First. Worst affected from the interlinkage of the four elements were central, eastern and south-eastern Europe – for the most part the poorest regions of the continent. Western Europe fared better (though Spain was an important exception).

The disintegration of the Austro-Hungarian and Ottoman empires at the end of the First World War, and the immense violent upheavals of the Russian Civil War that followed directly on the Revolution, unleashed new forces of extreme nationalism in which identity with the nation was usually defined ethnically. Nationalist and ethnic conflict was especially endemic in the poorer eastern half of the continent – the regions of long-standing ethnically mixed communities. Often nationalist hatred singled out Jews as special scapegoats for resentment and social misery. There were more Jews in central and eastern than western Europe, and they were mainly less well integrated and of a lower social class than their co-religionists in west European countries. These central and east European regions, far more so than Germany, were the traditional heartlands of vicious antisemitism. The greater ethnic homogeneity that generally existed in western Europe, and the fact that its nation states had usually evolved over a lengthy period of time, meant that the tensions there, though not completely absent, were less great than to the east.

The victors and most of the neutral countries in the First World War were, moreover, to be found in western Europe. Damaged national prestige and competition for material resources, the feeding-ground for aggressive ethnic nationalism, played a much greater role farther east. In the centre of the continent, Germany, the most important defeated country and the key to Europe's future peace, with borders stretching from France and Switzerland in the west to Poland and Lithuania in the east, harboured great resentment at its treatment by the victorious Allies and only temporarily quelled its revisionist ambitions. Further south and east, the ruins of the Austro-Hungarian, Russian and Ottoman empires gave birth to new nation states, often patched together in the least propitious circumstances imaginable. It is no surprise that the nationalist and ethnic hatreds that poisoned politics should make these regions the major killing-grounds of the Second World War.

Nationalist conflicts and ethnic-racial tensions were greatly intensified by the territorial settlement of Europe that followed the First World War. The architects of the Versailles Treaty in 1919, however good their intentions, faced insuperable problems in attempting to satisfy the territorial demands of the new countries formed out of the wreckage of the old empires. Ethnic minorities formed sizeable parts of most of the new states in central, eastern and south-eastern Europe, offering a potential base for serious political disturbance. Almost everywhere, borders were disputed and the demands of ethnic minorities, which usually faced discrimination from the majority population, were unresolved. These Versailles border reallocations moreover fostered dangerously simmering resentments in countries that felt themselves unfairly treated. Although Italy had no internal ethnic divisions (apart from the largely German-speaking population of South Tyrol, annexed after the end of the war), nationalists and fascists could exploit the sense of injustice that a country on the side of the victorious powers in the First World War should be deprived of the gains it aspired to in territory that would soon be called Yugoslavia. Far more dangerous for Europe's lasting peace, the deep anger in Germany – like Italy, lacking internal ethnic divisions – at the truncation of territory after the war, and the demands for revision of the Versailles Treaty, later fed into the growing support for Nazism, and outside the Reich's borders encouraged the resentment of German ethnic minorities in Poland, Czechoslovakia and elsewhere.

The shrill nationalism that emerged after the First World War gained momentum not just from ethnic rivalry but also from class conflict. A sense of national unity could be immeasurably sharpened by a focus on supposed class 'enemies' within and outside the nation state. The immense economic upheaval that followed the war and the dire consequences of the slump of the 1930s greatly intensified class antagonism throughout Europe. Class conflict, frequently violent, had of course punctuated the entire industrial era. But it was made far more acute, compared with the pre-war years, by the Russian Revolution and the establishment of the Soviet Union. This provided an alternative model of society, one that had overthrown capitalism and created a 'dictatorship of the proletariat'. Elimination of the capitalist class, expropriation by the state of the means of production, and land redistribution on a massive scale were attractive propositions after 1917 for wide sections of the impoverished masses. But the presence of Soviet communism also split the political Left, fatally weakening it, at the same time as it hugely strengthened extreme nationalist right-wing forces. Revitalized elements from the Right could direct the violent energies of those who felt threatened by Bolshevism – in the main the traditional propertied elites, the middle classes and the landholding peasantry – into new, highly aggressive political movements.

Counter-revolution, like the revolutionary appeal on the Left, exploited the bitterness and anxieties of class conflict. Counter-revolutionary movements gained their most widespread appeal where they were able to combine extreme nationalism with virulent anti-Bolshevism. Again, countries in central and eastern Europe, where the Bolshevik threat was seen to loom large, were particularly affected. But the greatest international danger arose where the combination of extreme nationalism and almost paranoid hatred of Bolshevism gave succour to the creation of mass movements on the Right, which in Italy and then later in Germany were able to take over power in the state. When in these cases the hate-filled nationalist and anti-Bolshevik energies that had propelled the extreme Right to power could be channelled into external aggression, the peace of Europe stood in great jeopardy.

The fourth component, underpinning and interacting with the other three elements, was the lasting crisis of capitalism between the wars. The massive disturbance to the world economy caused by the First World War, the serious weakness of the major European economies of Britain, France and Germany, and the reluctance of the one outstanding economic power, the USA, to engage fully with European reconstruction, spelled disaster. Europe's problems were compounded by the worldwide repercussions of the war. Japan expanded its markets in the Far East, not least in China – wracked by political chaos – at the expense of the Europeans. The British Empire faced mounting political as well as economic challenges, most obviously in India where the growth of an indigenous textile industry and consequent loss of export markets added to Britain's economic woes. And Russia effectively disappeared from the world economy in the wake of revolution and civil war. Capitalism's crisis was global, but especially damaging in Europe.

The inflationary crisis of the early 1920s and deflationary crisis of the 1930s bracketed an all too short-lived boom that proved to have been built on sand. The two phases, only briefly separated, of massive economic and social dislocation provided a climate in which both deprivation and fear of deprivation massively fuelled the political extremes.

Economic turmoil on its own was insufficient to produce major political upheaval. For that, the turmoil needed a crisis in the legitimacy of the state underpinned by an existing ideological schism and deep cultural divides that exposed weakened power-elites to new pressures from mass mobilization. Precisely such conditions were, however, present in many parts of Europe, especially where extreme integral nationalism, drawing on a wide-ranging sense of loss of national prestige and disappointed expectations of great-power status, could foster a strong movement that drew energy from the alleged strength of the diabolical enemies it claimed to face, and was in a position to challenge for power in a state with weak authority.

What was needed, therefore, to engender the comprehensive political, socio-economic and ideological-cultural crisis that brought Europe to the verge of self-destruction was the intermeshing of the four components of the crisis. In one degree or another, such interaction affected most European countries, even in western Europe. But in one country, especially – Germany – all four elements were present in their most extreme form, reinforcing each other with explosive effect. And when Adolf Hitler, exploiting the comprehensive crisis in masterly fashion and with ideas of overcoming it by use of force, was able to cement his dictatorial control over the German state, the odds on general catastrophe in Europe shortened markedly. Since Germany's military as well as economic potential was so great (if temporarily diminished after the First World War) and since its revisionist claims and expansionist ambitions directly impinged upon the territorial integrity and political independence of so many other countries, the probability that Europe's crisis would end in a cataclysmic new war became increasingly high. It was no surprise that the crisis would come to a head in central and eastern Europe, the most destabilized parts of the continent, nor that, once war had begun, the lands in the east would turn into the theatre of the greatest destruction and grotesque inhumanity.

The devastation of the Second World War plumbed new depths. The moral consequences of such a profound collapse of civilization would be felt for the rest of the century, and beyond. Yet, remarkably, the Second World War, in stark contrast to the mayhem engendered by the First, paved the way for Europe's rebirth in the latter half of the century. Where the First World War had left behind a legacy of heightened ethnic, border and class conflict together with a deep and prolonged crisis of capitalism, the Second swept away this concatenation in its very maelstrom of destruction. The Soviet Union's domination of eastern Europe forcibly suppressed internal ethnic divisions and unrest. The immediate post-war grand-scale ethnic cleansing reshaped the map of central and eastern Europe. Germany's dreams of domination in Europe were extinguished in the country's total defeat, devastation and division. There was a new readiness in western Europe to defuse nationalist antagonism in favour of cooperation and integration. Borders were now fixed by the presence of the new superpowers. The conversion into west European state ideologies of the earlier anti-Bolshevism that had bolstered the extreme Right fostered stable conservative politics. And not least the reformed capitalism (this time with an active lead provided by the USA) produced untold prosperity in the western half of the continent, thereby underpinning political stability. All these fundamental changes after 1945 combined to remove the matrix of crisis elements that had nearly destroyed the continent in the era of the two world wars.

Crucially, the Second World War broke once and for all the system of competing European great powers struggling for mastery of the continent, which stretched back beyond Bismarck's era to the end of the Napoleonic era in 1815. In a reborn Europe, though a Europe now ideologically and politically riven, the only great powers left were the United States and the Soviet Union, glowering at each other across the Iron Curtain and presiding over the rebuilding of states and societies in their own image. There was a further vital element: once both superpowers possessed atomic bombs, as they did by 1949, and within four years even more horrifically destructive hydrogen bombs, the spectre of nuclear war threatened a level of destruction that would have left the devastation of both world wars in its shadow. That concentrated minds and played its own part in creating what, in 1945, seemed a highly unlikely era of peace in Europe.

How these elements interwove to transform Europe, east and west, remains to be explored in the next volume. What follows in this volume is an attempt to understand how Europe sank into the abyss during the first half of such a violent, turbulent century, but then, remarkably, already within four years of reaching rock-bottom in 1945, how it began to lay the platform for astonishing recovery – for a new Europe to emerge from the ashes of the old and to embark on the road back from hell on earth.

I

On the Brink

We take pacifism very seriously! But we must get our artillery
budget through.

> *General Stumm, in Robert Musil,*
> The Man without Qualities *(1930–42)*

Even at the time, there were premonitions that descent into war would
bring an era to an end. Best known is the sense of foreboding expressed
by the British Foreign Secretary, Sir Edward Grey, on 3 August 1914:
'The lamps are going out all over Europe. We shall not see them lit
again in our lifetime.' The German Reich Chancellor, Theobald von
Bethmann Hollweg, had a similar intimation of disaster: 'I see a doom
greater than human power hanging over Europe and our own people,'
he exclaimed, as the prospect of war loomed ever closer towards the
end of July 1914. Three years earlier, in a speech in the German parliament, the Reichstag, the German socialist August Bebel had claimed,
to heated contradiction and objection, that the danger of a coming
European war was mounting, and that such a war would bring catastrophe to the continent. 'The *Götterdämmerung* of the bourgeois
world is approaching,' he declared. The war did not, as Bebel inti-
mated, lead to the collapse of capitalism and the triumph of socialism.
But he was prescient in foreseeing that it would usher in a new era.
The American diplomat, George Kennan, later described the war as
'the great seminal catastrophe'. He was right. It was certainly a catastrophe. And it inaugurated an epoch – the 'Thirty Years War' of the
twentieth century – in which the continent of Europe came close to
destroying itself.

A GOLDEN AGE?

The image of a glittering era of stability, prosperity and peace, tragically swept away in the horrors to come, was what lingered, especially in the memories of the privileged classes, after the First World War. 'The Gilded Age' was how Americans came to describe the pre-war years. But the term captured the way that Europeans, too, began to think of this era. The Parisian bourgeoisie remembered 'la belle époque' as the time when French culture was the envy of the world, when Paris seemed the centre of civilization. The propertied classes of Berlin looked back at 'the Wilhelmine era' as a period of wealth, security, grandeur and the national stature that befitted the recently united Germany. Vienna, too, seemed at a pinnacle of its cultural glory, intellectual brilliance and historic imperialist grandeur. Munich, Prague, Budapest, St Petersburg, Moscow and other cities across the continent shared in an efflorescence of culture. New, challenging, provocative forms of artistic expression embraced practically all forms of art, literature, music and theatre in an explosion of bold creativity.

In London, economics mattered more than culture. In the capital of a global empire, the generation after the First World War would hanker after a bygone 'golden age' of continued economic growth, flourishing trade and stable currencies. The great British economist John Maynard Keynes famously wrote after the war of 'the inhabitant of London' who could order 'by telephone, sipping his morning tea in bed, the various products of the whole earth, in such quantity as he might see fit, and reasonably expect their early delivery upon his doorstep'. This was of course a highly privileged perspective, by an upper-middle-class man of wealth and standing in the city that was the centre of world trade. Few in the shtetls of eastern Europe, the impoverished countryside of southern Italy, Spain, Greece or Serbia, or among the urban masses huddled in the slums of Berlin, Vienna, Paris, St Petersburg or London itself, would have recognized such an idyllic existence. Still, the image of a 'golden age' was not merely a post-war construction.

Despite Europe's internal divisions and nationalistic rivalries, all countries shared in the unimpeded movement of goods and capital as part of an interwoven, global international capitalist economy. The stability that permitted economic growth itself rested on recognition of the gold standard as a sort of world currency, rooted in the dominance of the City of London. In this the Bank of England held the key to the stability of the world economy. Invisible earnings from shipping, insurance, interest and exports more than matched Britain's import surpluses. There had been a big increase in the supply of gold in 1897–8, especially from South Africa. But the Bank of England neither built up excessive gold reserves, which would have damaged other countries, nor diminished them. The economies of the USA and Germany were more dynamic, growing faster than the British economy. American dominance of the world economy at some point in the future seemed probable. But Britain still had the biggest share of global trade (though this was shrinking) and was easily the largest exporter of investment capital. Rivalry for the economic exploitation of the globe among the great powers was certainly placing increasing stress on the stability of the international capitalist economy. Down to 1914, however, the system that had been of such benefit to Europe, particularly its industrialized parts, over previous decades, was still intact. Confidence in continued stability, prosperity and growth was widespread.

When the great World Fair opened in Paris in 1900, it was intended to exhibit a flourishing civilization, with Europe at its heart, and to sing a loud paean of praise to progress. An age of new technology was on show. Huge machines impressed people by their power and speed. The brilliance of the 'Palace of Electricity', lit by 5,000 light bulbs, quite literally dazzled its visitors. Twenty-four European nations, along with African, Asian, and Latin American countries and the United States, displayed their elaborate pavilions – visited over the next six months, often in awestruck admiration, by no fewer than 50 million people. Eastern Europe, most notably Russia with its nine pavilions, enjoyed a strong presence. And the European 'civilizing mission' featured prominently. With imperialism at its height, the lavishly exotic depictions of faraway colonial possessions conveyed an overwhelming impression of European world dominance. Commerce, prosperity and peace seemed to offer the unlimited continuation of this dominance. The future looked bright.

The optimism appeared justified. Compared with what had gone before, let alone with what was to come, the nineteenth century had been peaceful. There had been no general, continental war in Europe since Napoleon's era had ended in 1815. War in distant Crimea between 1853 and 1856, like the brief wars that had culminated in German and Italian unification in 1871, had not threatened the general peace of the continent. A decade after the great Paris exhibition a British writer, Norman Angell, published an international best-seller, *The Great Illusion*, in which he even went so far as to claim that the modern wealth flowing from commerce and a globally interwoven economy made war pointless. Many, not just in Britain, agreed. It was difficult to imagine that prosperity, peace and stability would not continue into the indefinite future, that they could be swept away so soon and so rapidly.

There was, however, another far less attractive face to Europe. The social fabric was changing fast, though very unevenly, across the continent. Regions of intense and rapid industrialization coexisted with great swathes that were still primarily, often almost primevally, agricultural. Around four-fifths of the working population of Serbia, Bulgaria and Romania still earned their living from the land in 1913. Across Europe as a whole, the proportion was over two-fifths. Only in Britain did it fall to little over a tenth. And in 1913 only in Britain, Belgium and, more surprisingly, Switzerland – not yet even in Germany – were over two-fifths of the working population employed in industry. Most Europeans still lived in villages or small towns. Standards of living continued to improve, though they were still miserable for the majority of Europeans, whether they had joined the teeming masses seeking work in the insanitary conditions of rapidly swelling cities such as Berlin, Vienna or St Petersburg, or whether they still eked out a precarious existence in the countryside. Many voted with their feet and left. Poverty and lack of opportunity drove many from their homelands. Far from seeing the benefits of prosperity and civilization, millions of Europeans simply could not wait to get away. Emigration to the United States of America peaked in 1907, when over a million Europeans crossed the Atlantic. The big upsurge after the start of the century – increasing threefold from the previous decade – was in those escaping from Austria-Hungary, Russia and, more than anywhere, from the impoverished south of Italy.

The rapidity of social change created new political pressures that had started to threaten the established political order. Political power in Europe remained in the hands of the few in the years just before the First World War. Landed elites, old aristocratic families sometimes intermarried with new dynasties that drew their vast wealth from industry and finance capital, still formed a governing class and military leadership in most countries. Europe was, not least, still a continent of hereditary monarchies. Only Switzerland (whose age-old confederation had adopted a modern federal republican constitution in 1848), France (since 1870) and Portugal (since 1910) were republics. In Austria-Hungary, Kaiser Franz Joseph, who had been on the throne since 1848 at the head of a sprawling multi-national Habsburg Empire of over 50 million subjects, seemed to symbolize the durability of monarchical rule.

A constitutional framework of government, pluralist political parties (though elected by an extremely restrictive franchise), and a legal system nevertheless existed practically everywhere. Even the Russian autocracy had been compelled to make concessions following an attempted revolution in 1905, when Tsar Nicholas II was forced to grant powers (that turned out in practice to be extremely weak) to the parliament, the Duma. But large sections of the population, even in Britain (viewed as the home of parliamentary democracy), still had no political representation. Some countries did have long-established systems of universal male suffrage. In Germany, for instance, the Reich constitution of 1871 granted all males over twenty-five the vote in Reichstag elections (though a highly restrictive franchise, guaranteeing continued landowner dominance, was retained for elections to the parliament of Prussia, an area of Germany comprising two-thirds of the entire Reich territory). In Italy the change to (almost) universal male suffrage came much later, in 1912. But women were not allowed to vote in parliamentary elections in any European country at the turn of the twentieth century. Feminist campaigns challenged this discrimination in numerous countries, though they had little success before the First World War other than in Finland (where, despite being part of the Russian Empire, it proved possible to introduce a level of democratic change following the abortive 1905 revolution in Russia) and Norway.

The key change, and one that elites in every country viewed as a fundamental threat to their power, had been the rise of working-class political parties and trade unions. The 'Second International' of European socialist parties had been instituted in 1889 as an umbrella organization to coordinate the programmatic demands of national parties. Most of these parties remained wedded in one form or another to the revolutionary doctrine enunciated by Karl Marx and Friedrich Engels. Their attack on the innately exploitative nature of capitalism, and their propagation of a new society based upon equality and the fair distribution of wealth, had obvious and growing appeal for large numbers of the poor and deprived industrial working class. Attempts by ruling elites to proscribe or suppress worker parties and the growing trade unions had failed. Workers were now organizing the defence of their interests better than ever before. The rapid expansion of trade unions reflected this. By 1914 trade unions in Britain had over 4 million members, in Germany more than 2.5 million, and in France about a million.

In most European countries, socialist parties and movements of different kinds had found a voice and gained increasing support by the beginning of the century. French socialists gave up their divisions and united in 1905, declaring that they were 'not a party of reform, but a party of class struggle and revolution'. By the eve of the First World War the Section Française de l'Internationale Ouvrière had won 17 per cent of the popular vote and 103 seats in the Chamber of Deputies of the French parliament. In Germany, Bismarck's attempts to suppress social democracy had backfired spectacularly. Since 1890, under a Marxist programme, the Social Democratic Party of Germany had grown into the biggest socialist movement in Europe, gaining over a million members before the war. In the 1912 election for the Reichstag (the German parliament), the Social Democrats were better supported than any other party, gaining almost a third of the seats, and sending a shiver down the spine of Germany's ruling classes.

In the more economically advanced parts of Europe, organized socialism, whatever the rhetoric, constrained outright militancy and channelled it into parliamentary, not revolutionary, action. Jean Jaurès in France gained a major following by advocating, despite the rhetoric of his Socialist Party, not revolution, but a parliamentary route to socialism. The German Social Democratic Party, though rhetorically bound to its Marxist doctrine, sought in practice to win power through the ballot box. In Britain the Labour Party (which adopted the name in 1906) had grown out of the trade unions and reflected their pragmatic concerns for worker interests rather than any revolutionary utopianism. The Marxist message was largely ignored in favour of the non-revolutionary message that capitalism did not need to be overthrown since it could be reformed, to the eventual benefit of the working class. State power, it was presumed, could be transformed by peaceful means to represent working-class interests. Workers in much of western, northern and central Europe were poor, but less outrightly impoverished and less militaristic than they had been in previous times. They had more to lose than their chains. They largely fell in line behind their reformist leaders.

In less well-developed parts of the continent, the situation was different. The confrontation with the power of the state was more stark. There was little or no diffusion of power through intermediary organizations or social structures that gave citizens a stake in their state. Power was largely despotic and top-down, based heavily upon coercion, with an entrenched ruling caste, corrupt officialdom, and weak or non-existent representative institutions. Notions of the seemingly unlimited progress of civilization built on benign state authority and respect for the law, which later formed part of the sense of a lost 'golden age' among the middle classes in central, northern and western Europe, looked bizarre from the southern and eastern periphery of the continent. Strikes, riots and localized insurrections against state power and 'bourgeois rule' increased in Catalonia and the Basque Country, for example, in the first years of the twentieth century. Anarchism, often involving sporadic anti-state violence, had much support among the landless labourers of Andalusia. In southern Italy, where corrupt state officials were in the pockets of the estate-holders, violent rural unrest was endemic. Bands of brigands roaming the countryside blended crime with popular protest in defending peasants and landless labourers against the power of the state and big landowners. Alarm among Europe's leaders at the threat they saw from a revolutionary working class was especially acute during a big wave of industrial strikes and upheavals in 1905. In Russia, faced with a revolution that came close to toppling the Tsar, the heavy hand of state repression turned into outright counter-revolutionary violence that year, when soldiers in St Petersburg massacred two hundred workers and injured hundreds more. The revolution was suppressed. Concessions, more cosmetic than transformational, were made to parliamentary representation, but power was retained by the Tsar and his appointed ministers. To the powerless, especially to those leading the socialist movement, whatever its doctrinal divisions, it seemed obvious. Tsarist autocracy could not be reformed. It had to be overthrown. The result was the intensified, raw radicalism of Russian socialism.

Not only in response to the perceived threat from left-wing movements, but also to help governments with little or no mass backing to widen the base of their support, populist counter-movements emerged. These were often sponsored directly or indirectly by industrialists or landholders keen to deflect potential class-based opposition into more controllable channels. They sought to 'nationalize' the masses, to instil in them assertive nationalist, imperialist and racist sentiments intended to benefit the political status quo. To some extent they were successful. Belligerent nationalism, vicious antisemitism and other brands of racism were commonplace outside the minority drawn to the doctrines of international socialism. The spread of basic education, the growth of literacy, and cheap popular newspapers offered the possibility of extending such influence. Mass politics was opening up to new forms of mobilization on the Right, as well as on the Left. Old certainties were starting to dissolve. The political establishment of the old conservative and liberal elites sensed new insecurity.

That mobilization of the masses could pose a serious threat to the existing political and social order had prompted the French psychologist Gustave Le Bon to publish in 1895 his analysis of mass behaviour, *The Crowd: A Study of the Popular Mind* (in its original version, *La psychologie des foules*). His claim that rationality disappeared when the individual was subjected to the irrational, emotional urges of the crowd was influential as the new century began – there were forty-five reprints and seventeen translations of the book, and it later became required reading for would-be fascist dictators. Across Europe, the emotional urges that Le Bon saw as characteristic of the masses could most easily be whipped up through appeals to nationalism. Europe's ruling elites did not see nationalism as anything like as

dangerous as socialism. Before the war, the dangers built into nationalist fervour were indeed containable. They laid the roots, nonetheless,
of forces that would come to undermine, then ultimately destroy, the
established order.

Political polarization as well as tension in foreign affairs or embroil-
ment in external conflict shaped relative levels of high-pitched
nationalist rhetoric. Attempts in Spain to build unity around notions
of 'national regeneration' were derailed following the disastrous
defeat and loss of colonies to the USA in what had initially been a
popular war in 1898. These attempts were in any event doomed to
failure given the deep internal divisions, regional as well as ideological, in the country. But the crusading zeal to forge a nation reborn
through struggle against internal enemies would eventually lead to
catastrophic conflict.

In most countries the imagery of enemies, internal as well as external, was built into rhetoric that was reaching new levels of aggression.
The mass media stirred animosities – usually intensely xenophobic and
often outrightly racist – that governments were glad to encourage. The
South African War of 1899–1902 gave a new boost to extreme nationalistic belligerence, dubbed 'jingoism', in Great Britain. In Germany
the conservative government whipped up nationalist fervour in the
so-called 'Hottentot election' of 1907 to besmirch the Social Democrat
opponents with alleged lack of patriotism. (That the Social Democrats
actually increased the size of their vote – though losing substantial
numbers of seats – indicates that, as in Britain, jingoism had far greater
currency among the middle classes than among workers.)

Nationalist organizations such as the Pan-German League, the
Navy League and the German Defence League – each of them largely
finding their appeal among the middle and lower-middle classes –
urged a more radically assertive and expansionist foreign policy.
Before 1914, they remained no more than significant pressure groups,
still outsiders to mainstream politics, let alone government. By now,
even so, assertive nationalist ideas had permeated practically the
whole of politics, beyond the socialist Left. In Italy the lingering sense
of national humiliation at the calamitous defeat of colonial Italian
forces (with the loss of over 5,000 Italian troops) by an Ethiopian
army at Adowa in 1896, and the feeling that the country was a

'proletarian nation' with no seat at the top table of Europe's imperialist great powers, boosted a nationalist feeling of almost religious fervour, emphasizing struggle and sacrifice, and advocating a strong anti-socialist state, military power and a more assertive foreign policy. For all the noise they made, Italian nationalists were far from representing majority opinion in a deeply divided society, and were still largely an irritant to government. Even so, nationalist pressure played its part in the decision of the Liberal government to gain a colony by invading Libya in 1911 – the first war in which aerial bombardment played a part, when the Italians bombed retreating Ottoman troops from a dirigible. In Italy, as in Germany, radical nationalism was still a minority taste. Maybe without the Great War it would have remained as such. But the seeds of later pernicious development had been sown.

Nationalism was increasingly defining 'the nation' not by territory, but by ethnicity – by those who should be permitted to belong to it. A French nationalist, Edmond Archdéacon, for instance, proclaimed himself in the 1902 election to be 'a declared opponent of internationalism. As an antisemite I demand that the 150,000 Jews and their lackeys, the 25,000 Freemasons, stop oppressing and ruining 38 million Frenchmen.' He represented, he said, 'the true Republic, the French republic'. In fact, in France as in other parts of Europe, nationalism as a political movement was riven with internal divisions, incapable of reaching out for state power, but nevertheless able to make governments more shrill in their foreign-policy assertions. And although nationalist politics were confined to the margins in France, the ideas at their heart – a nation defined by exclusion of those deemed not fit to belong to it, Jews quite specifically – remained undiluted as one part of a divided French culture. Similar arguments played out in much of Europe.

Antisemitism was a new term for an old phenomenon, widespread across the continent: hatred of Jews. Traditional Christian antagonism towards 'the killers of Christ', which had existed for centuries, remained prevalent, and was promoted by Christian clergy – Protestant, Catholic and Orthodox. Another deep-rooted element of the hatred came from age-old economic and social resentments, which had been strengthened as Jews benefited from recent freedoms to widen their involvement in business and cultural life. It swiftly found expression in the scapegoating of Jews during any economic down-turn. In the latter part of the nineteenth century, the long-standing, frequently vicious, forms of Jew-hatred had come to be overlain with something still worse. They were now intermixed with new, potentially lethal, race doctrines, which offered pseudo-scientific, biological justification for hatred and persecution. Older discrimination, certainly bad enough, had permitted (sometimes forced) Jews to convert to Christianity. Biological antisemitism ruled this out. Jews, in this thinking, were scientifically, racially, 'in their blood', different. A Jew could no more become a Frenchman or German, for example, than a cat could be turned into a dog. It was a doctrine that pointed not just to discrimination but to total exclusion. Beyond that, it was potentially the way to physical destruction.

Antisemitic rhetoric was appalling. German antisemites used the language of bacteriology to describe Jews. Vienna's popular and admired mayor, Karl Lueger, had called Jews 'beasts of prey in human form', and had earlier said the 'Jewish problem' would be solved if all the Jews could be put on a large ship to be sunk on the high seas. Whatever the rhetoric, antisemitism as politics seemed, at least in western Europe, to be declining during the 'golden age' before the First World War. This was partly deceptive, since antisemitism often became incorporated in mainstream conservatism. The spread of negative imagery did not die away. But before the war, its impact was politically limited. Despite antisemitism on the political fringes, most Jews could feel at home in Wilhelmine Germany. The atmosphere in France, which had so recently experienced the shameful Dreyfus Affair (when the wrongful conviction for treason of a Jewish army officer unleashed a frenzy of antisemitism), seemed to Jews more threatening. But there, too, the situation improved in the early years of the new century. Far worse was the situation of Jews in eastern Europe. Brutal pogroms, leaving thousands of Jews dead and injured, often instigated by the Tsarist police and administration, had sullied parts of western Russia between 1903 and 1906. Poland, Ukraine, Hungary, Romania and the Baltic regions were other areas where the visceral hatred of Jews was endemic. It was not just by chance that such areas would, later and in changed circumstances, become Europe's main killing-grounds.

The dark face of Europe's 'golden age' of civilization and progress showed itself in embryonic form in another mode of thought: 'eugenics', and its close relation 'social darwinism'. Its origins lay in the work in London of Sir Francis Galton, who applied the evolutionary theories of his uncle Charles Darwin to argue that ability was hereditary and that the human race could be improved by genetic engineering. Already before the First World War eugenics had been attracting attention in other European countries, including Scandinavia, Switzerland and Germany, as well as the USA. It was seen as a 'progressive' science. Supporters in Britain, for example, included leading thinkers associated with the liberal establishment or the nascent political Left, such as John Maynard Keynes, Lord Beveridge, H. G. Wells, Sidney Webb and George Bernard Shaw. In a private letter written in 1908, over thirty years before the Nazi 'euthanasia action', the widely acclaimed English novelist D. H. Lawrence even approvingly contemplated the building of a big 'lethal chamber' into which, with a band playing softly, 'all the sick, the halt, the maimed', would be gently led.

Eugenics appeared to offer the potential to 'breed out' of society the characteristics that produced criminality, alcoholism, prostitution and other forms of 'deviant' behaviour. It blended into the classic imperialist ideology of 'social darwinism', which rested upon assumptions that certain racial types were inherently superior to others. Galton himself wrote in 1908 that the first object of eugenics was to limit the birth rate of 'the unfit'. Elimination of the 'unhealthy' would over time, it was presumed, produce a fitter, healthier, 'better' society. Fears of racial degeneration through social welfare measures that encouraged procreation among the 'inferior' parts of society fed into notions of national efficiency.

A German magazine ran a competition in 1911 on the question: 'What do the inferior elements cost the state and society?' It was won by a Hamburg official of the General Asylum for the Poor (who incorporated almost all welfare costs in his answer). Sterilization of 'inferiors' was an idea that started to gain ground in medical circles. In Germany, Alfred Ploetz, a doctor, linked eugenics to 'racial hygiene', establishing a 'Society for Racial Hygiene' that had a small membership of 350 and four branches in German cities by 1914. That year the Society stipulated its demand for regulation of procedures 'where abortion or sterilization appear medically desirable'. Only weeks before the war, the Reich government prepared a draft bill that rejected social or eugenic grounds for sterilization or abortion, permitting action only if there was an 'immediate threat to life or limb'. Before the bill could become law, Germany was at war. Like antisemitism, eugenics – let alone its racial hygienist variant – might without the war never have attained the significance it was to acquire in a drastically changed climate. Even so, the intellectual foundations for later developments were laid in Europe's 'golden age' of civilization.

Europe before the First World War, despite its superficial peacefulness, bore the seeds of the later explosion of violence. Enmities and hatreds – nationalist, religious, ethnic, class – defaced practically every society. The Balkans and the Russian Empire were particularly violent parts of the continent. After the failed revolution in Russia in 1905, proto-fascist gangs, often supported by the police, took savage revenge on their enemies. Amid the wild outrages, Jews suffered worst. Over 3,000 murders of Jews in 690 pogroms were reported in October 1905. In Odessa the most appalling pogrom of all left 800 Jews murdered, 5,000 injured and more than 100,000 homeless. Counter-revolutionary reprisals resulted in the execution of 15,000 opponents of the Tsarist regime. Worse still was the situation in the Ottoman Empire, stretching over much of the Near and Middle East, ruled by the Turks since the fifteenth century, though now in terminal decline. Some estimates suggest that well over 80,000 Armenians were killed in the Ottoman Empire between 1894 and 1896 during the brutal repression under Sultan Abdul-Hamid II. The slaughter was prompted by Turkish fears of rising Armenian nationalism, fuelled also by economic discontent, religious and class antagonism, and was even tolerated by the police. Massacres of Armenians continued sporadically in the Ottoman Empire. In 1909 a further 15,000–20,000 were murdered.

Much of Europe's violence was, however, exported. Even where there was relative peace and growing prosperity at home, imperialist powers used considerable violence to enforce their continued domination of foreign territories and subjugated peoples in their colonies. Four-fifths of the globe was controlled, directly or indirectly, by Great

Britain, France and Russia. Where imperialist rule was challenged, reprisals were vicious. Kaiser Wilhelm II had urged German troops to behave like Attila's Huns in putting down the Boxer Rebellion in China in 1900. An international force drawn from several European countries with a vested interest in the economic exploitation of China, alongside American and Japanese troops, participated in widespread atrocities, looting and rape. According to some estimates, 100,000 Chinese fell victim to the accompanying massacres.

Immense cruelty was unconstrained in some colonial territories. Between 1885 and 1908 an estimated 10 million men, women and children of the native population of the Congo – effectively a personal fiefdom of King Leopold II of Belgium – were killed in uncontrolled atrocities perpetrated by their colonial masters as they exploited the global demand for rubber. The British, involved in a bitter three-year war from 1899 to 1902 to defeat the Boers and establish their complete control in South Africa, used ruthless scorched-earth tactics to destroy enemy possessions and established what became called 'concentration camps' to intern mainly Boer women and children. A quarter of the 28,000 or so prisoners (a large proportion of them under sixteen years of age) died in the appallingly overcrowded, insanitary and disease-ridden conditions. And according to some estimates, in South-West Africa (today's Namibia) 80 per cent of the Herero and Nama peoples (perhaps some 65,000 in total) perished between 1904 and 1907. German colonial troops, in systematic retaliation for rebellion against colonial rule, had driven them into the desert where most died of thirst and hunger. Many more were worked to death in slave-labour camps (which the Germans, taking over the English nomenclature, had started to call 'concentration camps').

As international tensions between the great powers began to mount, so did pressures to rearm and, with that, recognition that the destructive capacity of new weaponry would result in warfare unlike anything so far experienced. The Tsar of Russia, Nicholas II, no less, invited government representatives from twenty-six countries to a conference at The Hague in 1899 with the aim of preserving peace and limiting armaments as 'a happy overture to the century ahead'. The results – general conventions on settlement of international disputes, the laws of war, and banning of certain types of weapon for a period of five years – were soon enough proved vacuous. But they did indicate an awareness that the continuation of Europe's peaceful era could not be taken for granted, and unease about the capability of modern industrial weaponry. There was a growing sense that preventing war itself, but also the immense political and economic upheaval that would follow it, was an urgent task. The need to preserve Europe's peace, and to ensure continuing economic growth and prosperity, gained new currency. But Europe's leaders, while hoping for peace, prepared for the eventuality of war – and if there had to be war, then for a quick victory.

SLITHERING INTO WAR?

The British statesman David Lloyd George later famously wrote that in 1914 the nations of Europe had 'slithered over the brink into the boiling cauldron of war without any trace of apprehension or dismay'. The poignant phrase captures the unstoppable momentum towards war in the last week of July 1914, the sense that events were out of anyone's control. But it is mistaken in implying a general insouciance and lack of anxiety. Nor should it be taken to imply that war, when it came, was an accident, a tragic set of errors, an outcome desired by no one, an unforeseen and unpredictable occurrence. On the contrary, for all the genuine hopes of most decision-makers that a general conflagration could be avoided, for all the confusion, hesitation, prophecies of doom and last-minute cold feet – when it came to it, the will for war outweighed the desire for peace. Europe's leaders approached the prospect of war with their eyes wide open.

Lloyd George's phrase also carries the connotation that there was no obvious drive to war, that there was general, not specific, responsibility for the disaster. Certainly, European leaders and diplomats seemed collectively to behave like lemmings heading for the cliff. Certainly, there were misunderstandings and there was general distrust – the personalities of the key decision-makers played a part here – that helped to push the European major powers over the precipice. It is also true that there was no evident drive to war by a single country, as there was to be a generation later. And certainly, all the great powers bore some responsibility for what happened. France, as the crisis was reaching boiling point, encouraged Russia's increasingly warlike stance. Britain sent out ambivalent signals, failing to act to defuse the situation rather than comply with the ever more dangerous steps that finally culminated in war. But when all this is said, the responsibility for the fateful steps into a European-wide conflagration was not evenly shared.

The lion's share of the responsibility falls on those powers whose irreconcilable interests and ambitions were most geared to the risk of a general European war and whose diplomatic brinkmanship during the crisis rested ultimately on their willingness to use their military muscle. As breaking point was reached in July 1914, Germany, Austria-Hungary and Russia had been the decisive forces in the crisis. Germany's role was the most crucial of all.

Germany combined its own ambitions to be the dominant power on the European continent with a mounting, almost paranoid, fear of Russian ascendancy and eventual hegemony. To establish the former and prevent the latter, Germany was prepared to risk a general European conflagration. On 6 July 1914 Germany gave an unconditional guarantee of support to Austria-Hungary (the 'blank cheque', as it is usually known). This was on the assumption that limited action against Serbia would swiftly follow as punishment for the murder by Serbian nationalists of the heir to the Austrian throne, Archduke Franz Ferdinand, and his wife, Sophie, during a state visit to Sarajevo on 28 June. But it was *only* an assumption. The guarantee imposed no veto on Austria's retaliatory measures, though the danger of a wider conflict and the involvement of Europe's great powers were both evident. Germany's encouragement of an Austrian ultimatum to Serbia, delivered on 23 July and designed in advance to make acceptance impossible, was then decisive in converting an initially localized issue into a general European crisis. The ultimatum demanded action against Serbian officials and military personnel connected to the assassination plot, the arrest of two named officers, and the suppression of anti-Austrian propaganda. Most irreconcilable with protection of Serbian sovereignty were the demands that representatives from Austria-Hungary should collaborate in the investigation of the plot and the suppression of the subversive movement in Serbia.

Austria-Hungary, its control over the Balkans imperilled by Serbian ascendancy and its multi-national empire increasingly under threat of disintegration, was ready to embroil Europe in war to serve its own interests, but only as long as it could rely upon German backing. The deliberately impossible terms of Austria's ultimatum to Serbia (from whose territory the 'Black Hand' terrorist organization had provided the weapons for the Sarajevo assassins) were presented in full awareness of the likelihood that Russia would back the Serbs, again greatly heightening the chances of a general European war. And Russia, anxious to prevent dominance of the Balkans by Austria-Hungary (which would have blocked Russia's own ambitions), responded precisely in this way, offering outright backing to the Serbs in the knowledge that this made war, not just against Austria-Hungary but also against Germany, more likely; and that war with Germany would inevitably draw in the French (since it was known that German war plans envisaged striking against France as well as Russia) and, most probably, the British.

The high-risk strategy of Germany, Austria-Hungary and Russia – the willingness to escalate rather than to calm an essentially local conflict even if it meant a full-scale European war to serve their respective aims of power-politics – ultimately caused the catastrophe of 1914. And of these three powers, as noted, Germany bears especial responsibility. Without the 'blank cheque', in which Germany guaranteed its support, Austria-Hungary would not have been emboldened to issue Serbia with such an uncompromising ultimatum. And without Austrian aggressive intransigence, Russia would not have committed its support to Serbia, with all the consequences that entailed. The 'blank cheque' was the trigger that meant a general European war became more, not less, likely.

In 1914 the increasingly uneasy balance among the major powers of Great Britain, France, Russia, Germany and Austria-Hungary, bound up in rival systems of alliance, still held, but only just. One ominous long-term development, leading to growing tension, had been the emergence during the 1890s of Germany's ambitions to become a world power. The direct challenge was to Great Britain's world-power status. Rivalry between Germany and Britain intensified. But on the continent of Europe itself a strong Germany (which had been allied with Austria-Hungary since 1879 and with Italy since

1882) posed the biggest threat to France and Russia. Common interest brought a somewhat unlikely rapprochement between the latter two countries – one a republic, the other a monarchist autocracy – which led to an alliance signed in 1894 directly aimed at neutralizing Germany's challenge. Just over a decade later, Germany's position had been strengthened by the resounding defeat in 1905 – surprising to many at the time – of Russia at the hands of Japan, the up-and-coming power in the Far East, which shook the foundations of the Tsarist Empire. The autocracy only narrowly survived the internal turmoil that followed the defeat. Remarkably, however, under shrewd economic and political management, the following years were a boom time in Russia. With the help of large French loans, the economy grew impressively. Military rebuilding made rapid progress. And long-existing hopes of gaining control over the Bosphorus at the expense of the crumbling Ottoman Empire were revived – prospects enhanced by the hugely improved relations of Russia with Britain.

The two had traditionally been rivals. Britain had long been keen, to the point of war in the Crimea in 1854, to avoid Russian domination of the Turkish Straits – the Bosphorus and Dardanelles, crucial to control of the Mediterranean and entry to the Middle East – and to head off any potential threat to the vital colony of India that might arise from Russian expansion in central Asia. But Russia's weakness after the defeat by Japan brought a readiness to come to terms with Britain in a convention signed in 1907, which stipulated their respective spheres of influence in Persia, Afghanistan and Tibet – areas of potential conflict. Although this did not directly affect Germany, it certainly did so indirectly. The agreement between Russia and Britain, building upon the earlier Franco-Russian alliance and the Entente Cordiale of 1904 between France and Britain (aimed directly at German power), reshaped the structure of power-politics in Europe. Germany and its main ally, Austria-Hungary – Italy, not even a great power, even if its leaders harboured such a pretence, was a flakier ally – found themselves facing the newly created (and in the light of past enmities remarkable) entente of Britain, France and Russia. The understandable feeling within Germany that the Reich was encircled by its enemies grew ever stronger.

The opposing alliances, seen by the British Foreign Office as serving (like later nuclear weaponry) as a deterrent to aggression, came to determine that when war erupted, it would be general and not localized. The alliances did not, however, cause the war. There had been a number of serious crises over the previous decade, though these had not led to war. Tension between the great powers had been fairly swiftly defused when Germany had challenged French assertions of power in Morocco in 1905, again following the peremptory Austrian annexation in 1908 of Bosnia-Herzegovina (formally still part of the Ottoman Empire, though occupied by Austria for the previous thirty years), and in 1911 after the Germans had provoked the French by sending a gunboat to the Moroccan port of Agadir. When war did break out in the chronically unstable Balkans in 1912, as an alliance of Serbia, Bulgaria and Greece (a self-styled Balkan League) sought to take advantage of Ottoman weakness, followed by another war the next year between members of the Balkan League when Bulgaria attacked Serbia over the spoils of the first war, the great powers ensured that regional conflict did not lead to a general conflagration.

The tension between the great powers was nonetheless palpable. The Balkan Wars had destabilized this combustible region even more. Another flare-up was more than likely at some point before long. Moreover, while Ottoman influence in the Balkans had long been fading, the other major power in the region, Austria-Hungary, had been perceived as passive and weak during the two wars, even when its own interests seemed threatened. It was therefore left exposed to potential further trouble in the Balkans. Russian leaders, their hopes still alive of one day controlling the Turkish Straits and of securing their western borders by possession of Galicia (the part of Poland in Austrian hands), took note of Austrian weakness.

A European war was far from inevitable. But no one wanted to take chances through lack of preparation. Mutual suspicions prompted a sharp escalation of the arms race. Defence spending among the great powers was drastically increased – by 30 per cent in Germany, 50 per cent in Russia, between 1911 and 1913. Germany and Britain poured huge resources into new battle fleets in a competition to build the most formidable navy. Land armies were greatly increased in size. When the Germans extended the size of their army in 1913, the French did the same. The Russians, too, smarting from their defeat by the

Japanese in 1905, had gone far towards rebuilding their army by 1913 and, as the Germans were fearfully aware, planned for a further big increase in its size. Austria-Hungary lagged behind and was not well equipped to fight anything beyond a regional war. Its quota of conscripts had been fixed in 1889, and a new law to increase this in 1913 would prove too late to close the widening gap with other armies.

Even in Austria-Hungary, however, as across the continent, a remarkably high proportion of males of military age were trained for conflict. By 1914, millions of men, already serving or reservists, were ready or being made ready to fight. At full mobilization, Russia's army comprised 3.5 million men, Germany's 2.1 million, France's 1.8 million, and Austria-Hungary's 1.3 million. Great Britain was the only great power without a mass reserve conscript army. Its volunteer army of around 100,000 men, trained largely for colonial warfare, was puny compared with the size of the armies of the other great powers. But Britain had the Royal Navy, which allowed it to dominate the world's sea lanes and was the military basis of its imperial domination. It also had the potential to call upon huge numbers of recruits from its world empire.

Many presumed that the checks and balances that had kept Europe essentially peaceful over the previous century would continue in place. There were others, however, who thought war would before long be unavoidable. This was not just due to the increased militarization and heightened tension. These in themselves reflected the anxieties among the great-power elites that their countries faced an existential threat and that time was running against them. That in turn meant that a serious conflagration was indeed probable at some point. At any rate, a betting man would not have wagered much on Europe's fragile peace holding indefinitely.

That was even before the assassination of Archduke Franz Ferdinand on 28 June 1914. Serbian nationalism had sharply intensified following the Austrian annexation of Bosnia-Herzegovina in 1908. Radicalized nationalists, some of them army officers, had in 1911 formed a secret organization, the 'Black Hand', whose driving-force, Dragutin Dimitrijević (known as 'Apis'), became head of Serbian military intelligence in 1913. The plot to kill the Archduke took shape within the murky networks that 'Apis' controlled. A number of Bosnian Serb youths, one of them the eventual assassin, Gavrilo Princip, were recruited to carry out the assassination. The target, Franz Ferdinand, heir to the imperial throne, far from opposing Slav minorities, wanted to give the 'South Slavs' greater powers in order to stabilize the empire. But precisely this prospect was seen by Serbian radicals as a threat to Serbian nationalist ambitions. The assassination itself followed a bizarre incident during the state visit to Sarajevo of the Archduke and his wife. The chauffeur of the Archduke's open-top limousine had taken a wrong turning up a narrow street. When the car's engine stalled as he tried to reverse, he unexpectedly presented Princip with a golden opportunity to make amends for an earlier, bungled attempt by another member of the seven-strong group of fanatical Serbian nationalists. Even so, there was no obvious reason why the murder of Franz Ferdinand (and his wife) should spark a general European war. There had been other recent assassinations, even of kings, which had not triggered a major conflict. The French President, Sadi Carnot, had been assassinated in 1894, the Italian King Umberto I had been shot dead on 29 July 1900, the Serbian King Alexander and his wife were murdered on 11 June 1903, and King George I of Greece likewise was killed on 18 March 1913. That the assassination of Franz Ferdinand should provoke a general war seemed, in fact, unlikely until almost the end of July 1914.

It was over three weeks after the Sarajevo murders that the barometer of serious diplomatic tension began to rise sharply. Only in the last week of July did London's financial markets start to get jittery about the prospect of war. And even then there were still signs of confidence that the worst would be avoided. As late as 30 July the French Socialist leader Jean Jaurès, remarked: 'There will be ups and downs. But it is impossible that things won't turn out all right.' The following day, 31 July, he was shot dead by a deranged ultra-nationalist who claimed Jaurès was a traitor who had to be killed. His 'treason' had been to strive for international peace.

An obvious Austrian response to the assassination of Franz Ferdinand would have been to gain 'satisfaction' through a short retributive attack to 'chastise' Serbia – held responsible for the assassination – whose army had been seriously weakened by losses in the recent

Balkan Wars. The other powers would most likely have accepted this as a reasonable retaliation for the killing of the heir to the Habsburg throne. There was indeed almost a presumption that this would be a natural and justified reaction. In Vienna, but not just there, retaliation was regarded as a matter of prestige, necessary to confirm the status of the Habsburg monarchy as a great power. About three weeks after the assassination German leaders in particular thought that a localized war would be the outcome.

But even such a limited action would have taken too long to organize. The cumbersome governmental, diplomatic and military machinery of the multi-national empire took time to crank into gear. While the hawkish Chief of the General Staff, Count Franz Conrad von Hötzendorf, supported by the Austrian Foreign Minister, Count Leopold Berchtold, pressed for immediate war against Serbia, the head of government in the Hungarian half of the empire, Count István Tisza, urged caution, fearing 'the dreadful calamity of a European war'. This lack of unity among the rulers of the Austro-Hungarian Empire was the very reason that a guarantee of German backing was sought. The Austrians thought the German army was invincible; German backing was a solid guarantee, even if a European war were to arise from action against Serbia. And the Austrians had the impression from Berlin that if war was unavoidable, the timing could not be more propitious.

However, the Habsburg Empire knew only two speeds: slow and dead-stop. Many of the men needed for service in the army were at the time even more urgently required to get in the harvest. So an immediate response was impossible. It was pointed out, already two days after the assassination, that at least a further sixteen days would be necessary to mobilize the armed forces for a strike against Serbia. As it was, the protracted Austrian response amounted to a slow-burning fuse that eventually prompted all the great powers to become involved. As the crisis deepened, actions were influenced by mentalities, aims, ambitions and fears that had been long in the making.

Germany, a country united only since 1871 but with the strongest industrial economy on the continent, was ambitious, keen to acquire its 'place in the sun', to become a world power that could rival the British Empire in status and influence. At the same time Germany was most fearful that time was not in its favour and that the combined military might of its enemies threatened to block its ambitions. The Chief of the General Staff, Field Marshal Helmuth von Moltke, had already made clear as early as 1912, in the Kaiser's presence, that he saw war as inevitable, 'and the sooner the better'. He recommended that the press stir up anti-Russian feeling to make war popular when it came. Moltke remained the leading proponent of a preventive war – an early strike before Germany could itself be attacked, by Russia, France, or both in concert. In the weeks before the war, he continued to argue that Germany had to make sure that war, certain to break out anyway, should take place while it was in a position to win. Russia would have completed its armaments programme within two or three years, he was reported as saying in May 1914, and the military might of Germany's enemies would then be so great that he did not know how it could be mastered. The only option, he concluded, was 'to carry out a preventive war to smash the enemy as long as we could still to some extent prove successful in the struggle'.

But the gloomy, pessimistic Moltke, though holding the most crucial post in the German military hierarchy, did not determine government policy. And Bethmann-Hollweg, the German Chancellor, had real and growing anxieties about the consequences of a war. He saw it as a 'leap in the dark', and to be undertaken only as the 'gravest duty'. He even predicted, counter to what some German hawks were claiming, that war, far from destroying social democracy and eliminating its threat to the existing social order, would in fact strengthen it, 'and will topple many a throne'. Towards the end of July, as the crisis moved into its final phase and his own political initiatives had recognizably failed, Bethmann-Hollweg tried 'to apply the brakes with all his energy' as he visibly lost ground to the military leadership. Even so, his mind was not closed to the General Staff's argument that Germany's military position could only become less favourable over time, while Russia's would become immeasurably stronger, and that it was better, therefore, to have the war 'now rather than later', while victory could be quickly attained, than to wait and watch conditions worsen. Since Russia was allied with France, Germany's great enemy to the west, the fear of encirclement had by this time become pervasive.

The civilian, not military, leadership of Germany still retained the controlling hand on policy decisions until the Russian mobilization on 30 July, by which time war had become inevitable. In no other European country, even so, had the military such a degree of autonomy from the civilian government as in Germany. And when the crisis reached its climax at the end of July, the influence of Moltke and the General Staff proved decisive. Military imperatives took over from political initiative. The Kaiser, seeming at times to agree with Moltke's analysis, was, for all his belligerent bluster, a waverer who got cold feet during the crisis and sought at the last minute to back away from war. But the Kaiser was, in fact, in no position to control forces far more powerful than he was. German military planning was rigid in its long-standing strategy to defeat the French swiftly before turning on the Russians. So when on 30 July the Kaiser demanded that Moltke call off the attack on France (hoping this would ensure British neutrality) and redirect the entire army to face the Russians, his Chief of Staff replied in no uncertain terms that this could not be done. It would turn the well-trained army into little more than a 'chaotic rabble'. Army deployment, Moltke declared, was the result of years of planning and could not be improvised at short notice. During the crisis, far from dictating policy, the Kaiser could only react to the decisions of his government and, ultimately, to the imperatives of his military.

Until Moltke's stance was finally accepted, as events reached their climax at the end of July, the actions of the German government had been shaped by its earlier grave policy mistake – giving a free hand to Austria in dealing with the Serbian crisis – which had itself opened up the real risk of a European conflagration. This colossal error meant that Germany spent July mainly responding to events that were shaped by others – events that were rapidly spiralling beyond anyone's control.

Russian long-term interests were directed towards control of the Balkans and the Turkish Straits, vital to Russia's trade and, since they controlled access to the Black Sea, to its security in the south. No other power could be allowed to dominate the region. As the weakness of the Ottoman Empire became increasingly evident, the main threat to Russian interests in the Balkans plainly came from Austria-Hungary. Hawkish elements in the Russian naval leadership even mooted an early war to seize Constantinople (as the Russians still called Istanbul) and the Straits before the Turks acquired the five new Dreadnoughts they had on order (from the British). But such notions played little or no part in shaping Russian action during the July crisis. Russia's military preparations were not targeted for completion before 1917. No imminent showdown with Germany was contemplated in 1914 – until, that is, the terms of the Austrian ultimatum to Serbia became known on 24 July. From that point on, Russia's backing for Serbia meant the descent into a general European war was as good as impossible to halt. Considerations of prestige alone meant that no side could consider backing down.

Austria-Hungary, the weakest in the triad of major powers whose actions paved the way for war during July 1914, acted largely out of fear for its own future. The instability in the Balkans (enhanced by the erosion of Ottoman influence), the worries of losing dominance in the region to the Russians (known to harbour bitter resentment at the Austrian annexation of Bosnia-Herzogovina in 1908), and the growing assertiveness of Serbia, with the shadow of Russian support behind it, caused great anxieties in the corridors of power in Vienna. Crushing Serbia was, therefore, a tempting proposition in July 1914 – as long as German support was guaranteed and a limited war could be successfully, and quickly, executed. But quick retaliatory action for the assassination of Franz Ferdinand was not taken. Instead, the ultimatum of 23 July invited the involvement of Russia (and with that Germany and France) into the festering conflict.

Germany had voiced its unconditional support for Austrian action against Serbia, seen as entirely justified, as early as 6 July. Serbia would either back down or be militarily punished. The position of Germany's main ally in the Balkans would be strengthened as a result. It was not thought that Russia would intervene. The Tsar would surely not back assassins of royalty? And Russia, it was believed, was still militarily unprepared for war. The other powers would look on and accept the fait accompli. How shaky the German political calculations were would soon become clear. That they might indeed prove a serious miscalculation, and that they involved a great risk, was, however, recognized at the very time that the 'blank cheque' was issued. The Chancellor, Bethmann Hollweg, no less, acknowledged that 'an action against Serbia can lead to world war', and that this would turn 'everything that exists upside-down'.

Further foot-dragging in Vienna meant that German hopes of a speedy outcome to a localized crisis were effectively doomed from the start. The text of a tough ultimatum to the Serbs was not finalized until 19 July, and a further four days elapsed before it was presented. It was by now three and a half weeks since the murders in Sarajevo. Another forty-eight hours were to be allowed for the Serbian response. Remarkably, fearing the worst from an Austrian attack, the Serbs had initially been prepared to bow to the harsh terms. That was before the Russians, aware for days through a leak of the uncompromising terms of the ultimatum, stiffened Serbian resolve. Russian leaders had themselves been encouraged to take a hard line with Austria and to stand by Serbia, whatever the consequences, through the firm assurances of support from their French ally during the state visit to St Petersburg of President Poincaré and Prime Minister Viviani between 20 and 23 July.

The French President, who had as a boy experienced the Prussian invasion of his native Lorraine, had his own anti-German axes to grind. He had supported the notion of Russian intervention in the Balkans in 1912, aware that it could bring about conflict with Germany. Then, as now, a weakening of Germany's position in Europe through a military clash with Russia was in the French interest. In 1912 Russia had chosen to keep out of the Balkan conflict. This time policy-makers in St Petersburg thought it would be a mistake to hold back. Russia's strategic aims would be advanced by support for Serbia. If that meant war, then, with Germany committed to fighting on two fronts, the hawkish elements in the Russian leadership believed it was a war that Russia would win. That decision itself meant that options quickly narrowed. From the delivery of the Austrian ultimatum, events moved fast. A general war started to become more, not less, likely. Even then it could have been stopped. But there was not the will to prevent it.

'That means European war' was the immediate response next day of the Russian Foreign Minister, Sergei Sazonov, to the Austrian ultimatum. Shortly afterwards, Sazonov accused the Austrians of deliberately provoking war, telling their ambassador: 'You are setting fire to Europe.' However, as Sazonov knew only too well, the Russians' own actions were markedly ratcheting up the chances of inflaming conditions on the continent. Even before the Austrian ultimatum had expired, already on 24 July Russia had withdrawn all deposits of state funds in Berlin (amounting to 100 million rubles). More significantly, it had taken the decision to begin in secret the partial mobilization of the army (amounting to over a million men) and the Baltic and Black Sea fleets of the navy. By 25 July the so-called 'Period Preparatory to War' had started. Troop movements quickly made the Germans aware of the secret mobilization, even though it was not formally announced until 28 July. That was the date on which Austria finally declared war on Serbia.

The momentum for general war now proved unstoppable. Frantic and futile last-ditch diplomatic manoeuvres, some more genuine than others, were made to head off the descent into a full-scale European war. It was too late. German hopes that Austrian action against Serbia could be contained and localized had long since evaporated. Even so, five days after the Russian decision to begin mobilization in secret, Germany had yet to take any decisive military steps. On 29 July there was still hesitation in Berlin about ordering a 'State of Imminent Danger of War' (the last step before full-scale mobilization). But that evening the Russian leadership decided upon general mobilization. The following day, 30 July, after a delay when the Tsar first confirmed then, in a bout of nerves, cancelled the order, he agreed to full mobilization.

Military imperatives now finally overrode diplomatic considerations in Berlin. A 'State of Imminent Danger of War' was declared on 31 July. A central German concern was to ensure that the Social Democrats, whose spectrum of support embraced strong pacifist strains, would support war. It was essential, therefore, that Germany should be seen to be forced into a defensive war. The Russian general mobilization provided this justification. Chancellor Bethmann Hollweg expressed satisfaction that the Russians would now appear the guilty party, before adding fatalistically: 'things are out of control and the stone has started to roll'. At midnight on 31 July Germany issued a twelve-hour ultimatum to Russia stipulating German general mobilization if Russia refused to withdraw its mobilization order. When the ultimatum expired on 1 August, with no action taken in St Petersburg, Germany declared war on Russia. France mobilized in support of Russia the same day. Two days later, 3 August, Germany declared war on France.

Great Britain, preoccupied more by the prospect of civil war in Ireland than the mounting crisis on the continent, had not been among the hawks as the pressure for war grew. Of all the major powers, Britain had least to gain from a European war. The country's leaders were more than aware that, as Sir Edward Grey, the Foreign Secretary, had put it on 23 July, war would 'involve the expenditure of so vast a sum of money and such an interference with trade' that it would result in 'a complete collapse of European credit and industry'. 'Irrespective of who were the victors in the war, many things would be completely swept away,' he added, prophetically. Most of the British cabinet, like Grey, feared the consequences of war and hoped that peace could be preserved. During the following week the Foreign Secretary tried, hesitantly, to explore possibilities of a mediated settlement to the crisis. The terms of the entente with Russia and France did not bind Britain to intervention, and Grey continued to hedge British bets. A firm British declaration of neutrality, which the Germans were hoping for (though not expecting), might even at a late hour have prevented general war. But Grey's disastrous hesitation meant that the room for diplomatic initiatives vanished. And, ultimately, Britain could not take the risk of German domination of the continent. This was the chief reason why Britain was ready to fight. Moreover, there were those in the British government and also among the opposition who saw support for France and Russia as a matter of honour and prestige. Britain could not afford to stand aside from a major war, argued Sir Eyre Crowe, an influential voice in the Foreign Office, without seeing its standing as a great power diminished.

In the end, when German troops crossed the border into neutral Belgium and a British ultimatum demanding Germany respect Belgian neutrality was disregarded at midnight on 4 August, it provided the occasion for Britain to declare war. Ironically, Austria-Hungary, the state whose actions had precipitated the crisis, was the last of the great powers to enter the conflict, declaring war on Russia only on 6 August. France declared war on Austria-Hungary five days after that, and

Britain, finally, a day later still. Serbia, which had initially sparked the conflict, would not face war on its own soil for another fourteen months. But Serbia was by now a sideshow. The main event was about to begin.

Behind these fateful steps into war lay fear. Each of the powers harboured fears for its own future. These were partially shaped by internal pressures for democratization and socialism or, particularly in Austria's case, by shrill nationalist demands that, it was feared, could (and indeed would) end by splintering the empire. But the great powers were in the main highly fearful of each other. Germany feared encirclement by its enemies, France and Russia. It especially feared Russia and the consequences of the military might of the Tsarist regime overtaking its own, including future Russian domination of the Balkans, seen as vital to its own expanding influence. Russia in turn feared German control over the Balkans, the Near East, and over its crucial economic lifeline through the Bosphorus. France, invaded by Prussia only a little over forty years earlier, in 1870, harboured an almost paranoid fear of Germany. Britain feared the loss of its commercial dominance and German supremacy in Europe. German control of the Belgian and French coast, just across the Channel, was an intolerable thought. Fear drove the arms race. It also drove the readiness to act before it was too late, to seize the opportunity before the enemy did, to grasp the moment. And common to all the great powers was fear of loss of face from backing away from the brink.

The readiness to risk war was encouraged by the belief on all sides that it would be short. Perhaps it was less belief than hope dressed up as expectation, avoiding consideration of what would happen should it not be the case. Few decision-makers in each country – no more than a handful of individuals in every case – voiced apprehension about the grave consequences of war. Whatever their inner fears, they acted as if the war would be short. It was not that the leaders of European countries, or their military advisers, were ignorant about the highly destructive capacity of modern artillery or the high death-toll to be expected in a new war by sending infantry out to face machine-gun fire. The American Civil War had, decades earlier, given a foretaste of the heavy death tolls that could be expected. But little notice had been taken of this in Europe. Nor did the 184,000 dead in the Franco-Prussian

War of 1870–71 send any strong message. If anything, it suggested that the sheer destructiveness of modern warfare would bring quick results. After all, though that war lasted for ten months, the key battle, at Sedan, had taken place after only six weeks. More recently, observers had widely reported the high casualties in the Russo-Japanese War of 1904–5. But this war had also been short – not much longer than a year.

Based on relatively recent experience, another short war could be anticipated. So instead of being deterred by the prospect of a long drawn-out conflict and slaughterous stalemate, military thinkers in Europe were sufficiently impressed by advances in fire-power technology to imagine that a rapid, mobile offensive, even if accompanied by heavy casualties, would bring about a quick victory. German military strategists, in particular, operated along such lines. A lengthy war of attrition, they acknowledged, had to be avoided at all costs, given an enemy alliance superior in numbers and the potential throttling of the German war effort by a British naval blockade. The German General Staff, responsible for military planning, concluded, therefore, that the speedier and more devastating the offensive, the likelier it would be that the enemy would be overrun before it could mobilize adequate defence forces in time – and the sooner, therefore, the war would be over.

Moltke adapted a variant of the plan laid down by his predecessor as Chief of the General Staff, General Alfred Graf von Schlieffen, in 1905, which started from a premise of war on two fronts but aimed to move westwards first and at speed to knock out the French with a rapid offensive of enormous force, turning to defeat the enemy in the east before the Russians could attack. Schlieffen had thought a breakthrough to victory would be possible within about a month. But the French were hardly unaware of the danger, and, with a field army of comparable size, were preparing to meet attack with huge offensives of their own. The Russians also thought in terms of a swift, decisive offensive, into Austrian Galicia (an offensive against the Germans in East Prussia was, to the chagrin of the French, subordinate to this main aim) to reach the Carpathians. The Austrians, too, imagined that attack was the best form of defence. Yet they recognized that, while they could take on the Serbs, moving against the Russians could only be undertaken in tandem with a devastating German assault on the eastern foe. Each of the continental adversaries presumed the primacy of the offensive. That, they believed, was the way to decisive – and quick – victory. There was no fallback position. What would happen if speedy victory were not attained did not bear contemplation. It could only mean a long attritional war, and ultimate victory to the alliance with the greater economic as well as military capacity.

The belief that war was necessary and justified, and the self-consoling presumption that it would be short – a brief, exciting and heroic adventure – with victory swift and casualties few, went far beyond Europe's ruling classes and penetrated into wide sections of the population. It helps to explain why so many people in each of the belligerent countries were so enthusiastic, even euphoric, as tension – not experienced at grass-roots level before the last week of July – built up and finally burst into full-scale war. To be sure, such a belief was far from universal, and the enthusiasm far more limited than first impressions might suggest. In fact, there was a wide spectrum of emotions, differing among countries, regions, social classes and political allegiances, ranging from pro-war hysteria to fervent anti-war pacifism, from gung-ho exhilaration to deep anxiety. But there is no denying the widespread jubilation in at least some parts of the population of Europe's great capitals at the imminent prospect of war.

In Vienna the British ambassador reported 'vast crowds' in a 'frenzy of delight' parading through the streets 'singing patriotic songs till the small hours of the morning' when relations with Serbia were broken off. The Austrian pacifist writer Stefan Zweig later recalled how he had been captivated by an atmosphere in the city transformed into patriotic enthusiasm. 'There were parades in the street, flags, ribbons, and music burst forth everywhere, young recruits were marching triumphantly, their faces lighting up the cheering.' Zweig found his 'hatred and aversion for war' temporarily overcome by what he saw as 'majestic, rapturous, and even seductive'. The 'war mood', once the view that it would be a fight for protection against Tsarist tyranny had been accepted, also predominated over the initial protests in Austrian socialist ranks at moves that threatened peace.

In Berlin some 50,000 citizens – mainly middle-class and students – gathered in front of the royal palace on 31 July, as news broke of

Russian mobilization, to hear the Kaiser state that 'in the struggle ahead I know no parties among my people any longer. There are among us now only Germans.' In pubs, cafés and beer gardens, people rose to sing patriotic songs. Young men paraded in the streets, demanding war. In other German cities, too, there were jubilant demonstrations in favour of war. From the balcony of the Winter Palace in St Petersburg, Tsar Nicholas greeted a huge, cheering crowd which, as if following orders, knelt before him, waving their banners and singing the national anthem. In Paris there was an outpouring of patriotic fervour as President Poincaré proclaimed the overcoming of internal divisions in a 'sacred union' of Frenchmen. Socialists joined in. Working-class anger at the assassination of Jaurès was directed by the external threat into the need for patriotic duty and defiance against German aggression.

At the root of such extraordinary emotions, years of nationalist indoctrination in schools and universities, during military service, in patriotic organizations and lobby-groups, and in the popular press had done their job. In the upper and middle classes, especially, and among intellectuals and students, nationalist fervour was widely prevalent. For many, too, war was welcome as national regeneration, as a liberation from the perceived moral decadence of contemporary society. The Italian Futurist Manifesto had expressed this graphically and radically in 1909: 'We want to glorify war, the only source of hygiene in the world – militarism, patriotism, the destructive act.' War was seen as heroic, adventurous, manly – the antidote to national decline. There was a sense of national unity, with internal divisions temporarily overcome. For German intellectuals, the new unity seemed the embodiment of 'the spirit of 1914', almost a sense of religious awakening. It reinforced their feeling that German culture was not simply different from, but was superior to, French civilization with its roots in revolution and republicanism, let alone the materialistic democracy of Britain. The values of the superior culture had to be defended and, if need be, enforced upon the rest of Europe.

Neither this lofty, intellectualized sense of superiority, nor the broader enthusiasm for war, accurately or fully represented attitudes. The jubilation at the prospect of war was largely confined to big towns and cities. Even there, it was far from universal. In London the pacifist philosopher Bertrand Russell later claimed to have witnessed with amazement 'that average men and women were delighted at the prospect of war'. Contemporary indicators, however, pointed to a prevalent mood in London and other parts of Britain of anxiety and nervousness rather than jingoistic enthusiasm, which seems to have been largely confined to parts of the middle class, especially youths.

The patriotic fervour of groups of students in the centre of Berlin found no echo among the workers of industrial districts of the city. Anti-war feeling – at any rate, anxiety at the prospect of war coupled with the desire to maintain peace – predominated there. In the countryside, too, war enthusiasm had little currency. It was reported that 'many of our peasant families are weighed down with great sorrow', and that the rural population felt little to cheer about when fathers, sons, brothers or grandsons might lose their lives. Russian peasants often had no idea what they were being asked to fight for. In French villages there was shock, pessimism and fatalistic acceptance of the requirements of duty, but no sign of wild jubilation at Poincaré's declaration of 'sacred union'.

Within the industrial working class, too, particularly among workers associated with socialist parties and trade unions – strongly internationalist and tending towards pacifism – jingoistic ultra-nationalism and outright enthusiasm for war were relatively little in evidence. But even here there was as good as no opposition to the war. Resistance to conscription was minimal in every country. A sense of duty, or fatalistic acceptance, sufficed even where enthusiasm was lacking. Only 1.5 per cent of those mobilized in France resisted the call-up. The government had reckoned with a figure of 13 per cent. German trade unionists agreed to suspend strike action during the war. Socialists in the German, French and British parliaments voted to back government funding of the war. In Russia the socialists abstained (though the five Bolshevik members of the Duma did vote against and were later arrested).

What won supporters of international socialism to back nationalistic war was the belief that the war was defensive, and unavoidable. It was seen as a war that had reluctantly to be fought – and for freedom, not imperialist domination. Later generations would look back and see the war as a pointless squandering of human life on an immense scale. In August 1914 it did not seem pointless at all. Workers were ready to fight – and die – for their country alongside their compatriots and Allies in what they saw as a righteous war of self-defence against aggression from foreign enemies. As army conscripts they had been indoctrinated in patriotism and discipline. They now turned out to be patriots first, socialists second.

In Germany defence against the forces of the detested Tsarist autocracy motivated and united socialists. The Social Democrats had staged big anti-war rallies in German cities, attended in all by an estimated half a million peace-demonstrators, in the last days of July. They were nevertheless anxious to emphasize that workers were ready to defend the Fatherland in its hour of need. That need was a 'war against Tsarism'. When Germany declared war following Russian mobilization, the mood switched abruptly to one of patriotic defence. German-speaking socialists in Austria backed the war for the same reason. Russian socialists, too, ignoring the Bolshevik anti-war stance, rallied round the cause of defence of 'Mother Russia' against Germans viewed as 'trampling on all the rules of humanity'. Strikes were halted, pacifists and internationalists forced into exile. French socialists felt the same about defence of the *patrie* against invasion by the hated Germans. The British Labour Party also accepted that the war had to be fought till Germany was defeated.

Newspapers in every country whipped up anti-foreigner hysteria. Some people, to their credit, resisted it. But vivid imagination, inspired by the media, conjured up spies and fifth columnists everywhere. Anyone with a foreign accent or name was at risk. Those whose Germanic accent betrayed that they were from Alsace could find themselves attacked by Frenchmen. Two women overheard speaking French in Munich had to be rescued by the police. Patriotic mobs in St Petersburg wrecked the German embassy and looted German shops. The Tsar changed the name of the Russian capital to Petrograd in response to the frenzy. St Petersburg sounded too German.

Over a quarter of a million men rushed to volunteer in Germany in the first days of August – an impressive number given that almost the entire male population was covered by conscription, which exempted only persons under seventeen or over fifty years of age. In Britain, the only major power without conscription, 300,000 men volunteered for service in August, another 450,000 in September 1914. Many work-mates and neighbours in industrial towns and cities joined up together, and were formed into 'Pals battalions'. Social pressure to enlist was intense. Even so, as in other countries, and when every qualification has been made, the widespread enthusiasm was unmistakable and opposition minimal. At its outset, this was a popular war.

In each belligerent country, soldiers departing for the front were waved off from train stations by cheering crowds. The tearful farewells of mothers, wives and children were accompanied by patriotic songs and heady expressions of swift victory and early reunion. But many, perhaps most, of those reservists going off to fight, whatever outward show they put on for their families and friends, were leaving their homes, farms, offices and workplaces with some reluctance, and with some apprehension. They were consoling themselves, as well as their loved ones, with the dream that it would 'all be over by Christmas'. Few were as clear-sighted in their forebodings as the Austrian politician and historian Josef Redlich, as he watched thousands of reservists board trains for the front in Vienna's north station on 3 August 1914: 'The weeping mothers, wives and brides: what misery awaits them.'

Mobilization followed railway timetables. The Germans had 11,000 trains, the French 7,000, timetabled to take their troops to the front. Horses too – enormous numbers of them – had to be ferried to the fighting lines. The Austrians, Germans and Russians between them mobilized close to 2.5 million horses, the British and French hundreds of thousands more. In their dependence on horsepower, the armies of 1914 had changed little from Napoleon's time.

Uniforms had meanwhile become mostly drab khaki or grey. But the French went to war still wearing the bright blue tunics, red trousers and red-and-blue hats that belonged to an earlier age. And no soldier's kitbag in August 1914 included a protective steel helmet – issued to French and British soldiers only in 1915, to German troops the follow-ing year – or a gas mask, soon to be a necessary, if inadequate, protection against a new and deadly weapon.

The armies that went to war in 1914 were nineteenth-century armies. They were about to fight a twentieth-century war.

2

The Great Disaster

Silent crowds of people ... The regiments march past with their bands; remember that all these men are on their way to the slaughter.

Diary of Michel Corday,
a civil servant, Paris (14 July 1915)

After August 1914 nothing could be the same again. The new century was already fourteen years old. But the outbreak of what soon came to be known as 'the Great War' marked the real beginning of Europe's Twentieth Century. The years between the calendar date that registered the start of the century and the slide into calamitous war belonged to an earlier era. What came after August 1914 was the start of a new, more terrible, age.

A TRAGEDY UNFOLDS

Two years before the war, a Hamburg schoolteacher and anti-war writer, Wilhelm Lamszus, had grimly portrayed the horror and brutality of the well-oiled killing machines that would produce death on an unheard-of scale in a coming war in his novel entitled *Das Menschenschlachthaus (The Human Slaughterhouse)*. It was a tragically apt prophecy. Eight years later, Ernst Jünger, a passionately committed German officer who had served enthusiastically and with great courage as a troop leader at the front throughout almost the entire war, called his best-seller, one of the most extraordinary literary works on

44

the First World War, *In Stahlgewittern* (*In Storms of Steel*). He could have found no more appropriate title for what confronted the soldiers of Europe's countries at war over the next four years.

Both literary works, from before and after the catastrophic conflict, capture aspects of the war's essential character. More than any previous war, this was a war of industrialized mass slaughter. Human flesh stood against killing machines. Facing soldiers were heavy artillery, machine guns, quick-firing rifles, trench mortars, high explosives, grenades, flamethrowers and poison gas. Modern weapons deployed in ever greater numbers inflicted impersonalized death and destruction on an unprecedented scale. The colossal loss of human life was taken on board in the planning of massive offensives. Artillery and shrapnel were the most frequent agents of death on the battlefield, but countless thousands died of wounds and disease contracted through the atrocious battlefield conditions.

War as the driver of technological change introduced novel weaponry and methods of mass killing that marked the face of the future. Poison gas came into wide use from 1915 onwards after the Germans had deployed it in the spring of that year during the attack on Allied positions near Ypres. Tanks made their debut on the Somme as part of the British offensive in 1916 and by 1918 were being used in major battlefield formations. Submarines became from 1915 onwards a significant weapon in the German campaign against Allied shipping and changed the nature of the war at sea. Not least, rapid development of aircraft technology exposed civilians of towns and cities as well as fighting forces at the fronts to the terrifying prospect of aerial bombardment, of which the bombs dropped on Liège in Belgium by a German Zeppelin airship as early as 6 August 1914 were a foretaste. In their exposure to bombing, and in many other ways, civilians would from now on be incorporated in the war effort as never before, both in working for the war effort and as enemy targets. War propaganda used the mass media to instil hatred of entire peoples. Belligerent states mobilized their populations in new ways. War was becoming total. The French press coined the term 'la guerre totale' – total war – in 1917 to capture the fact that front and homeland were bound together in the war effort.

Moreover, though Europe was its epicentre, the war was for the first time a truly global conflict, affecting every continent. In part this reflected the global empires of Britain, especially, and France. Both mobilized their empires for war. The British dominions of Australia, Canada, New Zealand and South Africa entered the war in support of Britain in August 1914. Africans and Indians were enlisted to fight in a European cause, with high death rates. One million Indians fought on the Allied side, many of them in Africa and the Middle East. France enlisted over 600,000 men from its colonies, mainly in west and north Africa. Over 2 million Africans served as soldiers and labourers. Around 10 per cent of them did not survive. The death rate among labourers – deployed in huge numbers in east Africa to carry heavy supplies – was about twice that level, higher than the death rate for British soldiers during the war.

Like most wars, this one proved easier to start than to stop. Instead of being home for Christmas, as they had told their loved ones (and themselves) they would be, over a quarter of a million French soldiers by then lay dead. Total casualties (dead, wounded and captured) had gone beyond 450,000 already by the end of November. British losses by then were 90,000, more than had initially been recruited to fight. Austro-Hungarian casualties numbered over 300,000 in the very first battles, against the Russians in Galicia in August and September, and half a million men overall within the first five months of the war on the eastern front. Germany had lost 800,000 men by the end of the year, 116,000 of them killed (more than four times its total dead in the Franco-Prussian War of 1870–71). Russian losses in the first phase of the war were the highest of all. In the first nine months Russia lost just short of 2 million men, 764,000 of them captured. The casualties of the belligerent forces were higher in 1914, relative to the size of the armies, than at any other time of the war.

The inclusion of the civilian population in the killing, as the Germans attacked through Belgium, began immediately. Over six thousand civilians – including women and children – were killed, brutally maltreated or deported as German troops passed through Belgium in the first weeks of the war. German military training had instilled in soldiers a paranoid fear of guerrilla warfare. The soldiers, often consumed by hatred, viewed the civilians as collectively to blame for supposed (and mainly imaginary) actions of snipers or for incidents in which 'friendly fire' was mistaken for enemy attacks from behind. The collective 'punishment' was inflicted even when the soldiers knew that their victims were innocent.

When, at the crucial battle of the Marne, fought on 6–9 September, the French halted the German advance little over 50 kilometres from Paris, the entire strategy for rapid victory based on the Schlieffen Plan (by which the Germans had hoped swiftly to defeat the French before turning on the Russians) had failed. In the west, the time for swift offensives was over. Defence was the order of the day. Troops on both sides dug in and started to construct trenches – at first primitive, later becoming far more elaborate defensive formations. Before long these ran in an almost unbroken line from the Channel coast to the Swiss borders. Vast numbers of troops had to adjust to an unspeakable existence in the trenches – vermin-ridden quagmires of mud, built in zig-zagging rows, fronted by big reels of barbed wire, with adjunct trenches leading back to supply depots and field hospitals. By the end of September the stalemate on the western front that would last a further four long years, until 1918, was in place.

The immense early losses did not persuade any of the belligerent powers to try to end the war. They all had huge reserves of men to fall back upon. Since strategic thinking in essence on all sides amounted to wearing the enemy down until it was no longer able to fight, and since the main way to achieve this attritional end entailed pouring ever more manpower onto the battlefields to undertake ever greater offensives against well-entrenched defensive lines, the colossal bloodletting was set to continue indefinitely.

In the east, where the war, over a much longer and less densely populated front, never became so immobilized as on the western front, the situation had developed in more promising fashion for the Central Powers. Under the command of General Paul von Hindenburg, brought out of retirement and backed by an able, if sometimes impetuous, Chief of Staff of the Eighth Army, Major General Erich Ludendorff, in late August the Germans inflicted a heavy defeat on the Russian Second Army near Tannenberg in East Prussia. Germans were fighting on home soil here, repelling a Russian incursion. What they saw of Russian devastation during the fortnight's occupation of part of East Prussia confirmed existing anti-Russian prejudice and contributed to the ferocity of the fighting. Russian losses were high – almost 100,000 in all, 50,000 dead or wounded, another 50,000 taken prisoner. Only a short time later, between 8 and 15 September, in the battle of the Masurian Lakes, the Russians lost a further 100,000 men, 30,000 of them taken prisoner. Farther south, facing the Austrians, they had greater success in their attack on Galicia. The Austrians had found themselves overwhelmed by far larger Russian forces by 3 September, suffering huge losses and being forced into a humiliating retreat.

As with the Germans in Belgium, the belief – largely misplaced – that civilians were participating in attacks on troops fed the brutality that accompanied the Russian occupation of Galicia. Jews – Galicia had a Jewish population of almost a million – were particularly singled out. Cossacks were at the forefront of much of the violence. Large numbers of Jews, anticipating their plight, fled as the Russians advanced. Pogroms perpetrated by the invaders began as early as mid-August. Hundreds of Jews were killed as the occupiers' violence escalated. Robbery and rape were commonplace. Jewish villages were burnt down. Over a thousand Jews were taken hostage by the Russian army and released only on payment by extortion. Jewish property was confiscated. Up to 50,000 Jews – and as many non-Jews – were deported to Russia in the summer of 1915, many of them ending up in Siberia or Turkestan.

The Austrians had to endure yet another embarrassing defeat in the early weeks of the war, and this time not at the hands of another 'great power', but inflicted by the very country that had been at the core of the crisis that had spilled over into European war: Serbia. The campaign to 'chastise' Serbia for the assassination of Archduke Franz Ferdinand had been all but forgotten by the other belligerent powers by the time Austrian troops belatedly launched their infantry offensive on 12 August 1914. The 'punitive expedition' was not expected to last long. And at first it looked as if the Austrians would soon be entering Belgrade. But a counter-offensive by poorly armed but highly motivated Serbs managed after three days of ferocious combat to force the Austrians back. Heavy casualties were registered on both sides. Up to 10,000 Austrians were killed, three times that number wounded. Serbian casualties numbered 3,000–5,000 dead and

15,000 wounded. An exaggerated fear of snipers and of a hostile civilian population prepared to engage in guerrilla warfare against the troops prompted the Austrians to act with notable brutality. The number of civilian victims – most of them summarily executed – is estimated at around 3,500.

The war was set to widen. On 29 October Turkish ships, without provocation, attacked Russian naval bases in the Black Sea. When the Russians responded by declaring war on Turkey in early November, Turkish troops invaded Russia through the Caucasus, but by the end of the year were forced back. The defeat cost them at least 75,000 men, dead as much from disease and cold as through Russian arms. But the Turks enjoyed a major triumph the following year, 1915. This was in repelling an ill-fated, badly planned, ineptly executed attempt by the Allies, instigated by Winston Churchill as First Lord of the Admiralty (in effect, minister for the British Navy), to invade Turkey by landing a large force at Gallipoli in the Dardanelles in April of that year. Almost half a million Allied soldiers – including Indian, Australian, New Zealand, French and Senegalese troops – took part in the Gallipoli campaign. Turkish defence of the homeland, which established the heroic reputation of its commander, Mustapha Kemal Pasha (later better known as Atatürk), was ferocious and the heavily fortified shore proved impenetrable. For the Allies, it was an unmitigated disaster. By December, when they were forced to abort the operation and begin evacuation, their casualties were close to a quarter of a million, with around 50,000 dead (many of disease). The Turks lost a similar number.

The crisis faced by Turkey in 1915 motivated the worst atrocities during the First World War, in a region where horrific massacres built on competing territorial claims, ethnic conflict and religious antagonism between Muslim Turks and Kurds and Christian Armenians in eastern Anatolia had already been a dire part of pre-war history. The radical nationalist leadership, in control of Turkish domestic policy since a coup d'état in 1913, was already before the war seeking greater ethnic and religious homogeneity within Turkey. The large Armenian minority obviously posed an obstacle to this. War between the Ottoman and Russian empires had then sharply intensified tensions in the border regions of Anatolia and the Caucasus. Tension between Turks and Armenians in particular now reached near fever pitch.

Armenians, straddling the Russian border and hoping to free themselves from Turkish rule, mainly sympathized with Russia. They saw the war as the dawning of their day. They were encouraged by the Russians, and through spies in St Petersburg the Turks were aware of plans to provoke an Armenian uprising. This spelled danger to the Turks, not least because Armenians lived in a region of vital strategic importance. Turkish leaders saw them as collaborators with their enemies and as a threat to their war plans. The Armenians, beset by violent localized attacks, viewed collaboration with Russia as their best defence against worse massacres.

But when an Armenian rebellion began in the city of Van in mid-April 1915, accompanied by atrocities on all sides, by Armenians, Turks and Kurds, no help from the Russians was forthcoming. The Armenians were on their own. The Turks, faced with the western Allies attacking through the Dardanelles, paranoid at the threat posed by the Russians through the Caucasus, and viewing the Armenian minority as a Russian Trojan Horse, were ready to inflict savage reprisals. And the war had provided the opportunity to pursue the ideological goal of ethnic homogenization. Deportations began soon after the uprising, rapidly escalating in scale and accompanying violence. Within weeks, the Turkish leadership had ordered the entire Armenian population of eastern Anatolia – around a million and a half – to be deported to the heart of the Syrian desert. Many died from disease or maltreatment during deportation or in camps when they arrived. Many more died in horrific massacres, part of a terrible murderous programme, backed by Turkish leaders. Estimates of the numbers of Armenian dead range between 600,000 and over a million.

Despite increasing Allied superiority to the German army in troop numbers on the western front, an end to the stalemate was in the meantime nowhere in sight. The German Chief of the General Staff, Erich von Falkenhayn (who had replaced Moltke the previous September) set his hopes, therefore, on the east. Forcing the Russians to come to terms, he thought, was the key to winning the war in the west.

In the east, however, Germany had to cope with the ever more apparent military weakness of its main ally, Austria-Hungary. During a disastrous Austrian offensive in the depth of winter 1914–15 in the mountainous heights of the Carpathians some 800,000, including the

last well-trained reserves, were lost. Many froze to death or succumbed to illness. Tens of thousands went into captivity. Desertion
rates rose. The Central Powers were depending ever more on German
military strength, in both east and west.

For Austria the situation worsened still further when on 23 May
1915 Italy joined the war on the side of the British, French and Russian Entente, opening up a southern front. Remarkably, weakened
though they had become, the Austro-Hungarians held out well against
the Italians. The Germans were meanwhile inflicting serious defeats
on the Russians, in February in the Masurian Lake district of East
Prussia (with Russian losses of 92,000 men), then in spring and summer in Poland. Galicia was wrested from the Russians in June, most
of the remainder of Congress Poland (formerly ruled by Russia) in
July and August. Warsaw itself fell to the Germans on 4 August 1915.
When the great summer offensive eventually ran out of steam, the
Germans had also conquered the Courland (the coastal part of western Latvia) and Lithuania. Between May and September the Tsarist
forces suffered astounding losses of over 2 million men, more than
900,000 of them captured.

In the autumn the Central Powers also strengthened their position
in the Balkans. Serbia, the initial source of the conflict, was finally
invaded by German and Austro-Hungarian divisions in early October.
Bulgaria, which had committed itself to the war on the side of the
Central Powers a month earlier, also sent forces to join the Serbian
campaign. By the beginning of November, Serbia was under the control of the Central Powers. A land route for weapons supplies to the
Ottoman Empire had been gained. With Russia seriously weakened,
the Balkans under control and even the enfeebled Austrians holding
the Italians at bay in the south, Germany was now in a substantially
better position than had been the case a year earlier to try to force
victory in the west. Still, time did not favour the Germans. A push for
victory in the west could not wait long.

Falkenhayn's plan was to break the French by a massive assault on
Verdun, the centre of a big network of fortresses on the Meuse, about
200 kilometres east of Paris. To inflict a devastating defeat on the
French at Verdun, he thought, would be a major step towards overall
victory in the west. Verdun was under intense siege from February to

July 1916, and further heavy fighting continued until December. For the French, the defence of Verdun became the symbol of the fight for France itself. Losses were enormous: over 700,000 men – 377,000 French (162,000 dead) and 337,000 German (143,000 dead). But there was no German breakthrough. For the French, their country was saved. For the Germans, the huge losses had been for nothing. And by mid-July the scene of the greatest carnage had already shifted to the Somme.

Here, British and Dominion troops formed the mainstay of the 'big push'. If Verdun was seen later to symbolize the horror of the war for the French, the Somme acquired equally symbolic status in British memory. But there was a difference. Verdun could be remembered as a mighty but necessary patriotic sacrifice to save France. British and Dominion troops at the Somme were not fighting to stave off an attack on their homeland. To many, it was probably unclear just what they were fighting for. The plan of the offensive was largely the work of General (later Field Marshal) Sir Douglas Haig, since December 1915 the British commander-in-chief. The aim of the offensive had, in fact, been altered from its original conception. Initially foreseen as a mainly French-led offensive intended to produce a decisive break-through, it had been converted into a chiefly British-led attack to relieve the pressure on the French at Verdun. The Germans, it was hoped, would be worn down and significantly weakened. The crucial drive for victory would, however, have to wait. Whatever patriotic rallying-cries and morale-boosting addresses the troops about to go 'over the top' on the Somme heard from their officers, for most of them strategic aims were most likely less important than survival. But tens of thousands would not survive even the first day of the offensive. The Somme came for the British to symbolize the pointlessness of such immense loss of life.

After an intensive heavy bombardment lasting over a week, on 1 July 1916, the very first day of the battle, the British and Dominion forces lost 57,470 men, including 19,240 dead and 35,493 wounded. It was the most catastrophic single day in British military history. That it might bring the great breakthrough was swiftly revealed as a costly delusion. When the fighting on the Somme petered out towards the end of November in rain, sleet, snow and mud, British and Dominion troops had gained a strip of about 10 kilometres along a

35-kilometre stretch of the front, and the French about twice as much territory. For that, over a million men had been killed or wounded. British and Dominion casualties had amounted to 419,654 men (127,751 of them killed), while French casualties totalled 204,353 and German some 465,000. In the horrendous scale of its losses, and for so little, the Somme was the most terrible battle on the western front during the First World War.

A third huge offensive that year, this time on the eastern front, was named after a Russian general, Aleksey Alekseyevich Brusilov. It was a bold strike that began on 4 June 1916 against Austrian positions on a wide sector of the southern front between the Pripet Marches (straddling southern Belarus and northern Ukraine) and Romania. Brusilov's immediate and massive success owed something to his careful preparations. It owed still more to Austrian ineptitude, abetted by poor morale. Within two days, the Austro-Hungarian front was in a state of collapse. Reinforcements were rushed back from the offensive that had been opened up in northern Italy. German reserves, too, were brought in to head off a total debacle. But by the end of September the Central Powers had been pushed back some 90 kilometres on a broad front. The Austro-Hungarians had by then lost 750,000 men, 380,000 of them captured. German losses were also huge, around 250,000. Yet the Brusilov Offensive, though triumphant for the Russians, had also been at an enormous cost, with losses approaching half a million men during the first ten days, and around a million overall. The jubilation in Russia at the great victory hid the widening cracks behind the facade. Russia, as events were soon to prove, was nearing the end even faster than Austria-Hungary.

An immediate outcome of the Brusilov Offensive was to bring Romania into the war on 27 August on the side of the Entente. The Romanians were hoping for big gains at the expense of Hungary after what they took to be the increasingly certain defeat of the Central Powers. Such hopes were rapidly dashed when the Central Powers dispatched an army, under German leadership, which drove back the Romanians from the advances they had made. By the beginning of 1917, the Central Powers had occupied Bucharest and much of Romania, including the strategically important Ploesti oilfields.

Successes in the east were, however, no compensation to the

German leadership for their failure to make the decisive breakthrough in the west. In August Falkenhayn had paid the price for Verdun, when he was dismissed as Chief of Staff and replaced by the hero of Tannenberg, Field Marshal (as he now was) Hindenburg, a popular military leader in an increasingly unpopular war. His right-hand man, General Ludendorff, now appointed First Quartermaster General, soon turned into the actual driving-force of the new High Command of the Army.

This was the beginning of what quickly became tantamount to a military dictatorship, as Hindenburg and Ludendorff intervened ever more directly in government. One indication of this was the aim to end the war through unrestricted submarine attacks on Allied shipping, a strategy imposed over the opposition of the civilian government. The problem of the tightening Allied blockade had remained unresolved. But the German surface fleet had been able to do little about it. For all the money poured into the building of huge battle fleets both by the British and the Germans before the war, the sole major engagement at sea, the battle of Jutland on 31 May 1916, had proved inconclusive. The Germans sank more ships – fourteen, compared with eleven that they lost – and had fewer casualties (3,058 to 6,768 on the British side). But the losses crippled the smaller German fleet for months, effectively ruling out its deployment for the rest of the war, whereas the British fleet was capable of continuing the blockade. Attention, therefore, turned increasingly to the prospect of extending the use of U-boats not only to end the blockade, but to bring about a decisive shift in war fortunes. The German naval leadership reckoned that U-boats could sink 600,000 tons of shipping a month – a rate that would force Britain to a state of collapse within five months, before the USA could make any difference to the outcome of the war. But if the U-boat war did not succeed, and America joined the conflict, the prospects for Germany would significantly worsen.

The gamble was taken. From 1 February 1917, Germany began unrestricted submarine warfare. Allied and neutral shipping in British waters could now be attacked without warning. It was a catastrophic mistake. The US President, Woodrow Wilson, looking to cement American leadership in the post-war world, had up to this point wanted 'peace without victory' and had avoided committing his country to supporting one side or the other in the destructive European conflict. The German decision to unleash the U-boats abruptly terminated such a strategy. Within two days, Wilson broke off diplomatic relations with Germany. The inevitable sinking of American ships by U-boats helped to prompt the US declaration of war on Germany on 6 April 1917 (though it would be spring 1918 before the American Expeditionary Force was in a position to join the fighting on the western front). But only in April and June 1917 did the U-boats sink the required monthly tonnage, which in any event was based upon optimistic notions of British vulnerability. The U-boat war proved a failure. Even worse, Germany had a new and powerful enemy in the Americans.

The stalemate on the western front continued during 1917. The Germans, their manpower and resources severely stretched, settled temporarily for defending what they held. In the spring they withdrew to a shorter, more easily defendable new position. They called it the *Siegfried-Stellung*; for the Allies it was the Hindenburg Line. The shortened line had the additional advantage that it released about twenty German divisions. The Germans were as a result in an improved position to fend off the new Allied offensives that they knew were coming.

The first of the offensives, at Arras on 9 April, carried out in driving rain, sleet and snow, led to the usual costly attritional fighting for no further territorial gain. Losses numbered 150,000 Allied and 100,000 German soldiers. Arras was meant to weaken German defences for the major French offensive on the Chemin des Dames, a ridge running along the Aisne valley, east of Soissons and west of Rheims. This offensive was led by the new, assertive Chief of Staff, General Georges Robert Nivelle, appointed in December 1916 to replace General Joseph Joffre. But the Germans had gained intelligence of the forthcoming attack and heavy defences were in place. Nivelle's offensive was a disaster. Five days after it started on 16 April, with 130,000 casualties (29,000 of them dead) and no breakthrough, it was abandoned. On 29 April Nivelle was dismissed and replaced by General Philippe Pétain, the hero of Verdun.

Undeterred by this calamity, which confirmed his poor view of French fighting morale, and not discouraged by his own costly failure on the Somme the previous summer, Field Marshal Sir Douglas Haig still believed he could achieve a decisive breakthrough with a big offensive near Ypres in the summer of 1917. The aim was a drive through Flanders to eliminate the U-boat bases on the Belgian coast. This goal never came remotely close to realization. Instead, Haig's men became glued into the Flemish mud. The horrors of the third battle of Ypres, which to the British bears the single name 'Passchendaele' (after the village on a slight ridge a few kilometres east of Ypres), rivalled in notoriety those of the Somme.

The offensive, beginning on 31 July, was carried out in summer and autumn deluges of rain that, on low-lying ground already churned up by the preceding massive artillery barrage, turned the terrain into frequently waist-deep, glutinous mud swamps. When the offensive was finally called off, soon after the pitiful ruins of the village of Passchendaele were at last taken on 6 November (the village with the poignant name was to be evacuated again and regained by the Germans within five months), the British and Dominion forces had lost 275,000 men (70,000 of them dead), the Germans 217,000. For such losses the Allies had (temporarily) gained a few kilometres.

When the final offensive of the year in the west took place, at Cambrai, south-east of Arras, in November – partly an attempt at compensation for the failure at Ypres – it followed a familiar pattern. Early territorial gains by the Allies – 7 kilometres along a 15-kilometre stretch – could not be held. Losses amounted to 45,000 men on the British side, 41,000 on the German. Reserves that might have helped the Allies exploit the early German disarray were lacking, consumed as they had been in the muds of the Ypres salient. The battle of Cambrai did, however, offer a glimpse into the future. Following good air reconnaissance (another new development), British tanks – over 300 of them – for the first time attacked en masse in close formation, followed by infantry and artillery. They had been nearly useless in the morass of Passchendaele. On drier, firmer ground they here inaugurated a new method of attack. For the time being, the lumbering tanks could still be countered by heavy artillery. But their time would come.

If there was still military stalemate in the west, what was starting to alter was the sustainability of the conflict. War-weariness was palpable. For all the grumbling among troops, discipline in the British military nevertheless was upheld. Desertion rates and poor morale were worrying for the French government, however, even before some 40,000 French troops mutinied against Nivelle's orders – a mutiny quelled only when Pétain (after Nivelle's dismissal) addressed most of the soldiers' grievances.

For all the signs of mounting unrest, no government felt able to seek less than favourable peace terms to justify the horrendous losses suffered. With the war still at an impasse, these were unlikely to be forthcoming. Austria-Hungary was particularly keen to find an exit route. The new Emperor Karl I (successor to Franz Joseph, who had died in November 1916) had made half-hearted overtures towards peace to the American President, Woodrow Wilson, in December. But the German High Command had no intention of giving up Belgium, or other occupied territory. A peace through concessions was out of the question. Victory, whatever the cost, was still the goal. The German army remained ready to fight. Reorganization of armaments production, bringing a big increase in munitions output, enabled it to do so. And, just as deep political fissures within a war-weary Germany emerged and demands for peace grew louder, new hope arose – not in the west, but in the east.

In Russia the unrest, swelling for months in the wake of enormous losses at the front and ever worsening, deep privation at home, exploded into revolution in March 1917 (February in the old Russian calendar). The Tsar was toppled. The new Provisional Government that took office in such conditions of crisis felt it had to fight on, despite the evident war-weariness of the troops, to secure a 'peace without defeat'. Its Minister of War (later head of government), Alexander Kerensky, even gave his name to an ill-fated offensive in July across a long front in Galicia and Bukovina. This took place, however, amid continued political upheaval, gathering opposition to the war at home, and failing morale among the troops as revolutionary fervour filtered outwards from Petrograd to soldiers at the front. Following the failure of the Kerensky Offensive, weakened Russian forces were in no position to counter a German attack on Riga in September 1917 (August in the old calendar). The last Russo-German battle of the war ended with Riga under German occupation. By November (October in the old calendar) the Provisional Government, too, had fallen in a second revolution that brought the Bolsheviks to power. This would soon dramatically change the political constellation of Europe. More immediately, it promised to change war fortunes, for on 20 December 1917, five days after concluding an armistice with the Germans, the new Bolshevik leadership began the painful process of negotiating a peace treaty with Germany.

This formed the backcloth to President Woodrow Wilson's declaration on 8 January 1918 of his Fourteen Points – an idealistic outline of what he thought might bring an end to the war and serve as the basis for a durable peace in Europe. With the end to Russian involvement in the war imminent, Wilson saw an opportunity to press for an overall conclusion of hostilities and to offer the basis for a general negotiation of peace terms. Among his proposals were removal of economic barriers to free trade; disarmament; 'adjustment' (as he vaguely put it) of colonial claims; evacuation of occupied territories (including Russia, which was offered a 'sincere welcome into the society of free nations under institutions of her own choosing', and 'assistance also of every kind that she may need'); readjustment of Italy's borders 'along clearly recognisable lines of nationality'; opportunity for the 'autonomous development' of the peoples of the Austro-Hungarian and Ottoman empires; creation of an independent Polish state; and the association of nations to guarantee 'political independence and territorial integrity'. For all its apparent precision, much of Wilson's declaration was inevitably left open-ended, imprecise and subject to differing interpretation or dispute. The terms 'self-determination' and 'democracy' did not appear in the Fourteen Points. Nonetheless, they both soon came to be viewed as the cornerstone of the liberal vision that Wilson was advancing, and an encouragement for nationalist aspirations in Europe. For the immediate future, however, Wilson's Fourteen Points produced no moves to end the war in the west. And in the east, they played no part in the negotiations under way between the Bolsheviks and the Central Powers.

When these were concluded on 3 March 1918 at Brest-Litovsk (in today's Belarus), which had been German army headquarters in the east, the terms imposed on the powerless Soviet government amounted to some of the most punitive and humiliating in modern history. They were, however, among the most short-lived, for the Treaty of Brest-

Litovsk was annulled in November at the general Armistice that ended the Great War. The Baltic, Ukraine, the Caucasus and what had been Russian Poland were stripped from Russia under the terms of the treaty – a loss of a third of its population, and a greater proportion of its industry, agricultural production and natural resources of oil, iron and coal. The Caucasus fell to the Turks, while much of eastern Europe, including the Baltic, came henceforth under German influence (though Ukraine was in no position to provide the levels of grain supplies desperately needed both in Germany and Austria-Hungary).

The subsequent and almost equally savage dismemberment of Romania in May, in the Treaty of Bucharest signed between Romania on the one hand and Austria-Hungary, Germany, Bulgaria and the Ottoman Empire on the other, provided further major territorial gains for the Central Powers. If in this case the amputated territory went to Germany's allies, Austria-Hungary and Bulgaria (with minor gains to the Ottomans), the real winner was again, plainly, Germany itself, whose sphere of domination now stretched over most of central, eastern and southern Europe. It was to be of short duration. More than that, future trouble on a grand scale was in store across all these multi-ethnic regions, whose territories were treated like pieces on a chessboard.

The unexpectedly swift easing of the military situation in the east offered improved prospects for Germany in the west. The consequences would reveal themselves in 1918. More immediately, there was the possibility of intervention to clear up the inconclusive, but troublesome, Italian front. Since 1915, when they joined the war on the side of the Entente, the Italians had been battling more or less continuously with the Austro-Hungarian army, along the Isonzo River, running from the Alps to the Adriatic, near Trieste. In October 1917 the Germans sent down reinforcements to help the Austrians. The twelfth, and decisive, battle of Isonzo (which the Italians called the battle of Caporetto) began on 24 October. The Italians were routed and within a month had been relentlessly driven back around 80 kilometres. The Italian army, made up of conscripts – more than half of them peasants or agricultural workers from southern Italy – predominantly in the front-line infantry, simply had no stomach for the fight. They were badly led, ill-equipped and inadequately fed. By

10 November 1917, Italian losses were no fewer than 305,000. The casualty rate of dead (10,000) and wounded (30,000) was relatively low. The vast majority (265,000) had deserted or allowed themselves to be captured. It was little wonder that Caporetto became a day of infamy in Italian history.

Numerical superiority of men and weaponry on the western front had until now always lain with the Allies. And German losses had been far higher on the western than the eastern front. But the elimination of Russia from the war had freed no fewer than forty-four German divisions to be transferred to the west. Ludendorff, in effect running Germany, saw the chance of a conclusive victory in the west through a massive spring offensive in 1918, code-named Operation Michael, centred more or less on the line of the Somme, before the Americans could enter the fighting. The biggest artillery bombardment of the war, from 6,600 guns, began the offensive on 21 March. The shocked and outnumbered Allied troops were pushed back nearly 40 miles almost to Amiens. But there was no collapse. And the German infantry could make only slow progress, especially in the northern part of the front. Casualties were very high. The Germans lost almost 40,000 men, a quarter of them killed, on the first day of the offensive. British losses were only marginally lower. Taking German and Allied losses together, the bloodletting was the worst in a single day of the war, worse even than on the first day of the Somme. By the time the offensive was halted on 5 April, total German losses, by now irreplaceable, amounted to 239,000 men. The British and French had between them lost 338,000 men – nearly a quarter of them taken prisoner. The overall losses within two weeks matched those at Verdun over a period of five months.

This marked the beginning of the end for Germany. A follow-up offensive in April, in Flanders, aimed at capturing the Belgian ports, again ran out of steam after early German successes. Despite the losses (a further 150,000 men) the Allies could still find reserves. But the Germans were down to their last reserves, dredged up for final attacks in the spring and summer on old fighting territory – the Chemin des Dames once more, as far as the Marne (where the first great battle of the war had taken place). By June 1918 American troops had joined Allied ranks – and were arriving at the rate of 200,000 a month. A big

French counter-attack on the Marne, involving hundreds of Renault tanks backed by air cover, then swiftly mopped up 30,000 German prisoners. German morale started to crack, and before long it was collapsing. The gains in the March offensive were wiped out in Allied advances in late August and September. By early October the Allies were over the heavily fortified Hindenburg Line and the Germans were in full retreat. Germany was by now militarily as good as finished – not that the population at home was aware that defeat was imminent, since the worst had been concealed from it by propaganda that had continued to campaign for peace only after victory.

Hindenburg and Ludendorff recognized the writing on the wall. They were determined that peace should be negotiated before the German army collapsed and complete military defeat became obvious. The army's (and their own) standing in the state was at stake. They began to manoeuvre to extricate themselves from blame for the impending defeat and shift the responsibility for negotiations onto those political forces – predominantly the socialist Left – that had long been demanding parliamentary democracy. On 1 October, informing his staff officers that the war could no longer be won, Ludendorff told them: 'I have asked His Majesty [the Kaiser] now to incorporate those in government whom we have to thank for our situation. We will now see these gentlemen entering office. They must conclude the necessary peace. They have to swallow the soup they've cooked up for us.' It was the beginning of what would turn into the legend, with lasting baleful impact after the war, that the German army had been undefeated in the field, that the war effort had been 'stabbed in the back' by socialist forces fomenting unrest at home.

Germany's allies were meanwhile giving up, driven to do so by mass desertions from the army, growing revolutionary feeling and military defeat, together with the increasingly tangible prospect of peace. Bulgaria, faced with demoralizing defeat as Allied troops advanced unstoppably from the south-west, wracked by widespread desertions from the army, and amid growing revolutionary demands from soldiers' and workers' councils that had been established in a number of provincial towns and cities, signed an armistice with the Allies on 30 September. The last rites were being administered to the collapsing Ottoman Empire by the following month. Military defeats, an ignominious withdrawal from the Caucasus, and soldiers deserting in droves, accompanied by economic calamity and increasing lawlessness at home, led to Turkey signing an armistice with the Allies on 31 October.

In the early days of November, with the armies of the Central Powers in complete disarray and their governments in turmoil, it was obvious that the end of the great conflagration was fast approaching. When the Kaiser's regime fell on 9 November and the new German government indicated its readiness to accept President Wilson's Fourteen Points as the basis for peace negotiations, the war could at last be stopped. On 11 November at the headquarters of Marshal Foch, the Supreme Commander of the Allied Armies, in the forest of Compiègne, the Centre Party politician Matthias Erzberger, at the head of a German delegation, put his signature to the Armistice that finally put an end to the fighting. The guns fell silent at the eleventh hour of the eleventh day of the eleventh month.

LIVING THROUGH THE WAR

'You can't possibly imagine this horror. Nobody can, who has not gone through this,' wrote a German infantryman on 2 July 1916, describing the battle of Verdun. Countless others who fought in the First World War's bloodbaths on different fronts doubtless felt much the same way.

It is impossible to generalize about the experiences of the millions of soldiers who had to endure some or all of these four years of hell. Letters to and from the front provide some insights. They are, however, far more plentiful for the western than for the eastern front. And the letters often hid or diluted feelings and attitudes, since they had to pass by censors and, in any case, were frequently anxious not to alarm or upset loved ones reading them back home. Experiences of course also varied enormously. They greatly shaped attitudes towards the war. But these were also influenced by temperament, education, rank, social class, material circumstances, treatment by superiors, political allegiance, prior ideological formation and a myriad of other factors. Contemporary impressions can be amplified by the vast number of post-war recollections and memories gathered from those who had served. Such testimony, however, like any eyewitness accounts produced after the events they are describing – sometimes long after – is subject to the vagaries of memory as well as the influence, perhaps subconscious, of later developments. Post-war literary works, though often moving and offering deep insights, convey later constructed images, however realistic, of what mark the war experience made on the ordinary men and women who had to endure it at the time. So any attempt to summarize what it was like to live through the First World War can at best be only impressionistic.

It is, for instance, difficult to be sure how soldiers were affected psychologically, at the time or later, by living in such close proximity to the constant, cloying presence of death. There are numerous indicators that feelings rapidly became blunted. Little sentiment was elicited by the death of unknown soldiers. 'This indifference is perhaps the best condition for a man to be in in the midst of battle,' noted a French infantryman in the front line at Verdun, as the sight of yet another dead man left him unmoved. 'The long period of overwhelmingly powerful emotions has finally ended with emotion itself dying.' 'I saw some horrific things, but we were so disciplined that we took it all for granted, as though it was normal', was a former British private's retrospective summary.

The death, even of close comrades, seems to have swiftly acquired a matter-of-fact acceptance. 'Several hundred men have already passed through my platoon alone, and at least half of them have ended up on the fields of battle either killed or wounded', a Russian officer of peasant stock noted in his diary in April 1915. 'A year at the front has stopped me from thinking about this.' 'It was one continuous stream of wounded and dead and dying', one private in the British army recalled of the battle of the Somme. 'You had to forget all sentiment. It was a case of getting on with the job.' Another private spoke later of the losses in his unit on the first day on the Somme. 'We had no roll-call after we got back because there was [sic] only about twenty-five left out of eight hundred. There was nothing to count.' A corporal was shockingly frank. 'When I came out of the line, having lost a lot of men, I'm sorry to say that I didn't feel any sadness. The only thing I thought about was that there were less [sic] mouths to feed, and I should get all those men's rations for a fortnight before the rations were cut down.' 'As time went on I became quite callous,' remembered a sergeant from the Army Medical Corps. 'We had to get used to some very awful things.' It is impossible to be sure how representative such views were in the British army, let alone in other forces. But such accounts doubtless spoke for many.

There were, however, more humane sentiments. The Russian commander Brusilov, a strict disciplinarian, driven by a will to victory and conscious of what he saw as his 'hard and bitter task', was not immune to the human misery in a battlefield in Galicia 'piled high with corpses' that he described to his wife in the first month of fighting. 'It weighs terribly on my heart,' he remarked. A letter published in November 1914 in the German miners' newspaper, the *Bergarbeiterzeitung*, noted the horror of the writer at coming across the badly mutilated body of an infantryman. 'There is always this infantry man standing in front of me,' the letter ran, 'without a head and with a bloody lump of flesh on his shoulders instead. I cannot stop picturing this.' The writer noted that the 'sight was so terrible, so horrible, that I couldn't sleep the last two nights'.

Naturally, little pity was shown for enemy dead. 'The enemy is nothing but an obstacle which has to be destroyed', was one statement among many collected by the Institute for Applied Psychology in Berlin. 'We are turning into animals. I feel it in others. I feel it in myself', one French soldier admitted in a letter home in 1915. Not all soldiers were brutalized by their experience of war. But many were. It was brutal, but unemotional killing. Most of it was done by artillery, machine guns, grenades or other lethal weapons from some distance, against faceless enemies. Artillery fire alone was responsible for three-quarters of French casualties between 1914 and 1917. Soldiers commented at the time and later on about the ease of shooting an anonymous and impersonal enemy from a distance. Close fighting – jumping into an enemy trench and stabbing a man with a bayonet, for instance – was much rarer. Only 0.1 per cent of German casualties on the western front in the spring of 1917 arose from hand-to-hand fighting, compared with 76 per cent from artillery fire. For some soldiers close combat demanded that they overcome inhibitions or scruples. Still, it was done. And there were those who relished it. One young British major, who said he did not think much of the future, took it for granted 'that we would massacre the Boche in their front line'. Another British soldier described in his diary in June 1915 how he shot at close quarters a young German, hands in the air and begging for mercy. 'It was a heavenly sight to see him fall forward,' he wrote.

Some, though certainly a minority, saw the war as a cleansing process to destroy what they felt was rotten in their own society. One soldier in the German ranks, who had rejoiced when war was declared, wrote to an acquaintance early in 1915 that the sacrifices at the front would be worthwhile if they left behind a homeland that was 'purer and cleansed of foreignness (*Fremdländerei*)'. The world would soon hear more of this soldier. His name was Adolf Hitler.

National stereotyping of the enemy greatly helped the process of building hatred. It had largely done its job even before the war started. Once the fighting had begun, the stereotyping was greatly reinforced through propaganda at home and at the front. Official propaganda on all sides sought to demonize the enemy and to instil hatred in combat troops and the home population alike. Broadcasting accusations (real or contrived) of atrocities was one device. Stereotypes often worked. Left-wing German troops, highly critical of militarism, hyper-nationalism and the rule of the Kaiser at home, still accepted caricatures of Slavic inferiority and the need for a German civilizing mission to bring culture to the east. German soldiers entering Russia for the first time saw their existing caricatures confirmed. 'Asia, steppe, swamps . . . a godforsaken wasteland of slime', as one officer recalled, and 'without a glimmer of central European *Kultur*'. A German sergeant, given to verse, wrote in February 1918:

> All about my eyes still see the misery,
> Which the disgrace of the Russian army inflicted
> On their own land, on works of nature!
> That, which seemed forever lost, was created anew by –
> The German battalions of *Kultur*!

Propaganda images of Asiatic, backward, uncultured and barbaric Russians would feed into mentalities that would prepare the ground for boundless atrocities in a second great war – though the murderous racial conflation of Bolshevik and Jew was still to come. But hate propaganda in the First World War was not a complete success by any means, certainly on the western front. There was some fraternization in 1914–15 between German and British and French troops – including the Christmas unofficial 'truce' in no-man's-land in 1914 – until officers clamped down on it. Enemy soldiers were sometimes allowed to recover their dead and wounded. There were unofficial short periods of tacit truce resting on unannounced informal mutual understanding, or instances of soldiers on patrol deliberately aiming to miss. And there are indications of mutual respect among ordinary soldiers for the fighting qualities of their enemies together with a sense of common humanity taken up in a slaughter that defied understanding.

It would be as well, even so, not to exaggerate this. While ideological aims, overt or subliminal, that helped to make sense of the mayhem were more prevalent among officers and commanders, especially in the higher ranks, ordinary soldiers were also subjected to the national cultural forces that had shaped them in their education and training. More than that, the killing swiftly developed its own momentum. Soldiers became inured to it. Sometimes they saw it as simply 'kill or be killed'. They largely accepted what they had to do, saw no alternative, and thought above all of getting through it and surviving. 'Life is something good to eat and we chew it in silence with healthy teeth,' noted an Italian trooper in 1917 after surviving a torrid battle in which every second man had been killed or wounded. Grand ideals scarcely figured. 'We're here because we're here because we're here because we're here,' sang cynical British soldiers in the trenches.

Fear, like death, was a constant companion at the front, however much soldiers tried to hide it. The fatalism that naturally went with it was equally omnipresent. Soldiers were of course not always in the front line. Those who were there at any one time, in fact, constituted a minority. But the time spent behind the lines – recuperating, relaxing, recreation (playing football and visiting brothels seem to have been among the more popular pastimes for British troops), along with incessant drilling and training – always came with the thought that the next 'big push' was not far away. As word circulated that it was imminent, the apprehension and fear grew. When the moment arrived, some men were so terrified that they were incontinent. Others exuded confidence – no doubt in many cases to conceal their nerves. A few, often brave men who had been through the horror before were so frightened, sometimes in a state of nervous collapse, that they refused to go 'over the top', and paid the dreadful price of alleged cowardice or desertion at the hands of a firing squad.

Most knew they had no choice but to go through with it, and were fatalistic. Rum, schnapps or vodka, handed out copiously just before the offensive, often helped. 'When I went over, I didn't really think of anything. I just had to go. That was all,' recalled one private in a British regiment. Many accounts show soldiers less fearful of death than of being left badly mutilated. According to a German study into 'The Psychology of Fear in Wartime' published in 1920, 'to imagine being crippled is enough ... to make death seemingly desirable'. Many hoped for what the British called a 'blighty wound', the Germans a 'homeland shot' (*Heimatschuß*) – not crippling or life-threatening, but sufficient to have the soldier sent home, unfit for service. Some inflicted such wounds on themselves – but faced severe punishment along with the pain if they were caught.

Considering what they had to endure, morale on the western front held up surprisingly well. The French mutiny on the Chemin des Dames in 1917 was an exception, though censors looking through soldiers' letters noted signs of wavering morale as the epic battle at Verdun wore on, and desertions rose during the winter of 1916–17. The swift French response to placate the mutineering troops showed how seriously the government had taken the short-lived revolt. Morale was tested again during the big German military push in the spring and summer of 1918. But the French were fighting for their own country. That concentrated minds. When French tanks pushed the Germans back over the Marne in August, and the end was in sight, morale was buoyed anew. The British and Dominion forces also held out to the end with morale largely intact. Morale had been under strain at the German breakthrough in the spring of 1918, but then picked up again as the offensive faltered and reinforcements (not least, troops from the United States) arrived.

Of course, there was no lack in the British army, too, of complaints and grievances about the miserable conditions, poor food, meagre rations, the drilling, physical exertions and high-handed officers. Discipline was tough in all combat forces, ferocious in some (notably the

Russian and Italian armies). Coercion was intensified in all armies during the second half of the war period to try to counter wavering morale. But coercion alone cannot explain the readiness to continue fighting, and in fact could not quell serious and widespread disaffection in most armies towards the end of the war. Where morale held up, more positive forces were at work. Both French and British soldiers for the most part retained a belief in eventual victory and in the righteousness of their cause. Patriotism, defence of their country, continued to offer a positive reason for fighting to French soldiers. It played its part for British troops, too, if a less strong one (since Britain had not been invaded and they were not fighting on British soil). Censors scrutinizing letters from British soldiers saw no decline in the willingness to fight to the end, and little readiness to contemplate a compromise peace.

German morale crumbled only in 1918. For German troops, grievances – exacerbated by greater inequalities between officers and men than in the French or British armies – became increasingly politicized after 1916. Resentment at the discrepancy in pay between officers and men, the sense that officers in the rear echelons were still enjoying 'the good life' while troops at the front were dying in their thousands, anger at poor food and cuts in rations from 1916 onwards, and news from home about rising prices and deteriorating living conditions blended into a mounting belief among soldiers that the sacrifices were being made for nothing but the gain of capitalists and profiteers. There was growing talk in the last months that a revolution would be needed to put right the injustices. Many German soldiers by this time shared the view of the artist and sculptor Käthe Kollwitz, still heartbroken over the loss of her own son Peter in 1914, that the war, which had sent millions to the slaughterhouse, had been no less than a 'terrible swindle'. The demands for peace, socialism and revolution mingled and were voiced increasingly by soldiers at the front in those last weeks as they voted with their feet in a wave of desertions.

On the eastern front, other than in the German army, morale was shakier from a much earlier stage. Soldiers in the Russian, Austro-Hungarian and Italian armies often had from the outset little belief in the 'cause' for which they were said to be fighting. Many Russian recruits, over three-quarters of them from peasant backgrounds and the majority of these illiterate, 'had not the slightest notion of what the war had to do with them', or, apparently, that a country called Germany even existed, complained General Brusilov. Demoralization had set in early. Even after the first defeats in 1914 the Russian censors had reported that 'soldiers have no more confidence in victory'. Shortages of food, clothing and arms – many soldiers at the front were already reported as lacking weapons in 1915 – as well as military setbacks undermined morale. So did the brutal treatment by officers, who were widely hated as representatives of the landlord class and despised for their corruption and preference for creature comforts behind the lines. Increasingly soldiers asked who was to blame for their plight, and found the answer in betrayal. 'Perhaps we'll soon have to admit that our war campaign is lost and, above all, that it has been betrayed', was a view reported by Russian censors already in 1915. Defeatism – and the search for scapegoats and traitors – gathered pace in 1916, with damaging effects on the fighting front. A soldier listening to an NCO's 'explanation' that spies and traitors lay behind the most recent retreat remarked: 'A fish begins to stink from the head. What kind of a Tsar would surround himself with thieves and cheats? It's as clear as day that we're going to lose the war.' The road to revolution was opening up.

Desertion and voluntary surrender became widespread in the Russian army from 1916. As morale fractured, over twenty mutinies took place that autumn. The mutinies found much support and little condemnation among other soldiers at the front. War-weariness and deep despondency, once the short-lived success of the Brusilov Offensive had faded, blended with growing interest, fed by letters from families, in the worsening living conditions back home. The head of the Petrograd military censorship commission noted in November 1916 that rumours reaching the troops through letters from relatives 'cause depression in the soldiers' morale and much worry about the fate of relatives left at home'. The demand for peace – even peace without conditions – had been reported even in 1916. By the time of the February revolution of 1917 the groundswell had become a tidal wave.

Desertions on a major scale started early, too, among other combatant troops on the eastern front. In the Italian army, despite harsh punishment from the outset, desertions almost trebled between 1915 and 1917. More than 300,000 had deserted from the Ottoman army by November 1917. A readiness to surrender – far more prevalent than on the western front – was another sign that morale, which ultimately had to draw on commitment and self-discipline, was fragile.

Lack of national cohesion was a notable factor in the difficulties of sustaining morale in the Austro-Hungarian army. German-speaking Austrian officers often treated soldiers from other ethnic backgrounds – Croatians, Romanians, Bosnian Serbs, Czechs, Italians and others – with contempt. Such troops in turn not only detested high-handed officers, but viewed their superiors through the prism of ethnicity and the Habsburg cause often with indifference or hostility. Czechs and other ethnic minorities resented their treatment by what they saw as domineering and arrogant Austrian officers. The Austrians themselves thought the Czechs, Ruthenes (from eastern Hungary, south of the Carpathians) and, with some justification, the Bosnian Serbs to be unreliable. It was scarcely a recipe for good morale. Growing, and serious, Czech desertions pointed to the fact that ethnic nationalist tendencies were playing their part in weakening the Habsburg war effort.

On the eastern front, to a far greater extent than on the western front (except in its initial phase), civilians were directly engulfed by the fighting. Insight into the civilian experience of the war in one sector of the eastern front is provided by the remarkable memoirs of a Polish village mayor. Jan Słomka had been born in 1842 and his long life drew to a close in his eighty-seventh year in 1929. For forty years he was mayor of a poor village community in Dzików, near the town of Tarnobrzeg in south-eastern Poland, close to the Vistula and to the Carpathian mountains, in the part of Poland that before the war had been ruled by the Austrians. His vivid account of the impact of the war on his community bears more of a resemblance to the ravages, pillage and devastation wrought by advancing and retreating armies in the Thirty Years War of the seventeenth century than to the peculiar horrors of the static trench warfare that characterized the western front, where the huge attritional battles were effectively detached from civilian life.

Within a year of the war starting, Słomka's neighbourhood had seen Austrian troops pass through five times and Russian troops four times. Three big battles were fought in the vicinity. The Russians occupied the district twice, once for three weeks, the second time for eight months. The troop movements and battles caused huge devastation. Nearly 3,000 farms and homes were destroyed in the surrounding areas, mainly by shelling. Some villages were completely wiped out. Around 35,000 acres of woodland was burnt, cut down or destroyed by artillery fire. Anything left in the ruined homesteads was plundered. Much of the population – those who had not fled at the approach of the Russians – was reduced to penury. Many people were forced to live in makeshift homes among the ruins, their fields left untilled, wasted by infantry trenches and barbed-wire entanglements, their horses and cattle driven away by the Russians. Most of the adult males were deported to the Urals. Food, clothing and shelter were all in short supply. So was labour since there were no men left to work. Highly unpopular food rationing had to be introduced, but as the scarcity intensified so prices rose astronomically.

It had all started optimistically. Recruits in Dzików had rushed to join up when mobilization was ordered on 1 August 1914. The civilian population had warmly welcomed the troops as they passed by on the way to battle, singing as they went, their morale high. There was a general feeling that the Central Powers would be victorious, that the war would be decided on Russian territory, and that it would result in a new Polish state.

One significant division in the local population was, however, highlighted by the outbreak of war. Animosity and resentment among the Catholic population towards Jews (who formed the majority of the inhabitants of Tarnobrzeg, though not of Dzików itself or other nearby villages) found expression in allegations that they were evading military service and avoiding their share of providing billeting, horses and wagons for the troops, thus imposing a heavier burden on the villagers. Eventually, the Jews were rounded up and forcibly put to work.

The Russian withdrawal beyond the Vistula as the Austrians advanced confirmed people's confidence in an imminent Austrian victory, and with that victory for Poland. It was thought that the war would end within a few months. The early optimism was, however, soon shattered. The sound of guns close by on 9 September brought sudden alarm and panic to the population, confident until then that the Austrian army was on the way to victory. Within a few days it was clear that, on the contrary, it was in headlong retreat. Straggling, weary, hungry and wounded troops, a far cry from the splendid regiments that had left only weeks earlier, arrived back in the district, at first begging for food, then plundering property to get it. Many of the local Jews fled from the advancing Russians, and with good cause, since the enemy's treatment of Jews was 'very severe and ruthless'. Dzików's Jews were gathered together and publicly whipped. In a village nearby five Jews were hanged for allegedly hiding weapons. Two more from Tarnobrzeg were hanged by the roadside under suspicion of spying. When, in early October, the Russians were themselves forced to retreat, the population welcomed as their deliverers troops whom they took to be the Austrians, re-entering the village. In fact, the 'deliverers' turned out to be Hungarian regiments, and the 15,000 or so troops quartered in the area were as rapacious and hostile as the Russians had been. By the beginning of November the Russians were back again, their occupation – with further massive plundering and destruction – lasting this time until June 1915.

As economic circumstances deteriorated drastically in the later war years, as the plight of the local population worsened severely, and as the desertions from the army offered a clear indication of Austrian military weakness, hopes of independence for Poland faded. And when the eastern half of the Austrian province of Galicia was handed to the newly created Ukrainian People's Republic at a separate treaty between Ukraine, Germany and Austria-Hungary on 9 February 1918 (recognizing Ukrainian independence and offering military support against the Bolsheviks in return for foodstuffs), without any Polish representatives at the settlement, there was a widespread sense that Poles had been betrayed by Germany and Austria. As one of President Wilson's Fourteen Points listed the month before, the inclusion of the creation of an independent Polish state as part of Allied aims had already been an incitement to Poles to weaken their wavering allegiance to the Central Powers. But how, and whether, that state would ever materialize was highly uncertain.

On the last day of October 1918 throngs of deserters from the

Austrian army who had been hiding in the woods, supported by food from the local population, emerged to gather in the town square at Tarnobrzeg, their Austrian rosettes torn from their caps. Austrian insignia started to be removed everywhere in the first days of November, the Polish eagle put in their place. Soldiers rushed to the station to travel home as soon as they were able. Citizens at a mass meeting rejoiced that 'Poland is restored!' Local officials (including Słomka himself), who had been the face of intrusive and unpopular wartime regulations, were abruptly removed from their positions of authority. The police, frequently set upon and severely beaten, were particular targets of the population's wrath. Jews, accused of exploiting the misery of the population through money-lending at usurious rates, and of shirking front-line service, were also in the front line of the hostility, which occasionally erupted into outbreaks of violence as Jewish shops were plundered and their owners beaten up. Class hatred was manifest. Two-thirds of the land in the neighbourhood belonged to ten big landowners, while the other third was divided among about 14,000 mainly smallholding peasants. It was little wonder, then, that in the chaotic conditions at the end of the war, and often inspired by the Bolshevik Revolution, bands of peasants (sometimes assisted by estate servants), armed with clubs, pitchforks and guns, attacked the manor houses and large estates, raiding granaries and plundering food, livestock, hay, wagons and other possessions, on occasion beating and murdering estate administrators.

The war that had begun with such confident expectations ended in this part of Poland in bitter enmities, class conflict, heightened animosity towards Jews, a breakdown of authority, and widespread violence and disorder. The emerging state of Poland was anything but a united nation. At the time of the Armistice, the country did not have a government. When the existence of an independent Polish state was announced on 16 November 1918, its struggles to establish its frontiers and to build a unified infrastructure were only just beginning. And whatever the hopes that Jan Słomka's community in Dzików and the communities of countless other Polish villages harboured throughout the war for the restoration of a Polish state, its precise form when it came about owed little to their wishes and almost everything to the circumstances of the collapse of the three powers – Russia, Austria and Germany (before 1871 Prussia) – which had presided over its partition since 1795.

Everywhere, in western as well as eastern Europe, despite the differing characteristics of warfare on the two fronts, the population at home had to put up with new hardships, material and psychological, during the war. Women bore the brunt. They were often left to tend to peasant holdings, looking after small children at the same time, and in constant anxiety about husbands away fighting. In industrial regions women had to step in to do work that had earlier been done by men in armaments factories or keeping transport networks functioning. While looking after households amid growing food shortages and rapidly rising prices, women's constant dread was of the knock at the front door with news that a loved one had been killed in action. It was little wonder that there was growing anger and resentment. Queuing for food brought women into contact with each other, allowed news and rumour to be spread, and grievances to be ventilated. Letters from the front gave them an indication of how well or badly the war was going, and how the troops were responding. Their own letters to their menfolk at the front carried a sense of conditions at home. Soldiers would also gather what conditions were like on the home front from their infrequent periods of leave, and those memories accompanied them back to the trenches.

It was impossible for people at home to capture mentally in full measure the horrors of the front, even though in Britain millions of people had been given an inkling of what it was like through the official film *The Battle of the Somme*, which, if partly faked, did not disguise the grisly experience. This was the first time in history that a home audience had been offered a visceral experience of war. It was so harrowing that some people watching the film fainted with horror. The authorities were forced to realize that the population was not ready for such an exposure to war's grim reality. Most relatives at home wanted, or needed, to block out what their loved ones were enduring at the front. So it is not surprising that many soldiers returned to front-line duty with the sense that people at home had no understanding of what they were going through. The warm welcome that a British lieutenant received from his relatives when he went on leave in 1917 rapidly cooled. They eulogized about the British victory at Passchendaele. When he described the horrors of the battle and implied that the losses had been for nothing, he was shown the door.

Such insensitivity and incomprehension were not, however, necessarily typical. The interaction between home and front was closer and more important than this suggests. The sheer volume of mail, the vital lifeline with home, shows the strong desire for home leave (for those lucky enough to be able to enjoy it unlike, say, Canadian, Anzac or Indian troops, or many from far-flung regions of the Russian Empire). It seems, too, that attitudes towards the war at home and at the front increasingly merged as the conflict wore on, especially among those belligerent powers faced with the growing prospect of defeat.

The vast array of diverse experiences, at home and at the front, defies easy summary or generalization. What seems clear, however, and of historical significance, is that the countries which began the war with political systems enjoying a good deal of support, resting on relatively high levels of representation and widely accepted, established values – what could otherwise be termed 'legitimacy' – had a distinct advantage in sustaining morale at home and at the front, and therefore of maximizing the war effort. Of course, this was not enough in itself. These countries also needed superiority in supplies of weaponry, food and manpower. Britain and France were the powers that had these advantages, especially since they could rely upon support not only from their overseas dependencies but also from the United States, and late in the war had the direct backing from large numbers of American troops. This enabled the expectation of eventual victory to be sustained. And where hope in victory could be first upheld, then become increasingly realizable, the state system could retain its legitimacy, even in the face of horrific losses at the front.

But where the certainty of defeat grew, hope disappeared, and immense (and mounting) losses were seen to be in vain, the legitimacy of the state system held responsible for the calamity was undermined to the point of collapse. The plainest manifestation is in the scale of desertion in the armies of the Central Powers towards the end of the war. Where legitimacy was weakest, the war placed such burdens on the country that the regimes promoting it were increasingly endangered through mass unrest among both the civilian population and front-line soldiers.

THE STATE UNDER PRESSURE

The war placed all the belligerent states, even those that proved eventually victorious, under unprecedented strain. Whether new or hugely expanded, all tasks in a conflict on this scale became the responsibility of the state. Troops and resources for the front in ever larger numbers had to be mobilized. By the middle of the war a high proportion of each country's male population capable of bearing arms was conscripted for service. (Britain, which had begun the war with a volunteer army, moved to conscription in 1916.) Arms had to be mass-produced on a vast scale to give the soldiers weaponry to fight with. The state sponsored research into new technologies and the development of innovative types of weapons. The number of hospitals, improvised infirmaries and recuperation homes had to be increased hugely to cope with the large numbers of injured and mutilated returning from the front. The welfare, however inadequate, of widows and families robbed of their bread-earner had to be organized. Public opinion had to be orchestrated and morale sustained through state-run propaganda and censorship, and the dissemination of information was controlled by exerting direct or indirect influence over the press.

All of this necessitated controlled economies and greatly increased state spending. Military spending alone reached unprecedented levels towards the end of the war – 59 per cent of Germany's gross domestic product, 54 per cent of France's, 37 per cent of Britain's (though less advanced economies, such as those of Russia, Austria-Hungary or the Ottoman Empire could extract less). New or extended forms of taxation were imposed on citizens. Britain was relatively successful in financing war costs through taxation, though Germany and especially France were more reluctant to tax their citizens, imagining that the enemy would pay reparations for the conflict after victory. Most of the war financing came from loans. The Allies borrowed mainly from America. Austria borrowed to some extent from Germany. But, as the war went on, it became impossible for Germany to borrow from anywhere abroad. The German war effort had increasingly to be financed by domestic war loans. War-bond drives were deployed by all the belligerent states. Everywhere, state indebtedness hugely increased. When neither loans nor taxation sufficed, states printed money, storing up problems for a later day.

As state direction of the economy and intervention in civilian life intensified, the state apparatus grew in size. Bureaucracies expanded. So did levels of surveillance, coercion and repression. Enemy 'aliens' were interned. In some areas, particularly in eastern Europe, whole populations were displaced. When the Russians retreated from western Poland and Lithuania in 1915, leaving 'scorched earth' behind them as they went, they had deported at least 300,000 Lithuanians, 250,000 Latvians, 350,000 Jews (who were notably ill-treated) and 743,000 Poles into the Russian interior. By early 1917 some 6 million displaced persons in Russia – refugees from the Caucasus and borderlands in the west, as well as those deported by force – had been added to the masses suffering growing misery in Russian cities.

Everywhere, the state had to ensure the support, especially, of the industrial working class (now including large numbers of women in the armaments industry), whose militancy grew as material conditions worsened. Often, especially in more authoritarian systems, resort was more readily made to the stick rather than the carrot. In Britain, France and – until late in the war – Germany, however, workers were in essence bought off by increased wages (relative to other sections of society), promises for the future, and concessions to their wider organization in trade unions. In Germany the drastic measures introduced to mobilize labour under the Auxiliary Services Law of December 1916 – compulsory labour service in war industries for all males between seventeen and sixty – were coupled with the creation of works committees in factories with more than fifty employees, giving equal representation to workers and employers. Even so, and whatever the readiness to support the war effort, workers (including women) were prepared to strike to defend their material interests. In Britain, where conditions deteriorated less than in any other belligerent country during the war and where commitment to it remained relatively high, there were more strikes than in any other warring nation except Russia. Three times as many British workers went on strike in 1918 as in 1914. Outside Britain, strikes were relatively few in the first two war years, but then grew sharply in number (and with increased political content) in 1917–18.

As the seemingly endless suffering and hardship of the war intensified, so did the search for scapegoats held to blame for the misery.
Popular hatreds were fanned by state propaganda. Grass-roots resentment was widely directed at capitalists and financiers. But this was not
merely the obvious class hatred of war profiteers. It could also be
diverted with little difficulty into race hatred. Jews were increasingly
caricatured as exploiters of the toiling masses, as the embodiment of
finance capital. Hatred of Jews was, however, too long-standing among
much of Europe's population, and too chameleon-like in adapting its
colours to any prejudice, to be confined to a linkage only with capitalism. Deep antipathy often blended economic resentment with age-old
prejudice against Jews – still very prevalent, notably in central and
eastern Europe, and often promoted by Christian clergy – as the 'killers of Christ'. To this amalgam of hatreds was added another lethal
ingredient in 1917: the Jews as the cause of Bolshevism and revolution.
The multifaceted image of the Jew as the war approached its end defied
parody: enemy of Christianity, capitalist exploiter, shirker of military
duty, fomenter of internal unrest, driving-force of Bolshevism. It was
little wonder that a pre-war forgery by the Tsarist police, purporting to
show a Jewish conspiracy aimed at world power, the so-called *Protocols of the Elders of Zion*, increased its circulation sharply after
1917 as the backlash against the Russian Revolution began.

Changes in the society of each belligerent country were both
affected by, and in turn directly influenced, the effect of the war on
domestic politics and the viability of the respective state system. At
first, states tried to keep their political systems running as before the
war, or as close to it as possible. 'Business as Usual' was the slogan
coined in Britain by Winston Churchill in a speech in November
1914 to underline the need for continued normality, undisturbed by
hostilities abroad that were expected to be of short duration. Such
hope was to have a brief lifetime in every belligerent state. But politics, more or less as usual, continued until the states became to a greater
or lesser extent internally buffeted by the pressures of war.

In Britain and France, party-political differences were unabated
and often sharp, but did not override a sense of unity produced by
commitment to the war effort – a unity challenged only by minorities
who were at times vocal, though without mainstream influence.

Where change took place here it was after periods of adversity to put 'strong men' in charge of government to prosecute the pursuit of victory with relentless vigour. Following the huge losses at the Somme and in the wake of a serious rebellion in Ireland that threatened British rule on the island, the dynamic David Lloyd George became British Prime Minister in December 1916, at the head of a small but powerful war cabinet. His leadership succeeded in bringing new organization and drive to the war economy and in galvanizing the war effort. In France political crisis after the troubles of 1917 – serious mutinies at the front, strikes, anti-war demonstrations and demands for a compromise peace at home – led to the recall to government in November of that year of the veteran Radical leader Georges Clemenceau. A symbol of republican nationalism, he was appointed to embody energetic commitment, restore confidence, and symbolize 'the stubborn and patriotic struggle for a victor's peace'.

In neither Britain nor France did internal disputes over the running of the war and varying levels of social and political disaffection, mainly on the socialist Left, come close to a revolutionary challenge to the state. British morale at home was sustained in good measure by the confidence that the country would not be invaded, the prospect of victory and a relatively low level of material privation. Indirectly, the war of course affected everyone. But its direct effect was largely confined to those in military service. Attitudes in France were more divided. Pacifist protests and demonstrations for peace in early 1918, in which expressions of support for Bolshevism and revolution were voiced, led to a big strike of munitions workers in May. Such views might have been more widely held had the war not been fought on French soil. As it was, pacifism was more than countered by the urgency of fighting on to withstand the major German offensive. Once that had faded, and victory was in sight, French morale held up to the end. Overwhelmingly, in both Britain and France the socialist Left continued its support for the war effort. In neither country was there a serious threat to the legitimacy of the state itself. It could have been different here, too, had defeat loomed and the losses been viewed as in vain.

At the opposite end of the spectrum to the western powers was Russia. Only in Russia was there a revolution during the war itself.

Only in Russia did the revolution amount to a root-and-branch trans-formation of socio-economic relations as well as political structures. And only in Russia was the ruling class utterly destroyed.

The attempted Russian revolution in 1905 had failed because there had been no cohesion to link the discontents of striking workers, rebellious peasants and those of soldiers and sailors, only a relatively small number of whom mutinied. There had been a lack, too, of unify-ing revolutionary leadership. The Tsar had bought off the revolution partly through concessions towards constitutional government that soon proved to be little more than cosmetic. Repression did the rest. The Tsarist political police, the Okhrana, was efficient in arresting revolutionary leaders or banishing them to remote exile, infiltrating their organizations, closing down seditious newspapers, putting down strikes and executing peasant rebel leaders. The regime had, for now, staved off its destruction. Over the following years, communications were improved, the economy grew (in the last pre-war years at a faster rate than the United States), big advances were made in industrializa-tion, and state revenues were increased. But the big problem remained the sclerotic nature of the Tsarist autocracy. Perhaps, without the war, changes could have been introduced that would have transformed Tsarist rule into a parliamentary-controlled constitutional monarchy. This seems unlikely, however, given the stiff-necked resistance to sys-temic change in the ruling class and the extent of ingrained and organized (whatever the repression) hostility to the autocracy among the working class and peasantry. A revolution was more probable than not at some future point. By late 1916 it was looking likely in the near future.

During the bitter winter of 1916–17, while many Russian peasants hoarded food or sold it at high prices, the big industrial centres had suffered from an acute shortage of provisions and fuel. Transport was close to collapse. The state finances were in ruins. Inflation was ram-pant. Wages (apart from those of skilled munitions workers) could not keep pace with galloping prices. Many people were near starva-tion. But a privileged minority was still doing well out of the war – a source of intense resentment. Big protest strikes in January 1917 took place in Petrograd (formerly St Petersburg) and other cities in which anger about living standards was linked to anti-war feeling and opposition to Tsarist rule. When working women took to the streets on 8 March (23 February in the old Russian calendar) to protest that they had no bread, it sparked mass strikes and demonstrations by armaments workers. Soldiers and sailors supported the workers' insurrection in Petrograd. Firing on demonstrators in Petrograd could not end the strike of over 200,000 workers. And the government was powerless to defuse what was tantamount to a growing military strike within the armed forces. Orders to suppress the mutinies fell on deaf ears. The situation rapidly ran out of the control of the Tsarist authorities. In conditions of anarchy, workers elected their own form of representative government, a soviet (or council). Order rapidly collapsed. The soldiers also elected soviets to represent them, demanding the removal of the Tsar. When leading officers and politicians agreed that the Tsar had to go, he went, abdicating on 15 March. He and his family would be shot by the Bolsheviks in July 1918, though their bodies were only identified eighty years later, after the end of the Soviet Union.

The war had produced the conditions whereby the burning anger directed at the Tsar and the system of rule he represented, which was held to blame for their misery, transcended for the time being the divided interests of workers and peasants. The revolutionary forces in the industrial working class in 1917 temporarily linked with those among the peasantry. Even together, these may have proved insufficient to topple the system, as had been the case in 1905. But, crucially, the war allied their interests with those of the growing numbers of massively disaffected troops at the front. Once the disaffection spread to the front, once the soldiers were unwilling to fight any longer, and once their revolutionary fervour blended with that of the home front, the regime was living on borrowed time. The groundswell of discontent at the enormous losses and unbearable hardships coalesced into an explosion of opposition to the war that swept away the system held to blame for it. A regime that had relied upon repression and coercion, with few intermediary structures to integrate the mass of the population into unenforced support for it, found itself with hardly any friends as the pressures mounted before the dam-walls burst in 1917.

Even after the deposition of the Tsar and the establishment of the Provisional Government of 'revolutionary democracy' in March

1917, the situation remained highly unstable. The fluid conditions over the following months and the further prosecution of a war irredeemably lost created the climate in which a second, far more radical, revolution could take place.

By this point, in October 1917 (in the old Russian calendar) the organizational framework available for channelling and leading the revolution was at hand. This proved, in contrast to 1905, a decisive factor in the success of this revolution. The Bolshevik Party had as yet no mass base outside small parts of the working class. But it did have a tightly knit, fanatical leadership core with a preconceived programme that saw the destruction of the old system not as an end in itself but as merely the prelude to the building of an entirely new society. The Bolshevik Party had emerged as the larger faction of the divided Russian Social Democratic Labour Party, which had been founded in 1899 but had later split into a larger revolutionary (Bolshevik) and a smaller reformist (Menshevik) wing. Vladimir Ilyich Ulyanov, better known by his soubriquet Lenin (who had been exiled to Siberia in the late 1890s, and had then lived mainly outside Russia until 1917), had envisaged the party as the vanguard of the working class and advocated tight discipline and complete loyalty behind the aim of overthrowing the Tsar. Lenin's next objective was to establish, through ruthless deployment of terror against 'class enemies', a 'provisional revolutionary democratic dictatorship of the proletariat and peasantry'. In April 1917 the charismatic Bolshevik leader had been transported from his Swiss exile to the revolutionary chaos of Petrograd by the Germans, who were hoping to undermine the wavering Russian will to continue fighting by fomenting further unrest and agitation for peace. In the light of later events it was one of the great 'own-goals' of history. Amid government repression of the Bolsheviks, Lenin was forced to retreat in July to Finland (a semi-autonomous part of the Russian Empire since 1809 and, after the toppling of the Tsar, voicing ever more strident demands for independence). But as state power evaporated he returned to Petrograd to lead the second revolution.

What bound the close-knit Bolshevik Party leadership and its committed members together was a utopian ideology of salvation, the vision of a future classless society free of conflict. But what gave the

Bolsheviks the potential to reach out to a wider constituency was less ethereal and more pragmatic: the promise of peace, bread, distribution of land, ownership and control of the factories, and law in the hands of the people. Politically, the Bolsheviks demanded all power to the soviets (which had meanwhile been set up in all the major cities). The unpopularity of Alexander Kerensky's Provisional Government amid further acute shortages, rocketing inflation and huge bloodshed in the last disastrous offensive played into the hands of the Bolsheviks. Control of the Petrograd soviet (run by Leon Trotsky, born Lev Davidovich Bronshtein, a gifted organizer and demagogue who preached the need for permanent revolution) provided the launch pad for the October revolution, which eventually led to the complete Bolshevik takeover of the soviets. It would require ruthless internal terror against class enemies and over two years of the most brutal civil war imaginable before the powerful forces of reaction and counter-revolution were defeated and Russia was set firmly on the path to complete political, social, economic and ideological transformation. But it was plain from the start: the Bolshevik Revolution was an event of world-historical significance. What it had produced was an absolutely new kind of state and society. Reports of what was happening in Russia sent shock waves throughout Europe that would reverberate for decades.

Elsewhere in Europe the crisis of legitimacy came over a year after the Bolshevik Revolution, in the wake of looming defeat. In Germany war did not mean the end of party politics. On the contrary, the polarization of German politics, clearly established before the war but initially cloaked by the 'civil truce' of 1914, became fully exposed as the feeling of hardship, huge human losses for scant return, and of impending defeat grew. The ideological and class divisions that had been only temporarily glossed over at the beginning of the war soon resurfaced and from 1916 onwards in sharply radicalized form. As food supplies dwindled, prices increased sharply and living standards plummeted, the political divisions over peace or annexationist war aims intensified.

The main drive for drastic political change came from German left-wing elements. The Social Democrats had split in April 1917 over their stance towards the war. A radical minority, who rejected the war as an imperialist conflict that could only be overcome by socialist revolution, broke away and formed the Independent Social Democratic Party of Germany (the USPD, the core of which later became Germany's Communist Party). The larger body of Social Democrats, now calling themselves the Majority Social Democratic Party of Germany (MSPD), also condemned an imperialist war and German annexations, but they rejected revolution in favour of reform through the introduction of representative democracy, of government responsible to parliament, not to the Kaiser. (In Imperial Germany, political parties across the spectrum were represented in the Reichstag. But they did not control decision-making. Power lay in the hands of the Kaiser and of his appointed ministers and military leaders.)

On 19 July 1917 the MSPD was supported by some liberals (the Progressive People's Party) and the Catholic Centre Party in voting for a peace resolution in the Reichstag. But they faced powerful opponents on the Conservative and Liberal right wing who backed the military leadership and favoured not only the uncompromising prosecution of the war but also the drive for further territorial annexations. Pressure-groups, backed by big-business finance such as the Pan-German League and, especially, the huge rabidly nationalist and imperialist Fatherland Party (founded in 1917 and rapidly acquiring the backing of a million and a quarter members), popularized the case for fighting on to victory with extended territorial gains, and at the same time they rejected demands for parliamentary democracy. This political constellation remained in place down to the end of the war, intensifying as material hardship worsened and as defeat loomed. The radical polarization of German politics that followed the defeat in 1918 was already prefigured in the internal developments of the last two war years.

It was, however, only in the last few months of the war, after the failure of the summer offensive of 1918, that morale at the front collapsed, adding to the growing pressure at home to halt the fighting. Major strikes by German industrial workers in January 1918 had met with little sympathy at the front, where soldiers had been led to expect success in the spring offensive. The mood among the troops had been exultant at 'this elementary expression of German strength' when the big offensive was launched in March. When the realization dawned that it had failed, the welling anger started to turn into direct action. More than anything, soldiers who had fought with courage and conviction for almost four years wanted to survive what they now saw to be a hopeless contest. War-weariness turned into a mounting desire simply to stop fighting. In the last four months of the war 385,000 German soldiers surrendered on the western front – far more than in the previous four years of the war taken together. An estimated three quarters of a million soldiers deserted from August 1918 onwards. This blended into the growing unrest at home. In the huge strikes early in the year workers' protests had been mainly about living conditions. Now they had an unmistakably political edge. The demand was increasingly for peace, democracy and an end to the Kaiser's regime.

The longer the war went on, the more the nature of the German state itself had been called into question. The political system where ministers were responsible to the Kaiser, not to parliament, had already been rejected by socialists before the war but was upheld by strong forces that resisted any move towards democracy. Worsening war fortunes resulted in a growing clamour on the Left not simply to end the relentless bloodshed but to remove those held responsible and to introduce democratic parliamentary government. More and more Germans saw a system of rule resting upon militarism, class privilege and unchecked power, embodied by the divisive figure of the Kaiser – a system that had taken Germany into a disastrous war – as unreformable. It had to be replaced. Democracy had to be established. The people who had borne the pain, suffering and privations of the war had to have their political voice heard. By the autumn of 1918 the legitimacy of the state system in Imperial Germany had all but collapsed.

The Fourteen Point Programme that President Wilson had put forward the previous January, which foresaw among other things the restoration of territory that Germany had annexed or occupied, had previously been an anathema to Germany's leaders. In the rapidly changing circumstances, however, the newly appointed Reich Chancellor, Prince Max von Baden, who had personally long favoured political reform and peace without annexations, appealed on 5 October to Wilson, hoping for an armistice on terms amenable to Germany. Wilson would make no concessions, however, insisting on the introduction of parliamentary democracy (entailing the loss of power for Germany's ruling elites), renunciation of territorial gains and significant disarmament (including the handing over of the fleet). There was heated debate among Germany's leaders about the acceptability of what they saw as harsh terms. Ludendorff vehemently proposed continuing the war rather than yield to such humiliation. But he was no longer in a position to issue commands. And events were galloping beyond his, or anyone else's, control. On 26 October, blaming all but himself, he resigned.

During the night of 29–30 October mutineering sailors at Kiel defied the naval leadership's absurd orders for the fleet to put to sea to engage the British navy in a last great showdown battle. This would have invited a senseless sacrifice for nothing but the honour of the German navy. The sailors were having none of it. The mutiny rapidly spread and set the spark to full-scale revolution. Workers' and soldiers' councils sprang up, taking power at the grass roots into their own hands. The generals made plain to the Kaiser, the very symbol of the old order, that he had to go. Reluctantly, he went. During the night of 9–10 November, Kaiser Wilhelm II left the military headquarters in Spa, in Belgium, for exile in Holland (where he would remain until his death in 1941). His abdication was announced prematurely, since his formal renunciation of the throne only followed on 28 November. Even before he departed, a republic had been hastily proclaimed from the balcony of the Reichstag in Berlin. Equally without actual constitutional legitimacy, the Chancellor, Max von Baden, appointed his own successor, the Socialist leader, Friedrich Ebert. Constitutional niceties did not matter in the revolutionary moment. Germany was on its way, amid turmoil that would last for months, to the establishment of a fully fledged parliamentary democracy.

Ominously, still-powerful forces in the state, defenders of the old order, felt merely that they were biding their time, making necessary tactical adjustments until different circumstances could sweep away the concessions to democracy and parliamentary rule. Just before the Armistice, the view could be heard in the German military leadership 'that the parties of the Left have to take on the odium of this peace. The storm of anger will then turn against them. There are hopes then of later vaulting back into the saddle and ruling again in the old way.'

Democracy was viewed in such circles as 'the greatest misfortune' to befall Germany.

In Italy the growing crisis of the state system had been only slightly less profound than in Germany. Although Italy was on the side of the Entente, it did not feel as if the war was being won. The war had been imposed upon a deeply divided country in 1915 by a narrow political elite hoping after a quick victory for sizeable territorial gains in the Adriatic. Even the generals had been kept largely in the dark about the decision to intervene, and parliament had not been consulted. The majority of the population felt in any case that it had no stake in the existing limited political representation. Italians could drum up no enthusiasm for governments that changed frequently but always seemed the same – and to be looking after the same elite interests. Defeats, material hardship and heavy losses then polarized society and undermined support not just for a succession of weak governments but for the state itself.

The Italian parliament, symbolizing the weakness and division, seldom met. Governments ruled by decree. Moreover, though bearing the blame for what went wrong, they were unable to control General Luigi Cadorna, the austere, domineering and brutal commander of the Italian army until the humiliation at Caporetto in 1917 forced his removal. Before then, military imperatives had prevailed. Factory discipline was subject to military control. Censorship and restrictions on freedom of speech were increased. Repression intensified as protests against shortages and strikes took place in factories. Social and political divisions were greatly sharpened and focused on the inequities as well as the horrendous casualties of the war. As losses, defeats, material shortages and the sense of national humiliation mounted from 1916 onwards, unrest manifested itself in strikes, demonstrations and protests at food shortages. It fell short of an outright revolutionary mood – but not by much.

Opposition to the war and popular discontent was mostly voiced on the Left, though the socialist movement was itself split between those who rejected the war outright and wanted revolution and the majority who continued to provide patriotic, if unenthusiastic, support for the war effort. Ominously, the Italian government found itself even more vehemently attacked from the Right. The Nationalists extended the base of their support, increased their agitation for territorial expansion in south-eastern Europe and Africa, and, so the Minister of the Interior claimed, sought to gain control of the police and terrorize their opponents. They wanted to sweep away what they saw as sterile parliamentary rule and its attendant bureaucracy, advocating radical social change through a state and economy to be run on quasi-military lines even when the war was over. They were already at the forefront of the local defence formations that called themselves *Fasci*. Italy's post-war crisis was foreshadowed.

The house of Habsburg, rulers of Austria for centuries, was now also bearing the price for an increasingly and massively unpopular war. The conflict, sparked by a dispute with Serbia that had become all but forgotten, had never enjoyed complete support from the beginning. It could scarcely be portrayed as a defensive war. And the dependency on Germany, even for whatever victories could be mustered, was too obvious to be comfortable. The centrifugal forces threatening to split and destroy the Habsburg Empire were hugely reinforced as the disastrous war ground on. The strains were telling long before the last, catastrophic phase of the conflict. The aged Emperor Franz Joseph had for decades been almost the sole symbol of unity in the enfeebled multi-national empire (in which the Hungarian half was, in its institutional structures, already more or less a separate entity). When he died in November 1916 it was in the midst of a mounting crisis of legitimacy, both for the war effort and for the Habsburg throne. His grand-nephew and successor, Emperor Karl, had no chance of turning the tide, despite vain attempts to weaken the dependence on Germany and to seek a peace agreement with the Allies.

Briefly, after Caporetto, the Austrians dreamt again of glory. But the trains that had almost exclusively ferried provisions for the army were not available to transport fuel and food for the civilian population of the empire during the hard winter that followed. Huge protest strikes multiplied in various parts of the empire over the early months of 1918. Industrial unrest, anger at deplorable living conditions, nationalist separatist feeling, and anti-war disaffection blended in an unholy brew. 'Complete incapacity of the rulers, absolute demoralization and disorganization, general insecurity', was the view of the Viennese doctor and writer, Arthur Schnitzler. By October 1918, as food riots, strikes, protests, nationalist enmities and lawlessness spread, the situation, in the judgement of the head of the Austrian Food Office, Hans Loewenfeld-Russ, had become 'utterly desperate'. The Habsburg Empire was visibly falling apart.

Class divisions throughout much of the empire were in good measure subsumed into or overridden by the politics of ethnic nationalism. Outside the Austrian heartlands, where working-class protests at sharply deteriorating living standards threatened to develop into revolution, often taking inspiration from Russia, they were merged in demands for independence, for the dissolution of the empire, that were increasingly voluble among Czechs, Poles and south Slavs. In Hungary, despite the professed readiness of Emperor Karl to introduce liberal reforms and move to a more federally structured empire, pressure for independence from Vienna grew in the last war years, backed by socialists and many liberals. Unlike Hungary, where civilian rule and parliamentary debate had been at least nominally maintained, in the Austrian half of the empire the legislature, the Reichsrat, had been suspended and provincial assemblies closed down. Censorship and surveillance were stepped up sharply. Military law was introduced into non-German and non-Czech lands. Dissidents were arrested and imprisoned. But repression proved insufficient to quell the rising nationalist separatist movements, particularly strident among the Czechs, in the last war years.

After the remnants of the Austro-Hungarian army, with little on their minds but saving their own skins, were routed by Italians at Vittorio Veneto in October 1918, the empire was on its last legs. The army now disintegrated. Emperor Karl agreed in late October to troops joining their own national forces. It was no more than a recognition of what was happening on the ground, as Czechs, Poles, Hungarians, Croats and others deserted and left for home. By late October, with extraordinary speed, Czechoslovakia, Hungary and what would become Yugoslavia were proclaiming their independence. Austria's armistice with Italy on 3 November marked the end of its war effort. Emperor Karl reluctantly renounced his powers (though not his claim to the throne) on 11 November and spent the remaining three years of his life exiled in Switzerland and, finally, Madeira. Five centuries of Habsburg rule were over.

Revolution in Germany and in Austria-Hungary, the dismantling of their monarchies and replacement with republics (in the latter case in a number of 'successor states'), took place only at the point of defeat in the war. The dismembering of the Ottoman Empire to the south of Turkey itself – most of the former possessions in the Balkans had gained independence in the 1870s and the Balkan Wars of 1912 and 1913 brought the final loss of Ottoman territories in Europe – followed defeat, when the wartime Turkish leaders had fled on board a German submarine for Odessa, and eventually Berlin. Within the Ottoman Empire, too, however, growing adversity to the war had caused an insurmountable crisis of state legitimacy. The high level of desertion pointed to an increasingly parlous state of morale in the Turkish army. The shaky and unwieldy Ottoman Empire had overstretched itself in its war effort. It came away empty-handed in its attempts to make territorial gains in the Caucasus. And in the Middle East, an Arab revolt from 1916 onwards (greatly abetted by the British and French, keen to advance their imperialist interests) meant that Ottoman administration scarcely functioned in the southern part of the empire.

In the Turkish heartlands, meanwhile, the problems were mounting alarmingly. Losses at the front were massive. Estimates put Turkish deaths as high as 2.5 million, three times those of Britain. The scale of such losses, accompanied at home by a collapsing currency, soaring prices, and acute shortages of food and other commodities undermined the already tottering foundations of the Ottoman Empire. The Armistice brought no end to the suffering and violence in Turkey, which was soon plunged into a war of independence that lasted until 1923, when a wrecked country eventually emerged from the ruins as an independent sovereign state. And the takeover of Ottoman possessions in the Middle East by the western imperialist powers, Britain and France, was accompanied by huge anti-colonial unrest, waves of protest and endemic violence that equally saw no abrupt break with the end of the war. The consequences for the indefinite future were enormous.

The war left behind a Europe broken into pieces, scarcely recognizable from the continent that had entered the conflict four years earlier.

Even the victorious powers – Britain, France and (as a nominally victorious, nominally 'great' power) Italy – had been left shattered. Cleaning up the mess seemed most likely to fall to the one emergent great power, physically unscarred by the war and economically massively strengthened as the European powers were enfeebled: the United States. That America eventually left Europe with the task of clearing up much of its own mess played no small part in the unfolding crisis of the post-war era. But at the root of the catastrophic legacy lay something else. Crucially, out of the ruins of Imperial Germany, the Habsburg monarchy and Tsarist Russia an unholy constellation had been created that would have baleful consequences in the coming years.

The combination of ethnic nationalism, territorial conflicts and class hatred (now focused, in aspiration or in dread, on the new force of Bolshevism in Russia) would prove highly explosive. Ethnic nationalism was one of the war's main legacies. And it would be most lethal in precisely those parts of central and eastern Europe where mixed ethnic communities had for centuries lived alongside each other, but where new tensions, conflicts and hatreds, engendered in large part by the war, now found expression in bitter disputes over contested borders and divided lands, and where the poisonous hatreds had immeasurably increased due to the new ingredient: Bolshevism's triumph in Russia. Class conflict, most especially in eastern and central Europe, overlaid ethnic and territorial animosities to produce a boiling cauldron of violent animosity. This meant that the early post-war years were scarcely years of peace in these parts of the continent, where enormous violence continued unabated. The violence would leave deep enmities that would come to the fore when Europe was eventually plunged into another, even more devastating, conflict twenty years later.

The war had brought immense, unimaginable human losses. The military dead totalled almost 9 million, the civilian dead (largely caused by mass deportation, famine and disease) close to 6 million. Taking all the belligerents together, as many as 7 million combatants had been captured by the enemy and sometimes spent years in often primitive living conditions in prisoner-of-war camps (though most were fairly quickly repatriated after the Armistice). Victory had ultimately been attained by the combination of greater military power with superior economic resources. But what had it all been for? People's views on this naturally varied hugely, not least in accordance with their own experiences and the fate of their countries. Many, on all sides, had fought for ideals – often misplaced, but ideals just the same. These included defence of the homeland, national honour and prestige, freedom and civilization, patriotic duty, and, increasingly, national liberation as well as hopes of a better future. As the four years of slaughter drew to a close, the well-known Austrian writer Robert Musil cynically jotted in his diary in 1918: 'The war can be reduced to the formula: you die for your ideals, because it's not worth living for them.' By that time, probably only a minority among the millions of combatants still cherished the ideals – whatever they were – with which they had entered the war. For many among the legions of conscripted soldiers in Europe's mass armies there may indeed have been little in terms of abstract idealism to begin with. They often fought because they had no alternative. And for many of these, there had been no point to the slaughter.

The poignant words of a Frenchman, written at the western front in 1916 shortly before he fell, stand as a proxy for the sentiments of millions of ordinary soldiers in all combatant armies:

> I ask, hoping to understand
> This slaughter's purpose. The reply
> I get is 'For the Fatherland!'
> But never know the reason why.

The carnage had been colossal, the destruction immense. The legacy, in a dramatically changed Europe, would be profound. The long reckoning was about to begin.

3

Turbulent Peace

This is not a peace. It is an armistice for 20 years.

Marshal Ferdinand Foch's view
of the Treaty of Versailles (1919)

It was peace – after a fashion. But it often did not seem it. Huge turbulence, like a tidal wave after an earthquake, followed the war. The seismic upheavals took five years to subside. The soldiers returned home to a drastically altered political, social, economic and ideological landscape. The war had destroyed political systems, ruined economies, divided societies, and opened vistas onto radically utopian visions of a better world. It was labelled the 'war to end war'. Why, then, did it pave the way instead for another, even more devastating conflagration? Why did the hopes of millions for peace, and for a better society built on greater freedom and equality, so swiftly evaporate? How, instead, did Europe lay the foundations of a dangerous ideological triad of utterly incompatible political systems competing for dominance: communism, fascism and liberal democracy? Yet why, in these early crisis years and despite the immediate post-war traumas, did communism triumph only in Russia, Fascism only in Italy, while democracy survived in most of the remainder of Europe – not least in the country at the pivotal centre of the continent, Germany?

LANDS 'FIT FOR HEROES'?

During the British election campaign of 1918 the Prime Minister, David Lloyd George, hailed by many as 'the man who won the war', spoke of making 'a fit country for heroes to live in'. Even in what had before the war been Europe's richest country, and one left physically almost entirely undamaged by four years of fighting, the words would soon seem no more than a hollow mockery to many soldiers who had come home from the trenches.

Early demobilization of the soldiers in Britain had, in fact, been fairly smooth. From 3.5 million at the Armistice in 1918, the army fell in size to 370,000 men by 1920. An immediate post-war economic boom meant that by the summer of 1919 four-fifths of the soldiers had been discharged, and most of those had found work (sometimes at the expense of women employed during the war). But the boom ended as quickly as it had begun. By the autumn of 1920 it was over. Deflationary policies (following those in the USA), introduced to protect sterling, had a drastic effect on living standards. Wages, which had initially kept up with rising prices, fell sharply. Class tensions remained high. In 1919, 35 million days had been lost in industrial disputes. In 1921 the figure was 86 million. Unemployment doubled over the three months from December 1920 to March 1921. By the summer, 2 million were without work. Most of the unemployed lived in squalid, dilapidated accommodation. Homes for heroes had been promised in 1918. But by 1923, 822,000 new houses were needed just to cover the basic housing shortage – greater than in 1919 – let alone replace millions of desolate slum dwellings.

By 1921, countless former soldiers, many of them badly disabled, were living in dire poverty, begging on the streets or trying to eke out a living by selling matches and mementoes, eating at food kitchens, sometimes forced to sleep in doorways or on park benches. 'We were no longer heroes, we were simply "unemployed"' was one former officer's bitter commentary. 'Ex-servicemen were continually coming to the door selling boot-laces and asking for cast-off shirts and socks,' remembered Robert Graves, poet, writer and former front-line officer. 'Patriots, especially of the female variety, were as much discredited in

1919 as in 1914 they had been honoured,' recalled Vera Brittain, who had left a comfortable upper-middle-class background and volunteered to nurse the wounded at the front. She saw 'a world denuded of prospects and left arid and pointless'.

The situation in Britain, dismal though it was, was far from the worst in Europe, certainly among the countries directly involved in the fighting. Terrible though they were, the British casualties fell below the highest rates. The United Kingdom's military dead numbered 750,000 (a further 180,000 dead from across the empire), Italy's almost half a million, France's 1.3 million, Austria-Hungary's almost 1.5 million, Russia's around 1.8 million, Germany's just over 2 million. Some of the smaller countries suffered worst in proportionate terms. One in three Serbs and Romanians sent into battle was killed or died of injuries or disease. The proportion of the dead among the fighting troops from the major belligerent countries ranged between 11–12 per cent (Russia, Italy and the United Kingdom) and 15–16 per cent (France, Germany and Austria-Hungary). The wounded, disabled and incapacitated greatly outnumbered the dead in all countries. The overall death toll was more than twice as high as the combined total from all major wars between 1790 and 1914. The influenza epidemic of 1918–19 then caused deaths worldwide twice as high as those on European battlefields during the war. To add to the horrific toll were the victims of related post-war violence and border conflicts.

The economic cost of the war was immense – over six times the total of all countries' national debt from the end of the eighteenth century until 1914. In countries most directly affected by the fighting, production after the war was drastically reduced from what it had been in 1913. The United Kingdom, by contrast, fared much better. Its government indebtedness, even so, was nearly twelve times higher in 1918 than it had been in 1914, and its total net debt to the United States, the highest among the Allies, standing at nearly 4.5 billion dollars by 1922, now meant, as for most of Europe, lasting dependence on credit from the USA. Neutral countries were also economically buffeted by the war. Mostly, like Sweden, they had been able to expand their economies to cope with wartime demands. The impact on neutral Spain, however, was to intensify its economic problems and to deepen the social, ideological and political fissures already present in the country.

In western Europe physical devastation from the war was largely confined to Belgium and north-east France. These battleground regions suffered grievously. Hundreds of thousands of houses had been destroyed, industry was extensively damaged, vast acreages of land were left unfit to till, and a large proportion of livestock had been killed. The worst affected areas were, however, no more than 30 to 60 kilometres wide. Beyond the fighting zone, France, along with the rest of western Europe, suffered remarkably little destruction. In the east, where the war had been more mobile, it was a different story. Serbia, Poland and the regions that would become Belarus and Ukraine, trampled on and ravaged by advancing and retreating armies, underwent extreme devastation.

Victorious soldiers going home to a hero's welcome in London at least found a country recognizable from the one they had left. Soldiers returning – often in disarray – to Vienna, Budapest, Munich or Berlin were in contrast plunged into revolutionary upheaval and economic chaos. Oddly, defeated Germany coped better than victorious Britain (or for that matter neutral Holland) in managing the post-war labour market and keeping down unemployment – partly by forcing women out of the jobs they had entered during the war and replacing them by men. Inflation, too, helped. Deflationary economics at this point would have wrecked the German economy still further and made it impossible to find jobs for so many ex-soldiers. The rampant inflation that the government did nothing to curb was, however, a price which would soon be paid in other, seriously damaging, ways.

Inflation had gathered pace in Germany during the war, when the national debt rose almost thirtyfold, paper money in circulation over twentyfold. Prices were about five times higher in 1918 than they had been before the war, and the currency had lost about half of its earlier value. Germany was not alone. Austria-Hungary's wartime inflation and currency depreciation were even greater. Most countries experienced inflation on some level during the war. Prices were three times higher in 1919 than they had been in 1913 in France, the Netherlands, Italy and the Scandinavian countries, almost two and a half times as high in the United Kingdom. Especially in central and eastern Europe, however, price inflation galloped out of control in the post-war years. In Poland, Austria and Russia the currency was ruined amid hyperinflation. Jan Słomka (whom we met in Chapter 2), for many years the mayor of the village of Dzików in south-eastern Poland, recalled a few years later the impact of the rampaging inflation after the Austrian Crown had been replaced by the Polish paper mark in 1920:

> If anyone sold anything and did not at once buy something else with the money, he would lose heavily. There were many who sold house or field, or part of their cattle, only to keep their money either at home or in some bank. These lost all they had and became beggars. On the other hand, those who borrowed money and bought things with it made fortunes. There were endless heaps of money. One had to carry it in briefcases or baskets. Purses and the like were useless. For things for the house one paid in thousands, then in millions, and finally in billions.

Only the introduction in 1924 of an entirely new currency, the złoty, produced stabilization in Poland.

In Germany the descent into hyperinflation was part of the grave political crisis that gripped the country in 1923 after the French, retaliating for German defaults on reparations payments, had occupied the Ruhr industrial heartlands. But the roots of the hyperinflation lay in war financing, based on the gamble that Germany would win the war and recoup its costs from the defeated countries. The economic consequences of the defeat then offered little incentive to Germany to prevent inflation. The German war effort had been mainly financed by domestic war loans. Inflation offered the means to liquidate these domestic debts. Early post-war measures to check rising prices gave way, once the reparations bill (which could only be paid in gold marks, not depreciated currency) was known in 1921, to a strategic readiness to accept high inflation.

As well as paying off domestic debts and staving off serious labour militancy that deflationary measures had prompted, for example, in Britain, inflation helped German industry to make a quick recovery after the war and gave a major boost to German exports. Industrialists could borrow what they needed for investment and repay the loans in depreciated currency. And as the German currency lost value, goods could be exported at highly competitive prices. It was little wonder that Germany experienced enormous growth in industrial production and shrinking unemployment between 1920 and 1922, at a time when deflationary policies in the USA, Britain and France saw exactly the reverse – falling rates of production and rising unemployment.

The wages of skilled industrial workers in Germany could often keep pace with inflation, at least at first. Trade unions had been able to build upon employers' wartime concessions to secure improvements in pay and working hours. But for the unskilled, or those on fixed incomes or pensions, the inflation was a mounting disaster. In 1923, during the Ruhr crisis, it ran completely out of control and turned into an outright catastrophe. In 1914 the US dollar – by the end of the war the crucial hard currency in Germany – had been worth 4.20 marks, at the end of the war it had climbed to 14 marks, by late 1920 it stood at 65 marks, in January 1922 it had reached 17,972 marks, and in November 1923 it had rocketed to a dizzy 44.2 billion marks. What such scarcely comprehensible figures meant to ordinary individuals living on their modest savings is graphically highlighted by the fate of an elderly, well-educated Berlin man whose savings of 100,000 marks might in different times have provided for a reasonably comfortable retirement but, with the currency worthless, was enough only to buy a ticket on the underground railway. He took a trip on the underground around his city and, on returning, shut himself in his apartment, where he died of hunger.

Nowhere in post-war Europe was there a land 'fit for heroes'. Grieving widows, orphaned children, crippled soldiers mingled with the hungry, the unemployed and the destitute in towns and villages across the continent. The war had left around 8 million invalids in need of state support. In Germany alone there were over half a million war widows and over a million orphans. Among the 650,000 who had suffered serious injury were 2,400 men blinded in the war, 65,000 who had lost either an arm or a leg, and over 1,300 who were now double amputees. Medicine had made advances during the war. But surgery could not fully heal such terrible wounds. And beyond the crippled bodies were the damaged minds, traumatized by war experiences – numbers estimated at 313,000 in Germany, 400,000 in Britain. Many never recovered, suffering from inadequate psychiatric treatment and scant public understanding of their condition. War invalids faced economic hardship and social discrimination.

Employers did not want physically handicapped workers, while former soldiers psychiatrically damaged by the war were often seen as 'hysterics' or suspected of feigning illness to obtain a pension.

The prominent British socialist and pacifist, Ethel Snowden (whose husband, Philip, would become the first Labour Chancellor of the Exchequer in 1924), vividly captured the social misery in Vienna just after the war: 'Uniformed officers sold roses in the cafés. Delicate women in faded finery begged with their children at street corners. Grass was growing in the principal streets. The shops were empty of consumers . . . At the Labour Exchanges many thousands of men and women stood in long lines to receive their out-of-work pay . . . Gallant doctors struggled in clinic and hospital with puny children covered with running sores, with practically no medicines, no soap, no disinfectants.'

In eastern Europe the situation was even more dire. Hundreds of thousands of refugees fleeing from the Russian Civil War faced bleak prospects wherever they went and seldom a friendly welcome from people themselves suffering great hardship. Poland, much of it ravaged for years by fighting, was in a terrible state. Half the population of Warsaw was receiving unemployment relief of some minimal kind just after the war, disease was widespread, and in eastern Poland there was near starvation. 'The country,' reported Sir William Goode, head of the British relief mission to central and eastern Europe in 1919, 'had undergone four or five occupations by different armies, each of which had combed the land for supplies. Most of the villages had been burnt down by the Russians in their retreat [of 1915]; land had been uncultivated for four years . . . The population here was living upon roots, grass, acorns and heather.' The wonder is not that there were widespread political disturbances in much of post-war Europe, but that revolutionary upheavals were not more extensive.

Nearly everywhere people had to contend not just with severe material hardship, but also with personal loss. In a people's war, with such immense casualties, there had to be some national recognition of the magnitude of the suffering.

French families wanted their loved ones buried in the churchyards of their home villages. The government eventually yielded to public pressure and the state paid for the exhumation and reburial of

300,000 of the identifiable dead. This was possible, if a huge logistical and bureaucratic procedure, because the French dead had fallen mainly in their own country. For other nations, something similar was not feasible. The dead had to be commemorated where they had been killed, although victors and vanquished were kept separate. The French, especially, could not bear the thought of their loved ones lying alongside Germans. So where the German dead lay buried alongside the French and British, they were exhumed and reburied in separate cemeteries. The result was the establishment of war cemeteries, each country's uniform in somewhat different ways, on or near the former battlegrounds. The cemeteries symbolized immortal heroism and sacrifice for the nation. They also touched popular piety, evoking the sense that the sacrifice had not been in vain, and that the fallen would rise again in the presence of God. Among the serried white ranks of identical gravestones in the manicured lawns of the British cemeteries would sometimes lie a soldier whose identity could not be established, accompanied by the simple inscription: 'Known unto God'. Bringing home an unknown soldier and interring him in a national shrine soon became the focal point of a nation's collective mourning. In 1920, amid enormous pomp and ritual, the French interred an 'Unknown Soldier' beneath the Arc de Triomphe in Paris, the British in Westminster Abbey in London. Italy, Belgium and Portugal followed these examples soon afterwards.

What was possible in national commemoration for the fallen of the western front was not replicated in the east. No monument at all was erected in Russia. There, the war flowed without pause into the revolutionary struggles and the even greater losses of the horrific civil war. With Bolshevism's triumph the First World War – viewed as simply a conflict of rapacious imperialist powers – receded behind the heroic myth of the civil war. Ideological demands meant that the First World War could have no place in collective memory.

Nor could a feeling of national unity in memory of the fallen similar to that of the victorious western powers be expected for the defeated countries, where the war had been divisive and led not just to military disaster and immense loss of life, but to huge political upheaval and ideological confrontation. Germany inaugurated a national monument to the dead in Berlin only as late as 1931 (though many local war memorials preceded this). The meaning of the conflict and the German defeat were too bitterly contested to find unity in any war commemoration. At one end of the spectrum of public emotion lay grief, horror at the human cost of the war and pacifism, so movingly captured in Käthe Kollwitz's sculpture, conceived during the war, completed more than a decade later, and placed in a Belgian cemetery, of parents mourning the loss of their son. At the other end of the spectrum was the sense of national humiliation and anger at the defeat and accompanying revolution, which incorporated war heroism into hopes of national resurrection and rebirth. It was encapsulated in the 'myth of Langemarck'. Near this Flemish village with a German-sounding name, some 20,000–25,000 hastily assembled and badly trained young German volunteers had lost their lives in a futile battle with the British as early as autumn 1914. At the hands of German propaganda, this near senseless loss had acquired lasting legendary status as a demonstration of the sacrifice and heroism of youth that was the necessary basis of national renewal. The myth of the fallen remained in Germany a central focus of ideological dispute that would find its disastrous resolution in the 1930s.

The horror of the war made pacifists of many people. 'The War itself had turned me into an opponent of war', was the reaction of the German socialist playwright Ernst Toller to what he described as 'a catastrophe for Europe, a plague on humanity, the crime of our century'. From her revulsion at the death and suffering, and despondency at the loss of her fiancé, her brother and two close friends, the English writer Vera Brittain became a pacifist, socialist and ardent fighter for women's rights. In France, Madeleine Vernet, who before the war had run an orphanage, founded the 'League of Women against War', attracting support from feminists, socialists and communists. There, as in many parts of Europe, ideals of peace and an end to the social inequalities built into capitalist competition found ready ears. Idealistic pacifism remained, however, confined to a minority. Most of the soldiers returning home were not pacifists. They had fought, and would if patriotic duty and necessity demanded it reluctantly fight again. But they overwhelmingly wanted peace, security, a return to normality and a better future, without war. The vast majority wanted to get back to their farms, their workplaces, their villages and towns, above all to their families. This was the most commonplace reaction – certainly in western Europe – as people tried in different ways to reconstruct lives that had so often been upturned by the experience of this terrible conflict. The horror of what had happened produced the overwhelming conviction that there must never again be war.

CHAMPIONS OF
COUNTER-REVOLUTION

Not all, however, felt that way. There was an altogether different and competing legacy of Europe's great conflagration – a legacy that glorified war and welcomed violence and hatred. For many, the war simply did not end in November 1918. The culture shock of defeat, of revolution and the triumph of socialism, and the paranoid fears of 'Red Terror' in horror stories spread by refugees fleeing from the Russian Civil War fed a brutal mentality in which the killing and maiming of those viewed as responsible for the disaster became a duty, necessity and pleasure – a normal way of life.

New and frightening levels of intense political violence were a characteristic of much of post-war Europe. North-western Europe was not exempt, as testified by the high level of violence in Ireland between 1919 and 1923 during the struggle for independence from British rule – including sectarian killings, arbitrary brutality by British paramilitaries (the 'Black and Tans'), and eventually a brief but bloody civil war in 1922–3. The short-lived 'Easter Rising' against British rule in 1916 had been quickly suppressed, though it included counterproductive brutality towards prisoners and executions of the leaders of the insurrection that left an enduring legacy of bitterness. This fed into the guerrilla war for independence that, from 1919 onwards, was waged with much intimidatory violence by the Irish Republican Army (IRA). The British responded by deploying the Black and Tans. So called after their improvised uniforms – part police dark-green (not actually black), part army khaki – the Black and Tans comprised around 9,000 ex-servicemen, augmented by 2,200 former officers who formed an Auxiliary Division of the Royal Irish Constabulary, a force hated by Irish nationalists. The atrocities of the Black and Tans

and Auxiliary Division, including rape, torture, murder, and the burning down of houses of supposed insurgents, went a long way towards
poisoning Anglo-Irish relations for decades. Even Oswald Mosley,
who more than a decade later would go on to lead the British Union
of Fascists, was disgusted by their actions. Indeed their violence was
sickening – a lasting stain on British history.

But Ireland was an exception in north-western Europe – an exception even within the United Kingdom. The British government had
always regarded Ireland as a quasi-colony, to be treated differently
from other parts of the British Isles. Extremes of repressive violence
were otherwise reserved for Britain's colonial possessions (such as the
shooting by British troops under General Reginald Dyer of several hundred unarmed demonstrators in Amritsar in April 1919 as the struggle
for Indian independence gathered support, inspired by Mahatma Gandhi). At home, on the British mainland, the scale of post-war disorder
nowhere seriously threatened to turn into revolution. Civil defence formations were used in Britain and France to combat strikes in 1919 and
1920. But social and political unrest was contained by the state and fell
far short of gathering any revolutionary momentum. Paramilitary
mobilization became a significant concern only a decade or so later in
France, under different circumstances, and never threatened to upturn
the political order in Britain.

In southern Europe it was a different matter. Mounting political violence formed a backdrop to the rise of Fascism in Italy by 1922 and to
the establishment of a military dictatorship in Spain the following year.
And at the south-eastern tip of Europe the extreme violence that long
pre-dated the First World War, and which had included the deportation and massacres of hundreds of thousands of Armenians in 1915,
continued in the early post-war years. The worst occurred when, after
three years under Greek occupation, the Turks retook the multi-ethnic
Aegean port of Smyrna (now Izmir) on Turkey's western shores in September 1922, set fire to the parts of the city inhabited by Greeks and
Armenians, and massacred tens of thousands of them. The endemic
violence in the region finally subsided in 1923 with the end of catastrophic attempts by Greece to extend its territory to include western
Turkey. The Treaty of Lausanne that year ratified an exchange of
population (actually expulsions), the largest before the Second World

War, with the establishment of the new Turkish republic. It amounted to the first internationally agreed case of major ethnic cleansing – of over a million Greeks (most of whom had already fled from Anatolia the previous year) from Turkey and 360,000 Turks from Greece.

The epicentre of the new and extreme counter-revolutionary violence, greater than anything witnessed here since the Thirty Years War of the seventeenth century, was located nevertheless in central and eastern Europe. Here, whole societies, not just soldiers returning from years of exposure to killing and inured to bloodshed and suffering, had been brutalized. Scorched-earth policies and the deportation of civilians had been part of the war on the eastern front. And there the fighting did not stop in November 1918 but flowed without break into fierce border conflicts in Poland and into the Russian Civil War – of a horror that sent shock waves convulsing throughout eastern and central Europe.

Preventing Bolshevism from spreading to their own homelands was a crucial motive of counter-revolutionaries, some of whom readily participated in the anti-Bolshevik campaigns in the Baltic and elsewhere. But the violence was not simply a reaction to what was happening in Russia. The left-wing revolutions that swept the lands of the defeated Central Powers encountered opposition everywhere. Armed paramilitary organizations gathered strength amid the political chaos. Their leaders had invariably experienced the slaughter at the front, often in the east, during the First World War. What had horrified most Europeans had been for these men an exhilarating experience. They heroized fighting and extolled killing. When they came home, it was to a world that they did not understand, a world, as one put it, 'turned upside down'. They felt a sense of betrayal, or simply saw no future in a return to mundane, often poverty-stricken, civilian life. Many who felt like this found their way into the racial violence of paramilitary politics, burgeoning especially between the east of Germany and the west of Russia, and from the Baltic to the Balkans. The German *Freikorps* (freebooters, at government expense), often under aristocratic leadership, are estimated to have attracted between 200,000 and 400,000 men. They operated where border conflicts, radical ethnic nationalism, the threat of Bolshevism and a visceral hatred of Jews created a potent mix of violent emotions.

Around a quarter of the 225,000 German officers returning home in 1918, mainly lower-ranking from middle-class backgrounds, joined one or other of the paramilitary *Freikorps* units. So did a large number of unemployed former soldiers and landless labourers, hoping to acquire some land in the east and meanwhile contenting themselves with what they could plunder. War veterans were, however, outnumbered by activists too young to have fought in the war, though sharing a similar mentality with those disaffected by the peace – a 'war youth generation' fed on militaristic values and expectations of national glory.

The paramilitary recruits looked for ways to uphold – or try to recreate – the camaraderie, the 'trench community', the male bonds, and the sheer excitement of armed conflict. They recalled, or imagined, a sense of unity, of patriotic fervour, of commitment to a cause worth fighting and dying for. And this greatly magnified the bitterness they now felt towards those who, in their eyes, had demanded the enormous human sacrifice that had brought not victory and glory but defeat and humiliation. It enormously heightened the thirst for revenge that these paramilitary recruits felt against those deemed responsible for loss of parts of their homeland and those they viewed as creating a world opposed to all that they stood for – a world shaped by disorder, lack of authority, injustice, chaos (seen as fomented by the 'Reds') and 'effeminate' democracy. Their response was extreme violence.

The new upsurge of violence had no clear or coherent ideology. Greed, envy, thirst for material gain, desire to grab land all played their part. The violence itself owed far more to untrammelled activism than to a preconceived view of a future society or the form of the state. But it was ideological just the same; targeted and not random, aimed at the revolutionary forces – mainly perceived as internal enemies – that threatened to destroy the values they held dear.

Most prominent among these internal enemies were communists, socialists and, not least, Jews. For many of the champions of counter-revolution, these internal enemies blended into one another. When they saw Jews playing a prominent part in revolutionary movements – Leon Trotsky among others in Russia, Béla Kun in Hungary, Victor Adler and Otto Bauer in Austria, Kurt Eisner and Rosa Luxemburg in Germany, together with several leading figures in the short-lived 'soviet republic' in Munich in April 1919 – it just confirmed their fantasies, set in motion by that pre-war forgery of the Tsarist police, *The Protocols of the Elders of Zion*, of a 'Jewish world conspiracy' to undermine Europe's culture, morality and political order. Jews had for the most part welcomed the Russian Revolution as heralding emancipation. They had great hopes of a socialist future without discrimination and persecution. They joined the revolutionary movement in disproportionate numbers and came to play a significant role in Soviet administration and policing. As many as 75 per cent of the Kiev political police (the Cheka) in 1919 were Jewish, for instance. In eastern Europe, Jews became identified with Bolshevism – though most were, in fact, not revolutionaries. They were to pay a terrible price.

Many soldiers had soaked up the poisonous antisemitic propaganda that the Central Powers and the Russians had spread in the trenches as adversity deepened and defeat became ever more likely. The chaotic conditions in central and eastern Europe that followed the end of the war saw a cascade of anti-Jewish violence. 'Jews are hated everywhere,' wrote a Russian sociologist in 1921. 'They are hated by people regardless of their class or education, political persuasion, race, or age.' He saw hatred of the Jews as 'one of the most prominent features of Russian life today, perhaps even the most prominent'. The civil war led to an onslaught on Jews, at its worst in Ukraine. In some 1,300 pogroms there between 50,000 and 60,000 Jews were killed. The continued fierce fighting between Ukrainians and Poles in East Galicia spawned anti-Jewish violence in over a hundred townships, including Lvov, where seventy Jews were killed during a major pogrom when the Polish army entered the city in July 1919.

There was extensive anti-Jewish violence, too, in Hungary after the collapse of Béla Kun's short-lived communist regime in August 1919. A flavour of the intense hatred of Jews and their identification with Bolshevism was captured by the remarks of an otherwise refined and charming Hungarian aristocratic lady, recalled by Ethel Snowden in summer 1919: 'I would kill every Bolshevik if I could have my way; and they wouldn't die an easy death either. I would roast them in front of a slow fire. Think of what those dirty Jews have done to some of our best men. And all my clothes and jewels gone! ... Some horrid little Jewess is pulling [my beautiful white boots] on to her ugly feet this very minute, I am positive.' Given such a mentality, atrocities towards Jews in the wake of Hungary's post-war political turmoil were hardly surprising. In the parts of the country west of the Danube more than 3,000 Jews were murdered, according to a report in 1922.

Even in the new Czech republic, a beacon of emerging democratic freedom among the new states to emerge from the Habsburg Empire, there were pogroms, while student riots forced the Jewish rector of Prague University to resign in 1922. Germany and Austria experienced no pogroms. The violent antisemitic rhetoric did its work, nevertheless, in poisoning the atmosphere that led to the murder of Jews in prominent political positions, such as Kurt Eisner, the Bavarian Minister President, in 1919 and Walther Rathenau, the Reich Foreign Minister, in 1922.

The violence of the counter-revolutionaries knew few bounds. It invariably went far beyond the revolutionary violence that they claimed to be combating. 'Red Terror' is estimated to have taken the lives of five persons in Austria, up to 200 in Germany, and between 400 and 500 in Hungary. There were at least 850 victims of counter-revolutionary violence in Austria. The suppression of the Bavarian 'soviet republic' at the end of April 1919 brought a death toll of 606 persons, 335 of them civilians. And 'white terror' in Hungary, following the collapse of Béla Kun's soviet regime in Budapest, killed around 1,500 people, at least three times the number who had died at the hands of the Reds.

'No pardon is given. We shoot even the wounded,' wrote one student volunteer to his parents after participating in the repression of a communist uprising in Germany's Ruhr district in 1920. 'We slaughtered whoever fell into our hands ... There were no human feelings left in our hearts,' recalled another young German who participated in paramilitary fighting in the Baltic in 1919. Rudolf Höss, who later, as commandant of Auschwitz, presided over an unprecedented programme of orchestrated mass killing, remembered the fighting in the Baltic as more grim than anything he had witnessed during the First World War – 'pure slaughter to the point of complete annihilation'. The Baltic and Upper Silesia, where there was fierce fighting between Poles and Germans between 1919 and 1921, were the settings for a huge loss of life, perhaps as high as 100,000, at the hands of paramilitaries.

Paramilitary violence declined sharply after 1923. But those who had been at the forefront of the violence did not alter in character or attitude, even if they had to adapt to changed times. Many would find new opportunities in the fascist movements that gathered support across Europe during the 1930s. And in the regions of greatest violence there would be far worse to come – in no small measure as a reaction to the successful establishment of Soviet communism in Russia.

BOLSHEVISM TRIUMPHANT

It was inevitable that the Bolshevik Revolution in 1917 would not be accepted without a fight by those who stood to be dispossessed of land and other property. The result was a civil war of unimaginable savagery and bloodshed that raged for three years and cost the lives of over 7 million men, women and children, around four times Russia's losses in the Great War, the majority of them civilians. Huge numbers died from associated hunger and epidemic disease as well as actual fighting and terroristic repression.

What constituted the civil war was actually a series of wars, loosely interconnected through the common aim of the 'White' counter-revolutionary forces to try to strangle the new Soviet regime at birth. There was an international dimension. The 'Whites', led in the main by former high-ranking Tsarist officers and Cossacks, were backed by Allied troops, weaponry and logistical support. Some 30,000 Czech, American, British, Italian and French troops helped the White army fighting westwards from Siberia in 1919. The Allies provided munitions for the Whites equivalent to the entire Soviet production that year. Foreign support waned thereafter, however, and was of less importance than Soviet accounts of the civil war later claimed. For a time, especially in 1919, the outcome was far from certain. But by late 1920, Bolshevik power over practically the entirety of the vast territory of the former Russian Empire had survived. The final stages of the civil war merged with the war in 1920 of the increasingly victorious Red Army against Marshal Józef Piłsudski's Polish army. After the Poles had been driven out of Kiev (which changed hands a dozen times during the civil war) and the Red Army had been repulsed in August by Piłsudski's forces at the gates of Warsaw, an armistice in the autumn of 1920 produced a settlement that extended the Polish eastern border with the Soviet state. The Treaty of Riga in March 1921 guaranteed the new border – at least until the next great war.

The anti-Soviet campaigns, reaching their climax in 1919, took place largely in the peripheral regions of the former Russian Empire. The key to ultimate victory by the Reds, however, was their control of the large central core zone of Russia, together with superior organizational capacity and utter ruthlessness as well as divisions among their opponents. The vast territory gave the Reds access to huge manpower reserves (conscripted with the help of a good dose of terror in the countryside) and foodstuffs, ruthlessly extracted from an increasingly truculent but brutally cowed peasantry. This made possible the rapid expansion of the Red Army, which grew from a mere 430,000 men in October 1918 to 5,300,000 by the end of 1920. Badly equipped, ill-provisioned and often undisciplined though it was, the huge mass army, commanded by 75,000 former officers of the Tsarist army, marshalled by ferocious discipline, and fighting to defend the revolution, was more than a match for the numerically weaker and less cohesive White forces. Although the popularity of the Soviet state (which had been built heavily upon promise of land reform for the overwhelmingly peasant population) was rapidly declining, Bolshevik supremacy, the suppression of opposition parties, and ruthless terror against any who offered resistance meant that there was little alternative to compliance.

In any case, the Whites put forward little by way of a social programme that could favourably compete with that of the Bolsheviks. The White leaders, conservative Russian nationalists whose only objective seemed to be to turn the clock back to the pre-revolutionary period, were unable to win much support from non-Russian nationalists in peripheral regions. Ukraine, for instance, had a population of some 32 million, largely peasant, fervent Ukrainian nationalists who could not be mobilized for the Greater Russian cause. The Whites lacked not just a coherent programme; they were also organizationally weaker than the Soviets, could raise only smaller armies, suffered from poor communications, and had no coordinated military strategy. Yet the outcome of the civil war was far from a foregone conclusion. It took three years of the most bitter and bloody conflict before the Red Army was assured of outright victory. It would, nevertheless, have been against all the odds had Bolshevism not ultimately prevailed.

When the civil war ended the Soviet economy was in ruins. Industrial production had fallen by over 66 per cent compared with 1913, agricultural production by 40 per cent. Politically, too, the problems were enormous. By early 1921, under the extreme food shortages caused by peasants holding back their produce, industrial workers in Russia's big cities – the heartlands of Bolshevism – were in revolt against the coercive methods of the regime. Martial law had to be declared in Moscow and St Petersburg in the wake of huge strikes in February (new Russian calendar). Mounting danger for the regime reached a critical point in a rising by sailors – avid Bolshevik adherents in 1917 – from the naval base in Kronstadt, just outside Petrograd, in March 1921. The regime reacted with utter ruthlessness. Trotsky warned the rebel sailors that they would 'be shot like partridges' if they did not surrender within twenty-four hours. When they continued to resist, Trotsky was as good as his word. A major assault on the fortress at Kronstadt was launched by 50,000 troops from the Red Army. After a battle lasting eighteen hours, the uprising collapsed. Over 10,000 rebel sailors and Red Army soldiers lay dead. Thousands more rebels were executed or sent to concentration camps.

The uprising of one-time ardent supporters had shocked the Bolshevik rulers to the core. If that was a warning, the regime faced a much bigger challenge in winning over the vast majority of the population, the peasantry, whose hostility to Bolshevik land policy had become acute. Immediately following the revolution, in order to win peasant support the Bolsheviks had legalized the redistribution of land among the peasantry. But the forced requisitioning of peasant produce during the civil war and early attempts to introduce farming collectives had created a rebellious peasantry. The collectives were unproductive; the peasants deliberately sowed less. Sometimes the forced exactions of grain in any case amounted to no seed left to sow. The result was famine in 1921–2. Peasant revolts broke out in numerous regions, sometimes accompanied by gruesome violence against local Bolsheviks. Lenin saw the threat to the regime from the peasant wars as greater than that of the Whites in the civil war. The response was a massive use of force to put down the peasant risings during the summer of 1921. Thousands of peasants were shot, tens of thousands more sent to camps. But the big stick was not enough. Coercion alone, as the civil war had shown, would not produce food.

The Bolsheviks had not only completely alienated the major section of the population on whose cooperation they depended politically; they desperately needed the peasants to produce more. This brought a volte-face by the regime's leadership. Lenin bought off an increasingly rebellious peasantry by a 'New Economic Policy' introduced at the Tenth Party Congress in March 1921. This relaxed party control over agriculture and re-established a partial market economy while retaining state ownership of all major branches of industrial production, transport, energy and communications. Goods started to appear again. Economic recovery was soon under way – even if there was great resentment in the towns at the profiteers who shamelessly exploited the new conditions of supply and demand.

By the time of Lenin's death in January 1924 the economy had revived. The regime had weathered the major storm. Despite the buffeting it had taken, all parts of the Soviet state were by now in the hands of the Bolshevik Party. The party's organization, rigidly controlled from the centre by its General Secretary, Joseph Stalin, created a system of patronage and corruption that bought the allegiance of growing numbers of placemen and *apparatchiks*. The number of bureaucrats quadrupled to 2.4 million within four years of the revolution. And a huge influx of new party members – almost 1.5 million entrants by 1920, two-thirds of them from peasant backgrounds, hoping for better lives – helped the Bolsheviks to consolidate their hold on power, and to extend their penetration of the countryside.

Early idealistic notions of popular participation in the running of political, economic and social matters through elected representatives in the soviets, based upon worker control of production, had of necessity been reformulated. Communism itself would have to wait till the dawn of the utopia. Meanwhile, power in the socialist state would and could only be exercised by the avant-garde of the proletariat, the party. Any opposition could be dubbed 'bourgeois' and 'reactionary' and had to be destroyed. 'Bourgeois' law could not stand in the way of the merciless extirpation of class enemies.

Terror as an essential weapon in the class war was central to the Bolshevik revolutionary project. 'Let there be floods of bourgeois blood – more blood, as much as possible,' the Bolshevik press had urged in 1918. 'We must encourage the energy and the popular nature of the terror,' Lenin had written that summer. Turning the hatred of peasants, desperate for land, against *kulaks*, portrayed as land exploiters but often only marginally better-off peasants, was part of the strategy. Describing them as 'bloodsuckers [who] have grown rich on the hunger of the people', Lenin decried the kulaks as 'rabid foes of the Soviet government', 'leeches [who] have sucked the blood of the working people' and advocated 'death to all of them'.

By 1922, when the regime felt strong enough to attack religious worship and to destroy the hold of the Orthodox Church, Lenin encouraged 'merciless war' against the clergy. 'The more members of the reactionary bourgeoisie and clergy we manage to shoot, the better,' he stated. The early Soviet Union was already a regime in which conventional law had no place, one that gave licence to the unconstrained power of the Cheka, the state security police. 'The Cheka must defend the revolution and conquer the enemy even if its sword falls occasionally on the heads of the innocent,' declared its head, Felix Dzerzhinsky. This was a cynical understatement. Arbitrary imprisonment, torture and executions became commonplace. How many fell victim to the terror of the Cheka is not known. Estimates put the figure at several hundred thousand, including those thrown into prisons and camps. Inside the prisons, the torture methods deployed were hideous in the extreme.

The essential characteristics of Bolshevik rule had, then, emerged during Lenin's lifetime. What followed was continuation and logical consequence, not an aberration. Within the Bolshevik leadership, intense political, ideological and personal conflicts had been just about held in check as long as Lenin lived. But his death at the start of 1924, following a long illness, opened up a protracted and bitter power struggle. The winner, though this only gradually became obvious, turned out to be Joseph Stalin. Under his leadership, a new and even more terrible phase in the early history of the Soviet Union was to follow.

Despite the paranoid fears on the European Right, Bolshevism soon proved to be non-exportable. The Soviet leaders had at first reckoned with the spread of revolution across Europe. But during the civil war they had to accept that this was not going to happen. Lenin realized this no later than the autumn of 1920, when the Red Army was defeated by the Poles outside Warsaw. Conditions in Russia were completely unlike those in the rest of Europe. The very vastness of the country – the largest on earth, far greater in size than the rest of Europe put together, stretching 5,000 miles from east to west, and 2,000 miles from north to south – imposed its own peculiarities of political control. Uniquely in pre-war Europe, Tsarist rule had been unconstrained until 1906 by any constitutional restrictions, and thereafter only by fig-leaf constitutionalism. Russia had no independent basis of law and no representative framework of pluralist politics that could have worked for the gradual reform of state institutions elsewhere.

Compared with other parts of Europe, civil society in Russia was weak. Only a small property-owning middle class had emerged, and repression of political dissidence had produced an intelligentsia that was tiny but radicalized. Despite rapid modernization that had created an impoverished proletariat in the big industrial cities, Russia had remained intensely backward economically, a country in which the peasantry – more than 80 per cent of the population – lived largely in communes, often in the economic bonds of servility under the neo-feudal dominance of those who possessed the land, and they viewed the state and its officials with great hostility. Violence, brutality and scant regard for human life had been deeply embedded in this society. The Russian peasantry, as Lenin rightly adjudged, were a revolutionary class with no stake in property and order. Nowhere else in Europe was this true, even accounting for peasant antipathy towards estate owners in many parts of the continent and insurgent tendencies among agricultural labourers in some regions of Spain and Italy. Russia offered socially, economically, ideologically and politically propitious preconditions, even before the calamities of the First World War radicalized conditions and swept away Tsarism, for a fundamental revolutionary transformation that could not be replicated elsewhere.

Following the civil war, Soviet Russia became in effect an alien body, as good as quarantined from the mainstream of European politics, turned in on itself and subjected to the immense internal brutality that would accompany the building of the Soviet state and the modernization of its economy over the following years. As a million or so fleeing emigrés, many of them former supporters of the Tsarist regime, spread horror stories about Soviet Russia in European capitals, feeding the anti-Bolshevik hysteria as it spread across the continent, Bolshevism swiftly turned into a bogeyman to be feared and reviled, a negative focus for the politics of the conservative and radical Right.

During the deliberations of the leaders of the victorious powers, meeting in Paris in 1919 at the Versailles Conference to redraw the map of Europe, Russia already figured only as a negative entity. Militarily supporting the attempt to destroy Bolshevism and not prepared to recognize the Soviet Union, they had no option but to leave the thorny question of the validity and contours of Europe's eastern borders open.

THE GREAT CARVE-UP

The new map of Europe, when it took shape, looked very different to that of 1914. Four empires – the Russian, Ottoman, Austro-Hungarian and German – had vanished (though the new republic in Germany retained the name 'Reich', the symbol of a historic German Empire in Europe stretching back to Charlemagne). Their collapse amounted to a cataclysmic shift in the political structures of central, eastern and southern Europe. Ten new nation states (including, by 1923, Turkey) emerged in their wake.

The task of creating Europe's new order fell essentially on the four leaders of the victorious powers: the President of the United States, Woodrow Wilson, the French Premier, Georges Clemenceau, the British Prime Minister, David Lloyd George, and the Italian Prime Minister, Vittorio Orlando. The challenge facing them when they arrived in Paris to begin work in January 1919 was unenviable. Driven by Wilson's idealism, behind which lay the calculated aim of global economic dominance by the USA and a post-war world built in the American image, they had lofty ambitions. One was to set up a framework that would prevent Europe from again descending into war by establishing a League of Nations to guarantee collective security and international peace.

It was a noble ideal. After its foundation in January 1920 the League, comprising forty-eight member states by the end of that year with its headquarters in Geneva, sought to work for international cooperation, to protect ethnic minorities, and to do everything possible to mitigate the humanitarian crisis in central and eastern Europe. But most important of all was the commitment to uphold the post-war international settlement. This would prove a pipe-dream. Without military might to intervene, notions of an effective multi-national framework of collective security were illusory. And, for all that it was intended to be a truly global organization, the League remained in practice a largely European affair, dominated especially by the interests of Britain and France. Wilson's political opponents in the USA would ensure that America, which was meant to be the League's key player, was not even a member.

Wilson's central ideal, which underlaid the deliberations in Paris, was 'self-determination'. The term was susceptible to different meanings and Wilson was content to be vague about its definition, not least since its implications for maintaining power in the colonies were barely palatable to the major imperial powers, Britain and France. For Wilson, self-determination essentially meant government derived from popular sovereignty – the right of a people to have their own state, which would ideally evolve over time and not result from violent revolution.

In the disastrous conditions of post-war Europe, however, self-determination – a revolutionary concept – was a demand for the immediate future, not a long-term aspiration. The Bolsheviks had in fact been the first to use the concept. But their interest in self-determination was purely instrumental. Their support for nationalist movements was extended in order to undermine and destroy the existing multi-national empires in Europe and more generally to weaken or overthrow imperialism. However, in Stalin's words, 'when the right of self-determination conflicts with another, a higher right – the right of the working class that has come to power to consolidate that power', then 'the right of self-determination cannot and must not serve as an obstacle to the working class in exercising its right to dictatorship'. As this made abundantly plain, 'national self-determination' in the emerging Soviet Union was to become wholly subordinated to the centralizing power of the Bolshevik state.

The vision of self-determination that underpinned the deliberations at the Versailles Conference in 1919 (to which the Soviets were not invited) ran completely counter to the Bolshevik interpretation. It was to be the framework for a world order based on liberal democracy – government by popular consent in a state resting on popular sovereignty. The underlying problem, however, was that precisely in the most unsettled parts of the continent the claim to popular sovereignty was based on ethnic nationalism. And most of the territories of the fallen empires contained more than one nationality staking a claim to land, resources and political representation. In the countries of western Europe (as in the USA) the state had over time shaped the nation; association with the institutions of the state had gradually formed a national consciousness. But in most of central, eastern and southern Europe, national consciousness had emerged from the demands of a people defined by ethnicity, language and culture to establish a state that represented – often exclusively – their interests. How was self-determination to be squared with competing claims to a sovereign nation state?

It was obvious to the 'Big Four' from the outset that the complex ethnic mix of central and eastern Europe made national self-determination impossible to achieve. The peacemakers could only do their best – and hope that functioning nation states, in which ethnic differences were superseded by national unity in a multi-ethnic state, would emerge over time. However they adjusted Europe's boundaries, these were bound to include some sizeable national minorities, whose rights would be safeguarded (so it was thought) by appeal to the League of Nations. None of the new states, apart from the small rump of German-speaking Austria, was ethnically homogeneous. Three and a half million Hungarians, for instance, ended up living outside Hungary, many in territory handed to Romania, while 3 million Germans found themselves living in Czechoslovakia. When the new lines on the map were finally agreed, they had, in fact, less to do with the self-determination of nationalities than with the feasibility of satisfying some territorial claims at the expense of others, while trying to minimize any likely ensuing tension or hostility.

Almost everywhere there were hotly disputed territories. Claims resting on ethnicity were almost invariably spurious – merely a (sometimes transparent) cover for territorial ambitions, driven by economic, military or strategic reasons. Claims and counter-claims – between Greece, Bulgaria and Serbia (all wanting some of Macedonia), between Greece and Italy (over Albania), between Romania and Hungary (both staking claims to Transylvania), or between Poland and Germany (disputing Silesia) – were all made by paying lip-service to self-determination, but they were actually no more than attempts at traditional territorial aggrandizement. Some claims could barely even pretend to be about self-determination. These included Italy's demands for the predominantly German-speaking South Tyrol; the almost entirely Slav-populated Dalmatian coast; parts of Asia Minor settled mainly by Greeks and Turks; and, what became a cause célèbre for budding Fascists, the small port of Fiume (now Rijeka in Croatia), which had only a partially Italian population.

Trying to adjudicate on the complex disputes caused nightmares for the Big Four in Paris. Some artificiality behind the new state boundaries was inevitable. In a number of cases – Czechoslovakia, the Kingdom of the Serbs, Croats and Slovenes (renamed Yugoslavia in 1929), and Poland – it was a matter of recognizing existing reality in states created from the fallen empires at the end of the First World War. In other instances, it was to reward support for the Entente during the war and to punish the subjugated enemy. Romania, for example, was a major beneficiary, doubling its size, largely at the expense of Hungary. In central Europe, Austria, Hungary and Germany were major losers in the territorial redistribution.

Rejoicing among the winners from the territorial settlement was more than matched by dismay, anger and smouldering resentment among the losers. In Italy the fury over Fiume played into the hands of the rabid nationalists. The proto-fascist poet Gabriele D'Annunzio, who had himself coined the phrase 'mutilated victory' to imply that

Italy had been cheated out of rightful gains from the war, made the cause of Fiume his own and in mid-September 1919 led a motley paramilitary force into a bizarre occupation of the small Adriatic town, which lasted for fifteen months. In the Treaty of Rapallo signed between Italy and Yugoslavia in November 1920, Fiume was eventually designated a free city with land links to Italy. But Fiume remained a banner for the Fascists, who were gathering strength in Italy, and it was to be annexed by Benito Mussolini in 1924.

However difficult proved so many of the territorial issues arising from the war that the Big Four gathered in Paris had to deal with, their central and overriding priority was Germany. They were unanimous in holding Germany primarily to blame for the great conflagration. In their eyes the invasion of France (for the second time in just over forty years) and the breach of Belgian neutrality, accompanied by atrocities against the civilian population, pointed the finger of blame squarely at Germany. The questions of punishment and retribution for the exorbitant costs of the war were, therefore, the most pressing concerns of the Allied leaders. More crucial still was ensuring that Germany should never again be in a position to plunge Europe into war. German militarism and industrial muscle might, if not sufficiently tamed, again threaten Europe's peace. On the other hand, Germany's economic importance to a future Europe was obvious. Moreover, crushing Germany (which would have been popular in France, especially) might open the door for Bolshevism to spread into the heart of Europe.

A problem for the Allies was that many Germans did not recognize that their country had been militarily defeated. Germany was undestroyed after four years of war. No Allied troops had stood on German soil at the Armistice, though German forces at that time still occupied much of Belgium, and Luxembourg. German soldiers were welcomed home with festive flags and flowers. The Prussian War Ministry declared soon after the Armistice that 'our field-grey heroes return to the *Heimat* undefeated'. It was untrue. But the sentiment was repeated by the High Command of the Army; then in December 1918 by no less a person than the new Socialist head of government, Friedrich Ebert. The legend soon to be put about by the counter-revolutionary Right, that the troops at the front had been stabbed in the back by labour unrest fomented by revolutionary socialists at home, could germinate in fertile soil.

When the Allied terms were announced in early May 1919, the palpable shock in Germany was much greater than it would have been had its military defeat been obvious. The terms were severe – though not as harsh as those that the Germans had imposed on the Russians at Brest-Litovsk in March 1918, and too lenient for the liking of French public opinion, thirsting for much more draconian punitive measures. Germany was to lose some 13 per cent of its pre-war territory in Europe (including rich agricultural and industrial regions, mainly in the east), resulting in the exclusion of around 10 per cent of its pre-war population of 65 million. In economic terms, the losses were damaging but not irreparable. The real damage was political and psychological – the heavy blow to national pride and prestige.

The sense of humiliation was heightened by the Allied stipulations for demilitarization. The once mighty German army, which had still managed to put about 4.5 million men in the field in 1918, was to be reduced to a mere 100,000 men, and conscription was barred. The navy (whose ships and submarines had been taken into Allied hands or destroyed after the Armistice) was reduced to 15,000 men. No submarines were to be permitted in future. And Germany was banned from having a military air force.

The anger in Germany at the territorial changes was immense, and it crossed political and ideological boundaries. The Treaty of Versailles was denounced as a victors' *Diktat*. 'I am in no doubt that the Treaty must be revised,' wrote the diplomat Bernhard von Bülow in 1920. 'We must use the monstrosity of the Treaty and the impossibility of implementing so many of its stipulations in order to bring down the entire Versailles Peace.'

There were certainly some awkward hostages to fortune should Germany ever become powerful again. Danzig (today's Gdansk), for instance, an almost entirely German industrial port but now surrounded by Poland, was designated a League of Nations 'free city', with Polish access to necessary coastal trading facilities. Another fudge was produced to adjudicate on the Saarland, lying on the border with France and industrially important because of its coal and iron-ore deposits – so coveted by the French though mainly German populated. The French were given ownership of the mines, but the Saarland itself was placed under League of Nations administration for a fifteen-year period, after which the inhabitants could decide by plebiscite whether they wanted to belong to France or Germany or retain the status quo. Yet another uneasy arrangement was reached on the Rhineland. The French, desperate to ensure lasting security, wanted a permanent Allied occupation of the almost wholly German-populated area and Germany's western border to be fixed at the Rhine. France had to settle for occupation of the Rhineland for a period of fifteen years. The Germans were powerless to do anything about it – yet – but the deep sense of grievance did not go away.

Other painful amputations of German territory also played into the hands of nationalists who, even if forced to bide their time, kept alive hopes of a later revision of the terms of the Treaty of Versailles. In the west, the changes were relatively insignificant. The small, predominantly German-speaking border area of Eupen-Malmédy was given to Belgium. The northern part of Schleswig, mainly Danish speaking, went to Denmark. But in the east, the territorial losses were more acutely felt. What became known as the Polish Corridor took away West Prussia and Posen from Germany, incorporating them in the new state of Poland, but in the process it cut off East Prussia from the rest of Germany. German resentment at territorial losses was amplified in 1922 when, following an inconclusive plebiscite conducted amid heated nationalist agitation on both sides, the industrial belt of Upper Silesia, rich in coal and other minerals, was also assigned to Poland.

The deepest anger and resentment of all were reserved for Article 231 of the Treaty, and its implications. Article 231, later commonly known as 'the war guilt clause', deemed that Germany and its allies were responsible for the war. It provided the legal basis for Germany's liability to pay reparations for war damages – vehemently demanded by a baying public opinion in both France and Britain. The amount of reparations was left to an Allied Commission to determine and, in 1921, was eventually fixed at 132 billion gold marks. Huge though the sum was, it could have been repaid over time without crippling the German economy. In the event, most of it would never be paid.

Reparations were, in fact, not primarily an economic problem. The real damage was political. They remained for over a decade a cancer in German politics – sometimes receding, at other times recurring to attack the nation's political health through inciting further nationalist agitation. By the time the reparations were in practice written off, in 1932, Germany was in crisis again and a more dangerous nationalist menace than ever before was looming.

The Big Four had faced huge objective problems in attempting to rearrange Europe's boundaries. They were also subject to pressures from the public of their home countries. Unholy compromises were inevitable. Nevertheless, they had produced not so much a framework for lasting peace as a recipe for potential future disaster. The compromises left behind a Europe resembling a flimsy house of cards. For the time being the new order would hold, if only for the negative reasons that no force was powerful enough to destroy it. But Germany was the lingering problem. Should it ever again become militarily strong, the house of cards could easily come tumbling down. The Paris peacemakers had contained, but not eliminated, Germany's capacity to cause further problems. The militarism, aggressive nationalism and power ambitions that they had concluded to be the cause of the war were left dormant rather than eradicated. Neither the loss of territory and economic resources nor reparations were enough to cripple Germany permanently. Even the drastic reduction of the size and capability of the army and navy had left the military leadership intact. German military leaders, the economic and political elites, and significant sections of the population inwardly rejected both the terms of the Treaty and the representatives of the new democracy in Germany who had signed it. As such, they rejected Europe's new order. Given changed circumstances, they would want to alter it to Germany's advantage. For the time being Germany was helpless, but a wounded giant.

FRAGILE DEMOCRACY

A laudable principle had underlain the deliberations in Paris: the intention that the new Europe would be a continent of democracies, of government representing not the interests of unelected princes and landholders, but the will of the people, expressed in pluralist political parties, free elections and parliamentary assemblies.

In the first post-war years representative parliamentary democracy became the model for government everywhere outside the Soviet Union. Even in the Caucasus – a region beset by huge inter-ethnic violence – Georgia, Armenia and Azerbaijan hoped to become sovereign republics before they were conquered by the Red Army during the civil war and subsequently incorporated in the Soviet Union. Nine new democracies (Finland, Estonia, Latvia, Lithuania, Czechoslovakia, Yugoslavia, Poland, Austria and Hungary) emerged from the ruins of the former Habsburg and Tsarist empires. The Irish Free State was created as a democratic republic in 1922 when the larger southern part of Ireland secured effective independence from Britain (though formally remaining until 1949 a dominion of the British Crown). Turkey became a republic with a parliamentary constitution the following year after a war of independence, the expulsion of Allied occupying armies and the abolition of the Ottoman Sultanate.

European countries adopted democracy partly because the 'Big Four' leaders of the victorious powers, most of all President Wilson, insisted on democratic government as the basis of the new Europe. But even more so, the war itself had been a democratizing process, stimulating pressures for the introduction of democratic rule – mainly articulated by socialists, nationalists and feminists – from within the collapsing monarchical systems. People had been mobilized in vast numbers to fight the war. Once it was over, they demanded change, improvement, representation, hope for the future. The result was a major widening of the political base of society. It was an unstoppable trend. Mass politics were here to stay. The right to vote was extended almost everywhere to include all men and in some countries all women – though even then not to all women in Britain and not to women at all in France (thanks to the Senate rejecting a motion that had gained overwhelming backing in the Chamber of Deputies). Political parties were as a consequence able to mobilize far larger numbers of voters. The British electorate rose, for instance, from 8 million to 22 million voters between 1884 and 1918, the German from 14.5 million to just short of 36 million between 1912 and 1919. The increased potential for mass mobilization, of course, also created the potential for political movements to challenge and undermine democracy itself. Channelling, orchestrating and mobilizing public opinion was now a vital part of political life. The press had also gained increased power. The scope for manipulation of the masses, also to promote intolerance and authoritarianism, had been greatly widened.

Radicalized politics shaped the first turbulent years of peace. A multiplicity of parties emerged in many countries, drawing support from specific sectors of the population or particular interest groups. It was rare to find stability of the kind that underpinned the British political system, in which parliamentary power had long been contested by the Liberals (soon to be replaced as a major force by Labour) and the Conservatives. The British 'first past the post' electoral system, producing a single winner in each constituency, deterred the emergence of small parties, encouraged party discipline in Parliament, and made coalition government the exception rather than the norm (though coalitions had, in fact, existed between 1915 and 1922). Proportional representation, the system generally favoured in continental Europe, coupled with the major extension of the franchise, tended, by contrast, to result in irreconcilable parliamentary divisions and weak governments. The spectrum in most countries embraced support at varying levels for Communist and Socialist, peasant and nationalist, Catholic and Protestant, Liberal and Conservative parties. Fragmentation and governmental instability were the usual consequences.

Socialism made big advances among the working class of industrial areas, but it was almost everywhere divided, as the more militant sections of labour, inspired by events in Russia, became drawn to communism. In much of central, eastern and south-eastern Europe, where overwhelmingly peasant populations were concerned above all with the 'land question' (mainly involving redistribution of land from big estates), populist agrarian parties gained widespread, though fluctuating and unstable, support. These often blended into nationalist parties, representing significant ethnic groups in the emerging nation states, and frequently became a destabilizing factor where there were substantial ethnic minorities or disputed borders. Especially in the new states, trying in usually unpropitious economic circumstances to build a national identity and establish firm political foundations, democracy faced big problems. Mostly, in these early post-war years, democracy in fact survived the challenge. But it was a contested system of government – rejected by powerful elite groups and by some volatile, newly mobilized parts of the population.

Only in the economically advanced states of western and northern Europe that had proved victorious in the war (Britain and France) or remained neutral (the Scandinavian countries, the Netherlands, Belgium and Switzerland) was pluralist democracy an established and generally accepted system of government. Here, the problems of dealing with the post-war social and economic shock waves were serious and divisive, producing industrial unrest and working-class militancy (often inspired by the revolution in Russia). But the anti-democratic forces were relatively small and could be contained. Apart from Ireland, there were few destabilizing pressures from national minorities. And for all the turmoil in Ireland, which subsided only with the creation of the Irish Free State in 1922, there was consensus behind the idea of parliamentary democracy, leading to a stable two-party political system. With the partial exception of France, where minorities on the Left and Right rejected the liberal democracy of the Third Republic, the existing form of democratic government enjoyed almost universal backing. There was no crisis of legitimacy.

The main problems lay elsewhere. The parliamentary systems in Greece and Bulgaria, for instance, dated far back into the nineteenth century, though they had long provided scarcely more than a facade for factionalism and clientelism. Popular forces were exploited and manipulated by well-entrenched traditional power-elites and oligarchies. Violence and repression were regular occurrences. Post-war Greek governments, destabilized by the disastrous war with the Turks in Asia Minor, were beset by bitter conflict between rival factions of royalists and supporters of the divisive figure of Eleftherios Venizelos, leader of the Liberal Party and for long the key figure in Greek politics. But the dominant force, increasingly wielding decisive influence on state power, was the army leadership. A coup by anti-royalist army officers forced King Constantine I to quit the throne in 1922 after the defeat by the Turks. He was succeeded by his son, George II, who was himself forced out two years later – this time following a failed coup attempt by a group of royalist officers, who included the future dictator, Ioanis Metaxas. In March 1924 the monarchy was abolished and

Greece became a republic. The bitter divisiveness of internal politics thereafter subsided, though did not disappear.

In Bulgaria, exhausted and economically ruined by the war, the Agrarian Union, representing smallholding peasants (who had benefited from a substantial land redistribution), formed the largest party, followed at some distance by the Communist Party (founded in 1919) and the Socialists. Government under Alexander Stamboliiski, the Prime Minister and leader of the Agrarian Union, was, however, repressive and corrupt. He made powerful enemies, most dangerously among army officers. By 1923 they were ready to act to end the democratic experiment. Stamboliiski was deposed and the army took power.

Factionalism and violence, driven both by class conflict and traditional tribal loyalties, were even more evident central ingredients of what was merely a facade-democracy in the new state of Albania (created in 1913). The country emerged from wartime partition and occupation by its neighbours – Greece, Italy, Serbia and Montenegro – to enter a brief but troubled period of great instability. Political parties emerged, divided on questions of land reform and the framing of a constitution. But the interests of landowners and clan leaders dominated. Factions formed around two leading figures, Fan Noli, a graduate of Harvard University and bishop of the Albanian Orthodox Church, and Ahmed Bey Zogu, scion of one of the most powerful Muslim families. Torture, killings, bribery and corruption were regularly deployed by both men and their followers. In a political system closer to neo-feudalism than genuine parliamentary democracy, Noli ousted Zogu, who fled the country, in an armed revolt in June 1924. Six months later Zogu returned, backed by an army he had raised, including many foreign mercenaries, deposed the government and forced Noli and his followers to flee. In January 1925 the remaining members of parliament elected Zogu as President with extended powers for a seven-year term.

In Romania, where a pluralist system under a constitutional monarchy had existed since 1881 but where the state had been transformed by the great extension of territory (doubling its size) following the war, the powers of parliament remained weak while those of the ruling class – the aristocracy, military, Orthodox Church hierarchy and the upper levels of the bourgeoisie – were strong. Land reform (a response prompted by the threat of Bolshevism), incorporation of ethnic minorities, social mobility and increase in the urban proletariat led to overlapping conflicts and continuing internal crisis.

In each of these countries, post-war difficulties in overwhelmingly underdeveloped agrarian economies, border disputes and territorial demands, as well as nationality issues, brought with them political tensions. Newly enfranchized sections of the population, especially a politically inchoate peasantry, offered extended room for demagogic mobilization – and manipulation. Authoritarianism never lurked far from the surface.

There were equally grave difficulties in Spain, where, despite neutrality, the economy had been drastically disturbed by the war. Wracked by waves of strikes directed at the authority of the state itself, Spain seemed a country on the verge of revolution. Had it been a belligerent power, perhaps the war would indeed have tipped it into revolution. As it was, the constitutional monarchy, founded in 1876, which had long relied upon an oligarchy of liberal and conservative elites, held on in a grossly unrepresentative parliamentary system. The rapidly growing Socialist movement had more than doubled its membership since the end of the war, but electoral discrimination left it with a mere handful of seats. The control of the dominant elites was nevertheless weakening, their liberal-conservative political base fragmenting. And thirty-four governments between 1902 and 1923 contributed to widespread contempt for the feeble and ineffective parliamentary system. The ruling class saw that the state was too weak to uphold their interests; the opponents of the state, primarily within the working class, were however too weak to overthrow the system. The result was stalemate.

Castigating 'the weakness of Liberalism', there were calls in Spain for a 'civil dictatorship' to head off 'Bolshevist anarchy'. Demands for strong government and the restoration of order, coupled with fear of revolution, forged a coalition of interests ready by September 1923 to support a coup and takeover of power by General Miguel Primo de Rivera. Backed by the army, the Catholic Church, the landed elites, big business and the middle classes, the coup was opposed only by a feeble attempt at a general strike by a demoralized and divided working class. Martial law, press censorship, a single party of national unity and a corporate structure of labour relations were introduced, the anarcho-syndicalist trade-union organization was outlawed (to the satisfaction of its socialist rival), and some leading opposition figures were imprisoned. But Primo's dictatorship was relatively mild, and, through a programme of public works, it even briefly stirred a sense of growing prosperity in Spain. Above all, Primo succeeded temporarily in restoring order. For most Spaniards that was what mattered. Few wept tears over the death of what had been no more than a facade-democracy. Most people were indifferent. For the time being, counter-revolution triumphed.

In the successor states, parliamentary democracy was a fragile flower, planted in less than fertile soil. It faced challenges from the outset by powerful social groups and populist (usually nationalist) forces. But it survived the post-war crisis, even if only Finland and Czechoslovakia proved durable successes.

Finland's independence had been established in 1918 only after five months of bitter civil war between Reds and Whites (which left as many as 36,000 dead), and a parliamentary democracy was enshrined in the constitution of 1919. Despite government instability (reflecting ideological divisions between conservatives, social democrats, agrarians and Swedish nationalists), the determination to preserve that independence against the threat from the nearby Soviet Union underpinned the legitimacy of the new state. The Finnish President (Kaarlo Juho Ståhlberg in the first years of independence), a head of state with wide executive powers, also played a big part through his backing for the still unconsolidated parliamentary system.

The same was even more true of Czechoslovakia in the immediate post-war years. The President (and effective founder of the state), Thomas Masaryk, was a convinced democrat, helped by a loyal army, an efficient bureaucracy inherited from the Habsburg Empire, and an economy with a good industrial base pulling out of post-war recession. He was crucial in holding together a system that class and nationality interests in over twenty political parties threatened to undermine. In December 1918 and the first days of 1919 Masaryk used Czech troops to suppress moves to establish an independent republic in Slovakia. He called upon Allied assistance and proclaimed a state of emergency as he deployed new army units commanded by

French officers to repel an invasion to recover Slovakia by pro-Bolshevik forces from Hungary in May and June 1919. And he proved adept at appointing a cabinet of officials independent of divisive party allegiances to tackle a wave of serious disturbances that summer. The government then used martial law to counter a wave of strikes in November and December 1920, instigated by the pro-Soviet faction of the Socialist Party.

This was an important turning point. Thereafter the Czech parliamentary system held together, somewhat shakily at first, but with increasing authority. The revolutionary Left became isolated as most people wanted peace and order. A broad balance was struck between agrarian interests and those of the industrial proletariat, which was bigger in the Czech lands than in any of the other successor states but mainly supportive of parliamentary democracy, not communism. Political integration of the Slovaks and also of the sizeable German minority (which for now swallowed resentment at various forms of discrimination) kept separatist tendencies at bay. Democracy gradually became stabilized – though implicit tensions were held in check rather than eradicated.

In the Baltic states of Estonia, Latvia and Lithuania the importance of newly won independence and widespread hostility towards Bolshevism in the neighbouring Soviet state helped for the time being to sustain backing for parliamentary democracy despite unstable governments which, crucially, upheld the interests of the big agrarian lobbies while restricting the small communist parties. Democracy remained fragile, however, and government was dependent on the tolerance (which would not prove of long duration) of the military leadership and nationalist paramilitary organizations.

In Yugoslavia the parliamentary system (under the Serbian monarchy) established in the constitution of 1921 was an unpromising arrangement. It represented a narrow victory of centralism over federalism, but separatist tendencies continued to defy government efforts to propagate a sense of Yugoslavian identity in a country of some twenty ethnic minorities and significant divisions of the three main groupings of Serbs, Croats and Slovenes. The new state had to combat strong pro-Bulgarian paramilitary forces in Macedonia as well as separatist pressure for an independent Macedonia, and armed

Albanian rebels in Kosovo. It was chiefly threatened by Croat resentment at Serbian domination. No unifying identity could be created,
but Croat separatist tendencies were, if with difficulty, kept in check.
The Slovenes saw their own language and culture best protected in
the Yugoslavian state, other national minorities were weak and divided, and Italian expansionist ambitions stirred pro-Yugoslavian
sentiment along the Adriatic coast.

Acute though Yugoslavia's ethnic divisions were, the overwhelmingly agrarian country had no industrial proletariat to speak of and
the Communist Party, banned and persecuted from 1921 onwards,
was thereafter largely insignificant. The country's manifold corrupt
factional interests, often benefiting from land redistribution, had more
to gain by supporting rather than undermining the new state. Not
least, the very structural weakness of a parliamentary system in which
proportional representation produced forty-five parties, mainly
upholding ethnic and regional particular interests, and led to the
formation of twenty-four governments in eight years, in practice
bolstered the dominance of the royal court and its corrupt clientele,
the military (and paramilitary support organizations) and the security
services. For the time being, what in reality amounted to no more
than a facade-democracy could continue in existence.

In contrast to the manufactured, weak sense of Yugoslavian identity,
Polish national consciousness had gathered strength during the nineteenth century. The rebirth of Poland as a state in 1918 following
123 years of partition between Russia, Prussia and Austria, then the war
against the Soviet Union – one of six border wars the new state had to
fight between 1918 and 1921 – provided an initial sense of national
unity. This was embodied by Marshal Josef Piłsudski, widely viewed as
Poland's saviour, and by a nationalism enhanced by the Polish majority's
antipathy towards the country's large ethnic minority populations. But
unity rapidly gave way to deep and bitter divisions in a poor country
wracked by war and the ruinous effects of hyperinflation.

The divisions were partly along ethnic lines. Nearly a third of the
Polish population (and in some areas a majority) comprised ethnic
minorities – 14 per cent Ukrainians, 9 per cent Jews, 3 per cent
Belorussians, just over 2 per cent Germans, among others. Their
nationalist aims inevitably clashed and caused tension with the

assertive nationalism of the Polish majority. Class divisions were if anything even more politically polarizing. Land reform, in a country with a large peasant population, was a central priority for a grouping of parties of the non-communist Left, and steps towards a significant redistribution of land (though with compensation for big landowners) were eventually taken in 1925. But land reform was bitterly opposed by a right-wing bloc of parties, keen to defend the privileges of the propertied classes.

The democratic constitution introduced in Poland in 1921 drew especially on the model of the French Third Republic and, like its inspiration, led to weak government and an unwieldy, fragmented lower house (the Sejm) of a two-chamber parliament. A plethora of parties – peasant, worker, minority nationalities – jockeyed for influence. The main bodies were the Block of National Minorities (in which the concerns of the different nationalities often proved incompatible); the conservative National Democrats (upholding the interests of landowners, industry and a middle class seeking protection against 'foreign', especially Jewish, influence); the Peasant Party (seeking above all redistribution of land from the big estates); and the Socialists (anxious to preserve the substantial gains – including the introduction of an eight-hour working day – they had achieved in the near-revolutionary conditions at the end of the war). Frequent changes of government produced neither stability nor clear policy direction. Democratic government, in the eyes of much of the population, seemed increasingly incompetent – incapable of solving the country's huge problems through a parliament of squabbling politicians who put party interests above those of the nation.

The problems mounted when drastic austerity measures were introduced to arrest the hyperinflation (which in November 1923 reached 1.65 million Polish marks to the dollar) and again in 1925 when the recently introduced new currency, the złoty, itself came under pressure and brought about the fall of the government. Democracy in Poland had survived, with difficulty, the traumatic post-war years. But it had never stabilized and become a universally accepted system of government. At times Poland had seemed on the verge of civil war, or a military putsch. Disillusionment with democracy was widespread. There was talk of the need for an 'iron hand to lead us from this abyss'. By 1926 the national hero, Piłsudski himself, declared his readiness to fight against what he saw as the domination of Poland by political parties seeking only the material benefits of office and personal enrichment. It was the prelude to the coup he led in May 1926, and the beginning of authoritarian rule in Poland.

Most Austrians, now living in a tiny German-speaking nation state rather than a huge empire, placed their early hopes in union with Germany, but these were soon dashed by the Allies. Thereafter there was little basis for political unity. Deep fissures ran as a three-way split between the Socialists and the two major anti-socialist political forces, the Christian Socials (the largest party, close to the Catholic establishment, increasingly vehement in its Austrian nationalism) and the smaller, but vociferous German Nationalists (who favoured union with Germany). Big armed militias, largely peasant based and set up to defend Austria's vulnerable and disputed borders, particularly against Yugoslavian incursions in the south from Slovenia, were not just nationalist, deeply Catholic and strongly antisemitic, but also vehemently opposed to what they saw as socialist rule from 'Red Vienna'.

Even within Vienna, socialism was alien to much of the middle class, the state bureaucracy (with its strong continuities from the old empire) and the Catholic Church hierarchy. And outside Vienna, socialism struggled. Most of the new alpine republic was rural, conservative, patriotically Austrian, ardently Catholic – and fervently anti-socialist. After the initial, revolutionary phase, these forces, inherently authoritarian, would grow in strength. From 1920 onwards the Socialists, the main driving force behind the establishment of democracy, played no part in Austria's government. Democracy, associated above all with the Socialists, was pushed increasingly onto the defensive.

The one country outside Russia where it proved possible to set up a Soviet republic, though of brief duration, was Hungary. (A soviet-style government that assumed power in Bavaria in April 1919 did not break out of its temporary Munich base before being crushed by the army and right-wing paramilitaries.) In Hungary a weak coalition government of two small liberal parties and the Social Democrats (who relied upon support from only part of a relatively small working class) was unable to push through necessary social reforms or to tackle the urgent issue of land redistribution in a country where the Magyar nobility retained enormous privileges and ran vast estates with a near servile peasantry. Big demonstrations in towns demanded radical change. Communist propaganda fell on ready ears. Moderate social democrats lost influence. Workers' and soldiers' councils increasingly challenged the power of the government. Agricultural labourers took over some former royal estates. The last straw was when the Allies demanded withdrawal of Hungarian forces facing the Romanians, with the certain loss of territory that this would involve. Refusal of the government to accept the ultimatum on 21 March 1919 produced a communist-led government that proclaimed a Soviet Republic and 'dictatorship of the proletariat' in Hungary.

The four months of this regime were a catastrophe. Hasty and draconian state intervention to nationalize the economy and confiscate bank deposits was accompanied by forced requisition of food, persecution of the Church, and, amid mounting state-sponsored terror, the arbitrary arrest of hundreds of property-owners. Some of these were released only on payment of large ransoms, others were shot. Several hundred Hungarians fell victim to the 'Red Terror'. As the country descended into anarchy, Hungary faced attack from Romanian, Czechoslovakian and Yugoslavian forces. By August 1919 the regime was in desperate trouble. It had alienated the middle class, the peasantry, and even the bulk of the working class. The fact that the regime's leader, Béla Kun, and most of the communist Commissars behind the 'Red Terror' were Jewish stoked up antisemitism. Only help from Soviet Russia could have saved the Hungarian communist regime – and then, perhaps, just temporarily. But Soviet Russia, fighting for its life in a civil war, could offer no military aid. The failure to export communism to Hungary was the clearest sign that notions of world revolution, radiating from the Russian example, would have to be abandoned.

Béla Kun's hapless government resigned on 1 August 1919, just before Romanian troops, by now occupying most of Hungary, entered and looted Budapest. Kun fled, eventually to Russia, where he was to end his life as yet another Stalinist victim. Within months, right-wing nationalist conservatives had reasserted their control in Hungary. Land reform was curtailed; estate-holders were able to hold on to their property, and to their power. The military, the bureaucracy, business leaders and the better-off sections of the peasantry, all horrified by Kun's regime, also welcomed what they saw as the restoration of order through conservative authoritarianism. The war hero, Admiral Miklos Horthy, was consequently able to preside from 1920 as head of state over authoritarian governments that were to last for almost the next quarter of a century. The immediate response to the 'Red Terror' of Kun's regime was the unleashing of a far wider 'White Terror' (claiming about 5,000 lives and imprisoning thousands, according to some estimates), in which right-wing officer detachments of the National Army carried out a wave of atrocities directed mainly at communists, socialists and Jews.

Hungary, like Spain, was an exception to the trend in the first post-war years. Democracy, if sometimes narrowly, was generally able to endure the enormous upheavals of this turbulent period. This was in part because across Europe it had idealistic, enthusiastic backing, mainly from the socialist and liberal Left who had long and passionately sought to throw off the shackles of traditional elitist, authoritarian rule and envisaged a fairer, more prosperous society in a democratic future. It was mainly, however, because the old order had suffered a shattering defeat at the end of the war. Its adherents were too weak to challenge the establishment of democracy or to overthrow such a new system of government that could call upon extensive, if unstable, popular backing, arising from a combination of social and political interests. The weakness of the elites, coupled with their extreme fear of Bolshevism, meant they were ready to tolerate, if not warmly support, a pluralist democracy that they could often manipulate to their advantage. This could usually be achieved by latching on to populist nationalism, which could be whipped up by heated disputes over border territory. But nationalist parties and movements were themselves mostly divided. The absence of unity on the nationalist as well as the elite Right meant that a coherent challenge to democracy could rarely be mounted in the early post-war years.

Weakness among the former ruling classes was mirrored to some extent by the weakness and splits on the Left. The revolutionary supporters of Bolshevism were nearly everywhere outside Russia in a minority among socialists, who in their great majority backed parliamentary democracy. Often, therefore, what materialized was uneasy survival where neither the counter-revolutionary Right nor the revolutionary Left was powerful enough to upturn a newly created democracy.

The major exception to the pattern of democratic survival, other than Primo's takeover of power through a coup in Spain, was Italy, the first country – and the only one during the post-war crisis – in which liberal democracy collapsed to be replaced by Fascism.

FASCISM VICTORIOUS

A pluralist parliamentary system of government had existed in Italy since Unification in 1861. To call it democratic, however, would be to stretch the meaning of the term. Resting on an extremely limited electorate, Italian politics were factional and corrupt, dominated by a small oligarchy of Liberal notables. Reform of the suffrage in 1912 almost tripled the size of the electorate, from under 3 million to nearly 8.5 million voters (most of them still illiterate). But little significant change to the government system followed. Then came the divisive and traumatic war, which Italy, after much wavering and secret negotiations, eventually entered in 1915 on the Allied side. Immediately after the war, in December 1918, all adult Italian males were given the vote – a reward to the soldiers – and the following year a new electoral law introduced proportional representation. The hope was to bolster support for the government. But the reform backfired massively.

Amid the post-war turmoil, the newly enfranchised population turned their backs on the old liberal politics and voted in large numbers for the newly founded Italian People's Party (Partito Popolare Italiano), representing Catholic interests, and the Socialist Party, which declared its aim to be 'the violent conquest of political power on behalf of the workers' and the establishment of a 'dictatorship of the proletariat'. The Socialists professed their allegiance to the Communist International (Comintern) that Lenin had founded in March 1919 in Moscow. At the election in November of that year they trebled their seats in the Chamber of Deputies, while the Populists almost quadrupled theirs. Support for the Liberal establishment was strongest in poorer, largely agricultural southern Italy, where clientelist politics still prevailed. But the Liberals and their supporters were now in a minority in parliament. Party politics fragmented. Government became destabilized – there were six changes of government between 1919 and 1922 – and increasingly paralysed. Italy seemed on the verge of a red revolution.

Throughout 1919 and 1920, which came to be dubbed the *biennio rosso* ('the two Red years'), Italy experienced huge social and political conflict. In industrial cities there were large numbers of strikes (over 1,500 in each year), factory occupations, worker demonstrations, and looting of shops by crowds angry at price rises. In parts of rural Italy recently demobilized peasants seized land from large estates and more than a million agricultural labourers joined strikes. As disorder grew alarmingly, as the government was plainly unable to restore order, as fear of revolution and anxieties of the propertied classes about Socialism mounted, and as the fragmentation of party politics offered no way through the morass, political space opened up for a new political force. It was to be filled by the Fascists.

A number of small paramilitary movements prosaically calling themselves *Fasci* – 'groups' (or, literally, 'bundles', the name deriving from the Latin term for the set of rods that had been the symbol of order in ancient Rome) – sprang up in the cities and towns of northern and central Italy amid the political disorder, attracting mainly lower-middle-class ex-servicemen (especially demobilized officers) and many students. There was no central organization. But what the various movements had in common was the relative youth of their members, their militant ultra-nationalism, their glorification of war, their violence, and their visceral dislike of what they saw as the discredited, divisive, weak and corrupt parliamentary politics of the Liberal establishment. Italy's heroic war effort, in their eyes, had been undermined by the political class. Italy could never be great under the leadership of the old notables. They should be swept away. What the Fascist militants offered was radical action to renew Italy. This was implicitly revolutionary in that it was directed towards violently and fundamentally changing the existing state. What exactly would replace it was left open.

Among the myriad *Fasci* was one founded in March 1919 by Benito Mussolini, a former editor of the official socialist newspaper, who had broken with the socialist Left when he fervently advocated intervention in the war in 1915. He viewed the war, in which he had fought and been wounded, as a heroic period in his own and Italy's past. The programme presented at the foundation of his *Fasci di Combattimento* in 1919 was little different to that of the other *Fasci*, and distinctly revolutionary in tone. Many of its proposals could have been advanced by the Left: universal suffrage; suppression of all noble titles; freedom of opinion; an educational system open to all; measures to improve public health; suppression of financial speculation; introduction of an eight-hour working day; workers to be organized in cooperatives and to share profits; the abolition of the political police, the Senate and the monarchy; and the foundation of a new Italian republic based upon autonomous regional administration and decentralized executive power. The aim was 'a radical transformation of the political and economic foundations of collective life'.

Mussolini was later, however, to disavow what seemed concrete social and political aims, declaring that these had been not an expression of any doctrine but merely aspirations to be refined over time. Fascism, he stated, was 'not the nursling of a doctrine worked out beforehand with detailed elaboration; it was born of the need for action and it was itself from the beginning practical rather than theoretical.' This was a rationalization, almost twenty years after its beginnings, of the fundamental change that his own movement had undergone within no more than two years. For Mussolini, the supreme opportunist, the programme announced in Milan was there to be ignored, bypassed or adjusted as political needs determined. The 'socialism' of his movement was always subordinated to the aim of national rebirth, a vague but powerful notion that was capable of uniting, at least superficially, quite disparate interests. Principles meant nothing to him, power everything. So his movement turned from revolution to counter-revolution. Early backing for workers' strikes gave way by autumn 1920 to the deployment of Fascist paramilitary squads to break strikes in the interests of landowners and industrialists. The violence of the squads escalated sharply over the following months. Mussolini had recognized that he could not defeat socialism and communism by trying to compete for the same base of support. To gain power, he needed the backing of those with money and influence. He had to win over the conservative establishment and the middle class, not just disaffected ex-servicemen and violent thugs.

Why Mussolini, at first only one of numerous Fascist leaders and regional chieftains, came to dominate the early Fascist movement owed less to his forceful and dynamic personality – all Fascist bosses had in some way to be forceful personalities – than to his use of the press and to the connections he forged with industrialists to maintain his newspaper, *Popolo d'Italia*. His brand of radicalism – the emphasis on national unity, authority and order, the readiness to impose order through violence against those who stood in its way (the socialist Left, revolutionaries, striking workers) – was not only compatible with the interests of the conservative ruling class, but directly served them. With order breaking down and the liberal state incapable of restoring it, the Fascists became an increasingly useful vehicle for Italy's political and economic elites.

By mid-1921 the government was assisting the Fascists with money and arms to combat growing disorder. The police were told not to intervene. In the May election, the Liberal Prime Minister, Giovanni Giolotti, incorporated Fascists alongside nationalists, liberals and agrarians in a 'national bloc' in the hope of taming them and weakening the opposition of the Socialist Party and Italian People's Party. The national bloc gained the most votes overall (though the Fascists themselves won only 35 seats out of 535). But the Socialists and People's Party were not sufficiently weakened. The chronic government instability continued. And the existing state system had only minority support in parliament. The Fascists, though electorally still small, were a growing force. From a mere 870 members at the end of 1919, they now numbered 200,000.

The breakthrough came not in the economically backward, overwhelmingly agricultural south, nor in the northern cities such as Milan, where Mussolini's movement had begun. It was in the more commercially developed countryside of central Italy, in Emilia-Romagna, Tuscany, the Po Valley and Umbria, that Fascism gained strength. Landlords and leaseholders, facing socialist unions, agrarian cooperatives, and domination of local councils by the Socialists or

People's Party, would pay for lorry-loads of Fascist thugs, often transported in from local towns, to beat up their opponents, force them to drink castor oil, drive them from office, destroy their property and otherwise terrorize them – with the police standing by. Former 'red' provinces were turned within weeks into Fascist strongholds. Newly erected Fascist 'syndicates', the worker or peasant members 'encouraged' by the threat of terror to join, replaced the former socialist unions. By June 1922 the syndicates had half a million members, mainly peasants. Unruly agitation was transformed, to the liking of landowners and industrialists, into docile compliance.

The *squadristi* – paramilitary bands of thugs, usually a dozen or so strong – were controlled by powerful regional Fascist bosses. Mussolini, if the most important of the Fascist leaders, was far from dominating the movement. In fact, when he tried in 1921 to tone down the anti-socialist violence, to show his credentials to the governing elite as a patriotic 'moderate' seeking constructive national unity and even proposing to come to terms with the socialist unions, the regional Fascist bosses rebelled. Mussolini was forced to resign as leader and only reinstated after he had given in to the radicals and renounced any notion of pacification of the socialists. His national standing, control of the Fascist press, and links with industrialists and other powerful figures made the regional bosses, divided among themselves and mutually distrustful, willing to reinstate him. He returned the favour by demonstrative support for the squads, which took control in numerous northern towns over the following months. And in October 1921 he formally established Fascism as the National Fascist Party.

The organizational framework was widened to 2,300 local sections (each providing regular party subscriptions) over subsequent months, giving Mussolini an extended political base. The middle classes, increasingly disenchanted with weak liberal government, flocked into the party. By May 1922 the membership stood at over 300,000 – a 50 per cent increase in under six months. A disproportionate number of landowners, shopkeepers, clerical workers and, especially, students swelled the socially disparate movement, which generally had the sympathies of local elites, the police and judges.

By autumn 1922 Fascism had penetrated the social and political establishment and had acquired a strong basis of popular support. A general strike called by the socialist unions in August had been an abject failure, but had increased the fear among the middle classes. In contrast to the evident weakness of the Left, a big rally of 40,000 Fascists in Naples on 24 October appeared a manifestation of strength. Mussolini was ready to swallow another of the initial demands of his movement, that Italy should become a republic, and now declared that he did not want to abolish the monarchy. He proclaimed the readiness of his movement to seize power, and demanded a new government with at least six Fascist ministers.

In fact, the 'March on Rome' on 28 October was nothing of the sort. The King, faced with the resignation of the government, was misinformed that 100,000 Fascist militia were marching unstoppably on Rome. Actually there were no more than 20,000 poorly armed 'blackshirts' who could easily have been repulsed by the army – had the army wanted to turn them back. When a last attempt to form a liberal government failed, the King invited Mussolini to become Prime Minister. Far from leading a march of triumphant Fascists into Rome, Mussolini arrived by train, dressed in a black shirt, black trousers and a bowler hat. He was constitutionally appointed, and the government he led was a broad coalition, including ministers from the Liberals, the Nationalists, the Democrats and the People's Party as well as Mussolini and three other Fascists. In mid-November the new government received a resounding vote of confidence from parliament. But given the chronic governmental instability of recent years, few expected it to last long.

That soon changed. Careerists now rushed to join the Fascist Party, which swelled to 783,000 members by the end of 1923 – well over double its membership at the time of the 'March on Rome'. Fascism was becoming institutionalized. Its initial *squadristi* core of brutal fighters and fanatical believers was being diluted by the intake of opportunists looking for jobs and advancement – including former nationalist rivals, many of them monarchists and conservatives. Mussolini still had no clear plans for a one-party dictatorship. But he was gaining in confidence and, compared with the traditional gerontocracy of party notables, he already cut a more dynamic figure. In November 1923 he engineered a vital change to the electoral system to give the leading party in an election two-thirds of the seats if it polled more than a quarter of the votes. Ostensibly, the change was to ensure governmental stability. In practice, it guaranteed that, to stay in power, liberals and conservatives would have to support his government. In the election of April 1924 under the new allocation system, the national bloc, most of them Fascists, won two-thirds of the votes anyway, giving them 375 seats out of 535, thanks in no small part to a campaign of violence against their opponents. Opposition parties remained in existence. But the Socialists and People's Party had lost much of their former strength. Outside the working class, most Italians were, with varying degrees of enthusiasm, ready to accept Mussolini's leadership.

A dangerous flashpoint occurred in June 1924 when the Socialist leader Giaocomo Matteotti, who had denounced the election result as fraudulent, disappeared and was later found dead – murdered, as all rightly presumed, by Fascists, almost certainly on the orders of Mussolini or leading members of his entourage. A first-rate political crisis ensued. The Socialists withdrew from parliament in protest – a move whose only effect was to strengthen the position of the government. Opposition remained divided and impotent. Mussolini, meanwhile, played the moderate. He made concessions to bring some nationalists, monarchists and rightist Liberals into government posts, and incorporated the Fascist militia into the armed forces. Fearful of any revival of socialism, the 'big battalions' – the King, the Church, the army and major industrialists – backed Mussolini. But the Fascist provincial bosses made their own support conditional upon their leader moving to a fully fledged Fascist regime. A new wave of violence emphasized the point.

As throughout his rise to power, Mussolini faced both ways, manoeuvring between conservatives who were needed to establish political control, and his Fascist radicals, unhappy at any steps towards moderation. Forced to accommodate his party bosses, while adamantly refusing during a speech in parliament in January 1925 to acknowledge his complicity in Matteotti's murder, Mussolini publicly accepted full responsibility for what had happened. Placating the radicals, he stated: 'If two irreconcilable elements are struggling with each other, the solution lies in force.' The principle was put into practice. Political opponents were arrested, opposition parties suppressed, the freedom of the press was abolished and government left almost completely in the hands of the Fascists. The 'foundations of the totalitarian state were laid,' Mussolini later wrote. The Matteotti crisis might have broken Mussolini. It ended by strengthening him. Fascist power was secure.

Why did Fascism break through in Italy but nowhere else during the post-war crisis? Crucial to Mussolini's success were the existing, and rapidly worsening, crisis of legitimacy of the liberal state, the impact of the war, and the perceived revolutionary threat. Nowhere else apart from Spain was the crisis of legitimacy so profound in the immediate post-war years. And Spain had not participated in the war. The impact of the war in Italy, by contrast, can scarcely be exaggerated.

The Italian state, recently unified, but still for the most part economically backward and socially divided, rested upon a narrow base of oligarchic politics before the war. This could no longer be sustained after the war. Intense social and ideological divisions had been glaringly exposed by intervention and magnified by the calamitous losses during the conflict. Millions of Italians had been mobilized to fight. Many were now open to political mobilization. The belief that, in the eyes of countless thousands of ex-servicemen and many others, victory had been 'mutilated', that Italy had been cheated out of the promises of national glory and imperialist expansion, that the sacrifice had not been worth it, fed a vitriolic rejection of the existing state and its representatives.

The sense that the ruling oligarchy had betrayed Italy's heroic war veterans provided an initial base for Fascism's core support. The emotional appeal to nationalist commitment, to national rebirth, and to the destruction of the weak and decadent liberal state held strong attractions to many in this atmosphere of resentment, disunity, disorder and socialist revolutionary threat. Big electoral gains for a Socialist Party preaching the need for a violent seizure of power by the workers, and the early growth of a Communist Party after its foundation in 1921, made the threat of revolution, so soon after the Bolshevik takeover in Russia, seem very real.

The post-war changes to the franchise had completely destabilized government. The fragmentation of politics in the centre and conservative Right, and the patent inability of the government to combat the threat that the new strength of the Socialists, in the eyes of property-holders, posed, provided the political space in which Fascism could mobilize support. Extreme violence against perceived internal enemies extended this support, especially in the commercially developed areas of the countryside of northern and central Italy.

But for all its radicalism, Fascism could not have attained domination without the support of the ruling elites, who threw in their lot with Mussolini's movement. Mussolini did not seize power; he was invited to take it. Thereafter, the conservative, monarchist, military and Church elites, fearful of Socialism, were happy to back the methods of intimidation and manipulation that, by 1925, gave Fascism close to monopoly control of the state.

The European country where conditions seemed closest to those that encouraged the rise of Fascism in Italy was Germany. So why, when democracy collapsed in 'victorious' Italy, did it survive the post-war crisis in defeated Germany?

DEMOCRACY SURVIVES IN GERMANY

North of the Alps, Mussolini's 'March on Rome' had an immediate effect on the extreme radical Right in an increasingly troubled political scene in Germany. Since 1920 a racist-nationalist hothead with remarkable demagogic talents, Adolf Hitler, had been making a stir in Munich's beer halls, though scarcely beyond. In 1921 he had become leader of the National Socialist German Workers' Party (NSDAP), which in some ways, including the build-up of a violent paramilitary arm, resembled Mussolini's early Fascist Party. The Nazi Party (as the NSDAP became dubbed) differed little from that of similar extreme racist nationalist movements in Germany. But Hitler could draw the crowds like no other speaker. Although still small, his party had rapidly built a following, mainly in Bavaria – a state with considerable regional autonomy within the German federal system and since 1920 the bastion of nationalist opposition to what was portrayed as 'socialist' democracy in Prussia, by far the largest German state.

Hitler's movement had grown from 2,000 or so members in early 1921 to 20,000 by the autumn of 1922. And when one of his leading acolytes announced to the roars of a big beer-hall audience a few days after the 'March on Rome' that 'Germany's Mussolini is called Adolf Hitler', it gave the nascent personality cult developing around the Nazi leader a substantial boost. As Germany descended into economic and political crisis in 1923, following the French occupation of the Ruhr, Hitler's power to mobilize the violently anti-government nationalist extremists was sufficient to propel him to a leading position in the maelstrom of Bavarian paramilitary politics that was developing into a force ready and prepared to move against the elected Reich government in Berlin. Democracy was gravely endangered.

The anti-democratic nationalist Right – conservative as well as radical – had, in fact, begun to recover remarkably quickly from the shock of defeat and revolution in November 1918. In the fear (exaggerated, as it turned out) of the revolution becoming radicalized along Bolshevik lines, the new Socialist interim government in Berlin had even before the Armistice struck a fateful deal with the leadership of the defeated army that allowed the officer corps to get a second wind. In essence, the revolutionary government had agreed to support the officer corps in return for backing for the government in combating Bolshevism. The split on the Left between those favouring parliamentary democracy and the minority that, looking to Moscow, had formed the German Communist Party and sought a root-and-branch Soviet-style revolution, would prove a lasting hindrance to the new democracy that emerged in 1919. The serious threat to democracy came, however, from the Right – temporarily undermined by the defeat and revolution, but subdued, not destroyed. By the spring of 1919, the revival of the anti-socialist, anti-democratic Right was already under way. Strong support came from the middle class and landholding peasantry, whose visceral detestation of Socialism and fear of Bolshevism was accentuated by the month-long attempt to impose a Soviet-style government in Bavaria in April 1919.

By March 1920 an extremist group within right-wing military circles, headed by Wolfgang Kapp, a founding member of the annexationist pro-war lobby organization, the Fatherland Party, and General Walther von Lüttwitz, the inspiration behind the paramilitary *Freikorps*, felt strong enough to try to overthrow the government. Within a week their putsch attempt proved a fiasco. Kapp, Lüttwitz and their chief supporters fled to Sweden. Significantly, however, the army had taken no action to suppress the rising. The attempted coup had been foiled by a general strike called by the trade unions and by the refusal of the civil service to carry out Kapp's orders. The Left was still capable of defending democracy.

However, when serious clashes in the aftermath of the Kapp Putsch took place between armed socialist and communist self-defence units and government-supported *Freikorps* groups in Saxony and Thuringia, and especially in the big industrial area of the Ruhr (where workers had formed a 'Red Army'), the army was called in and brutally restored order. Dubious though its loyalty to the new democracy was, the army had turned into its essential prop. Right-wing extremists took refuge in Bavaria. Meanwhile, democracy was weakening. The mainstays of the new democracy, the Social Democrats, the Catholic Centre Party and the Left Liberals, saw their support dwindle from almost 80 per cent to only 44 per cent of the seats in the Reichstag between January 1919 and June 1920. The core democratic parties had lost their majority, and at national level only once, in the elections of 1928, briefly came close to regaining it. It was said, inaccurately but with pardonable exaggeration, that Germany was now a democracy without democrats.

The reparations issue more than anything else kept political tensions high during 1921–2, and it was like oxygen to the nationalist Right. Political violence was never far away. Right-wing terrorists carried out 352 political murders between 1919 and 1922. Parliamentary democracy was attacked from the Left as well as from the Right. An attempted communist rising in Saxony's industrial belt in the spring of 1921 led to fierce fighting for a few days before it was put down by Prussian police. Despite their defeat, the communists continued to gain support in industrial areas. In Bavaria, by contrast, where the state government refused to implement the Law for the Protection of the Republic, passed by the Reichstag in 1922 to combat political extremism and violence, the extreme nationalist Right was winning new backing.

In 1923, as hyperinflation destroyed the currency – and the savings of middle-class Germans – politics polarized. The spectre of communist revolution was again glimpsed. The army was sent in to suppress a communist 'October Revolution', in one case by shooting on demon-strators, in Saxony and Thuringia. A short-lived communist rising in Hamburg collapsed after clashes with police, leaving over forty dead. But the threat from the Left passed quickly. That from the Right was more dangerous, and focused on Bavaria. The large and by now com-bined paramilitary armies were a force to be reckoned with. General Ludendorff, no less, had become their symbolic figure, Hitler their pol-itical spokesman. But the paramilitaries, important though they were in Bavarian politics, stood little chance of toppling the government in Berlin without the backing of the German army – the Reichswehr.

The army leadership had taken an ambivalent stance since the foundation of the republic, supporting the state in the abstract though merely tolerating the new democracy without enthusiasm. The head of the Reichswehr, General Hans von Seeckt, sent unclear signals. He refused to intervene to restore order in Bavaria while at the same time, as rumours of a putsch grew stronger, warning the Bavarian political leaders against supporting the increasingly loud and shrill nationalist clamour on the extremist paramilitary Right. The Bavarian Reichs-wehr leadership had favoured a march on Berlin and proclamation of a national dictatorship – echoes of Mussolini's exploits in Italy. But when von Seeckt blew cold on the idea, and stated that he would not move against the legal government in Berlin, the Bavarian army retreated from backing a coup.

Pushed into a corner, Hitler felt he had no choice but to act or see his support drain away. The attempted putsch, theatrically launched by Hitler in a big Munich beer hall on 8 November 1923, collapsed ignominiously next morning in a hail of police gunfire in the centre of the city. The threat from the Right, as well as that from the Left, had been contained. The collapse of the beer-hall putsch was the lancing of a boil in the body politic. The putschists were rounded up and, a few months later, the ringleaders, including Hitler, were tried and sentenced – unduly leniently – to terms of imprisonment. The extrem-ist Right fragmented. The crisis subsided. The currency was stabilized soon afterwards and a new, more amenable, framework for repayment of reparations established. Democracy had survived – but only just.

War, defeat, revolution and the peace settlement had traumatized and polarized Germany. Governments were unstable. The middle classes feared and hated Socialism, giving sustenance to shrill nationalist agitation and brutal paramilitary violence on the anti-democratic Right. In all this, there were similarities to post-war Italy. Unlike Italy, however, democracy retained strong, well-organized support, not just among the large Social Democratic Party but also among the Catholic Centre Party and the Left Liberals. Pluralist politics, if not parliamentary democracy, drew on a lengthy history. Political participation had well-established deep roots and could draw upon more than half a century of universal male suffrage. Moreover, unlike Italy, Germany was a federal system. Although the main democratic party, the Social Democrats, retreated into opposition at Reich level, and though Bavaria developed into a stronghold of the anti-democratic, nationalist Right, Prussia, by far the biggest state, remained under the government of staunchly democratic parties. This in itself would not have been enough to save democracy had the power elites – lukewarm at best towards the new republic – turned their backs on it.

But, most crucial of all, the army leadership, whose attitude towards parliamentary democracy had from the beginning been ambiguous, supported the state at the height of the 1923 crisis, whereas Mussolini's movement could reach for power only because it had the backing of the Italian military. This was decisive in allowing democracy to survive the post-war crisis in Germany at a time when it collapsed in Italy. The German military leadership plainly had serious doubts about the putschists' chances of success – memories of the ignominious failure of the Kapp Putsch in 1920 were still fresh in the mind. Beyond such doubts, the unwillingness to underwrite a putsch reflected the worry that the military would not be able to master the daunting problems which would face them both at home and abroad should they be forced to take political responsibility in Germany.

The country's crippling economic woes and international weakness were sufficient reason in themselves to avoid lending support to a dilettante attempt to topple the elected government. A right-wing dictatorship, following a successful putsch, would have been from the outset in a precarious military and economic position. It would have had no obvious way of resolving the economic crisis. Whether the Americans would have provided financial aid for a regime run by the German military is extremely doubtful. And a further default on reparations under an assertive national government might have led to renewed French intervention and the loss of the Rhineland. Gravely weakened in the post-war settlement, the German army would have been in no position to offer armed resistance. The time to back an authoritarian solution to the problem of democracy, as the army leadership saw it, had not come.

Until reparations could be terminated, loosening the shackles of Versailles and rebuilding the army would have to wait (though secret arrangements with the Soviet Union following the Treaty of Rapallo in 1922 offered some degree of cooperation in the training of officers, evading restrictions imposed at Versailles). But without army support, the extreme nationalist Right in Germany had no possibility in 1923 of emulating the rise of Fascism to power that had taken place in Italy the previous year. The danger to democracy passed. New and better times were about to arrive. But the threat had only subsided, not disappeared.

By 1924 the post-war crisis was over. But beneath the surface of the calmer times to follow, the outcome of the First World War and the post-war settlement had left trouble brewing. The main threat to Europe's lasting peace would come from the unholy combination of hyper-nationalism and imperialism. A world of nation states was emerging. In Europe a new order based on nation states, many of them unstable, had been a crucial outcome of the war. But the imperial dream among Europe's major powers was still very much alive. The victorious Allied powers, Great Britain and France, saw their future prosperity and prestige continuing to rest on their empires. They were the great winners in the post-war settlement, significantly expanding their imperial possessions outside Europe by taking control of former German colonies around the world and the territories of the former Ottoman Empire in the Middle East.

A secret deal struck in 1916 between Sir Mark Sykes and François Georges-Picot had carved up much of the Arab Middle East between Britain and France. In all, Britain added another million square miles to its empire, France around a quarter of a million square miles. The new creations of Syria and Lebanon were handed to France, mandates for Palestine (including Transjordan) and Iraq to Great Britain (turning the Middle East in the process into the future cornerstone of imperial defence). In 1917 the British Foreign Secretary, Arthur Balfour, supporting the aims of the still small Zionist movement, had announced that the British government favoured 'the establishment in Palestine of a national home for the Jewish people'. The announcement was partly intended to gain Jewish support in the USA for the war – America had yet to enter the conflict – and also to ensure that the strategically important area of Palestine would not, as had been foreseen, later be handed to the French. The consequences of both the Sykes-Picot Agreement and the Balfour Declaration would reverberate not just through Europe but throughout the entire world, especially during the second half of the twentieth century – and beyond.

The one-time or would-be great powers, Germany and Italy, also still harboured imperialist pretensions. Humiliated by the loss of colonial possessions or failure to gain them, they felt themselves to be thwarted 'have-not' nations. For now they could do nothing. But the foundations for future trouble had been laid. There was no unbroken umbilical cord that tied a second great world conflagration to the first. Things could have turned out differently. Nevertheless, the legacy of the Great War made another major war in Europe more, rather than less, likely. Meanwhile, thinking the worst was over, Europeans began to entertain realistic hopes of future peace and prosperity.

4

Dancing on the Volcano

If we were to ask them about the meaning and purpose of life, the only answer they could give would be: 'We don't know what the purpose of life is, and we're not interested in finding out. But since we are alive, we want to get as much out of life as we possibly can.'

A Protestant clergyman commenting
on 'proletarian youth' in German cities (1929)

By 1924 the prospects for Europe looked brighter than they had done for more than a decade. Ravaged economies were recovering. Living standards were starting to improve. International peace was less threatened than at any point since 1914. Violent upheavals on the continent had subsided. Cultural creativity and innovation flourished. As the horror of the war started to recede into memory, it was as if the continent were starting to come to life again – spring after a long, dark winter. For the young, especially, a new and more carefree age appeared to have dawned. Jazz, the Charleston, the 'flapper': the imports from the USA symbolized for many contemporaries, as they have done subsequently, Europe's own 'roaring twenties'. Others came to call them the 'golden twenties'. The future could at last be viewed with more hope and greater optimism. The worst was over. Or so it seemed.

But only five years later the Wall Street Crash in New York triggered a global crisis of capitalism, unprecedented in its severity. The crisis swept through Europe, plunging the continent into an extraordinary spiral of economic depression, destroying hopes of peace and prosperity in its wake, undermining democracies, and paving the way for a new war, even more terrible than the last one had been.

Was Europe emerging from catastrophe in ways that held great promise for future peace and prosperity before the havoc brought by economic depression descended as an immense, unforeseeable and unavoidable force? Or did post-war recovery conceal more ominous traits in Europe's development, latent but only to be fully exposed when economic crisis engulfed the continent?

With the recovery at its height in 1928, Gustav Stresemann, Germany's Foreign Minister, offered a stark warning against undue optimism. The German economy, central to Europe's recovery, had indeed undergone a transformation since the dark days of hyperinflation. Yet, remarked Stresemann, it was still in a precarious state. It was like 'dancing on a volcano'. Not just with regard to Germany, this seems a fitting metaphor for the years when much of Europe danced the Charleston, blissfully unaware of the disaster about to erupt and plunge the continent into an era of mounting crisis.

BOOM

There is no need to be a disciple of Karl Marx to recognize the extent to which economic forces determined the course of Europe's post-war development. These were understood by few, if any, economists and practically no political leaders, let alone by the mass of ordinary people whose lives they determined. Even today, economists disagree about the precise causes of the Great Depression, and why it was so widespread, so deep and so long-lasting. The essentials seem nevertheless clear enough. The direct cause of the crash was the greatly overheated American economy during the boom of the 'roaring twenties'. The overheating had its roots in cheap money that flowed into consumer spending – sales of automobiles and electrical goods led the way – and eventually into stocks and shares that seemed to be on an endless upward curve. When the bubble burst in 1929, the fallout in Europe reflected structural economic weaknesses that had left the continent extremely vulnerable. In particular, the post-war economic dependence upon the United States was part of a highly disturbed global economy, in which the pre-war controls and balances no longer operated.

Before the collapse, Europe's economy had been showing evident signs of recovery from the enormous upheavals of the early post-war crisis. Economic revitalization depended in no small measure upon rebuilding Germany's damaged but strong industrial potential. And indeed there was remarkable recovery as Germany rebounded from the trauma of the hyperinflation of 1923. Industry's debts had been largely eradicated by inflation. But industrial capital was mainly outmoded. The problem was tackled through a rigorous programme of modernization and rationalization of industry, which produced impressive technical advances in production and substantial increases in output. It was, however, far from an unqualified success story. In fact, it highlighted some of the underlying structural weaknesses in the European economy, which left Germany extremely exposed when the crash came in America in 1929.

A vital basis for Germany's recovery had been the stabilization of the currency, ruined by the hyperinflation. Linked to this stabilization was regulation of the thorny issue of reparations, which lay at the root of so much of the economic and political turmoil of 1922–3.

The key step to replace the completely valueless currency had already been taken at the height of the crisis with the introduction of the new *Rentenmark* in November 1923. This temporary currency, backed by assets in land, property and industrial capital, swiftly gained public confidence and the following year, supported by a big American loan, was put on a secure footing, converted to the gold monetary standard, and renamed the *Reichsmark* (converted from the old mark at a trillion to one). Also in the autumn of 1923 an international committee of experts, chaired by the American banker Charles G. Dawes, had set about re-examining reparations and by April 1924 was ready to make its recommendations. Under the Dawes Plan, stages of gradually increasing instalments made the payment of reparations far more manageable. It was intended as an interim arrangement. Once Germany's economy was fully flourishing again, reparations would lose their sting. That was the presumption.

The problem was that the money to repay the reparations came mainly from foreign loans, mostly from the USA, which now poured in. American investors saw rich pickings in a vibrant German economy. Big American firms such as General Motors, Ford and General Electric planned factories in Germany. Foreign credits to Germany amounted to around $5 billion by 1930. German industry was the initial major beneficiary. But business was soon complaining that too much investment was being diverted to German municipalities to build parks, swimming pools, theatres and museums, or to renovate public squares and buildings. These were undoubtedly good for the quality of life in German towns and cities. But long-term investments were being funded with short-term loans. It was imagined that the good years would continue. What would happen if, instead, the short-term American loans were recalled and lending was curtailed? It did not seem an issue at the time.

The Dawes Plan was the most obvious indication that in the post-war world economic primacy had shifted irrevocably to the United States – by far the biggest winner from the enormous disturbance to the world economy brought about by the war. In the Far East, Japan had also emerged as a powerhouse. Britain's global economic dominance was, however, over. Within Europe the number of countries, currencies and customs barriers had increased, sharpening the tendency to protectionism – in effect, economic nationalism – through the imposition of import tariffs. The countries that had thrived before the war, Britain at the forefront, thought they could turn the clock back. Before 1914, the 'gold standard' – fixed exchange rates related to the internationally agreed price of gold and centred on the Bank of England – had been the hallmark of economic stability. The gold standard had been suspended during the First World War, and when it was restored, piecemeal, during the 1920s, this occurred in a very different economic and political climate.

Conditions were now highly unstable, with the United States economically preeminent and London's one-time financial supremacy challenged by New York and Paris. But in 1925 Britain took the major step of returning to the gold standard. France followed three years later, by which time all the most important European economies had returned to the gold standard. For prestige reasons, Britain (accompanied by a number of other countries) insisted on pre-war parity against the dollar. It was thought to be a 'return to normalcy' – the economic security of the pre-war era. But it was a changed world. Fixed exchange rates, in which the position of Britain, a country with serious economic problems, was pivotal, were now a source of weakness, not strength. What they did was store up trouble for the future.

These problems were not foreseen in the mid-1920s, when the European economy was recovering strongly. Industrial production rose by over 20 per cent between 1925 and 1929. There was above-average growth in Germany, Belgium, France, Sweden, Finland, the Netherlands, Luxembourg and Czechoslovakia; also (from a modest base) in Hungary, Romania, Poland and Latvia. Growth in France and Belgium was helped by currency depreciation. France's expansion built upon the extraordinarily quick economic recovery it had made in the early 1920s. Industrial production increased by more than a quarter between 1925 and 1929, while per capita income was nearly a fifth higher. On the eve of the Great Depression French exports were about 50 per cent higher than before the war. Belgium, too, saw an impressive rise of about a third in industrial production, and a big increase in exports. The most remarkable growth, after the calamities of its civil war, took place in the Soviet Union, though here, of course, the market forces of the international economy did not operate.

In the United Kingdom, Italy, Spain, Denmark, Norway, Greece and Austria, however, economic growth remained sluggish. Fascist Italy suffered from a significant overvaluation of the lira, pushed through by Mussolini for prestige reasons. Unemployment and wage cuts, only partly offset by public works and agricultural subsidies, followed. Primo de Rivera's dictatorship in Spain also brought trouble upon itself. High tariff protection, largely cutting off Spain from international markets, and the overvalued peseta left the Spanish economy in worsening difficulties by 1929. Denmark and Norway, too, suffered from overvalued currencies. The British economy showed a spurt in growth in 1928–9. However, although there had been expansion in newer industries such as car manufacturing, chemicals and electrical goods, the traditional industrial heartlands of coal, steel, textiles and shipbuilding had remained depressed throughout the 1920s. In Europe as a whole, nonetheless, by 1929 recovery from the immediate post-war blight had been a success story. Driven especially by the American boom, international trade had risen by over 20 per cent.

The pace of change was greatest in the more industrialized and urbanized parts of northern and western Europe. In poorer, less well-developed rural areas – the norm in eastern and southern Europe – change was much slower and more limited. Automobile production was one important agent, both of economic stimulus and of social change. Cars, first mass-produced in the USA by Henry Ford, had been a luxury item before the war. Buying one was still beyond the reach of most people. By the early 1930s there were still only about seven private cars for every thousand people in Europe compared with 183 cars in America. But car production in Europe, too, was starting to be aimed at a mass market. The British-manufactured Austin 7, first built in 1922, led the way. Fiat in Italy, Citroën then Renault and Peugeot in France, were also soon producing smaller, lower-priced cars. Opel (bought by the American giant, General Motors, in 1929) began to do the same in Germany, though little headway was made anywhere in Europe in the boom years of the 1920s to produce a car that less well-to-do people could afford.

Even so, cars and motorcycles were no longer an unusual sight in Europe's cities. By the middle of the decade, there were about a million cars on Britain's roads, half a million in France, and a quarter of a million in Germany. Italy built the first motorway in the middle of the 1920s and within a few years had a network of about 3,000 miles. Roads elsewhere were far less developed, but most in western and central Europe were fit for motor vehicles by the end of the 1920s. In European towns and cities, goods vehicles, buses and taxis were no longer pulled by horses. The street-scene was changing fast. The motorization of Europe was under way.

Electric lighting, too, was changing the urban landscape. Entire districts could be lit at the press of a switch in a power station. Gas lamps, and the jobs of men who walked the streets to light and extinguish them, were becoming obsolete. With electricity came modern household appliances, already becoming commonplace in the USA. Vacuum cleaners slowly began to make their appearance in middle-class homes in Europe, though washing machines, fridges or electric ovens remained a rarity, and for working-class households domestic work continued to be pure drudgery. Office work was changing with the spread of the telephone. There were said to be a million and a quarter conversations a day on Berlin's half a million telephone lines. As yet, though, few private homes had a telephone. Sweden led the way by the end of the 1920s with eighty-three telephones per 1,000 inhabitants, compared with fifty in Germany and only seven in Italy. Electricity also enabled the beginning of the first communications revolution, with the start of national radio broadcasting networks. The BBC, only two years after radio programmes began, had a million registered listeners by 1924. Close behind Britain in the rapidity of radio's expansion was Germany, where the number of listeners rose from 10,000 in 1924 to 4 million by 1932 – one home in four.

It looked to many as if Europe was on the way to prolonged prosperity. It proved a false dawn. It probably did not even feel like a boom to many people. Mostly, as before, it was a matter of getting by, not of becoming prosperous. If poverty was not so utterly grinding as it once had been, it was still near ubiquitous. Large parts of the population still lived in primitive conditions in the countryside or in atrocious housing in big cities and industrial areas, where there was chronic overcrowding. Often an entire family had to share a single room in a slum with primitive sanitary arrangements. New and better housing was an urgent requirement. There were certainly improvements – sometimes on an impressive scale, especially when the state intervened. By the end of the 1920s, the German democratic state was building over 300,000 new homes each year, many of them publicly financed. Big new estates, intended for the working class, arose in Berlin and Frankfurt. Public spending on housing during the pre-war monarchy had been practically zero. By 1929, house construction was the area of the largest increase in state expenditure compared with 1913. Between 1924 and 1930 some 2.5 million dwellings were built in Germany, one in seven dwellings was new, and over 7 million people were the beneficiaries. The city government of 'red' Vienna, controlled by Social Democrats, also made impressive advances, rehousing 180,000 people in new apartments. The most spectacular achievement was the huge Karl-Marx-Hof, completed in 1930, which contained 1,382 apartments for the city's poorer population.

But such developments were exceptional. And they were far from sufficient. A million German families were still without their own home in 1927 amid a continuing chronic housing shortage. The increase in house-building in Sweden in the 1920s did little to address the serious overcrowding in urban areas. Unplanned urban sprawls of high-density, insanitary dwellings in the suburbs of Paris and other French cities awaited migrants from the countryside or beyond France's borders, drawn to find work in expanding industries. In Britain, too, housing misery, especially in industrial areas, remained a huge social problem. Immediate housing needs after the war had been estimated at 800,000 homes. But the post-war housing programme, which produced 213,000 new houses, petered out as the cost of borrowing rose sharply in 1920–21. The Conservative government in 1923 favoured subsidizing private building, but most of the 362,000 houses constructed by private enterprise over the following six years were beyond the reach of poor working-class families and went in the main to lower-middle-class buyers. The new Labour administration in 1924 introduced the first social housing programme through subsidizing controlled rents for dwellings built by municipalities. The big expansion of what were called 'council houses' saw 521,000 homes erected by 1933 for mainly working-class people. It was a start, but little more. Millions still lived in dire circumstances. In the cities of southern and eastern Europe, appalling housing conditions were the norm, exacerbated by the influx of people from poor areas of the countryside, where most peasant dwellings remained primitive.

Trade unions – greatly expanded in size and exploiting labour's new bargaining power in the war – had successfully pressed (in the face of employer resistance) for the forty-hour working week which, beginning in France, Germany and Italy, was in many countries becoming the norm. This reduced workers' long working days, even if in practice overtime meant that more than the forty hours a week were actually spent working. Skilled workers, especially, saw their wages rise, though at a rate that lagged for the most part far behind the growth of business profits. There were, however, notable variations. Workers in newer, expanding industries could do well. Real wages at the huge Renault factories in France, employing thousands of workers to feed the growing output of motor vehicles, grew by 40 per cent over the 1920s. But if their wages were rising, the work itself was for the most part sheer monotony – repetitive, assembly-line production, enforced with iron discipline. Much of it was carried out by immigrants – by 1931, close on 3 million (7 per cent of France's population) – who had to endure a great deal of discrimination and bad treatment. France took in 400,000 Russian refugees in the 1920s, more than four times as many as any other country. Many other immigrants came from Poland, Italy, Armenia and Algeria.

In older industries wage levels told a different story. By far the biggest strike of the mid-1920s, the General Strike in Britain between 3 and 13 May 1926, arose from the attempt – successful as it turned out – by employers to reduce wages in a coal industry suffering from serious overcapacity. Over 1.5 million workers from various branches of transport and industry came out on strike in support of about 800,000 miners locked out by their employers. Attempts to break the strike gathered momentum and within ten days the Trades Union Congress (TUC) called off the dispute, accepting government terms that were little less than humiliating. The miners continued their defiance, but were eventually driven back to work after six months – impoverished, completely defeated, and forced to accept the longer hours and lower wages imposed by the mine-owners. German employers took an equally aggressive stance in November 1928, when they locked out the entire workforce of the Ruhr iron and steel industry – around 220,000 workers – to enforce new wage rates in the teeth of a national arbitration award. These major conflicts were the most obvious signs of a weakening position of industrial workers (especially those in the older, heavy industries) and their trade unions, and a corresponding increase in the bargaining strength and militancy of employers amid high rates of unemployment – and this even before the Great Depression.

France, like Germany, was among the countries most advanced in adopting in large-scale industry the modern management methods pioneered in the USA by Frederick Winslow Taylor soon after the turn of the century and the mass-production techniques introduced into car manufacturing by Henry Ford in 1913. A consequence in Germany of the far-reaching rationalization of industrial production was that unemployment, which had remained low during the early 1920s, more than trebled in 1925–6 to over 2 million (10 per cent of the working population). Similar levels of unemployment were not uncommon elsewhere in Europe. In countries where growth was slow, such as Denmark and Norway, unemployment reached 17–18 per cent. It was high, too, in the older branches of heavy industry and textiles, which faced increased competition in world markets and where rapid expansion had led to overcapacity. Unemployment in Britain never fell below 1 million even before the slump.

Unemployment insurance, first introduced in 1911 under the National Insurance Act, was extended after the war to cover around 12 million British workers (though in practice only about 60 per cent of the workforce). Women were included, but their weekly benefit payments were lower than those for men. Domestic servants, agricultural labourers and civil servants were excluded. The scheme headed off the worst. But it had been intended to cover short-term, not long-term, structural unemployment. The insurance fund proved insufficient and had to be subsidized by the state out of taxation. In Germany the problem was similar, but worse. The safety net of unemployment insurance, introduced in 1927 (and a notable addition to the insurance scheme against illness, accident and old age brought in under Bismarck in the 1880s), was already under strain by the time the Depression beset the economy, and became overwhelmed thereafter. In any case, less than half of the working population had a claim on unemployment relief. Although other parts of Europe had followed Britain's early lead and introduced systems of unemployment benefit, the proportion of the workforce covered was even smaller.

If the boom was both limited and uneven in its effect on industrial parts of Europe, in the countryside, where most of Europe's population still lived, many peasants on smallholdings barely providing subsistence hardly noticed a boom at all. Many farmers had done well out of the war, and the post-war inflation often allowed them to wipe out their debts. Low land prices at the end of the conflict enabled those who could afford it to add to their holdings. But agriculture soon faced harder times. Increased production in Europe, as post-war recovery gained ground, encountered markets already glutted through produce from non-European countries whose output during the war had expanded to fill gaps and cover shortages. By the later 1920s the Soviet policy to export grain in order to be able to import vitally needed industrial equipment added to the glut. The result was falling prices. International prices for agricultural products had by 1929 dropped by over a third compared with the years 1923–5. Countries in eastern and southern Europe, heavily dependent upon agricultural production, were particularly badly hit.

Agriculture remained largely unmechanized. Post-war land reforms broke up many big estates, but created large numbers of small, less productive farms and fragmented holdings. Farm subsidies in Czechoslovakia and elsewhere helped to promote improvements, while a shift to dairy and livestock products enabled Baltic countries to increase their exports. But for most of those who made their living from the land the problems were mounting long before the slump. Farm indebtedness grew alarmingly. Many producers were on the edge before the Depression tipped them into insolvency. Flight from the land into the squalid living conditions of overcrowded towns increased as the gap between urban and rural incomes widened and as young people saw no future for themselves in the countryside. They could no longer emigrate in great numbers to the USA, once far stricter immigration controls had been introduced there in the early 1920s. But they moved within countries. In France alone, 600,000 people left their smallholdings between 1921 and 1931 to try their luck in urban workshops and factories.

For those living in the countryside, the later 1920s scarcely constituted a boom period. The Depression struck regions already blighted over much of Europe. The 'crisis before the crisis' left a rural population already before the slump susceptible to political radicalization. Many landless labourers were attracted by communism. Peasants who possessed land, on the other hand, tended to find appeal in the gathering forces of the authoritarian Right.

Although the economy in most of Europe had recovered strongly in the second half of the 1920s, the underlying problems left the continent exposed to grave difficulties in the event of a downturn in fortunes. Few were aware of them. There had been modest improvements in the standard of living for many people, certainly compared with the previous decade. Many, perhaps most, people felt they could look forward to still better times in the future. Optimistic voices, some cautious, others more heady, predominated over the prophets of doom. But optimism vanished practically overnight as the drastic impact of the stock-market crash in New York between 24 and 29 October 1929 enveloped Europe.

THE ALTERNATIVE MODEL

Even before the onset of the economic crisis, those who were prophesying the certain and imminent end of capitalism could turn with admiration, and for inspiration, to one country: the Soviet Union. Cushioned from the vagaries of the international economy, the model of the Soviet Union – a system of state socialism preparing the ground for the final goal of communism, a society without private property and freed from class divisions and inequalities – appeared to many to be the utopian hope for the future. There was an attractive alternative to the market economy, the Soviet Union seemed to show – a better model for society than the grossly unjust, economically outdated and inferior capitalist system. State planning, resting on ownership of the means of production, and autarchy – economic self-sufficiency – appeared to point the way forward. Both ideas were gaining supporters across Europe.

Within the Soviet Union economic growth had indeed been impressive – if from a low platform, the result of the upheavals of the First World War and revolution, followed by the ravages of the civil war. Recovery had been remarkably swift. By 1927–8 both industry and agriculture had reached levels of output comparable to those of 1913. The New Economic Policy, the Soviet policy between 1921 and 1928 that gave peasants a vested interest in cultivation and offered them limited opportunities to profit from marketing their produce, had proved a success. But by 1927 the policy was creating its own problems. And industrially the Soviet Union still lagged far behind the advanced countries of western Europe.

How to tackle the problem of economic backwardness had remained an issue of heated debate among the leadership. Overcoming this huge weakness was seen primarily as crucial to averting the threat from rapacious imperialist powers, but also to improving living standards as the basis of securing the future of socialism in the Soviet Union. These, it was taken as axiomatic, would at some point embroil the country in war. 'Either we do it, or we shall be crushed,' Stalin told the party's Central Committee in November 1928 at a vital economic and political turning point for the Soviet Union. But the path to this decisive moment was far from straightforward. After Lenin's death in January 1924, economic policy had increasingly become the central issue in the bitter internal political struggle that would end in Stalin's outright dominance and a huge, fateful shift in the direction of the Soviet economy.

The New Economic Policy had been contested from the outset in 1921. Some prominent Bolsheviks, Trotsky more than any, had seen it as merely a temporary expedient to get over the worst and were soon pushing for increased state economic planning and more rapid industrialization at the expense of the peasantry. Trotsky also continued to insist upon the need to export Bolshevism and promote world revolution. Stalin, on the other hand, had announced in December 1924 that the party's goal had to be 'Socialism in One Country'. By this time, Trotsky's influence was waning fast. Whatever the force of his arguments and his striking personality, he had made too many enemies. Moreover, his control over crucial levers of power within the party was weak. Stalin, backed by other leading figures – Grigory Zinoviev, Lev Kamenev and 'the darling of the party' (as Lenin had dubbed him), Nikolai Bukharin – was able to outmanoeuvre him. In 1925 Trotsky resigned as Commissar for War and later in the year was removed from the Politburo. In 1927 he and his followers were expelled from the party for their 'heretical' views, and the following year Trotsky was sent into exile 3,000 kilometres from Moscow. Lenin had warned on his deathbed that Stalin was not a fit personality to remain as the party's General Secretary – the position he had held since 1922. But Stalin had ensured that the warning was not circulated and used his pivotal position at the heart of the party's organizational machine to engineer his own supremacy. Zinoviev and Kamenev made it easier for him. In 1926 they had reversed their former stance, joining Trotsky's opposition to what they viewed as an economic policy that was too favourable to the peasantry.

In fact, steps towards comprehensive industrial planning had already been taken, though as yet without any official weakening of the New Economic Policy. Stalin, firmly backed at this stage by

Bukharin, the leading advocate of the policy, was able to undermine, then oust from their positions of power, both Zinoviev and Kamenev. They too were expelled from the party in 1927 (though, condemning Trotsky and recanting their opposition, they were readmitted, contrite and humbled, the following year). Only Bukharin now stood in Stalin's way.

Stalin, pressing for extensive requisitioning of food supplies and a harder line towards the peasantry, was now increasingly at loggerheads with his former ally, Bukharin, who strongly favoured maintaining the New Economic Policy. By mid-1928 the two had become irreconcilable political enemies. Stalin was adamant that small-scale production posed an insuperable block to economic growth. It was essential to guarantee the provision of food for an expanding industrial population. And that could only be achieved through large-scale production run by the state. He moved deftly in winning support in the party for an ambitious plan to maximize rapid industrial growth – at the expense of those in the countryside. Controlling the party's apparatus, he denigrated Bukharin as a 'deviationist'. By 1929, Bukharin was yesterday's man. Stalin was the winner of the power struggles, the Soviet Union's supreme leader, finally unchallenged in claiming Lenin's mantle for himself.

Already by then, the New Economic Policy, though not publicly disavowed, was obsolete. In the winter of 1927–8 peasants were hoarding grain rather than selling it at the official depressed price. Serious food shortages started to build up, just at the time when major industrial projects had been set in motion. Middlemen – racketeers able to exploit the shortages – were buying up agricultural produce and selling it at black-market prices. Stalin, the self-styled 'man of steel' – he had been born Josef Dzhugashvili – lived up to his soubriquet and responded in characteristic fashion: through brutal coercion. He journeyed to the Urals and Siberia in January 1928 and peremptorily requisitioned stocks of grain, much as had been done during the civil war. Any opposition to what was dubbed 'the Urals-Siberian method' received short shrift. Bukharin tried in vain to prevent the extension of the requisitioning and to head off Stalin's increasing hold on power.

By the middle of 1928 Stalin had won the conflict over future economic policy. A draft programme of rapid industrialization was put forward that year and accepted by the Party Congress in April 1929 as the first 'Five-Year Plan'. Much of the Plan was in fact fairly chaotic in its implementation, and the targeted extraordinary increases in production were achieved only in fabricated official output figures. Even so, the advances were impressive – all the more so with the rest of industrialized Europe now slumping into the throes of a severe Depression. Huge new industrial complexes sprang up. An enormous hydroelectric plant was established on the lower Dnieper, sprawling metallurgical factories were built at Magnitogorsk in the Urals and Kuznetsk in Siberia, and large-scale tractor manufacture expanded in Stalingrad and Kharkov. Peasants left the countryside in droves to join the swelling numbers of workers in industry, whose numbers doubled within four years. Industrial output grew, even by sceptical estimates, at over 10 per cent a year, with roughly a doubling in the production of coal, oil, iron ore and pig iron by 1932.

The human price was, however, horrendous – a price that no country in the rest of Europe could have contemplated for a second. Working conditions, rates of pay and living standards of industrial workers were appalling. Discipline in factories was draconian, with severe punishment for 'slackers'. But the Five-Year Plan had far worse consequences for those in the countryside. The regime had recognized from the start that the industrial programme had to be pushed through on the backs of the peasantry. The failure to extract sufficient grain from the peasants to prevent shortages and rationing of bread in towns in 1929 prompted the adoption that year of a programme of forced collectivization of agriculture. The intention was that within two years a quarter of the sown area would be held by collectives – big factory farms, worked by a rural proletariat of peasants who had been deprived of their own holdings. In fact, collectivization went ahead faster than this. Nearly 60 per cent of the 25 million peasant households were collectivized already by March 1930.

But the peasants did not comply readily. Almost three quarters of a million took part in revolts, which broke out in several parts of the Soviet Union. 'We had grain and potato requisitions, and they took them from us by force, both from the poor peasants and from the middle peasants. Simply speaking, it was robbery,' complained one smallholder, asking for the reversal of collectivization, pleading for 'freedom, and then we will be glad to help the state'. The regime temporarily acknowledged the problem. Stalin blamed the excesses on local functionaries 'dizzy with success'. The proportion of the peasantry in collectives fell back sharply, to 23 per cent. It was a brief lull. Pressure soon resumed. By the harvest of 1931 more than half of the households had once more been dragooned into collectives, which produced nearly all Soviet grain. Three years later and collectivization had triumphed almost everywhere.

Enforcement was ruthlessly carried out by brigades of party zealots sent out from the towns. A policy of 'dekulakization' – 'liquidating the kulaks as a class' – was proclaimed to encourage an assault on the supposed better-off peasants, accused of being rural capitalists. 'Kulak' meant, however, whatever party activists wanted it to mean. Anyone resisting collectivization could be dubbed a 'kulak' and imprisoned, deported to a far-off labour camp, or simply shot. From Ukraine alone as many as 113,637 'kulaks' were deported by force in the first months of 1930. Those voicing objections to the coerced collectivization but plainly too poor to be 'kulaks' were dubbed 'sub-kulaks' and subjected to the same punishment. Many 'kulaks' fled, selling their property if they could, or simply abandoning it. Some killed their wives and children, then took their own lives.

Grain production had been expected to double. In fact, it fell – not drastically, though since state procurement of grain more than doubled, the rural population was left desperately short of food. And as the peasants were forced into collectives, they slaughtered their own cattle or left them to starve rather than surrender them to the state. The numbers of cattle and pigs fell by half, sheep and goats by two-thirds. Meat and milk were, as a result, also scarce. Collectives that had not met requisition targets were deprived of produce from elsewhere in the Soviet Union and ordered to hand over their seed corn – thereby guaranteeing a repeated harvest disaster the following summer.

Famine, worse than in 1921–2 and a direct consequence of Soviet agricultural policy, was widespread in the terrible year of 1932–3. Kazakhstan and North Caucasus were among the areas worst affected. The impact was most terrible of all in Ukraine, which should have been a fertile crop-growing area. A party official, entering one village, was told 'we've eaten everything we could lay our hands on – cats, dogs, field mice, birds', even the bark from the trees. Over 2,000 people were punished for cannibalism in 1932–3. The death toll from the famine in Ukraine cannot be known with accuracy. The best estimates are around 3.3 million deaths from starvation or hunger-related diseases. For the whole of the Soviet Union, the figure can be nearly doubled.

Some news of the horror trickled out. But admirers of the Soviet Union downplayed the stories that emerged or rejected them as anti-communist propaganda. Most people in western Europe knew nothing of the famine. Few foreign observers were able to witness the disaster. One, the British journalist Malcolm Muggeridge, described it as 'one of the most monstrous crimes in history, so terrible that people in the future will scarcely be able to believe that it happened'. He was right. The people on the eastern fringe of the European continent had suffered more than most even before the First World War, then in the post-war turmoil and the Russian Civil War, and now under the Soviet regime. The vale of tears was already deep. But the full depth of the abyss was yet to be plumbed.

THE CULTURAL MIRROR

What sense did people in Europe make of the world they were living in, of the forces that were inexorably shaping their existence? A generalized answer is of course impossible. Patterns of life and the reflections they provoked depended on many variables. These included accidents of geography and family background as well as social class, political culture and the vagaries of historical development. Far-reaching reflective insights were in any case inevitably confined in the main to a well-educated elite – an elite with access to the higher levels of education denied to the overwhelming majority of the population. The most innovative talents in the creative arts both mirrored and shaped what, in the broadest understanding, could be described as the *Zeitgeist*, or 'spirit of the age'. For those, mainly in the upper classes or the educated middle classes, who were used to imbibing the products of this 'high culture', important traits of social thought and artistic creativity could prove, if only indirectly, extremely influential. For much of the population, however, this 'high culture' was inaccessible; it lay beyond the parameters of normal life.

What remained for most people at the end of the working day or week were avenues of popular culture – entertainment films, dance halls, and not least (for men, at any rate), visits to the pub or bar – that offered not reflection on the world around them but escapism and momentary excitement, temporary release from the drab, often depressing, reality of daily life. Going to the cinema offered the greatest chance of escapism. New 'picture palaces' shot up in Europe's towns and cities. Germany had more than anywhere, over 5,000 by 1930 (double the number a decade earlier), with 2 million seats in total. Cinema attendance grew even more once 'talkies' started to replace silent films towards the end of the 1920s. Cinemas provided what audiences wanted. Most films were comedies, dramas, adventure or romance. Professional sport – football especially – offered the other big escape for working men, though hardly at all for women. Football's popularity had extended from Britain to other European countries long before the First World War. Major leagues had been established in Germany, Italy, Spain and elsewhere. Huge attendances were commonplace. In England, the first Wembley Cup Final of 1923, when Bolton Wanderers beat West Ham United 2–0, had attracted a crowd officially put at 126,000, though usually thought to have been double that number.*

'High' and 'popular' culture rarely met. But in different ways, they were both central to the *Zeitgeist* of interwar Europe. It was not merely a question of alternative forms of culture. The extremes of cultural creativity and artistic innovation that were reached in the first post-war decade were inevitably the taste of a small minority. Not only were avant-garde cultural forms – too varied to be easily summarized – remote from the lives of most of the population, but,

---

* My grandad – long before I was born – and his two elder sons were among the crowd. They had travelled down 200 miles from Oldham together by train, but arrived back separately, and on different days. Uncle Jimmy was found asleep in a railway siding at Reading three days after the match. The Kershaws had enjoyed themselves!

where they were seen most acutely to challenge 'traditional' culture and values, they faced hostile rejection.

Belonging to the avant-garde meant attachment to the artistic ideals, forms and expressions of cultural modernism. From about the beginning of the twentieth century – though the ideas themselves went back two decades or so earlier – practically all branches of cultural creativity turned away from earlier classical, realist and Romantic forms of expression and self-consciously embraced 'modernism'. The diffuse, aesthetic concept of 'modernism' covered a huge range of differing modes of artistic expression. What united them was the revolt against previous forms of representation, which they regarded as outmoded, superficial, devoid of inner meaning. The manifesto, presented in 1906, of the Dresden group of Expressionist artists who called themselves 'Die Brücke' – the name was meant to imply 'the bridge' to a new artistic era – proclaimed that 'as young people, who carry the future in us, we want to wrest freedom for our actions and our lives from the older, comfortably established forces'. All that was conventional, or 'bourgeois', was rejected. It was replaced by boundless aesthetic experimentation with the new, the 'modern'. It amounted to revolutionary destruction of the old in order to rebuild in completely new ways according to artistic imagination and creativity. Earlier ideals of beauty, harmony and reason were radically discarded in modernism. Fragmentation, disunity and chaos were the new leitmotifs – a remarkable anticipation in cultural forms of the political and economic rupture left by the First World War.

After the war, as before 1914, Paris was a magnet for cultural energy and creativity, a centre of modernist vitality. Pablo Picasso, already famous as the creative force behind Cubism – new forms of three-dimensional abstract representation – who had made his home there before the war, was the most glittering star in the firmament. Artists from across the continent and beyond were drawn to the vibrancy of the French capital. So were modernist writers, including James Joyce, Ernest Hemingway and Ezra Pound. Artistic innovation flourished on the Left Bank. Dadaism (created in Zurich in 1916) and Surrealism (originating in France the following year), the two, closely related, most novel and revolutionary art forms, thrived in Paris in the 1920s. They had emerged chiefly in reaction to the bourgeois society that had produced the horror of the First World War and extended from the visual arts to literature, theatre, film and music. Rejecting reason and logic, both emphasized the absurd, the nonsensical, the illogical and the irrational, depicting strange leaps of imagination. Direct or indirect stimulus came from the insights into psychoanalysis and the primal urges of the unconscious by Sigmund Freud and Carl Jung. Behind the superficial order of the world, experimental art aimed to show, lay inexplicable chaos. Beyond apparent coherence was absurdity, weird flights of fantasy of the hidden psyche. The intention was to shock the sensibilities, to stimulate the search for unknown possibilities of meaning.

The forms of cultural 'modernism' varied greatly and crossed the continent in different, but often overlapping, ways during the 1920s. Russian 'Constructivism' and the Dutch De Stijl movements emphasized geometrical abstraction in design. Italian 'Futurism', its pre-war heyday now past, used abstract painting to depict speed, dynamism, the triumph of technology. In writing, self-conscious 'modernism' underlay James Joyce's *Ulysees*, the poetry of T. S. Eliot (most notably his epic 1922 composition *The Waste Land*) and the novels of Virginia Woolf, a central figure in the London 'Bloomsbury Group'. The 'Second Viennese School' gave its name to the experimental 'atonal' music of Arnold Schoenberg, Alban Berg and Anton Webern, which used fluid varieties of twelve-tone constructions to break way from classical harmony.

Whatever form modernism took, it was characterized by a rejection of conventional artistic realism. Fragmentation, irrationality, fragility, dissonance were its main features and accorded with a post-war world in which certainties had dissolved. Even physics, following Albert Einstein's revolutionary development in 1905 of the Theory of Relativity, had lost its certainties, while Werner Heisenberg's 'uncertainty principle', introduced into quantum mechanics in 1927 and demonstrating that the position and speed of particles around a nucleus could not be known with precision, seemed to cement the view that rationality could not explain the world.

All the features of modernism were present in avant-garde culture before the war, but the horrors of 1914–18 greatly accentuated the artistic assault on rationality. And from being the 'outsider' movement before the war, modernism had now entered Europe's cultural mainstream – though its popular acceptance was another question altogether.

Nowhere, not even Paris, eclipsed German linguistic and cultural innovations in 'modernist' brilliance. Because of its lasting importance, it would be easy to exaggerate how representative 'Weimar culture' (as the remarkable German cultural avant-garde of the era has become known) was in its time. Most cultural expression, even in Weimar Germany, remained conservative and conventional. (The name 'Weimar Republic' had been taken from the town in Thuringia, the traditional centre of German culture, closely associated with Goethe and Schiller, where the constitutive assembly had met in 1919.) Only 5 per cent of nearly 3,000 exhibits at the Munich art exhibition of 1930, for instance, were 'modern' works. Nevertheless, Weimar Germany, whatever its political travails, and Berlin quite especially as its focal point, witnessed in a brief few years an extraordinary efflorescence of avant-garde cultural and intellectual creativity that has few parallels in history. And in Germany, perhaps more than anywhere, art and social thought matched closely the changing temper of the age as the explosion of creativity of the 1920s gave way to its violent rejection in the 1930s.

The war brought no rupture in the German cultural avant-garde. Expressionism, which deliberately distorted form and deployed unusual combinations of striking colour to transcend superficial appearance and expose the feelings and anxieties that lay hidden within, had been the most vibrant and significant artistic style in the decade before the war. Some of its leading exponents, harbouring utopian dreams, had even welcomed the war as a cathartic experience that would destroy the old bourgeois order. The first experiences of the fighting underscored the exhilaration. 'I wish I could paint this noise,' Max Beckmann had written in 1914. The euphoria was fleeting. By the end of the war, Beckmann, Ernst Ludwig Kirchner and Oskar Kokoshka, all of whom had volunteered for military service, had been discharged from the army because of physical or psychological breakdowns. August Macke and Franz Marc had been killed. Expressionism had outlasted the war, though it was already being overtaken both by Dadaism, as a more overt form of social and cultural protest, and by a new realism that graphically represented the 'truthfulness' of the horror of war and revolutionary violence.

The idealistic exuberance of pre-war Expressionism was shifting to a bleak pessimism about human nature. In March 1919 Beckmann completed his large painting *Die Nacht* ('The Night'), a frightening depiction of street-violence and political chaos entering the home. Otto Dix, an enthusiastic volunteer in 1914, sketched crippled war victims and, under Dadaist influence, surrounded them with collages of newspaper cuttings and banknotes as scattered fragments of reality. Anti-war feeling was most plainly politicized in Georg Grosz's grotesque compositions of disfigured dead soldiers and war invalids, starving beggars and prostitutes soliciting at sordid city street corners, or gloating war profiteers, bloated industrialists and self-satisfied militarists.

By the mid-1920s the dominant cultural trend seemed to mirror the more stable conditions that had taken hold in Germany. Preoccupation with the inner psyche, emotions and idealism that had characterized Expressionism and its related forms gave way to a search for clarity and order in aesthetic form, a 'new objectivity' or 'new matter-of-factness' (*Neue Sachlichkeit*), which took its name from an artistic exhibition held in 1925 in Mannheim. Modernism was now adopted in practical design, architecture, painting, photography, music and theatre. At Weimar, then Dessau, the Bauhaus founded by Walter Gropius in 1919 brought together artists, sculptors, architects and graphic designers to create a novel style marked by rationality and functionality. Among the leading artists associated with the Bauhaus was Wassily Kandinsky, who before the war had been the dominant figure in the Munich-based *Der Blaue Reiter* ('The Blue Rider') group of Expressionists. Now, back from Russia, he had turned to brilliantly striking, more angular, abstract geometrical compositions. The Bauhaus had a practical as well as an idealistic artistic purpose. Gropius believed in harnessing technology to create new forms of rationally planned housing that would overcome social misery and class distinction. Cleanliness, comfort and efficiency in the use of space were its hallmarks. Simplicity of style and beauty were indivisible in this utopian vision. It would be 'new objectivity' in its most practical and socially valuable expression.

One of the outstanding products of architectural innovation was the Weissenhof Estate, built for an exhibition in Stuttgart in 1927. The sixty buildings, constructed by a team of outstanding architects (including Le Corbusier) under the direction of Ludwig Mies van der Rohe, epitomized a new modernist style dominated by geometrical lines, unadorned facades, flat roofs and open-plan interiors. The machine age, modern technology and mass production found their artistic exploitation in the use of steel, glass and concrete. 'Form without Ornament' was the maxim. It was far from universally welcomed. Vehement opponents decried it as 'cultural Bolshevism'. In fact, little of the avant-garde architecture and town-planning had a direct impact upon the housing plight of German cities during the 1920s, even if architects were called upon to design apartment blocks in Berlin, Frankfurt and elsewhere. However, much of the modern design (like the related Art Deco, first created in France during the 1920s) was gradually to find its way into a variety of more commonplace usages, in Germany and far beyond.

The richness of literature and social thought in the German cultural sphere did not completely or neatly fall within the categories of neo-expressionism and 'new objectivity', however broadly these terms are defined. Possibly the most influential German novel of the inter-war years was among the finest works of one of Germany's most renowned authors, Thomas Mann, whose conservatism had gradually led to a rational, if not instinctive or emotional, commitment to the new German democracy. *Der Zauberberg* (*The Magic Mountain*), which Mann had actually begun writing before the war, appeared to great acclaim in 1924. He had interrupted its composition during the war before completing it more than a decade after starting it, under the influence of humanity's capacity for self-destruction in the great conflagration, and in a form that bore little resemblance to its initial conception. The highly complex work is rich in symbolism, its main focus the sickness of bourgeois society. The rarefied setting of a tuberculosis sanitarium in the Swiss Alps offers a metaphor for a world that is sick and decaying. Two of the main characters (Settembrini and Naphta) represent the conflict between reason and frightening irrationality. The third (Castorp), torn between the two, seems finally to side with the values of the Enlightenment, only, as the novel draws towards its close on an ambiguous note, to declare himself 'for the principle of unreason, the *spirituel* principle of disease, under whose aegis I had already, in reality, stood for a long time back'.

Unreason, in this case a claustrophobic, threatening inexplicability of determining forces that held the individual in an iron cage, and which he was incapable of combating, was at the centre of the mysterious, seemingly prophetic works of Franz Kafka – works that were less known in the 1920s than long after his death in 1924. The striking originality of the gaunt-looking, hollow-eyed and psychologically tormented Kafka is all the more extraordinary given his relative detachment from the main literary exponents of the German avant-garde (even if he was well acquainted with many of their productions). Kafka was no more able to foretell the future than anyone else. But his writing – modernist literature at its bleakest – seemed supremely able to capture the helplessness and total, bewildered alienation of the individual in the face of modern social and bureaucratic mechanisms of power and repression. The brilliant German sociologist, Max Weber, had regarded bureaucratic power as the very essence of modernity, writing of 'the disenchantment of the world' in a rationalized society, though one where disciplined reason would uphold freedom. In Kafka's hands there was no room for such implicit optimism.

Confronting a reality beyond the seemingly ordered facade of daily routine, Kafka depicts an unfathomable world of bureaucratic rules, orders, laws and persecution in which all attempts to find a path through the labyrinth are met with closed doors and never lead out of the chaos to the craved distant goal of redemption.

In *The Trial*, published in 1925 after Kafka's death, Josef K. is arrested on charges that are never explained, and faced with a menacing, seemingly omnipresent, inescapable, though unseen, court. When he tries to protest his innocence, he is told 'that's the way guilty people talk'. His protracted 'trial', though there are no formal proceedings, forces him to gradual acceptance of his guilt, ultimate submission, and eventually to acquiescence in his barbaric execution at the hands of two silent executioners in a lonely and desolate quarry. In *The Castle*, published in 1926, a land surveyor arriving in a remote village, on presumed orders from the never-to-be-seen castle-owner, encounters unremitting hostility from a closed community, subservient to the undefined (though real in their own minds) authority of the nebulous castle. The outsider, increasingly and destructively obsessed with the castle's authority, comes up against a dense network of social control. This even rules out an approach to a perhaps purely imaginary high official to discover why the surveyor has been called to the castle that is forever out of his reach. Willing submission to incomprehensible regulation in Kafka's work offers what seems – though the extraordinarily complex writing is susceptible to varied interpretations – a preview into the totalitarian societies of the following decades.

Astonishing though the output of 'high culture' was in so many different fields and in numerous European countries during the 1920s, it nevertheless hardly touched the lives of most ordinary people in any direct fashion. German theatre provides a case in point. The flourishing of the theatre in the 1920s even in small towns (thanks in good measure to generous public funding, largely made possible by the short-term loans coming from the USA) was a central element of the extraordinary Weimar culture. Most famously, Bertold Brecht experimented with novel forms of theatrical presentation, partly through using montage, sparse settings and disconnected scenes, to produce alienation from the action rather than identification with it, and thereby to stimulate a critique of capitalist society. But most theatre-going Germans avoided the experimental works by Brecht and other avant-garde creations. Experimental theatre comprised no more than 5 per cent of the typical repertoire of the 1920s. Most theatre was conservative in character. Furthermore, most audiences wanted musicals, comedies, farces and other light entertainment. In any case, regular theatregoers were themselves a small minority of the population and largely, because of the cost, middle class. Most German workers, as a survey in 1934 indicated, never went to the theatre at all.

Other media show a similar disjunction between 'high' and 'popular' culture. The spread of the gramophone and still more so of the radio meant that people did not even need to leave home for their entertainment – which was more often than not light in character. Young people especially were more likely to listen to ragtime, jazz, dance music or popular songs that had crossed the Atlantic than to Beethoven or Wagner, let alone Schoenberg or Webern.

Reading patterns, too, often bypassed the modern literary classics. Books were still expensive enough to be bought largely by the better off. The network of public libraries was expanding, though how much this directly benefited the working class is not clear. The 'educated bourgeoisie', a relatively large section of the German population, might rush to read (or at least talk knowingly about) Thomas Mann's *Der Zauberberg*, but most German workers appear to have read little more than newspapers and magazines. British readers were more likely to devour the detective thrillers of Edgar Wallace and Agatha Christie or enjoy the scrapes of P. G. Wodehouse's Jeeves and Wooster then immerse themselves in the complexities of Virginia Woolf's 'modernist' writing. The Parisian intelligentsia might excite themselves about André Breton's 1924 *Manifeste du surréalisme* (*Surrealist Manifesto*), the latest works of Marc Chagall or Picasso, or Marcel Proust's extraordinary (not least for its length) seven-volume epic novel, *À la recherche du temps perdu* (*In Search of Lost Time*), but it is unlikely that the passion was shared by the peasants deep in provincial France or toiling workers in the big factories of the north. Even a sympathetic critic of Fritz Lang's dystopian vision of human enslavement to machines in his brilliant, futuristic 1927 silent film *Metropolis*, saw it as a failure 'because it simply is not like life, neither the life of yesterday nor of tomorrow'. Rapidly growing cinema audiences wanted for the most part to laugh at Charlie Chaplin's silent-film antics rather than ponder the meaning of life in thought-provoking artistic avant-garde masterpieces.

The two spheres of 'high' and 'popular' culture, of art and entertainment, rarely coincided or overlapped. Avant-garde modernist culture may have seemed an irrelevance to most Europeans, something that they did not encounter and which had no effect on their daily lives. Yet it had a massive significance, just the same: only a few years later in 1933 the Nazi burning of books outlawed by the cultural and racial ideology of the regime and the frontal attack on 'degenerate art' were to demonstrate this in the most brutal way possible.

The Great Depression of the early 1930s had by then proved a cultural watershed. As the critique of all that was new, threatening and 'modern' swelled under the impact of the crisis, the assault on 'degenerate' cultural forms became a powerful part of the armoury of fascism. This reaction was most extreme in Germany, not least because the artistic experimentation there during the 1920s had been so radical. However, the appeal of the fascist Right, not just in Germany, was culturally anchored not in the attempt to turn the clock back to some mythical traditional era, but to harness an image of 'traditional' cultural values – in practice often much distorted – to the vision of an alternative, utopian future. This vision was itself 'modern' in its way, certainly in its exploitation of technological progress for political ends. But its version of 'modernity' was one that utterly rejected the ideas of liberal pluralism, individualism, democracy and freedom which had spread throughout Europe since the French Revolution of 1789. Central to the utopian vision of fascism was national rebirth through redemption from the 'decadent', 'diseased' forms of modernity. This meant the ruthless expunging of the avant-garde artistic creativity of a pluralist society.

A disjunction between avant-garde and popular culture is common to most societies. More ominous was the cultural pessimism – more pronounced in Germany's large educated bourgeoisie than anywhere else, though certainly not confined to that country alone – which condemned both strands as expressions of decadent, corrosive modernity and symptoms of national decline. Modern art forms offered plenty of targets at which conservatives could aim their fire, while the hedonism of Berlin society was a ready target for aggressive denunciation in staid middle-class homes, small-town café conversation, or at the locals' table in a rural pub. Such 'decadence' could be seen as a threat to the nation's moral and cultural fibre.

Rejection of 'Americanism' became shorthand for all the ills of modernity that the German middle classes felt they faced. Jazz was decried as 'negro music', the product of an inferior civilization to that which had produced Bach and Beethoven, while the erotic rhythms of 'American' dancing were considered a threat to the sexual morals of young girls. Their bobbed 'American' hairstyle, said one cleric, was 'truly bereft of metaphysics'. The debasement of culture seemed epitomized by Josephine Baker, an African-American singer and dancer from St Louis, Missouri, who was taking Berlin by storm (as she had done Paris) with her exotic (and erotic) dancing, clad in little more than bunches of bananas. Hollywood films, attracting millions of viewers by the late 1920s, were said to be 'swallowing up not just individuals but the personalities of whole peoples' in their mediocrity. Mass-produced industrial goods, considered a threat to traditional German crafts, and consumerism, symbolized by the large department store that undermined the existence of small shops, were further manifestations of 'Americanism', which was understood as posing an assault on the cultural essence of the nation.

Attacking cultural decadence in Germany went further than an attack on 'Americanism'. Socialism, Marxism, Bolshevism, liberalism and democracy could all be co-opted into the critique of modern society. And there was an unmistakable racial dimension. It was easy to portray Jews, prominent in cultural life and the mass media, as the chief purveyors of the modern 'asphalt culture' of the big city, the antithesis of the 'true' German culture embedded in the 'blood and soil' of the countryside.

Hopes of creating a new elite could also gain strength amid the cultural pessimism, which provided fertile ground for the cultivation of ideas of national regeneration through eugenics and 'racial hygiene'. The First World War, and the dramatic changes that it had unleashed, had heightened greatly the sense of lost values and cultural decline. The losses suffered in the war sharpened in particular the worries about falling birth rates, much commented on and widely felt as a threat to the family, the values it represented, and to the virility of the nation. War invalids with missing limbs and the sight of young widows grieving for husbands killed at the front seemed to symbolize the demographic dangers for the nation's future. Not just declining birth rates but also the quality of the population preoccupied influential figures in the medical profession and promoted ideas of eugenics.

It was not a German peculiarity. The Eugenics Society in Britain, founded in 1926, quickly gained about 800 members, mainly from elites in science, culture and politics, who were obsessed with the biological improvement of the population and whose influence ran beyond their numbers. Eugenics societies existed also in Scandinavia, Spain, the Soviet Union and elsewhere. Sterilization of mental patients to improve the quality of the population – and to save money at the same time – was mooted beyond German borders. A Swedish Institute for Racial Biology had been founded, for example, in Uppsala in 1922. But the obsession with racial quality was nonetheless especially marked in Germany. As early as 1920 a criminal lawyer, Karl Binding, and a psychiatrist, Alfred Hoche, had mooted what was then still the extreme view of a small minority, that 'the destruction of life not worth living' should be legally permitted. 'The emphasis on quality rather than quantity in the composition of the nation is psychologically connected with the reduction in our food-producing area', it was claimed in an address to the German Association for Psychiatry in 1925 – linking population policy with a lack of 'living-space' (*Lebensraum*, a term later associated with Nazi ideology). Two years later the declining German birth rate was described as 'the most fearful of the many symbols of the decline of our culture', brought about by 'the victory of the city over the peasantry' and the emancipation of women, and bound to lead eventually to 'the fall of the white race'.

Highly influential in promoting cultural pessimism was Oswald Spengler's *Der Untergang des Abendlandes* (*The Decline of the West*), the first volume of which had appeared in 1918, just before the end of the war, and the second four years later. Spengler's laboriously developed comparison of historical cultures used a biological analogy of life cycles to argue, in somewhat mystical terms, that Western culture was condemned to decline under the impact of materialism, which could only be combated by the power of a strong state united in the hands of an elite. The German middle classes had bought more than 100,000 copies of the convoluted work by 1926. Easier reading than Spengler, but again promoting the mood of cultural pessimism and exploited by the political Right, was Hans Grimm's 1926 novel *Volk ohne Raum* (*People without Space*), which implied that overpopulation was at the root of Germany's economic woes and could only be overcome through a 'struggle for existence' to conquer new land (which, touching on nostalgia for empire, he envisaged as being in Africa). The novel sold over 200,000 copies between 1926 and 1933, many, no doubt, to supporters of the growing Nazi Movement.

Only a relatively small minority of Germany's population of 60 million were avid readers of Spengler or Grimm. Nonetheless, the influence of such writers, and others with opportunities to expound their views in newspapers or other publications, or, like clergymen and schoolteachers, serving as 'multipliers' of opinion, should not be underrated. Nor should their potential to shape attitudes that could later be popularized by fascism.

Most of the German population was old enough to recall – if often with distorted, wistful memory – what seemed increasingly with the passage of time a wonderful era of peace, prosperity and civilization that had been destroyed by the war, leaving a disastrous, chaotic aftermath. In the eyes of cultural pessimists only the shadow of former glory remained. And to them what was left of European civilization and the values of the Christian 'West' (*Abendland*) was imperilled not just by decadence within but by importing external moral and political 'disease'. There is little doubt about the nature of their paramount anxiety: the existential threat from the potential spread of Bolshevism throughout Europe and, above all, its corrosive effect in Germany itself.

Cultural pessimism was more widespread and acute in Germany than anywhere else in Europe. No other state was as riven with anxiety about national decline – though France ran it close, and few if any countries were devoid of cultural pessimists. The manifestations of cultural pessimism in Germany indicate that in the most important and advanced country in central Europe, ideas were being articulated even during the 'golden twenties' which could become a potent force in a drastically changed political and ideological climate. That time had not yet arrived. Cultural pessimism and its ancillary trends were still a minority taste. But that would all alter with the onset of the Great Depression.

BRIGHT PROSPECTS?

The acceptance in 1924 of the Dawes Plan opened the door to a potential new basis of relations between France and Germany. This formed the crux of all hopes for Europe's lasting security. The new British Foreign Secretary, Austen Chamberlain, whose aloof, austere figure in morning coat, complete with top hat, carnation and monocle, made him, if unfairly, appear a mere caricature of the English upper class, voiced the hope in January 1925 that a 'new Europe' could be 'built on foundations that may give peace and security to the nations of the old world'. The hope seemed realistic. The key to European stabilization was to overcome the inherent blockage posed by the incompatibility of German demands for revision of the Versailles Treaty and French insistence on impenetrable security against any further aggression from their neighbour east of the Rhine.

Chamberlain was to be an important broker in putting Franco-German relations on a new footing in 1925–6. Britain's global interests, involving costly defence expenditure (especially on the navy) to protect overseas possessions, required the defusing of tensions in Europe, which meant establishing some sort of equilibrium between France and Germany. But the two main players in reordering relations were Chamberlain's counterparts in those countries, their Foreign Ministers Aristide Briand and Gustav Stresemann.

Briand – eloquent, charming, a cigarette invariably on his lips beneath a bushy moustache – was the archetypal French diplomat and a statesman of vision, even contemplating at such an early juncture a future European federal union independent of American power. Briand recognized that French interests lay in marrying the indispensable need for security with a rapprochement that could form the basis of lasting peace and prosperity for both France and Germany. His difficulty was in persuading French public opinion that any rapprochement with the old enemy would not undermine security.

The German Foreign Minister, Gustav Stresemann – a solid figure in appearance, his face slightly porcine with a thin moustache and balding head, a forceful, ambitious, imposing personality – was equally far-sighted in looking to secure foundations of lasting peace in a Europe. He had at one time been a fervent monarchist and, during the war, a pronounced annexationist. But the conflict, Germany's post-war experience and the traumatic year of 1923 (during part of which he had been Reich Chancellor) had convinced Stresemann of the need to place relations with France on a new footing if his professed aim of 'a peaceful Germany at the centre of a peaceful Europe' was to become reality. 'The new Germany and its recovery,' he told the conference of the German People's Party in 1926, 'can only be based on peace.' 'But how will this peace be possible,' he asked, 'if it is not founded on an understanding between Germany and France?'

Stresemann was both a shrewd pragmatist and an unremitting nationalist. There was no contradiction. Crucial to him was the need to re-establish Germany's predominance in Europe. But Germany was diplomatically isolated and militarily weak. To make German reascendancy possible, the restoration of the country to full equality of 'great-power' status alongside Britain and France, leading to a revision of Versailles and solution of the reparations question, was the absolute prerequisite. It could be obtained, in his view, only through peaceful negotiation, which meant rapprochement with France. Like Briand in France, Stresemann had his hands full in keeping at bay the sizeable and aggressively critical parts of the nationalist Right, who were demanding a more assertive foreign policy. But for five years he managed it.

The decisive step in establishing Franco-German détente was the Treaty of Locarno signed on 16 October 1925. The terms had been negotiated by Stresemann, Briand and Chamberlain on board the *Orange Blossom* during a five-hour boat ride on Lago Maggiore. Germany, France and Belgium undertook not to attack each other. Great Britain and Italy stood as guarantors. The central component was the guarantee by the five powers of Germany's western borders and the demilitarized zone of the Rhineland. The treaty paved the way for Germany's accession to the League of Nations in 1926, while the improved international relations created by 'the spirit of Locarno' offered hope among West Europeans for lasting peace. The French were happy that Britain was now formally guaranteeing their security. For Briand, this was the vital gain. Britain welcomed the détente and the confinement of its future responsibilities in Europe to the Rhine frontier. For Stresemann, Locarno was a necessary step towards a longer-term goal of German resurgence. With diplomatic isolation removed, the prospects of bringing about the early withdrawal of Allied troops from the demilitarized zone in the Rhineland (scheduled for 1935) were brighter. Beyond that, it might now prove possible to win back Eupen-Malmédy from Belgium, acquire the Saar again, ease reparations and end Allied military control in Germany. The loss of Alsace-Lorraine had to be accepted, it was true, but Stresemann pointed out that this was an inevitable corollary of German military weakness. And he had conceded nothing on the question of Germany's eastern borders.

Each of the western powers had grounds for satisfaction in the outcome of Locarno. In eastern Europe the response was different. Poland in particular felt let down by the western powers, especially by its ally, France. Poland's position was significantly weakened, the country more isolated than it had been, precariously squeezed between the Soviet Union and Germany. There had been no 'eastern Locarno'. Germany had explicitly ruled out any guarantee for Poland's frontiers. Neither Britain, which wanted no engagement in eastern Europe, nor France, despite its alliances, dating back to 1921, with Poland and with the 'little Entente' of Czechoslovakia, Romania and Yugoslavia, had strong enough motives to insist upon such a guarantee. Both had greater interest in binding Germany more closely to the west and ruling out any likelihood of it strengthening ties with the Soviet Union – advocated by some voices in Germany, recalling the merits of the Rapallo Treaty of 1922 which had established flourishing trading relations (as well as hidden military cooperation) of significant benefit to both countries. Germany's strident nationalists were predictably unhappy with Locarno. Stresemann himself sought to assuage his right-wing critics by leaving open the question of 'correcting' the eastern frontiers, with the prospect that at some point Danzig, the Polish Corridor and Upper Silesia would return to Germany. He gave assurances that force would not be contemplated. His own presumption was that patient diplomacy alone would bring this about in time.

On 10 September 1926, Germany was accepted into the League of Nations as a permanent member of the council. Stresemann spoke of Germany's place alongside former enemies, denoting the potential for a new direction for mankind. Chamberlain saw it as the end of the war chapter and a fresh start for Europe. Briand was the one who provided the effusive rhetoric. 'Away with the rifles, machine guns, cannon! Clear the way for conciliation, arbitration, peace,' he declared. (Two years later Briand, his idealism undimmed, was to instigate, together with the American Secretary of State, Frank B. Kellogg, the singularly vacuous Briand-Kellogg Pact, renouncing war as an instrument of national policy and a means of settling international disputes – a dead letter from the moment it was signed.)

The heady 'spirit of Locarno' soon sobered up. The gap between French and German interests remained wide, once the euphoria dissipated. French security fears were not easy to overcome. Correspondingly, German hopes of an early end to the foreign occupation of the entire Rhineland swiftly evaporated (though Allied troops left the Cologne zone in 1926). A proposal in 1926 to purchase the attainment of German goals, by marketing railway bonds deposited with the Reparations Commission and worth 1.5 million gold marks, came to nothing. Germany had pressed for evacuation of the Rhineland (where 60,000 Allied troops were garrisoned on German soil), return of the Saar and Eupen-Malmédy to Germany, and removal of the Inter-Allied Military Control Commission. But the French saw little or no gain from a greater security risk (although Allied supervision of the German disarmament was, in fact, handed over to the League of Nations in 1927). Moreover, American bankers opposed the commercialization of obligations under the Dawes Plan. At a League of Nations meeting two years later, in 1928, Germany formally demanded the evacuation of the Rhineland, this time offering nothing in return. France and Britain, predictably unimpressed, insisted that the Rhineland question be bracketed with finally resolving the reparations issue.

By this time, reparations were once more becoming a prominent concern, since German repayment instalments, under the Dawes Plan, were set to rise in 1928–9 and so would present an increased burden on the German economy. A new reparations committee, headed by the American businessman Owen D. Young, began work in January 1929 on a revised framework of regulation. Its recommendations, presented five months later, were accepted by the governments involved in August that year. Under the Young Plan, Germany would have to pay significantly less, especially in the early years, than under the Dawes Plan. But the burden would be lengthy. The last instalment would be due only in 1988. The outraged nationalist Right in Germany organized a petition to reject the Young Plan and forced a referendum on the issue. But when this was held, in December 1929, six out of seven voters supported acceptance. Stresemann, though he did not live to see the referendum, had favoured the Plan since it meant the attainment of one of his immediate goals: the Allies undertook to evacuate the Rhineland if Germany accepted it. The German parliament ratified the Young Plan in March 1930. And on 30 June that year the Allies pulled their troops out, five years earlier than stipulated under the Versailles Treaty.

By then Stresemann, the architect of peaceful revisionism, was dead. He had achieved much in a short time, although he did not live to see the fruits of all his efforts: the ending of the Ruhr occupation, the end of supervision by the Allied Military Commission, the stabilization of the economy, the regulation of reparations, and the early evacuation of the Rhineland, quite apart from the Locarno Treaty and German entry into the League of Nations. But he had long been suffering from serious health problems, exacerbated by his exhausting diplomatic efforts. With the clouds gathering over Germany, and economic crisis about to sweep across the European continent, Stresemann's death was a serious blow to the chances of continuing along the path that he had laid out – one of compromise, caution and negotiated restoration of German power. The loss was compounded by Briand's declining influence, following what was widely interpreted in France as his weakness in the negotiations to expedite the evacuation of the Rhineland and his perceived inadequate defence of French security interests. Briand had been the French Premier a record eleven times. In this his last term (a position he had held only since July, as well as being Foreign Minister), he left office within a month of Stresemann's death.

The Hague Conference in August 1929, which had met to reach agreement on the reparations and the evacuation of the Rhineland, bore the title: 'The Conference on the Liquidation of the War'. It sounded like the commencement of a bright new future. In fact, 1929 proved to be the exact halfway point between the two vast conflagrations that shaped Europe's modern history.

FALTERING DEMOCRACIES

The calming of international relations from the mid-1920s onwards had been brought about by democratic governments. As long as they survived, there were fair prospects for peace in Europe. But the years of economic recovery in the mid- and later 1920s did not result in a general strengthening of democracy throughout Europe. Some democracies were already giving way to authoritarian regimes. This was more likely in backward, agrarian societies, with shallow democratic roots, which had deep ideological fissures or faced major problems of national integration. Only in northern and western Europe did democracy remain strong. Across the continent, the picture was chequered.

In central Europe democracy existed merely as a facade in Hungary and faced serious internal difficulties in Austria, but survived well in Czechoslovakia. In Hungary political parties, elections (with a highly restricted franchise, without secret balloting outside urban areas) and a parliamentary system continued in existence. But the system was pluralist in appearance rather than substance. It was controlled from above by a strong executive, supported by an unchallenged governing party that represented largely elite interests, and was aided by much popular apathy and a politically emasculated working class.

Austria's democracy remained intact, though its foundations were insecure and its problems daunting. There was little common ground between Social Democrats and the dominant Christian Socialists who, usually backed by the right-wing Pan Germans, controlled the national parliament (though not the capital of Vienna) throughout the 1920s. The unbridgeable ideological gulf grew, rather than diminished, in the years of stabilization. A flashpoint occurred in 1927. When two members of the Social Democrat 'Republican Defence League' were shot dead by the right-wing 'Home Defence', and the perpetrators were then acquitted in court, a working-class crowd burnt down the Courts of Justice building in Vienna. The police fired on stone-throwing demonstrators, killing eighty-five and suffering four dead themselves. Hundreds more were injured. An uneasy calm returned, but the main profiteers were the right-wing home-defence organizations, which gained both new supporters and increased financial backing from industrialists. Ominously, too, the German nationalists were gaining support. The political fronts were becoming radicalized. Economic crisis, when it hit in 1930, struck a democracy built on shaky ground.

In contrast, Czechoslovakia overcame ethnic divisions and fragmentation of its party structure to defy the trend and sustain democratic rule without serious threat. The Czech lands (though not Slovakia) were industrially well developed. There was a large, well-educated bourgeoisie and an experienced civil administration. The threat of communism – the Communist Party won almost 14 per cent of the vote in 1925 (an election contested by twenty-seven parties) and more seats than any other party – was a unifying factor across the remainder of the political spectrum. Whatever their divisions, the major parties (apart from the Communists) supported the democracy. It proved possible to build functioning coalitions, whose vested interest in making democratic government work was enhanced by strong economic growth from 1923 onwards and a sharp fall in unemployment. The hard-won and still fragile national unity of Czechoslovakia depended on internal stability, which also assisted the readiness of the political parties to sustain the democratic system, while conciliatory noises towards conceding greater autonomy to the large German minority and the Slovaks defused potential opposition in those constituencies.

Czechoslovakia was a rare success story. But already before the onset of the Great Depression, in much of eastern Europe, in the Balkans and across the Mediterranean as far as the Atlantic, democracy had collapsed, was collapsing, or was struggling.

In Poland the hero of Polish independence, Marshal Piłsudski, out of patience with the inadequacy of successive administrations to bring stability to a country facing daunting problems, launched a coup d'état on 12–14 May 1926 and over the following years took Poland increasingly towards authoritarianism. Integration within a short time of a country that had had six currencies, three legal codes, two railway gauges, a plethora of political parties and sizeable ethnic minorities (each facing heavy discrimination), was as good as impossible. The economy was recovering after the hyperinflation of 1922–3 – the introduction of a single currency, the złoty, in 1924 was a major step forward – but the country was still facing serious problems (exacerbated by a tariff war with Germany), made all the harder to surmount by a permanent political crisis. Land redistribution was, more than any other issue, politically divisive. Governments had come and gone in short succession.

By 1926, with neither political nor economic improvement in sight and government effectively stalemated by unresolvable parliamentary differences, Piłsudski had had enough. Gathering support from parts of the army that had remained loyal to him, and following a short military struggle in Warsaw, he forced the resignation of the government. The trappings of constitutional government continued in existence. But restrictions on democratic freedoms were increased and authoritarianism was extended, including mounting repression against political opposition.

Similar structural conditions to those that brought authoritarianism to Poland – serious problems in a predominantly agrarian economy, tension over the land question, unbridgeable party-political divides, sizeable ethnic minorities, unattainable national integration and a powerful military – bedevilled the chances of establishing secure democracy across much of eastern Europe. In Lithuania the collapse into authoritarianism did not take long to materialize. The Lithuanian military, defeated by Piłsudski's army in 1920 but now inspired by his coup in neighbouring Poland, instigated a putsch in December 1926, which led to a decade-long suspension of parliament and concentration of power in the hands of the President. Elsewhere in the Baltic, in Latvia and Estonia, and Finland, parliamentary systems, despite internal instability, managed to hold out against authoritarian pressures from Left and Right – though only Finnish democracy proved capable of lasting survival.

In the Balkans clientelist politics and raw violence invariably went hand in hand behind the semblance of representative government. Corruption was rife. Political rivalries often mirrored clan hatreds in overwhelmingly poor, agrarian countries with high levels of illiteracy. Border and nationality issues contributed to chronic instability. The military usually played a determining role.

Greece lurched from monarchy to republic to short-lived military dictatorship and back to a republic between 1923 and 1927, when a third constitution in three years was introduced. Thereafter, four years of relative stability followed until the drachma lost three-quarters of its value as economic crisis set in and Greece plunged into a further spiral of disastrous governmental incapacity before the facade-democracy finally collapsed into authoritarianism in 1936.

The lawless, violence-ridden Albania could hardly lay claim even to be regarded as a state. Here the paranoid, vicious Ahmed Zogu, the victor of numerous blood-feuds and vendettas, seized power in December 1924 at the head of a military coup. Four years later he declared himself King Zog, ruling through patronage backed by armed force, and initiated fourteen years of personal dictatorship..

In Bulgaria, too, political violence was extreme and endemic. When the Prime Minister, Alexander Stamboliiski, was assassinated in 1923 by a group of officers backed by King Boris III, his body was dismembered and his head sent to Sofia in a tin. An attempted communist uprising was then bloodily repressed, the numbers of victims counted in the thousands. Another wave of horrific 'white terror' followed a bomb explosion in Sofia's cathedral in 1925 that left 160 dead and hundreds more badly injured (though the King and his ministers were unscathed). Backed by such repression, a superficial form of parliamentary rule, under a dominant government party, was stabilized and survived until the Depression years.

In Romania deep tensions revolved around the land question – the bulk of the overwhelmingly rural population were peasant smallholders – and the issue of national identity. The nation was seen to be threatened by the Hungarians' hopes of recovering territory taken from them in the Versailles Treaty, by Bolshevism (though the tiny Communist Party, outlawed in 1924, posed only a shadowy threat), and by ethnic minorities, above all Jews. During the 1920s the tensions were controllable. The new constitution of 1923 bolstered the executive power of the government. Electoral manipulation enabled the ruling Bratianu family to exercise a near monopoly of power, resting on the parliamentary dominance of the National Liberal Party, which they controlled. The death of King Ferdinand in 1927 after a fourteen-year reign, however, undermined the Bratianu family's hold on power and ushered in political instability. The following year, in the wake of mounting difficulties in the agrarian economy, the National Liberal Party was defeated in elections by the National Peasant Party. Unable to master the economic problems, however, the latter soon lost support. In a bloodless coup in 1930, Carol II, who had been forced in 1925 to renounce his right to the throne because of his part-Jewish mistress, reneged on his renunciation and was proclaimed King. The following years would see lasting political crisis amid the rise of a violent, intensely antisemitic, fascist movement, against the backdrop of severe economic difficulties, and the road to eventual dictatorship.

In the Kingdom of the Serbs, Croats and Slovenes, a shaky construction from the start, the expropriation of major landholders (with compensation) and redistribution of land to the peasantry remained a source of great friction. The country also faced border issues on all sides – towards Italy, Greece, Hungary and Albania. But the structural problem of trying to reconcile the insoluble competing interests of the Catholic Croatians and the majority Orthodox Serbs was what tipped the unmanageable democracy into authoritarianism. The assassination in parliament of three Croatian deputies by an uncontrollably outraged Serb in 1928 triggered the moves that saw King Alexander dissolve parliament and suspend the constitution the following January. Press freedom was abolished, political parties were banned, and a more centralized state was introduced. (In October 1929 it was given the supposedly unifying name of 'Yugoslavia' – land of the Southern Slavs.) These steps were cemented in the new, authoritarian constitution of September 1931.

In the Mediterranean, pluralist parliamentary government had long since been on the defensive, or had collapsed altogether. With the Lateran Pacts of 1929, recognizing the sovereignty of the Vatican, regulating relations with the papacy and reaffirming Catholicism as Italy's state religion, Mussolini consolidated his grip on power over the Italian state by eliminating any potential opposition to his regime from the Catholic Church. The last sphere of relatively autonomous power in the Fascist state had been neutralized. In Spain, Primo de Rivera continued the relatively benign dictatorship that he had established in 1923, though he was facing mounting difficulties in holding his flimsy regime together by the time the Depression struck.

In 1926 Portugal followed these Mediterranean countries into authoritarian rule. The First World War had destabilized the old oligarchical power-structure in Portugal. Chronic governmental instability produced forty-five administrations of different types between 1910 and 1926. A military government had taken power for a few months in 1915. A further brief military dictatorship, with some proto-fascist traits, followed in 1917–18. Political violence, never far from the surface of Portuguese politics, became endemic in the early 1920s. The military, though disunited, constituted a potentially insurrectionist force that barely tolerated a dysfunctional pluralist system. A badly organized coup in 1925 was foiled. The following year military factions overcame their divisions and civilian government, lacking any fervent support from an apathetic public, offered no resistance to a coup headed by General Gomes da Costa. The conservative elite and the Catholic Church welcomed the coup. The Left was too small and too weak to pose any challenge. Costa swiftly gave way to General Antonio Carmona, whose rule rested on military backing. He became President in 1928 and remained in office until his death in 1951. But the key figure was soon to be Antonio de Oliveira Salazar, Professor of Economics at Coimbra University, appointed Finance Minister in April 1928, who became Prime Minister two years later. He would be the decisive voice in Portugal's authoritarian regime for forty years.

Only in northern and western Europe – the most economically advanced parts of the continent – was democracy secure in the late 1920s. There, the conditions that went far to undermine democracy in the south and east were absent. Democracy was either already well established or was on the way to firm consolidation in the years of strong economic growth before the Depression. The state rested upon extensive consensus at elite and popular levels, and parties of extreme Left and Right were marginalized. Whatever the variants, a number of general factors played a part in sustaining democratic legitimacy: the continuity of political and social institutions despite the turbulence of the war and its aftermath; forms of government that were capable of incorporating the interests of broad sections of society and of making pragmatic adjustments to policy; territorial integrity and cultural homogeneity; and the weakness of communism, which left relatively strong social democracy as the main representation of the working class. National integration in these countries had been for the most part a fairly lengthy, gradual process. This was the case in Britain, France, Scandinavia, the Low Countries and Switzerland. The new Irish Free State, comprising the larger, southern part of Ireland, was an exception in that it had emerged only after six troubled years of the struggle for independence from British rule. Yet in southern Ireland too it quickly proved possible to consolidate a newly created nation state and a functioning two-party democracy, based in good measure on a homogeneous culture, underpinned by deeply ingrained Catholicism, and widespread antagonism towards Britain.

The failure of democracy in much of Europe had consequences for the population of the countries concerned, sometimes too for their near neighbours. But it was not likely to threaten the peace of Europe. Such a threat could only come about if democracy were to collapse in one or more of the great powers – Great Britain, France, Germany – whose stability was essential for the continuity of the shaky post-war equilibrium.

Britain's economy was in the doldrums for much of the 1920s, yet compared with practically any other country in Europe it proved a model of political stability. This was despite the fact that its electoral system of majority voting, which militated against fragmentation of parties and formation of coalitions, had not prevented three changes of government between 1922 and 1924. Ramsay MacDonald, the son of a Scottish farm labourer and housemaid, had defied the social handicap of illegitimacy to rise to the leadership of the Labour Party. In his first of two terms as Prime Minister, MacDonald formed a short-lived administration, which lasted from January until November 1924. Government then passed for the next five years into the hands of the Conservatives. The new Prime Minister, Stanley Baldwin, from a wealthy Midlands steel-manufacturing family, cut a solid, reassuring figure. The government had to surmount the social divisions and political turmoil that accompanied the General Strike of 1926, and by the following year was on the wane. But crisis in Britain was managed by adjustment within the system. Communism, supported by under 1 per cent of the electorate, and the tiny nascent fascist factions backed at this point mainly by cranks and eccentrics, could make no impact on mainstream politics. Britain's socio-economic problems in the 1920s were substantial. But they did not undermine democratic legitimacy. When the Depression heaped a crisis on the minority Labour government of Ramsay MacDonald in 1930–31, there was no crisis of the state.

Stability was less assured in France, though democracy faced no serious problems until the Depression years. The rapid turnover of cabinets – six different governments amid the currency crisis between

April 1925 and July 1926 – did not call into question the legitimacy of the Third Republic. Stability returned under Raymond Poincaré's premiership between 1926 and 1929, and seemed consolidated by the shift to the conservative Right in the 1928 elections. On the surface, all seemed well.

In contrast to Britain, however, the political system was not uncontested. A sector of French society, influential beyond its still small numbers, had never accepted the Republic, or merely tolerated it under sufferance. When the communists, who had lost a good deal of their support, took part, alongside the socialists, in a huge parade in Paris on 23 November 1924 to accompany the transfer of the ashes of the socialist hero Jean Jaurès (assassinated in 1914) to the Pantheon – at a time when France had a left-wing government and was in the throes of a financial crisis – the 'forest of red flags' conjured up the spectre of Bolshevik Revolution. It was portrayed by the Right as 'the funeral of the bourgeoisie', 'when the revolutionary menace became clear to everybody'. Within days a number of 'patriotic movements', calling themselves 'Leagues' of different kinds – one of them, the Faisceau, showing its leanings in its very name, borrowed from Italian Fascism – sprang up, recruiting tens of thousands of mainly young Frenchmen almost overnight.

Not all of the Leagues were fascist; some, in fact, outrightly rejected the association. And not all of France's extreme Right was attracted to the Leagues. As elsewhere, the boundaries between the extreme and the conservative Right were fluid. The moment passed. Poincaré's stabilizing hand, and the sense of restored security for owners of property, defused the crisis. The Leagues lost support – for the time being. With conservatism dominant, the perceived need for an extreme Right diminished. But it had not vanished. Given a renewed crisis – more prolonged, more destabilizing, more dangerous – the menace of the extreme Right could return, in stronger shape, to threaten the French Republic.

If Britain was solidly stable and France not much less so, Germany was more enigmatic. It fitted neatly into neither the model of relatively well-established democracies of the more economically advanced north-western Europe, nor the model of the newly created, fragile democracies of eastern Europe. In many ways Germany was a hybrid.

It looked both west and east. It had both an extensive industrial proletariat, like Britain and France, but also a large peasantry, especially
in its eastern regions, whose values were rooted in the land. Germany
had a long tradition of democratic idealism and pluralistic party-
politics, a highly developed bureaucracy, a modern, industrial economy,
and a well-educated, culturally advanced population.

But its democratic system was new. It had emerged from the trauma
of defeat in the war and revolution, and was vehemently contested
from the outset. Political unity in Germany was still little more than
half a century old, and was overlain by a much older sense of cultural
identity that stretched far beyond the borders of the nation state.
Unlike Britain, France and the other countries of north-western Europe, German nationality was defined by ethnicity, not territory. And
Germany's intellectual elites, however varied their views, mainly
rejected the values of what they called 'western' democracy, whether
the French traditions dating back to the Revolution of 1789 or the
free-trade capitalism and liberalism that had shaped the British development. The German state, as the embodiment of German cultural
values, was in their eyes not only different from, but superior to, the
products of western civilization. Germany's national humiliation at
the end of the First World War, its post-war economic and military
weakness, its loss of status as a great power, and the divisiveness of its
parliamentary system were in their minds a temporary disaster, not a
permanent state of affairs.

Germany's political stability was not simply a matter of concern to
its own citizens; it was vital to the peaceful future of the European
continent. Germany's geographical position, straddling Europe from
west to east, its economic and military potential, and its revisionist
expectations in eastern Europe, made the survival of democracy, and
with it the continuation of Stresemann's policy of international
cooperation, essential if the uneasy equilibrium of power on the
European continent was to be sustained.

There seemed no undue cause for worry in Germany during the
'golden years' of the later 1920s. There was strong economic growth.
Living standards were improving. Germany was now part of the
League of Nations. The western borders had been settled at Locarno.
Four changes of government between 1925 and 1927 did not affect

the sense that, after the huge upheaval of the early 1920s, democracy was bedding down. The political extremes had lost support. Communist backing had fallen to 9 per cent in 1924, with a corresponding rise in votes for the moderate Social Democrats. The extreme Right had fragmented after Hitler's attempted putsch in November 1923. Although, on leaving prison the following year, he had refounded his Nazi Party, it remained on the outer fringes of politics. In the opinion of one observer in 1927, it was no more than a 'splinter group incapable of exerting any noticeable influence on the great mass of the population and the course of political events'.

The general election of 1928 reflected more settled times. The conservative Right, much of it half-heartedly democratic at best, lost heavily. That the Nazis were finished as a political force seemed proven by their miserable return of only 2.6 per cent of the popular vote, giving them only twelve seats in parliament. The chief winners were the Social Democrats, who gained just short of 30 per cent of the votes and were by far the largest party in a 'grand coalition' with the two Catholic and two liberal parties. Under Hermann Müller, the Social Democrats headed the government for the first time since 1920. Democracy in Germany seemed to face good prospects.

Beneath the surface, the situation was less rosy. Müller's coalition was flimsy from the start, with deep divisions soon to surface between the Social Democrats and their unlikely coalition partners, Stresemann's German People's Party, the representatives of big business. The first issue to put the parties at loggerheads was the building of a big warship. The Social Democrats had campaigned before the election with a slogan 'not armoured cruisers but food for children'. So when the building of a cruiser was pushed through by ministers from the coalition's centre and right wing, Social Democrats were outraged. The Ruhr industrialists' lockout of almost quarter of a million iron and steel workers then caused a further big rift among the coalition partners. And the incompatibility of the coalition's members was fully revealed in a protracted and irreconcilable dispute over the proposal to introduce a small increase in employer contributions to unemployment insurance – the issue that finally brought the unwieldy coalition down in March 1930.

By then, economic difficulties were mounting. Unemployment in

Germany had reached the 3 million mark in January 1929, up a million from the previous year and accounting for 14 per cent of the working population. The Communists, who had increased their support at the polls to over 10 per cent in the 1928 elections, were finding ready backing among many of the unemployed and, following the new Stalinist line adopted by the Comintern, were turning their fire on the Social Democrats, ludicrously vilified as 'social fascists'. In the countryside, the crisis in the agrarian economy was causing a great deal of political disaffection.

Somewhat to their own surprise, and without any sustained agitation on their part, the Nazis found that they were garnering considerable support in the countryside of northern and eastern Germany. The party membership had been growing, in fact, even during the years in the political wilderness, and now stood at over 100,000 – a good activist basis with which to exploit the growing unrest. The favourable publicity they received in the conservative press for their shrill campaign against the revised reparations scheme presented in the Young Plan also helped their cause. The Nazis, though still far from a mainstream party, increased their share of the vote in a number of regional elections in 1929. The following June, with the Depression now biting, Hitler's party won over 14 per cent of the vote in state elections in Saxony – nearly six times higher than its vote in the 1928 Reichstag election.

Shortly afterwards, Müller's successor as Chancellor, the Centre Party politician Heinrich Brüning, dissolved the Reichstag after it had rejected his proposals for swingeing cuts in public expenditure. No attempt was made to find a democratic solution to the financial difficulties. Instead, Brüning sought to push through his deflationary measures by presidential decree. The absolutely crucial position of the Reich President had been held since 1925 by the war hero Field Marshal von Hindenburg. Although sworn to uphold the democratic republic, Hindenburg, a pillar of the old monarchist regime, was no democrat but saw himself rather as a type of ersatz-Kaiser. Replacing the Social Democrat Chancellor, Müller, with Brüning, known from soundings to be favourably disposed to governing with the backing of presidential decree, had in fact been planned months earlier as part of a strategy to undermine Social Democracy and introduce government without parliamentary pluralism. Hindenburg, Brüning and the conservative elites who backed their move, were not for a moment contemplating a government run by the Nazis – seen as primitive, vulgar, loud-mouthed populists, not the sort to manage the German state. What they wanted was essentially to turn the clock back, with or without the monarchy, to a type of Bismarckian constitutional arrangement in which government was beyond the control of parliament – most of all beyond the control of the hated Social Democrats. The aim of Hindenburg, Brüning and the conservative elites was a sort of anti-democratic semi-authoritarianism managed by those elites.

With Brüning's accession to the Chancellorship, and Hindenburg's readiness to bypass parliament, a serious blow had been inflicted to the democratic state in Germany already before the slide into Depression. A further major blow followed in the Reichstag election on 14 September 1930. Brüning's decision to go to the country backfired spectacularly. Hitler's party achieved an astonishing electoral breakthrough, winning 18.3 per cent of the vote and gaining 107 seats in the new Reichstag. All at once the Nazis were on the map, now the second largest party in the German parliament. A vote for the Nazis was no longer a wasted ballot for a minor fringe party. Mass support, bringing an inflow of funding to engage in further radical agitation, grew rapidly. The bandwagon was rolling. A Hitler Chancellorship still seemed a remote possibility. But with the fateful decision to move to rule by presidential decree, and with the election success of the Nazis in 1930, the death knell for German democracy was sounding. And with that, uncertainty in Europe as a whole was bound to be magnified. The uneasy equilibrium of the past few years would be in jeopardy.

Of course, the future is always open, never a clear, predetermined path down a one-way street. Perhaps, without the Depression imported from the USA, Europe could have progressed along the road of undisturbed economic growth, liberal freedom and democratic rule to the broad sunlit uplands of international peace and harmony. But a betting man would not have placed much money on it. Although the deepening crisis of subsequent years was neither inevitable nor preordained, it did not come out of thin air. Europe's 'golden twenties' were, beneath the surface glitter, a tarnished, troubled time.

Serious economic weaknesses within an unstable and imbalanced global economy, magnified by nationalist protectionism and glorified self-interest, offered no firm basis for staving off the shock waves from across the Atlantic. Cultural divisions fostered extensive levels of prejudice and vitriol that could easily be exploited should there be a downturn in the social and intellectual climate. Democratic, liberal ideas were everywhere on the defensive. And by the time of the Depression much of Europe had already collapsed into authoritarianism, or was on the verge of doing so.

One country was more crucial than any other to Europe's destiny. Hopes for a brighter future for the continent rested above all on Germany. And in Germany, quite especially, even before the Wall Street Crash, there were grounds for concern. Economic growth concealed mounting problems. The cultural divide was more acute than anywhere else. And the signs of potential political danger were already visible before the descent into full-scale crisis. The survival of German democracy was the best safeguard of Europe's future peace and stability. What would happen if democracy in Europe's pivotal country collapsed? The consequences of the Depression over the next few years would be decisive not just for Germany but for the whole of the continent.

Europe had danced on the volcano during the seemingly carefree Charleston years. The volcano was now about to erupt.

5

Gathering Shadows

Down the slippery slope, sunk without trace, utterly destroyed.
Order and cleanliness, gone; work, material security, gone;
making progress and hope, gone.
>   *Hans Fallada,* Little Man – What Now? *(1932)*

The Great Depression, tightening its hold from 1930 onwards, was nothing less than a catastrophe for Europe. It did not strike evenly across the continent. Some countries, depending on their economic and political structures, escaped its impact fairly lightly. And within individual countries, not all regions were equally affected. There were some areas of growth even in severely depressed economies. Even so, the damage wrought by the slump can scarcely be exaggerated. It was widespread and massive. Nowhere escaped the consequences altogether.

The political fault lines in Europe opened up during the Depression. The continent split largely in two. Other than in Finland, Czechoslovakia and Spain (and in the latter two countries not for long), democracy survived only in north-western Europe. Everywhere else, authoritarianism in one form or another triumphed. The shadows were forming over an economically and politically broken continent.

SLUMP

The huge American boom that had brought increasingly risky investments in consumer durables, cars, steel production and building construction, collapsed from 24 October 1929 when the speculative bubble burst. 'The market seemed like an insensate thing that was wreaking a wild and pitiless revenge upon those who had thought to master it,' one observer commented. Panic selling of shares gripped Wall Street. Share prices plummeted. Thousands of speculators were ruined. Business confidence collapsed. Industrial production and imports went into sharp decline. Commodity prices fell. Unemployment shot up. Foreign lending had already dropped before the crash. Earlier short-term loans, from which European countries, especially Germany, had benefited, were called in.

In an imbalanced international economy, already faced with strong deflationary tendencies, Europe was inevitably sucked into rapidly widening economic disaster. The contagion spread. By 1930 manufacturing in Europe had slumped. Mass unemployment had followed across the Atlantic. By the early summer of 1930 there were already 1.9 million unemployed in Germany alone, and the unemployment insurance system was not coping. Average income per person across the whole country was already dropping and by 1932 would be only around two-thirds of what it had been in 1929. A deflationary cycle spread across the continent. As demand fell, prices dropped. People bought less. Even spending on absolute necessities was cut back to a minimum. Wages and salaries were cut, although, with falling prices, wages – for those still in work – could buy more; so 'real wages' often increased. Government revenues were placed under greater strain as receipts from taxation fell.

Attempts to balance budgets through cutting state expenditure simply worsened the dismal situation. The only effort to try to provide an internationally coordinated response, the much-trumpeted World Economic Conference of 1933 in London, failed miserably. Governments reacted with attempts to protect their own economies. By the summer of 1930, the USA had already turned strongly towards protectionism. Other countries retaliated with their own tariff protection. Average tariffs on imported goods in France, for example, were increased to 38 per cent in 1931, in Czechoslovakia to 50 per cent. Britain broke its tradition of Free Trade by imposing a general tariff of 10 per cent in March 1932 and reached a deal with its Dominions four months later to ensure preference for British goods. International trade, already struggling, was further damaged as exports fell sharply.

Worse was to come. The banking system was under growing strain in a number of European countries. The collapse in May 1931 of Austria's biggest bank, the Creditanstalt in Vienna, as depositors feared the loss of their savings and withdrew funds, was a major shock to Europe's financial system. The second largest German bank, the Darmstädter und Nationalbank, was dragged into the slipstream and amid panic withdrawals went bankrupt two months later. As European banks sold sterling to bolster their gold reserves, there was a run on the pound. Britain vainly attempted to uphold the exchange rate but lost £2.5 million a day in the second half of July. Withdrawals from London between mid-July and mid-September totalled over £200 million, the Bank of England's reserves fell to a dangerously low level, and on 21 September Britain was forced to abandon the gold standard. The pound lost a quarter of its value on foreign exchanges in the immediate aftermath.

By 1932, the slump across Europe was at its worst – an unprecedented collapse of the capitalist economy. Gross national product fell practically everywhere. The rates of decline – in Britain, Sweden and Italy by under 7 per cent, in Belgium by just over 10 per cent, but in Germany and Yugoslavia by over 17 per cent and in Poland by almost 25 per cent – nevertheless varied in accordance with the differing economic structures of these countries together with the level of dependency on American finance markets. One of Europe's biggest economies, that of France, was at first little affected, partly because the franc was undervalued before 1931. A big agricultural sector, with a relatively high level of subsistence farming on small peasant farms, and a good deal of small-scale craft and artisanal production wedded into the local and regional economy, initially helped to stave off any dramatic inroads from the Wall Street Crash. Measures taken in 1929 to protect agricultural prices, keeping domestic markets buoyant, also contributed to early French resilience. The government proudly claimed that its 'policy of prosperity' would continue while other countries faced economic failure. 'Whatever the cause of world depression, France can face it with relative serenity', a leading French daily newspaper announced. 'The happy balance of the economy and the virtues of the French people have made France a pillar of the world economy.'

Hubris was soon followed by nemesis. As late as 1931, France's unemployment figure still stood at only 55,000. But by then the country could no longer avoid being sucked into the international slump. And when the Depression set in, beginning in 1931, it lasted longer than in most other major economies. Production did not recover to its 1929 level for a decade. French exports were by 1936 only a half of what they had been in 1928. The number of business failures shot up in 1932 and continued to rise. Unemployment officially peaked at around 1 million in 1935. Unofficially, it was much higher. The sluggish recovery was exacerbated by France's reluctance, for prestige reasons, to devalue the franc. Once sterling and the dollar had been devalued, this left France's exports uncompetitive.

Although the lasting image of the Great Depression is of mass unemployment in industrial towns and cities, those who earned their living from the land – farmers, peasants and agricultural labourers – also suffered grievously from the economic blizzard. Eastern Europe, with a high dependency on agriculture, was especially hard hit. Extreme poverty and deep social misery were widespread. Nowhere were they worse than in Poland, a heavily agricultural economy with a small industrial sector, whose government compounded the severe problems by deep cuts in state expenditure and retaining an overvalued currency. One contemporary's summary of the Depression's impact on the Polish countryside ran as follows: 'It is easier in summertime, but in winter one comes across children huddled up in huts and swathed up to the neck in bags filled with chaff, because without this clothing they would freeze in the cold, unheated dwelling ... Life has become so wretched for all.'

As agricultural prices collapsed, lending dried up and interest rates remained high, indebtedness reduced many to penury. Farms were sold or auctioned off. Forced sales of farms in Bavaria between 1931 and 1932, for instance, rose by more than 50 per cent. Land labourers often struggled to find work. Smallholders survived on subsistence farming. Sometimes it was bare survival. Families in a poor village in southern France were reduced to a main meal each day consisting of nothing more than chestnuts, olives, radishes and a few garden vegetables that they were unable to sell. Anger directed at any that farmers thought were to blame for their plight – the state, bureaucrats, townspeople, financial exploiters, foreigners, Jews – unsurprisingly mounted in rural France and in many parts of Europe, feeding the radicalism of the extreme Right.

In industrial regions the devastation of the economy was even more evident. Austria's production fell by 39 per cent between 1929 and 1932, while unemployment almost doubled. In Poland industrial production in 1932 was down by 30 per cent from 1929, with a doubling of unemployment. The biggest economy on the European continent, that of Germany, saw production almost halve between 1929 and 1932. As factories and workshops closed their gates, millions were thrown out of work. Levels of unemployment rocketed. By the end of 1932 over a fifth of employees in Britain, Sweden and Belgium had no work. In Germany almost a third of the workforce was jobless – 6 million according to official figures. Adding part-time workers and hidden unemployment takes the figure to over 8 million, meaning nearly half the country's workforce was wholly or partially unemployed. The figures, unmistakably awful as they are, mask the realities of human misery and suffering.

Those out of work had to exist on whatever meagre unemployment pay they received in state systems overwhelmed by the numbers. The British government cut unemployment relief by 10 per cent in 1931. Many of the long-term jobless could in any case make no claim on it and had to survive on poor-law relief, which was provided only after a rigorous, much-hated 'Means Test' to assess income. As was said at the time, the Means Test could only have the effect of making the poor poorer, for it reduced the unemployment pay for one family member if other members were working. The unemployed father of a family of four in Wigan saw, as a result, his unemployment benefit reduced from 23 to 10 shillings a week because his two sons between them earned 31 shillings. A Blackburn family, in the woefully depressed textile area of Lancashire where the cotton mills had laid off most of their employees, was existing in 1932 only on the unemployment pay of a single member. When he turned down a job in Cornwall, more than 250 miles away, he was peremptorily deprived of his dole, and so his family of their sole source of income. It is little wonder that memories of the detested Means Test were to cast a shadow over social policy in Britain for the remainder of the twentieth century and beyond.

This was soul-destroying poverty, blighting family lives, leaving hopelessness in its wake. In early 1936 George Orwell, one of the most influential English writers and social commentators of his era, stayed for a time in Wigan, in north-west England, to experience at first hand living conditions in a depressed industrial area.*

As he left Wigan a few weeks later 'through the monstrous scenery of slag-heaps, chimneys, piled scrap-iron, fouled canals, paths of cindery mud criss-crossed by the prints of clogs', he spotted 'the usual exhausted face of the slum girl who is twenty-five and looks forty, thanks to miscarriages and drudgery; and it wore, for the second in which I saw it, the most desolate, hopeless expression I have ever seen.' A year or two earlier Orwell had chosen to witness dire poverty in Paris. 'You discover what it is like to be hungry. With bread and margarine in your belly, you go out and look into the shop windows . . . You discover the boredom which is inseparable from poverty; the times when you have nothing to do and, being underfed, can interest yourself in nothing.'

Of the German unemployed in 1932, only 15 per cent received the full benefit, meagre enough though that was. Another 25 per cent had emergency allowances, as many as 40 per cent were dependent on poor relief, and a further 20 per cent received nothing at all. 'The whole nation is enveloped in distress; official interference is of no avail; the people live in a veritable hell of meanness, oppression and disease' was how one observer, travelling through some areas of dire poverty, described it. Thousands of the homeless in Berlin and other towns and cities found their way each day in the winter months to big, improvised halls set up to provide warmth, basic food and overnight accommodation. The effects were debilitating for whole families. 'My father has been unemployed for over three years,' wrote a fourteen-year-old German girl in December 1932. 'We used to believe he would get a job again one day, but now even we children have given up all hope.'

---

* Surprisingly, such a perceptive observer of the working class missed the opportunity to witness an archetypal proletarian sport, Rugby League, in Wigan. On his first Saturday in the town, 15 February 1936, and close to where he was staying, Orwell could have seen the mighty Wigan team humbled 17 points to 10 on their own ground by the minnows of Liverpool Stanley in front of 15,000 spectators.

The apathy, resignation and profound sense of despair caused by long-term unemployment were demonstrated in a classic sociological study of the Austrian village of Marienthal, about 25 miles south of Vienna, where three-quarters of the population suffered from the closure of the textile factory, the only major employer in the locality. 'He has no hope left and just lives from one day to the next without knowing why' was the assessment of one poverty-stricken unemployed worker, in his mid-thirties with a wife and two undernourished children. 'The will to resist is lost.'

The effect on family life was often disastrous, as a report on conditions in Poland indicated. 'The crowding of several people into a single room where soon there is not enough furniture for them to sit down or sleep, and where there is less and less food to be divided, and the atmosphere becomes more and more hopeless and depressing – all this cannot but lead to constant quarrelling ... The break-up of family life is accelerated and the road lies open to a life of vagrancy and prostitution.' One dire indicator of misery in Poland was a sharp rise in suicide caused by unemployment.

Worst affected were those employed in heavy industry – coal-mining, iron and steel production and related branches such as ship-building. Textile areas (such as Marienthal), where the staple industry was in long-term decline, were also devastated. But the impact of the Depression varied. Unemployment in Germany as a whole quadrupled between 1928 and 1932. In predominantly agrarian East Prussia it doubled (though the plight of the rural economy nonetheless meant widespread misery). In industrial Saxony, by contrast, unemployment increased more than sevenfold. By 1932 unemployment in Britain was twice as high on average in the north as in London. But such averages themselves hid wide divergences. In Bishop Auckland and Jarrow, in the north-east, more than one in two workers had no work. 'Wherever we went there were men hanging about, not scores of them but hundreds and thousands of them,' observed a shocked J. B. Priestley on his 'English Journey' in autumn 1933. In Merthyr Tydfil in the industrial region of South Wales over two-thirds of workers were unemployed. But in St Albans, to the north of London, unemployment stood at no more than 3.9 per cent of the working population.

There were nonetheless also areas of notable growth even in the midst of such a far-reaching depression. The relative prosperity of the southern half of the United Kingdom attracted a slow movement of those from the blighted parts of the country in search of work, adding to the demand that fed into growth. The construction industry flourished in meeting the demand for new houses, schools, shops, cinemas and other facilities. Extended suburbs needed new roads. Building spawned further areas of growth. The electrical industry, based mainly in the south of England, continued to grow as the use of household appliances spread. The almost tenfold increase in electricity consumption between the wars created demand for electrical goods even during the Depression. More people, too, mainly in the upper and middle classes, were able to afford a car. The market for motor vehicles continued to expand despite the slump, and the Midlands, where much of British car manufacturing was located, escaped the worst of the economic devastation that afflicted northern England, Wales and Scotland, the homelands of the older industries. The north–south gap widened economically as a result. So did the divide between the employed and the unemployed. The mass unemployment of the worst-hit regions seemed a distant problem to many middle-class families in the more prosperous south. Those who worked in the expanding industries, and the consumers with the income to take advantage of their products, were indeed the fortunate ones.

The economic crisis greatly sharpened already existing sources of anger and resentment, and also deepened anxieties and worries about the future. It made societies meaner, less tolerant. One indicator, amid the mass unemployment, was the increased prejudice against women in work holding 'men's jobs'. 'Double-earners', where a man and his wife both worked, attracted high levels of public opprobrium in Germany as unemployment soared. In France, too, the Depression intensified prejudice against women. The place for them was seen to be at home, on the farm, as wives and mothers, at best doing 'women's work' like welfare or nursing. As the Depression tightened its grip, women were forced out of many workplaces, had career openings blocked, were unwelcome in universities, and faced discrimination at practically every level (not least in French politics, where they were denied the vote until

1944). Where women could find jobs – such as shop assistants, secretaries or other clerical positions – it was a matter of course that their wages were below those of male equivalents. Only Scandinavia did not follow the general European trend towards further discrimination against women's employment, Sweden indeed legislating (in 1939) that marriage was no longer a bar to employment.

The exceptional path taken by Scandinavia regarding women's employment was part of broader thinking on welfare and population policy. But here, too, the preoccupation with population decline, and what was seen as the inevitable consequence of deterioration in the quality of the population, fitted wider currents of thought in Europe that were enhanced by the climate of economic crisis. The worries about population decline – commonplace in most of Europe since the war, and particularly acute in France and Germany – produced a backlash against contraception, which had been increasingly promoted in the 1920s. The reactionary trend was widespread, had much popular support, and was especially strongly backed in Catholic countries by the Church's unceasing and vehement opposition to birth control. Abortion had already been outlawed in most of Europe, but here, too, attitudes hardened. Britain, for example, made abortion a statutory offence in 1929. Any person convicted of 'intent to destroy the life of a child capable of being born alive' (defined as a pregnancy of twenty-eight weeks or more) was to be punished by penal servitude for life. Hundreds of thousands of women in Britain and across the rest of Europe, married as well as unmarried, continued even so to have abortions, risking not just severe punishment by the law but serious injury and death through illegal operations.

When Marie Stopes, an English botanist, had promoted birth control in the 1920s, it had been in the context of measures to improve the quality of the population. Questions of heredity, genetics, decline of racial stock and the desperate need for superior breeding had become an obsession among Europe's intellectuals since the war. Eugenics, or its more ominous-sounding equivalent, 'racial hygiene' – breeding out 'defectives' and improving 'national efficiency' through racial improvement – gained support as the Depression crisis intensified doubts about the 'health of the nation'. The cost of looking after 'unproductive' members of society had taken on a sharper edge as states tightened their belts during the slump. In Britain, not just distinguished scientists, psychologists and doctors but also leading intellectuals, such as the economist John Maynard Keynes and the dramatist George Bernard Shaw, were among the supporters of the eugenics movement. Just before publication in 1932 of his dystopian novel *Brave New World* (depicting a society whose stability rests on biological engineering and mental conditioning to achieve maximum social and economic utility), Aldous Huxley spoke of eugenics as a means of political control, indicating his own approval of measures to prevent 'the rapid deterioration ... of the whole West European stock'. Some of the more extreme eugenicists, believing that the British 'race' was faced with inevitable degeneration and eventual extinction of its biological quality unless drastic measures for racial cleansing were introduced, even contemplated the painless extermination of 'undesirables' or, failing that, compulsory sterilization. Although such ideas were confined to a minority of eugenicists and taken no further in Britain, they showed the way the wind was blowing during the Depression, even in a democracy.

In Germany draft proposals for *voluntary* sterilization of those suffering from hereditary defects were introduced with the support of doctors in 1932, before the Nazi takeover. Hitler's government promptly went much further. But it could be certain of much popular support for its law of 14 July 1933 to introduce *compulsory* sterilization for an extensive range of hereditary illnesses, serious physical deformities and chronic alcoholism, which over the following years would produce around 400,000 victims. ('Lethal chambers' to exterminate the mentally ill in Germany would have to wait a further six years.) Compulsory sterilization was not, however, confined to the actions of an inhumane dictatorship. All the democratic Scandinavian states passed laws in 1934, with widespread public backing, to introduce compulsory sterilization for certain citizens, resulting in tens of thousands of victims. Nor was statutory sterilization confined to Europe's 'dark continent'. By the eve of the Second World War, some 42,000 citizens in thirty American states had been sterilized, mainly compulsorily, on the grounds of 'feeblemindedness' or 'madness'. Throughout Europe (and the wider Western world) state intervention in the lives of citizens was becoming acceptable in ways that would have been inconceivable before 1914.

Across Europe the disastrous worsening of the economic situation radicalized not just social thinking but political action. As class tensions sharpened, politics polarized. The Left, split in most countries between mutually antagonistic more moderate Socialist and Moscow-aligned Communist parties, sought, usually vainly, to fend off drastic cuts in living standards for the working class. Militancy on the Left was in no small measure also a response to the dangers of a rising tide of extreme anti-socialist movements on the Right. In practically every country outside the Soviet Union, the Depression brought a surge in support for fascist movements that aimed to destroy the Left and reorder societies through manufactured and enforced national unity. The more comprehensive the crisis, the greater was the likelihood that large parts of the population could be mobilized by the extreme Right. The crisis was most comprehensive in Germany; unsurprisingly, the reaction to it was more extreme there than anywhere else in Europe.

The most disastrously affected economy in Europe was the most important on the continent. Germany was a country with a fragile democracy, feeling its culture under threat, utterly divided ideologically and politically, and still bearing the deep scars of the war. As the economy collapsed, social misery intensified and democratic government imploded amid mounting violence and political polarization. Democracy, already embattled as it entered the crisis, was too weak to survive. A shift to authoritarian rule became inevitable. Some democracies in Europe had already collapsed. Others would soon do so. But Germany was by far the most crucial of them. Not just its size, powerful industrial base (if temporarily severely damaged by the slump) and geographical centrality in Europe, but also its extensive ambitions to revise the territorial stipulations of the Versailles Treaty, made Germany an exceptional case – and a potential threat to European peace should an authoritarian government follow an assertive foreign policy.

As the Great Depression tightened its grip, the social fabric cracked and the ideological gulf widened to a chasm. The sense of a formerly great nation now crisis-ridden, its very existence in danger, humiliated, helpless and hopelessly divided among itself, massively intensified.

Under such pressure, the structures of parliamentary democracy gave way. Political space opened up. And as it did, one political force, in the eyes of increasingly large numbers of Germans, alone offered the hope of national salvation: Hitler's Nazi Party.

The result would be Hitler's takeover of power in Germany on 30 January 1933, a date that would prove a disastrous turning point in European history. Of all the ways that the Depression reshaped European politics and society, what happened in Germany would prove the most fateful – not just for the people of Germany, but for the entire continent of Europe and, eventually, for much of the world.

THE WORST POSSIBLE OUTCOME

Germany's crisis was not just, or even primarily, economic, but amounted to a complete crisis of state and society. Acute economic calamity in the USA did not lead to a crisis of the state. A less acute, but nevertheless extremely severe, economic downturn in Britain brought a notable strengthening of the conservative establishment. In both America and Britain the dominant elites saw their interests served by the existing political system, while the overwhelming majority of the population supported existing structures of rule and the values that underpinned them. The state in France, where consensus was less secure, underwent more of a shock, but withstood it. Sweden's economic crisis actually bolstered the social-democratic basis of the state.

In Germany, by contrast, the Depression fully opened up the festering wounds that had been only superficially bandaged since 1918. The shallow level of acceptance of democracy among the political, economic and military elites was now glaringly exposed. And the belief among the masses in a democracy that, in the eyes of a growing majority, was responsible for Germany's plight shrivelled more and more as the Depression worsened. Undermined by the elites and faced with rapidly collapsing popular support, German democracy was actually on a life-support machine from 1930 onwards. As politics polarized and the extremes profited, Hitler proved the ultimate beneficiary.

The Reich Chancellor during the worst of the economic crisis,

Heinrich Brüning, had pinned his entire political strategy to the removal of reparations by demonstrating that Germany, wracked by an ever-worsening Depression, was unable to pay. The deepening of social misery at home was, in his eyes, a necessary price to pay in order to rid Germany of the reparations burden. By June 1931 his goal had come within reach when the US President, Herbert Hoover, in the face of French opposition, pushed through a one-year moratorium on German reparations payments. By the end of the year a committee established under the terms of the Young Plan to determine Germany's ability to pay concluded that it would not be able to do so once the moratorium had expired. The committee proposed the cancellation of German reparations payments, and also of inter-Allied war debts. At a conference in Lausanne the following summer, the proposal was adopted. Germany agreed to pay a small final instalment (which, in fact, was never actually handed over). With that, reparations, since 1919 a political more than an outrightly economic millstone around Germany's neck, were written off. Brüning was, however, no longer in a position to reap any credit. He had lost the confidence of Reich President Hindenburg, who had dismissed him as Chancellor just before the Lausanne conference. Brüning had served Hindenburg's purpose, and was now surplus to requirements.

With the end of reparations, revisionists could start to muse more realistically about removing the shackles of Versailles, the army about rebuilding its strength, and anti-democratic elites about firmer authoritarian rule. Hindenburg started to show his true colours. Government in Germany moved further to the Right under the Chancellorships, in quick succession, of Franz von Papen (June–November 1932) and General Kurt von Schleicher (December 1932–January 1933). But, lacking mass support, neither was able to come close to solving the rapidly worsening crisis not just of the economy but of the German state. Their problem was that any solution needed Hitler.

The increasing fragmentation of the political system between 1930 and 1933 created an enormous vacuum that the Nazis filled. As the existing state system lost almost all popular support, a tidal wave of disaffection swept voters into the arms of Hitler's movement. Hitler himself increasingly became the magnet for the angry and fearful masses. The propaganda machine behind him was able to manufacture an image that embodied not only popular fury at Germany's existing condition but also the hopes and dreams of a better future. People projected onto Hitler their own beliefs, wishes and desires. He incorporated them in a vision of complete national rebirth.

Not all, by any means, were attracted. The Left held on to over 30 per cent of the vote down to 1933. A further steady 15 per cent went to the two Catholic parties. But the deep rancour between the Social Democrats and the Communist Party (the latter almost entirely a party of the unemployed) ruled out any united front against the Nazis. This fateful division contributed to the looming catastrophe for the German Left. But the split did not cause it. The parties of the Left had no access to power. The main problem lay not on the Left but on the Right. Government authority was crumbling and public disorder spreading. Violent clashes between Nazis and Communist paramilitary organizations were multiplying. Panic at the growing support for the Communist Party (largely at the expense of the Social Democrats), and the wildly exaggerated prospect of a communist revolution, had gripped the middle classes. The 'bourgeois' parties of the centre and right duly collapsed, along with over thirty small regional or interest parties (their proliferation facilitated by an electoral system of unrestricted proportional representation). The Nazis hoovered up the bulk of their dwindling support.

Nazi agitation stoked the fires of elemental rage and hatred, drawing on disparate resentments and prejudice. The appeal was, however, not all negative. Nazi propaganda linked the demonization of political and racial enemies to a vaguely couched, though extraordinarily powerful, emotional call for national regeneration and unity. It evoked the national unity that had (briefly) existed in 1914, and the 'trench community' of front-line soldiers during the war, aiming, it said, to create a 'people's community' of ethnic Germans that would transcend all internal divisions. It was effective symbolism.

An eighteen-year-old clerk, who joined the Nazi Party in 1929 after attending meetings of other parties, expressed the attraction in his own way after being fired up by the stirring address of a Nazi speaker:

> I was swept along not only by his passionate speech, but also by his sincere commitment to the German people as a whole, whose greatest

misfortune was being divided into so many parties and classes. Finally a practical proposal for the renewal of the people! Destroy the parties! Do away with classes! True people's community! These were the goals to which I could commit myself without reservation. The same night it became clear to me where I belonged: to the new movement. It alone gave hope of saving the German fatherland.

Hundreds of thousands like him, whatever their individual motives, streamed into the Nazi Movement between 1930 and 1933. By the eve of Hitler's takeover of power, party members numbered nearly 850,000 – over four-fifths of whom had joined since the start of the Depression. The paramilitary stormtroopers' section alone (the *Sturmabteilung* or SA) numbered around 400,000, many of whom were not actually members of the Nazi Party.

Voters were not for the most part looking for a coherent programme, nor for limited reforms to government. Hitler's party was attractive to them because it promised a radical new start by clearing out the old system entirely. The Nazis did not want to amend what they depicted as moribund or rotten; they claimed they would eradicate it, and build a new Germany out of the ruins. They did not offer to defeat their opponents; they threatened to destroy them completely. The message was attractive precisely because of its radicalism. Respectable middle-class Germans, who had imbibed the expectation of 'peace and order' with their mother's milk, were now prepared to tolerate Nazi violence – as long as it was directed at the detested socialists and communists, or at the Jews (widely viewed, not just by ardent Nazis, as too powerful, and a malign force in Germany). The middle classes saw the violence as a by-product of an entirely positive goal: the cause of national renewal. That the appeal to a sense of national unity to overcome internal division involved intolerance and violence was no deterrent. When Hitler made a virtue out of intolerance, declaring in a speech in the summer of 1932, 'we *are* intolerant. I have one aim, to clear the 30 parties out of Germany', the huge crowd of 40,000 bayed their approval.

The loose amalgam of phobias and nationalistic sloganeering that stood behind the violent rhetoric allowed many critics to dismiss Nazism as merely an inchoate protest movement that would fall apart once conditions improved and if ever it was forced to take a responsible part in government. The Nazis *were* a huge, unwieldy, factionalized protest movement, it was true. But there was more to them than simple protest and propaganda. Their leaders, Hitler above all others, were not just gifted demagogues and propagandists, but determined, committed and utterly ruthless ideologues.

Hitler had hardly kept quiet about his aims. His book *Mein Kampf*, written between 1924 and 1926 (the first part while he was in Landsberg prison), had advertised in the plainest terms his anti-Jewish paranoia, and his view that Germany's future could be secured only by gaining land at the expense of the Soviet Union. Few beyond Nazi adepts had taken much notice of what seemed a deranged dystopia of a failed putschist on the political margins.

Nor did his personal ideology play much part in winning over the masses to Nazism in the early 1930s. Antisemitism, so central in Hitler's thinking, was in fact less prominent in Nazi propaganda in the early 1930s, as voters were flocking to the Nazi banner, than it had been in the early 1920s, when relatively few had been won over to Nazism. Jews served of course as a catch-all scapegoat for Germany's ills. But what drew voters in the Depression was the promise of an end to the misery which, in their eyes, Weimar democracy had created, the destruction of those responsible for Germany's plight, and the creation of a new social order resting on a national 'people's community' that would build future power, pride and prosperity for Germany. Propaganda emblazoned Hitler's image as the only man who could achieve this, 'the hope of millions', as a Nazi election slogan of 1932 put it. He was the embodiment of the party's ideology, and of the popular yearnings for national salvation.

Hitler's exceptional demagogic talent coupled with his ideological certainty (though tactical flexibility) had enabled him to consolidate his supreme power within the Nazi Movement. His ideological vision was broad enough to subsume the differing individual strands of right-wing thinking or potentially divisive interest that one or other of his subordinate leaders, each wedded to a specific fetish, might passionately (if impractically) advance. Those who wanted, for instance, to put the emphasis on winning over workers through a 'national' brand of socialism, or who sought to stress 'blood and soil' to gain the support of the peasantry, found their specific programmatic aims incorporated within a nebulous but powerful appeal to national unity, while particular social grievances could be diverted into anti-Jewish rhetoric. The Leader in this way became the embodiment of the 'idea'. And the leadership cult erected around Hitler amounted to a barrier against the inherent tendency – common to fascist movements – to fragment into warring factions, as had been all too evident in the early Nazi Party.

In the Depression years, the Nazi Party had mounting success in undermining the tottering remains of Weimar democracy. By 1932, only the fifth or so of voters who still supported the Social Democrats, together with the few remaining liberals and some adherents of the Catholic Centre Party, wanted to retain the democratic system. Democracy was dead. As to what should replace it, opinion differed considerably. About three-quarters of Germans wanted some form of authoritarian government, but there were various possibilities. A dictatorship of the proletariat, a military dictatorship, a Hitler dictatorship were among the variants. For all their ceaseless clamour and relentless agitation, the Nazis had by the summer of 1932 reached the limit – just over a third of voter support – of their possible success in free elections. And when Hitler, in August 1932, demanded to be made head of government (just after his Nazi Party, with 37.4 per cent of the electorate behind it, had become easily the largest party in the Reichstag), he was firmly rebuffed by Reich President Hindenburg. The form of authoritarianism that Hindenburg wanted – something like a reversion to the system of Imperial Germany – did not countenance a Hitler Chancellorship. Within five months, however, Hindenburg had changed his mind – and at a time when the Nazi vote was sagging, not rising.

When Hitler was eventually appointed Chancellor, on 30 January 1933, it followed an electoral defeat. In the election of November 1932 the Nazis had actually lost votes for the first time since their surge had begun in 1929. It looked as if their bubble, amid an internal crisis of the party's leadership, had burst. That election – the second Reichstag election of 1932, coming on top of two rounds of the presidential election and a series of regional elections – had been caused by the continuing and deepening crisis of the state. Increasing violence in

Germany's cities expressed in clashes between Nazis and communists gave rise to real fears that the country was slipping into civil war. The army was fearful of becoming embroiled. Successive governments of the conservative Right were too weak to offer any solution. An impasse had been reached. The national conservative elites were unable to govern without enlisting the mass support that the Nazis controlled. But the Nazis were unwilling to enter government unless Hitler was made Chancellor. Machinations behind the scenes by those with the ear of the Reich President eventually broke the deadlock by persuading Hindenburg that the only way out was to give Hitler the Chancellorship but hedge him in with a cabinet predominantly of conservative ministers. This was the fateful deal that finally gave Hitler the power he wanted.

He knew how to use it. Mussolini had needed three years to establish complete control over the Italian state. Hitler established his total domination in Germany within six months. Open terror against opponents was the main method, alongside heavy pressure to comply with the new regime. Tens of thousands of communists and socialists – 25,000 in Prussia alone – were arrested in the first weeks of Hitler's government, thrown into makeshift prisons and camps, and grievously maltreated. Emergency decrees legitimated unconstrained police power. An Enabling Act passed in a menacing atmosphere in the Reichstag on 23 March freed the government from any possible parliamentary constraints. German society, partly cowed and intimidated, partly enthusiastic, fell into line. New members swarmed to join the Nazi Party, and the myriad social and cultural organizations, clubs and associations that existed at national, regional and local levels swiftly nazified themselves. Beyond the 30 per cent or so of Germans who had been adherents of the Left (and of course the already persecuted small Jewish minority, a mere 0.76 per cent of the population), there were many who had not voted for the Nazi Party but who could nevertheless find some appeal at least in what it claimed to offer during what the party called the 'national uprising'. Those who failed to find anything appealing about the party were well advised to keep their views to themselves. Intimidation was the constant accompaniment of the heady atmosphere of national renewal.

Potential organized opposition to Nazi rule was systematically eliminated. The defiant Communists were ruthlessly crushed, the Social Democratic Party – the oldest and biggest working-class movement in Europe – was banned. With its demise, and with the forcible liquidation of the huge trade union movement at the beginning of May, Germany's democracy – of a mere fourteen years' duration, though drawing on the existence of lengthy democratic ideals – was all but extinguished. All that remained were the flickering remnants that persisted in perilous underground opposition. The 'bourgeois' and Catholic political parties were also banned or dissolved themselves. On 14 July the Nazi Party was officially declared to be the only party legally permissible.

Hitler, in the early part of his rule, had to bear in mind not just his huge army of followers but pillars of the conservative establishment, represented by the revered figure of Reich President Hindenburg. In a spectacularly staged display of unity on 21 March (the 'Day of Potsdam'), Hitler won their backing by offering national renewal based upon the bonds of the old and new Germany, symbolically harnessing the Prussian militarism dating back to the glory days of Frederick the Great to a vision of future national greatness. Many doubters were impressed. Hitler seemed more statesmanlike than in his rabble-rousing days. He was on the way to converting his image from that of a party leader to that of a national leader of stature.

A serious crisis had arisen early in 1934 over the ambitions of Ernst Röhm, the leader of the stormtroopers, to radicalize still further the Nazi revolution, and to subordinate the army to control by the paramilitary wing of the party. The threat to the position of established elites in the state was obvious. Hitler was forced to act, and he did so on 30 June in brutal fashion by authorizing the massacre of the stormtrooper leaders in the 'Night of the Long Knives'. Röhm and other SA leaders were shot dead. Others who had crossed Hitler at some point, including Gregor Strasser (seen as a traitor for his opposition in the autumn of 1932), and the former Reich Chancellor, General Kurt von Schleicher (regarded as continuing to intrigue against the regime), were also murdered. The total number killed has been estimated at 150–200 persons.

Hitler's position was immeasurably strengthened, remarkably, by his sponsoring of mass murder 'in defence of the state'. Ordinary people saw him clearing out the Augean stables of an overbearing and corrupt presence – an 'ulcer' in the body politic. The army were gratified by a 'cleansing action' that had removed a major threat to their power and cemented their own indispensability to the state. And those who might have thought of posing a challenge to Hitler's regime were given a stark warning of its readiness to strike against even the mightiest subjects with brutal force. Hitler was now unchallengeable. When Hindenburg died at the start of August 1934, Hitler himself took over the authority of head of state. With this move, his total power in Germany was cemented. State power and Führer power were one and the same.

The consolidation of the dictatorship was accompanied by the revitalization of the economy, and by rapid steps towards the rebuilding of military strength – at the very time when the Western democracies, buffeted by the Depression, were revealing their weaknesses and divisions. As European countries struggled to overcome the economic crisis, democracy was almost everywhere forced onto the defensive, while authoritarianism of one kind or another was advancing. It was a deeply worrying development for the peace of Europe.

ROUTES TO ECONOMIC RECOVERY

By 1933 the Great Depression had touched rock bottom in much of Europe and the first feeble signs of patchy recovery could be dimly spotted. For many of the worst affected industrial areas, early improvement – if there was any – was barely visible to the naked eye. And France was slipping deeper into Depression just as Europe's other major economies had turned the corner. In the summer of that year, the newly elected President of the United States of America, Franklin Delano Roosevelt, pulled the plug on the World Economic Conference that had aimed to stabilize currencies and end tariff wars. It had been the sole attempt to reach international agreement on measures for recovery. Roosevelt unsurprisingly gave outright priority to American national interests in stimulating the US economy. He promptly devalued the dollar against sterling. It sealed the already existing pattern for dealing with the crisis. Countries had to find their own way out of the

Depression. They did so in different fashion, and at different paces. The failure to agree on an international system of trade undoubtedly prolonged it. Democracies for their part stumbled towards recovery. John Maynard Keynes acknowledged that the economy was in 'a frightful muddle' even to professional economists. It was little wonder that government leaders seldom had a clear idea of where they were going.

By 1933, Britain's economy – the largest global economy outside the American – was starting to come out of the Depression. The following year Britain was the first country to surpass its industrial production level of 1929 – though this was largely a reflection of the low growth of the 1920s. Falling unemployment was another indicator that the worst was over. Unemployment fell from 3 to 2.5 million during 1933. However, it remained stubbornly high, declining only slowly from 17.6 per cent of the working population in 1932 to 12–13 per cent in 1935. In the most depressed regions it was still over 50 per cent. 'Hunger marches' by thousands of unemployed workers from Scotland, Wales and the north of England in 1932, backed by the Communist Party, had encountered hostility from Ramsay MacDonald's National Government, and led to major disorder and violent clashes with police. A well-supported petition to abolish the Means Test had been confiscated by the police to prevent it even reaching Parliament. In 1936 the march of some 200 poverty-stricken, unemployed workers from the devastated shipbuilding town of Jarrow, in the north-east, to London, nearly 300 miles away, evoked more public sympathy. But the government refused to accept their petition, signed by 11,000 local inhabitants, asking for government help for the stricken town.

The government stuck to financial orthodoxy, aimed at a balanced budget. Theories of combating the Depression through unorthodox methods of deficit financing were still in their infancy. Keynes, who had embarrassingly predicted soon after the Wall Street Crash that there would be no serious consequences for London and that 'we find the look ahead decidedly encouraging', had still not finalized his counter-cyclical economic theory. When the Depression set in, the most ambitious blueprint for a planned economy regalvanized through borrowing to finance growth came from Oswald Mosley, whose political ambition, impatience and rootlessness matched his undoubted ability. Mosley, from an aristocratic background, had once been a Conservative. Disenchanted with the Conservatives, he had left the party in the early 1920s to become an Independent Member of Parliament, before joining the Labour Party. His stance on social and economic policy was distinctly on the Left. When his ideas for stimulating the economy through deficit financing were rejected out of hand, he led a secession from Labour and created the New Party. And when his New Party failed to win any worthwhile support at the 1931 general election, he moved to the extreme Right, openly expressed his admiration for Mussolini, established the British Union of Fascists in 1932, and set out on the path to political oblivion.

The National Government, which had come into office during the financial crisis in the summer of 1931, included ministers from the three main parties, Labour, Conservative and Liberal, in a small ten-man cabinet. The dominant figures were soon to become the former Conservative Prime Minister, Stanley Baldwin, and Neville Chamberlain, the son of the former prominent Liberal politician, Joseph, and half-brother of Austen, the British Foreign Secretary who had helped forge the Locarno Treaty of 1925. But Ramsay MacDonald, Prime Minister in the Labour government between 1929 and 1931, retained his office and Philip Snowden remained initially as Chancellor of the Exchequer. By joining the National Government, MacDonald and Snowden split the Labour Party, which, amid much acrimony and talk of betrayal, expelled them from its membership, forcing them to form a new party; they called it 'National Labour'.

Snowden's emergency budget, driven by the imperatives of sound finance, predictably met with fury within his former party. But the National Government, backed by a huge majority in the House of Commons, could now push through the expenditure cuts, rise in income tax, and reduction in public service workers' pay and unemployment benefit that, when they had first been proposed (since many of the cuts fell disproportionately on the poorest in society), had prompted the fall of the Labour government. Restoration of confidence in the faltering pound had been a pre-eminent motive. But a consequence had been to reduce demand and invite deflation. What pulled Britain gradually out of the Depression was above all the cheap money resulting from the reduction in the costs of short-term borrowing. One consequence was to encourage a big expansion in house-building, which spurred demand for building materials, household furnishings, electrical goods and other ancillary by-products. Even in 1930, the worst year, 200,000 new houses had been built. Between 1934 and 1938 the average was 360,000 a year.

Alongside slum clearance, which demolished about a quarter of a million houses unfit for habitation between 1934 and 1939, the government subsidised the building of social housing (known in Britain as council houses). In Scotland the majority of the housing demolition and rebuilding was undertaken by municipal authorities. Over 300,000 homes for the working class were built overall in Scotland in the interwar decades, though 66,000 houses were still in 1939 deemed unfit for human habitation and a further 200,000 houses were needed to alleviate overcrowding. In England and Wales, too, some progressive municipal authorities introduced major house-construction programmes. But far more new homes – around 2 million out of 2.7 million in all – were built in the 1930s without government assistance, three-quarters of them financed by building societies, which offered mortgages and whose capital had greatly expanded since the war. Private house-building prospered, especially in the suburban developments in southern England. Land was relatively plentiful, building costs were low, houses affordable and mortgage loans for buyers cheap. The economy was also boosted by the growth in domestic demand and in exports from the new electro-chemical and car industries. The expansion of motoring brought in valuable income for the government. Tax on motor vehicles produced five times more revenue for the government in 1939 than it had done in 1921.

Like Britain, France tried to heal its ailing economy through orthodox methods of financial retrenchment. Government expenditure was severely cut. Big reductions were made in school-building, worker-housing and other construction work. A swollen bureaucracy offered an easy and popular target. But when cuts, imposed by government decree that bypassed parliament, affected salaries, pensions and benefits of all state employees, forcing up unemployment and starting to impinge on war veterans and other sectors of the public, resentment swiftly grew and brought increasing political turbulence. Political considerations ruled out a resort to the devaluation that other countries had deployed to boost exports. When Belgium, which had continued alongside France in the depleted group of countries still on the gold standard, finally left it in March 1935 and devalued its currency by 28 per cent, production and exports soon started to recover, while unemployment fell sharply. France still refused to devalue. Eventually, and inevitably, in September 1936 devaluation came – forced on the left-wing Popular Front government, which had promised to defend the franc but was driven into heavy expenditure on rearmament. Another devaluation followed in June 1937, and a third in 1938. By then, the franc had lost a third of its value in under three years. Only at this point did the economy begin again to grow significantly.

While practically all of Europe thought no further than classical liberal financial orthodoxy as the way to manage the economic crisis until the markets adjusted to produce renewed growth, the Scandinavian countries took a different path. Denmark, Sweden and Norway had all been badly hit by the Depression. Unemployment was high – over 30 per cent in Denmark and Norway, over 20 per cent in Sweden. Denmark had also been particularly affected by the fall in agricultural prices and drop in exports. Governments since the war had generally been unstable. Further fragmentation and a move to the political extremes seemed likely. Instead, starting in 1933 in Denmark and quickly followed by Sweden and Norway, there was political consolidation between the parties, which provided the platform for a high level of consensus in adopting economic policies that greatly assisted the nascent recovery.

Denmark paved the way in January 1933 when the need for agreement on devaluing the krona produced a deal by which the Social Democrats backed protectionist measures to assist farmers in return for the readiness of the Agrarian Party to support measures to alleviate unemployment and welfare policies. Similar arrangements followed in Sweden and Norway. In Sweden especially, the new, pragmatic basis of consensus was used to introduce counter-cyclical economic policy aimed at combating unemployment through state spending on public works. Just how important such schemes were in economic recovery is not altogether clear. Levels of deficit financing in the early years of recovery were low, and recovery itself was already beginning before the schemes set in, aided by devaluation and rising exports, and only gradual in pace. Even so, the agreements reached as a way out of the crisis had lasting significance in laying the basis for welfare policies that rested on political stability and popular acceptance. The similarity in policies adopted by the Scandinavian countries reflected new levels of cooperation that were prompted not just by the need to defuse internal tensions but also by growing international worries, especially about developments in Germany.

Dictatorships had their own routes to recovery. The existence of a Fascist regime in Italy had in itself been no bulwark against the inroads of the Depression. In fact, the deflationary policy introduced in 1927 had weakened the economy even before the impact of the Wall Street Crash. Deflationary measures followed the revaluation of the currency, now fixed at an overvalued exchange rate of 90 lire to the pound since Mussolini regarded what he saw as a previously undervalued lira (150 to the pound) as an insult to Italy's national prestige. The revaluation was meant as a display of strength and political will. But in economic terms it had damaging consequences. Industrial production fell by nearly 20 per cent between 1929 and 1932, while unemployment trebled. Earnings, for those in work, dropped, though between 1932 and 1934 the drop was more than compensated by the sharp fall in prices and by the introduction of family subsidies. The working week was reduced in 1934 to forty hours, mainly to cut unemployment, though there was no adjustment of hourly rates to compensate for the fall in earnings. Real wages fell again from 1935 onwards and by the eve of the Second World War had still not reached their 1923 level.

Mussolini's government responded to the Depression by increasing state intervention in the economy. Expenditure on public works was massively extended. State spending on land reclamation was in itself nothing new in Italy. But while during the half a century after 1870 this had amounted to 307 million gold lire (at 1927 prices), between 1921 and 1936 it rocketed to 8,697 million gold lire. This helped to reduce unemployment, though it did nothing to keep costs down, improve productivity or enhance technological progress. The drive for self-sufficiency in food was also given high priority. The 'battle for grain', accompanied by high protective tariffs on agricultural goods, increased wheat output, improved crop yields, and forced down wheat imports by 1937 to a quarter of what they had been in the late 1920s. One consequence was, however, rising food prices and a fall in average consumption of most staple foodstuffs.

During the Depression, too, the Fascist regime in Italy moved, belatedly, to give practical shape to ideas of a corporate state, culminating in the establishment in 1934 of twenty-two corporations, each representing a specific sector of economic production and together meant to provide an integral, planned economy. Goals and reality, however, remained detached from each other. The corporate state proved an unwieldy, over-bureaucratized structure that stifled, rather than promoted, enterprise. Behind the veneer, real economic power remained in the hands of big business. Trade unions had lost their independence already in 1926, leaving industrial relations in control of industrialists, organized within the General Confederation of Italian Industry. Cartels in the main industrial sectors ensured that the interests of business were upheld. The regime's economic measures during the Depression also aided big business, despite the appearance of bringing the economy under rigorous state control. The regime established in 1931 a state corporation to buy up the shares of failing banks, leading to increased control of the banking sector and the nationalization of the Bank of Italy in 1936. A further state corporation (Institute of Industrial Reconstruction) was created in 1933 to stimulate failing industries. Gradually, the state extended its direct involvement in important sectors of industry such as shipping, engineering and armaments production.

The moves towards autarchy, strengthened in the later 1930s, increased the measure of state intervention and took Italy further from the path of liberal economies. State regulation imposed limits on the freedom of action of business leaders, who were increasingly subordinated to bureaucratic controls. Industrialists' initial fears of losing control to the state were, however, never fully realized. Although relations between the Fascist state and big business were not free of friction, there was more than enough common interest – not to mention soaring profits for industry from armaments production – to ensure their close collaboration well into the Second World War.

Overall, in the decade following the onset of the Depression, the

Italian economy remained largely stagnant, with economic growth far lower than in the period 1901–25 and with enterprise stifled by state restrictions, by individuals' worries about losing their jobs, and by possible reprisals for any show of political nonconformity. The standard of living for much of the population fell, and had only slightly improved by the advent of the war. The same was true of industrial production. Italy's route out of the Depression, despite the heavy hand of a repressive state, proved to be both more cumbersome and less efficient than was the case for Europe's democracies. And it was far more dangerous. By 1935 it was overshadowed by Mussolini's quest for imperialist glory, launched by the invasion of Ethiopia in October. Although the roots of the colonial conquest were ideological, there was certainly a feeling among prominent fascists that at a time of severe economic difficulty colonial expansion into Africa could revitalize the regime. For fascism, economic recovery was part of a wider agenda.

This was even more clearly the case in Germany. Here the most remarkably rapid economic recovery took place exactly where the Depression had been deepest. The speed of recovery astonished and impressed contemporaries, within and outside Germany, helped to consolidate the support for Hitler's dictatorship, and gave rise to the notion of a Nazi 'economic miracle'. The Nazis had come to power without any clearly formulated blueprint for economic recovery. At his first speech on becoming Reich Chancellor, on 1 February 1933, Hitler had promised two big 'four-year plans' to rescue German farmers and to eliminate unemployment. How these aims might be achieved he did not disclose, and did not know. Economics for him was not a matter of technical finesse, but – like everything else – of will. In his crudely deterministic mind, political power, not economics, was decisive.

What Hitler and his regime did in the early months of Nazi rule, as he had promised the leaders of big business before taking power, was to reshape the political conditions within which the economy could function. The destruction of the parties of the Left and of the trade unions gave industrialists what they wanted. Labour relations were restructured, providing employers with dominance in the workplace. State repression underpinned the new freedom given to economic enterprise. Wages could be held down and profits maximized. In return, however, industrialists were left in no doubt that the interests of the state, not the liberal market economy, had to determine the framework of economic enterprise. Hitler was content for financial experts in the state bureaucracy and for economic leaders to devise plans to get the economy moving again. For him, the *image* of new dynamism, of revitalization, was the key factor. And in instilling the confidence that recovery was taking place, he made his most personal contribution to making it happen.

The Nazis were fortunate in that their takeover of power coincided with the bottom point of the Depression, so that some cyclical recovery would have taken place under any government. However, the speed and scale of the German recovery – reviving faster than the world economy in general – went beyond any normal rebound from recession. Early recovery owed much to ideas that had already been developed (and were in some stage of implementation before the Nazis came to power), which were now picked up and greatly expanded. Work-creation schemes had been introduced in 1932. But they were insignificant, without any hope of making an impact on the scale of unemployment. Where the Papen government in 1932 had provided 167 million Reich marks for job creation, the Nazi regime made 5 billion Reich marks available by 1935. In itself this still accounted for only 1 per cent of gross national product – far too small to restimulate the economy. But the propaganda impact was much greater than implied by the limited sum involved. Germany seemed to be working again.

The work-creation schemes – local road-building, ditch-digging, land reclamation and the like – were highly visible, whatever their actual economic value. Columns of those on the voluntary Labour Service (compulsory from 1935) added to the impression of a country starting to pick up. Pay was miserable, but those disinclined to undertake back-breaking work for minimal recompense found themselves in a concentration camp, brutally compelled to reconsider their attitude towards work. Those on the various emergency schemes were struck off the unemployment register. The rapidly falling level of unemployment – the fall was genuine, but smaller than the statistics seemed to demonstrate – again instilled confidence in a country revitalizing its economy through dynamism and energy.

Work creation, alongside significant expenditure on construction projects, tax concessions for the motor industry, and further measures to strengthen agricultural protection against low prices and so benefit farmers (whose earnings rose at three times the level of weekly wages over the following five years), all added up to a major step by the Nazi regime towards economic stimulus. This was well before high levels of expenditure on rearmament from the mid-1930s started to take the recovery onto a new level, wiping out unemployment entirely and leading to a labour shortage. The car industry received a boost through Hitler's instinct for effective propaganda. At the very beginning of his rule he promised tax relief on car manufacturing, a major road-building programme and the production of a cheap 'people's car' (though the Volkswagen was never actually to be available to the civilian population until after the war). Car production was 50 per cent higher in 1934 than it had been in 1929, the peak year before the Depression. Road-building – including the initiation of motorways, a great propaganda success – was expanded in spectacular fashion. Expenditure on roads was 100 per cent higher in 1934 than at any time in the 1920s. State investment in the construction industry also spurred private house-building, creating business for innumerable small firms that produced the goods and services needed both by construction firms and by the consumers wanting to furnish their houses.

The policies adopted to stimulate the German economy had obvious consequences for foreign trade. Demand could not be satisfied by German resources alone. But the refusal to contemplate any devaluation of the Reich mark, not just for prestige reasons but also because of the bitter memories of the great inflation of 1923 when money had lost all its value, meant that imports were expensive and that the balance of trade was running against Germany. The effect was to enhance a move away from reintegration into the world market economy towards bilateral trade agreements and an increasing drive towards autarchy. Under Hjalmar Schacht, President of the Reichsbank and, from 1934, Economics Minister, earlier measures that had initially followed the bank crash of 1931 to control foreign exchange and regulate debt repayment were greatly extended. By 1934, a critical shortage of foreign exchange and a worrying fall in currency reserves prompted a concentration on bilateral trade deals, especially with countries in south-eastern Europe that provided raw materials on credit set against delivery (invariably belated) of finished goods from Germany. The strategy emerged pragmatically from Germany's economic weakness rather than from any preconceived calculation of establishing dominance over central and south-eastern Europe. It helped recovery in those parts of the continent. Over time, however, as the German economy strengthened, the economic dependency of such regions grew and they became increasingly sucked into Germany's orbit.

Economic recovery in Germany was not an end in itself, but was subordinated to a political programme directed at rapid rearmament and eventual expansion through military might. By 1936, government expenditure was not far short of double what it had been in the pre-Nazi years, and was on course to double again during the following two years. And the largest proportion of public expenditure – well over a third by 1936, almost a half by 1938 – now went on rearmament, which had become the central driver of the economy. At first, the army had been unable to spend all that Hitler wanted to give them. But from the beginning, the primacy of rearmament had been plain. From 1934, backed by vast sums of camouflaged funding that Schacht provided by 'creative accountancy' outside the state budget, the building of big and powerful armed forces swiftly gathered momentum. Spending on capital goods and raw materials greedily soaked up by the rapidly expanding armaments industries substantially outstripped the growth in consumer goods.

But an obvious problem loomed ominously by 1935. Paying for sufficient food imports as well as coping with the rapidly rising demands of rearmament was impossible at a time when foreign exchange was in short supply and currency reserves were dwindling. A poor harvest in 1934 and the inefficiency of the over-bureaucratized Reich Food Estate (established in 1933 to energize agricultural production and boost the standing of farmers) led to serious food shortages by the autumn of 1935. Growing unrest caused such worry for the regime that Hitler felt compelled to intervene to ensure that foreign exchange was allocated for food imports instead of the raw materials for which armaments firms were desperately clamouring.

By early 1936 an economic impasse had been reached, an inexorable consequence of Germany's way out of the Depression under the Nazi regime. Removing the impasse could be achieved in one of two ways: either Germany scaled back rearmament and took steps towards re-entering the international economy; or it pressed on with rapid remilitarization, which meant a drive for autarchy that could only be partially accomplished without territorial expansion. And territorial expansion would be impossible without war at some point. In 1936 Hitler had to decide. It was obvious which way his choice would fall. Implicit from the outset of the Nazi regime, the shift confirmed it: the primacy of economics gave way to a primacy of ideology. From 1936 onwards the clock towards a new European war was ticking.

POLITICS LURCHES TO THE RIGHT

During the Depression years the politics of Europe moved sharply to the right. Remarkably, while capitalism was undergoing what many contemporaries thought was its terminal crisis, in a period of mass unemployment and widespread social misery the Left lost ground practically everywhere. Even in Spain, where the Socialists had been the driving-force in establishing the Second Republic in April 1931, Socialism was from 1933 onwards increasingly on the defensive, while the socialist-led Popular Front government in France, which gained power in 1936, proved to be of short duration. The success of social democracy in Scandinavia was the exception. Elsewhere, the Right was on the march – often quite literally. Why was this the case? What determined whether democracy survived or collapsed? How extensive was fascism's appeal? Why did Europe overwhelmingly shift to the political Right, not the Left? And to what extent was the economic crisis itself responsible for this ominous development? Sometimes the move to the Right strengthened conservatism, whether in the relatively benign form to be found in West European democracies, or in the reactionary authoritarian regimes dominated by anti-democratic political elites in eastern and south-eastern Europe. But the Depression also provided conditions in which populist movements of the radical Right were able to garner support and in some instances further destabilize already fragile systems of rule.

The Allure of Fascism

Some of the movements of the extreme, radical Right explicitly copied the methods, symbols and language used by the followers of Mussolini and Hitler, and proudly called themselves 'fascist' or 'national socialist'. Others shared some, even most, of the ideas of the openly fascist movements while rejecting the label for themselves. The issue is largely one of definition – and trying to define 'fascism' is like trying to nail jelly to the wall. Each of the myriad movements of the extreme Right had its distinctive features and emphasis. And since each of them claimed to represent in 'true', 'real' or 'essential' form a specific nation and based much of their hyper-nationalist appeal on the presumed uniqueness of that nation, there could be no genuine international organization representing the radical Right, equivalent to the Comintern on the Left. When an attempt was made, at a meeting of representatives of the extreme Right from thirteen countries (Austria, Belgium, Denmark, France, Greece, Ireland, Lithuania, the Netherlands, Norway, Portugal, Romania, Spain and Switzerland) in December 1934 on the shores of Lake Geneva, to establish a framework for collaborative action, the most important country, Nazi Germany, boycotted the gathering – which found itself unable to agree even on the basis of a common doctrine.

Some common ideological features of the extreme Right, whether or not a movement called itself 'fascist', nonetheless existed: hypernationalist emphasis on the unity of an integral nation, which gained its very identity through the 'cleansing' of all those deemed not to belong – foreigners, ethnic minorities, 'undesirables'; racial exclusiveness (though not necessarily biological racism like Nazism's variety) expressed through insistence on the 'special', 'unique' and 'superior' quality of the nation; radical, extreme and violent commitment to the utter destruction of political enemies – Marxists quite especially, but also liberals, democrats and 'reactionaries'; stress upon discipline, 'manliness' and militarism (usually involving paramilitary organizations); and belief in authoritarian leadership. Other features were important, indeed sometimes central, to the ideology of a specific movement, but not omnipresent. Some movements directed their nationalism towards irredentist or imperialist goals, with devastating effect, but not all were intrinsically expansionist. Some, though not all, had a strong anti-capitalist tendency. Often, though not invariably, they favoured reorganizing the economy along 'corporatist' lines, abolishing independent trade unions and regulating economic policy by 'corporations' of interests directed by the state.

This amalgam of ideas, with varying emphasis, was generally consonant with the aim of establishing mass support for an authoritarian regime of an essentially reactionary, non-revolutionary kind. Some of the radical Right movements, those that were avowedly fascist, went further. They wanted more than just to overthrow or dismantle the existing state and replace it with a nationalist, authoritarian government. They sought total commitment to the collective will of a united nation. They demanded soul as well as body. They looked to create a 'new man' (the language was invariably macho), a new society, a national utopia. This total claim, more than anything else, was ultimately what made fascism revolutionary and distinguished it from related parts of the Right that were authoritarian and nationalist but looked essentially to conserve the existing social order. Fascism sought a revolution not in terms of social class, as Marxists advocated, but a revolution nonetheless – a revolution of mentalities, values and will.

Scholarly exactitude of terminology was a matter of supreme indifference to those who suffered at the hands of the extreme Right, and to those on the Left who mobilized resolute opposition to movements that they themselves had no hesitation in dubbing 'fascist'. And, indeed, the finer points of definitional clarity should not obscure the broader issue of the shift to the Right – in one or other of its manifestations – during the Depression era.

Whether the shift was to the conservative or to the radical Right, it was advertised as essential to protect and regenerate the nation. As class conflict intensified – now no longer primarily economic but overtly political and ideological in nature – national unity was advanced as the essential bulwark to the threat of socialism. Where that threat was perceived as low, mild or seen to be distant, as in Britain, conservatism – wedded to upholding the existing political and social order – prevailed and the space for the breakthrough of the radical Right barely existed. At the opposite pole, as in Germany, where the threat was seen as high, conservatism – itself looking to overthrow the existing political and social order – splintered and its constituency was largely swallowed up by the fascist Right. Other countries fell somewhere between these polar opposites.

The allure of fascism was never greater than at this time. Fascism's message of national renewal, powerfully linking fear and hope, was diverse enough to be capable of crossing social boundaries. Its message enveloped an appeal to the material vested interests of quite disparate social groups in a miasma of emotive rhetoric about the future of the nation. It touched the interests of those who felt threatened by the forces of modernizing social change. It mobilized those who believed they had something to lose – status, property, power, cultural tradition – through the presumed menace of internal enemies, and especially through the advance of socialism and its revolutionary promise of social revolution. However, it bound up these interests in a vision of a new society that would reward the strong, the fit, the meritorious – the deserving (in their own eyes).

Given an appeal that self-consciously attempted to transcend the conventional sectoral boundaries of interest politics (which intensified as crisis conditions increased political fragmentation), it is not surprising that the social base of fascist movements was quite heterogeneous. Some sectors of society were, it is true, more prone than others to succumb to the allure of fascism. The emotional, romanticized, idealistic side of fascism, its violent, adventurous activism, held disproportionate appeal for young males who had been exposed to such values in middle-class youth movements – if they were not already bound up in left-wing or Catholic youth organizations. Anti-establishment 'generational revolt' could easily be channelled into fascist hyper-nationalism and paramilitary racist and anti-Left violence. The membership of fascist parties was predominantly male, though in Germany, where it can be measured, women came increasingly to vote for the Nazi Party as it approached the threshold of power, and probably for the same reasons that men supported it.

The disaffected middle classes were generally drawn to fascism out of proportion to their numbers in society. White-collar workers, businessmen, those in the professions, former officers or NCOs, state employees, shopkeepers, craftsmen, owners of small workshops, farmers and students (usually from middle-class backgrounds) were normally overrepresented in fascism's base support. But, though middle-class recruits tended to dominate among party functionaries and in leadership positions, fascism cannot be defined (as used to be the case) as simply a middle-class movement, or, indeed, in unequivocal class terms at all. Workers, skilled and unskilled, supported fascism in far greater numbers than once thought. Around 40 per cent of new recruits to the Nazi Party between 1925 and 1932 came from the working class. More than a quarter of Nazi voters were workers – possibly as high as 30–40 per cent if working-class households as a whole are taken into consideration – and more workers probably voted Nazi than either Socialist or Communist by 1932. Among the paramilitary stormtroopers, a macho street-fighter organization, young working-class males were the majority, forming well over half of the membership between 1925 and 1932, and an even higher proportion once the Nazi Party had come to power.

Not many of these workers had been won over from the Socialist or Communist parties. Some had indeed switched allegiance, but the vast majority had not previously belonged to the institutionalized working-class milieux of the parties of the Left. The Nazi Party, not least in its huge size (even by the beginning of 1933 it was well over three times as big as the Fascist Party had been in Italy before Mussolini's 'March on Rome' eleven years earlier), was in many respects atypical of the radical Right as a whole. But the structure of support in smaller fascist movements – with a middle-class core, but a sizeable component of workers not previously attached to the parties of the Left – was often broadly similar. This was the case, for example, in France, Spain, Austria, Switzerland and Britain (as well as Italy before Mussolini's 'seizure of power').

There was no direct correlation between the Depression and the chances of success of the radical Right. The Depression crisis had, it is true, led to Hitler's triumph. But Mussolini had come to power in Italy almost a decade before the slump, while in some countries fascism only emerged when the Depression was subsiding. Furthermore, other countries (notably Britain and, outside Europe, the USA), although suffering severely from the Depression, still did not produce any significant fascist movement. Only where the social and political tensions created by the Depression interacted with other prevailing factors – resentment about lost national territory, paranoid fear of the Left, visceral dislike of Jews and other 'outsider' groups, and lack of faith in the ability of fragmented party politics to begin to 'put things right' – did a systemic collapse occur, paving the way for fascism..

Italy and Germany turned out to be, in fact, the only countries where home-grown fascist movements became so strong that – helped into office by weak conservative elites – they could reshape the state in their image. More commonly (as in eastern Europe), fascist movements were kept in check by repressive authoritarian regimes, or (as in north-western Europe) offered a violent disturbance to public order without the capacity to threaten the authority of the state.

Fascism's triumph depended upon the complete discrediting of state authority, weak political elites who could no longer ensure that a system would operate in their interests, the fragmentation of party politics, and the freedom to build a movement that promised a radical alternative. These preconditions were present in post-war Italy between 1919 and 1922 and in Depression-ridden Germany between 1930 and 1933. They hardly existed anywhere else, other than Spain, where the increasingly violent confrontation of Left and Right (each factionalized) led eventually to civil war in 1936–9 followed by military dictatorship, not to a fascist 'seizure of power'. Where, in contrast, a democratic state retained the broad allegiance both of the dominant elites and the mass of the population, as was the case in north-western Europe, or where authoritarian elites could rigorously control a state system that operated in their interests, curtailing civil liberties and organizational freedom, as in much of eastern and southern Europe, fascist movements were not strong enough to gain power.

The Right in Western Europe: Resilient Democracy

Britain provides the clearest example of a state whose political system left no space for the radical Right to break through. The dominant social and political values – resting on the monarchy, the nation, the empire, parliamentary government and the rule of law – were widely accepted. The state system of constitutional monarchy based on parliamentary democracy was as good as unchallenged as the slide into Depression took hold. No major Marxist party existed to pose a threat, real or imagined, to the political order. The Labour Party (which during the 1920s had replaced the Liberal Party as the main opposition to the Conservatives) was reformist, not revolutionary, as were the trade unions that formed its backbone. The Conservative Party, unlike conservatives in some other European countries, had a vested interest in upholding the existing order. When the banking crisis led to the fall of the Labour government in 1931, the subsequent general election, on 27 October, saw the Conservatives triumph in the biggest landslide in British parliamentary history. The National Government won 521 seats with over 60 per cent of the vote. As many as 470 of these seats were won by the Conservatives. Despite the unifying sound of the name, the 'National Government' was in practice a Conservative administration. In the depth of economic crisis the British parliamentary system had, then, not simply held firm but had if anything solidified. There was no crisis of the state. No danger came from the Left. Labour was in opposition, but state-supportive. The political extremes were marginalized. Throughout the Depression there was not a single communist or fascist in Parliament.

The strength of conservatism blocked any opening to the extreme Right. Oswald Mosley's British Union of Fascists (BUF), founded in 1932, never had a chance of breaking through. At its height the BUF had around 50,000 members, a motley clientele of disgruntled middle-class professionals, ex-army types, small-businessmen, shop-keepers, clerks and unskilled workers from some of Britain's depressed areas and London's poor East End (a traditional immigrant area that housed a third of Britain's Jewish population). The style of the BUF always resembled a crude import. The fascist black-shirted uniforms and marches, the political style and imagery, not least the sickening public violence against Jews and political opponents, did not fit well with British political culture. Clashes with the anti-fascist Left caused increasing disturbances of public order. Support – including that of Lord Rothermere, the owner of the widely read newspaper, *The Daily Mail* – collapsed after a big rally in London in June 1934 had been accompanied by nauseating thuggery against Mosley's opponents, hundreds of whom had infiltrated the crowd of around 15,000. Mosley was so certain of his party's electoral humiliation that the BUF did not even contest the 1935 general election. By October 1935, membership had plummeted to a mere 5,000, and only slowly recovered to around 22,500 by the eve of the Second World War. At the outbreak of the conflict Mosley and other BUF leaders were interned, and the party was dissolved. The British Union of Fascists was a menace to those it deemed to be its racial or political enemies, and a sizeable public-order nuisance. But its impact on mainstream British politics was minimal.

Elsewhere, too, in north-western Europe, whose countries had been either victorious or neutral in the First World War and where feelings of national humiliation or irredentist ambitions scarcely existed, the radical Right found the route to power blocked by the resilience of the existing political structures. Fascist movements gained derisory popular backing in Denmark, Iceland, Sweden and Norway. There was more support in Finland, but 8.3 per cent of the vote in 1936 marked the fascist high tide of electoral success. In some of the German-speaking Swiss cantons, the fascist National Front gained up to 27 per cent of the vote between 1933 and 1936, though it fell sharply thereafter, while elsewhere in Switzerland fascism found only minuscule levels of support and encountered great opposition.

The Irish Blueshirts – officially, the Army Comrades Association, renamed in 1933 the National Guard – were a short-lived affair. They were formed in 1932 and, following his dismissal as Irish Police Commissioner, came under the leadership of Eoin O'Duffy, a former IRA Chief of Staff, temperamentally erratic and politically extreme. By 1934 they had claimed a membership of around 50,000, mainly from the economically hard-hit south-west. But support rapidly disintegrated following a government ban and the end of a trade dispute with Britain that had badly affected Irish agriculture. The Blueshirts abandoned their fascist radicalism and identity, and merged into the new mainstream political party, Fine Gael. By 1935 they had ceased to exist. O'Duffy had meanwhile resigned from Fine Gael – the party had become increasingly embarrassed by his presence – and subsequently led an Irish Brigade to fight briefly for General Franco in the Spanish Civil War.

In the Netherlands, despite unemployment as high as 35 per cent in 1936, the radical Right could make few inroads into political structures that remained heavily wedded to the Protestant, Catholic and

Social Democrat subcultures. Governments came and went, but there was actually much continuity in personnel, and a good deal of pragmatic adjustment and compromise among the governing parties. The growing fear of Nazi Germany also contributed to a sense of national unity that aided the cohesion of the existing parliamentary system. Fascism was both 'foreign' and viewed as a national danger. The high point of the main fascist movement, the *Nationaal Socialistische Beweging*, was reached in 1935, when it won just short of 8 per cent of the vote. Within two years, however, this had fallen to only 4 per cent and support for the extreme Right remained low in the remaining pre-war years.

Belgium saw a brief flurry of support for a Catholic, authoritarian, corporatist movement that bordered, at the least, on fascism. In 1936 the Rex Party (taking its name from a Catholic publishing house, Christus Rex, which derived its own name from the recently established Feast of Christ the King) won 11.5 per cent of the vote – largely a protest by the French-speaking middle classes in the industrialized parts of south-eastern Belgium against perceived corruption in the establishment parties. This vote soon shrivelled, however, to leave no more than a small rump of support. As in the Netherlands, the strength of existing social and political milieux – Catholic, socialist and liberal – closed off the political space that new movements of the extreme Right might have occupied. A hindrance in Belgium, too, was the absence of a genuine *Belgian* nationalism; Rex had relatively low levels of support in Flanders, where separate nationalist and proto-fascist movements existed (though without mainstream support).

France's Third Republic seemed for a time more seriously menaced by the far Right. The French political system produced not just frequent changes of government (often amounting to little more than musical chairs with the same personnel around the cabinet table), but also shifting pragmatic alliances of parties. These more often than not involved the Radicals, who formed the core party of the Republic. The Radicals were anti-clerical, attached to liberal economic principles, drawing heavily on middle-class support, and ready to do a deal with either the moderate Right or Left in order to stay in power (which they generally did). The 1932 elections, as the Depression was just setting in, brought sizeable gains for the Socialist Party and for the Radicals, who formed an uneasy alliance of the moderate Left. The defeat of the right-wing bloc of conservative parties triggered an exaggerated reaction on the Right in a climate of increased xenophobia, shrill nationalism, antisemitism, anti-feminism and fears of a 'red threat' (though the Communists had managed to win only 12 seats out of 605 in the Chamber of Deputies). The febrile atmosphere was heightened by the drama of events across the Rhine. The extra-parliamentary paramilitary Leagues on the nationalist Right, incorporating large veterans' associations, some of them with at least partly fascist traits, gained a new breath of life after their support had sagged during the financial stabilization under Poincaré's government.

Amid mounting tension, the overwhelmingly right-wing Parisian press lost no opportunity to berate the government with unconstrained venom. The French political scene was notoriously venal and corrupt, but a scandal exposed at the end of 1933 was seized upon by the press with particular relish and contained ingredients that could be cooked up to pose a threat not just to the government, but to the republic itself. This corruption scandal arose from a public-finance swindle perpetrated by Alexandre Stavisky, an unsavoury character, and an embezzler who happened to be of eastern European Jewish origin – an ideal fit for right-wing prejudice. The scandal involved figures in high places, mostly in the Radical Party; some rumours suggested that no fewer than 132 politicians were on Stavisky's payroll. When the swindler was said to have committed suicide, the rumour-mill went into overdrive. Jews and freemasons were said to have been implicated in a cover-up to silence Stavisky, whose death sparked off growing disorder on the streets of Paris. On 6 February 1934 large bands of supporters of the nationalist and racist extra-parliamentary Leagues – some estimates suggest as many as 30,000 – marched on the French capital. The culmination was a night of violence, involving clashes between the police and thousands of demonstrators that ended with 15 dead and over 1,400 injured.

The scale of the organized violence – the worst experienced in Paris since the Commune of 1871 – was a major shock to the French political establishment. The government (which had only been in existence a few days) was brought down – in effect by street violence and paramilitary force. The resulting political turbulence heightened the

Left-Right confrontation that characterized French politics for the remainder of the 1930s. But any threat of substance to the existence of the state proved a mirage. The existence of the French Republic was not seriously endangered – though that was not how it seemed at the time. The Leagues, though they shared extreme nationalism, fierce anti-communism and authoritarianism (often favouring a form of corporatist state) as ideologies, were divided among themselves in terms of leadership and their aims. The largest of the Leagues, the Croix de Feu (Cross of Fire), with perhaps 40,000 members by early 1934, generally maintained discipline during the February riots, compared with the violence from members of Action Française and other right-wing organizations – something that gained the Croix de Feu plaudits from the conservative press. Its leader, Colonel François de la Roque, later distanced himself from the antisemitism of some of his followers.

Moreover, a direct result of the events of 6 February 1934 had been to unify the divided French Left in the struggle against fascism. Had that not been the case, the threat to the republic could have been much more serious. As it was, the Left responded rapidly and with counter-force. The Communists had mobilized their supporters already by 9 February. Clashes with the paramilitary Right left nine dead and hundreds injured. Three days later over a million trade unionists brought Paris to a standstill in a day-long general strike. During the next two years there were over a thousand demonstrations of one kind or another, mainly by the Left against the threat of fascism. At precisely the point that Hitler's triumph in Germany had finally persuaded Stalin, in 1934, to abandon the absurdity of the Comintern's 'social fascist' attacks on social democratic parties and call for a common front of the working class against fascism, the violent confrontation concentrated minds in France and paved the way for the government of the Popular Front, formed in 1936. After the events of February 1934, a divided Right was met for the first time by a united Left.

The Leagues, banned in June 1936 by the Popular Front government, in some cases reformed themselves as parliamentary parties. The Croix de Feu metamorphosed into the Parti Social Français, and greatly extended its support. By 1937, it had around three-quarters of a million members, more than the Socialists and Communists combined. In the process, however, it moved further away from fascist-style mobilization towards conservative authoritarianism. A genuine fascist party, the Parti Populaire Français, did emerge in June 1936, led by a renegade communist, Jacques Doriot. The growing menace of Nazi Germany, the collapse of the Popular Front government in 1938 and, with it, any internal threat from the Left, and the increased emphasis on national solidarity as war loomed, all undermined Doriot's party, which by then was in steep decline. Even so, in its myriad forms – some outrightly fascist, others verging on fascism – the French Right had established an extensive base of popular support. The ready backing for the Vichy regime after 1940 would have been unimaginable without it.

For all its travails, republicanism in France had an extensive base of long-established popular support. The situation in Spain was quite different, and the forces antagonistic to a democratic republic were far more powerful. Initially, however, the prospects for the authoritarian Right appeared to have diminished, rather than increased, as growing economic problems beset a country whose deep-seated social and political fissures meant that it was never far from crisis.

Primo de Rivera's military dictatorship, which had lasted since 1923, had run out of whatever steam it ever had by early 1930. Amid growing discontent and fading authority, as the economic boom that had underpinned his early success ended, Primo was forced to resign, left the country for exile in Paris, and died soon afterwards. Within months, he was followed into exile by King Alfonso XIII, and elections in April 1931 ushered in a new democratic republic. At a juncture when democracy in much of Europe was moving to the Right, Spain went in the opposite direction – at least for the time being. The overwhelming victory of the Left in the 1931 elections was, however, deceptive. Although many Spaniards, disenchanted with Primo and the monarchy, were prepared to give the republic a chance, their support was often lukewarm, tentative and conditional. The republic lacked a genuine mass base of reliable support outside the industrial working class – a relatively small sector of the population, and concentrated in a number of big cities and specific regions, notably in Catalonia, the Basque Country and Asturias. And there were serious divisions within the republican parties. The Left was itself irredeemably split between the socialists, the mainstay of the republic, and the anarcho-syndicalists (with significant strength in the countryside, especially in southern Spain), who saw the republic as no more than the first stage of a continuous violent struggle, led by the trade unions, against state authority. The strong regional identities and antagonism towards Madrid in Catalonia and the Basque Country, especially, also hindered the creation of a united Left. The Right, meanwhile, was defeated, disorganized and in disarray after the 1931 elections. But the parliamentary defeat belied the underlying strength and resilience of the deeply conservative, anti-republican forces. The establishment of the republic reignited, in fact, the ideological fires that had only temporarily and partially died down under Primo's dictatorship.

The new democracy was a violently contested system from the start. Within two years, legislation for agrarian reform, protection of workers, and a significant reduction in the powers of the Catholic Church from a coalition government of socialists and liberals prompted an increasingly shrill reaction from a broad, though fragmented, militantly anti-socialist and stridently Catholic authoritarian Right. Landlords, employers, the Catholic Church and the military were implacable in their opposition to the republic, while the slow, partial and limited progress of social reform frustrated and alienated many of the republic's own followers. In new elections in November 1933, the Left suffered a heavy defeat, the parties of the Right triumphed, and in the following two years the reforms of the early republic were reversed or blocked as power shifted back to landlords and employers. The embryo of civil war was forming.

The Spanish Right was far from united in its aims. Some sectors were outrightly reactionary – seeking a restored monarchy and an authoritarian, corporate state, backed by the military. A much bigger part of the Right – in fact the biggest party in Spain, claiming 735,000 members – came together in 1933 to form the CEDA (*Confederación Española de Derechas Autónomas*, or Spanish Confederation of Autonomous Right-Wing Groups), a huge conglomerate of populist Catholic conservatism. The CEDA claimed to be defending Christianity from Marxism, addressed the head of the party, Gil Robles, as 'Leader', and adopted other outward forms of fascism such as rallies, uniforms, a type of Fascist salute, style of mobilization, and organization of an increasingly fascistic youth movement. It differed from radical fascism in rejecting paramilitarism and adhering at least formally to existing state institutions and to legal and non-violent parliamentary methods. In practice, however, the CEDA increasingly backed anti-republican violence and leant towards the adoption of a corporatist, authoritarian state. Its democratic credentials were at best ambivalent. 'When the time comes, either parliament submits or we will eliminate it,' Robles declared.

Amid this large, but fragmented, body of support for the authoritarian Right, much of it conservative authoritarianism with fascist overtones, genuinely radical fascism had little of a following. The most important fascist movement, the *Falange Española* (Spanish Phalanx), established in 1933 by José Antonio Primo de Rivera, son of the former dictator, attacked the bourgeois Right as well as the Marxist Left. Predictably, José Antonio made little headway. The Falange gained a membership of no more than 10,000 in a country of 25 million, and won only 44,000 votes (0.7 per cent of votes cast) in the 1936 Spanish election. In that year the Falange was banned and its leaders were jailed. José Antonio himself was sentenced to death and executed in November. By then, the rebellion against the Spanish Republic, launched in Morocco under the leadership of General Francisco Franco, had begun. Only when Franco took over the Falange in April 1937 and made it, at least nominally, the cornerstone of the conglomerate of right-wing nationalist forces that supported his rebellion, did fascism in Spain become a mass movement – eventually, after the civil war, as the state party of a military dictatorship that it served but did not control.

Before the civil war, the Falange was competing in very crowded territory. Moreover, its social revolutionary message was guaranteed to alienate much of the middle class as well as the Catholic establishment. In the conditions of pluralist democracy before the civil war, attempts to build a fully fascist mass movement in Spain were a failure. Did it matter? In the eyes of their bitter opponents on the varied sections of the Left, there was little to distinguish the small Falange party from the mass of rightist support. Whatever the niceties of definitional distinctions, the CEDA seemed to them as fascist as the

Falange. Were they mistaken? From the perspective of those who suffered appallingly at the hands of the Right before, during and after the
civil war, fascism in Spain had huge support, and was not confined to
the small numbers who supported the Falange.

Whereas in Italy and Germany, political space opened up as the
established parties of the conservative and liberal Right collapsed,
leaving big populist fascist mass parties to fill the vacuum and unite a
new Right around a programme of national renewal that destroyed
the threat from the Left, no such vacuum existed in Spain. There, the
political space was filled by a number of conservative-authoritarian
movements of differing strength, some of them with distinctly fascist
overtones, most notably the CEDA. The anti-democratic Spanish
Right was very large, but the very strength of conservative reaction
blocked the chances for radical fascism. By the time of Franco's uprising in July 1936, the crisis of Spanish democracy had deepened. But
the Spanish Left was ready to fight. It took a bitter three-year civil war
to bring democracy down.

Fertile Ground for the Right: Central and Eastern Europe

Spain was an exceptional case in western Europe. In central and eastern Europe, the lurch towards the extreme Right was commonplace.
The biggest fascist movements arose in Austria, Romania and Hungary. In the case of Austria, Hitler's rise to power next door in
Germany was a special determining feature. In Romania and Hungary, the lasting disturbance from the post-war territorial settlement
in Europe was a major precondition.

Much of the non-socialist allegiance in Austria was already
proto-fascist by the time of the Depression. The banking collapse of
1931 and soaring unemployment gravely damaged the country's
economy and the living conditions of much of the population. Under
the impact of the Depression, the three-way split in Austrian politics
deepened and became further radicalized. Two large fascist movements, the home-grown *Heimwehr* (Home Defence) and the rapidly
growing Austrian Nazi Party, inspired by events across the German
border, both faced a big Socialist Party that retained its solid support

in the industrial working class. In 1930 the *Heimwehr* still had double the support of the Austrian Nazi Party, seen by many as a foreign import. But the Nazis were fast gaining ground. In regional and local elections in Austria in 1932 the Nazis were able to win over 16 per cent of the vote.

Once Hitler took power in Germany in January 1933, the Nazi threat in Austria was obvious. In response, the Austrian Chancellor, the tiny but energetic thirty-nine-year-old Engelbert Dollfuss, abolished parliamentary rule and established what he called a 'social, Christian, German state of "Austria" based on [corporate] estates and strong authoritarian leadership'. His regime, backed by most of the non-socialist parties, the *Heimwehr* and the Catholic establishment, restricted freedom and suppressed opposition. In February 1934 it bloodily crushed an armed socialist uprising that it had provoked, and it outlawed socialism. The forces of the Left had proved no match for those of the Right, even though, unlike the situation in Germany and numerous other countries, the Austrian Left had not been split into rival social democratic and communist parties. A new constitution abolished parliament in favour of a corporate state, based on top-down selection of an elaborate arrangement of 'corporations' and advisory councils backed by a single political organization, the state-supportive Fatherland Front. Real power in the authoritarian state rested in the hands of the Chancellor. Dollfuss himself was assassinated by Nazis in July 1934. But the authoritarian regime – more repressive conservative-reactionary than fascist, or at any rate embracing a relatively mild form of partial fascism compared with what was to come – lasted under his successor, Kurt von Schuschnigg, despite mounting Nazi pressure. Von Schuschnigg attempted to reassert Austrian independence in a plebiscite to be held on 13 March 1938. But he was thwarted by the German invasion and annexation of Austria (the *Anschluss*) on 12–13 March.

Since Romania had done so well out of the war, more than doubling its territory (especially at Hungary's expense, though with gains, too, from Russia, Bulgaria and Austria), it is not at first sight obvious why fascism should have proved attractive there. The backdrop was a lengthy and crippling agricultural depression that saw peasant income fall by little short of 60 per cent. As economic difficulties on the land worsened, resentment deepened towards ethnic minorities – Magyars, Germans, but above all Jews – who were dominant in industry, commerce and finance. With the expansion of territory, non-Romanians made up around 30 per cent of the total population. And Romania, where Jews had been deprived of citizenship rights until 1918, had long been one of the most antisemitic parts of Europe. It was not hard, in the prevailing conditions, to link economic hardship to prejudice and hatred against minorities, nor to construct nationalist imagery in which the 'true' Romanian people could be portrayed as threatened by foreigners.

The ultra-violent (even by fascist standards) and ultra-antisemitic Romanian fascist movement, the 'Legion of the Archangel Michael' – otherwise called the 'Iron Guard' – under the leadership of the charismatic Corneliu Zelea Codreanu, a former law student, grew to attract 272,000 members by 1937 and won 15.8 per cent of the vote in that year's election, making it Romania's third largest party. Codreanu garnered support through a heady brew of extreme and romanticized ethnic-racist nationalism. This was fermented by a doctrine of cleansing violence aimed at the purification of the nation from all alien elements (especially Jews, who were associated both with a perceived threat to Romania's borders from Bolshevik Russia and with rapacious capitalism). Stirred into the brew was the evocation of 'true' Romanian moral values rooted in Christian purity and the peasant soil – the 'spiritual revolution' of 'National Christian Socialism' that would produce 'the new man'. Teachers, civil servants, lawyers, Orthodox clergy, ex-officers, journalists, students, intellectuals, and of course peasants constituted the backbone of the party's support. Peasants were not won over purely by irrational 'back-to-the-soil' romanticization of the countryside, but by the way this emotional appeal was linked to their economic resentments, deepened in the protracted agrarian Depression, and by the promise of land to be gained through confiscating Jewish wealth.

Despite fascism's growing appeal in Romania during the 1930s, it remained an opposition movement, incapable of grasping power in the state. The success of Codreanu's movement in the 1937 elections in Romania alarmed the monarch and ruling class. Backed by the army, the bureaucracy and much of the establishment National Liberal Party, and able to exploit divisions among the other parties, King Carol dissolved parliament in early 1938 and established a royal dictatorship. The Legion of the Archangel Michael was banned, while Codreanu was arrested and then murdered in prison. Much of what fascism offered – including its extreme antisemitism – was incorporated in the monarchist regime. It was a pyrrhic victory. Fascist organization was forced underground and, despite the execution of hundreds of followers, re-emerged in the Second World War to participate in government for a short time, though in very different circumstances.

In Hungary, where serious irredentist grievances after losing so much territory in the post-war settlement remained a festering sore, the Depression, which saw a slump in agricultural production and a third of the industrial workforce unemployed, greatly exacerbated social and political tensions. However, particularly during the premiership from 1932 to 1936 of Gyula Gömbös, whose own extreme rightist leanings divided and for a time disarmed the small fascist forces, the ruling elites, having regathered their strength in the conservative restoration of the 1920s, were able to manipulate their domination of a controlled parliament and adapt to crisis management so that no major fascist party emerged before 1937. The weakness of the socialist Left, which had never recovered after being crushed following the collapse of Béla Kun's regime in 1919, and the subsequent years of limited mass participation in the facade-democracy of Miklós Horthy's authoritarian regime, played their part in denting the chances of fascist mobilization. Only from 1937 onwards, influenced by events in Germany and by the rapidly changing constellation of international politics, did a big fascist movement emerge. The Hungarian National Socialist Party – an amalgam of eight extreme nationalist groups – arose from the Party of the National Will that had been founded by a former staff officer, Ferenz Szálasi, in 1935, and eventually in 1939 it became the Arrow Cross. The party began to recruit strongly among public-sector professionals, army officers, and also workers in Budapest industrial districts, gaining as many as 250,000 members by 1939–40. The Arrow Cross's brief moment of triumph – though a time of horror for its victims – would come only late in the war, with Hungary under German domination and defeat looming.

Elsewhere in eastern and in south-eastern Europe, the control of the state by reactionary-conservative authoritarian elites, not least the military, who saw populist mobilization as a threat to their power, was the biggest obstacle to the breakthrough of fascist movements. Sometimes, indeed, the latter were suppressed, though their aims and ideas were usually stolen by the prevailing strongly nationalistic, often viciously racist authoritarian regimes. As governments turned to authoritarianism (such as Estonia and Latvia in 1934, Bulgaria in 1934 and Greece in 1936), or in places where the hold of existing state-supportive elites strengthened existing authoritarian regimes, the space for fascism to organize and mobilize, and even the need for a fascist movement to do so, was severely limited.

By the eve of the Second World War, democracy was confined to eleven north-western countries (Britain, Ireland, France, Switzerland, Belgium, the Netherlands, Denmark, Norway, Sweden, Finland and tiny Iceland). All had been either victorious or neutral during the First World War. About three-fifths of Europeans (leaving aside for now the people of the Soviet Union) lived in sixteen states under some form of repressive, authoritarian rule where civil rights were strongly curtailed and minorities faced discrimination and persecution: Italy, Germany (now incorporating Austria), Spain, Portugal, Hungary, Slovakia, the former Czech lands (now the Protectorate of Bohemia and Moravia, under German rule), Romania, Bulgaria, Albania, Greece, Yugoslavia, Poland, Lithuania, Latvia and Estonia. Of the democracies created after the First World War to succeed the Austro-Hungarian Empire, only Czechoslovakia had survived – until it was destroyed by German invasion in March 1939. The failure of democracy in the successor states to the Austro-Hungarian Empire was the clearest indicator of the bankruptcy of the post-war settlement.

The two countries, Italy and Germany, that produced fascist parties powerful enough to take power in the state and form dictatorial regimes, were exceptional, even among all of Europe's authoritarian regimes, not just in the character and comprehensive scale of their internal control, but in their expansionist aims. However, there was a major imbalance in the threat to Europe's peace. Italy sought to control the Mediterranean and belatedly attain a colonial empire in Africa. This threat could have been contained and in any case, in itself, is extremely unlikely to have caused a general European war. The larger, more dynamic, more brutal and more ideologically radical of the two regimes, Hitler's Germany, was a different matter. It looked to the heart of Europe for its expansion. That posed a threat to the whole continent. The precarious balance of power was mortally endangered by the menace of German hegemony. Europe's peace was from now on existing on borrowed time.

6

Danger Zone

'Experience teaches,' said Gletkin, 'that the masses must be given for all difficult and complicated processes a simple, easily grasped explanation. According to what I know of history, I see that mankind could never do without scapegoats.'
Arthur Koestler, Darkness at Noon *(1940)*

By the time the worst of the economic crisis was over, around 1934, Europe had changed – and in menacing fashion. The post-war settlement was collapsing. The three-way ideological conflict between fascism, bolshevism and liberal democracy was intensifying. The fascist regimes were asserting their strength, the democracies revealing their weakness. Dictators were gaining the upper hand, shaping the agenda. Out of the ruins of a global economic crisis, a global conflagration was looming.

THE INTERNATIONAL ORDER CRUMBLES

Europe's post-war international order had from the beginning been an extremely flimsy edifice resting on the shakiest of foundations. National self-interest, ethnic tensions and nationalist resentments fostered by the post-war settlement had always threatened to trigger its collapse. These were at their most acute in the eastern half of Europe. In the west, the 'spirit of Locarno' had for a few brief years in the late 1920s offered hope of stability and reconciliation. But the hope had evaporated completely in the climate of economic depression. The consolidation of fascism's conquest of the state in Italy, and most recently Hitler's takeover of power in Germany, presented the most unsettling challenge. Italy, after a decade of Fascist rule, was no longer the feeble, divided country that it had been before the Great War, and was already envisaging its own chances of acquiring an empire and dominating the Mediterranean and north Africa. The most disturbing new entity that emerged during the Depression, with enormous potential to upturn the international order, was, however, a revitalized, confident and strongly assertive German Reich under Nazi leadership.

These new forces would soon reshape a constellation of 'great powers' much changed since the war: the demise of the Austria-Hungarian Empire had given rise to a belt of unstable states in central and eastern Europe; the western democracies, Great Britain and France, had been significantly weakened; while the Soviet Union was still heavily preoccupied with its violent internal reconstruction. The international arena was becoming dominated almost entirely by the changing balance of relations between the big and powerful countries, while the smaller nations were increasingly drawn into their slip-stream. The national assertiveness of the fascist countries, Italy and, especially, Germany, was the new, dynamic factor that endangered the international order. The other powers, including a Soviet Union whose overriding priority was to strengthen its defences against what it viewed as the threat from western capitalist imperialist aggression, were largely compelled to react to forces that they did not fully comprehend. Given their mutual suspicions and competing interests, these powers were also too divided among themselves to contest such forces.

Offering a feeble parry to the powerful centrifugal elements in the European international order was the one major body that had been designed to transcend national interest, the League of Nations. Without American involvement, the effectiveness of the League had been impaired from the outset. During the 1920s the League had nevertheless played a part in providing aid for the tens of thousands of refugees streaming across eastern Europe. It had also been instrumental in staving off national bankruptcy in Austria and Hungary by providing big loans to help stabilize currencies wrecked by hyperinflation. The League continued, even during the Depression years and afterwards, to carry out work in diverse areas such as combating epidemic diseases, preventing human trafficking and improving conditions for world trade, all of which necessarily transcended national boundaries and, in varying ways, would feed into positive developments after the Second World War. But in its central aim, to uphold and, where necessary, enforce peace (though without presiding over any international military means to do so), the League would prove a complete failure. It was no match for the predatory, rapacious national assertiveness of Italy and Germany, and it proved unable to surmount the divisive and self-defeating policies of national self-interest of the western democracies.

The first disturbance to the international order actually emerged far away from Europe, with the Japanese occupation of Manchuria in September 1931. When China appealed for international support to condemn this outrage, the League belatedly set up a commission to explore the entire background to the conflict and make suggestions for a settlement. The commission took nearly a year to report, finally denouncing Japan's action though at the same time pressing China to acknowledge what the commission regarded as legitimate Japanese interests in Manchuria. However cautious, the judgement was in any case out of date by the time it was delivered. By 1932 a Japanese puppet state in Manchuria, renamed Manchukuo, had been established in the large, economically vital region. The League had no coercive power to force Japan to give up its conquered territory, and China was too weak and divided to attempt an armed reconquest. Japanese aggression was vilified in world opinion. But that was to no avail, other than to ensure that, alienated by international condemnation, Japan withdrew from the League of Nations in February 1933. The country's diplomatic isolation encouraged the rise of shrill nationalism there as Japan tilted sharply towards rule by a military oligarchy set on expansion. Manchuria had laid bare the feebleness of the League of Nations. This in turn advertised the weakness of Britain and France, the two dominant countries in the League. Upholding British naval strength in the Far East meant further pressure on Britain's already overstretched defence resources. It was an inducement to appeasement, both in the Far East and in Europe.

The League's central concern, to reduce the prospects of international conflict through a system of collective security based on an agreement to disarm, had by then proved an unmitigated failure. The great hopes and ideals evinced at the establishment of the League in January 1920 had led to few or no results in that decade. It was not that disarmament was unpopular with much of public opinion – where that could be freely registered. Ten years after the Armistice that had ended the First World War, a revival of interest in the catastrophe and the memories evoked of the horror of the conflict blended into gathering fears of the apocalyptic disaster that a new war would bring. Pacifist movements, if invariably embracing a small proportion of the population, gained increasing support in western European countries such as Britain, France and Denmark. Far more numerous were those who did not embrace pacificism but actively campaigned for peace and disarmament. Socialists, trade unionists, intellectuals, liberals and clergymen were prominent among them, and women were disproportionately represented. Anti-war feeling had been strong, too, in Germany in the late 1920s on the political Left. Erich Maria Remarque's anti-war novel, *Im Westen nichts Neues* (*All Quiet on the Western Front*), had become an immediate best-seller when it appeared in 1929, selling over a million copies in Germany.

The anti-war feeling on the German Left was confronted with undimmed militarism and glorification of war on the extremes of the Right. The appeal of Ernst Jünger's war-glorifying memoir *In Stahlgewittern* (*In Storms of Steel*) in Germany during the 1920s had already given a plain indication of how divided the German population was in its views of the First World War. It was not surprising, then, that the publication of *Im Westen nichts Neues* provoked outrage on the Right, especially among members of its emerging standard-bearer, the Nazi Party. When the American film of the novel was released in Germany in December 1930, it attracted such storms of protest from the Nazi-led Right, which saw it as an insult to German honour, that public showings were banned for 'endangering Germany's international standing' and 'disparagement of the German army'.

Only with the rise of the Nazis, however, did the militaristic view of the war – a glorious struggle in which victory was denied through the

'stab-in-the-back' by Marxist revolutionaries at home – come to triumph over anti-war feeling. The largest militaristic veterans'
organization, the *Stahlhelm* ('Steel Helmet'), which glorified the
front-line experience, had in the 1920s been far smaller than the
anti-war veterans' association of the Social Democrats, the *Reichs-
banner* ('Reich Flag'). As late as 1932, only a year before Hitler took
power, German socialists organized peace rallies attended by over
600,000 people. And even after Hitler had become German Chancellor, much of the German population, especially those who had lived
through the First World War, retained a pathological fear of another
war. Where Hitler pulled a masterstroke was in persuading them for
years that he was striving for peace, not war, that rearmament was the
best way to secure German defence, and that he wanted no more than
'equal rights' with the western powers in terms of military strength. If
these would not disarm, he argued, basic equity as well as the pride
and prestige of a great nation demanded that Germany should be
permitted to rebuild its armed forces, reduced to puny levels at the
1919 Treaty of Versailles, to similar levels. For many, not just in Nazi
ranks, it was a compelling argument.

This turned out to be the decisive issue that vitiated all attempts by
the Disarmament Conference, which first met in Geneva on 2 February 1932 (after years of preparation), to arrive at an international
settlement. There were, of course, many daunting technical problems
involved in attempting to regulate a global trade in arms, restrict arms
spending by national governments and persuade countries to put their
faith in security through disarmament. But a bigger obstacle by far
was that some major countries – Japan, Soviet Russia, Italy and Germany among them – simply lacked the will to disarm. This problem
was compounded by a further major difficulty that preoccupied
France and Great Britain especially: what was the permissible level of
armaments in Germany? Understandably, having been invaded twice
in living memory from over the Rhine, France's paramount national
interest was in security. No disarmament was acceptable that would
jeopardize this in the slightest. Britain on the other hand, the main
driving-force behind disarmament proposals, took the more idealistic
view that general disarmament would actually create security. The

French were unconvinced, and were not likely to change their stance given Britain's avoidance of a guarantee to put its own army in the field to aid France in the event of German attack.

The fundamental division between the two major western powers on disarmament policy played into Hitler's hands. It offered a prime opportunity for him to exploit what he could portray as a basic unfairness of principle behind the high-minded rhetoric of the Disarmament Conference: the western democracies were themselves unwilling either to reduce their own armament levels to those imposed upon Germany, or to permit Germany to rearm to the levels that they were demanding as a prerequisite for their own security. Unbending national interest (also on the part of the smaller countries), with each country rooted to guarantees of security that it was impossible to provide, wrecked any hope of a general agreement.

The Conference was already on the way to arguing itself into oblivion when Hitler, fully in line with the wishes of the German army leadership and Foreign Office, seized the moment to withdraw Germany both from the Conference and from the League itself on 14 October 1933. With his unerring eye for a propaganda coup, he did not miss the chance to follow up the withdrawal with a plebiscite that brought him an official 95 per cent vote of support for his move, greatly strengthening his standing among the German people. After the German withdrawal, disarmament was a dead letter, even though the Conference staggered on in an exhausted fashion until it was finally put out of its misery in June 1934. Hitler was triumphant. The League had suffered a major blow. The chances of disarmament were zero. Europe was bracing itself for a new arms race.

In March 1935 Hitler felt confident enough to announce the creation of a new and large Wehrmacht of thirty-six divisions (about 550,000 men), and the reintroduction of general military service. The existence of a German air force – already as large, Hitler claimed (with notable exaggeration), as Britain's – was also made public. Both steps were in plain defiance of the Versailles Treaty. The western democracies protested; but that was all. Hitler's move had nevertheless unnerved them. They stepped up sharply their own spending on rearmament.

Alarmed by German rearmament, the leaders of Britain, France and Italy, meeting in April 1935 in Stresa, northern Italy, had agreed to uphold the Treaty of Locarno of 1925. But no more than two months later, Britain undermined even this fig leaf of international solidarity by agreeing to a bilateral naval treaty proposed by Germany, limiting the relative size of their fleets. The British hoped that the Naval Agreement would be a step towards a wider regulation and curtailing of German rearmament. It was a vain hope. In fact, the Naval Agreement amounted to a further nail in the coffin of Versailles, this time with the direct connivance of one of the major powers behind the post-war settlement. Germany rejoiced. France, in particular, grimaced as Britain independently and unnecessarily gave Hitler a further boost to his prestige.

As Germany emerged newly strengthened from international isolation, and with the post-war European order visibly crumbling, countries scrambled for new alliances to try to bolster their security. Poland had been the first state (after the Vatican, which had signed a Concordat with Germany shortly after Hitler had come to power) to seek a new basis of understanding with the awakening giant in central Europe. Hitler had obliged with an agreement to conclude a ten-year non-aggression pact with Germany's eastern neighbour in January 1934. It served both German and Polish interests to stabilize relations between the two countries. Poland gained security to its west. Germany blocked off any potential trouble from the east at a time when, driven by Nazism's vehement anti-Bolshevism, its relations with the Soviet Union were deteriorating sharply.

The Soviet Union had been largely preoccupied with its own internal convulsions during the early 1930s. But once Hitler had assumed power in Germany, Soviet leaders, well aware of the new danger that potentially faced them, saw the need to collaborate with the western democracies in building a system of collective security in Europe. Diplomatic ties were established with the United Kingdom, France and the USA in 1933. In September 1934 the Soviet Union joined the League of Nations – earlier denounced as an 'imperialist conspiracy'. New alliances had to be forged. The following year, the Soviet Union signed a mutual assistance pact with France and a further pact with Czechoslovakia, already bound to France in a defence alliance. Far from deterring Hitler, the new pacts made him all the more determined to break any bonds of constraint.

In fact, events not in the centre of Europe but far to the south were to undermine the international order, fatally wounding the League of Nations and laying the path for closer ties between Italy and Germany. On 3 October 1935 Italy invaded Abyssinia (Ethiopia as it was later more commonly called). It was old-fashioned imperialism with modern methods. Mussolini was the decisive advocate of the war – aimed in no small measure at enhancing his own prestige. Victory would provide revenge for the humiliating defeat of Italian forces by the Abyssinians at Adowa in 1896. It would show the western powers that Italy was no longer the feeble country that in 1919, though on the victorious side in the war, had been deprived of what many Italians regarded as its 'rightful' share of African colonies. It would demonstrate, through military conquest, Italy's standing as a dynamic imperial power at a time when the colonial might of Britain and France seemed on the wane. Not least, Ethiopia would be a stepping stone on the way to the building of a latter-day Roman empire resting on Italy's dominance of the Mediterranean, the Adriatic and Dalmatia, Greece and the Aegean, north and east Africa.

The war was barbaric. Italian bombers made widespread use of poison gas to terrorize the population. But the Ethiopians held out for months against greatly superior forces. The war was effectively ended with the flight of the Ethiopian Emperor, Haile Selassie, and the entry of Italian troops into Addis Adabba in May 1936, though it was a further seven months before the Italians, at great cost, declared Ethiopia 'pacified'. The King of Italy was proclaimed emperor. Mussolini could glory in the eulogies of the Italian public. His popularity had never before reached such heights, and would never do so again. But for now his prestige at home was immense.

Internationally, the war in Ethiopia sounded the death knell of the League of Nations as an international vehicle to promote European peace and security. The League imposed economic sanctions on Italy. They were limited indeed. The export of foie gras to Italy was banned, for example, whereas export of iron, steel, coal and oil was not. When news leaked out of a proposed deal, by which the Foreign Ministers of Britain and France, Samuel Hoare and Pierre Laval, agreed to reward Mussolini's aggression by giving Italy around two-thirds of Ethiopia, the outcry, especially in Britain, was enormous. The two most important members of the League were agreeing to the carve-up of another member state that had been invaded by a further member state in an unprovoked act of war.

Relations between Britain and France were temporarily strained. But the damage to the standing of the League was far greater. The smaller nations of Europe saw the powerlessness of the League. They reconsidered their own commitment and looked to alternative routes to security. Switzerland confirmed its neutrality though in effect it looked to Italy as a counter-weight to the influence of France and Germany. Poland, Romania and Yugoslavia lost faith in France's reliability. Scandinavian countries, together with Spain, Switzerland and the Netherlands, no longer saw merit in committing themselves to a sanctions regime when the League's main players were seeking to reward aggression with territorial gains. Following Ethiopia, the League was reduced to idealistic irrelevance. As an instrument intended to uphold and secure the peace of Europe, it was dead – even if, bizarrely, its last publication under the heading of 'disarmament' was to appear only in June 1940 at the very moment when German armed might was in the process of destroying France.

The main beneficiary from the Ethiopian War was Germany. Mussolini had up to this point been distinctly cool towards Hitler. The Italian leader was as wary as the western powers about German expansionist aims, especially towards Austria. In 1934, on the assassination of the Austrian Chancellor Engelbert Dollfuss, he had even moved Italian troops to the Brenner Pass in the Alps as a warning to Hitler. As late as April 1935, Italy had aligned itself with the western democracies in the 'Stresa Front', aimed at containing any German western expansion, and particularly any moves to dominate Austria. But during the Ethiopian War, Italy found itself largely friendless, facing sanctions, and making only hesitant military progress. Hitler kept Germany neutral during this war. But he offered no backing to the League. Mussolini needed friends; Hitler could use them. In January 1936 Mussolini shifted ground. He signalled that Stresa was dead in his view, that he would not oppose Austria falling under German sway, and that he would offer no support to France and Britain should Hitler wish to react to the ratification, forthcoming in Paris, of the mutual assistance pact with the Soviet Union. Hitler was alert. It meant he could contemplate an early move to remilitarize the Rhineland – an essential step in German western defence and important for rearmament, but a flagrant assault on the 1925 Locarno Treaty that had guaranteed the post-war settlement in western Europe.

Sooner or later any nationalist German government would have sought to remove the stipulation of the post-war settlement, endorsed at Locarno, that a 50-kilometre strip of German territory on the right bank of the Rhine should remain demilitarized. To most Germans, not just extreme nationalists, this amounted to an intolerable limit on German sovereignty and a lasting stigma of the victors' diktat of 1919. The likelihood is that patient diplomacy would have negotiated an end to the demilitarization over the next couple of years. Hitler himself had 1937 in mind. But patient diplomacy was not Hitler's way. He saw the big advantages, to his domestic prestige as well as international standing, of a dramatic coup. The ratification of the Franco-Soviet pact offered the pretext. The disarray of the western democracies over Abyssinia, the loss of credibility of the League of Nations, and Mussolini's green light provided the opportunity. The moment had to be seized. There was some last-minute hesitation and nervousness. But Hitler did not waver for long. On 7 March 1936 a force of 22,000 German troops entered the demilitarized zone. A mere 3,000 men out of the assembled force of 30,000 troops had been ordered to advance deep into the Rhineland, backed by police units. There was no military confrontation. As Hitler had guessed, the western democracies protested after the event, but otherwise did nothing. He had got away with his biggest triumph to date.

This proved the last chance, short of war, for the western democracies to stop Hitler in his tracks. Why did they not do so? After all, only a small German force advanced into the Rhineland, and with orders to retreat if challenged by the biggest army in western Europe. If the French had stopped the advancing troops with a show of military force, the blow to Hitler's standing would have significantly weakened him in the eyes of the German military and public. What the consequences might have been is impossible to know. It is distinctly feasible that Hitler may well have proved incapable of pushing ahead with subsequent moves, seen by powerful figures in the military leadership as reckless and dangerous, had he failed ignominiously in attempting to remilitarize the Rhineland in 1936. However, as Hitler knew from what had been gleaned from French intelligence, there was little chance of France taking military measures to stop the German action. French politicians had, before Hitler's move, all but ruled out the use of force to remove German troops from the Rhineland. Mobilization would have been financially and politically disastrous at a cost of 30 million francs a day. Even as it was, financial panic in Paris was only narrowly averted. Moreover, France's army was not capable of immediate action. It needed a sixteen-day period of mobilization. And this was to defend France's borders, not to fight on the Rhine. French public opinion was also opposed to military retaliation. Even those who wanted to see Hitler punished did not think the Rhineland worth fighting for.

In any case, the French were unwilling to act without British support. There was, however, no chance of any British backing for military action over the Rhineland. British leaders were well aware – and made it clear to the French – that Britain was in no position to take military action against Germany in the event of a breach of the Locarno Treaty. British opinion would certainly not have favoured any such action. The mood in Britain in the wake of the Abyssinian crisis was, if anything, more anti-French than anti-German. There was absolutely no appetite for taking on Hitler when, after all, in the eyes of so many people he was simply entering 'his own back yard'. In contrast with British popular reactions to the Italian invasion of Abyssinia, there were no protest marches, demonstrations or demands for sanctions against Germany.

So neither Britain nor France did anything beyond trying to cover up their own disagreements about how to proceed, wring their hands, appeal to the League of Nations' Council – a move certain to cause Hitler sleepless nights – and eventually put forward half-hearted diplomatic proposals for a settlement of the Rhineland question which Hitler, having already settled matters in his own way, had no difficulty in rejecting. Anthony Eden, by now British Foreign Secretary, told the House of Commons that his objective had been to seek a peaceful and agreed solution. 'It is the appeasement of Europe as a whole that we have constantly before us,' he stated. 'Appeasement' was a term that would soon come back to haunt the British government.

At the end of March 1936 Hitler staged a plebiscite to ratify the Rhineland action. It brought him the 99 per cent vote of support so dear to dictators. Of course, it was a contrived result. But there can be no doubt that in reality an overwhelming proportion of the German population enthusiastically welcomed Hitler's move – certainly once it was clear that it would not lead to war. The dictator's popularity at home soared to new heights. This boosted his dominance over the traditional German ruling elites. His boldness had paid off. Their doubts had proven to be mistaken. The army, in particular, was further beholden to Hitler. The dictator's own egomania knew no bounds. He thought himself practically infallible, while for those who had wavered during the tense days preceding the march into the Rhineland he had nothing but contempt.

Germany's military strength now unquestionably constituted the supreme factor in the European constellation of power. It was an astonishing turnaround from the situation a mere four years earlier when, with the country on its knees, the western powers had agreed to the effective termination of reparations. The remilitarization of the Rhineland gave the coup de grâce to the Versailles and Locarno Treaties, and finally demolished lingering hopes of a lasting basis of security on the Franco-German borders. A confrontation of the western democracies with Hitler's Germany at some point seemed ever more likely. Over the past three years Hitler had repeatedly grasped the initiative while the western powers had dithered, revealing only weakness and lack of resolve.

As Britain and France continued to try to wrestle with diplomatic partners who did not play by established rules, the dictators of Germany and Italy edged closer together. At the beginning of 1936 relations between the two had still been far less than cordial. By the autumn, the creation of what Mussolini, on 1 November, proclaimed as the Rome-Berlin Axis was forged. Mussolini, though he did not yet see it, was moving from senior dictator to junior partner. The two expansionist powers, each ruled by unpredictable leaders wielding near absolute power in their countries, posed a mounting dual threat to Europe's peace. Now deprived of Italian support, Austria had agreed in July to terms that heavily increased German influence on the country. And, even before it had been formally constituted, the Axis was at work in Spain. Both Hitler and Mussolini had already decided to provide military support to the nationalist rebellion led by General Francisco Franco.

A significant factor in bringing the dictators closer together was anti-Bolshevism. Hitler was here plainly the driving-force. For Mussolini, anti-Bolshevism had been in the main a propaganda weapon at home. Russia was of little strategic importance to him. Hitler's anti-Bolshevism was more radical. The intrinsic link in his mind between Jews and Bolshevism had been a personal obsession since the 1920s. But the Soviet Union had played at best a subordinate role in shaping his moves in foreign policy since taking power. This was changing in 1936. In that year the notion of a coming showdown with the key ideological foe, something that had never left Hitler's mind, started to solidify. He was becoming preoccupied by the Bolshevik threat. Hitler saw real danger for Germany arising from possible communist domination in France and Spain. He was well aware of the big advances in industrialization in the Soviet Union and the plans for extensive rearmament. Time, in his view, was not on Germany's side. He saw Europe as divided between two irreconcilable camps. The danger had to be confronted at some point over the next few years, before it was too late.

By the end of August 1936, Hitler had completed a lengthy memorandum laying down the direction of the German economy over the following four years, stipulating a programme aimed at maximizing domestic production geared towards a rapid acceleration of rearmament. The background was the mounting economic pressure within Germany over previous months. Food imports had temporarily taken priority over imports of raw materials needed for rearmament. Prominent voices were pressing the leadership to curtail rearmament and reorientate the economy. A decision was needed.

Hitler made it. He chose guns over butter. His reasoning was political, not economic. His memorandum on the 'Four-Year Plan' began by asserting that Bolshevism would be at the centre of a new worldwide conflict. Even though it could not be known when it would take place, a showdown with the Soviet Union, he declared, was inevitable. He ended the memorandum by setting out two tasks: 'I. The German armed forces must be operational within four years. II. The German economy must be fit for war within four years.' It was not a timetable for war. But from now on, Germany could not free itself from the track on which it was travelling. Short of removing Hitler from power, there could be no reversal to a peacetime economy built upon international trade. The choice had been for an intensive programme of economic autarchy to build up armed strength in readiness for conflict. The points were set. The track led towards war. The dictators were starting to shape Europe's destiny.

DICTATORSHIP

Reactionary Regimes

The 1930s were the decade of the dictators. Some dictatorships had been formed in the 1920s. Others would follow as occupation regimes in the 1940s. But the 1930s were the decade above all in which dictators thrived. By 1939 more Europeans lived under dictatorships than democracies.

All dictatorships shared a number of features – the elimination (or severe restriction) of pluralist forms of political representation, limits on (or abolition of) personal freedoms, control over the mass media, the termination (or strict limitation) of any judicial independence, and heavy-handed repression of political dissidents through extended police powers. And all dictatorships resorted to forms of pseudorepresentation. Apart from the Soviet Union, where 'dictatorship of the proletariat' based its claim to legitimacy on class, dictatorial regimes invariably asserted that they represented 'the nation' or 'the people', that they embodied popular sovereignty and were acting in the national interest. Some form of national assembly or parliament, however rigged, controlled or manipulated, was normally retained. Actual power invariably resided, however, in the rule of a 'strong man', whose authority rested on the backing of the military and security forces. In all dictatorships the role of the military was decisive. And apart from the Soviet Union, the military was without exception ideologically national-conservative and vehemently anti-socialist in character. For most dictatorships, essentially negative aims of quelling internal unrest, restoring 'order', and sustaining the existing power of elites, sufficed. They posed no international danger.

The authoritarian regime, for example, established in Estonia in 1934 by the Prime Minister and former leader of the Farmers' Union, Konstantin Päts, had the declared aim, amid deep political unrest and parliamentary instability, of upholding internal security. The Veterans' Union (*Vapsen*) – a radical right-wing populist movement, quasi-fascist in character – was held responsible for the growing political disorder and banned. The election of its deputies was annulled, some of its leading members were arrested, and political demonstrations were forbidden. Some newspapers were silenced. Päts then dissolved parliament. Thereafter, oppositional activity was prohibited and national unity promoted through state-run propaganda. But there was no large-scale political persecution, no concentration camps were set up, the arts and literature were not restricted (as long as they were not 'seditious'), and there was even little interference with the judiciary. Päts called his regime 'directed democracy'. It was distinctly less than democratic. But it was at most an undynamic dictatorship and, after the early clampdown, compared with most authoritarian regimes of the era, even relatively liberal.

A relatively mild form of authoritarianism (in its early years, at least) also existed in Poland. External forms of democracy had been retained after Marshal Piłsudski's coup of May 1926. A parliament (the Seym), pluralistic parties and trade unions continued to exist. The press remained relatively free. However, the executive power of the state was greatly strengthened. The 'strong man', Piłsudski himself, controlled government from his formal position as War Minister. In 1930 over 5,000 political opponents were arrested and some of the more important severely maltreated in prison. With this notable exception, repression at that stage was not extensive. In March 1933, with Poland beset by economic crisis, the Sejm gave the government powers to rule by decree. Real power, behind Piłsudski, lay in the hands of the military. Leading governmental positions were held by those dubbed 'the colonels', all proven Piłsudski loyalists. Repression became sharper. A concentration camp was erected by presidential decree in 1934 in Berza Kartuska. Internment for three months (and a possible extension for three further months) did not require sentence by a court of law. The first prisoners, in July 1934, were Polish fascists. Most internees before 1939 were, however, communists. In all, around 3,000 individuals were sent to the camp in the pre-war years. Around a dozen died there – bad enough, though compared with the victims of many authoritarian regimes a small number. The authoritarian character of the state was confirmed in the new constitution of April 1935, which accorded wide powers to the President as head of state and greatly diminished any basis of parliamentary independence.

Piłsudski's death, shortly afterwards in May, brought no fundamental change. Amid continued factionalism, political disunity, and awareness of the growing threat from Nazi Germany, a big state-supportive organization, labelled the Camp of National Unification, was set up in 1937 and came to rally support for the dominant Polish figure of the later 1930s, General Edward Śmigly-Rydz, referred to as 'Leader of the Nation'. Poland became more stridently nationalist, more virulently antisemitic, less tolerant of ethnic minorities. But ideology remained confined to little more than the vague aim of national unity. And a significant fascist movement did not exist. There was nothing dynamic about this form of authoritarianism. No major attempt was made to mobilize the population. The regime was content to control society. It had no great ambitions to change it. Preservation of order, to serve primarily the interests of the conservative elites that had traditionally dominated Polish society, was enough.

Mass mobilization remained a limited vehicle in most authoritarian dictatorships. In Greece the distinctly uncharismatic General Ioannis Metaxas had no mass organization at his disposal. Before taking power in April 1936, he had enjoyed the support of no more than 4 per cent of Greeks. However, with the backing of King George II – the monarchy had been restored in 1935 – and the military, and amid serious political upheaval, bitter power struggles and parliamentary deadlock, he was able to establish a dictatorship in August 1936. The declared aim was to set up a government free of parties and factions to save Greece from communism. Parliament was dissolved, the constitution abolished, martial law declared, parties and oppositional organizations were suppressed and political liberties curtailed. The military and police were strengthened. Several thousand prisoners were incarcerated in brutal prison camps. Metaxas tried to imitate fascist methods, creating a fascist-style National Youth Organization and staging big parades to glorify the Leader. But there had been little fascist influence in Greece before Metaxas took power and his attempts to mobilize a mass base of support along the lines of Italian Fascism – plainly directed at forging a genuine base of personalized power – were a failure. Nor was there anything resembling a coherent ideology. Metaxas remained in power until his death in 1941. But he was wholly dependent upon the king and the military. His dictatorship was another variant of repressive authoritarianism that constrained and controlled but did not mobilize society, and it lacked any ideological drive.

Most other interwar dictatorships shared similar features, shaped in each case by national determinants. In Hungary, Miklós Horthy's authoritarianism, coming increasingly under German influence during the 1930s, retained the outer trappings of a pluralist system but in practice depended even more heavily than ever on the army and big landowners rather than the mobilized masses. The fascist mass party was viewed as a threat to the regime, not a basis of support. Its leader, Ferenc Szálasi, was imprisoned and his movement (the Party of the National Will, then the Hungarian National Socialist Party) banned before again being permitted to operate, reconstituting itself in March 1939 as the Arrow Cross and gaining a quarter of the votes cast in the elections of May that year. Even so, despite the growth of fascist influence and its own increasingly extreme nationalist and anti-Jewish colouring, Horthy's regime remained essentially undynamic – reactionary, not revolutionary.

On the other side of Europe, António Salazar's Portugal was possibly the least dynamic of all Europe's dictatorships. His 'New State' (*Estado Novo*), founded in 1933, was based on a corporative constitution that embodied the values of reactionary Catholicism. These, and sustaining the Portuguese colonial possessions overseas, more or less amounted to the sum of the vague unifying ideology of the regime.

There was a restricted franchise, press censorship, a ban on strikes and lockouts, and the usual apparatus of repression – a political police and special courts, widespread denunciation and a network of informers. A state-organized party, the 'National Union', a youth movement and a paramilitary organization (which used the Fascist salute) provided mass backing for the regime. However, Salazar had no wish at all to become dependent on a fascist mass movement and actually suppressed the National Syndicalists – the fascist 'Blueshirts'. This most dull of dictators wanted no leadership cult, and also turned his back on assertive militarism and imperialist expansionism. His brand of conservative authoritarianism offered the sharpest contrast to Europe's dynamic dictatorships.

Dynamic Dictatorship: Ideology and Mass Mobilization

Even for contemporaries it was abundantly plain that three dictatorships – those of the Soviet Union, Italy and Germany – stood out from all the rest. By the mid-1930s their ideological confrontation – that of Soviet Bolshevism facing Italian Fascism and German National Socialism – was hardening visibly. The confrontation was by this time, as the leaders of the western democracies recognized, taking Europe into a danger zone. The amber lights warning of increasing likelihood of European war were starting to flash brightly. None of the conventional authoritarian regimes posed a threat to European peace. But each of the three exceptional, dynamic dictatorships, especially Stalin's Russia and Hitler's Germany, was viewed with mounting apprehension by the western democracies. Many on the conservative Right feared communism more than fascism or Nazism and from the 1920s onwards started to bracket the regimes together, labelling them 'totalitarian', to distinguish them from merely 'authoritarian' forms of rule. For most on the Left, not just communists, it was a gross error to conflate Soviet communism with the regimes in Italy and Germany, which had to be seen as variants of a common evil – fascism.

Undeniably, despite their ideological differences, there were notable similarities in the methods of rule of the three dynamic dictatorships – their complete regimentation of society, their terrorization of opponents and minorities, their adulation of a leader and their relentless mobilization by a monopoly party. They were different forms of a completely new, modern type of dictatorship – the complete antithesis to liberal democracy. They were all revolutionary, if by that term we understand a major political upheaval driven by the utopian aim of changing society fundamentally. Correspondingly, they all made in principle (the practice varied) a 'total claim' on the individual. They were not content simply to use repression as a means of control, but sought to mobilize behind an exclusive ideology to 'educate' people into becoming committed believers, to claim them soul as well as body. Each of the regimes was, therefore, dynamic in ways that 'conventional' authoritarianism was not. But how alike in practice were these dictatorships?

Stalinism: Idealism, Terror and Fear

By the mid-1930s, the Bolshevik system of rule had become Stalinism. Collective leadership, not altogether fictional in the early years of the Soviet system, had evaporated completely since Lenin's death in 1924. The factional struggles that had accompanied the last phase of the New Economic Policy and the introduction of the first Five-Year Plan in 1928 had produced a clear winner. The self-styled 'dictatorship of the proletariat' was turning into the dictatorship of Joseph Stalin.

In 1936 a new Soviet Constitution was promulgated (replacing the first constitution of 1924). Stalin proclaimed it 'the most democratic of all the constitutions in the world'. It offered universal electoral franchise, civil rights, freedom of thought, the press, religion, organization and assembly, and guarantees of employment – all 'in accordance with the interests of the working people and for purposes of strengthening the socialist system'. Seldom has a constitution lied so monumentally. In truth, the Soviet Union was by this time an utterly ruthless dictatorship based heavily upon fear, servility and careerist ambition. Freedom – even in the limited way in which it had existed under Lenin's New Economic Policy – did not exist. Nor did any protection under the law. Soviet citizens were in practice fully exposed to the unlimited and arbitrary power of the state. This was the product in the main of the intensely forced process of breakneck industrialization and modernization imposed on a backward country,

combined with growing fear of war and, not least, the extreme auto-
cratic, relentlessly brutal and outrightly paranoid proclivities of the
ruler, Stalin himself.

What happened during the First Five-Year Plan between 1928 and
1932, at its heart the compulsory collectivization of the peasantry,
was labelled by Stalin a revolution from above. By the end of 1932,
the Plan was proclaimed fulfilled, a triumph. Much had indeed been
achieved, even if the statistics were often fabricated. But the Plan had
been pushed through by extreme coercion. And it had been massively
unpopular, especially among the peasantry. Agricultural regions –
most of the vast country – were impoverished. But in towns, too, there
was much discontent. There were food shortages, a severe lack of
housing and rising prices. Dissatisfaction was tangible at every level –
also and not least within the Bolshevik Party, and among the ruling
strata of party and state. Not all Bolshevik leaders, many of whom
were veterans of the old Leninist times, approved of what Stalin was
doing, or the way he was doing it. And many of them remembered the
Stalin of Lenin's days, recalling him as no more than a mere acolyte of
the great man, and far from his best-liked or most able underling.
They knew the man before he had become elevated to something
approaching the status of a demigod. For Stalin, that knowledge was
less than comfortable.

There was, however, not just dissent and opposition to what was
happening. There was also idealism and commitment. The vast and
rapid industrialization programme mobilized millions across the Soviet
Union. Countless party members, and young communists being
groomed for party activism in the youth movement, the Komsomol (in
contrast to the youth movements in Italy and Germany, still at this
time an elite body rather than the mass organization it was to become
by the late 1930s), worked ceaselessly to spread the vision of a coming
socialist utopia. Of course, the image of a united people striving to
attain such a future paradise was contrived, and could scarcely offer
great compensation or comfort to the huge majority of the population
struggling under the yoke of daily anxieties, material deprivation and
oppression. Even so, there was no shortage of enthusiasts. Young
urban workers, intellectuals and Jews (disproportionately drawn
across Europe to socialism as the path to freedom from discrimination

and persecution) were particularly likely to be attracted to the vision of the brave new world under construction. The enormous building projects – dams, power stations, the Moscow underground, even new cities such as Magnitogorsk in the Urals – were seen as a hugely positive, visible sign of an astonishing transformation that was under way, a tangible indicator of progress, of what Soviet society could produce. The idealism that participation in building the new utopia produced was not a phantasm.

The feeling of integration in the building of a new society was coupled with real, material, here-and-now expectations, not just distant utopian advantages that commitment to the regime could bring. The immense mobilization behind the industrialization programme demanded huge numbers of activists who could build careers, improve their living standards and, not least, wield substantial power in their striving to make the system work. Half a million party members were recruited between 1934 and 1939. Most were poorly educated and inexperienced. These newcomers now moved in great numbers into the lower ranks of administrative authority – and they liked the taste of power, as well as the status and privileges it brought them. Supervisors, foremen and managers were needed in the factories, not just workers. (Nearly 30 million peasants poured into towns from the countryside during the 1930s, attracted by the chance of increased income but unaware of their forthcoming subservience to brutal authority.) The often unbridled ambitions of low-ranking administrators could be served if they in turn served the regime. Ruthlessness for the cause merely mirrored what was happening above them. Despotic managers could, and often did, treat their charges like dirt, knowing that this would bring no sanction, indeed would be welcomed, as long as targets were met. And careers depended on those targets being met. Failure, however arbitrarily it was defined, was too grim to contemplate. It was the core of a system reliant upon millions of 'little Stalins' who made the regime work at the grass roots. Localized rule operated, however, only on a one-way basis: through orders from the top and responsibility from the bottom.

Stalin's control of the party apparatus as General Secretary ensured rigid centralization of command. All the crucial levers of power and organization were in his hands. A formidable bureaucratic apparatus – more and more at the arbitrary whim of Stalin's growing despotism, but increasing in size despite unbureaucratic inroads into its work – was capable of micro-management from the very centre. Telegrams from Stalin himself dealt even with trivial matters; he could, for instance, order someone in a party or state agency at the other end of the enormous country to supply desperately needed nails to a building site. The party dominated the state in the Soviet Union; and Stalin dominated the party. In fact, his autocracy completely undermined the party's institutional framework of collective rule at the top.

The Party Congress met only twice during the 1930s – in 1934 and again in 1939. The party's Central Committee, in theory its sovereign body, had become by the mid-1930s merely a pliant instrument of Stalin's will. The Politburo, the party's key decision-making body that under Lenin had met weekly, had ever fewer meetings across the 1930s. Its membership, once fifteen-strong, became reduced to a handful of Stalin's closest cronies, the most important of whom was his faithful lapdog, Vyacheslav Molotov (who was also Chairman of the Council of People's Commissars, in effect Prime Minister). This group of loyal lieutenants – their servility to the dictator guaranteed both by a sense of their own insecurity and by the inducements and rewards of power – played an important role in transmitting and implementing orders in varying spheres of Stalinist rule. Their meetings were often informal, sometimes dinners at Stalin's dacha or on visits to his holiday residence on the Black Sea. Decisions were rubber-stamped; there was no voting. Often a decision followed a proposal by Molotov to Stalin, which would be returned with amendments then dispatched as an order to party offices or even to the supposedly sovereign state body, the Council of People's Commissars (*Sovnarkom*).

At the grass-roots level, Stalin's autocracy prompted a huge turnover of party membership. An army of new party officials replaced the older cadres. They owed their positions to the openings offered to them by the drastic changes in Stalin's 'revolution from above'. This in turn encouraged servile acceptance of his untrammelled authority, which was bolstered from the early 1930s onwards by the manufacture of a 'heroic' personality cult around the leader.

A Stalin cult had to be built carefully. This was not just because the man himself was so physically unprepossessing – diminutive and squat, his face dominated by a big walrus-moustache and heavily pitted from smallpox – or that he was a secretive, intensely private individual who spoke in a quiet, undemonstrative voice, his Russian couched in a strong Georgian accent that never left him. The real problem was the giant shadow of Lenin. Stalin could not be seen to be usurping the legendary image of the great Bolshevik hero and leader of the revolution. So at first Stalin trod cautiously. The celebrations for his fiftieth birthday in December 1929 brought public eulogies. But the cult was still in its embryonic stages. Stalin professed modesty, publicly disowning attempts to put him on a pedestal with Lenin, and disavowed expressions of personalized devotion. It was no more than a front. Tacitly, he allowed his own elevation – amid outright falsification of his role during the revolution, in reality a fairly minor one – first to equal status with Lenin in a sort of dual cult, then to outright supremacy.

Untold numbers of minions, time-servers and sycophants rushed to embellish in myriad ways the heroic image of the 'people's leader'. By 1933 there were more than twice as many busts and images of Stalin to be seen in central Moscow than of Lenin. And by now Stalin, no notable philosopher of Marxism, had been elevated into its preeminent theorist, his works published in numbers far exceeding those of Marx and Engels, greater even than those of Lenin. When Stalin made a (relatively rare) public appearance, dressed as usual in his dull party tunic, at a Moscow congress in 1935, the frenetic applause by over 2,000 delegates lasted fifteen minutes. As it finally subsided, a woman shouted out 'Glory to Stalin', and it all began again.

Of course, much of the cult was invention. But there was genuine popular resonance as well. Countless ordinary Russians revered him. 'The Russian people need a tsar,' Stalin is alleged to have exclaimed in 1934. A populist 'father tsar' evoked for many Soviet citizens, especially for peasants from a countryside still rooted in belief and ritual, the picture of a stern family patriarch, the guarantor of order and the well-being that derived from it. It was undoubtedly an important component of the increasingly all-pervasive Stalin cult. The image of strong, resolute leadership matched the qualities that millions of

Soviet citizens yearned for after years of intense upheaval. And though the Soviet Union was officially an atheistic society, traditions deeply embedded in popular religion – 57 per cent of Soviet citizens still claimed to possess religious belief in a 1937 census, later suppressed – encouraged quasi-sacral elements of the Stalin cult, a belief in him as prophet, saviour or redeemer.

The cult doubtless established for Stalin a basis of genuine popularity, even if this cannot be quantified. It was of unquestionable importance in consolidating his dominance. But far more important was another factor: fear. Stalin's personal rule rested, above all, on the precariousness of all subordinate authority, increasingly subject to his arbitrary decisions over life or death. The regime relied primarily upon all-pervasive insecurity that ran throughout Soviet society. This reached new levels altogether during the 'great terror' that accompanied the purges of 1937–8.

Already during the First Five-Year Plan there had been huge levels of state violence and massive numbers of arrests. Even by 1933 over a million 'anti-Soviet elements' found themselves in camps and prisons. Stalin's extreme displeasure at what he took to be opposition at local level to the drastic pace of economic change led to over 850,000 members being thrown out of the party in 1933. There were tensions high up in the leadership, too. Some party leaders wanted to reduce the pressures on the economy. There were indications that Stalin could no longer depend upon the undiluted backing of the highest echelons of the party. Some pinned their hopes on Sergei Kirov, the popular Leningrad party boss and member of the Politburo. However, in December 1934 Kirov was shot dead in his office in Leningrad.

The young assassin, Leonid Nikolaev, had once been associated with Grigory Zinoviev, whose earlier opposition to Stalin and support for Trotsky, by now a demonized arch-enemy, the dictator had not forgotten. Nikolaev's motives may well, in fact, have been personal, not political; Kirov had been flirting with Nikolaev's wife. But Stalin was on the lookout for political plots. The assassin was swiftly interrogated, then shot. Whatever the lingering suspicions, Stalin's involvement in the assassination was never proved. But he was quick to turn the murder of Kirov to his own advantage. He gave the state police (NKVD) authority to arrest, try and execute at will. Zinoviev and Lev

Kamenev, who had also earlier supported Trotsky, were sentenced to long periods in prison. More than 30,000 real or supposed opponents in Leningrad were deported to Siberia or other remote areas. Nearly 300,000 party members were expelled over the following five months. Stalin's mounting paranoia would not have been lessened if he read police reports soon after Kirov's assassination. 'They killed Kirov. We will kill Stalin' was a refrain doing the rounds, along with other expressions of the desirability of getting rid of Stalin.

The dictator's suspicions by now knew no bounds. The NKVD told him in 1936 that Trotsky had links from abroad with supporters of Zinoviev, Kamenev and another former adversary, Nikolai Bukharin. Stalin had Zinoviev and Kamenev taken from prison, retried now in public – the first show trial – for alleged 'terrorist activities' including assassinations, which had Stalin himself next on the list after Kirov. Zinoviev and Kamenev were sentenced to death and shot in August 1936. These were the first of the early Bolshevik leaders, one-time members of the party's Central Committee, to be purged – but far from the last. Bukharin's own show trial and inevitable execution were to follow in 1938. Members of the Central Committee themselves now lived in dread, and with good reason; no fewer than 110 out of 139 members, deemed 'unreliable', were arrested – a move that usually led to execution or an unenviable fate in the Gulag. Also arrested were party and state leaders practically all over the national republics of the Soviet Union. Of 1,966 delegates at the 1934 Party Congress, 1,108 were arrested. Stalin was destroying the Communist Party itself as an independent power base. Managers, scientists and engineers also fell victim in large numbers to the purges – one reason why economic growth came to an end after 1937.

The purges, once unleashed, took on their own momentum. In 1937 the NKVD gave the Politburo a target of quarter of a million to be arrested. Over 70,000 would be shot, the rest sentenced to long spells in prison or a labour camp. By the end of 1938, when the purges subsided (possibly because the enormous disruption was damaging industrial production), the target had been massively exceeded. Arrests had reached close to a million and a half, and nearly 700,000 had been shot. Even the purger-in-chief, Stalin's head of police since 1936, Nikolai Yezhov, nicknamed the 'Iron Hedgehog', was arrested in

1939 and executed the following year. By 1939 the total number of prisoners in gaols and in labour camps and colonies, where conditions were closer to death than life, was almost 3 million. The death rate through starvation, overwork and arbitrary execution was colossal.

Stalin was a deeply vengeful, coldly cruel individual. (He even purged his parrot, hitting it on the head with his pipe, when its imitation of his crude spitting finally got on his nerves.) He was also given to paranoid fantasy. But the paranoia itself fed on developments that did, in fact, give Stalin rational grounds to doubt his own security. Nor was the extraordinary orgy of terror that enveloped the Soviet Union in the 1930s simply an extreme expression of Stalin's paranoia. Millions of ambitious apparatchiks and servile citizens made the terror effective at all levels of society. For every victim of the terror there were winners, those who profited from serving the regime. Unquestionably, too, there was a widespread belief, encouraged by the regime, that the Soviet Union was infested with 'wreckers', 'saboteurs', 'nationalists', 'kulaks', spies and enemy agents. Terror to root out 'oppositionists' was, therefore, welcomed by many, reinforcing their sense of identification with the epic task of building a socialist society, and underpinning their faith in Stalin. Even many who suffered persecution and discrimination desperately sought to belong, associating themselves with Soviet values.

Denunciation at all levels was encouraged. The slightest 'deviationist' remark could bring the dreaded knock on the door in the middle of the night. 'I wake up in the morning and automatically think: thank God I was not arrested last night', a Leningrad woman entered in her diary in November 1937. 'They don't arrest people during the day, but what will happen tonight, no one knows.' Another Leningrad citizen, a factory worker, would lie awake at night dreading the sound of a car engine. 'They have come for me!' his son remembered him saying, whenever he heard a car at night close by. 'He was convinced that he would be arrested for something he had said – sometimes, at home, he used to curse the Bolsheviks.' The arrival of the police was terrifying. 'Suddenly, several cars would drive into the yard,' recalled the son of Osip Piatnitsky, a veteran Bolshevik and once a trusted comrade of Lenin, recounting his father's arrest. 'Men in uniform and plain clothes would jump out and walk towards staircase entrances ... In those days many people expected to be arrested, but they did not know when their turn would come.' Fear of denunciation made for a silent society. 'People talk only in secret, behind the scenes and privately. The only people who express their views in public are the drunks', one man confided to his diary in 1937.

Denunciation was not necessarily political. It could bring career advancement or direct material rewards. It was also a godsend for settling personal scores – perhaps a conflict with neighbours, a work-place argument, or the break-up of an intimate relationship. An army of informers – some paid or bribed, some blackmailed into cooper-ation, often simply voluntary collaborators – reported their fellow citizens to the police. Imprisonment, exile, labour camp or execution invariably followed. The prison population – much of it in ignorance of their 'crime' – represented all sections of society. By 1937–8 no one was safe in Soviet society, from the lowliest peasant to members of the Central Committee. The party elite were, in fact, disproportionately unsafe. Even Stalin enthusiasts could never be sure that at some point the nocturnal hammering on the door would not be for them.

Stalin's mounting anxiety about the looming danger to the Soviet Union might well have lain behind the outright explosion of terror in the great purges. Sensing 'fascist spies and enemies' everywhere as an immense 'fifth column' within his own country, Stalin left no stone unturned in the attempt to eradicate all internal opposition before war could strike. Ethnic minorities close to Soviet borders were subjected to mass deportations and executions. Poles (along with many Belorus-sians and Ukrainians regarded with suspicion) in the western regions of the Soviet Union were particularly endangered. Fearing Poland would join with Hitler's Germany in attacking the Soviet Union, in August 1937 Stalin ordered the round-up of 140,000 Soviet Poles who were either shot or sent to labour camps over the following months.

Nor did Stalin spare the Red Army. With deepening awareness of the threat from both west and east – Hitler's Germany and Japan had come together in signing an Anti-Comintern Pact in November 1936 – the last thing he needed (it might have been thought) was any disturbance to the strengthening of the Red Army. Astonishingly, however, in 1937–8 Stalin practically demolished his military high command. The most outstanding strategist, Mikhail Tukhachevsky, who had earlier more than once crossed Stalin, was arrested, forced into a confession of conspiring to overthrow the Soviet Union, and executed. Over 30,000 officers in all were purged, at least 20,000 executed. The higher the rank, the greater was the likelihood of arrest. The 'decapitation' of the Red Army left it gravely weakened, under the command of the incompetent Stalinist favourite, Kliment Voroshilov, and in no position to contemplate a major war.

In recognition of the alarming gap to be made up, Soviet defence expenditure increased at a frenetic pace in the later 1930s – rising from 9.7 per cent (just short of 5,400 million roubles) to 25.6 per cent (39,200 million roubles) of the state budget between 1934 and 1939. As it did so, material conditions for Soviet citizens, which had improved somewhat during the Second Five-Year Plan of 1933–7, again fell sharply. Measures to extract higher delivery quotas of agricultural produce, increase taxes, and intensify work on the collective farms were hugely unpopular in the countryside. Urban workers were outraged at restrictive labour laws introduced in 1938.

This was no popular dictatorship. There were many committed individuals, idealists and ideological zealots, to be sure. But the population at large, beyond the real or feigned Stalin-worshippers and regime-enthusiasts, was cowed into truculent quiescence. There were no major disturbances or displays of unrest. And, so far as is known, there was never an attempt to kill Stalin. He was loved by many, but feared by far more. Terror had done its job. Terror was the defining characteristic of Stalin's regime. Never before had any government terrorized so many of its own people so wantonly and callously.

Mussolini's Italy: The 'Totalitarian' Dream

In June 1925 Mussolini had lauded 'the fierce totalitarian will' of the Fascist movement. Like much of what he proclaimed, it was bombast. He was well aware that 'will', however 'fierce' and however 'totalitarian', could by itself provide no solid basis for rule. Activism and thuggery, which comprised a good deal of what this 'will' amounted to in practice, might disarm opponents, but could in themselves build nothing. Despite his own radical instincts, Mussolini was astute enough to see that he needed support, as in the 'seizure of power', from forces beyond his ill-disciplined streetfighters. He needed the backing of the established elites in the land. And he recognized that a solid platform for power had to rest not on the party, but on the state.

He had been either clever enough, or perhaps just lucky, in February 1925, while still pandering to the extremists in his movement, to alight on a solution to the problem of his unruly, radical party bosses. He had made Roberto Farinacci, the most radical of all the provincial party bosses (the *Ras*), National Secretary of the Fascist Party. Farinacci was a vicious, utterly ruthless individual, though possessed of poor political antennae. He did purge some of the most disruptive radicals, helping Mussolini in the process. However, the public violence that he condoned, even directly encouraged, provoked a backlash, allowing Mussolini to dismiss Farinacci in 1926 and distance himself from the unpopular actions of the party. During the following years, under less radical but more administratively competent party secretaries, the Fascist Party greatly expanded (by 1933 it was nearly a million and a half strong, in a population of about 42 million) but lost all semblance of a 'fierce totalitarian will'. It was transformed into an establishment party, shedding its revolutionary élan in the process.

Certainly, there were those in the party, most prominently Mussolini himself and also some of the regional bosses, who still harboured revolutionary ambitions. They guaranteed that there would be no retreat into merely conventional authoritarianism. In essence, however, the party had turned into little more than a propaganda instrument, a vehicle to orchestrate the adulation of Mussolini, an apparatus for social control, and an organization to uphold the power of the state. For in Mussolini's Italy, in stark contrast to the Soviet regime, the monopoly party – no other parties were permitted after 1928 – was the servant, not the master, of the state.

'Everything in the state, nothing outside the state, nothing against the state'. Those had been Mussolini's words in October 1925. The extent of state social and economic controls introduced by every belligerent country during the First World War had encouraged a growing belief, not just in Italy, that national strength could only be sustained through total control of society by the state. The subsequent demonstrable weakness of liberal political systems to cope with the immense problems that were the legacy of the great conflagration had bolstered such views. Mussolini's most prominent theorist, Giovanni Gentile, professor of philosophy in Rome and since 1923 the regime's Education Minister, spoke not of the Fascist movement's 'totalitarian will' but of the 'totalitarian state'. For Gentile, nothing beyond the state had significance. It embraced all facets of society. It was the embodiment of the national will. The 'totalitarian' essence of Italian Fascism concerned itself 'not only with political organization and political tendency, but with the whole will and thought and feeling of the nation'. However vague and however unrealizable in practice, the idea was novel for its time.

The construction of this 'totalitarian state' had taken shape gradually, not overnight, in the later 1920s. It rested, inevitably, on suppression of opposition. Political opposition had been quashed early in 1925. By this time, with opponents already cowed, that did not take much to achieve. Only about a hundred individuals were arrested. Most opposition leaders fled the country. The press was swiftly brought under government control the same year and strict censorship imposed. None of this provoked much protest, though the Senate, which retained a measure of independence, held up the press law for some time. In 1926, after four foiled assassination attempts on Mussolini had been exploited to create a fervour for imposed order, all opposition parties were banned. So were strikes and lockouts. The communists kept their underground organization going for some years, though it petered out to no more than a couple of hundred members by 1934. In 1929 the Catholic Church was placated by the Lateran Treaties. No trouble was to be expected from that quarter. As a sign of the new accord, Pope Pius XI exulted Mussolini as a man sent by 'providence' to liberate his country from the false doctrine of liberalism.

Although the Italian Fascist state had been made possible by the violence of the paramilitary armed units, the *squadristi*, the systematic repression needed to contain potential opposition was the task of the police and judiciary – neither of them in the hands of radical Fascists or party activists. Earlier forms of state repression were extended and sharpened rather than revolutionized. The political police – in practice beyond judicial control – were centralized, a large network of agents and informers (many of them voluntary) built up. Tight surveillance of dissent was introduced. Denunciation, usually anonymous, was commonplace. Thousands of police actions, often aroused by the denunciation of minor, if not imaginary, 'offences', took place regularly. 'Subversives' could be punished by lengthy terms of imprisonment or by banishment to remote provinces in the south of Italy or islands off the coast. Communists were the most frequent victims. (The former Communist leader, Antonio Gramsci, wrote his *Prison Notebooks*, containing some of the most important theoretical reflections on Marxism, while serving a twenty-year jail sentence, during which he died.) The death penalty was instituted for attacks on Mussolini or members of the royal family. A 'Special Tribunal for the Defence of the State' was established in 1927, applying military law, beyond normal legal constraints, and it dealt with over 5,000 cases in the following years.

All this was certainly repressive enough to erase any real prospect of serious opposition to the regime from within. Yet compared with some other authoritarian regimes – not just Nazi Germany or the Stalinist Soviet Union – domestic repression was mild. Franco's Spain, for instance, was soon to prove far more bloodthirsty. Fewer than 20 per cent of the cases brought before the Italian Special Tribunal resulted in a conviction. Most of these were communists. Freemasons were also heavily targeted. Before the war, there were only nine sentences of capital punishment; the death penalty for eight others was commuted. About 14,000 anti-fascists were punished – often simply on police orders – by exile (*confino*), sometimes for long terms though in practice often amnestied after shorter periods.

For much of the population, it was a matter of coerced conformity, rather than enthusiasm for the regime. Conformity was necessary to obtain a job or to acquire welfare benefits. Corruption and bribery of officials were its inevitable accompaniment. Those who were critical did well to keep their views to themselves. However, Italians who toed the line did not need to live in dread of the knock at the door by the political police in the dead of night. Instead of being arbitrary and unconstrained, the repression was mainly targeted at anti-fascist opponents. That largely sufficed. Dissent was contained, opposition neutralized. There was much apathy and dulled acceptance of what could not be changed. But this was not a terrorized society, like Stalin's Soviet Union. The worst of the terror was exported, deployed not against the majority Italian population but against their presumed racial inferiors in the African colonies.

The traditional props of Italian state power were coopted for Fascism. Mussolini had promised to reduce state bureaucracy; in fact he extended it. The dictator had himself taken over eight government ministries by 1929. He needed career civil servants to run them for him. Of course, they joined the party. But most of them were civil servants first, fascists second. In the provinces, too, the state prefects not the fascist regional bosses were in charge – and they kept local fascist activists as well as potential 'subversives' under surveillance. More often than not, quite especially in the south, notables from the established ruling class, most of whom were again fascists only on paper, continued to run the localities.

The army, too, had to be kept on board. Plans in 1925 to reduce its size were abandoned, and the Minister for War who had proposed them was fired. Mussolini himself took on the Ministry (and soon afterwards the Navy and Air Ministries). In practice, this meant that the armed forces ran themselves – with minimal coordination and efficiency. There was little that Mussolini could do to improve matters. The officer corps remained for the most part conservative, hardly fascist in true allegiance. The monarchy itself provided a bond of loyalty for conservative officers who were inwardly not enthusiastic about Mussolini. The generals and admirals, even more died-in-the-wool national conservative, were, in any case, more than happy to accept the imposition of fascist 'order', the repression of the Left, and the manufacture of national unity – as long as it did not interfere with the armed services.

By the 1930s, the Fascist regime had fully consolidated its hold on power. No worthwhile opposition remained. The support of the power-elites – monarchy, military, Church, captains of industry, big landowners – was assured. In practice, the idea of the totality of state and society never came close to realization. Fascism proved unable to win over large sections of society, not least the old socialist milieux in the big cities and wide swathes of the rural southern provinces. But where inward commitment was lacking, there was at least quiescence. People accommodated themselves to the regime. In its early days, Fascism had found its main support in the middle classes. The middle-class basis of backing for the regime became even more pronounced in the 1930s as fears of the Left receded, internal order was assured, expectations of improved status and material conditions were aroused, and the prospects of national grandeur magnified. The middle-class character of the Fascist Party itself was enhanced by recruitment of the large numbers of clerks, white-collar workers and supervisory staff. For these and others in any form of public employment, party membership became compulsory in 1933.

Whatever people inwardly thought of the regime, the quality that set Italian Fascism apart from other more conventional authoritarian regimes at the time, and won it many admirers, even in the western democracies, was less its repression and coercion – common to some degree in all dictatorships – than its relentless mobilization of the population, its overt vitality and dynamism. This was represented in a new aesthetics of power that attempted to harness art, literature and, not least, monumental architecture to its service. To many outside observers, fascism seemed the modern face of government, a rational organization of society. It appeared to combine order with state-organized social welfare.

The fascist idea of the 'totalitarian state' aimed to embrace all facets of life, from cradle to grave. It aimed to create a 'new man' who would embody the spirit of Italian Fascism, backed by 'the new Italian woman', committed to her duty for the nation, largely envisaged as providing domestic happiness and bearing babies. 'The thoughts and wishes of the Duce must become the thoughts and wishes of the masses,' said Gentile. The Fascist Party itself extended its tentacles into almost all avenues of daily life. But mobilization went much further than the activities of the party itself. Almost half of the entire population was a member of some type of fascist affiliation by 1939. Welfare organizations were set up to look after pregnant women and new babies, provide food, clothing and emergency shelter for the needy. A youth organization with numerous sub-branches, founded in 1926 and with over 5 million members by 1936, indoctrinated young Italians with the requisite martial values. Apart from pre-military training, it ran popular youth clubs that offered wider opportunities and better facilities for sport than had earlier existed. Youth hostels were built. Half a million children, many from poorer families, were sent on camping holidays in 1935. Schools and universities reinforced the indoctrination in a new value system. Most impressive, in the eyes of many Italians (and foreign observers), was the novel creation in 1925 of a big leisure organization, the *Opera Nazionale Dopolavoro* ('National After-Work Organization'), which had 4.5 million members by 1939 (around 40 per cent of industrial workers). This offered blue- and white-collar workers in factories opportunities for sport, entertainment and travel that they had never previously enjoyed. Much of this was popular – though that did not mean it readily translated into popularity for the regime itself, let alone the Fascist Party.

Sport, in particular, was highly popular. The regime turned it into an evocation of national pride and prestige. Cycling and skiing became popular mass sports, strongly encouraged by the regime. One of the most prominent Fascist leaders, Italo Balbo, showed off the courage and skill of the airman by flying across the Atlantic. Primo Carnera was world heavyweight boxing champion from 1933 to 1935. Motorcar racing, fostered by famous names such as Maserati, Bugatti and Alfa Romeo, thrilled the masses, drawn to speed and power. Above all, football was well on the way to becoming the dominant Italian sporting passion and a propaganda window for the regime when Italy won the World Cup in 1934 and again in 1938. Italy's sporting prowess was advertised to the nation in newsreels in the most popular form of popular entertainment, the cinema, which could subtly – and sometimes overtly – transmit the values of Fascism to its big audiences. The spread of radio, too, was a boon to Fascism. For those without a radio – still most Italian families in 1939 – thousands of loudspeakers were set up in town squares to make sure that, dragooned into attendance by the party, they did not miss one of Mussolini's speeches.

Mussolini himself was the regime's greatest single asset. Foreigners admired him not least as a bulwark against communism. No less a person than Winston Churchill lauded him, describing him in 1933 as the personification of Roman genius. The Duce cult was a careful construct. Only from the mid-1920s, with opposition suppressed and the mass media mobilized in the service of the regime, could propaganda give full expression to building up an almost superhuman image of a new Caesar. Among Italians, Mussolini's popularity by the mid-1930s greatly outstripped both that of his regime in general and the Fascist Party in particular.

The Duce was widely idolized by many who were quietly critical of much of Fascism and detested the party's overweening and often corrupt local bosses and functionaries – though even he did not escape the growing political apathy and disillusionment with Fascism in the later 1930s. What practically amounted to a deification of Mussolini in wide sections of the population could draw upon a transmuted form of naïve popular religious faith. 'When you are looking around and don't know who to turn to any more, you remember that He is there. Who, but He, can help you?' intoned the leading newspaper *Corriere della Sera* in 1936, speaking not of God but of Mussolini. The article asked when people should write to the Duce, and gave the answer, 'practically on every occasion, at a difficult time in your life'. 'The Duce knows that when you write to him it is out of genuine sorrow or real need. He is the confidant of everyone and, as far as he can, he will help anyone.' Many Italians believed this. Around 1,500 of them sent him letters every day: 'I turn to You who does all and can do everything.' 'For us Italians you are our God on earth, and so we turn to you faithful and certain of being heard.' 'Duce, I venerate you as the Saints should be venerated.' These were some of the effusive outpourings from peasants in one province that had once been a socialist stronghold.

The quest for imperial glory had been a hallmark of the regime from the beginning. The propaganda fanfare that greeted the invasion of Abyssinia in 1935, and the depiction of Italy as a country unjustly treated by the League of Nations, intensified the patriotic fervour in the land. Unsurprisingly, therefore, the victory in Abyssinia in 1936 sent Mussolini's popularity into the stratosphere. Tributes showered in from all sides, describing him as 'divine', 'infallible', a 'genius', a 'Caesar', and the 'founder of a religion' whose name was 'Italy'. This was, however, the pinnacle of his popularity. Internal police reports revealed it to be on the wane in the last years before the war as the gap between propaganda and the experience of reality widened. Beset by material problems of everyday life, worried about the prospect of another war that they doubted the country was in a position to fight, and disliking the increasing dependency on Germany, many had by this time lost their belief in Fascism.

To revive the visibly flagging dynamism, and to show that Fascism did not lag behind Nazism in radical drive, the regime intensified its ideological zeal in the later 1930s. The Fascist salute with outstretched arm was made compulsory in all forms of greeting; civil servants had to wear uniforms; the army was told to adopt the goose-step. The most visible sign of the new radicalism was the introduction of vicious anti-Jewish legislation in 1938. There had been no pressure from Germany for the legislation, yet even so it was the model. At one time the Nazis had looked to Fascist Italy as their exemplar. Now it was the other way round. Mussolini had no wish to be seen as Hitler's acolyte. He wanted to prove that he was just as radical as the German dictator. Moreover, he thought that, as in Germany, singling out the Jews as an 'enemy within' could help to cement national unity. Racism in Italy had traditionally been largely directed at black Africans rather than the tiny Jewish population of under 50,000 (scarcely 0.1 per cent of the total population of the country). But antisemitism, though not a central feature, had always been present in the Fascist movement. And once Italy bound itself to Germany in the Axis, it became more prominent, culminating in the racial laws of 1938 that rested on the premise that 'the Jews do not belong to the Italian race'. There was no notable protest. The anti-Jewish fervour was not shared by most of the population. But few felt strongly about it and some, certainly, were won over by anti-Jewish propaganda. In this, as in other facets of Fascist rule, the regime put down shallow roots in the population but could reckon with the passivity and conformity of the masses.

The internal affairs of the dictators, however distasteful, were seen by the western democracies as their own business. Internationally, however, Mussolini and Hitler were by now viewed by those democracies as 'mad dogs' threatening Europe's peace. Before the invasion of Abyssinia, Italian Fascism had not been regarded as a grave danger. From 1936, linked with Nazi Germany as part of the Axis, it was a different story. The real menace, even so, was plainly the revitalized, unified and strengthened German Reich.

Hitler's Germany: The Racial Community

The rise to power of Fascism in Italy, and above all the figure of Mussolini as the embodiment of the strong, authoritarian leader who had crushed Marxism and united his country through force of will, had fascinated German nationalists long before Hitler's 'seizure of power' in 1933. Mussolini was one of the few individuals who elicited Hitler's own admiration. Personal connections were built up between some leading Nazis and the Italian Fascist leadership. The 'German Greeting' with outstretched arm, compulsory within the Nazi Party after 1926, was 'borrowed' from the Fascist salute. The 'deal' between the Nazi leadership and the national-conservative ruling elites that brought Hitler to power was reminiscent of that which had sealed Mussolini's takeover in Italy eleven years earlier. And long before Mussolini and Hitler bound together the fates of their countries in the Axis, the affinities of Italian Fascism and German National Socialism were plain to see.

The Nazi regime's big leisure organization, 'Strength through Joy', set up as a subsection of the German Labour Front (the state-run substitute for the smashed trade unions) to provide an array of cultural and leisure activities for workers, was modelled on the *Dopolavoro* in Italy, created in 1925. The motorway (*Autobahn*), soon regarded as the emblem of the new Germany's economic recovery and modernization, took its inspiration from the first motorway, the *autostrada*, which was built in Italy between 1924 and 1926. The German cult of the fallen in the First World War, the inculcation in the population of a militaristic ethos, the staging of huge rallies and parades as part of the attempt to construct a new aesthetics of mass mobilization, the creation of a youth movement to build a generation that imbibed Nazi values from early years, a panoply of welfare organizations, and, inevitably, the dominance of a huge, monopoly party bound together by unquestioned allegiance to the leader – all had parallels in Fascist Italy. The suppression of the Left and, of course, anti-Bolshevism were also traits that the two regimes had in common. So (in contrast to the radical state socialism in the Soviet Union) was the promotion of big business, as long as it served the regime's interests. Both dictatorships were also not just stridently nationalistic and militarist, but quintessentially imperialist.

For all the parallels, however, the regimes were inherently more distinctive than similar. That the Nazi regime was more radical, more dynamic, more aggressive, more ideologically driven in all it undertook reflected crucial structures of the German dictatorship that bore only superficial similarity to Italian Fascism.

The exceptionality of the Nazi regime hinged in no small measure upon the ideological hopes, expectations and opportunities that were embodied in Hitler's supreme and unchallengeable position as Germany's leader. The cult that invested 'heroic', almost superhuman, qualities in Hitler, turning the one-time beer-hall demagogue into the object of almost deified veneration, was, of course, fabricated, just like the Duce cult in Italy, the Stalin cult in the Soviet Union, and leadership cults elsewhere. However, Hitler did not have to transcend an earlier source of ideological legitimacy, as Stalin had to do in his nominal allegiance to the legacy of Lenin and the tenets of Marxism. Nor did Hitler have to build his leadership cult only years after taking power, as did Mussolini. The roots of the Führer cult were less shallow, of longer standing, and of greater consequence for the ideological dynamism of the dictatorship.

Already by the mid-1920s Hitler had established his complete preeminence within the Nazi Movement. By the time he was appointed Reich Chancellor in 1933, he had long embodied the utopian vision of national renewal and future greatness that had won over millions to support his party. Not for nothing was National Socialism known as 'the Hitler movement'. In 1933 his dominance within the party was transferred to the workings of a modern, advanced state. And from 1934 he had total power in that state, unlike Mussolini who remained nominally at least subordinate to the king. The fixed points of Hitler's vision, distant and imprecise future goals though they were, could now infuse all parts of the state, driven on as they were by the unswerving allegiance of the myriad affiliations of the monopoly party, the efficient repressive machinery of the police and surveillance organization, and supported in broad outline by the national-conservative elites and millions of ordinary Germans. The personalized vision of Hitler – one premised on war to attain national salvation through erasing the shame of the capitulation in 1918 and the destruction of those he considered responsible for it, the

Jews – offered 'guidelines for action' that could now be turned into state policy.

The twin aspects of 'removal of the Jews' (an idea that meant different things to different people at different times) and 'living space' (*Lebensraum*), entailing preparation for military conflict at some point in the foreseeable future to secure Germany's future economic basis and supremacy in Europe (an idea capable of embracing various notions of German expansion), served to sustain a relentless ideological dynamic. This ideological drive was not remotely matched in Mussolini's Italy and was completely different in essence from what underpinned the manic upheavals in the Soviet Union. It followed no coherent plan or timetabled blueprint. But both the direction and the inexorable momentum of radicalization were intrinsic to the Nazi system.

Central to the radicalization was racial cleansing. The racism of Italian Fascism, even after the introduction of the anti-Jewish legislation of 1938, matched neither in centrality nor in intensity the mobilizing drive to impose racial purity that ran through the entire Nazi regime. The racism went far beyond antisemitism. Hatred of the Jews was, however, at its core, The Jews held a unique place in the Nazi panoply of phobias. For Hitler and many of his ardent followers the Jews amounted to an all-pervasive danger that threatened Germany's existence. Internally they were seen as poisoning its culture, undermining its values and corrupting its racial purity. Externally, they were viewed as a malign international power through their presumed domination of both plutocratic capitalism and of Bolshevism. The elimination of all imagined Jewish power and influence was, therefore, the very pivot of the utopian vision of national renewal built on racial purity.

These pathological delusions could, from 1933 onwards, be turned into practical state policy. A nationwide boycott of Jewish businesses on 1 April 1933, followed by a first tranche of legislation to exclude Jews from the civil service and discriminate against them in the legal and medical professions, signalled to many Jews at the very outset of the regime that they had no future in Germany. A second big wave of persecution in 1935 culminated in the Nuremberg Laws of September 1935, outlawing marriage between Jews and 'those of German blood' and excluding Jews from Reich citizenship – the basis for a turning screw of further discrimination during the following years. A further wave – the worst – was to come in 1938 and would explode in the nationwide pogroms of 9–10 November (sarcastically dubbed *Reichskristallnacht* because of the shards of broken glass from Jewish businesses and homes). This resulted in further tens of thousands fleeing from the country. Before then, Jews had been increasingly forced out of the economy, robbed of their livelihoods, and driven as pariahs to the fringes of a proclaimed 'people's community' constructed on the basis of racial discrimination and persecution, and gaining its very identity through exclusion of those deemed not fit to belong to it.

As well as Jews, an array of perceived social 'outsider' minorities – gypsies, homosexuals, the mentally ill, alcoholics, beggars, the 'workshy', 'habitual criminals', 'antisocials' of one kind or another – were excluded from the mainstream 'aryan' community. The medical profession, welfare experts and law-enforcement agencies needed little encouragement from the Nazi Party to play their own part in implementing the exclusionist agenda. Welfare and pro-natalist measures directed at the majority population – such as marriage loans, maternity aid, child support, even sterilization of 'degenerates' (already begun in 1933) – had their counterparts in other European countries. But nowhere else were such measures so radically and comprehensively driven by principles of 'racial hygiene' to create a racially pure, genetically strengthened society – one being prepared (not that this was loudly stated) for war.

Within the enormous, hydra-like Nazi movement, the racial ethos of the 'people's community' was axiomatic. The Nazi Party itself, neither subordinated to the state as in Italy nor superior to it as in the Soviet Union but existing alongside and intersecting with the state in an uneasy dualism, saw to it that the pressure to exclude 'inferiors' from the 'people's community', and the anti-Jewish momentum especially, never sagged for too long. The most crucial institutional driving-force of race policy, however, had no direct parallel, either in Italy or in the Soviet Union. This was the SS (*Schutzstaffel* – literally, 'Protection Squad'), the elite section of the Nazi movement, and its most ideologically dynamic sector, committed to the pursuit of 'racial cleansing' both to improve the 'political health of the nation' and to provide the basis for future German domination of Europe.

From 1936 the SS, already running the concentration camps (which lay far beyond any legal constraints), took over the leadership of the security and criminal police, constructing a huge surveillance network and eventually also developing a military wing (the Waffen-SS). By the mid-1930s the repression to quell any genuine opposition to the regime, vicious though it had been, had achieved its goal. At the beginning of 1935, the population of the concentration camps, still mainly from adherents of the former left-wing parties, had dwindled to about 3,000, the lowest figure during the regime's existence. The camps, having served their initial purpose, could have been wound up at this time. That would not, however, have suited Hitler, or the SS leadership. A plain indication that the mission of the combined SS-police apparatus involved a never-ending, upward spiral of control, eradication of 'internal enemies of the nation', and the racial purification of the 'people's community', was that plans for the expansion of the camps were being laid at this precise time. The exclusion from the 'people's community' of those on the margins of society deemed to be 'harmful to the people' (*volksschädigend*) saw the number of concentration-camp inmates swell sevenfold within four years to stand at 21,000 by the eve of the Second World War.

Alongside race policy, the drive to build powerful armed forces, militarize the 'people's community' and direct the economy towards rapid rearmament ensured a relentless tempo that was never allowed to subside. From 1936 the momentum sharply accelerated. Hitler had not wavered, as his memorandum to launch the Four-Year Plan had demonstrated, from the vision of racial imperialism he had advanced in *Mein Kampf* a decade earlier – the premise that a conflict to acquire 'living space' would at some point be necessary. And the empire would be won not in colonial Africa or elsewhere overseas, but in Europe itself.

The idea remained at present just that: an indeterminate notion in the mind of Hitler and some other Nazi leaders. There were different interpretations of what 'living space' might mean, different presumptions of the character of any mooted expansion. Some generals thought in terms of a strong army as a deterrent to secure Germany's defence. Others envisaged conflict at some point in the future to establish German hegemony in central and eastern Europe. Few, if any, in 1936 imagined war against France and Britain or an invasion of the

Soviet Union in the near future. But, even if little concrete thought was given to scenarios of future conflict, a big army was not being built up so as to sit indefinitely in barracks. And, unlike the undynamic Italian army, capable of eventually winning an imperialist campaign in Abyssinia but not much more, Germany's military leaders were efficient, experienced, skilled and determined.

They had imbibed a culture in which a strong army, national aggrandizement and empire were taken for granted as the attributes of a great power. They had experienced war, conquest and the occupation of territory in Europe between 1914 and 1918 before having to swallow the bitter pill of harrowing defeat, national humiliation and devastating loss of great-power status. They had been contemplating major war, anticipating all the modern machinery of death and destruction, even in the mid-1920s, once a new, strong army could again be built. Hitler's aims and achievements to re-establish German strength, overthrow the Versailles Treaty, and pour countless millions into rearmament were certain of a warm reception among such military leaders. After the western democracies had shown their weakness and divisions in 1935 and 1936, over the breaches of Versailles and Locarno, German expansion became increasingly likely. The second strand of Hitler's ideology, expansion for 'living space', like the first, 'removal' of the Jews, was starting to come into focus.

By every indication the Nazi regime could reckon with wide popular support in the mid-1930s. Just how extensive the support was, as in other dictatorships that brutally suppressed hostile opinion and monopolized the mass media with regime propaganda, is impossible to quantify. But without doubt the economic recovery, elimination of unemployment, restoration of political 'order', re-establishment of national unity and strength, above all the patriotic triumphs (especially the defiance of the western powers in the remilitarization of the Rhineland), were widely popular. Hitler's own popularity was immense, even among many who disliked the party and its local representatives, or were alienated by the attacks by party radicals on the observances, institutions and clergy of the major Christian churches, Catholic and Protestant. Even bitter opponents of the regime had to resign themselves to depressed acceptance of the widespread adulation for Hitler. The march into the Rhineland took his virtual deification to new heights. 'What a fellow, Hitler. He had the courage to risk something', was commonly heard even among the working class of industrial areas, who otherwise had nothing good to say of the regime but hugely approved of his actions to tear up the hated Versailles Treaty. Hitler was seen as the symbol of Germany's new standing in the world. There was 'simply wonderful' trust that he would 'succeed in bringing everything to a good end for Germany'.

Propaganda could build upon pseudo-religious sentiment and naive popular piety as well as belief in patriarchal values that would guarantee discipline and order. Each year more than 12,000 Germans from all walks of life sent Hitler letters of praise and sycophantic veneration approaching adoration. Younger Germans of both sexes, even those who had grown up in former communist or socialist milieus, were disproportionately won over to the regime, soaking up nazified values in the Hitler Youth movement (which, as the state youth movement, became near compulsory by 1936). Many found excitement, adventure and an impression of a community that transcended all class divisions. They had a sense of fascination, of a world of new and enticing opportunities and experiences that awaited them, and a feeling of entitlement as members of a special, and superior, people. 'I thought it was a good time. I liked it,' admitted one elderly lady many years later, looking back on her teenage years. She was not alone. Many Germans who had experienced since the war of 1914–18 rampant inflation, then mass unemployment and deep political division during the Weimar years, later recalled the 1930s as 'good years'.

For the rest, terroristic repression had done its job. By 1935 the last flickering embers of opposition from the Left were all but snuffed out. Socialist opponents, those who had not gone into exile, did what they could to retain clandestine contact with each other, but beyond this did little or nothing to disturb the regime. Communist cells continued to be rebuilt, infiltrated and smashed, the cycle of courageous but futile resistance repeating itself to the very end of the Third Reich. But beyond the tiny minorities who were still committed to the perilous world of underground opposition, most Germans inevitably had to find ways of accommodating to dictatorship, complying with varying degrees of enthusiasm to the demands of the regime. Surveillance, snooping, denunciation – all the accoutrements of a rigidly controlled society – were omnipresent. It was unwise to stand out from the crowd, for instance, by refusing to return the 'Heil Hitler!' salute. People were always on their guard. The pressure to conform was constant. But those who did conform were unlikely to find themselves in trouble with the Gestapo. Beyond the minorities seen as 'enemies of the people' – Jews, the widening band of social outsiders ('community aliens' as they were starting to be called), and political opponents – terror played a far more restricted role in the 1930s than it did in the Soviet Union under Stalin.

Most were content to be reminded that they were part of a unified 'people's community', with prospects of a glorious future resting on their racial exclusivity and superiority. Most shed no tears for 'outsiders' debarred from the 'community', least of all for Jews. Constant vilification and demonization of Jews in relentless propaganda did not fail to have an effect. 'The National Socialists really have brought about a deeper gulf between the people and the Jews,' adjudged a clandestine agent of the exiled Social Democratic leadership, reporting from Berlin in January 1936. 'The feeling that the Jews are another race is general nowadays.' It was widely accepted that Jews had no place in the German 'people's community' and should leave Germany or be forced out. There was no shortage of 'comrades of the people' (as ordinary Germans were now known) ready to acquire Jewish businesses at knock-down prices, obtain Jewish possessions or move into their apartments when they left.

That ethnic Germans from other parts of Europe should join the 'people's community' was welcomed. But few wanted to risk war to bring it about. For now, they suppressed their fears and hid their heads in the sand. It would soon enough be obvious to them that they were deep in the danger zone.

DYNAMIC DICTATORSHIPS IN COMPARISON

The three dynamic dictatorships – Stalin's Soviet Union, Mussolini's Italy and Hitler's Germany – were in practice quite distinctive forms of rule even though they had a number of structural features in common. Stalin's regime stands out plainly from the other two, which share more similar characteristics (and some 'borrowings' by Nazi Germany from Fascist Italy) though also displaying crucial differences. Each made a 'total claim' on its citizens. This was not realized in practice and most weakly accomplished in Fascist Italy – paradoxically the only one of the three regimes explicitly to declare that it was building a 'totalitarian state'. However, the 'total claim' unquestionably had huge consequences for the behaviour of citizens in such heavily orchestrated and controlled societies. 'Political space' and forms of organized social activity, even compared with those in other dictatorships of the era let alone liberal democracies, effectively ceased to exist outside what was permitted and managed by the regime itself. A ceaseless attempt was made in each of the three regimes to mould attitudes and behaviour according to exclusive ideological tenets. Identity with the regime was underpinned and reinforced through emphasis on the 'enemy within' – the 'outsiders' whose very existence shaped the creation of a community of 'insiders', of those who 'belonged'.

The penetration of society by regime values was lowest in Italy, in all probability greatest in Germany. The success of indoctrination was variable, though most apparent in all three regimes among the young. In each instance, the regime had substantial success in mobilizing large numbers of idealists and gaining extensive popular support. Quantifying the support is impossible, given the repression of all opposition on which each regime rested and the lack of freedom of expression. From the imprecise indicators available, Nazi Germany had the greatest level of popular support, Italy was some distance behind, while the Soviet Union was the most coerced population, suggestive of the least authentic support.

Each deployed the heavy hand of terroristic repression. For those terrorized by the police state, the ideological or structural differences between the regimes were a matter of the purest indifference. Even so, they mattered. The Soviet Union exerted an extraordinary level of terror directed at its own citizens, far more than the other two regimes, an arbitrary, unpredictable deterrence not replicated elsewhere. Nazi terror focused on quashing organized political opposition then, increasingly, on weak and small minorities – Jews, especially, and other racial or social 'outsider' groups. The worst of Fascist terror was reserved for Italy's African colonies. At home, once the early street violence of castor oil and the cudgel had waned, the application of terror was mild in comparison with that of the other two regimes, concentrating on eliminating known opponents but otherwise largely content with a strategy of containment.

Where Fascist Italy was also weakest was in its ideological dynamism and its militarization. Much of the mobilization of society was little more than superficial. After more than a decade of Fascist rule, the gap between rhetoric and reality was sizeable. The aim of a totality of state and society had remained illusory. There was little underlying driving purpose behind the regime. Even colonial war and victory in Abyssinia, popular though the triumph was, had only a superficial hold over Italian mentalities and could mobilize the population only for a short time. Whatever the belligerence of Mussolini and the Fascist leadership, there was little fixation among the Italian people on the prospect of war and military glory, and certainly little willingness to endure war's hardships and suffering. The Italian armed forces were capable at best of brief campaigns against inferior opponents, but they were completely unequipped for a major war. A technologically backward armaments industry was not capable of keeping up with the pace of rearmament in other countries.

The ideological driving-force in the Soviet Union was, in contrast to Italy, extremely strong. Enormous advances, at colossal human cost, had been made to mobilize the state-run economy, restructure agricultural production and industrialize at breakneck speed. The presumption of war at some point before too long lay behind the extraordinary pace of these developments. Unlike Germany, and even Italy, however, the focus was on preparing the economy and society for the military defence of the Soviet Union, rather than external aggression (though, admittedly, occupation of the Baltic countries and, perhaps, western Poland was envisaged as part of building a defence cordon). As Stalin knew only too well, rearmament was only in its early stages. The Soviet Union was nowhere near ready for a major conflict, while he himself inflicted grave damage on the Red Army's leadership through the great purges.

The ideological dynamism of Hitler's regime stands out from the other two regimes both in the sharpness of focus of its intensifying persecution of internal 'enemies', most obviously Jews, and in its heated preparations for military conflict in the foreseeable future – preparations that were plainly aggressive, not defensive, in nature. Germany had the most advanced economy on the European continent, one being increasingly and rapidly tailored for war. And it had the most efficient military leadership.

Although, between them, all three dictatorships were to play a disproportionately large role in shaping the future of the European continent in the years that followed, the leaders of the western democracies unsurprisingly and correctly saw Germany as the overwhelming menace. Stalin was at this stage regarded as mainly a danger to his own people. Mussolini was chiefly a danger to the subjugated peoples of Italy's colonial territories in Africa and a source of unpredictability in the Mediterranean. Hitler was a danger to German Jews – but from an international perspective above all a huge and growing danger to the peace of Europe.

The British government, especially, was mistrustful of and antagonistic towards the Soviet Union, detesting its social system and mystified by Stalin's purges. Italy was regarded as a manageable problem in the Mediterranean, increasingly hostile to western interests though not, on its own, a great threat. The main, and mounting, worry was Germany, a united people led by a ruthlessly determined dictator, rearming fast, and with strength in armed forces already close to outstripping its military power during the First World War. In 1914 Great Britain had gone to war chiefly to prevent German dominance in Europe and to protect its empire from Germany's pretensions to world-power status. It was looking all the more likely that there would be a replay before too long.

Meanwhile a chance presented itself in 1936 for a prior clash of the most powerful dictatorships in a conflict that many soon saw as a harbinger of a greater showdown to come. In July 1936 General Franco launched his rebellion against the Spanish republic. Within a short time he had gained military support from Hitler and Mussolini, while Stalin provided military backing for the republican forces. The dictators, on opposite sides of the Spanish Civil War, were flexing their muscles. The western democracies would once more come to reveal their weakness. The involvement of the major powers in the Civil War was the clearest sign, beyond the national tragedy for Spain's people, that Europe's international order was collapsing. The danger of the continent becoming engulfed in a new conflagration was growing ever stronger.

**AU COURS D'UN COMBAT SOUS LES MURS DE TRIPOLI
UN SOLDAT ITALIEN S'EMPARE D'UN ÉTENDARD VERT DU PROPHÈTE**

1. Colonial violence. During the invasion of Libya in 1911, an Italian soldier seizes a Muslim flag from vanquished Ottoman troops near Tripoli.

2. A German caricature of belligerent Europe in 1914. Germany and Austria-Hungary point their weapons at the threatening monster of Russia. A German boot prepares to stamp on the French. Britain (in the figure of a Scotsman), Italy and Turkey look on with some alarm, while a British bulldog seems to reside in Ireland.

3. German troops on their way to the battle of the Marne in September 1914, perhaps not greatly encouraged by the procession of ambulances returning from the front.

4. The 'Ravine of Death' just below the French fortress at Douaumont during the battle of Verdun in 1916.

5. A French poster showing Serbs fleeing after the disastrous defeat by the Austrians and Bulgarians in Autumn 1915 and proclaiming a 'Day of Serbia' on 25 June 1916 to raise money for Serbian refugees.

DER WAHRE JACOB

○ ○ ○ Abonnementspreis pro Jahr Mt. 2.60 ○ ○ ○ | ○ ○ ○ ○ ○ ○ Erſcheint alle vierzehn Tage. ○ ○ ○ ○ ○ ○ | Verantwortlich für die Redaktion: B. Heymann in Stuttgart.
Anzeigen pro 4 geſpaltene Nonpareille-Zeile Mt. 2.50 | Preis bei Poſtbezug vierteljährlich 65 Pfg. (ohne Beſtellgeld). | Druck und Verlag von J.H.W. Dietz Nachf. G.m.b.H. Stuttgart.

Die Erde im Jahre 1916 vom Mond aus geſehen.

6. 'The Earth in 1916 seen from the Moon' – a German magazine's striking image of the world dripping with blood.

7. A speaker from the Independent Socialist Party of Germany (USPD) addresses the crowd on 29 December 1918, as the funeral procession of sailors killed by government troops during the revolutionary upheavals in Berlin passes the former royal palace. The USPD left the government in protest at its action. Many of its members joined the newly formed Communist Party of Germany.

8. 'What We Have to Lose'. A poster shows what Germans claimed Allied demands at the Treaty of Versailles would mean for Germany: loss of 20 per cent of its productive area, 10 per cent of population, a third of coal, a quarter of agricultural produce, four-fifths of iron core, all the colonies and the merchant navy.

9. French suffragettes in 1919 demanding the vote. They were not successful. Women in France had to wait until 1944 before they were given the right to vote.

10. German propaganda during the Upper Silesian Plebiscite Campaign in 1921: 'in Germany lasting prosperity, in Poland poverty and emigration'. Upper Silesia was eventually partitioned, with most of the important industrial region going to Poland.

11. A British tank in Cologne, headquarters of the British Rhine Army, *c.* 1920, as part of the Allied occupation of the Rhineland between 1919 and 1930.

12. Signatures of those who negotiated the Treaty of Locarno in 1925 – including Briand, Stresemann, Austen Chamberlain and Mussolini – engraved on the pendulum of the clock in Locarno's court building.

13. A Kulak family is expelled from its farm in the Odessa region of Ukraine at some date between 1928 and 1937 during the brutal Stalinist drive to collectivise agricultural production.

14. A poster from about 1930 advertising the UFA-Palast cinema in the entertainment complex of Wilhelmshallen am Zoo in Berlin. The advent of 'talkies' brought a boom in cinema attendance throughout Europe in the 1930s.

15. Some city councils made determined efforts to combat appalling housing conditions. The socialist government of 'Red Vienna' commissioned the building of the Karl-Marx-Hof, which, on completion in 1930, contained 1,382 apartments for the city's poorer inhabitants.

16. A huge crowd attends a Nazi election rally in Frankfurt am Main – probably to hear Hitler's speech on 28 July 1932. The Nazi Party won 37.4 per cent of the vote in the general election three days later – the high point of its electoral success before Hitler became Chancellor the following January.

17. A guard stands outside the Karl-Marx-Hof in Vienna, after a socialist uprising on 12 February 1934 against the repressive authoritarian regime in Austria had been bloodily suppressed by government troops.

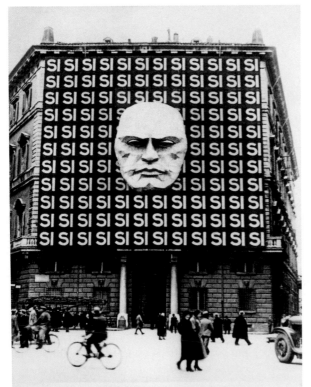

18. Fascist propaganda for the Italian 'election' – no more than a plebiscitary farce – on 26 March 1934. An enormous 'Big Brother' image of Mussolini is superimposed on the repeated single word 'Si', hammered home to encourage a 'yes' vote. Italians could vote only for a single-party list. Unsurprisingly, the National Fascist Party won 99.84 per cent of the vote.

19. Troops from General Franco's Army of Africa await their flight to Spain in a Junkers-52 supplied by Nazi Germany, during the first days of August 1936. The provision by Hitler and Mussolini of transport for nationalist troops was crucial to Franco's early successes in the civil war.

20. Polish men under German guard in Autumn 1939, perhaps being assembled to be sent to work in Germany – certainly awaiting an unenviable fate.

21. Members of a German propaganda company take photos of abandoned British war material after Allied troops had been forced to evacuate Dunkirk at the end of May 1940.

22. London citizens take shelter in an Underground station, sleeping on the escalators, during a German air raid on the British capital on 7 October 1940.

23. A recruiting poster for the Norwegian legion of the Waffen-SS, probably around the time of its formation on 29 June 1941, with the slogan 'against the common enemy... against Bolshevism'.

24. An unending column of German, Italian and Hungarian soldiers taken captive by the Red Army in early 1943 following the Battle of Stalingrad.

25. Prisoners in the concentration camp at Mauthausen in Austria in 1943, forced to carry heavy granite blocks up 186 steps to the top of the quarry.

26. Anti-Bolshevik propaganda poster for the 'service of obligatory labour' (*service du travail obligatoire*) in France in 1944. 'Each hour working in Germany is a stone for the rampart that protects France', runs the slogan. But the labour duty was hated and many conscripts fled to join the growing resistance movement.

chaque heure de travail en Allemagne c'est une pierre apportée au rempart qui PROTÈGE LA FRANCE

27. Italians watch American tanks pass by the Colosseum in Rome after the liberation of the city on 4 June 1944.

28. A Soviet photograph of Warsaw in ruins at the end of the Second World War. 'Here is a burial ground. Here is death,' one Polish woman remarked on seeing the devastated city.

29. A surprisingly cheerful looking group of Sudeten Germans near Liberec (Reichenberg) in Czechoslovakia on 6 May 1946, perhaps feeling that they were over the worst as they waited to be sent to Germany. They were among around 3 million Germans expelled, often in extremely brutal fashion, from Czechoslovakia by the Autumn of 1947.

30. 'Make Way for the Marshall Plan' runs the slogan of a poster advertising the American aid programme that symbolized the path to new prosperity for Western Europe. Stalin rejected the plan for the Eastern Bloc.

7

Towards the Abyss

The principle must not prevail that one can accommodate oneself to the circumstances and thus shirk the solution of the problems. The circumstances must rather be adapted to suit the demands. This is not possible without 'breaking in' to other countries or attacking other people's possessions.

Adolf Hitler, addressing military
commanders, 23 May 1939

War again, only a generation after millions had bled to death on the killing fields of the great conflict of 1914–18, was a fearsome prospect to most Europeans. Yet few contemporaries were blind during the later 1930s to the gathering, inexorable momentum towards another war. This time there would be no question of 'slithering over the edge' or 'sleepwalking' by political and military leaders into a catastrophe that they only dimly foresaw. This time there was an obvious aggressive power whose actions increasingly closed off all options other than war – or acceptance of domination of the European continent by the tyrannical might of Nazi Germany. 'The road to Hell', as the saying goes, 'is paved with good intentions.' That is the best gloss that can be placed on the way the western democracies tried to deal with Hitler. Their flawed attempts to accommodate the German expansionist drive allowed Hitler to dictate events to which they could only weakly react. His blackmailer's response to their concessions was to ask for more. The rest of Europe looked on, with ever greater anxiety. Everywhere, preparations were being made for a war that was greatly feared, but increasingly expected.

THE DEFEAT OF THE LEFT

The defeat of the Left in Germany during the Depression years, and its destruction in 1933 after Hitler's takeover of power, now came into full perspective. Both German parties of the Left, the Social Democratic Party and the Communist Party, had, if from quite different ideological positions, utterly opposed the militarism of the Right that they rightly foresaw would lead ultimately to war. Had the Left not been destroyed after Hitler's takeover of power, and had democracy – the mainstay of which had been the Social Democratic Party – survived in Germany, the odds on a new European war would have dropped sharply. Instead, the way was open for an assertive foreign policy, favoured by the national-conservative power-elites, backed by shrill populist nationalism, and subject to the increasingly high-risk gambles of Hitler.

The Left's tragic demise in Germany was only part of its much wider defeat in most of Europe. Outside the Soviet Union, the Left was almost everywhere powerless by 1935. Social democracy had held on to a stake in government in the Scandinavian countries, though these carried little weight in shaping the international constellation of power. Elsewhere the forces of the Right, invariably backed by the military, the police and the surveillance services, proved far too strong. Most of Europe by the mid-1930s was under some form of repressive nationalist regime, whether reactionary or outrightly fascist, leaving the Left impotent and in the grip of the forces of fierce persecution. In the most powerful western democracies, Great Britain and France, conservative-driven government had dominated in the Depression years. Here too, therefore, the Left's political influence had been greatly diminished.

The defeat of the Left took place on a continental scale, even if national structures had conditioned its specific nature. It was partly a reflection of crippling divisions, the decisive one between its social democratic and its communist wings (though unity on the Left did not prevent its defeat in Austria). The communist Left was itself disunited, sometimes broken into rival fractions, and its major representation completely dominated by the interests of the Soviet Union. The defeat of the Left also reflected the visceral detestation of socialist ideology and intense fear of communism in the upper and middle classes, the peasantry and parts of the working class itself. Whereas nationalists of whatever variety held out an appeal to all sections of society, the Left, whether socialist or communist, looked in the first instance to advancing the interests of a specific social group, the industrial working class. But the class politics of socialism, let alone the communist aim of a 'dictatorship of the proletariat', had self-evidently limited appeal to all those – the majority of the population – who saw themselves as certain losers should the Left triumph.

The fear of the Left, particularly of Bolshevism, was hugely out of proportion to the Left's actual power, or even potential for power, in most of Europe. But it is scarcely surprising, given the slogans of class hatred mouthed by the extreme Left in the parts of Europe where it still had a voice, the horror stories seeping out of the Soviet Union, and the dominance almost everywhere of a right-wing, anti-socialist press, that so many Europeans were prepared to place their trust in those they imagined would maintain 'order' and uphold national interests and not the interests of one specific class.

False Dawn in France

Amid all the deepening gloom for the Left in Europe, one particular election offered a flicker of light. The French general election of 1936 produced a result that seemed an outright triumph for anti-fascism, a reversal at last of what had for years been a European-wide trend towards the militant, extreme Right. When the ballots of the second round of voting were counted on 3 May 1936 (the first round had been a week earlier, on 26 April), the Popular Front of Socialists, Communists and Radicals had won an astonishing victory with 376 seats, far exceeding the 222 of the Right's National Front. The euphoria among supporters of the Left – workers but also most intellectuals, writers and artists – was immense. Manes Sperber was a Jewish writer born in 1905 in Poland but exiled in Paris since his brief experience of German imprisonment in 1933 and an increasingly critical member of the Communist Party (which he would quit in 1937). He later wrote of his elation at the election result. For him and for many others, he recalled, it was more than an election victory. It was as if a fresh wind had dispelled an oppressive, stifling air. A goal long seen as unreachable had come within grasp. 'Never had fraternity seemed so close as in the May days of 1936,' he wrote. 'From all avenues men, women and children poured into the squares of the *Bastille* and the *Nation*', their songs and cries of joy reaching adjoining streets, calling everyone to unite in the quest for justice and freedom – and all made possible without revolutionary violence. Sperber's humanitarian hopes soon revealed themselves to be a wildly optimistic dream.

France remained a completely divided country. The hatred of the nationalist Right for the Popular Front went far beyond conventional political opposition. Special vitriol was directed at its leader, Léon Blum, a Jewish intellectual who had been an early supporter of Dreyfus. Blum had been physically assaulted by a nationalist mob in February 1936. And the previous spring, the leader of the far-right *Action Française*, Charles Maurras, had appallingly denounced Blum as 'a man to be shot – in the back'. The Left's electoral triumph did not lessen France's ideological polarization. In reality, the victory had been far less sweeping than it seemed at first sight. The Left's proportion of the votes, 37.3 per cent, was only marginally higher than the 35.9 per cent won by the Right. The major shift had been within the Left itself – though this only increased the antagonism of the Right. The Radicals, the centrist mainstay of the Republic, had lost ground, down from 157 seats in 1932 to only 106 seats in 1936. The Socialists, the largest party in the Popular Front, had climbed from 131 to 147 seats. Various small left-wing parties had won 51 seats, an increase of 14 compared with 1932. Most worrying for the Right, the Communists had been the biggest winners – a leap from 10 to 72 seats.

The victory had been made possible once Stalin, in June 1934, had abandoned with a suddenness 'like scene-shifting in the theatre' (as Blum put it) the Comintern's denigration of social democrats as 'social fascists'. The growing strength of Hitler's Germany necessitated a complete reversal of earlier communist strategy throughout Europe. The revised strategy entailed working for collective security together with previously decried 'bourgeois' states. At the national level, Stalin now actively encouraged collaboration of Communists with Socialists and even 'bourgeois' parties in the building of 'popular fronts' of the Left to combat the increasing menace of fascism. The move was confirmed at the Seventh Congress of the Communist International in the summer of 1935.

Within France, pressure for a 'popular front' against fascism had come from below, from grass-roots level, at first articulated by trade unions, then adopted by the French Communist Party. The pressure had mounted during the course of 1935. By the autumn, when the Radicals joined forces with the Socialists and Communists, the Popular Front had become a reality.

Its election promises included a public works programme (marking the end of deflationary economic policy), reduction in the working week, retirement pensions and the establishment of an unemployment fund. Reflecting the strong anti-fascist mood, paramilitary organizations were to be banned. But radical measures likely to scare the middle classes were avoided. Social revolution would have to wait. The Socialists retreated from their advocacy of nationalization of the economy; the Communists dropped all talk of soviets or peasant collectives. The running of the Banque de France was to be broadened to eliminate control by a tight oligarchy of shareholders. But the bank was not nationalized. The value of the franc was to be upheld – a reassurance for those in the middle class who had lost savings under the previous left-wing coalition government – though this soon proved an unwise commitment. The right of women to work was guaranteed, but, anxious to avoid opening up debate on a possible change to the constitution (advocated by much of the extreme Right), there was no mention of their right to have the vote.

Blum, France's first Socialist and first Jewish premier, led a government of ministers – including three women – from the Socialist and Radical parties. The Communists (and a number of minority parties) provided support though they chose to stay out of government. Even before the new government took up office, the biggest wave of strikes France had ever known – often spontaneous, and carried out in high spirits, in a carnival-like, festive atmosphere – swept across the country. Nearly 2 million workers, many non-unionized and including large numbers of women on low pay, took part in thousands of strikes, factory occupations and sit-ins, overwhelmingly in the private sector.

Restaurants and cafés shut their doors, hotel guests had to manage without room service, there were no shop assistants to attend to customers in the big Paris department stores, and closed petrol stations meant motorists could not refuel their cars. The exhilaration of the strikers and their supporters was one part of the picture. The other was the widespread condemnation of social disorder by middle-class adherents of the Right, fearing it was the portal to communism. Political polarization was enhanced.

The massive strike wave concentrated the minds of employers. Within a single afternoon, on 7 June, in a meeting at the Prime Minister's residence at the Hôtel Matignon, they conceded to the main demands of the trade unions. Industrial relations were transformed overnight. The right to join a union, collective bargaining, recognition of shop stewards, a ban on punitive action against striking workers and wage rises of around 15 per cent were all agreed. The forty-hour working week and two weeks of paid holiday each year (which, supported by cheap rail fares, began the summer exodus from Paris and other cities that became a permanent feature of French society) was law within days. The strike wave gradually subsided. The blizzard of legislation continued with the ban on paramilitary leagues on 18 June, calming political disorder and street violence (though forcing parts of the extreme Right underground). Further laws introduced the reform of the Banque de France, raised the school-leaving age to fourteen, nationalized armaments industries and placated farmers by fixing big increases in grain prices. A new ministry of sport and leisure was established with the aim of democratizing access to outside activities (countering the militarization of leisure in fascist organizations), providing attractive forms of relaxation for the working class, and improving public health. As a consequence, cycling, hiking, youth-hostelling and popular tourism were all boosted, sporting facilities improved, general interest and participation in sport promoted. All in all, the level of intervention undertaken by the Popular Front government in such a short time was remarkable.

So was the euphoric mood on the French Left. Eric Hobsbawm, later one of Europe's most eminent historians, experienced as a nineteen-year-old revolutionary the extraordinary atmosphere in Paris on 14 July 1936, anniversary of the storming of the Bastille in

1789. He recalled how 'the red flags and tricolours, the leaders, the contingents of workers ... passed before the serried masses on the pavement, the crowded windows, the hospitably waving café proprietors, waiters and clients, the even more hospitable enthusiasm of the assembled and applauding brothel staffs'.

The summer euphoria swiftly faded, the carnival atmosphere evaporated, the cares and worries of everyday life returned. The government was soon in difficulties. Blum's limited socialist experiment rapidly ran into powerful headwinds from international market forces. The refusal to devalue the franc revealed itself as a mistake, hampering the government's room for manoeuvre. Big business moved its investment out of the country. The increased cost of the forty-hour week was passed on in price rises, fuelling growing inflation that was not matched by greater productivity. Pressure on the franc and gold reserves mounted. By September 1936 the government was forced to acknowledge its earlier error and devalue the franc by around a third. Even this did not remove the pressure on the currency. Workers' earnings and middle-class savings were eaten up by inflation. Support for the government waned. When the conservative Senate refused to grant the government emergency powers in June 1937 in order to combat the country's financial difficulties, Blum resigned and was replaced by the Radical, Camille Chautemps. Socialist ministers (including Blum) remained in the government. But the socialist impetus was gone. Government was now dominated by the Radicals, whose political inclinations were moving them rightwards, towards greater conservatism.

Chautemps, empowered by parliament to legislate by decree (powers that had been refused Blum), raised taxes and ended social reforms. Much of what had brought down Blum's government was unchanged. Prices continued to rise. Public debt continued to grow. The franc continued to lose value (eventually compelling further devaluation). Productivity continued to stagnate. Unrest continued to foment. The Popular Front continued to wither away – wracked by intransigent economic problems, facing implacable opposition on the conservative and fascist Right, and confronted by increasing danger in international affairs.

Blum returned as premier March 1938, but in a drastically changed international climate following the incorporation of Austria into the German Reich. By now, France, beset by worries about foreign policy, was impatient of social and economic experimentation. Blum was swiftly disabused of any hope of making progress with new attempts at state-directed investment, exchange controls and a wealth tax. Rising expenditure on rearmament imposed its own constraints on government spending for civilian purposes, while the flight of capital and plunging gold reserves necessitated further cuts in public expenditure and an eventual third devaluation of the franc. Blum's first administration had lasted 382 days; his second ended after only 26. With his removal for a second time, politics shifted to the conservative Right under the leadership of the new Prime Minister, the Radical Édouard Daladier. He was seen as a 'safe pair of hands', the very epitome of small-town provincial France, backed by both small and big capital, and lauded by the Right for reversing much of Blum's social legislation, thus terminating 'the revolution of June 1936'.

The construction of a Popular Front, bringing Socialists, Communists and the political centre as represented by the Radicals together in an attempt to confront and defeat fascism in France, was a rational and sensible strategy. At the very least it halted the threat to the Republic from the paramilitary Right. But if a Popular Front was necessary, it is equally clear that its failure to establish itself was almost guaranteed from the outset. A revolutionary social programme, such as the Communists would have favoured, stood no chance of being adopted. With the backing of no more than 15 per cent of the population it would have been impossible to push through. The middle-class clientele of the Radicals would have been horrified at any threat to their property. And the Socialists were compelled to tread a careful line that did not squander support to either their left or right. But piecemeal social reforms introduced in the face of opposition from much of the population, wrung out of the representatives of big business, and buffeted by international market forces, had the odds stacked heavily against their success.

The creation of the Popular Front was only possible through compromise amounting to a shotgun marriage between ideologically incompatible partners. The compromise temporarily painted over the deep divides in face of a common enemy. But it was a fragile construction whose foundations were undermined by the daunting problems facing the government. Relations between the two left-wing parties were themselves severely tested. Socialist antipathy towards the Communists was heightened by widely publicized negative accounts of conditions in the Soviet Union and by reports of Stalinist show trials. The Communists, for their part, regarded Blum as 'the killer of workers' after police had opened fire on communist protesters, killing 6 and wounding 200, at a demonstration in Clichy, a working-class district of Paris, in March 1937.

The Spanish Cauldron

The failure of the Left in France was about to recede into the shade of a much greater tragedy for the Left in Spain, as the travails of the Popular Front government were overtaken in public consciousness by events unfolding across the Spanish border. The Spanish Left, with extensive popular backing and the resources of the state at its disposal, was ready to fight to defend the Republic. It was seriously weakened, nevertheless, by bitter factional divisions, internecine conflicts and ideological rifts, overlain by regional separatist feeling stronger than anywhere else in western Europe (especially in the economically relatively advanced Catalonia and in the Basque Country). Even more damaging for the Left was the long-standing deep polarization of Spanish society. In contrast even to France, a chasm separated the ideological groupings of Left and Right in Spain. Republican loyalties were not as deep-rooted as in France. Nor were they tied to an epochal, symbolic event in the nation's history equivalent to the French Revolution.

The Second Republic in Spain was of very recent foundation, dating back only to April 1931. It had been brought about by the Left, and was fundamentally rejected by practically all on the increasingly extreme Right, whose anti-socialism was profound, visceral and widespread. The detestation of the Left was easily woven into the fabric of untarnished Catholic values that blanketed much of provincial Spain and which the Right had incorporated into their imagery of the Spanish nation. This hostility was backed of course by the traditional power-elites, who had most to lose from feared socialist rule – the landowners, leading industrialists, the Catholic Church and, most importantly, significant sections of the army's officer corps. Their power was in retreat, but still unbroken. Removing the Republic by force was for them an option. After all, Primo de Rivera's dictatorship had only ended a few years earlier, in January 1930, and the *pronunciamiento* (or military coup) had long held a place in Spanish politics. By March 1936, Spanish generals were conspiring to launch a new attempt to overthrow an elected government.

The triumph of the socialist and republican Left in the 1931 elections had, as was noted in Chapter 5, proved short-lived. By November 1933, when new elections took place, the Right had regathered strength. The Left were heavily defeated by a right-wing coalition of the CEDA and the Radicals under their leader Alejandro Lerroux, who became Prime Minister. The following two years then ended, often upturned, the modest social advances made since the foundation of the Republic. For the Left these were the *bienio negro*, the 'two black years' of growing fascist threat and heavy repression. A two-week strike in the northern region of Asturias in October 1934 by miners armed with whatever they could lay hands on and taking on the police, had ended when it was bloodily suppressed by notably brutal troops specially brought in from Morocco by none other than the future dictator, General Francisco Franco. The repression was savage, often barbarous. Some 2,000 civilians were left dead, 4,000 injured and 30,000 jailed, many of them tortured while in prison. Spain was already verging on civil war.

When the right-wing governing coalition fell apart, beset by financial scandals and political wrangling, new elections were called for February 1936. The Left had meanwhile formed a Popular Front, an electoral pact of Republicans (whose backing was largely middle class) and Socialists – the two major forces – supported, with varying degrees of enthusiasm, by the Communists, Catalan separatists, and socialist and anarchist trade unions. Opposing them in the election was a national bloc of right-wing groups. The country was split down the middle, and more radicalized than ever. The election was portrayed as a contest for Spain's future. For the Right it was a choice between good and evil, Catholicism or communism, 'the Spain of ancient traditions' or 'the anti-Spain of demolition, church-burning and . . . revolution'. Left-wing voices threatened 'to do in Spain what has been done in Russia'. When the votes were counted, the Popular Front had won a historic victory – narrow in the numbers of votes cast (4,654,111 to 4,503,524), yet overwhelming in the distribution of parliamentary seats (278 to the Right's 124).

The Popular Front's unity lasted no longer than the election. The government, comprised only of Republicans, was feeble from the outset. The Socialists, themselves disunited, refused to participate. The party was split between its reformist wing, headed by the moderate Indalecio Prieto, and the increasingly revolutionary General Workers' Union, led by Francisco Largo Caballero, who revelled in the appellation 'the Spanish Lenin' bestowed upon him by the Soviet press. The Socialist Youth Movement, like the trade union organization, also saw the future in terms of full-scale revolution, not piecemeal reformism. The attractions of the Communist Party, still small but growing fast, were evident.

The government started to restore the social and economic changes of 1931–3, released political prisoners, expropriated land from big estates and gave back autonomy to Catalonia (promising it, too, to the Basques). But the government's control was weak. Poor peasants and agricultural labourers occupied big estates in southern Spain. Strikes broke out in urban centres. The burning of churches – symbols of the oppressive hand of Catholic power – was more widespread than it had been in 1931, and a propaganda gift to the Right. Numerous murders were perpetrated by both the Left and Right. Both were moving further to the extremes. The Falange, previously a small faction on the Right, suddenly found itself winning new recruits, many from members of the youth movement of the 'Spanish Confederation of the Autonomous Right' (CEDA), who backed a more aggressive anti-republican stance than many older supporters of the party. And meanwhile, with the government unawares, the conspiracy was brewing.

Some army leaders, including Franco, had contemplated a coup directly after the election. But the time was not ripe. Instead the generals watched and waited. The government had sought to neutralize potential trouble from the military by removing Franco from his position as Chief of Staff and dispatching him to the Canary Islands. General Emilio Mola, known to be bitterly hostile to the Republic (and in fact the prime mover behind the planned coup), was also demoted. Remarkably, however, Mola was brought back from a command in Spanish Morocco and placed in charge of a garrison in Pamplona, in northern Spain – a prime location from which he could forge close links with clandestine supporters of an uprising. Some Falangists were arrested, though they were still able to organize even from within jail. But a weak government took little other action to preempt trouble.

On 17 July 1936 the uprising began in Spanish Morocco and the Canaries, spreading to mainland Spain over the next two days. The conspirators had expected a swift coup and military takeover. But it was soon apparent that this was not going to happen. In some areas mainland garrisons and much of the population backed the rebels. Three prime ministers within two days was a clear sign of government panic. Mola felt confident enough to turn down a request for a compromise truce. Elsewhere, however, even though they were often hedging their bets, the army and police remained loyal to the Republic. Workers in Madrid, Barcelona, San Sebastián in the Basque Country, and elsewhere took up arms. Within a matter of days Spain was completely divided, much as it had been in the February election.

The east and south remained mostly on the republican side. The rebels had, however, made rapid gains in the south-west, the west and much of central Spain. Militarily, the forces of the Republic and the rebels were fairly evenly balanced; economically, the most important industrial regions were still in government hands. People, down to village level, took sides: Left or Right, the Republic or fascism. Violence spiralled. Even in the first days, there were serious atrocities on both sides. In the areas they conquered, the rebels killed and summarily executed large numbers. The exact number killed is impossible to establish, though it certainly ran into the thousands. On the republican side, too, there were widespread acts of revenge against supporters of the uprising or class enemies. Scores were settled. 'Revolutionary justice' in improvised tribunals led to numerous executions. Horrific violence was directed at the clergy. Over six thousand members of the clergy – priests, monks and nuns – were murdered, churches burnt down, religious images destroyed. It was already turning into a full-scale civil war. But no outright winner was in sight.

An important shift in the balance of military power began in late

July and August when Hitler and Mussolini – keen to prevent communism gaining a foothold on the Iberian peninsula – provided the planes to transport Franco's crack Army of Africa, more than 30,000 hardened, experienced fighters, from Morocco to mainland Spain. This was the start of increasing aid to Franco's troops from Germany and Italy. Both Hitler and Mussolini hoped eventually to have backing from a nationalist Spain and in the meantime welcomed the opportunity to try out their firepower well away from home. Salazar's Portugal, fearful of Bolshevism triumphing next door, also supplied men and supplies for the rebels.

As a result, the rebel nationalists had a marked advantage. It could have been more than countered had the western democracies supplied arms to a fellow democracy. However, in August, Britain, closely followed by France (where Blum was mentally torn and conscience-stricken about depriving Spanish socialists of aid), led the way in reaching international agreement not to provide war materials to republican Spain. They were anxious to prevent the deepening conflict there turning into a full-scale European war. But as a result the struggle became sharply tilted towards the prospect of nationalist victory. Stalin responded in the autumn to a plea for military aid from the republican government, but the imbalance in arms supplies continued. Eventually, twenty-four countries signed the Non-Intervention Agreement. Germany, Italy and the Soviet Union all signed it, cynically paying lip-service to non-intervention while providing arms in great quantities.

In spite of official policies of non-intervention, at least 30,000 volunteers (a fair number of them Jewish) from various European countries – mostly socialists, communists and trade unionists organized by the Comintern into International Brigades – travelled to Spain from the autumn of 1936 onwards to try to save the Republic. Most of them, in one way or another, were idealists, fighting as they saw it in a class war and in a struggle to defeat fascism. Thousands of them lost their lives in the attempt. Their military contribution was exaggerated by Soviet propaganda at the time, and often has been since. But the Brigades certainly played their part in some of the big battles, starting with the fight to save Madrid from the rebel forces. In the judgement of one British journalist, Henry Buckley, who saw the

Brigades in action, 'by and large they were heroes in the way they fought. Their weapons were bad, discipline was hard to obtain, they spoke a dozen different languages and few of them any Spanish. They worked miracles by sheer heroism.' For the European Left, the beginning of the Spanish Civil War was a source of inspiration. Gradually, it turned into a source of demoralization.

Once Franco's troops, pushing northwards towards Madrid, had failed to take the Spanish capital after a lengthy siege in November 1936, the civil war descended into a lengthy attritional struggle fought with boundless savagery. A pattern developed of slow but relentless advances by the nationalists while the republicans, though capable of producing short-lived counter-offensives, were mainly forced into resilient but increasingly desperate defence. The spring and summer of 1937 saw nationalist forces make major advances in the north. By the autumn, after they had secured the northern coast, including the Basque Country (giving Franco access to vital raw materials and a crucial industrial region), the republican government's control was confined to a large block of territory stretching south-east of Madrid to the coast and, in the north, little more than Catalonia.

The civil war presented the Germans with the opportunity to carry out bombing experiments 'without responsibility on our part' (as Wolfram Freiherr von Richthofen, commander of the 'Condor Legion', the German bomber-fleet, put it). The bombing of a number of southern Spanish towns followed raids on Madrid. Richthofen found the results 'very good'. The Italians were by the spring of 1938 also bombing Spanish towns and villages in the nationalists' northern offensive, while the Germans stepped up their attacks to support the offensive by dropping 600 tons of bombs on Bilbao. The terrible attack on the Basque town of Guernica by about thirty German and three Italian bombers on the afternoon of 26 April 1937, which shocked and appalled the world, did not stand in isolation. That very morning German bombers had left 'no house intact' in a raid on Guerricaiz, 8 kilometres away. The sustained attack on Guernica itself, lasting three hours and aimed at demoralizing the Basques, in German eyes 'a complete technical success', left the small town a smouldering ruin with around 300 of its citizens dead. A priest who had arrived just in time to witness the devastation vividly described the screams as people fled in terror from the marketplace with the town in flames. Pablo Picasso's famous painting, displayed in the Spanish pavilion at the Paris World Exhibition in 1937, immortalized the destruction of Guernica in a graphic depiction of the barbarism of modern war. Despite worldwide condemnation, heavy German bombing in Spain continued. Towards the end of the fighting in Asturias that autumn, the Condor Legion command took the decision 'to deploy the squadrons ruthlessly against all places and methods of transport in the reduced Red living-space'.

The war was far from over in the autumn of 1937. But it had taken an inexorable course. The nationalists' conquest of Spain was slow, but relentless. The slowness was partly because of strong republican defence. It owed much, however, to Franco's conduct of the war. The war was for him a crusade to restore the greatness of Catholic Spain. This demanded the eradication, not just the defeat, of those he saw as Spain's inner enemies. Franco was, consequently, in no hurry to win a quick but superficial victory.

Francisco Franco, born in 1892, had spent all his formative years in the army. A combination of first-rate skills as a military commander, burning ambition and unwavering determination had taken him to the top of the army. Although late to join the conspiracy against the Republic, his command of the Army of Africa was crucial to its success. By the end of September 1936 he was accepted by nationalists as supreme commander of the army and head of state. The following April he unified the various factions of the Right in a single party whose title was such a mouthful – *Falange Española Tradicionalista y de las JONS (Traditional Spanish Phalanx of the National-Syndicalist Offensive Groups)* – that it was as good as never used in full and invariably shortened to *FET*.

Franco had none of the populist charisma of Hitler or Mussolini. He was a military product through and through. He had not arrived at his pre-eminent position through rabble-rousing speeches and political manoeuvring but through the army ranks, and through his undoubted military talent. In personal appearance he was unprepossessing – small, with a shrill, high-pitched voice. He was, however, ice-cold in his ruthlessness towards his enemies – who, in his eyes, were many. He saw Freemasonry, communism and separatism as the evils that had brought decadence, corruption and decline to Spain since its Golden Age in the sixteenth century. His caution as a military commander was inseparable from his determination to consolidate the nationalist conquest of Spain through the complete and lasting elimination of the enemy that stood in his way. He personally read through the death sentences following mass trials of his opponents and signed them. His forces carried out in all around 200,000 executions. A million prisoners were stuffed into his jails and labour camps. It was intended to serve as a lesson for evermore to the Left and his other enemies.

That the Republic was able to resist Franco's forces with such resilience and for so long is in itself remarkable given the divisions, infighting, rancour and ideological incompatibility that beset the government side. Socialists (themselves bitterly split), anarchists, socialist and anarchist trade unions, communists following Stalin's line, factions of communism that rejected Stalin's line, and the Catalan Left with its own agenda – all were united by little more than their overriding determination to defeat fascism. (Purist definitional differences over whether the nationalist forces were genuinely fascist are immaterial. For republicans, they *were* fascists. Who is to say that they were wrong in this?) Anti-fascism was the most powerful of unifying forces. Beyond it lay only splits and factions.

The Republic had seemed close to disintegration in the early months of the war. The government itself left beleaguered Madrid in November 1936 and moved to Valencia (retreating the following October still further, to Barcelona in Catalonia). By then state authority had often been replaced by anti-fascist committees that had sprung up following the nationalist rising and had expropriated powers in their localities. Basque nationalists declared an autonomous Basque Republic. Catalonia, too, went its own way, as did Aragon. The anarchist and socialist trade unions pushed through what amounted to a spontaneous social revolution. Landed property, industries and businesses were turned into collectives, local militias set up, government was taken over by local revolutionary councils. Much of it was fairly chaotic, though it functioned after a fashion – at least in the short term.

George Orwell described the conditions in Barcelona, where he had joined the militia of a small, non-Moscow-aligned communist organization, the *Partido Obrero de Unificación Marxista*, the Workers' Party of Marxist Unification, usually abbreviated to POUM: 'Practically every building of any size had been seized by the workers and was draped with red flags or with the red and black flag of the Anarchists; every wall was scrawled with the hammer and sickle and with the initials of the revolutionary parties; almost every church had been gutted and its images burnt ... Every shop and café had an inscription saying that it had been collectivized ... Practically everyone wore rough working-class clothes, or blue overalls or some variant of the militia uniform.' The social revolution was unlikely to endear itself to many beyond committed Marxists, though there was little choice but to comply with the new order.

The militia themselves were inadequately armed and badly organized – 'a complete rabble by any ordinary standard', as Orwell saw it. It was improbable that such forces would win a war against Franco's well-armed, disciplined troops. Central government had to adapt – and swiftly. Socialists and Communists entered a genuinely Popular Front government in September, headed by Largo Caballero – now seen (temporarily) as a unifying, not divisive figure. The government was in agreement that social revolution had to wait for another day. In the meantime there was an urgency in replacing militias with a properly organized army. Gradually, central authority was asserted. A unified army, backed by a centralized economy, conscription, rationing and organized civil defence took shape.

Some of this was under increased Soviet influence. With the arrival of Stalinist arms the influence of the Communists in the government grew – and the Communists were not at heart interested in a 'bourgeois' republic, but only in saving it from fascism in order to direct a 'genuine' revolution at a later date, and meanwhile in eliminating all rivals, such as Trotskyists and Anarchists, on the radical Left. In May 1937 Largo Caballero was forced out of office and replaced by Juan Negrín, a shrewd politician and competent administrator (he had previously been Finance Minister) who regarded a more dominant communist role as the acceptable price and best chance of defeating Franco. In Catalonia and Aragon the social revolution was brought to an end and the POUM crushed in a ruthless purge. The Republic was able to fight on, though the increased influence of the Communists was far from welcomed by many in the republican zone, and contributed to declining morale.

By 1938 the final agony of the Republic was approaching. A last big republican offensive failed on the lower Ebro River in eastern Spain. Morale was deteriorating fast, war-weariness widespread. Food supplies were running low. Catalonia finally fell in early 1939. Huge numbers of prisoners were captured – and left to the tender mercies of the nationalists. Half a million refugees fled into France and an uncertain, often miserable, future. What was left of republican control crumbled in March. On 26 March the nationalists at last entered Madrid. By the end of the month the remainder of republican territory was in their hands. On 1 April Franco declared the war over. Over 200,000 men had died on the battlefield. Well over a million (from a population of 25 million) suffered death, torture or imprisonment. Many more fled into exile.

Franco and his followers showed no mercy after victory. Typifying the spirit of a redemptive purge to purify Spain was the man appointed as president of the national Tribunal of Political Responsibilities, Enrique Suñer Ordóñez. A former professor of paediatric medicine in Madrid, he had described republicans in 1938 as 'devilish ... sadists and madmen ... monsters'. Behind them he saw Freemasons, socialists, anarchists and Soviet-backed Jews whose plans in the *Protocols of the Elders of Zion* were being realized. In his warped mind, the purpose of the war was 'to strengthen the race' and 'to bring about the total extirpation of our enemies'. Such attitudes characterized the vindictive approach to a demonized Left. Some 20,000 republicans were executed after the war had been won. Thousands more died in prisons, camps and in forced-labour battalions. The killing went on well into the 1940s.

Silence now descended over the half of Spain that had defended the Republic against Franco's nationalist rebels. Discrimination, hardship and suffering, together with bitter accommodation to the new, repressive dictatorship, were all that was left to them. The silence would last for over thirty-five years until Franco's death in 1975 brought a new start for Spain.

Could the civil war have been avoided? It seems unlikely. The chances of avoiding it were low by 1936. The country was completely divided and the government, in the first months after the election in February, was fast losing control. When in May Prieto was asked to form an administration but was blocked by his left-wing rival, Largo Caballero, the last chance of avoiding a civil war had probably gone. A strong, but moderate, Socialist government at this point might have headed off at least some of the middle classes who were frightened of the extreme Left and shifting rightwards to support the nationalists. As it was, Largo Caballero ensured that the government remained weak and the Left divided, while most of the middle classes looked to the rebels rather than the Republic. Nor could Prieto's plans to limit the powers of the police, disarm fascist terror squads and appoint a trusted head of state security be put into practice. It is extremely doubtful, however, whether Prieto could have introduced reforms that would have defused the situation, given how little faith much of the Left now had in a 'moderate' solution and how determined the Right was to overthrow the Republic. It is equally doubtful whether he or any other republican leader could have wielded sufficient power to arrest right-wing leaders or remove significant military leaders whose loyalty to the Republic was known to be dubious. The attempt was, in any case, not made. Those wishing the Republic greatest harm were allowed their freedom to plot the military uprising intended to bring it down.

Could the civil war have been won by the Republic? Once the uprising had taken place, Mola had refused truce terms, Franco had transported the Army of Africa from Morocco to Spain and the nationalists had consolidated early substantial territorial gains, a victory for the Republic became increasingly unlikely and by mid-1937 was as good as impossible. The divisions and conflicts on the Left did not help the Republic. However, they did not cause the defeat. Government forces were, if never altogether efficiently, gradually able to fight a lengthy defensive war. At no point, though, did they look capable of ultimate victory. They might have done so had not the lopsided nature of foreign intervention, in a conflict that rapidly acquired the character of a surrogate ideological contest between the international forces of fascism and communism, given a distinct advantage to the nationalists. As it was, while Soviet aid enabled republican forces to prolong the fight but little more, arms to the rebel nationalist forces from Fascist Italy and Nazi Germany were vital in helping ensure military success. Crucially, the non-intervention policy of the western democracies – and the USA's determination to observe strict neutrality – meant that, apart from Soviet aid, the republicans were feeding off scraps while the nationalists were in receipt of regular flows of arms from the fascist powers. Such an imbalance practically ruled out a republican victory and made Franco's eventual triumph practically certain.

The war left Spain mourning its dead (though with many of its most bitter wounds concealed for generations), its society still utterly riven even if the deep divides were now concealed beneath a thin veneer of declared national unity, its economy in ruins, its prospects of much-needed modernization delayed for years to come. For the Left in Spain the war was a disaster that would last for decades, a catastrophic defeat whose scale is hard to exaggerate. But did the human tragedy in Spain have wider political consequences for the rest of Europe? How, if at all, did the defeat of the Left affect the wider course of European history? Would a victory for the Left in the Spanish Civil War, however improbable, have done anything to prevent another general European war?

It seems highly unlikely. How Spain would have turned out under republican rule after a defeat of Franco's nationalist forces is impossible to gauge. Conceivably, the ultimate beneficiaries might well have been the communists, taking Spain down the route towards left-wing dictatorship. Had the more moderate Left triumphed, probably a less likely outcome, it would have given a boost to socialists in western Europe and offered the West a potential ally in a coming conflict. A possibility might have been to improve the prospects of the mooted 'grand coalition' of international forces, including the Soviet Union, to deter Hitler. At least as possible, however, is that a triumph for the Left in Spain (and France) would have provoked more than deterred Hitler – the prime danger to Europe's peace. Spain might even have found itself at a later date the target of German invasion. These are unknowable scenarios. As it was, events in Spain left socialists demoralized: tens of thousands from over fifty countries, the majority of them communists, who had been fired by idealism to join the

International Brigades to fight for the Republic, were left bitter at what they saw as the betrayal of the cause by the western democracies. Spain, however, contributed to the deepening acknowledgement on the Left that a lingering belief in pacifism and disarmament could not be sustained. Only force of arms could defeat fascism.

The civil war that many had feared would be the precursor to the showdown of fascism and Bolshevism in a new European war did not turn out that way. For all that Germany, Italy and the Soviet Union engaged in a proxy conflict in Spain, none was yet ready for a major European war (though Germany was certainly taking steps that would make one inevitable). The Germans, especially, had learnt important tactical lessons about air strikes in support of ground troops and the need to improve their tanks. They and the Italians had seen what their bombers could do to the civilian population of towns and cities; the Soviets had recognized they could not rely on the western 'bourgeois' powers in defence against the growing menace of fascism. The western democracies, for their part, felt vindicated that they had not been drawn into the conflict. Although the result was a nationalist Spain that could develop still closer ties with the fascist dictatorships, that was better in their eyes than a triumph of Bolshevism close to home.

The civil war lasted a terrible three years, blighting Spain for decades to come. It was, however, largely detachable from the main developments that were shaping the continent. Spain had been on the European fringes before the civil war. For a brief, traumatic period the cataclysmic events in Spain held much of Europe's attention. After 1939, however, Spain once again subsided into a European backwater – important strategically once a much bigger war had eventually broken out, but apart from that receding in wider interest until greatly altered circumstances during the Cold War turned Franco into a prized asset to the West.

For the rest of Europe, the events that were leading directly towards another great continental conflagration had little to do with Spain. They were taking place in the pivotal danger area of central Europe. And they were shaped by a force that the terrible civil war in Spain did not significantly affect: Germany's relentless drive to expansion.

THE ARMS RACE

In Berlin on the dark and dreary late afternoon of 5 November 1937 the commanders-in-chief of Germany's army, air force and navy – General Werner von Fritsch, General Hermann Göring (also head of the Four-Year Plan) and Admiral Erich Raeder – made their way to the Reich Chancellery to learn Hitler's decision on the allocation of steel to the three services. At least, that is what they thought they were going to learn.

Hitler addressed them for two hours, though not about the allocation of steel. At first there was little new. They had heard many times from him before that Germany's future economic security could be assured not by dependence on the vagaries of international markets but only through the acquisition of 'living space' (*Lebensraum*). The idea itself, a variant of imperialist ideology reinforced by Germany's exposure to economic blockade during the First World War and one of Hitler's obsessions since the mid-1920s, implied, of course, expansion and the risk, if not the certainty, of armed conflict at some point. This in itself worried neither the military leaders nor the others present, the War Minister, Werner von Blomberg, the Foreign Minister, Konstantin von Neurath, and Hitler's Wehrmacht adjutant, Colonel Friedrich Hossbach. What 'living space' meant in practice had been left open. It covered various notions of future expansion. None necessarily signified war in the near future. What Hitler went on to say, however, was that he was contemplating precisely that possibility. Time was not on Germany's side. The current advantage in armaments would not last. He was determined to act by 1943–4 at the latest, but under certain circumstances much earlier.

He raised the possibility of attacking Austria and Czechoslovakia even during the coming year, 1938. That worried some of his small audience a great deal. It was not that they were concerned about asserting German supremacy in central Europe or economic dominance of the Danube region (specially favoured by Göring). It was the prospect of war between Germany and the western powers that triggered their alarm. Germany was nowhere near prepared for a major war, and they knew it. What they had heard left Blomberg, Neurath and, above all, Fritsch nervous. Three months later the sceptics were gone. Hitler had removed all of them from their posts.

As 1937 drew to a close, the arms race among Europe's most powerful countries was an increasingly crucial determinant of the actions of governments. Hitler's meeting with his military leaders had ostensibly been about steel allocation. And, indeed, the shortages of steel were creating major difficulties for the German rearmament programme. Steel production was far too low for the demands of the army, it was imposing drastic constraints on aircraft production, and it left the building of warships lagging far behind the navy's projected targets. The growing steel crisis had led in the latter months of 1937 to the ousting of the Economics Minister, Hjalmar Schacht, who had masterminded the economic recovery after 1933 but had more recently raised weighty objections to a military spending programme that was running out of control. Göring, head of the Four-Year Plan – the crucial rearmaments programme laid down in autumn 1936 – was now effectively in charge of the economy and interested in economic management solely to maximize rearmament production and make Germany ready for war in the shortest possible time, regardless of cost. When the industrial barons of the Ruhr baulked at the costs of smelting the low-grade iron ores to meet his targets of domestic production, he commissioned three state-owned steelworks to do precisely that.

Leaders of German big business, not for the most part enthusiastic about Hitler before he had gained power, had been swift converts thereafter, eagerly eyeing the vast profits to be made from a revitalized economy, an armaments boom, and the anticipated domination of eastern and south-eastern Europe. Reluctant though the Ruhr steel barons were to invest in low-grade iron ores, they were nonetheless major beneficiaries of the vast state expenditure on rearmament. A huge concern such as the chemicals giant IG Farben had already seen its profits soar under the demands of the Four-Year Plan, and eye-watering possibilities lay in store as booty from German conquest. Its bosses could be certain to favour expansion into Austria and Czechoslovakia, both of which offered the prospect of major economic gain in the near future – acquisition, not least, of raw materials and industrial potential, ever more urgently needed to sustain the armaments drive in an economy under massive strain.

Supply bottlenecks and acute labour shortages were already building up. Over subsequent months the problems would become increasingly severe. Eventually, they would even bring warnings of an imminent collapse in the Reich's finances. Any 'normal' government would have felt compelled to address the difficulties by reining in expenditure to avoid economic disaster. But the Nazi regime was in no way 'normal'. Hitler's own unchanged view, coming to be shared by weighty sections of the military-industrial complex, was that only war – and the acquisition of new economic resources – would solve Germany's problems. Far from acting as a brake on Hitler's drive to war, Germany's mounting economic problems reinforced his conviction that war was an urgent necessity.

The other European country rearming for the purpose of external aggression was Germany's Axis partner, Italy. The pace of its rearmament was, however, crassly different from that in Germany. Steel production, as in Germany, imposed sharp restrictions on the scale of rearmament. So did dwindling currency reserves. Italian industrialists were happy to maximize their profits from producing arms, but unwilling to risk long-term investment for short-term gain. Poor management and bad mistakes in the commissioning of weapons led to weaknesses both in technology and performance. And many of Italy's scarce resources were wasted through involvement in the civil war in Spain, which was lasting much longer than Mussolini had foreseen when he had been so quick to provide aid to Franco. By the end of 1937, the combination of problems in the Italian economy was beginning to impose significant constraints on rearmament. The state lacked both the industrial capacity and financial strength to push through a rapid increase in rearmament. In fact, as other countries were intensifying their rearmament programmes, Italy actually saw a drop of 20 per cent in military spending in 1937–8 compared with the previous year. Mussolini was envisaging up to five years before Italy would be prepared for war. Even that reckoning was optimistic.

The Soviet leadership had from 1936 reacted ever more allergically to the growing danger to their country from Germany, allied most likely, it was presumed, with other 'fascist' and 'imperialist' powers. With all branches of industrial production in the hands of the state in a closed economy and under a brutal dictatorship, there were no constraints on an all-out rearmament drive. Output was nonetheless hampered by inefficiencies, disputes over areas of competence between industry and the army, and structural problems in converting civilian to military production. On top of that came the disastrous purges – themselves at least in part a reflection of Stalin's paranoia about 'internal enemies' who were allegedly threatening Soviet defences. Unsurprisingly, foreign Kremlin-watchers took it as axiomatic that the Soviet Union had been seriously weakened and was, certainly for the foreseeable future, not a force to be reckoned with. Despite the massive advances in the rearmament drive, on the basis of the intelligence they were receiving the Soviet leaders deemed that the gap with Germany, especially in the critical sphere of the quality of air armaments, was widening, not narrowing. It was a worrying thought.

For the western democracies, rearmament was a necessary evil, a reaction to the mounting threat from Italy and, especially, Germany (as well as, in the Far East, Japan). Their international finance, trade and business could only be damaged by war and huge continental, if not global, disruption. Their interests lay in sustaining peace. This priority was reinforced in British eyes by the mounting and costly difficulties they faced in sustaining control over some of their overseas possessions. India, where they had to contend with continued pressure for independence, remained a major problem. Beyond this, beginning in 1936 (and lasting for fully three years), they were engaged in the brutal suppression of a big Arab insurrection against colonial rule and Jewish settlement in the mandated territory in Palestine.

It was not that the resources needed for the defence of the United Kingdom were hugely diverted to the empire; French resources for the defence of their own colonies were even more subjugated to the pressing requirements of building up home defences against the obvious growing danger from across the Rhine. Nevertheless, imperial defence still meant that men and resources had to be provided. Britain's political and military leaders fully realized that the country's global defence commitments were greatly overstretched. Simultaneous war in three separate theatres, against Italy, Germany and Japan, would present the nightmare scenario. This dire prospect drove the policy of appeasement – assuaging potential enemies – in which Britain took the lead and France followed.

The ability to match Germany's accelerating rearmament programme was a great source of anxiety. The state of air defences in
particular was acutely worrying. Stanley Baldwin, the dominant figure in the British National Government and, from June 1935, Prime
Minister for the third time, had three years earlier done nothing to
diminish the public fear of attacks from the air in the event of another
war when he had stated that 'the bomber will always get through'. It
had been at that time, in 1932, an expression of the futile hope that
Britain might take the lead in outlawing bombing as part of international disarmament. As such hopes evaporated and large-scale
German rearmament had to be recognized as an ominous fact, fears
were already voiced by the autumn of 1934 that British defences had
been neglected and would not be capable of matching a growing dis-
parity in armed strength, especially in air power. Then, at a meeting in
Berlin in March 1935, Hitler (with more concern for the effect than
accuracy) had told the British Foreign Secretary, Sir John Simon, and
Lord Privy Seal (a minister without portfolio), Anthony Eden, that
Germany had already gained parity in air power with Britain. The
result was great alarm in London. From this point onwards, those
who still favoured disarmament – including most Liberals and Labour
supporters – were gradually placed on the back foot. In June
1935 Baldwin replaced the ineffective Air Minister, Lord London-
derry, with the more energetic and forceful Sir Philip Cunliffe-Lister.
The expansion and modernization of the air force now acquired new
urgency as part of a general (and increasingly substantial) extension
of British rearmament.

On their assessment of the German lead in armaments, British military planners looked to 1939 as the year of maximum danger, when
Britain must be militarily ready to confront Germany. Some thought
such timing illusory. There were dire warnings from within the
military – keen, of course, to press the case for massively increased
expenditure on rearmament – and within the high echelons of the Foreign Office that Britain would by then be in no position to contain the
threat of Germany. They pointed to a growing, not diminishing, dis-
parity in arms, especially in the air. Worries were also expressed that
tilting the economy too rapidly towards rearmament might necessitate
tax rises and an increased cost of living. These in turn might threaten

social stability, possibly even opening the door to a socialist-style state-run militarized economy. Opinion varied among political and military leaders on the severity of the threat from Germany, the point of gravest danger, and the intensity with which the effort to overcome the gap in military build-up had to be undertaken. The dominant view, however, was that it was crucial to play for time, avoid premature war, and, with luck, avoid war at all through clever diplomacy – implicitly meaning, without doubt, reaching an accommodation with Germany. The predominant economic as well as military arguments advanced pointed in the same direction – towards appeasement.

The economic case for appeasement appealed even more to French ministers following the fall of Blum's Popular Front government in 1937. The austerity policies introduced in the attempt to stabilize state finances were incompatible with an expanded armaments programme. The Finance Minister, Georges Bonnet, indicated that it was impossible to provide both guns and butter. Big rearmament programmes would have to be cut back. France's liberal economy, he argued, could simply not compete with Germany's unconstrained spending on armaments. The defence budget for 1938 was actually reduced as a result. Armed forces chiefs complained in vain.

The threat from the air, viewed in France as elsewhere as the greatest danger in any future war, was especially worrying. The restructuring of France's recently nationalized aircraft industry created production problems to add to the financial constraints. Only 370 aircraft were built in 1937, compared with Germany's 5,606. The Air Minister, Pierre Cot, widely viewed as a left-wing radical and unpopular because of his advocacy of a close alliance with the Soviet Union, said he needed a 60 per cent increase in his budget to galvanize aircraft production. Given financial constraints, that was out of the question. Unsurprisingly, the French air force was gloomy about its prospects in a coming war. Its chief predicted in early 1938 that should war break out that year 'the French air force would be annihilated in a few days'. Acutely aware of both economic and military weakness, France's leaders were temperamentally attuned to the policy being forged in London of buying time through finding a way to come to terms with Hitler's Germany.

By late 1937 the arms race that had been unleashed by Germany was taking on its own momentum and restricting political options among all the major powers. The contours of the extraordinary drama that would unfold over the following two years were taking shape. And in that drama, as the room for manoeuvre became objectively curtailed, the role played by a small number of key individuals would prove decisive.

HAWKS AND DOVES

In London in November 1937, around the time that the meeting in the Reich Chancellery was taking place, Lord Halifax, Leader of the House of Lords and soon to become British Foreign Secretary, was preparing to visit Hitler. He hoped to arrive at an accommodation with the German dictator over central Europe. It was the first step in a more active appeasement policy that reflected the initiative of the new British Prime Minister, Neville Chamberlain, who had replaced Baldwin on 28 May.

Baldwin might be thought to have retired from the premiership at a good moment. The previous December he had deftly handled the abdication crisis, when King Edward VIII had renounced the throne in favour of his brother, George VI, to marry an American divorcee, Mrs Wallis Simpson. Two weeks before Baldwin's resignation the coronation of the new king had seen a momentary display of patriotic unity in the country, which was recovering from economic depression and had avoided the political extremism that had beset much of Europe. And Baldwin, increasingly worried about the prospect of war, resigned before he would have had to contend with the grave and prolonged international crisis that was about to grip Europe.

When he met Hitler on 19 November, Halifax himself suggested that the British government would accept a change through 'peaceful evolution' in the current status of Austria, Czechoslovakia and Danzig, though it was keen to avoid 'far-reaching disturbances'. This was music to Hitler's ears. He told Halifax he had no wish to annex Austria or reduce her to political dependence – and went on behind the scenes working towards exactly such an eventuality. Halifax noted in his diary that he found Hitler 'very sincere', wanting friendly relations with Britain. The cultured British aristocrat was plainly out of his depth with a political leader whose expressed solution to the problems that Britain was encountering in India was to shoot Gandhi and several hundred members of the Congress Party until order was restored. When he reported back to the British cabinet, Halifax assured ministers that Hitler had no 'immediate adventure' in mind and suggested giving him some colonial territory to make him more amenable in Europe.

Chamberlain thought Halifax's visit had been 'a great success'. He told his sister in a private letter that, though the Germans wanted to dominate eastern Europe, he did not see why agreement could not be reached as long as Germany rejected the use of force to deal with the Austrians and Czechoslovaks and Britain gave assurances that it would not act to prevent change by peaceful means. The minister most opposed to this new, more active form of appeasement – the search for accommodation with Germany through bilateral relations and concessions of territorial change in central Europe – the Foreign Secretary, Anthony Eden, was from January 1938 ill and recuperating in the south of France. While he was away, the direction of foreign affairs was in Chamberlain's own hands. Worn out, and in continuing conflict with Chamberlain, Eden resigned on 20 February 1938. His successor was the arch-appeaser, Lord Halifax.

A British government only too aware of its defence weaknesses and overstretched global commitments, and looking actively to find accommodation with Hitler, was by now the chief obstacle to German expansion in Europe. It was not an encouraging thought. In Paris there was recognition by the time that Chautemps, the Prime Minister, and his Foreign Minister, Yvon Delbos, travelled to London in November 1937 to hear an account of Halifax's meeting with Hitler, that French foreign policy was heavily subordinated to that of Britain. When the French asked whether its ally, Czechoslovakia, could reckon with British as well as French support in the event of the country becoming a victim of aggression, Chamberlain avoided any commitment, stating that Czechoslovakia was 'a long way off' and a country 'with which we had not a great deal in common'. Chautemps privately in fact acknowledged the inevitability of extended German influence in central Europe at the expense of Austria and

Czechoslovakia and was not unhappy to let Britain make the running in appeasement.

In Rome, Benito Mussolini could reflect in November 1937 on how he had been bedazzled by his state visit to Germany only a few weeks earlier when Hitler had left no stone unturned in the successful endeavour to impress his Axis partner. Early in the month Italy had signed the Anti-Comintern Pact, linking itself with the agreement signed the previous autumn between Germany and Japan. The Pact was directed ostensibly against the Soviet Union. However, in his dealings with the Italians prior to them joining the Pact, Hitler's foreign emissary and currently ambassador in London, Joachim von Ribbentrop, had indicated what was really behind the move. The British, he explained, had rejected the overtures to an Anglo-German rapprochement (the hope that had been behind Hitler sending Ribbentrop as his ambassador to London). The Pact, he led Mussolini and his Foreign Minister, Count Galeazzo Ciano, to understand, was 'in reality clearly anti-British', the preliminary basis of closer military ties between Germany, Italy and Japan. Italy was being gripped ever more tightly in Germany's iron embrace. In January 1938 the Italian army was given a directive, for the first time envisaging an alignment of Germany and Italy against Britain and France. The Italian armed forces, well aware of the inadequacies of their rearmament programme, could only hope that war would not come soon.

In Moscow, Stalin had spent much of 1937 demolishing the Red Army's leadership through his great purges. It seemed sheer madness to outside observers. This was Hitler's view. 'Must be exterminated,' he remarked ominously to his Propaganda Minister, Joseph Goebbels, that December. The Soviet Union was, however, not yet on his immediate agenda, and had not figured in the scenarios he had painted to his military leaders a month earlier. Within the Soviet leadership, war with the capitalist powers – among which they included Germany and Italy (viewing fascism as the most extreme and aggressive form of capitalism) – was seen as inevitable. There was a growing conviction that the western democracies were encouraging Hitler to turn eastwards, to fight the war against communism for them. On his own eastern borders, Stalin also had concerns. Japanese militarism along the uneasy border between Manchukuo and the USSR was starting to pose a significant threat. The only question was when war would come. The longer it could be postponed, the better it would be for the Soviet Union. There was a long way to go before the Soviet military machine would be ready.

In the meantime, Stalin's options were narrowing. Collective security, the policy advocated by his Foreign Minister, Maxim Litvinov, became ever less attractive in view of the evident weakness of the western democracies and their readiness to contemplate accommodation with Hitler. An alternative, which would gradually gain weight, was to try to return to a form of rapprochement with Germany. The arrangement in the 1920s, following the 1922 Treaty of Rapallo and using mutual economic advantage as a lever, offered a sort of precedent. But Hitler's visceral anti-Bolshevism, which he had again demonstrated as recently as the Nazi Party rally in September 1937, stood in the way of even indirect overtures. Stalin's third possibility was to accept Soviet isolation and increase still further the pace of rearmament, hoping that there would be no early descent into war. For the time being, this offered the only way forward.

In the capitals of countries in central and eastern Europe political leaders in the late autumn of 1937 were more than aware of a drastically shifting balance of power and their own limited options. Their dependence on actions of the major European powers that they could not control was obvious. Collective security through the League of Nations, as Abyssinia had shown, was long dead. France, once the guarantor of protection through its network of alliances, was gravely weakened, its internal divisions and economic problems plain to see. Britain, it was clear, had no major interest in preserving the status quo in central Europe. German political as well as economic influence was filling the vacuum. National interest and mutual distrust or enmity posed barriers to military cooperation. And meanwhile German strength was growing visibly, central Europe being the obvious target for any expansionist moves. Nervousness and apprehension were tangible. In Vienna and Prague there was particular cause for anxiety. Both Austria and Czechoslovakia were short of friends; the French, their foreign policy becoming heavily tied to Britain's, were less reliable allies of the Czechs than had once been the case. Austria, no longer with Italy's protection, was most likely to be Hitler's first target. A move would surely come soon.

Far from Europe, too, there were momentous developments – eventually to have a profound impact on the continent. Since July 1937, Japan, increasingly militaristic and aggressive, had been fighting a bitter war in China. The atrocities perpetrated, among them the horrendous slaughter of Chinese civilians by rampaging Japanese troops in Nanking in December, shocked the world. They contributed to a gradual, if slow, decline in isolationist sentiment in the United States, where President Roosevelt had already signalled, three months earlier, the need to 'quarantine' the aggressive powers that were threatening world peace. As yet, to the frustration of the British (whose interests in the Far East would be most directly endangered by Japanese aggression), no action followed from the USA. Even so, 1937 saw the beginning of the growing confrontation between Japan and America in the Pacific that would eventually bring both countries into a global conflict. And it saw the start of Roosevelt's awareness of the need to persuade American public opinion that any German aggression in Europe was not without consequences for the USA.

On 4 February 1938 sweeping changes in the political and military leadership of the German Reich were suddenly announced in Berlin. Blomberg, the War Minister, and Fritsch, the commander-in-chief of the army, had been dismissed. Hitler himself had taken over at the head of a restructured high command of the Wehrmacht. His own supremacy was as a result even further enhanced. The position of the military leadership was significantly weakened. Those voicing fears of being plunged into war against the western powers were greatly outnumbered by Hitler loyalists, won over by huge spending on rearmament, restored prestige and Germany's enhanced international standing. Other powerful elites in the economy or in the high ranks of the state bureaucracy, whose hopes of a resurgent German dominance had never vanished, had overwhelmingly aligned themselves with Hitler's regime. The assertive foreign policy, exploiting the weakness and divisions of the western democracies, had made Hitler a hugely popular dictator. The masses gave him the plebiscitary backing that enormously boosted his standing at home and abroad. An enormous,

multi-layered Nazi Movement provided the organizational underpinning of his rule and the apparatus to ensure the constant mobilization
of mass support. The dictatorship was strong, secure, and not threatened by any significant opposition. The potential for organized
resistance had long ago been quashed. Only a military coup could
effectively challenge Hitler's mastery. Of that there was as yet no sign.

In the major restructuring of the regime's leadership in early February 1938 the other big departure, alongside the military figures
Blomberg and Fritsch, was that of the conservative Neurath, replaced
as Foreign Minister at a critical juncture by the hawkish Ribbentrop.
He was known to echo Hitler's own views and, since his failure as
ambassador in London, was bitterly anti-British. Further widespread
changes were made in the upper ranks of the officer and diplomatic
corps. Hitler now had personnel in key positions who were attuned to
his high-risk foreign policy. Possible constraints on any decisions he
might make had dwindled to insignificance. The likelihood of one
bold move to be undertaken very soon was surmised by those around
Hitler. The Austrian Chancellor, Kurt von Schuschnigg, ought to be
'trembling', one high-ranking officer in Hitler's entourage noted
privately in his diary.

Little over a month later the Austrian government capitulated to
intense pressure from Berlin, German troops crossed the Austrian
border, and legislation to incorporate Austria into a Greater Germany
was hastily drawn up. On 15 March, before a vast, ecstatic crowd in
Vienna's Heldenplatz, Hitler announced 'the entry of my homeland
into the German Reich'. As he had foreseen, the western democracies
lamely protested but otherwise did nothing. Nor did the subsequent
ferociously brutal persecution of Austrian Jews and political opponents of the Nazis elicit any reaction from Paris or London, or deter the
hopes of Neville Chamberlain that it might be possible 'some day for
us to start peace talks again with the Germans'.

Czechoslovakia, its borders now exposed, was certain to be Hitler's
next target. Britain and France had practically written off Austria
long before it fell to the Germans. Czechoslovakia was a different
matter. Its geographical position made it pivotal. It had an alliance
with France, another with the Soviet Union. And France was Britain's
ally. An attack on Czechoslovakia might well unleash a general

European war. From a German perspective, Czechoslovakia's ties with both the west and the east from a key position in central Europe posed a potentially serious strategic problem. Its raw materials and armaments would certainly be extremely valuable to German war preparations. But attacking Czechoslovakia was a high-risk enterprise. It could take Germany into war against the western democracies – a war that some among its military leaders, not least the Chief of the Army's General Staff, General Ludwig Beck, were sure it could not win.

Czechoslovakia, however, lacked powerful friends. Even as Germany was swallowing up Austria, the French government were being told by the Defence Minister, Édouard Daladier, that France could offer no direct military assistance to its Czech ally. France's military leaders dismissed at the same time any prospect of the Red Army coming to the aid of Czechoslovakia. A few weeks later French leaders learnt that Britain would provide no guarantee to take military action should the Germans attack Czechoslovakia. The stance of the western powers throughout the summer of 1938 was set. France, whatever noises were made about standing behind its Czech ally, would not act without Britain. And Britain would offer no prospect of military intervention. The Czechs were on their own.

Their unenviable plight was made worse, in not dissimilar fashion to that of Austria earlier, by unrest from within Czechoslovakia. Konrad Henlein, the leader of the increasingly nazified German minority in the Sudetenland (badly treated by the Czech majority, though nowhere near as much as German propaganda claimed), was primed by Hitler to pose demands for autonomy that could never be satisfied by Prague. For the western powers, some at least of the demands seemed reasonable. And when Hitler claimed to want no more than to bring persecuted Germans 'home into the Reich', it appeared that he was once more merely a nationalist politician, if an extreme and utterly intransigent one, who was pursuing the limited aim of incorporating another German ethnic bloc within the Reich. The lack of comprehension of Hitler's motives was a crucial component of the growing tragedy of Czechoslovakia. German ruthlessness, Czech helplessness and Anglo-French feebleness all played their part in the drama that took Europe to the verge of another war.

In a summer of bluff, brinkmanship and unbearably mounting tension, Hitler was ready to risk war against the western powers in order to destroy Czechoslovakia by force. Preparations for attack laid down the date of 1 October at the latest. For public consumption Hitler turned up the volume of his ever more frenzied verbal assaults on the Czech government and openly stated that he had no further territorial demands in Europe beyond the solution of the Sudeten problem.

Believing that Hitler wanted the incorporation of the Sudetenland into Germany but no more, Neville Chamberlain flew twice to Germany in mid-September for talks with Hitler. Chamberlain returned from his first visit, on 15 September, optimistic that a deal was within reach. It amounted to the Czechs ceding the Sudetenland to Germany and Hitler renouncing the use of force. Chamberlain privately expressed the view that Hitler, though harsh and ruthless, 'was a man who could be relied upon when he had given his word'. The British Prime Minister would be swiftly disabused of his presumption of Hitler's good faith. Britain and France had in the meantime exerted huge pressure upon the hapless Czechs, indicating that they could not rely on British or French support if it came to war, and compelling them to agree to territorial concessions. On 21 September the Czechs finally capitulated, with the deepest reluctance and profound sense of betrayal, to the Anglo-French diktat. But for Hitler it was not enough. At his second meeting with Chamberlain, on 22 September, he reneged on what the Prime Minister had taken as an agreement they had reached only a week earlier. He now demanded that they accept German occupation of the Sudetenland by 1 October, otherwise he would take it by force. He claimed to be indifferent to warnings from Britain that this could lead to war with the western powers.

Privately, however, Hitler was retreating from his intention to use military might to destroy Czechoslovakia in its entirety. The British and French were, after all, forcing the Czechs to give him what, ostensibly, he had wanted. With the Czechs browbeaten into accepting the mutilation of their country, the areas of disagreement with the western powers were by now relatively minor. 'You can't carry out a world war on account of modalities' was how Hitler's Propaganda Minister, Joseph Goebbels, succinctly put it.

It very nearly came to war just the same. Hitler had pushed some in

Chamberlain's cabinet, including the Foreign Secretary, Lord Halifax, too far. On 25 September they opposed acceptance of Hitler's ultimatum. The French and British agreed on the sending of an emissary to Berlin to warn Hitler that, should he attack Czechoslovakia, it would mean war. The French started to mobilize. The British mobilized their fleet. The Soviets, too, were mobilizing. War looked ever more likely. Frantic efforts were made to summon a conference to work out a settlement. The breakthrough came when Mussolini intervened to broker a four-power conference of Germany, Italy, France and Britain. (The Soviet Union, distrusted on all sides, was left out in the cold.) With that, the way was open for the climax of the drama in the Munich Agreement, signed on 30 September 1938. The Czechs were not represented at the gathering of the big powers that proceeded to break up their country. The two western democracies had forced another democracy to submit to the bullying of a dictator.

'The Government of the Czechoslovak Republic', ran the official announcement of the capitulation issued in Prague, protested 'to the whole world against the decisions of Munich, which were taken one-sidedly and without Czechoslovak participation.' The German humanist writer and publicist Frederic W. Nielsen, who had left Germany in October 1933 for exile in Prague in disgust at an inhumane regime, as he already saw it bent on war (he was later forced to move to Britain then the USA), undoubtedly expressed the bitterness of the entire Czech population of his adopted country in the open letters he sent to Chamberlain and Daladier. 'Don't deceive yourself!' he wrote to the British Prime Minister. 'The same voices that give praise to your name today will curse you in the not too distant future when it becomes clear what poison stems from the seed of this "act of peace".' His condemnation of Daladier was no less pungent: 'The greatness of France, founded in the storm on the Bastille, has now through your signature become the laughing-stock of the world.'

Hitler had gained what, on the surface at least, he had wanted. The occupation of the Sudetenland was to be carried out at once; the rest of Czechoslovakia, he had no doubt, could be taken at a later date. Peace had been preserved – but at what price?

Both Chamberlain and Daladier returned home to delirious

receptions. Only gradually did the shame of the capitulation to German bullying at the expense of the Czechs become widely acknowledged. Was there an alternative? On this views differed at the time and have remained divided across the decades. Hitler held the aces in his high-stakes gamble. And Chamberlain had a poor hand. On this there is little dispute. But how badly did he play his poor hand?

Chamberlain's weakest card was the state of British rearmament. For Daladier, across the Channel, the position was even worse. In both cases, the military leadership had made plain that the armed forces were not equipped to fight a war against Germany. In fact, both the French and the British exaggerated German armed strength. But their sense of gross inferiority in arms, especially in the air, was based on contemporary intelligence, not the benefits of hindsight. (A strategic bombing campaign of the type so feared was actually quite beyond Germany's capability at the time.) Other intelligence reports, emphasizing Germany's lack of raw materials and inadequate preparations for a major war, were ignored or downplayed. The military chiefs saw the outright priority in winning time to rearm.

Even so, at the height of the crisis, on 26 September, the French commander-in-chief, General Maurice Gamelin, informed French and British leaders that, taken together, their military forces, added to those of the Czechs, were greater than those of the Germans. On the French border with Germany, should an offensive be required to draw the Germans away from Czechoslovakia, France had twenty-three divisions compared with only eight for Germany. If Italy joined in, Gamelin had notions of attacking to the south, launching an offensive across the Alpine border into the Po valley, defeating the Italians, then marching north to Vienna and on to help the Czechs. Less reassuring was Gamelin's indication that, when facing the Germans, French troops would advance until they encountered serious opposition, then return to the Maginot defensive line. The French, especially, but the British military too, suffered from a misplaced inferiority complex towards the Germans. The underlying problem throughout, however, had been in essence political, not military.

It had begun well before 1938. The British and French had advertised their weaknesses and their difficulties both in comprehending

Hitler's aims and in how to deal with him on numerous occasions over the previous five years, most plainly during the remilitarization of the Rhineland in 1936. They had done nothing to prevent Hitler's Germany becoming militarily strong. That was what Chamberlain had to contend with on becoming British Prime Minister in May 1937; that, and the legacy of years in which Britain had sought to disarm rather than rearm, together with the balancing act, during years of severe economic constraints, of spreading the armed forces for duties in the Far East and the Mediterranean as well as in home waters. Chamberlain was easily the most dominant figure in the western democracies given the internal turmoil and economic problems of the French. Moreover, he had not just a more proactive way of trying to accommodate German expansionist demands, but also an extraordinarily misplaced self-confidence that he knew what Hitler wanted, could handle him, and could cajole him into a peaceful settlement of Europe's problems.

Chamberlain's personal imprint on British foreign policy, sometimes against the advice of experienced figures within the Foreign Office, reflected this conviction. A sign of his self-confidence was that on his first visit to Germany, in mid-September, he negotiated alone with Hitler, one to one. His Foreign Secretary, Lord Halifax, had not even accompanied him on the trip. In a later age, extensive international diplomacy would surely have been deployed in an attempt to defuse the critical situation. But this was long before transcontinental shuttle diplomacy. And with the League of Nations more or less defunct, there was no international body to intervene. The Dominions, having bled in one European war, had no appetite for another, and supported appeasement. The United States, still to emerge from its isolationism, watched from afar. Roosevelt had appealed for peace during the summer of 1938, but did no more than that. Chamberlain, his anti-American feelings never far beneath the surface, was dismissive of the prospect of any help from the USA. In any case, American military weakness left the United States in no position to intervene, even had the willingness been there. As it was, Roosevelt cabled 'Good man!' to Chamberlain on hearing that he was going to the Munich conference. The President, inconsequentially, then compared the outcome, which had been utterly predictable, to Judas' betrayal of Jesus.

The centre of the drama focused, therefore, heavily upon the personal duel of Hitler and Chamberlain — a historic mismatch if ever there was one. Chamberlain's belief that he could negotiate a peaceful outcome with Hitler had wavered only when he encountered the opposition of the loyal Halifax and others in his cabinet on return from his second visit to Germany. That belief had returned by the time of the Munich Conference, to the point where Chamberlain thought that by obtaining Hitler's signature on a worthless piece of paper, flaunted on his return to England, he had attained 'peace in our time'. He later regretted his exuberance, expressed under the influence of the rapturous crowds in London, and was hard-headed enough to imagine that he had only deferred, rather than prevented, war. He insisted until his death in 1940 that to have fought in 1938 would have been far worse than postponing if not averting war. Britain was not ready, he insisted; he had to gain time.

Whether, despite the warnings of military leaders, Britain and France would have been better off fighting in 1938 than waiting another year has been endlessly debated. It was indeed only in 1939 that British and French military spending came close to matching that of Germany, and only in that year that the two democracies began serious wartime planning. But Germany, too, had been rearming strongly that year on top of the four previous years of intensive rearmament and was also far better equipped to fight than it had been in 1938. This was reinforced by the destruction of Czech military power and the acquisition of new sources of raw materials and armaments from former Czechoslovakia. The balance of forces had, in fact, in some respects by 1939 tipped somewhat towards Germany.

Whether the Munich debacle could have been avoided has also been debated since those very days. Winston Churchill, the long-standing but largely isolated opponent of appeasement, had been the most outspoken voice in 1938 pleading for a 'grand alliance' with the Soviet Union and eastern European countries to deter Hitler. He later argued strongly that war would not have been necessary had deterrence, not appeasement, been the strategy. The Labour Party and many others on the Left supported the idea of the 'grand alliance'. The deep distrust, as well as embedded detestation, of the Soviet Union, embellished by gruesome reports of Stalin's purges, meant, however, that such a strategy never had a chance of winning the support of the British, or the French, government.

The prospect of a 'grand alliance' had indeed been the best option of deterring Hitler. Whether it could have translated into action is another matter. The Soviet Union's position was that it would fulfil its treaty obligations to the Czechs once the French had acted to fulfil theirs – something hardly likely to happen. Even had the Soviet Union acted, the Romanians and Poles would not have permitted Soviet troops to cross their soil. The Romanians had indicated, however, that they would allow Soviet planes to overfly their territory. The Soviet air force was positioned to offer assistance to Czechoslovakia, had the French engaged in the defence of the country, and a partial mobilization of Red Army troops did take place. But Stalin remained cautious throughout the crisis, awaiting developments, wary of becoming involved in a clash of 'imperialist powers'. The potential threat to Germany from east as well as west that a 'grand alliance' would have posed never materialized.

Deterrence through a 'grand alliance' could also have encouraged the nascent opposition within Germany. A plot to arrest Hitler in the event of an attack on Czechoslovakia had been taking shape over the summer, centred on the military leadership and high officials in the Foreign Ministry. The Munich Agreement blew away any prospect of the plotters acting. The best guess is that the plot would have come to nothing anyway, or, even if it had been carried out, would not have succeeded. But there is at least the possibility that had Hitler – against some weighty military advice – struck against Czechoslovakia, resulting in a much-dreaded war on two fronts, he would have emerged significantly weakened if he had not been overthrown.

Whether that would have prevented a general war in the long run is impossible to say. More likely is that war would have proved unavoidable at some point. Nevertheless, had Hitler been blocked, or even toppled, in 1938, it would have been a different conflict in different circumstances. As it was, after Munich the road to the war that did occur was a short one.

LAST RITES OF PEACE

Hitler had been irritated, rather than delighted, with the dividend his aggression had gained him at Munich. He had been compelled to back away from what he had wanted, to yield to the pressure for a negotiated settlement over the Sudetenland when he had wanted to destroy Czechoslovakia by armed might. 'That fellow [Chamberlain] has spoiled my entry into Prague,' he is reputed to have exclaimed on returning from Munich. The exultant crowds in Germany were cheering less a territorial triumph won at the high risk of war than the preservation of peace (which many credited to Chamberlain). Some weeks after the Munich Agreement, on 10 November, Hitler admitted in a speech (not for publication) to a meeting of German journalists and editors that having to dissemble for years about Germany's peaceful aims had insufficiently prepared the German people for the use of force.

The day before this candid admission, Germany had been convulsed in a terrible night of violence (*Reichskristallnacht*). Horrific pogroms had seen nearly a hundred Jews murdered (even by official government figures, and probably an underestimate) and countless others grievously molested by rampaging Nazi mobs, who had burnt down synagogues and destroyed Jewish property the length and breadth of the country. It was the culmination of an appalling spiral of anti-Jewish violence – surpassing the waves of 1933 and 1935 – which had followed the takeover of Austria in March and gathered momentum during the rising tension of the summer. Hitler, scornful of the weakness of his foreign opponents after Munich, approved the unleashing of the Nazi hordes at the prompting of his Propaganda Minister, Joseph Goebbels.

The aim of the pogroms was to speed up Jewish emigration. In this they succeeded. Half a million Jews, most of them completely assimilated before the Nazis gained power, had remained in Germany, despite the horrendous climate of growing persecution. Now tens of thousands of them poured over neighbouring borders to find refuge in western Europe, many of them then across the Channel to England or over the Atlantic to the safety of the United States. Despite immigration policies that remained restrictive, around 7,000 Jews crossed into the Netherlands, 40,000 eventually settled in the United Kingdom and around 85,000 in the USA. Some 10,000 children were taken in by Britain in the refugee action known as the *Kindertransport*, which the British government introduced days after the pogroms.

The Jewish immigrants would over subsequent decades make a significant contribution to the scientific and cultural life of their adoptive countries. For Germany the self-inflicted loss was immense. Tens of thousands more Jews, however, who were refused entry to European countries, the USA and Palestine (still under the British Mandate), were less fortunate. And many Jews remained in German hands, with vast numbers more likely to fall into their clutches in the event of war. Less than three months after the pogroms, Hitler issued a baleful warning – a 'prophecy' he called it – to the outside world: another war would bring about the destruction of Europe's Jews.

Germany was not the sole beneficiary from the dismemberment of Czechoslovakia. There was no love lost in Poland for its neighbour, and the Poles, eyeing up potential territorial gain from the break-up of Czechoslovakia, had remained neutral during the summer crisis in 1938. Losing no time after Munich, they had annexed Teschen, a sliver of south-eastern Silesia with a divided population, claimed after the First World War by both Poland and Czechoslovakia but awarded in 1920 to the Czechs. The Poles soon learned, however, that the ten-year non-aggression pact with Germany, signed in January 1934, meant nothing if they stood in Hitler's way.

The first sign of difficulties came when the Poles refused in the autumn of 1938 to accede to German proposals for the return to Germany of Danzig (a free city under the aegis of the League of Nations since 1920, though almost entirely ethnic German in the composition of its population), and for a transport route through the 'Corridor' that separated East Prussia from the remainder of the Reich. Poland's obstinacy over these issues continued into 1939. Hitler's irritation was contained for the time being. He could wait. Only in the spring of that year did his attention begin to focus on Poland.

That was after German troops had completed what Hitler had wanted the previous summer – the invasion of the remainder of Czechoslovakia on 15 March. A 'Protectorate of Bohemia and Moravia' was established. The Slovaks set up their own autonomous state. Czechoslovakia, the most successful of the new democracies that had emerged from the demise of the Austro-Hungarian Empire, disappeared from the map. After the German entry into Prague there could be no further illusions about Hitler as merely a nationalist politician aiming to incorporate ethnic Germans within an extended Reich. This was plain imperialist conquest. The western democracies at last saw Hitler in his true colours. Appeasement was dead. It was clear to all but the wilfully blind that Hitler would stop at nothing. It was equally clear that when the next time came, as it surely would, he would have to face armed resistance. There would be war.

On the rebound from the German occupation of the leftovers of Czechoslovakia and feeling deeply that he had been duped, Chamberlain on 31 March 1939 offered Poland, viewed as Germany's likely next victim, a guarantee of British military support should it be attacked. The French, effectively without a foreign policy of their own, went along with the British move. The Soviets were still not considered suitable allies in any attempt to confront Hitler with the possibility of a two-front war. Given notice of the guarantee only hours before it was announced, angry Soviet leaders were more than ever convinced that Chamberlain was playing a long game that would ultimately result in what he wanted: a war between Germany and the Soviet Union.

Deterrence was the key intention of the guarantee. Chamberlain had finally come round to trying to deter Hitler from further acts of aggression. His hope was that even now Hitler would see sense and settle his territorial demands without force. But Chamberlain had chosen a poor basis and relinquished Britain's initiative at the same time. He knew that Britain could do nothing militarily to prevent the Germans overrunning Poland, which, his advisers were telling him, would be accomplished within three months of an invasion. But after refusing the previous summer to give a similar guarantee to a democracy that had been ready to fight and was allied with France and the Soviet Union, he now bound Britain to the fate of Poland. Yet Poland (as Churchill put it) 'with hyena appetite had only six months before joined in the pillage and destruction of the Czechoslovak State', and was a country geographically exposed and militarily ill-equipped to withstand a German onslaught. Whether Britain entered a new war would from now on lie in the hands of Germany and Poland.

The guarantee was never going to deter Hitler. Its effect, indeed, was to provoke him. Raging against the British, he promised to 'cook them a stew that they'll choke on'. By early April he had authorized a military directive for the destruction of Poland any time after 1 September 1939. Polish obduracy on Danzig and the Corridor did the rest. The contours of the crisis that would reach its climax in the high summer of 1939 were set.

Meanwhile Mussolini, feeling upstaged by Hitler's Prague coup and not to be left out of land-grabbing, showed off what there was of Italian armed might by annexing Albania in April. Britain and France responded by extending their guarantee to Romania and Greece. Badly executed though the Italian attack on Albania had been, it was paraded as a great triumph that, as Dino Grandi, a leading Fascist, put it, would 'open the ancient paths of the Roman conquests in the east to the Italy of Mussolini'. The roads that the Italians started to build in the small, poverty-stricken country led towards Greece. Should war come, Italy's intention was that the British were to be driven from the Mediterranean. Tensions in southern Europe, too, were starting to foment.

The ordinary people of Europe could only look on anxiously as the leaders of the most powerful countries, as if moving pieces on a chessboard, determined their fate. The general mood in the summer of 1939 differed from that of the previous summer. At the height of the Sudeten crisis, the dread that Europe was teetering on the edge of the abyss, about to plunge into war, had been widespread and palpable. The euphoria that greeted Chamberlain, Daladier, Mussolini and Hitler when they returned from the Munich Conference expressed sheer relief that war had been avoided. The moral implications of what had been done to preserve peace had sunk in only later – where they did so at all. During the Polish crisis in 1939 the mood was more resigned, strangely less fearful.

In Germany the 'war psychosis' that internal reports had registered the previous year was largely absent. The feeling was that if the western powers had not been prepared to fight over Czechoslovakia, they would scarcely do so over Danzig (the overt German aim in the Polish crisis). 'The people in the streets are still confident Hitler will pull it off again without war' was the judgement in late August of William Shirer, an American journalist and broadcaster based in Berlin. 'It'll work out all right again' was a view that Viktor Klemperer, a Jewish academic living in endangered seclusion in Dresden but an acute observer of the hostile environment around him, took to be general opinion. As the crisis rapidly heated up, there was still hope that war would once more be avoided, together with resigned readiness to fight should Britain and France force war on Germany (the message that propaganda was hammering home). There was a wish that the problem of Danzig and the Corridor be solved in the German interest, though many people, possibly most, thought those issues were not worth a war. Contemporaries remarked on how different the mood was to 1914. There was no enthusiasm this time anywhere.

In France, too, the mood had altered. Fear of what war might bring, above all fear of bombing, was undiminished. But since Hitler's march into Prague, there was greater resilience, deeper resolve to stand up to further German aggression – a sense that enough was enough. Three-quarters of those asked in a French national survey in July 1939 professed themselves ready to use force in defence of Danzig. A type of false normality existed. Cinemas, cafés and restaurants flourished as people 'seized the day' and shut out the thought of what might be coming. Doom-mongers were largely to be found in intellectual circles. Next month the big cities emptied as people left in their droves for coastal resorts or the countryside, often clutching the latest best-seller, their translation of Margaret Mitchell's *Gone with the Wind*, to enjoy their holidays with pay in the lovely summer weather – perhaps the last opportunity to do so for some time, so not to be missed.

It was much the same in Britain. Germany's occupation of the rest of Czechoslovakia had altered public attitudes. 'There was a sea-change in the country's attitude toward pacifism and conscription,' William Woodruff later recalled. He was then a young man from a northern, working-class background who had managed to gain a place to study at Oxford University. Students debated 'whether they would have to fight this year or next. Rearmament was no longer a dirty word.' In an opinion survey carried out in Britain in July an almost identical proportion to that in the French survey – around three-quarters – thought Britain should fulfil its pledge to fight alongside Poland if the Danzig conflict led to war. As in France, people clasped at illusions of normality, shutting out of their minds the ominous beat of war drums. Dance halls and cinemas were booming, the sporting population was taken up with cricket Test matches between England and the touring West Indian team (the third Test was completed at The Oval in London little over a week before the start of the war), while the exodus to the seaside from northern mill towns during 'wakes weeks' took place as usual. In the English countryside, peaceful and beautiful that lovely summer, the horrors of war seemed far away. Many believed, in any case, that Hitler was bluffing over Danzig, that he would pull back in the end from attacking Poland if it meant war against Britain.

In Poland itself the guarantee had transformed attitudes. Feeling had suddenly become pro-English and pro-French. Hostility towards Germany was plain. The growing certainty that there would be war hung in the air, overshadowing everything. The atmosphere was one of mounting nervousness. The novelist Maria Dąbrowksa, famous since her family saga *Nights and Days* had won Poland's most prestigious literary prize in 1935, was recuperating from surgery and enjoying the beauty of a retreat in southern Poland in July, pondering whether she should return to Warsaw but reluctant to leave. 'The weather is so wonderful, the prospect of war so close, perhaps this is the last idyll in life,' she thought. There was a sense that time was precious. When she was back in Warsaw, a colleague persuaded her in early August to move to a spa resort in north-western Poland. 'Don't think about it for long,' he advised. 'It's the last possibility, the last opportunity. What's to talk about? At the latest in a few weeks there'll be war.' In the last days of the month there was a hasty mobilization of men, wagons and horses. Households hurried to stock up provisions. There was a hunt for gas masks, which the authorities had not made available in sufficient numbers. Attempts were made to seal off gas-proof rooms, windows stuck up with strips of paper. As everyone knew, the chances of peace hung by a thread. 'Poland faced a terrible catastrophe.'

The bombshell struck late in the evening of 21 August. Germany and the Soviet Union, the ultimate arch-enemies, were on the verge of an extraordinary deal. After years of being told that fascism was the ultimate evil, Soviet citizens were astonished to find Hitler was now their friend. It was, as one woman living at the time in Moscow later put it, 'the world turned upside down'. After years of being harangued about the diabolical nature of Bolshevism, German citizens were equally astonished at the barely credible turnaround. But most of all they were relieved. It meant 'that the dreaded nightmare of encirclement' had been destroyed.

Germany had first made tentative feelers towards the remarkable rapprochement with the Soviet Union several months earlier. Stalin's dismissal on 3 May of Maxim Litvinov, the proponent of collective security, and his replacement as People's Commissar for Foreign Affairs by Vyacheslav Molotov, had signalled a shift in thinking in the Kremlin. Ribbentrop saw a possible opening to a new understanding that would rule out any conceivable anti-German alliance of the Soviet Union with the western democracies (again being mooted, if without enthusiasm, in London and Paris) and at one fell swoop totally isolate Poland. For weeks, no more than hesitant steps towards a trade agreement ensued. Then indirect signs from Moscow gave Ribbentrop the encouragement he had been looking for to press for a political understanding involving mutual territorial interests.

The timing Hitler had in view for an attack on Poland – the end of August, before the autumn rains set in – imposed its own pressure. On 19 August Stalin finally signalled that he was prepared to reach an agreement with Germany. Hitler made arrangements without delay to send Ribbentrop to Moscow. Four days later Molotov and Ribbentrop put their signatures to a non-aggression pact between the Soviet Union and Germany. A secret protocol delineated spheres of interest in the Baltic, Romania and Poland with a view to 'a territorial and political transformation' in these regions. It was the most cynical deal imaginable. It made eminent sense, however, to both parties. Germany had sealed its eastern front. The Soviet Union had bought precious time to consolidate its defences.

With that, nothing stood in the way of an imminent German invasion of Poland. Hitler still harboured faint hopes that Britain and France would back away from their commitment to the Poles. But he was prepared to go ahead anyway, even if it meant war with the western democracies. His contempt for them had been confirmed the previous summer. 'Our enemies are small worms,' he told his generals. 'I saw them in Munich.' His chief concern was to avoid any last-minute intervention that might result in a second 'Munich' and prevent his demolition of Poland.

When Hitler's high-risk policy had threatened war with the western powers during the previous year, an embryonic opposition had emerged among the elites in the military and Foreign Ministry. The Munich Conference had then undermined whatever chances of success such opposition might have had. A year later those who continued secretly to oppose Hitler's headlong rush towards war and, they prophesied, ultimate disaster, lacked any prospect of challenging him. Army leaders, divided in their views on war in 1938, now said and did nothing, where they entertained any doubts at all. Fatalistically, if not enthusiastically, they backed Hitler. That was crucial. Internally, nothing stood in the way of Hitler's determination to go to war.

Since 22 August the British ambassador in Berlin, Sir Nevile Henderson, had endured a number of extremely tense meetings in the Reich Chancellery during which Hitler had seemingly held out hope of a peaceful settlement to the crisis, while secretly preparing to invade Poland. Göring had in addition sent a personal emissary, Birger Dahlerus, a Swedish industrialist, three times to London with offers of German good intent. But from the German side, the negotiations were a mere charade. There was not the slightest intention of holding back from the planned attack on Poland. The attack should, in fact, have taken place on 26 August. Hitler had given the mobilization orders for the army the previous afternoon, but he was forced to cancel the attack a few hours later after Mussolini had informed his Axis partner that Italy was currently in no position to enter the war alongside Germany. If embarrassing for Mussolini, it was no more than a passing setback for Hitler. He soon fixed a new date for the attack. Early on the morning of 1 September 1939 German troops crossed the Polish border.

The British had hoped until the last that Hitler would negotiate, and the attack took them by surprise. Two days of hesitation followed in which Britain and France did not act in unison while Hitler's troops started to devour Poland. Mussolini offered to mediate with Hitler to convene a conference on 5 September. The French were more ready than the British to countenance the suggestion. Predictably, however, it cut no ice at all with Hitler. The French Foreign Minister, Georges Bonnet, viewed by Churchill and others in London as the 'quintessence of defeatism', sent confused diplomatic signals, sought to play for time, and was reluctant to commit France to the final, dreaded step. As late as the afternoon of 2 September, Chamberlain and Halifax, too, were still prepared to contemplate a conference if German troops withdrew from Poland. That evening in Parliament, Chamberlain was left in no doubt, however, that the prospect of any further negotiations with Hitler would bring down his government. Facing a revolt in his cabinet, he committed himself to sending an ultimatum that Germany withdraw its troops from Poland forthwith, to be presented in Berlin at 9 a.m. the following morning. Hitler was given two hours to respond.

Next morning, at 11.15 a.m. on 3 September 1939, people throughout Britain clustered around their radio sets to hear Chamberlain, in a mournful monotone, tell them that no response had been received to the ultimatum 'and that consequently this country is at war with Germany'. A wail of air-raid sirens immediately afterwards turned out to be a false alarm, but gave a foretaste of what was to come. Largely as a result of Bonnet's foot-dragging, the declaration of war was not synchronized. Instead there was a lag of nearly six hours before, at 5 o'clock that afternoon, the French eventually followed suit.

The road to the hell of another war had been a twisted one. It had indeed been 'paved with the good intentions' of the appeasers. Chamberlain told the British House of Commons on 3 September: 'Everything I have worked for, everything that I have hoped for, everything that I have believed in during my public life, has crashed into ruins.' If from the best of motives, appeasement had been, as Churchill put it, a 'sad tale of wrong judgements formed by well-meaning and capable people' amounting to 'a line of milestones to disaster'. The appeasers, in Britain and in France, were no doubt 'well-meaning'. But their upbringing, experience and political schooling left them utterly unprepared to encounter a gangster on the international stage. They were simply no match for Hitler. *They* thought they could negotiate a deal for peace, even at the expense of throwing another country to the wolves. *He* wanted war throughout. Only conquest, according to the world view he had harboured for the best part of two decades, would satisfy German needs. So the end of the road was always the most likely one: it was war again in Europe.

'In a sense, there is relief; doubts resolved' was the lapidary reaction of Sir Alexander Cadogan, Permanent Under-Secretary at the British Foreign Office. The English working-class Oxford student, William Woodruff, gave up his pacifist convictions that day: 'To fight was the lesser of two evils. I would arrange my Oxford affairs and join up.' Countless others rushed to volunteer for war service. Woodruff encapsulated, probably correctly, the view of most people in Britain, that war was unavoidable and that Hitler had to be tackled: 'They were glad that the deceit had ended and the life-and-death struggle had begun.' The Jewish writer Manes Sperber was among the long queues of volunteers in Paris, fearful of what awaited him but relieved that his parents and brothers were safely in England. 'No wild enthusiasm. There's a job to be done; that's all,' noted Pierre Lazareff, the editor of *Paris Soir*, in his diary. Conscious of the carnage on their soil only a generation earlier, the French troops called up – soon 4.5 million of them from France and its colonies – were, as prefectoral reports pointed out, resigned to fighting, but with no sign of the enthusiasm witnessed in 1914.

It was little different in Germany. William Shirer noted the atmosphere in Berlin on 3 September: 'On the faces of the people, astonishment, depression ... In 1914, I believe, the excitement in Berlin on the first day of the World War was tremendous. Today, no excitement, no hurrahs, no cheering, no throwing of flowers, no war fever, no war hysteria.' By contrast, in Warsaw, recalled Marcel Reich-Ranicki, later a famous literary critic in Germany, the mood on hearing that Britain and France had declared war on Germany was one of scarcely containable happiness. A delirious crowd gathered outside the British Embassy shouting 'Long live Britain!' and 'Long live the fight for liberty!' Later in the day they sang 'La Marseillaise' outside the French Embassy. They thought help was on the way. Soon enough, as German bombs rained down on Polish cities and their martyrdom began, they would realize that no help was coming.

Whatever the myriad feelings across the continent on 3 September, practically everyone recognized that their lives would now drastically change. What, exactly, war would bring, nobody knew. There were grounds enough to view the coming years with the greatest anxiety. Many people sensed that they would have to endure hell's fires once more. Few, however, perhaps felt the depth of foreboding noted in his diary (written in imperfect English) by the Austrian Jewish writer, Stefan Zweig, exiled in England. The new war, he wrote on 3 September 1939, would be 'a thousand times worse than 1914 ... We have got no idea what *new* horrors on poisining [sic] and boiling this war will bring. I am expecting everything from those criminals. What a breakdown of civilization.'

8

Hell on Earth

It seemed to us that we were witnessing a total break in the evolution of mankind, the complete collapse of man as a rational being.

Heda Margolius Kovály, Under a Cruel Star:
A Life in Prague 1941–1968 *(1986)*

For millions of Europeans the Second World War, more even than the First, was the closest they came to hell on earth. The death toll alone – over 40 million just in Europe, more than four times as high as in the First World War – gives a sense of the horror. The losses defy the imagination. The Soviet Union's alone were more than 25 million. Germany's dead numbered around 7 million, Poland's 6 million. The bare figures convey nothing of the extremities of their suffering, or the misery inflicted on countless families. Nor do they give any impression of the geographical weighting of the immense casualties.

Western Europe came off relatively lightly. In Britain and France far fewer died than had done during the First World War. Total Allied military deaths for the Second World War as a whole were just over 14 million. Britain (and its overseas territories) suffered around 5.5 per cent of these, France (with its colonies) about 3 per cent, the Soviet Union some 70 per cent. Excluding the war with Japan, the Soviet proportion would be even higher. Civilian deaths in Britain, mainly from bombing, were under 70,000. Civilian deaths in the epicentre of the killing – Poland, Ukraine, Belarus, the Baltic countries and the western parts of the Soviet Union – numbered about 10 million.

Unlike the First World War civilian deaths in the Second greatly outnumbered those of the fighting troops. This was, much more than the earlier great conflict, a war that enveloped whole societies. The high death rate among civilians was not least a consequence of the genocidal nature of the Second World War. For, unlike the war of 1914–18, genocide lay at the heart of the later great conflagration. This war brought an assault on humanity unprecedented in history. It was a descent into the abyss never previously encountered, the devastation of all the ideals of civilization that had arisen from the Enlightenment. It was a war of apocalyptic proportions, Europe's Armageddon.

The second war within a generation was the unfinished business of the first. Beyond the millions mourning loved ones, the earlier war had left a continent in convulsion. Immense nationalist, ethnic and class hatred, interwoven with each other, had created a climate of extreme political violence and polarized politics out of which Hitler's regime had emerged to endanger Europe's peace. For Germany more than any other country, the first war had left unfinished business. But a grab for continental, eventually even world dominance, through another war was an enormous gamble. The odds, given Germany's resources, were stacked heavily against the gamble succeeding. Other countries, rearming fast, would do all they could to prevent German hegemony, and with greater resources at their disposal once these were mobilized. Germany's opportunity to achieve victory before its enemies could stop it would be brief.

For Hitler himself, and for others in the Nazi leadership, another war had a powerful underlying psychological motivation. It was to be a war to undo the outcome of the first war, to expunge the disgrace of defeat and the humiliation of Versailles, to eradicate the legacy of the 'November criminals' (the leaders of the Left who in Hitler's eyes had brought about the revolution of 1918). Not least, as Hitler had 'prophesied' in his speech in January 1939, it was to be a war to destroy what he saw as the baleful power of Jews throughout Europe. In sum: a new war would rewrite history.

The western democracies, Britain and France, whose weakness had been so fully exposed by Hitler, had been ready to accept the extension of German influence in central Europe – accommodating the mutilation of Czechoslovakia in the process – as the price of peace. This in itself was a concession to a significant shift in the balance of power within Europe. The prospect of unlimited German conquest was another matter altogether. It threatened not just to disturb the balance of power in Europe and destabilize British and French overseas possessions, but to endanger France, and even Britain, directly, by German conquest. A Europe dominated by Hitler and his inhuman regime was infinitely worse to contemplate than a Europe under the Kaiser might have been. For the British and the French, the time had come, therefore, to resist the expansion of German power. Few in Britain and France wanted another war. The pain of 1914–18 was still raw. The armed forces were not ready for a major conflict. The economies, just recovering from the Depression, were in no fit state to finance one. The City of London and big business, in France as well as in Britain, could scarcely wish for a repeat of the economic earthquake that the first war had produced. The people, remembering the immense bloodshed of the previous war, certainly did not want another. But it was plain: this war had to be fought. National interest and a moral cause conveniently blended together. If ever there was a just war, this was it. Hitler had to be defeated if Europe was to have peace.

If the first great war was the seminal catastrophe, the second was the culmination of this catastrophe – the complete collapse of European civilization. It marked the ultimate clash of all the ideological, political, economic and military forces that had crystallized during the first war and caused the instability and tensions on the continent during the subsequent twenty years. It became the defining episode that reshaped the twentieth century. With the Second World War, the Europe that was the legacy of the First came to an end. The continent almost destroyed itself. But it survived. A drastically changed Europe would ensue.

A CONTINENT IN FLAMES

What eventually became a world war, joining the conflict in the Far East to that in Europe, fell into three main phases and afflicted the European continent in widely differing degrees and at different junctures. Sweden, Switzerland, Spain, Portugal, Turkey and Ireland remained officially neutral. They took no part in the fighting, though they did not escape indirect involvement in the hostilities. All other European countries were in one way or another enveloped by the war.

The first phase saw the war spread from Poland to the Baltic, then Scandinavia, western Europe, the Balkans and north Africa. It followed the path of German and Italian aggression, but also that of Soviet expansion into Poland and the Baltic, aimed at extending Soviet power to consolidate a defensive cordon. The eastern part of Poland, as agreed with Germany, was occupied by the Soviet Union in mid-September 1939. The Baltic states of Estonia, Latvia and Lithuania were forced to become Soviet republics in April 1940, followed in July by the annexation of Bessarabia and northern Bukovina, hitherto parts of Romania. Finland had held out in a courageous war against the might of the Red Army during the winter months of 1939–40, but was ultimately compelled to yield territory to the Soviet Union to form part of its defensive barrier in the Baltic.

Poland was quickly crushed in the autumn of 1939. In the spring of 1940 the neutral states of Denmark, Norway, the Netherlands, Luxembourg and Belgium were overrun. Then, almost incredibly, France itself (which possessed the largest army in Europe) capitulated after a campaign that had lasted scarcely more than five weeks. Over a million and a half captured French soldiers were transported to Germany, where most remained prisoners of war for the next four years. The following spring Yugoslavia and Greece also swiftly succumbed to German armed might.

In the catalogue of German triumphs, one major failure stood out starkly. Britain, backed by its world empire, remained unconquered. This owed much to the refusal by Winston Churchill, Prime Minister since 10 May 1940, in tense discussions towards the end of the month and while the British army was stranded on the beaches at Dunkirk, to contemplate the suggestion of his Foreign Secretary, Lord Halifax, that Britain should consider exploring terms for a peace settlement. (The Royal Family and many in the Conservative Party would have preferred Halifax as the country's leader.) With Britain determined to fight on, Germany faced the uneasy prospect of the British benefiting from American economic and perhaps military support. Ending the war in the west had been Hitler's prerequisite for turning on the Soviet Union in the war he had been set on fighting for the best part of twenty years. But he was unable to force Britain to its knees and conclude victory in western Europe. Invasion was briefly considered in 1940. The logistical difficulties were, however, daunting. Invasion was never likely, and the idea was soon abandoned. Bombing Britain into submission proved far beyond the capabilities of the Luftwaffe, despite extensive damage to British cities and tens of thousands of lives lost in the air raids of 1940 and early 1941.

By the spring of 1941 the astonishing series of lightning German attacks, combining in new and devastating fashion air power with fast-moving tank units that gave the Wehrmacht fearsome military superiority, had ensured German domination stretching from Norway to Crete. Italy had fared less well. Joining the war at the point of the German conquest of France in June 1940, it soon revealed embarrassing military weaknesses in Greece and north Africa, necessitating German military intervention to aid its struggling Axis partner.

Obsessed by time racing against Germany's best chance of success in its great gamble for European, then world, domination, Hitler turned initial thinking on its head. The way to defeat Britain, he told his generals, was first to defeat the Soviet Union. Grotesque underestimation of Soviet military capacity (encouraged by the Red Army's struggle to crush the small Finnish forces in the 'Winter War' of 1939–40) encouraged acquiescence by German generals in the belief that victory in an eastern campaign could be gained in a matter of weeks. In December 1940 the directive was issued for an invasion of the Soviet Union the following spring. Victory in that campaign would gain Germany the 'living space' that Hitler had claimed it needed. It would at the same time fulfil the second of the objectives that he had harboured for two decades: it would provide a 'final solution to the Jewish question' that had irrationally obsessed him and the Nazi leadership from the outset.

The second phase of the war began early on the morning of 22 June 1941 when, without any declaration of war, German forces invaded the Soviet Union. More than 3 million German troops advanced across the Soviet borders. In the west of the Soviet Union almost as many soldiers of the Red Army stood facing them. Thus started the most gigantic – and what would prove by far the most deadly – armed struggle in history.

There was a high premium on complete victory being rapidly attained in this colossal operation. The rich resources of the Soviet Union were vital if Germany was to achieve total mastery on the continent. And this itself had to be the prerequisite to end the threat from the west, where Britain was edging closer to a full-scale war alliance with the USA. Hitler envisaged America being ready to enter the war on Britain's side by 1942. Germany, he was adamant, had to attain continental dominance before then. These concerns were scarcely lessened by the vote taken in the US Congress on March 1941 to pass the Lend-Lease Bill, a device to ensure that aid to Britain would be massively increased. President Roosevelt still did not dare take any proposal to enter the war to Congress. The policy of isolationism had declined but still posed a significant influence. Lend-Lease confirmed, however, that the United States was now committed to adding its massive economic power to the attempt to defeat the Axis powers. For Germany it was a race against time to defeat the Soviet Union before American economic power – and, most likely, direct military might at some point – could decisively affect the conduct of the war.

The German three-pronged attack that constituted the invasion of the Soviet Union – 'Operation Barbarossa' – initially advanced at a staggering pace in the north, centre and south of the immensely long eastern front stretching for about 1,800 kilometres. Stalin had catastrophically ignored all the warnings, many of them accurate, of an imminent invasion, regarding them as deliberate disinformation. Many units of the Red Army had been left in exposed forward positions and had fallen easy prey to fast-moving panzer attacks spearheading massive encirclements, which resulted in the capture of hundreds of thousands of prisoners. Within two months, however, it was plain that the extraordinarily ambitious objectives of 'Barbarossa' would not be realizable before winter – for which scant provision had been made. The enemy had been grossly underestimated and the logistics of conquering such a huge country were too great. The rich agricultural land of the Ukraine was won, but it proved impossible to advance as far as the oilfields of the Caucasus, or to destroy Leningrad in the north. The advance on Moscow started late, only at the beginning of October. Stalin was prepared to contemplate surrender of territory for a peace deal with Hitler. The German dictator was uninterested; he thought Germany was on the verge of victory. The inhabitants of Moscow started to panic in mid-October as German forces approached.

Stalin thought of leaving the city, but then changed his mind. Soviet morale, after wavering, recovered. The German advance was meanwhile bogged down in autumn rain, then in the snow and ice of early winter as temperatures plummeted to minus 30 degrees Celsius. By this time two-fifths of the population of the USSR and nearly half of its material resources were under German control. Some 3 million soldiers had been taken captive. But German losses had mounted alarmingly. Almost three-quarters of a million – nearly a quarter of the eastern army – were registered as dead, wounded or missing since the start of 'Barbarossa'. Reserves of men were already running short. Stalin, on the other hand, appeared to have an endless supply. The Soviet counter-offensive, beginning on 5 December 1941 with the German forward troops no more than 50 kilometres from the gates of Moscow, brought the first major crisis of the war for Germany. Hopes of quick victory had been replaced by the recognition that it faced a long and bitter war.

The Japanese attack on Pearl Harbor on 7 December, and the American declaration of war on Japan the next day, transformed the war into a global conflict. Hitler saw a strategic opportunity. War against the Japanese would tie down the Americans in the Pacific arena. German U-boats, held back for months while the USA was pursuing an 'undeclared war' in the Atlantic, could be let loose on American shipping to break the crucial umbilical cord to Britain and win the war at sea for Germany. With such hopeful notions in mind, on 11 December 1941 Hitler took Germany into war against the United States. Whatever Hitler's rationale, the odds were now stacked against Germany winning the war in Europe.

Hitler had, in fact, grossly overestimated Japanese military power. Pearl Harbor was a shock to the USA, but far from a knock-out blow. Japanese expansion, though initially successful, reached its limits during the first half of 1942. But the big American naval victory at Midway in June 1942 marked the turning point of the war in the Pacific.

The shift in fortunes in the Atlantic came a year later. But Hitler had also overestimated the destructive capacity of his U-boats. The success that they had enjoyed during 1942 could not be sustained, largely because British intelligence was eventually able, after a lengthy struggle, to decode German communications sent through the Enigma encrypter, and to locate the position of the submarines. Improved defence against the U-boats meant vital Allied supplies could cross the ocean in increased security. By 1943 Hitler was losing the battle of the Atlantic.

Germany had meanwhile reached the limits of its expansion. The battle of El Alamein, stretching over three weeks in October and November 1942, ended the German advance in North Africa and paved the way for complete Allied victory in that theatre the following year. In the Soviet Union the second huge German offensive (though with depleted numbers, compared with 1941) in the summer of 1942 had aimed to secure the oil of the Caucasus, but it ended in catastrophe at Stalingrad – an attritional five-month battle in the depths of a Russian winter that ended in February 1943 with the complete destruction of the German Sixth Army and the loss of over 200,000 men (and some 300,000 of their allies). The fortunes of war had turned irreversibly during 1942. There was still far to go but the leaders of the Allies were now confident of ultimate victory. And when Roosevelt and Churchill met for talks at the Casablanca Conference in January 1943 it was agreed that victory would only follow the unconditional surrender of the Axis powers.

The Allied landings in North Africa in November 1942 had opened the path for the capitulation of the Axis forces there the following May. In July 1943 the Allies crossed to Sicily – a move that triggered the toppling of Mussolini by his own Fascist leadership the same month. This was followed in September by an Italian armistice with the Allies, leading to the occupation of much of the country by German troops. The slow struggle northwards began for the Allied forces. It was a second front – though not the one that Stalin had been pleading for. Nor was the bombing campaign against German cities and industrial installations that gathered destructive momentum during 1943. The British policy of 'area bombing', envisaged by Air Chief Marshal Arthur Harris as the means to destroy German morale and win the war, had begun the previous year. A huge raid had destroyed much of Cologne in May 1942. Other cities in northern and western Germany had been attacked. But nothing came close in destructive power to the devastation of Hamburg in late July 1943 in raids that killed at least 34,000 civilians – a figure amounting to more than half of all the British victims of air raids during the entire war. Even this was far from the climax of the bombing campaign, which would be ramped up massively in the last year of the war as Allied air superiority became practically complete.

The last big German offensive on the eastern front, in July 1943, lasted little more than a week. 'Operation Citadel' was called off after a colossal tank battle – over 5,000 tanks in all were involved – at Kursk. Immense Soviet losses far outweighed those of the Germans. But German troops were needed in southern Italy to strengthen defences following the Allied landing in Sicily. With the end of 'Citadel', the initiative passed irrevocably to the Soviets. July had proved a disastrous month for Germany. Extraordinary resilience meant there was no collapse, but German strategy by now amounted to no more than fighting a protracted and tenacious rearguard action against hugely superior forces and hoping that the 'Grand Alliance' of capitalist Britain and America with the communist Soviet Union would fall apart. With the gulf between German and Allied resources widening inexorably, the writing was on the wall. A sign that the tables had been turned was the Soviet taking of Kiev in November. That same month, at the Tehran Conference, Allied leaders agreed that Britain and the United States would launch an invasion of German-occupied western Europe the following year.

The successful Allied landing in Normandy on 6 June 1944 (D-Day), and two weeks later the huge and devastating breakthrough by the Red Army in 'Operation Bagration', opened the third and final phase of the war in Europe that ended with the German capitulation. This was the bloodiest phase of all. A quarter of all the European dead of the war, equivalent to the total military dead of the entire First World War, can be accounted to these months. Most British and American military deaths, a high proportion of Soviet deaths, half of all German military deaths in the entire war and a majority of civilian deaths occurred during the last eleven months of the conflict. Many of the civilian dead were the victims of Allied air raids that laid waste to German cities in a crescendo of devastation in the closing months. The destruction in February 1945 of Dresden, with the loss of 25,000 mainly civilian lives, stood symbolically for a terror from the skies that rained down on German towns and cities as air defences collapsed. British planes dropped more bombs in March 1945 alone than in the first three years of the war.

German losses in the east during and following 'Bagration' dwarfed those at Stalingrad or in any other battle, and could not be made good. Germany fought on to the very end. Fear of conquest by the Soviet Union (in awareness of the horrors that German soldiers had perpetrated on Soviet soil), intensified repression of all dissidence at home, comprehensive controls by the Nazi Party and its agencies, the impossibility of organizing any resistance after an attempt to kill Hitler had failed on 20 July 1944, recognition on the part of Nazi grandees that they stood or fell with Hitler, and lingering belief in the dictator within the military and civilian leadership – all contributed to the vain struggle to hold out when rationality spoke loudly in favour of surrender.

However, it was by now just a matter of time. With the collapse of the eastern front, Finland, Romania and Bulgaria turned against Germany in September 1944. Romania and Bulgaria were occupied by the Soviets. Poland – with Warsaw in ruins following German destruction after the rising of August 1944 – was in Soviet hands by the end of January 1945. After lengthy intense fighting, Hungary likewise was under Soviet control by March. By then the western Allies had forced their way over the Rhine – the overture to the advance into northern Germany, the taking of the vital Ruhr industrial belt, and relentless progress into southern Germany. The Soviet steamroller was equally unstoppable in the east, pressing forward to the Baltic coast and the Oder, poised for the final assault on Berlin that began on 16 April 1945. The Soviet advance into Germany, and now its conquest of the Reich capital, had been accompanied throughout by horrendous cruelty towards the German population, the rape of countless women one of the paramount hallmarks of the savage revenge for the earlier unspeakable atrocities by the German occupiers on Soviet territory.

On 25 April the large forces converging on Germany from both east and west met at the river Elbe. Soviet and American troops shook hands. The Reich was split in two. Berlin was encircled the same day by the Red Army. By 2 May the battle of Berlin was at an end. Hitler had committed suicide in his bunker two days earlier. A brief but bloody postscript followed before Grand Admiral Karl Dönitz, Hitler's chosen successor, finally bowed to the inevitable. Complete German capitulation on all fronts was signed in the presence of representatives from Great Britain, the United States and the Soviet Union on 8 May 1945. The most horrific war in the history of Europe was over. The cost – material and in lives – was still to be counted. The political and moral consequences would shape future decades.

THE BOTTOMLESS PIT OF INHUMANITY

All wars are inhumane, modern wars especially so. Modern weaponry means that killing in warfare has become impersonal as well as enormous in scale, with civilians increasingly drawn into the slaughter. The Great War of 1914–18 had amply demonstrated these characteristics. Terrible though that war had been, however, it was left in the shade by the bottomless pit of inhumanity into which mankind plunged during the Second World War.

The unprecedented descent had been waiting to happen in a Europe riven by ethnic and class hatreds, extreme racism, paranoid antisemitism and fanatical nationalism. Entering war driven by hatred and being set on eradicating – not just defeating – the enemy was the recipe for the collapse of all standards of basic humanity. This was widely the case among soldiers in the war in the east, though far less so in western Europe. Total war was the ingredient necessary to convert such lethal antagonisms into actual mass killing on a scarcely imaginable scale.

In all wars battlefield killing takes on its own momentum. The Second World War was no exception. In the campaigns in western Europe and in north Africa, however, the fighting was for the most part relatively conventional. In eastern Europe it was different. There the cruelty, callousness and sheer contempt for human life defies belief. There the fighting was part of a racial war. This derived directly from the joint objective of colonial-style conquest and racial cleansing of the National Socialist leadership in Germany.

The resulting hell on earth, not just for the fighting troops but also for civilians, was primarily a product of ideology. That is, who should live and who should die was in the first instance an ideological question. The terror and killing inflicted upon the civilian population in Poland and during the eastern war clearly reflected that from the very beginning. The clearest demonstration of the ideological priority was the singling out of Jews, among all the countless victims of the extreme violence, in what soon turned into all-out genocide.

Ideology nevertheless went hand in hand with economic imperatives. This was already plain within Germany itself, in the so-called 'euthanasia action' that began in 1939. This was primarily directed at the elimination of 'racial degenerates', an essential principle of eugenics. Hitler had earlier said that any such action would have to await war. In October 1939 he backdated his signed secret authorization of the 'euthanasia action' to 1 September, a clear sign that he saw the start of the war as the moment to begin such a fundamental breach of the basic humanitarian principle of the right to life. The 'action' was equally secretly halted in August 1941, after knowledge of it had become public and led to its denunciation by the Bishop of Münster, Clemens August Graf von Galen. By then, some 70,000 patients of mental asylums had fallen victim to it. This total exceeded what the doctors had foreseen, despite their recommendations of patients deemed suitable for the 'euthanasia action'. The 'halt order' of August 1941 was, however, by no means the end of the process of exterminating the 'useless' mentally ill. Their killing now moved into the secrecy of the concentration camps. The victims of the 'euthanasia' killings are estimated to have numbered over 200,000 in all. Doctors and nurses were heavily implicated in the deliberate killing of their patients. Although the killing of the mentally sick was ideologically driven, it also aimed to make economic savings by removing those deemed to be 'useless lives'. Precise calculations were made on the savings to be achieved. 'The mentally ill are a burden on the state' was how the head of the Hartheim asylum, near Linz in Austria, put it.

The steps towards genocide against the Jews also had an important economic component. When it became obvious that the mass 'cleansing' of Jews from the conquered territories, at first taken for granted, could not quickly be attained, the ghettos established in Poland became highly profitable enterprises for the German occupiers. As a result some of those running them later, when Jews were set to be deported to their deaths, did not want to see the ghettos closed. But what about the Jews who were unable to work? Already in July 1941 the head of the German Security Service in Posen, within the German-annexed part of western Poland, was suggesting that since 'the Jews can no longer all be fed', thought should be given to 'finishing off those Jews not capable of working by some sort of fast-working preparation'. Five months later Hans Frank, the Nazi boss of the central German-occupied Polish zone known as the General Government, when outlining the urgency of exterminating 3.5 million Jews in his domain, told his underlings that the Jews were 'extremely harmful to us through the amount of food they gorge'. Later, when the Jews were being murdered in their millions, the biggest of the Nazi concentration camps, at Auschwitz in another part of Poland, Upper Silesia, combined extermination with industrial profit. The huge complex included twenty-eight sub-camps – industrial installations operating on the slave labour of 40,000 prisoners generating in all about 30 million marks of profit for the German state. When the prisoners were no longer fit for work they were sent to the gas chambers.

Ideology also blended closely with economics in the way the German leadership viewed conquest and occupation. Securing food for the German population was imperative. The 'turnip winter' of 1916–17 had gone far towards breaking morale during the First World War. There could be no repeat. It was immaterial if the rest of Europe starved. It was taken for granted that between 20 and 30 million Slavs and Jews would die of starvation from German occupation of the Soviet Union. The only consideration, Göring told Nazi leaders from the occupied territories, was that there should be 'no German collapses from hunger'. There were cases of cannibalism among the desperate Soviet prisoners sometimes crammed together so tightly that they could hardly move, even to relieve themselves, and dying at a rate of 6,000 a day. Of 5.7 million Soviet prisoners of war in

German hands, 3.3 million died a terrible death from starvation or related disease from lack of food or the freezing conditions. Meanwhile Germany was taking 20 per cent of its grain, 25 per cent of its fats and almost 30 per cent of its meat from occupied Europe.

Measly rations were eventually provided to the Soviet captives, since the absurdity slowly dawned on the Nazi leadership of starving prisoners to death in camps when labour was ever more urgently required for war production. Even so, the majority of Soviet prisoners did not survive captivity. In the case of the Jews, there was an obvious contradiction between ferrying them halfway across Europe to their deaths while there was an acute labour shortage. But here, ideology retained its clear primacy.

Poland was from the start of the German occupation an ideological experimental ground. The western parts of the conquered country – West Prussia, the province of Posen (now renamed 'Reichsgau Wartheland, from the name of the river running through the region) and Upper Silesia – were annexed to the Reich, not just restoring but considerably extending the territories that had before the First World War been part of Prussia. These areas, though their population was overwhelmingly ethnic Polish, were now to be ruthlessly 'germanized'. Central and southern Poland, the most densely populated part of the country under German occupation, was dubbed the 'General Government' (*Generalgouvernement*) – in colloquial usage dismissively referred to as 'Rest of Poland' (*Restpolen*) – and seen as a dumping-ground for 'racial undesirables' from the annexed territories. Hitler, as always, set the tone. It was going to be a 'hard racial struggle,' he declared. There would be no place for legal constraints. All this added up to unbelievable misery and suffering for the subjugated Polish population and the antechamber to genocide for the lowest of the low within that population, the Jews.

Contempt for the Poles was widespread in Germany. Hitler himself described the Poles as 'more animals than human beings'. He was far from the only German who thought that way. With few exceptions, members of the German army serving in Poland had no objections to the licensed killing, merciless persecution and large-scale economic plunder that they witnessed or in which they participated. The Poles were treated as subhumans, far beyond the protection of the law, to be deprived of any form of education, imprisoned or executed on a whim, and no more than a reservoir of slave labour. Near-starvation rations were imposed. Polish culture was to be eradicated, all sense of Polish statehood extinguished. The Polish intelligentsia as purveyors of culture and statehood were to be liquidated or sent to German concentration camps. Auschwitz was a place of utmost terror for Poles long before it became an extermination camp for Jews. In the annexed regions of western Poland, Catholic churches were closed and large numbers of the clergy imprisoned or killed. Public executions were commonplace, the victims often left hanging for days to deter others.

But underground resistance was never completely crushed. In fact, it grew in size despite the horrific reprisals to form a substantial, extraordinarily courageous illegal movement that, however draconian the repression, caused increasing problems for the occupiers. Collective retribution frequently followed individual acts of resistance. One estimate, resting on a far from complete record, counted 769 instances that took the lives of almost 20,000 Poles in reprisal actions. Some 300 villages were destroyed during the German occupation. The terror even increased during the course of the occupation as the war fortunes changed, German hold over the country became more precarious, and resistance more emboldened. 'There was never a moment when we did not feel threatened,' one woman recalled. 'Every time we left home, we never knew whether we would ever see it again.' Everyone feared the round-ups of people for deportation to forced labour in Germany. By 1943 a million Poles were working for the German war industries. Their relatives often had no idea where they were. Many never saw their homeland again.

It had been rashly presumed that the forcible removal of Jews from the annexed regions could rapidly be achieved. Ultimately, the intention was to remove the Jews from the General Government as well. Between 1939 and 1941, however, they were deported *into*, not out of, the General Government. During the depths of the winter of 1939–40 over 100,000 Christian and Jewish Poles were given a few minutes' notice to pack a few belongings, then herded into unheated cattle-wagons and dumped in the General Government. Hundreds of thousands more followed during 1940. By March 1941 over

400,000 had been deported and a similar number sent to Germany as forced labour. The deportation of a further 831,000 was prevented only by the preparations for 'Operation Barbarossa'.

The deportations were intended to make room for the settlement of ethnic Germans from the Baltic and elsewhere. Jews were to be confined in a huge reservation in the Lublin district of south-eastern Poland. At least, that was the initial aim. But the Germans had grossly underestimated the logistical difficulties involved. Hans Frank was soon refusing to allow more Jews into his domain in the General Government. With Nazi leaders pressing to have the Jews from their areas deported, but nowhere to transport them to, and millions more Jews in Nazi hands since the conquest of Poland, alternatives to a reservation in the General Government became ever more urgently sought. After the German victory over France in 1940, the French colony of Madagascar was for a brief time considered as a destination for Europe's Jews. That possibility, too, soon proved impracticable. Deporting them into the icy wastes of the Soviet Union eventually emerged as a possibility during the planning of 'Barbarossa'.

Poland, after a mere twenty years of independence, had been partitioned yet again in September 1939. East of the demarcation line agreed by Germany and the Soviet Union for the division, the Polish population was subjected to a different kind of ideologically determined horror. Here the aim was Sovietization, not Germanization. A social revolution was soon imposed on eastern Poland. The land was collectivized in 1940, landowners were evicted from their property. The banks were nationalized and savings confiscated. Much industrial machinery was dismantled and sent to the Soviet Union. Private and religious schools were closed, the teaching of religion and history was banned and the catechism according to Marx and Engels introduced. Eradication of Polish nationalism was axiomatic, as was the elimination of all who were imagined to pose a threat to Soviet interests. The Polish elite were particularly at risk.

Stalin and the other members of the Politburo personally signed the order on 5 March 1940 to kill more than 20,000 members of the Polish elite in eastern Poland. Among them were 15,000 Polish officers who disappeared in May of that year. The corpses of more than 4,000 of them were discovered by the Germans in Katyn Forest, near

Smolensk, in April 1943. Who killed them was long disputed. It is now beyond all doubt, however, that they had been shot by the Soviet secret police, the NKVD. The other 11,000 almost certainly suffered a similar fate as part of the registered total of 21,857 people executed under Stalin's order.

Waves of arrests followed the Soviet occupation. Over 100,000 Polish citizens were seized, most sentenced to years of penal servitude in the Gulag, over 8,500 sentenced to death. Poles settled close to the former Soviet border were in special danger. In some places local Ukrainians and Belorussians were incited to plunder the property of Poles and even murder Polish neighbours. Local militias spearheaded the violence. Those Poles seen, usually in a mere figment of the imagination, as a particular threat to the Soviet Union, were rounded up for deportation. The vast deportations were carried out with utmost brutality. Almost 400,000 Poles – by some estimates far more – were sent to concentration camps in the wilds of Siberia or Kazakhstan in sealed, unheated, windowless wagons on winter train journeys of up to 6,000 miles. Around 5,000 died during the transports; another 11,000 were dead of hunger and disease by the following summer.

One of the NKVD men involved in the round-ups for deportation later offered an insight into his mentality at the time: 'I was responsible for the deportation of one or two villages,' he recounted:

> Now I think about it, it's really hard to take the children away when they're really small . . . Of course, I knew that they were our enemies, enemies of the Soviet Union, and they had to be 'recycled' . . . I regret it now, but at the time it was different . . . Stalin was much like a god for everybody. And all of his words were the last word on any subject. You couldn't even think that it wasn't right. One did not doubt it at the time. Every decision that was made was correct. That wasn't only my opinion – we were all thinking like that. We were building communism. We were obeying orders. We believed.

Unsurprisingly, given their intense persecution by the Germans, many Jews welcomed the Soviet occupation of eastern Poland. They had also often experienced discrimination in pre-war Poland. The arrival of the Red Army seemed to promise liberation. Jews sometimes greeted their presumed liberators by displaying red flags. They not infrequently took up administrative positions with the Soviet occupiers, the readiness to collaborate prompting much resentment among Catholic Poles. When the Germans came to occupy the region after their invasion of the Soviet Union in June 1941 and discovered the corpses of thousands of victims of NKVD atrocities in jails in eastern Poland, they had no difficulty in whipping up hatred not just for the Bolsheviks but also for the Jews who had been widely viewed as acting in their service. In fact, most Jews had soon come to realize what Soviet occupation meant – and it was not liberation. Many had been robbed of their property, while intellectuals and professionals had been arrested in great numbers. A third of the deportees had been Jewish.

The brutality of the sovietization in eastern Poland had parallels in Estonia, Latvia and Lithuania after they were annexed by the USSR in 1940. The savagery of the German occupation of Poland had, on the other hand, no remote counterpart in the German treatment of occupied western Europe.

In Croatia, a newly created state (incorporating Bosnia and Herzegovina) after the German invasion of Yugoslavia in April 1941, the Germans found others to do the dirty work for them. The regime they installed under Ante Pavelić, the leader of the Ustaša fascists, instigated a rule of terror that practically defies expression. His was a fanatical movement with probably no more than around 5,000 supporters before gaining power but bent on 'cleansing' the country of all non-Croatians – almost half of the entire population of 6.3 million. The aim of Pavelić was to solve the 'Serbian problem' by converting a third of the nearly 2 million Serbs in Croatia to Catholicism, expelling a third and killing a third. It was lethal lunacy.

Whether Pavelić was entirely sane – he is said to have kept a basket full of human eyes on his desk as souvenirs – is perhaps open to doubt. There is, however, no doubting the sanity of most of his followers. Yet the atrocities perpetrated by his death squads as they massacred sometimes entire communities, targeting Serbs, Jews and gypsies especially, with the aim of wiping out all non-Croatian influence, plumbed the depths of sadistic horror. In one instance around 500 Serbian men, women and children from a small town not far from Zagreb were shot dead. When 250 people from nearby villages gathered to offer to convert to Catholicism to avoid being killed, six members of the Ustaše locked them inside a Serbian Orthodox church and murdered them one after another by hitting them on the head with spiked clubs. Other orgies of killing involved obscene measures of humiliation and torture. Even in a region where political violence had long been endemic, such a human catastrophe had never been remotely experienced before. By 1943 the Ustaše had murdered around 400,000 people.

The Ustaše were certainly able to exploit ethnic antagonisms in former Yugoslavia when they took over Croatia. But their gross barbarity spawned far more and deeper ethnic hatred than had been present at any stage before the war. It was also counter-productive for the Germans. In Croatia the Ustaše had explicit German backing for their actions. (This was unlike Romania, where the orgy of violence perpetrated by the fascist Iron Guard led the Germans, anxious for stability because of the importance of Romanian oil, to support their suppression by the Romanian leader, General Antonescu.) Their atrocities fed both anti-Axis feeling and the growing strength of Josip Broz Tito's emerging communist partisan movement.

With much of eastern and southern Europe already falling ever deeper into the pit of dire inhumanity, the German invasion of the USSR in the summer of 1941 began a wholly new chapter. The war in the east – Hitler's war – was drastically different from all preceding campaigns, even though the untold savagery during the German occupation of Poland since September 1939 prefigured the descent into boundless inhumanity in the Soviet Union, in Nazi eyes the breeding ground of 'Jewish Bolshevism'. Hitler himself was indispensable both in promoting and in authorizing the barbarism. But he was its driving-force and radical spokesman, not its prime cause.

He himself told his army leaders that the war in the Soviet Union was to be a 'war of annihilation'. Communist soldiers were not to be regarded as honourable adversaries. The German army leadership was complicit in orders drawn up to liquidate Soviet commissars on capture without trial and effectively to declare open season on the shooting of Soviet civilians. Unsurprisingly, given encouragement of this sort to act without mercy against an enemy repeatedly portrayed as 'bestial' or 'criminal' in what the army's own leadership described as a struggle of 'race to race', extreme barbarism in the Soviet war was widespread from the beginning. It rapidly came to characterize the behaviour of German troops, inviting retaliatory barbarism by the Soviet defenders and a swift spiral of unconstrained inhumanity on both sides. There had been nothing like it during the campaigns in western Europe, where the very speed of the conquest had meant that casualties, even among the defeated, were relatively low and the treatment of the population in the occupied countries was far less harsh than in the east. During the attack on the Soviet Union the destruction of human life was enormous from the start. And here, unlike the west, huge numbers of civilians were slaughtered as part of the assault.

The war in the east was outrightly genocidal. It had been planned that way. Months before the launch of 'Barbarossa' and with Hitler's express backing, the head of the SS and Chief of Police, Heinrich Himmler, and the head of the Security Police, Reinhard Heydrich, had seen the 'final solution of the Jewish question' to be attainable by the deportation of all Jews in German hands – an estimated 5.8 million – into the lands to be conquered in the Soviet Union. There they would have died through starvation, overwork, disease, or exposure to the Arctic cold. Since Germany could not bring the war to a speedy, victorious conclusion, the policy of deportation into the Soviet Union proved unrealizable. Nevertheless, the killing of Soviet Jews was an implicit part of the German conquest. Close to the launch of the invasion, four big 'task forces' (*Einsatzgruppen*) of men from the security police were instructed to accompany the army and to eradicate all 'subversive elements'. This meant, in the main, Jews.

As the German army advanced into the Baltic countries at the start of 'Barbarossa', it had no trouble in finding willing collaborators among nationalists in Lithuania, Latvia and Estonia who saw the Germans as liberators from the yoke of Soviet rule. Tens of thousands of citizens of those countries had been deported to the Gulag by the Soviets when the countries were annexed in 1940. Soviet oppression had laid its heavy hand on entire communities. Jews had been prominent among the Soviet administrators and police. Many in the Baltic countries were prepared to believe that the Jews and the Bolsheviks were indistinguishable, that the Jews were responsible for their suffering at the hands of the Soviets.

The Germans and their collaborators were easily able to whip up anti-Jewish hatred among extreme nationalists. Soon after the Germans arrived in Lithuania, within days of the start of 'Operation Barbarossa' on 22 June 1941, mobs killed around 2,500 Jews in pogroms. Lithuanian units helped the German security police task forces in their grisly operations, which in the Baltic, even by Nazi standards, were extraordinarily murderous in the early months of the occupation. It was little different in Latvia, where the Germans, with Latvian assistance, had killed nearly 70,000 out of 80,000 Jews by late 1941. In Estonia, where there were very few Jews, local units working under German orders killed all 963 they could lay their hands on, and a further 5,000 or so non-Jewish Estonians for presumed collaboration with the Soviets. The task forces kept a careful count of their killings. By the end of the year the task force operating in the Baltic region could proudly record, with bureaucratic exactitude, a precise total of 229,052 Jews killed (along with another 11,000 or so other victims).

Far to the south, in Ukraine, Jews had by then also been slaughtered in vast numbers. But, unlike the Baltic, the non-Jews in Ukraine, deemed to be the 'inferior' Slavs, were themselves mercilessly treated by the German conquerors. As in the Baltic, Ukrainians had at first welcomed the Germans with open arms. 'We were all so happy to see them,' one woman remembered. 'They were going to save us from the Communists who had taken everything and starved us.' The terrible famine of 1932 was still a searing memory. The heavy hand of Stalinist oppression had not receded since then. When the Germans invaded, many Ukrainians deserted the Red Army or disappeared to avoid mobilization. As the Soviets retreated to try to escape German capture, the NKVD emptied the jails by shooting thousands of Ukrainian prisoners. Countless Ukrainians were left to struggle as Soviet 'scorched-earth' measures destroyed livestock and industrial machinery. Within days of the Germans arriving in Kiev on 19 September 1941, the city centre was rocked by explosions from mines that the Soviets had planted, starting a huge fire that killed many and left over 20,000 homeless. There was, then, good reason for the deep and widespread hatred for the Soviets among the Ukrainian population, and little wonder that the Germans were welcomed as liberators. Only downright idiocy could have converted that into even greater hatred of the Germans than the Soviets. But that is what the German conquerors achieved.

Even some ardent Nazi ideologues argued for turning the Ukrainians into allies and the Ukraine into part of a ring of satellites to ensure lasting German rule in the east. Hitler, however, saw the Ukrainians as 'nihilistically asiatic', just like the Russians. He backed utterly ruthless domination in the Ukraine, a policy put into action by his representative there, the abnormally brutal Reich Commissar Erich Koch. The view of Himmler was that the Ukraine had to be 'cleansed' for future German settlement. The fate of the mass of the Ukrainian population was intended to fall within the 'General Plan for the East', which envisaged over the next twenty-five years the 'removal' of some 31 million people, overwhelmingly Slavs, from conquered eastern territories.

This much vaster genocide could not be put into practice because the war turned against Germany. Even so, the occupation, in which the Germans were helped in their cruel repression by police units of Ukrainians, Latvians, Lithuanians and other collaborators, was so brutal that it engendered an all-pervasive fear in the population. Corpses on the streets, arbitrarily shot by the occupiers, were a frequent sight. Victims of public executions were, as in Poland, left hanging for days as a deterrent. Incidents of sabotage led to reprisal executions of hundreds. Whole villages were burnt down for not providing requisitioned food or for allegedly supporting partisans. 'Whenever we saw a group of Germans, we would hide immediately,' recalled one inhabitant of Kiev.

One huge source of fear from 1942, with Germany by now desperate for labour for war industries, was being rounded up for deportation to the Reich. It was seen as tantamount to a death sentence. Nearly every family was affected as those deported swelled in number to a million by June 1943. The deportations and the brutality with which they were carried out served as a great recruiting sergeant for partisan activity. Out of an initially welcoming population, German occupation had created a nation of enemies. But the Soviets were also the Ukrainians' enemies. Ukrainian Nationalist partisans found themselves in violent conflict not just with the Germans, but also with the Soviet partisans. One Ukrainian partisan later recalled what it was

like: 'The Germans just killed us, but with the Red partisans the bes-
tialities were different . . . They have this Asian way' (so he put it) 'of
torturing people – cutting your ears and tongue off . . . But, of course,
we were quite cruel . . . We didn't take any prisoners of war and they
didn't take any prisoners either, so we killed each other. That was
natural.'

Ukrainian Jews (numbering some 1.5 million, about 5 per cent of
the population, though around a quarter of Kiev's), unlike non-Jews
in Ukraine, had naturally feared German conquest. Even in their
worst nightmares, however, they could scarcely have imagined what
fate immediately awaited them under German occupation.

Antisemitism, often vicious, was widespread in Ukraine long before
the Germans arrived. Once the occupation began, Ukrainian Jews
found themselves within a friendless society facing a murderous
onslaught from the conquerors. A small minority of Ukrainians did
help their Jewish neighbours. A much bigger minority was ready to
denounce Jews to the German occupiers or to join in massacres. Most
Ukrainians, however, stood by and did nothing. Envy of Jewish
wealth, property and position played a significant part in Ukrainian
antisemitism. So did, as in other parts of the east, the belief that Jews
had been agents of Soviet oppression. When the Red Army retook
Ukraine in 1943 the view was frequently heard that 'these Jews are
here again'.

By the time the Germans entered Ukraine, not just Jewish men but
women and children, too, were being slaughtered throughout the east.
In the Babi-Yar ravine, on the edge of Kiev, in a colossal massacre over
two days, 29–30 September 1941, 33,771 Jewish men, women and
children were mown down by machine guns. Tens of thousands more
were murdered across Ukraine, in Belarus, and in other parts of the
former Soviet territories in the autumn and winter as German conquest extended its hold. Genocide was by this time total in the east. It
would soon be coordinated into a programme for total genocide
across the whole of German-occupied Europe.

In January 1942 the target figure for the number of Jews to be
exterminated in the 'final solution' was 11 million (though the estimates of the Jewish population in the various European countries
were sometimes highly inaccurate). The total included Jews in

England, Finland, Ireland, Portugal, Sweden, Switzerland, Spain and Turkey – areas not under German control but presumed at some future point to be incorporated in the 'final solution'. The target could not be met. Even so, when the course of the war brought the killing to a close, around five and a half million Jews had been murdered.

Amid the immensity of the horrific slaughter of non-combatants during the Second World War, there should be no hierarchy of victims. Whether an individual was starved or worked to death, shot or gassed, by Hitler's or Stalin's men, whether he or she was a 'kulak', a Jew, a homosexual or a 'gypsy' (of whom around half a million were murdered by the Germans), this was a person with loved ones, not an unfortunate casualty of fighting but someone deliberately killed. None should be placed higher or lower in a ranking order. There were differences, however, in the motivation behind the killings, and in the essential character of the murderous programmes. No social or ethnic group other than Jews had been encapsulated in ideology, long before the war began, as a cosmic enemy of diabolical power to be eradicated. Only Jews were carefully slated for destruction through the machinery of a meticulous bureaucracy. No other people – not even the Sinti and Roma (demeaningly labelled 'gypsies') – were then so relentlessly destroyed in a systematic programme, not just in mass shootings but increasingly in an industrialized system of mass annihilation.

In the entire catalogue of destruction, devastation and misery that made up the Second World War, the murder of Europe's Jews was the lowest point of mankind's descent into the abyss of inhumanity. The fires of the death-camp crematoria were almost literally the physical manifestation of hell on earth.

During the autumn of 1941 the killing of Jews in separate, murderous actions in different regions of eastern Europe was initiated by local Nazi leaders operating under a broad mandate from Berlin. They were inspired by Hitler's own drive to bring about the most radical 'solution' to the 'Jewish question'. These actions in eastern Europe accelerated the move to total genocide. The move gathered pace that autumn because the aim of deporting European Jews to Russia, where genocide was already raging, had to be abandoned when the expected early German victory in the Soviet Union did not materialize. With the mounting pressure, stirred for months by Nazi leaders, to declare their own provinces 'Jew-free', somewhere else had to be found for the 'final solution of the Jewish question'.

By early 1942 a programme of mass deportation to killing locations in Poland was emerging. Mobile and stationary gas chambers were by now preferred to mass shooting as the killing-method. Gas vans – resembling furniture vans, but modified to discharge carbon monoxide into the sealed rear compartment – at Chełmno in western Poland began operating in December 1941 and by the time they had finished had killed about 150,000 Jews. By March and April 1942 Polish Jews were being conveyed to their deaths in the stationary gas chambers at Belzec and Sobibor in eastern Poland. Treblinka, near Warsaw, followed suit in June, the third of the trio of extermination camps that by the summer operated within 'Aktion Reinhard', aimed at wiping out the whole of Polish Jewry.

There was no labour component in these camps. Actually, 'camps' is a misnomer. There were no residents apart from guards and the few prisoners temporarily held back as 'special detachments' (*Sonderkommandos*) to do the dirty work of handling the corpses at the gas chambers and crematoria. The 'camps' of 'Aktion Reinhard' existed for one purpose only: to kill the Jews sent there. Few lasted longer than a few hours after their arrival. When these camps were wound down in autumn 1943, they had overseen the murder of about 1.75 million Jews, mainly Polish. Around 2.7 million were murdered in the year 1942, almost half of the entire total killed during the war. Most perished in the 'Reinhard' camps.

The main killing-centre in 1943–4, however, was Auschwitz. Unlike the camps of 'Aktion Reinhard', Jews were transported to Auschwitz as slave labour, not just to die. Also unlike the 'Reinhard' camps, the vast majority of Jews sent to Auschwitz from 1942 onwards came from outside Poland. Auschwitz was already an enormous concentration and labour camp – initially for Polish prisoners – when the deportation of Jews from across Europe, starting with Slovakia and France, then Belgium, the Netherlands, and soon extended to other countries, began in March 1942.

The deportees were mostly sent to Birkenau, an auxiliary camp 2 kilometres away from the parent camp at Auschwitz itself, but vastly bigger. From May 1942 onwards those Jews incapable of working were separated from those capable of slave labour, and sent straight to the gas chambers, whose killing capacity was hugely extended when new crematoria (which could burn nearly 5,000 corpses a day) were built in 1943. By then, the tentacles of the genocidal programme had stretched to the farthest corners of Nazi-occupied Europe. Even in the western outpost of the Channel Islands, the only possessions of the British Crown to fall under German rule, three Jewish women (two Austrian, one Polish) were deported, initially to France, then to Auschwitz. Their subsequent fate is not known; but none survived the war.

The biggest deportations to Auschwitz were the last: those of the Hungarian Jews in the spring and summer of 1944, following the German occupation of Hungary. The Germans needed the labour and wealth of the Hungarian Jews. But economic motives blended with the ideological imperative of destruction. Hitler told his military leaders in May 1944 that the entire Hungarian state was 'undermined and corroded' by Jews, who were a 'seamless web of agents and spies'. Their destruction was essential to German victory. His military commanders responded with storms of applause when he told them that he had intervened to 'solve the problem', emphasizing that only the maintenance of the German race mattered. The consequence was the mass deportation to Auschwitz of the Hungarian Jews. By July, 437,402 of them had perished in the Auschwitz gas chambers.

Around 1.1 million people were murdered at Auschwitz – about a million of them Jews, 70,000 Polish political prisoners, more than 20,000 Sinti and Roma, 10,000 Soviet prisoners of war, along with hundreds of Jehovah's Witnesses and homosexuals. The Red Army liberated Auschwitz's prisoners at the end of January 1945. Even hardened Soviet soldiers had been shocked in July the previous year when they had come across the part-extermination camp at Lublin-Majdanek, where about 80,000 Jews were among the estimated 200,000 victims. What they discovered at Auschwitz was worse still. But even now the torment of the Jews was not over. About a quarter of a million camp prisoners, overwhelmingly Jews, perished on death-marches in the final months of the war when the remaining camps, first in Poland and finally in Germany itself, were evacuated as the enemy approached.

Each of those sent to Auschwitz and the other death-camps had once had a name. The bureaucracy of mass-killing turned the names into numbers. For the killers, the victims were anonymous. It was a very modern way of killing. Primo Levi, an Italian Jewish chemist captured by Fascist militia, who found himself by February 1944 sent to work in the slave-labour camp at Auschwitz-Monowitz, recalled what it was like to be deprived of identity. It amounted to 'the demolition of a man'. 'We had reached the bottom,' he continued. 'It is not possible to sink lower than this; no human condition is more miserable than this, nor could it conceivably be so. Nothing belongs to us any more; they have taken away our clothes, our shoes, even our hair . . . They will even take away our name.' They did. He soon learnt that he was Prisoner Number 173417, the number tatooed on to his left arm. He commented: 'This is hell. Today, in our times, hell must be like this.'

But some retained an identity beyond the concentration-camp number, and they kept their human dignity even as they prepared to enter the gas chambers. Chaim Hermann wrote a remarkable last letter to his wife and daughter, truly a voice from the gas chambers, which was found in February 1945 beneath human ashes near one of the Auschwitz crematoria. He depicted his life in the camp as 'an entirely different world' to any his wife could imagine, 'simply hell, but Dante's hell is incomparably ridiculous in comparison with this real one here'. He assured her that he was leaving this hell 'calmly and perhaps heroically (this will depend on circumstances)'.

Not all were as stoical. A poem written in Czech that survived the death of its author in Auschwitz epitomises the deep anger at the perpetrators of the horror, the inner rebellion against the degradation and death, the feeling, surely shared by many of the victims, that a day of reckoning must sometime dawn:

> And there are more and more of us down here;
> we swell and grow day by day;
> your fields are already bloated with us
> and one day your land will burst.

And then we'll emerge, in awful ranks,
a skull on our skulls and bony shanks;
and we'll roar in the faces of all the people
We, the dead, accuse!

HELL ON EARTH'S MANY MEANINGS

For the anonymous Czech poet, and countless others, it was difficult to find meaning in the pointless slaughter of so many innocent victims. Many Jews asked where God was while the boundless suffering and death was taking place. If there was a God, why did He permit such horror? Christians, in many parts of Europe subjected to unimaginable misery, frequently asked the same question. Others, in contrast, clung to their belief. It was, it often seemed, all they had left. Whether the hundreds of thousands of Sinti and Roma victims could find succour in religious belief, or felt just hopelessness and pointlessness in their persecution and murder, is harder to know. There were no poets in their midst. Most were illiterate and left no written accounts for posterity of their suffering – countless human lives purposefully obliterated, and leaving little trace beyond memory and oral tradition.

Genocide and 'ethnic cleansing' on a gigantic scale were an intrinsic part of the meaning of the war to the German leadership and to the host of subordinates in the military, police and bureaucracy who sought to implement racial policy. For their millions of victims, there could often be no more than blank incomprehension. The bleakest pessimism about humankind would have been, and sometimes was, a perfectly natural response to what they had to endure. Yet, astonishingly, there was more than nihilism. Even in Auschwitz, Beethoven's 'Ode to Joy' was sung. Even in this man-made hell, there was still humanity, still a sense of transcendence that music, if not religion itself, could evoke.

People found their own meanings, or lack of them. Is it possible to speak of the 'meaning' of the war for the millions who lived, fought and died during the titanic conflict? What did they make of the maelstrom of events that had swept through their lives, changing them forever, often in most traumatic fashion? Plainly, each individual experienced the war in some way that was unique. The war had many meanings, or often none at all. Circumstances, widely differing, dictated experience and, from experience, sometimes a sense of what meaning the war might have. Experiences were not purely individual. Many were shared, common experiences, often shaped in part by the accident of nationality, others extending beyond nationality, even if frequently conditioned by it and perceived through national lenses.

Millions served on widely differing fronts, at sea or in the air, some in occupying forces, others in the shadowy guerrilla war of national resistance. Women joined the armed services in high numbers, hundreds of thousands of them providing essential auxiliary services, playing significant roles in resistance movements, and in the Red Army and among Yugoslav partisans fighting in the front line. Civilians, trapped in war as never before, experienced daily anxieties about loved ones far away in combat. In most of Europe they also had to adjust to enemy occupation, suffer heavy material privations and often face the terror of bombing and the traumas of forced evacuations. The character of occupation shaped wartime experience in many decisive ways. The grotesque levels of inhumanity in eastern Europe were not directly paralleled in the west. But there too, although differing from country to country, the years of occupation left a searing mark on mentalities. Life itself was everywhere more precarious than it had been. For millions the war was about little more than survival. Certainly that is what it meant in the first instance for countless fighting troops of all nationalities.

Fighting Troops

For soldiers, sailors and airmen at the point of gravest danger survival was most usually the sole thought and concern. In the heat of battle there was no room for reflection. Fear and apprehension were overwhelming sentiments as the guns started firing. Thoughts of loved ones back home, of the need to protect them, and of the need to live to return to them, were strong motivating factors. So too, often, was the need to take revenge for what the enemy had done to loved ones. Beyond fighting for self-survival, loyalty to immediate comrades closely followed as a motive. When loss of life was on such a massive scale as it was during the war on the eastern front, and when entire military units were being repeatedly destroyed and reconstituted, 'group-loyalty' could not have the meaning that it had, for instance, for the 'pals battalions' that had marched into the First World War from Britain's industrial towns and cities. Nevertheless, self-survival depended in great measure upon the actions of immediate comrades. Self-interest determined, therefore, that the fight for survival was also a fight for the survival of those fighting alongside. Fear of the consequences of *not* fighting also played its part. Soviet and German soldiers, in particular, could expect no mercy from their own side for refusal to fight, or for desertion.

Away from the heat of the battlefield, those in the armed forces, even if they were not reflective individuals, often gave at least hints, in letters home or sometimes in diaries, of what, beyond personal survival, they imagined they were fighting for. A subliminal sense of meaning was, through training, upbringing, background and long-imbibed shared cultural values, superimposed upon the immediate, personal reasons for fighting.

The belief that they were part of a crusade to defend Germany from a dire threat from Bolshevism undoubtedly drove the actions of most Wehrmacht soldiers as they poured over the Soviet frontiers in June 1941. It gave them seeming justification for their subsequent barbaric conduct of the war, against civilians as well as the Red Army, and involving the massacre of Jews. 'Here Europe ends,' one cultured German soldier wrote home to his friend as he stepped onto Soviet soil. Germans were there, in his view, to defend the cultured Christian Western world from the repellent, atheistic vandalism of Bolshevism. And though no ideological antisemite, the same soldier had imbibed Nazi propaganda about 'Jewish Bolshevism'. He did not hide his disgust at the Jewish population of some of the villages his unit marched through. A German reserve policeman, a shopkeeper in civilian life, wrote to his wife in August 1941 about the shooting of 150 Jews, men, women and children. 'The Jews are being completely exterminated,' he commented. 'Please don't think about it, that's how it has to be.' Many soldiers watched impassively as mass executions took place. Some took photos. 'We watched the show and then went back to work, as if nothing had happened,' one told his wife. His justification followed quickly: 'Partisans are enemies and blackguards and must vanish.' The sentiment assuaged consciences, at first sometimes troubled but soon acclimatizing to what was required, when hundreds of villages were burnt and the inhabitants slaughtered (or burnt to death) – 600 villages in Belarus alone – as reprisal for real or alleged partisan activity.

There were exceptions to the inhumanity, of course. The courageous officers who came to form the backbone of the German resistance that sought on a number of occasions in 1943 and 1944 to kill Hitler were galvanized in their conspiracy by the knowledge of the gross atrocities perpetrated against Jews and others in the east. Misfortune more than anything foiled their efforts. But the names of General Henning von Tresckow and Colonel Claus Schenk Graf von Stauffenberg stand proxy for many others nauseated by the knowledge of the inhumanity of Hitler's Germany.

Some ordinary soldiers, too, felt uneasy from the start about what was happening. Some from religious conviction inwardly rebelled again the barbarism, or even on rare occasions helped Jews. Wilm Hosenfeld, a one-time Nazi Party member and stormtrooper who had admired Hitler and fully believed in Germany's cause in the war, became so appalled by what he saw and heard as a low-ranking officer based in Warsaw that he took it upon himself, prompted by his strong Catholic beliefs, to help Jews where he could. Among those he helped to save were the Polish-Jewish musician, Władysław Szpilman, whose story much later became well known through Roman Polanski's film, *The Pianist*. 'Has the Devil taken on human form?' Hosenfeld asked in a letter to his wife in July 1942, after mentioning that Jews were being killed in their thousands. 'I don't doubt it' was his answer to his own question. History knew no precedent, he remarked. He described it as 'such a terrible blood-guilt that you want to sink to the ground in shame'.

The number of those who behaved so nobly has been estimated at perhaps a hundred. Perhaps the actions of some others have not been registered for posterity. But at any rate the number is small, compared with the figure of over 18 million who served in the Wehrmacht.

Most of these swallowed to some degree what they were told was the purpose of the war. All the indications are that the unvarnished views outlined by Field Marshal Walter von Reichenau, an outright Nazi and one of Hitler's favourite generals, percolated down at least in some degree to the army's grass roots. Reichenau clarified the duty of German soldiers in the east in a general order on 10 October 1941:

> The main aim of the campaign against the Jewish-Bolshevist system is the complete destruction of its forces and the extermination of the Asiatic influence in the sphere of European culture. As a result, the troops have to take on tasks which go beyond the conventional purely military one. In the eastern sphere the soldier is not simply a fighter according to the rules of war, but the supporter of a ruthless racial [*völkisch*] ideology and the avenger of all the bestialities which have been inflicted on the German nation and those ethnic groups related to it. For this reason soldiers must show full understanding of the necessity for the severe atonement being required of the Jewish subhumans.

What such German soldiers thought they were fighting for amounted to an opaque vision of a future utopia, a 'new order' in which German racial superiority and dominance over crushed enemies would guarantee their families and descendants peace and prosperity. By 1944–5 such vague hopes had vanished. But the war still had meaning. That it was fought so resiliently to the end now rested predominantly upon a different ideological imperative: 'defence of the Reich'. The phrase encapsulated not simply an abstract political or geographical entity, but defence of family, home, property and cultural roots. And knowing what crimes they and their fellow soldiers had committed, above all in the east, fighting on meant holding out at all costs against the Red Army whose vengeful victory would surely bring the destruction of all that they held dear. The ideological meanings of the war helped, alongside discipline, training and good leadership, to sustain remarkably high fighting morale in the Wehrmacht until practically the end.

For Germany's military allies the meaning of the war was far less clear, morale far more difficult to uphold. Around 690,000 non-German troops, mainly Romanian, had joined the invasion of the Soviet Union in 1941. In the offensive that met such a catastrophic end at Stalingrad, Romanians, Hungarians, Croatians, Slovakians and Italians all participated. Nearly 300,000 non-German Axis troops were caught in the Soviet counter-offensive. Hitler had nothing but angry contempt for their lack of fighting spirit. In truth, this did lag way behind that of the Germans, and for understandable reasons. Hatred of the Soviet Union was widespread, but did not suffice on its own to provide motivational meaning for Germany's allies as it did for the German troops themselves. Germany's allies had no clear future vision of a society or regime for which they thought it worth fighting, and perhaps losing their lives. Desertion was commonplace, lack of morale rampant, leadership dismal. Romanian officers treated their rank-and-file, ill-equipped and under-strength troop units little better than dogs. It was no wonder that many of them fought only under duress. 'Romanians didn't have a real goal – what were they fighting for?' was a pertinent question posed by a former Red Army soldier who had faced them and observed their weakness as a fighting force. Italian troops fighting on the River Don also often wondered what they were doing there. They were far from home, in appalling conditions, in a war that meant little to them. It was hardly surprising that they lacked fighting morale. When an Italian sergeant was asked by a Soviet interpreter why his battalion had surrendered with not a shot fired, he answered: 'We did not fire back because we thought it would be a mistake.'

Most Italians had not wanted to fight. They increasingly felt that Mussolini had dragged them into a war that suited only the detested Germans. Without plain or pervasive ideological meaning, the war lacked for them any strong motivating purpose. It was completely rational that they preferred surrender, and survival, to fighting on in a lost cause. But with their country occupied by the Germans in the north and the Allies in the south, once Italy dropped out of the war in September 1943, Italians showed that they were ready to fight ten-aciously – against the occupiers and against each other – for an ideological cause that directly affected themselves, their families and their homes: what sort of post-war country was Italy going to be, fascist again or socialist?

For the soldiers of the Red Army, a huge multi-ethnic fighting body, the war had an altogether different meaning. Most came from uneducated backgrounds and had lived in primitive conditions. Three-quarters of the infantry were peasants. Some boys from backwoods villages had never even seen an electric light before they entered the military. Reflections on a deeper meaning to the war they were fighting are unlikely to have come readily to most of them. Many doubtless fought because they had to, because they had been left with no choice, because failure to do so would have meant certain death. But fear alone could not have sustained such astonishing fighting power and morale of the Red Army from the verge of catastrophe in 1941 to complete victory four years later.

In fact, morale in the Red Army was close to cracking completely as the seemingly unstoppable German advance went from triumph to triumph in the summer of 1941. Desertion rates were high. So were the rates of murderous retribution on those deserting. But a non-stop barrage of propaganda, the endless stories of German butchery of those they conquered, and, at last, a tale of heroism as the Red Army triumphed before the gates of Moscow, eventually stopped the rot. Soviet soldiers, like those of the Wehrmacht, saw meaning in the war, even if they could not articulate it. Underestimating the role of ideology in their motivation would be a mistake. It was not necessarily the official ideology of the regime, though this was now attuned to an emphasis upon patriotism. When Stalin addressed the troops on the morning of the great Red Army offensive on the Don in November 1942 that culminated in the victory at Stalingrad, he couched it in patriotic terms: 'Dear generals and soldiers, I address you my brothers. Today you start an offensive and your actions decide the fate of the country – whether it remains an independent country or perishes.' One witness recalled his emotions that day: 'Those words really reached my heart ... I was close to tears ... I felt a real upsurge, a spiritual upsurge.'

But it was not just patriotism. Patriotism and Marxist-Leninist ideology reinforced each other. The troops had been schooled in Bolshevism. Those who fought at the gates of Moscow, at Stalingrad, at Kursk, knew nothing else. They had since childhood soaked up visions of a new, better society for all. One Red Army veteran who admitted to dreaming of Stalin 'like a father' and likened hearing his voice 'to the voice of God', said that, whatever the repression, 'Stalin embodied the future, we all believed that.' This future utopia of the communist Motherland was now under dire threat. It could still become reality – but only if Hitler's fascists who were descending like hyenas to ravage Soviet homelands, kill its citizens and lay waste to its towns and villages, could be destroyed. It was a powerful message that even gained in potency by the added ingredient of vengeance once the tables had been turned and the Red Army had the frontiers of the Reich in its sights. For Red Army soldiers what they were fighting was a defensive war, a just war – one that had to be fought and won, whatever the human cost. It was strong motivation. The war had real meaning.

For the fighting troops of the west European Allies the war could not be reduced to a single meaning. The initial western Allies, Great Britain, France and Poland, were swiftly joined after the outbreak of war by the British Dominions. British and French colonial possessions supplied huge numbers of troops. India alone provided 2.5 million men, mainly deployed in fighting the Japanese, while colonial north Africa came to provide the base for the re-establishment of French military strength after 1942. Czechs, Belgians, Dutch and Norwegians were among the many other Europeans who fought with the Poles and French alongside the British from an early stage of the war. The USA and many other countries later joined the war on the Allied side. In 1942 the alliance against the Axis powers constituted twenty-six countries, calling themselves the 'United Nations'. The war inevitably had varied meanings for the men and women of such a disparate fighting force, engaged not only in Europe but also, after the Japanese had entered the war, in the Far East, as well as on the seas and in the air. Nor were Allied troops any better than other soldiers at articulating what it was they thought they were fighting for. Letters home usually dealt with more mundane aspects of life in the armed services, mostly sparing loved ones the worst of the hardships, pain, fear and trauma that the troops had to endure. Comradeship was crucial, longing to return to home and family near universal; ultimately, personal survival was what mattered. Even if mostly unspoken, there were, however, cultural values and subliminal motivational beliefs that sustained morale and made this a war worth fighting.

For the exiled Poles and the Free French, based in Britain, and for the citizens of other European countries who joined the Allied forces, the cause was an obvious one: liberation of their homelands from

German occupation. But General de Gaulle, leader of the Free French, did not for a long time speak for most French citizens. For the people of France, at home and abroad, the war had no single meaning. For the exiled Poles, too, the war had more than one meaning. The cause was not just freedom from the German yoke but, gaining in importance as the war progressed, seeking to ensure that a post-war Poland would not exchange one form of servitude for another and fall under the dominance of the Soviet Union.

Under General Władisław Sikorski, commander-in-chief of the Polish armed forces and Prime Minister of Poland's exiled government, some 19,000 Polish soldiers and airmen had been evacuated to Britain from France in 1940, though three-quarters of the number of Poles fighting on French soil had been killed or captured. Polish pilots then made a disproportionate contribution to the Battle of Britain. Less well known is that the Polish cryptographers were also instrumental in working with the British and French to break the Enigma code – they had already broken an earlier Enigma model in the 1930s – which enabled the Allies to read German signals, a crucial factor in eventually winning the battle of the Atlantic.

From 1942 onwards, after Stalin had released tens of thousands of Polish prisoners from the Gulag and re-established Soviet-Polish diplomatic relations, some 40,000 Polish troops under General Władisław Anders fought alongside the British in north Africa, then with the Allies in Italy. Anders himself had been captured by the Soviets and suffered grievous torture at their hands while in prison. Unsurprisingly, he remained after his release virulently anti-Soviet. The gruesome discoveries at Katyn in April 1943 were the plainest of reminders to Poles in exile of the horrors not just of German but also of Soviet occupation. The crushing of the Warsaw Rising in August 1944 saw hopes of establishing an independent Poland extinguished. The agreement of the British and Americans at the Yalta Conference the following February, that Poland, with reordered boundaries, should be assigned to a post-war Soviet sphere of influence, completed the Polish sense of betrayal. For non-communist Poles, the vast majority of the population within Poland as well as in exile, the war started and ended in national disaster.

Charles de Gaulle was a little-known junior officer in the French army before 1940. Elevated to the rank of general during the German invasion of Belgium, and soon afterwards appointed Under-Secretary for Defence in the French government, he had, with British backing, established himself by the summer of 1940 as the leader of the exiled Free French, a tiny force of only around 2,000 men and 140 officers. In a series of ringing radio addresses to the French people from London, de Gaulle asserted that the Free French represented the true France. He sought to embody defiance, both to the Germans and the Vichy regime (the government of the non-occupied zone of France following the defeat in 1940), to which he denied any claim to legitimacy. But he had little success until the middle of the war. Many in France, influenced by the Vichy press, saw him as a traitor.

The sinking of the French fleet at Mers el-Kébir in Algeria on 3 July 1940, on Churchill's orders (to prevent it being made available to the Germans) and with the loss of life of 1,297 French sailors, did little to win support for the Allied cause either in France itself or in its colonies. Along with the colonial authorities, French troops in the colonies, far outnumbering those in France itself, were initially loyal to the Vichy regime, repulsing an abortive landing by the Free French at Dakar in September 1940. Only gradually, as war fortunes swung against Germany and Vichy lost popularity, did colonial support move to support the Free French. De Gaulle's fractious relationship with Churchill and Roosevelt and internal wrangles among the Free French leadership were a hindrance to a consolidated opposition to Vichy until well after the Allied landings in north Africa in November 1942. At that point the Free French forces still numbered a mere 50,000 compared with 230,000 who had until then been at least nominally loyal to Vichy. Only by the summer of 1943, having moved his headquarters to Algiers and gained in standing through his support for the growing resistance movement within France, was de Gaulle recognized as, effectively, the uncontested head of a government in waiting. He now represented a rival, growing in power and support, to the Vichy regime which, from November 1942 when the Germans had taken over what had been the previously non-occupied zone, was more than ever a puppet to the increasingly hated German rulers.

British troops were unique among their European allies in not fighting to free their country from foreign occupation. The cause for which they were fighting, the meaning of their war, was in this sense more abstract, less obvious. Overwhelmingly they backed Churchill as a war leader. But beyond the elites, represented within the officer corps, not many shared Churchill's own belief in the meaning of the war, that beyond the fight for freedom and democracy it was to preserve the greatness of the British Empire. Many colonial troops who fought alongside the British hoped, in fact, for exactly the opposite, for independence of their homelands from colonial rule. Even troops from the British mainland, fighting thousands of miles away in the Far East against a brutal and merciless Japanese enemy, had little sense that they were there to sustain British imperialism. Surviving jungle hell-holes as well as Japanese onslaught and, all too often, the indescribable horrors of barbarous treatment in captivity, was for most all that mattered. Few of the troops spoke in their letters home about any meaning of the war beyond their own survival. One who did, a British officer, wrote to his parents shortly before he was killed in north Africa, expressing vague ideals that nonetheless almost certainly had fairly wide currency. He was prepared to die, he wrote, for what he depicted as 'the heart-felt longing of all the "middling folk" for something better – a world more worthy of their children'.

This sense that the meaning of the war was to pave the way for a better future was widespread, if often unspoken, among the British forces. It gained voice at home with the publication in November 1942 of the report by the Liberal William Beveridge, laying out the framework for a system of social security that would offer all British citizens forms of state welfare from cradle to grave. The Beveridge Report was widely discussed among the troops overseas, an indication in itself that the war was seen as the gateway to a new society. The pervasive sense that the war was not just about defeating and destroying the menace of Nazism – though that was the obvious, foremost objective – but about breaking with the old world at home once the main job was done, gave the British troops purpose and helped to maintain morale. It would gain expression at the British general election in 1945, when the war against Germany had been won, that against Japan was still raging, yet the war hero, Churchill, was nevertheless rejected by the votes of millions of servicemen as representing the old class order of privilege, wealth and position, finally to be replaced by a fairer society. Utopian hopes, as well as the fight against Hitler's Germany, gave meaning to the British war effort.

For some who had served in the armed forces, however, and had started with high hopes, the war had brought disillusionment – in politics, in a better future, in mankind itself. William Woodruff had gone from working-class Lancashire during the slump to Oxford University, a pacifist socialist who had become converted to the necessity of fighting Nazism to secure an improved, changed society. Yet he came back from the war inwardly changed himself, his optimism dissipated on the battlefield. 'Before the war I had talked about building a new civilization,' he later wrote. 'At the end I knew how fragile civilization is ... It took a long time for the memory of other men's deaths to fade.' Many other returning soldiers doubtless felt the same way.

Home Fronts

The gulf between the fighting and home fronts was smaller in the Second World War than in any previous war. Often, there was no gulf at all; the fronts more or less merged. In parts of eastern Europe the rampaging backwards and forwards of Hitler's and Stalin's armies and the spreading activities of partisans largely erased any separate meanings for fighting and home fronts. In other parts of Europe there was more of a distinction. In differing fashion, the peoples of all the belligerent countries endured a hell on earth, mostly under the jackboot of German occupiers.

Only the six neutral countries – Switzerland, Sweden, Spain, Portugal, Turkey and Éire (known until 1937 as the Irish Free State) – along with the mini-statelets of Liechtenstein, Andorra and the Vatican State, managed to escape relatively unscathed. But even they were not left untouched by the war. The population of each suffered privations on account of economic disruption and in some instances direct blockade, and were even subjected to occasional air attacks (for example, the Swiss towns and cities of Schaffhausen, Basel and Zurich) through misplaced Allied bombing, causing death and injury to civilians. Nevertheless, each of the neutral countries avoided the worst. The path of their neutrality differed in each case. It was only in part shaped by ideological proclivities. To a much greater extent it was a consequence of strategic necessity and economic advantage.

Switzerland, three-quarters of its population German-speaking, worried about the prospect of German invasion and eventually exposed on all its borders to the Axis powers, was inevitably drawn indirectly into the conflict. Both the Germans and, later the Allies, repeatedly violated Swiss airspace. And both sides made use of Swiss banking. The need for food and fuel imports meant it was vital for Switzerland to retain its trade links with Germany. The export of precision instruments helped the German war effort. Swiss banks held large amounts of German gold, much of it plundered from the occupied countries and used to purchase vital supplies of raw materials for the war effort from other neutral countries. And despite Allied pressure, supplies of coal, iron, building materials and, in the first stages of the war, weapons and military equipment crossed Switzerland en route from Germany to Italy. On the other hand, Switzerland's proximity to Germany meant that it was a ready goal for refugees and escaped prisoners of war. The country took in, though not always willingly, several hundred thousand military and civilian refugees. However, it turned away many others, including over a third of Jewish refugees fleeing Nazi persecution.

Swedish neutrality, like Switzerland's, was heavily compromised. Trade was badly hit by a British blockade. This contributed to the substantial increase in Sweden's trade with Germany – already the country's major trading partner – in the early phase of the war. Crucial to German steel production were the imports of Swedish high-grade iron ore. Swedish ball-bearings were also important to the German war effort (though, bypassing the blockade, almost as vital to the British war economy). Coal, desperately needed in Sweden, was imported from Germany in large quantities. Neutrality was overridden in allowing the passage of troops and armaments. German troops were transported through Sweden to Finland before the attack on the Soviet Union in 1941. Over 2 million German soldiers in all passed through Sweden between Norway and Germany. And thousands of goods wagons containing armaments and military equipment were conveyed through Sweden, to Finland as well as Norway. Especially later in the war, however, Sweden took in thousands of refugees (including Jews fleeing from Denmark and Norway). Sweden also, like Switzerland, provided the Allies with important intelligence.

On the Iberian peninsula Spain and Portugal, though both officially neutral, differed in their stance towards the belligerent powers. Portugal, Britain's oldest ally, favoured the Allies over the Germans in its neutrality, especially once the war had inexorably turned against Germany. In particular, permission to use airbases on the Azores, reluctantly granted in 1943, meant greater protection for the Allied convoys crossing the Atlantic. In contrast, Franco, despite his later assertions that his astute leadership had kept Spain out of the conflict, had actually been keen to join it on the Axis side. But his price for entry had been too high. He not only had expectations of territorial gains in north Africa at the expense of the French, but also put forward such huge demands for foodstuffs and armaments that Germany could not contemplate meeting them. Franco did not change his ideological preference for the Axis. Important exports of raw materials were sent to Germany, U-boats were allowed to refuel in Spain, and nearly 20,000 of Franco's countrymen volunteered to fight for the Germans on the eastern front. But as eventual German defeat became a certainty, and as Allied blocking of desperately needed food and other imports concentrated minds, Franco gradually changed his tune and allowed his neutrality to serve the interests of the Allies.

Turkey's anxiety not to be drawn into another ruinous war, and the country's geographical exposure to widening conflict in the Mediterranean, underpinned its neutrality. Early in the war, encouraged by loans and credits of over £40 million to purchase military equipment, Turkey favoured the Allies, though it resisted all pressure to enter the war. And, like Spanish neutrality, Turkey's stance indirectly helped the Allied war effort in the Mediterranean and north Africa. With the German expansion in 1941 reaching to its very borders, however, Turkey entered upon a treaty of friendship with Germany. It was a necessary insurance bet against Germany winning the war. Germany exerted heavy pressure in 1943 to ensure that Turkey delivered increased quantities of chromite, necessary for the war economy. But Turkey still maintained its neutrality. It maintained this stance, against renewed Allied pressure once the war had turned against Germany. Purely symbolically, since it continued to avoid involvement in any fighting, Turkey finally declared war against Germany on 23 February 1945.

In spite of widespread anti-British feeling among Irish nationalists, Éire's neutrality was tilted heavily towards support for the Allies. Britain was, it is true, deprived of the use of ports – finally ceded to Ireland as late as 1938 – that would have shortened shipping lines to the USA. But British ships were repaired in Irish shipyards. Irish airspace was used for coastal patrols. Allied aircrews who were picked up were returned, while Germans were interned. And there was much cooperation between the Irish and British governments around the joint interest in the defence of the island of Ireland. Moreover, whatever the official position, many Irish families had close ties with relatives in Britain. Despite neutrality, an estimated 42,000 citizens of Éire volunteered to serve in the war (several thousand of whom lost their lives wearing British uniforms), while around 200,000 crossed the Irish Sea to work for the British war economy. Éire's neutrality had a bizarre coda: the Irish Prime Minister (*Tsaioseach*) and veteran of the fight for independence, Éamon de Valera, little more than a fortnight after expressing his condolences on the death of President Roosevelt, joined an extremely small club of those offering formal condolences to Germany on the news of Hitler's death in 1945.

British civilians were the most fortunate of any belligerent country in Europe. It would not have seemed that way to the citizens of London's East End or the people of other British cities (among them Coventry, Southampton, Bristol, Cardiff, Manchester, Liverpool, Sheffield, Hull, Glasgow and, in Northern Ireland, Belfast) suffering under the hail of German bombs in 1940 and 1941 – then again in 1944–5 when under attack from flying bombs (or V1s) and V2 rockets. The civilian population of Britain, like people in other countries, had less to eat, had to work longer hours, endure hardship and anxiety about loved ones away fighting, and homelessness in bombed-out areas. They had to bear the deep sense of loss when the knock on the door brought the dreaded telegram to say that a husband, son, father or brother had been killed or was missing in action. Women in particular had to bear the brunt of the new material hardship. They were left to cope with the stringent rationing of everyday foodstuffs that had been part of a staple diet, with looking after children while husbands were away, and often having to balance family commitments with long hours at work. Women who had not previously been employed, or had been housewives, contributed 80 per cent to the addition to the workforce – which grew by half a million – between 1939 and 1943.

The pressures on civilian life in Britain, considerable as they were, nevertheless fell far short of those experienced in practically all other European countries. Above all, Britain was not an occupied country. There was no ruthless drain on the economy by German occupiers. There was no forced labour, driven off to an uncertain future to work for German industry. Outside the big cities there was little physical destruction by the war, and even within the cities the damage caused by the bombs, though severe, was limited to relatively confined areas. Thousands were made homeless, though there was nothing to compare with the flood of refugees and evacuees across much of the continent. Food rationing had a significant impact on living standards, but it did not remotely approach the famine conditions inflicted by German occupation (abetted by Allied blockade) on Greece and the German blockade on food-supply lines in Holland near the end of the war, let alone the horrific starvation of the population of Leningrad. The black market thrived, though less than in other countries where the material shortages were greater. Not least, the fact that Britain remained unoccupied meant, crucially, that there were no pressures to conform with the demands of conquerors, no gulf between those who collaborated (at numerous levels) and those who chose to resist (in various ways).

Britain was quite possibly a society more united during the war than it had ever been before or would be again. The dwindling minority of those wanting to make peace with Hitler's Germany – most prominent in the upper-class establishment – soon kept their own counsel, or were interned like Sir Oswald Mosley and other prominent fascists. But the majority voice was not coerced or fabricated, as in repressive authoritarian systems. A broad consensus behind the war effort existed in reality. Morale fluctuated, of course, rising and dipping with war's fortunes, and affected by material concerns such as the availability of foodstuffs. Bombing, too, shook morale (contrary to much later legend), though it did not destroy it. Around

300,000 people were injured by bombing over the course of the war (mainly in 1940–41 and 1944–5), a fifth or so of those numbers, over 60,000 people, killed – horribly high figures, of course, but far fewer than anticipated and not enough to undermine the morale of the population in general.

There were the usual grievances and grumblings of everyday life, even growing numbers of industrial disputes and strikes, with over 2,000 stoppages and more than 3 million days lost to production in 1944. But, though hardly welcome to the government, the strikes were generally short and for the most part about wages and working conditions. They were not a protest against the war. Whatever the ebbs and flows of morale, there was for the British civilian population, as for the servicemen at arms, an underlying sense of the justice and necessity of fighting the war. Propaganda naturally played its part in boosting this sense of a just cause. The success of propaganda lay, however, in its ability to build upon a consensus that was already present. Churchill, a highly divisive figure as a reactionary pre-war politician, embodied the consensus, basking in approval ratings sometimes of over 90 per cent. His powerful speeches may not have played the decisive role in boosting morale that has often been presumed; but at crucial moments (such as the retreat from Dunkirk in May and June 1940) they undoubtedly lifted spirits, reinforcing the sense of meaning invested in the war, as vital for the survival of freedom and democracy. Churchill's significance can be measured in simple terms by imagining what Britain's fate might have been had its war leader been Lord Halifax, as was so nearly the case.

The war also had a unifying effect in the vast hinterland of the Soviet Union that remained unoccupied, well beyond the reaches of the Wehrmacht. The Stalinist regime's shift in propaganda to emphasize patriotic defence, appealing especially to Russian national feelings, even promulgating a concordat with the Russian Orthodox Church, was not without effect in helping to stimulate a willingness to suffer immense hardship in the cause of repulsing such a cruel and ruthless enemy. Wartime mobilization of the civilian population was inevitably accompanied by heavy coercion and repression (though the numbers interned in labour camps fell). Where there was any doubt about the loyalty of the population, draconian measures were taken.

When a minority in some of the national minorities – the Volga Germans, the Crimean Tatars, the Kalmyks, the Chechens – favoured the invaders, Stalin did not hesitate to deport the entire ethnic community, amid appalling suffering and great loss of life, to the inhospitable wastes of remote parts of the Soviet Empire. Nevertheless, terror and repression cannot in themselves account for the extraordinary war effort of the Soviet civilian population.

The hardships endured and the scale of difficulties that Soviet citizens had to face are scarcely describable. Around 25 million citizens were left homeless in the wake of the German invasion in 1941. Food, apart from potatoes, was drastically rationed, and almost all civilians had to cope with acute food shortages. Around a million people in Leningrad actually starved to death. Even in the rest of the Soviet Union, the urban population existed at little more than starvation level. The black market in unofficial peasant surpluses held back from the drastic state requisitioning was, however draconian the penalties, crucial to survival. Despite the near constant hunger, morale did not collapse. The working day was lengthened, with harsh penalties for any labour misdemeanours. But huge numbers of new workers – housewives, students, pensioners – volunteered for work. Women, especially, were incorporated within the workforce as never before, making up 57 per cent of industrial workers by 1943 and no fewer than 80 per cent of workers on collective farms.

New productive norms, sometimes double or triple what had earlier existed, were agreed. It took the best part of two years for Soviet production to recover from the catastrophe of 1941. But when it did, it provided the platform on which military victory could be built. People accepted the intense privations because they saw that husbands, fathers or sons were fighting for the country's very survival. Even where death on a large scale had long been part of the culture, the war brought new dimensions of loss. Scarcely a family escaped it. The sacrifice, material and human, might have undermined morale in a society less accustomed to hardship and death. As it was, the peril that all of them faced should the war be lost created a new sense of community capable of endurance and will that no powers of coercion alone, however strong, could produce.

The experience of German occupation varied greatly from one

country to another. The Czech lands – the 'Protectorate of Bohemia and Moravia' as they were labelled – had been under German rule since March 1939, and there was no fighting on Czech soil until almost the end of the war. The economic importance of the Protectorate and reliance on Czech workers were so great that the Germans felt compelled to avoid the draconian racial solutions – expulsion or even extermination of the Slavic population – desired by SS 'race experts', and to refrain from imposing at first too harsh a regime on the subjugated population. But the climate worsened when, in the autumn of 1941, the head of the Security Police, Reinhard Heydrich, was appointed Reich Protector to quell growing signs of unrest and opposition. Repression now sharply intensified. It reached a high point after Czech patriots flown in by the British Special Operations Executive (SOE) succeeded in fatally wounding Heydrich during an assassination attempt in Prague on 27 May 1942. His death on 4 June prompted ferocious reprisals. Heydrich's killers escaped by committing suicide. But 1,300 Czechs, including 200 women, were executed in retaliation for the assassination. The entire village of Lidice – the name had been found on a Czech agent – was destroyed. Hitler threatened to deport huge numbers of Czechs to the east if there were further trouble. The Protectorate remained thereafter relatively quiet until near the end of the war, when with the Red Army on the doorstep Prague erupted in rebellion.

In contrast to the early occupation of the Protectorate, Hungary was occupied only in March 1944. When, in October that year, with the Red Army advancing on Hungary, the head of state (though since March merely at German behest), Admiral Horthy, announced that the country was quitting its alliance with Germany and concluding a separate peace with the Soviet Union, Hitler immediately had him deposed and replaced by another puppet ruler – Ferencz Szálasi, the fanatical leader of the Arrow Cross fascists. The Szálasi regime lasted only until, after weeks of ferocious street-fighting in Budapest, Hungary surrendered to the Red Army in February 1945. But it was deadly for Hungarian Jews, as Szálasi's ferocious Arrow Cross exposed them to a reign of terror that provided a horrific coda to the martyrdom they had suffered under the Germans.

In some parts of occupied Europe, far from promoting unity among the subjugated population, the war was bitterly divisive. So acute were the divisions in southern Europe that they gave rise to civil-war conditions which overlapped with the war against the occupiers.

The brutality of the German occupation in Yugoslavia, the massacres and huge reprisal actions, alongside the sickening atrocities of the unspeakable Ustaše, fostered the growth of two separate big partisan movements: the Chetniks, led by nationalist army officers who wanted a restoration of Greater Serbia under a restored Yugoslavian monarchy, and the communists, led by the Croat Josip Broz Tito. The partisans, however, fought each other as well as the Germans, the Ustaše, Bosnian Muslims, and Montenegran and Albanian separatists. Only as the war entered its last phase did Tito's communist partisans, meanwhile supported by British munitions and weapons, come to dominate resistance and establish the basis of post-war leadership in a new Yugoslavian state, the one country in Europe where partisans (aided by the Red Army) could eventually gain control and form a government.

For Greeks, the outright plunder, ruination of the currency, and size of the material tribute taken by the German and Italian occupiers led directly to famine. The drastic food shortage was greatly exacerbated by the prohibition of food exports from eastern Macedonia and Thrace, under Bulgarian control since the German invasion, where nearly a third of Greece's grain had previously been grown. War meant for most Greeks a daily struggle to survive. The immense privation, alongside the ruthlessness of German reprisals for acts of sabotage, nourished as in Yugoslavia the guerrilla activities of rapidly growing, but bitterly divided, partisan movements. By 1943 the communist resistance movement, the largest in Europe, was violently opposed by non-communist, nationalist republicans, who would eventually gain British backing. The roots of the devastating post-war civil war were firmly embedded.

In Italy, too, the collapse of Mussolini's regime in July 1943, followed by the German occupation of the north and the far more benign Allied occupation of the south, created conditions that came close to forming a civil war within the war itself. The Fascist regime had merely papered over the deep fissures in Italian society. The war, never hugely popular from the outset, brought growing internal disaffection and collapsing morale. This was accentuated by acute food shortages (accompanied by steeply rising prices and a thriving black market), then by Allied bombing which, far from unifying the population behind the government, stirred huge anger at the Fascist authorities that had exposed people to the air raids.

After the Germans had reinstated Mussolini as head of a puppet regime with its headquarters at Salò on Lake Garda in September 1943, the underlying divisions took on sharply radicalized form. Increasingly desperate followers of Mussolini, many of them hard-line fanatics and idealists who looked to the possibility of completing the Fascist revolution, formed vicious death-squads, hanging or shooting partisans or any who got in their way. Meanwhile the various partisan organizations, frequently settling old scores, assassinated hundreds of Fascists each month wherever they found them as well as engaging in sabotage in the war against the German occupiers. The combination of war and, in effect, civil war made the months of Mussolini's so-called Salò Republic the most bitter and violent in the entire conflict for Italians in the north of the country. Up to 40,000 partisans are estimated to have been killed in fighting, a further 10,000 anti-fascists fell victim to reprisal killings, and around 12,000 fascists or their collaborators were wiped out in 'cleansing' actions. Anti-fascist resistance, dominated by communists but incorporating fighters of different political colours, could reckon with the support of over a quarter of a million activists by April 1945.

Unlike Yugoslavia or Greece, however, they were able to unite against a common enemy in what they saw as a war of national liberation, mounting insurrection on such a scale against retreating German forces that they controlled many northern towns and cities before the Allies arrived. In the very last days of April, they were able to capture and shoot Mussolini, leaving his corpse to hang in the centre of Milan. In the south of the country, meanwhile, Allied occupation from September 1943 onwards had meant that the civil war of the north was avoided. Instead, under the cloak of the first reawakening of pluralist politics following the Allied entry into Rome in June 1944, there was a swift return to the age-old clientelism of southern Italian society. The war had left the north-south divide in Italy as great at the end as it had been at the start.

In northern and western Europe, German occupation produced nothing like the conditions of civil war in the south. Compared with eastern and southern Europe, the occupation of these parts of the continent was at least in the early stages of the war relatively mild. Nevertheless, the war meant primarily coming to terms with the realities of life in a conquered country. Invariably, the Germans found cooperation from existing state bureaucracies and from a minority keen to collaborate out of political conviction. Another minority, growing in size as it became clear that the days of German occupation were numbered, entered the perilous world of active resistance. But most people were neither outright collaborators nor resistance fighters. They wanted to see their country liberated, but, as there was no knowing how long the occupation was going to last, some manner of adaptation to the new regime in whatever form was unavoidable. How the people of north-west European countries adjusted shaped not only what the war meant to them, but also had a lasting legacy. The character of the occupation, the prevalent political culture of the occupied country (conditioning in good measure the behaviour of both the elites and the masses), and the change from early, comparatively benign, administration to increasing harshness and imposition of intense material hardship on the population, were fundamental in shaping the varied responses to German rule.

The Netherlands, Belgium, Norway and Denmark had differing wartime experiences, though the trajectory of occupation was often relatively similar. The Germans were keen, initially, to keep western Europe quiet. Cooperation, not rebelliousness, was what they wanted. Military conquest was not directed towards turning the subjugated people into helots, as in eastern Europe, especially since there were vague notions of incorporating the Germanic peoples of the Low Countries and Scandinavia within the Reich in the distant future. In each country there was a minority of home-grown fascists or national socialists who positively welcomed German rule. The prime minister of Norway's puppet government, Vidkun Quisling, even lent his name to the general term, 'quislings', given by the western Allies to collaborators. Each of the four countries provided small contingents of fanatics who joined the foreign legions of the Waffen-SS. About 50,000 Dutch and 40,000 Belgians (both Flemings and French-speaking Walloons),

6,000 Danes and 4,000 Norwegians served. Since ideologically committed fully fledged collaborators were generally detested as traitors by
most of the population, they were often seen as largely counter-productive
by the occupiers. The willing cooperation of the bureaucracy and
police, on the other hand, was essential to the effectiveness of the
occupation.

After 1942, as it became ever clearer that occupation was not going
to be indefinite, and as German demands for food, other material
provisions and labour sharply intensified, popular opposition in
numerous and various forms greatly increased. There were, nonetheless, substantial differences in the pressure of occupation even within
western Europe.

German rule in Denmark, for instance, was for most of the war far
less repressive than in the other occupied parts of northern and western Europe. This was mirrored in the relatively low number of lives
lost – Danish civilian deaths totalled about 1,100 – during the occupation. Denmark had almost immediately surrendered on the invasion
in April 1940, King Christian X remained in the country, and the government continued to administer the country under a German
governor. The collaboration worked at first. Food rations were better
(despite the Danes delivering large quantities of foodstuffs to Germany), forced labour was never introduced, there was no direct
plundering of the country, and occupation costs amounted to only
22 per cent of national income per year, compared with 67 per cent in
Norway and 52 per cent in Belgium. From August 1943, however,
policy in Denmark changed. This followed a rebellion against collaboration, forcing the resignation of the Danish government. Thereafter
the occupation became harsher, the role of the German police much
more assertive, the level of reprisals significantly higher, and both
non-cooperation and outright resistance more evident. Cooperation
gave way to truculence, which in turn fostered a resistance movement
that reached its highest levels of activity in 1944–5.

Out of widespread compliance at the beginning, the character of
German rule in all north-western countries ultimately led to implacable disaffection. In the Netherlands, for example, drastic rationing
already in 1940 brought severe food shortages, especially for city
dwellers, accompanied by soaring prices and a rampant black market,

while curfews and transport restrictions reduced public life to a minimum. Law-abiding people were effectively forced into breaking the law to keep warm and fed. The trawl for labour to be coerced into working in Germany for war industries, as the German labour shortage became acute, quickly turned into a further source of mass unrest.

In the Netherlands, as elsewhere, only few joined the underground resistance movement. Resistance was an intensely perilous activity, continually subject to betrayal and treachery, creating terrible dangers for families, then to horrendous torture and death for those captured. Those directly involved probably numbered around only 25,000 in the Netherlands before the autumn of 1944, with maybe another 10,000 or so joining thereafter. The attritional rate was high. Over a third of Dutch resisters were arrested, nearly a quarter did not survive the war.

A somewhat higher proportion of the Norwegian population of around 3 million was actively engaged in resistance. Resistance fighters there, often trained in British exile, sabotaged German shipping, fuel supplies and industrial installations as well as, later, railways to prevent troop movements. They built close links with the British SOE, sustaining their activities in part through the 'Shetland Bus' – boats shuttling between Bergen and the Shetland Islands. Some 40,000 Norwegians were actively involved in resistance by the end of the war. For acts of sabotage or attacks on members of the occupying forces, entire communities could face ferocious German reprisals. These were indeed terrifying. The small Norwegian fishing village of Televåg, for instance, was completely destroyed and its male inhabitants were sent to the concentration camp at Sachsenhausen near Berlin (where thirty-one of them died), for shielding resistance fighters who had killed two Gestapo agents.

Those involved in active resistance within countries under German occupation were united only by the desire to see the end of it, but they were otherwise often sharply divided ideologically between conservative nationalists, socialists and communists. With all the perils, resistance nonetheless gained broadening networks of support as the war neared its end. The harsher the German occupation became, the more the strength of anti-German feeling served to cement the sense of national unity and the desire for liberation. The suffering of the population from German punitive measures was, nevertheless, often extreme. When Dutch resistance halted the railways to assist the Allied landing at Arnhem in September 1944, German reprisals by blockading food supplies subjected the whole population to starvation and an extreme shortage of heating materials in the freezing-cold 'hunger winter' of 1944–5. Relief only came through with Allied air-drops in the last days of the war. For the Dutch, the war meant above all the trauma of such suffering in the last months of the conflict.

Whatever solidarity occupation engendered among the conquered peoples of north-west European countries, it rarely extended to the Jewish communities – small in the main, by comparison with those of eastern Europe. Virulent antisemitism did not have to be widespread. Even so, Jews were usually seen as 'outsiders', all the more so when forced to wear the 'yellow star'. The resolute determination of the German rulers to round them up for deportation, coupled with fears that any help given to Jews might bring harsh recrimination, meant that the section of society facing the gravest danger was also the least protected and most exposed.

The non-Jewish population was, however, not wholly passive or hostile. The first attempts to round up Amsterdam Jews for deportation in February 1941 even prompted a short-lived mass strike, though this may have backfired into encouraging greater readiness on the part of Dutch bureaucrats and police to cooperate with the occupiers. Such cooperation, at times even anticipating the presumed wishes of the Germans, helped to ensure that proportionally more Jews – some 107,000 out of 140,000 designated by the Nazis as 'full Jews' – were deported, most of them to their deaths, from the Netherlands than from any other western European country.

There were, however, those prepared to take risks themselves, from Christian principles and a variety of other motives, to help Jews. About 25,000 Dutch Jews, including half-Jews and those in mixed marriages who had a degree of protection from summary deportation, benefited from such help from individuals or rescue networks in evading capture and disappearing into a precarious underground illegal existence – though 8,000 of these were caught in hiding. Belgian networks for helping Jews to escape the clutches of the occupiers were more extensive, especially the illegal organizations of the Jews themselves. About 24,000 Jews were deported from Belgium to Auschwitz. But a further 30,000, the great majority of them recent immigrants living in Brussels and Antwerp who had fled poverty and pogroms in eastern Europe in the 1920s and from Germany during the 1930s, found some form of refuge and managed to survive the occupation. Hundreds of Jews, over half of the small Norwegian Jewish community, were helped to get away to neutral Sweden, though most of those who stayed eventually perished. In Denmark in 1943 non-Jews warned Jewish neighbours – Jews constituted a tiny proportion of the overall population, and were well assimilated – of the imminent round-up planned by the German occupiers and helped them escape. As a result, the great majority of the Jews designated for deportation to their deaths were spirited away across the Sound to the safe haven of Sweden. Although Jews had much better chances of survival in western than eastern Europe, huge numbers still fell victim to the relentless German drive to complete the 'final solution of the Jewish question'.

The population of France, by far the biggest of the conquered countries of north-western Europe, shared some of the experiences of their northern neighbours. There were, however, significant differences. Some arose from the division of France into two zones: an occupied zone covering approximately two-thirds of the country (northern France, including Paris, and a strip down the whole of the Atlantic coastline); and an unoccupied quasi-autonomous zone with its capital in the central French spa town of Vichy. What the war meant to people varied over the duration of the war, and according to geographical location – not just Vichy or the occupied zone, but even region and locality – as well as ideological predisposition and personal experience.

This time there was no sense of the 'union sacrée' that President Poincaré had successfully evoked in 1914. The catastrophe of defeat in the summer of 1940, which saw three-quarters of the panic-stricken population of northern towns fleeing southward from the oncoming German invasion, had left the French people divided and humiliated. Alongside the shock, however, the French Right which, whatever its divisions, was united at least in its detestation of the Third Republic, welcomed defeat as the chance to bring about national rebirth.

There were collaborators of the first rank out of ideological conviction, such as the former socialist Marcel Déat who became Minister of Labour, responsible for conscripting French workers to serve in Germany; and there was the fascist leader Jacques Doriot, who later joined 4,000 other French volunteers to fight in the 'crusade against Bolshevism' on the eastern front. One of the most prominent faces of collaboration was that of Pierre Laval, Vice-Premier in the Vichy regime, a skilful pragmatist and political manipulator who publicly declared his wish for a German victory, 'because otherwise Bolshevism would install itself everywhere'. Such overt collaboration was not typical of the mass of the French people. But nor was active resistance – certainly not in the early years of the occupation. Most people, like those in the other occupied countries of western Europe, had to find ways of accommodating (though seldom enthusiastically) to occupation – cooperating with the new rulers when unavoidable, generally keeping their distance, adopting a stance of 'wait-and-see', and displaying mounting detestation as the occupation became harsher and as the prospect of liberation loomed larger.

As elsewhere in north-western Europe, German occupation was at first relatively mild, but it became more draconian as Germany started to face adversity. The economic demands on France were heavy – 55 per cent of French government revenue to cover occupation costs, 40 per cent of France's total industrial output to go towards the German war effort, 15 per cent of its agricultural produce to assist in keeping food on German tables, and, by 1943, 600,000 men drafted for work in Germany. Most French families in cities and towns, like those in other parts of north-western Europe, experienced the war as a constant struggle to obtain food, often via the black market.

French experience of severe privation and material hardship stretched over both zones. But the demarcation line between the zones did have real meaning. In the southern third of France, government was in French, not German, hands. Although bearing the scars of defeat, materially and psychologically, the French largely controlled their own destiny in the non-occupied zone. Vichy provided yet another meaning to the war for millions of Frenchmen: rejection of the Republic which, in many eyes, had become discredited as corrupt and decadent long before the military defeat of 1940, and a restoration of 'traditional' French values of 'work, family, country'. The 'French state', as the authoritarian Vichy regime headed by Marshal Pétain after the fall of France called itself, was widely popular at first (though its popularity ebbed sharply after the first year or so). About 1.2 million veterans rushed to join the Légion Française des Combattants – an organization with some resemblance to a fascist-style acclamatory body – swearing allegiance to the Marshal and forming the base of the flourishing personality cult built up around Pétain. As the representative of patriarchal authority and Christianity, the figurehead of the reaction against atheism, socialism and secularization, Pétain also enjoyed the backing of the Catholic hierarchy.

The octogenarian Marshal scarcely embodied the symbolism of youth common to fascist movements. Even so, his regime had fascist traits in its evocation of a mythologized past, its glorification of the countryside and 'return to the land', its idealization of an organic society, its emphasis on youth, motherhood and natalist polices to 'renew' the population – and not least in its persecution of 'internal enemies'. Even in Vichy's early days, left-wing mayors had been ousted, Freemasons dismissed from all state employment, and trade union organizations dissolved. Dozens of internment camps for foreigners, political prisoners, social 'undesirables', Roma and Jews were set up. Vichy authorities extended the 'aryanization' programme of the occupied zone to expropriate thousands of Jewish firms, bought for knock-down prices by French companies. The regime introduced anti-Jewish statutes to restrict Jewish employment. In 1942 and afterwards Vichy bureaucrats and police collaborated avidly in the round-up and brutal deportation of foreign Jews (around a half of France's total Jewish population of 300,000) to add to the deportations from the occupied zone. Of the 75,721 Jews deported from France to the death-camps in Poland (of whom only 2,567 survived), foreign Jews comprised 56,000.

Non-Jews, too, had to contend with increasing repression. Already by the autumn of 1941 the first assassinations of German personnel resulted in up to fifty hostages executed in reprisal. Other mass reprisal shootings soon followed. The reprisals drastically intensified in number and scale after the Allied landings in June 1944. In the most infamous action, carried out by the Waffen-SS, the entire village of Oradour-sur-Glane, north-west of Limoges, wrongly assumed to be concealing a cache of arms for the Resistance, was laid waste. Its 642 inhabitants were shot or burnt to death. The French blackshirted paramilitary police, the Milice, established in the Vichy zone in 1943, were feared as much as the Gestapo as an agent of repressive terror. However, repression, as elsewhere, became increasingly counter-productive once it became obvious that the days of German rule were numbered. It went a long way towards creating unity where none had earlier been present – unity behind the goal of liberation.

Active resistance – itself divided between communist (regalvanized once Germany had invaded the Soviet Union) and conservative (gradually congealing under de Gaulle's leadership) – became more, not less, extensive, despite the dread of fearsome retribution if captured. Whereas most French people avoided active participation and still preferred a 'wait-and-see' stance, the levels of support grew for those engaged in resistance. Like almost nothing else, the law introduced on 16 February 1943 by the Vichy regime and signed by Prime Minister Laval, to enforce compulsory labour in Germany, created a climate of popular disobedience that fed into the growth of active resistance. Large numbers of those conscripted simply disappeared, often into the mountains or remote countryside, where they were taken in and sheltered by locals, not infrequently joining the swelling Resistance movement as liberation approached after the Allied landings in Normandy in June 1944.

After the war, resistance came to symbolize more than anything else what the conflict had meant to the French. This was intended to, and did for long, draw a veil over the less palatable side of the French experience after defeat during the 'black years', especially in the unoccupied zone that they themselves had (at least at first) controlled. It would be many years before the French were ready to confront 'the Vichy syndrome'.

For the 'home front' in Germany, the war acquired meanings not shared by the people of any other country. What the American journalist William Shirer, who experienced the war at first hand in Berlin from the outset until the start of hostilities with the USA in December 1941, somewhat cynically noted as the basic reaction to the brief campaign in Poland, had general application until major anxieties started to mount in the autumn of 1941: 'As long as the Germans are successful and do not have to pull in their belts too much, this will not be an unpopular war.' By the winter of 1941–2, however, despite plundering much of Europe for food and other resources, privations at home had sharply increased and belt-tightening among the civilian population became necessary as food rations were sharply cut. The popularity of the war – and the regime that had taken Germany into it – declined dramatically.

The drastic deterioration in the military situation, symbolized more plainly than anything in February 1943 by the disastrous defeat at Stalingrad, brought the mounting realization among the domestic population that the war could well be lost. This necessitated in turn contemplating what a lost war would mean. Propaganda played upon the fears not just of military defeat but of the entire destruction of Germany, and of the German people, should the unholy coalition of the Reich's enemies – the western Allies and the dreaded Bolsheviks – prevail.

People were broadly aware, even if they consciously or subconsciously suppressed the knowledge in a conspiracy of silence, that Germans had perpetrated terrible crimes in the occupied east, especially against Jews. Although few knew details, there are numerous indications of extensive awareness of the fate of the Jews. Betraying the success of antisemitic propaganda, many expressed fear of 'Jewish revenge' in the event of defeat. They also knew they could expect no mercy if the Red Army entered Germany. Dread of the consequences of defeat did much to sustain the readiness of the population to hold out, despite the rapidly worsening military situation.

The last two years of the war saw the horror that the Nazis had inflicted on most of Europe rebound upon ordinary Germans themselves. For the German civilian population, the last phase of the conflict was their hell on earth. What characterized the trauma for millions was fear of Allied bombs. Goebbels called it 'terror bombing'. In this case propaganda did not lie. The bombing was meant to terrorize the population, and did so, as people were left defenceless while their towns and cities were obliterated. More than 400,000 people were killed and 800,000 injured by bombing raids on towns and cities, attacks that were increasingly pointless from a military perspective.

Around 1.8 million homes were destroyed, nearly 5 million people left homeless.

The civilian population of Germany's eastern provinces, less exposed to the bombing, faced a different sort of terror. People had to flee from their homes in icy conditions in temperatures of minus 20 degrees Celsius to join the flood of refugees pouring westwards in fear and dread as the Red Army drove into the Reich. Close on half a million civilians, many women and children, died in the desperate flight from the doomed German east. For many German women in the path of the Red Army, the last phase of the war meant violence against their bodies as an estimated 20 per cent of them were raped by Soviet soldiers. More than 10,000 German soldiers were meanwhile being killed on average *every day* in the last months of the war.

As the death toll of civilians as well as soldiers rose astronomically, the war acquired new meaning for Germans. They saw themselves as victims of the conflict. They blamed Hitler and the Nazi leadership for inflicting the catastrophe on Germany, the Allies for the devastation of their country, and yet again – this among a minority core of recalcitrant antisemites – even the Jews for bringing about the war. 'We believe ourselves to have been fooled, led astray, misused,' a former general put it soon after the war, expressing a common sentiment. In the search for scapegoats and the perception of themselves as victims, traumatized people often overlooked the fact that they had in their millions cheered Hitler's earlier successes and rejoiced in the victories of the Wehrmacht – even as countless Europeans suffered penury and slavery, death and destruction under the Nazi yoke. But, if the full dimensions of the moral catastrophe would take years to gain recognition, at least this time, compared with 1918, the defeat was total, unmitigated and final.

LASTING MEANING

For those who lived through this hell on earth, the immediacy of their experience, in its varied manifestations, shaped what the war meant to them. Later generations can see the lasting significance of the war somewhat more clearly, can see more plainly that it marked the decisive caesura in the history of the twentieth century in Europe.

The definitive ending of fascism as a major political force was one obvious consequence. Out of the First World War had emerged a triad of competing ideologies and constellations of power – liberal democracy, communism and fascism. After the Second World War only the first two were left as rival political systems. Total military defeat and the increasing revelation of fascism's unprecedented crimes against humanity now discredited that ideology completely, other than in the eyes of dwindling and politically largely impotent admirers.

An overriding consequence of the Second World War was the recasting of Europe's geopolitical structure. The First World War had ended with Russia (soon to become the Soviet Union) convulsed by revolution, then civil war, and the United States distancing itself from Europe through its unwillingness to join the League of Nations and its shift to isolationism. The Second World War ended with the boundaries of Soviet influence, largely decided at the Yalta Conference in February 1945, greatly extended throughout eastern Europe, even into Germany itself. On the back of its military victory, the Soviet Union was now well on the way to becoming a superpower. The United States, which the war had already forged into a superpower on the basis of its mighty military-industrial complex (itself a product of the conflict), had established its own dominance throughout western Europe and, unlike 1918, was destined to stay on the European continent in the long term. Whereas the First World War had broken empires and replaced them with crisis-ridden nation states, the Second World War produced a Europe divided down the middle between the two blocs dominated by the USSR and the USA, in which national interests were swiftly becoming subordinated to the geopolitical concerns of the emerging superpowers.

For the peoples of eastern Europe, those who had suffered most in the six-year conflagration, the war came to mean the replacement of one tyranny by another. The countries of the east, which had seen the Red Army as their saviour from Nazi terror, now fell under decades-long Soviet oppression. Stalin was not going to give up his gains, made through the shedding of so much blood. That was plain. The western Allies agreed to his new division of Europe. Short of turning on their former ally and fighting another war, which they were not militarily, economically or psychologically capable of doing, they had little choice. For the peoples of eastern Europe, that was cold comfort.

For western Europe the war brought a new start – one that was difficult to discern, peering through the ruins of 1945. Even as the bombs wrought their destruction, planning was under way for the rebuilding of Europe and avoiding the mistakes that had bedevilled the continent after 1918. While eastern Europe battened down under Soviet domination and state-run socialist economies, the rebuilding of western Europe reinvigorated capitalist enterprise. In economics as well as politics, the war had divided Europe.

The reordering of Europe also saw the fundamental weakening of the three one-time 'great powers', Britain, France and Germany, which had previously dominated the continent. Britain had been bankrupted by the war, its status as a great power massively eroded. Its empire had backed it in the war, but the peoples of the colonies, perceiving imperial weakness, increasingly looked to their independence. The already shaky foundations of colonial rule were now undermined more than ever. France had suffered an enormous blow to its national pride through the defeat of 1940, a blow by no means compensated by the much emblazoned courage of the Resistance. French colonies, too, were eyeing independence, no longer prepared to contemplate an indefinite future of rule from Paris.

Germany, defeated but not destroyed in 1918 and carrying simmering resentments that later paved the way for Hitler's rise to power, was this time utterly crushed. Divided into the four zones of occupation agreed at Yalta – British, American, Soviet and, a late addition, French – Germany was a completely ruined country, economically as well as politically destroyed, its sovereignty as a nation eliminated. This marked the end of the 'German question' that had preoccupied European politicians since the days of Bismarck. In the aftermath of defeat the state of Prussia, the dominant force in the Reich, was dissolved, the German armed forces were disbanded (thus ending any threat of German militarism), and the industrial base that had provided the economic framework for Germany's dominance was placed under Allied control. The big landed estates in the eastern provinces, the homelands of so much of the German aristocracy that had played a major part in the army and the state for so long, were lost in perpetuity as the frontiers were shifted westward. Once internationally admired for its culture and learning, Germany was morally now reduced to pariah status, though the reckoning with the German leadership was still to come, in the war-crimes trials that the victorious Allies were soon to stage.

It would take many years before the immensity of the collapse of civilization would come to be fully recognized, would take its due central place in the understanding of the Second World War's legacy. German genocidal policy had reshaped much of the ethnic pattern of settlement, especially in eastern Europe. The destruction of the Jews, in particular, had wiped out centuries of a rich cultural presence. 'Ethnic cleansing' actions by Germans and by their allies had also had a lasting impact – and sometimes left a legacy of grievance, as in Yugoslavia, that decades of communist rule would not efface. The ethnic German presence, too, in eastern Europe was eliminated both by Stalinist brutality and then by the savage 'cleansing' actions by Poles, Czechs, Hungarians and Romanians in the immediate post-war years. Above all, however, the collapse of civilization was denoted by the German attempt to destroy physically the Jews of Europe on grounds of race alone. That this vast war had a racial project – one of genocidal destruction – at its very heart would come over time to be seen as its defining feature.

The moral question of how this conflagration could have been possible, how Europe could have plunged into this bottomless pit of inhumanity, would preoccupy the continent for generations. The war had revealed more plainly than ever before the terrible crimes of which human beings are capable when all legal constraints on behaviour are removed or warped to serve inhumane purposes. The concentration camp came to symbolize more than anything else the nightmare of a world in which human existence counted for nothing, in which arbitrary will determined life or death. Increasingly, it became clear that in creating this hell on earth for so many of its citizens, Europe had come close to destroying itself. The realization that the continent had been on a suicidal path meant there was the need for an entirely new start.

Although the European war ended with the German capitulation on 8 May 1945 (VE Day), European troops were still fighting in the Far East for another three months until the Japanese, too, surrendered unconditionally. The total defeat of the Japanese brought the world conflict to an end. This was hastened by the event that, more than any other, would shape Europe's future, and that of the rest of the world, in the coming decades: the dropping of the atom bomb on the Japanese city of Hiroshima on 6 August, followed three days later by a similar devastating attack on Nagasaki. The Americans had for four years been pouring huge resources as well as employing the pioneering research of nuclear scientists into producing the atom bomb. The Germans, mercifully, had lagged far behind in their own research. The dropping of the atom bomb at once dramatically changed the basis of political and military power, and refashioned the ways in which war could be conceived.

It would be impossible in the future to fight a war through attritional mass slaughter as at the Somme in the First World War or as at Stalingrad in the Second. But a future war in Europe would mean destruction on a scale not remotely reached even in the Second World War. The atom bomb now gave its possessors a terrible weapon – one that, as nuclear weaponry became even more devastating, would have the power to destroy an entire country at the push of a button. The ultimate legacy of the war was to leave Europe, and the rest of the world, under the permanent threat of weapons of unprecedented destruction. From now on, Europeans would have to learn to live under the shadow of the bomb, to face the threat of nuclear annihilation. The bomb's mushroom cloud would be the symbol of a new age. It was the point when the world turned.

9

Quiet Transitions in the
Dark Decades

> History resists an ending as surely as nature abhors a vacuum;
> the narrative of our days is a run-on sentence, every full stop
> a comma in embryo.
>
> *Mark Slouka,* Essays from the Nick of Time:
> Reflections and Refutations *(2010)*

The thirty years in which Europe seemed bent on self-destruction were so disastrous, and characterized by such massive ruptures, that continuities of long-term socio-economic value systems and cultural trends of development seem scarcely conceivable. Yet beneath the surface of Europe's dark age people's lives did continue to be shaped or reshaped in quiet transitions, unbroken if not untouched by the trauma.

Beyond the impersonal long-term determinants of social and economic change lay the values and beliefs by which people led their lives, predominantly the preserve still of the Christian Churches. A good deal of the most important political and social thought of the era nevertheless stood outside, or even in opposition to, the influence of the Churches. How did Europe's intellectual elite respond to what they perceived to be a crisis of civilization? When work, reflection and (sometimes) prayer were done, a fourth sphere was left: leisure, and enjoyment to be had from the rapidly changing field of popular entertainment. Each of these four areas – economic and social change, the role of the Christian Churches, the reaction of intellectuals and the 'culture industry' – reveals both continuities and transitions that would leave a significant mark on the post-war world.

ECONOMY AND SOCIETY: DYNAMICS OF CHANGE

Throughout all the horrors that afflicted Europe between 1914 and 1945, the economies and societies of European countries were, in fact, growing somewhat more like each other. Of course, major differences – especially national, ethnic, regional and (often interspersed with these) religious– remained. These were above all what shaped a sense of identity, even more so than social class. Opportunities for foreign travel, apart from for the upper classes and leaving aside service in the military, were extremely limited, enhancing the sense of national identity (and the prejudices that often accompanied it). The fragmentation after the First World War into a continent even more dominated than before by nation states (often driven by extreme nationalism), and the establishment – most notably in Russia, Italy and Germany – of systems of rule with quite different (and incompatible) economic models, tended to drive countries apart, rather than closer together. The two world wars, it goes without saying, produced their own distortions and divergences.

Yet there were important underlying patterns of development that transcended (or at best were only temporarily interrupted by) political distinctiveness and division. The long-term impact of industrialization, affecting different parts of Europe in varying degrees and at dissimilar tempos, was the determining dynamic force. The ensuing changes affected practically the entire continent, and were not confined by national boundaries. Even the least developed countries were touched in some ways – importing, copying or assimilating change that was already under way elsewhere. The gap between the wealthier, economically more advanced parts of western and northern Europe and the poorer south and east barely diminished over the first half of the twentieth century. Even so, the trends in development – in demography, urbanization, industrialization, employment patterns, social security, literacy and social mobility – were broadly similar.

Population

Despite two world wars, numerous civil conflicts, politically induced major famines, economic depression and large-scale 'ethnic cleansing', Europe's population continued to grow substantially during the first half of the twentieth century (if less rapidly than during the preceding half-century). In 1913 almost 500 million people lived in Europe. By 1950 this figure had reached almost 600 million. The growth was, of course, not uniform. Political and military factors obviously exerted their influence in some parts of the continent. The Soviet population was 26 million smaller in 1946 than it had been in 1941. German population statistics also plainly show the damaging impact of both world wars, and also of the Great Depression of the 1930s. In both countries, however, the drop in population proved temporary, even if for years women greatly outnumbered men. Economic backwardness also played its part in demographic patterns. The Irish population, for instance, dropped as large numbers of young people left their homeland for work, mainly in Britain.

The general population trend was nevertheless upwards. The main cause was the steep decline in death rates, continuing a trend that had begun in the second half of the nineteenth century but accelerated sharply in the first half of the twentieth. Birth rates were also declining, but at a far slower pace than death rates. In 1910 life expectancy at birth in north-western Europe was around fifty-five years, in Russia about thirty-seven years and in Turkey under thirty-five years. Forty years later, most people across the continent could expect to live to the age of sixty-five or more. At the start of the century, the highest birth and mortality rates were to be found in eastern and southern Europe. By 1950 the gap with northern and western Europe had narrowed considerably. Even in Russia, despite the horrors the country was forced to endure, the mortality rate dropped remarkably, from 28 per 1000 head of population under the Tsar to 11 per 1000 in 1948.

The fall in the mortality rate was largely the result of the greater emphasis attached to public hygiene, better housing, health education and corresponding improvements in the health of mothers (which greatly assisted the decline in child mortality). Generally, if at different rates largely related to levels of economic advancement, European countries experienced greatly improved health over the first half of the twentieth century. The big housing boom of the 1920s (referred to in Chapter 4), often sponsored by government spending, reduced some of the most squalid overcrowding and brought improvements in sewerage, water supplies and personal hygiene. Modestly increasing real income and better diet (as the ratio of meat to cereal consumed rose) also contributed to the fall in mortality. Awareness of the importance of public health spread from the relatively advanced countries of north-western Europe to the east and south of the continent. But where little was done to overcome the backwardness of poor sanitation, deficient personal hygiene and lack of medical facilities, as in Albania, Macedonia, southern Italy and Turkey, mortality rates remained disproportionately high.

Advances in medical knowledge and care contributed to falling mortality rates by greatly reducing the chances of premature death through infectious diseases. The medical advances were less in surgical techniques (though reconstructive surgery had made some headway in the First World War) than in treatment of wounds and development of medicines to combat killer diseases such as tuberculosis and influenza. The influenza epidemic at the end of the First World War had led to far more deaths than the military carnage itself. Infants had been especially prone to enteric diseases, and birth-related child mortality had remained high. But sulphonamides started to be used increasingly to control infectious diseases, as were immunization against tetanus and diphtheria, and anti-malarial drugs. Penicillin, initially developed to prevent wound infection, became available, though only to the western Allies, towards the end of the Second World War. Immunization then went on to have much wider usage in the post-war world. In rural areas of southern Europe, where states had done little to improve living conditions and public health, malaria continued to be a substantial problem, sometimes until well after the Second World War. But even here infectious diseases were coming under control. Cases of malaria, for instance, fell in Italy from 234,000 in 1922 to under 50,000 by 1945, and by 1950 the disease had been almost totally eliminated.

The poorer, less developed parts of the continent also continued to flout the general trend towards declining fertility. In Russia, Spain and Portugal the decline only began in the 1920s, in southern Italy and

Turkey even after the Second World War. In Turkey between the wars the fertility level was over five births per mother. In most of Europe it had fallen by then to about two and a half births per mother, and in some countries to under two (or less than the rate necessary to reproduce the population, short of immigration). This prompted great anxiety about falling birth rates and national decline, especially in France (where the low rate had set in early), the Scandinavian countries, and not least, playing into fascist ideology, in Italy and Germany. The spread of birth control and greater education in family planning (itself helped by increasing literacy) played a big part in the declining fertility. In western Europe around 90 per cent of births fell within marriage (illegitimacy still carried a social stigma) and marriage rates remained fairly stable (apart from a short-lived boom in the late 1930s), so the decisive factor was that couples were simply choosing to have fewer children – a trend encouraged by the greater numbers of younger women entering paid employment. Catholic regions of Europe and the poorer rural areas of eastern and southern Europe only gradually fell into line with the general pattern of declining fertility – in western Europe the relative size of the rural population of Ireland was an exception to the general trend – though the direction was the same and the speed of convergence tended to increase alongside greater levels of modernization of the economy.

Significant social and economic shifts within Europe were intensified, where they were not directly caused, by war. The move from rural to industrializing regions, from south and east to western Europe, was one characteristic – a long-term trend that the pressures of war hugely exacerbated. The massive displacement of population through war and 'ethnic cleansing' was a more short-term outcome of political upheavals, though with long-term consequences.

Before the First World War emigration to the United States had offered one escape route from the grinding poverty of the poorest regions of Europe. But once the USA introduced strict immigration quotas in the early 1920s, the exodus fell to little more than a trickle. Most people looking for a better life, or fleeing from persecution, had to find new homes within Europe itself. For economic migrants this meant in the main looking for employment in the burgeoning industrial areas. The flow of migrants from the countryside to the towns, a strong feature of the economic recovery during the 1920s, declined but did not stop during the Depression of the 1930s.

Everywhere the population working on the land shrank. In 1910 agriculture had in Europe as a whole accounted for about 55 per cent of production. By 1950 this had fallen to 40 per cent. The biggest shift from the land to industry was in Russia, accounting for as much as half of the overall drop in the agricultural share. But in all countries the size of the rural population was falling. Industrialized Bohemia drew in workers from rural Slovakia. Milan and Turin attracted migrants from southern Italy. Poles moved from the south and east of the country to the more rapidly industrializing western regions. And large numbers from eastern and southern Europe found permanent work in the growing industries of Germany, France and the Netherlands. France, with its stagnant population levels (which would, in fact, be ended during the Second World War, when there was a sharp rise), saw the greatest need for foreign labour between the wars. By 1931 about 8 per cent of the French population, some 3.3 million people, were recent immigrants.

The long-term shifts – rural to urban areas, agriculture to industry, south and east to north and west – were sharply boosted by the Second World War. Germany, with full employment, had by 1939 close to half a million foreign workers, despite its xenophobic state ideology. Nearly 50 per cent of them – including Poles, Italians, Yugoslavs, Hungarians, Bulgarians and Dutch – worked, often seasonally, on the land (where there was an acute labour shortage), but industry too was swallowing up larger numbers of foreign workers, from Czechoslovakia especially. The increasingly desperate German demand for labour during the war brought a huge surge in the number of foreigners (about a third of them women) – most of them conscripted for intensely cruel forced labour – especially from 1942 onwards. By mid-1944 the 7,651,970 foreigners (1,930,087 of them prisoners of war) comprised more than a quarter of the German labour force.

Germany was able to exploit a continent-wide empire for its labour needs (and did so in utterly ruthless fashion). But in all belligerent countries war brought a massive increase in demand for labour. Much of the shortfall, as men were called to the front, was made up by women. This had happened in the First World War, but the change had then proved short term. Women were soon removed from the labour market as men returned from military action. In the Second World War, the change became more enduring. Unemployment in Britain, which had seemed endemic between the wars, was wiped out. Women – housewives and those previously not employed (or who had left domestic service) – comprised more than three-quarters of the added labour force. In the Soviet Union, where women were already widely employed before the war, more than half the labour force was female by 1942.

The most sudden and violent internal shifts in Europe's population in the first half of the twentieth century were, of course, not simply a consequence of long-term trends in the labour market, even when boosted by the demands of wartime economies. Far more drastic were the population upheavals caused by political and military action. These were most dire in eastern Europe, though the Spanish Civil War produced some 2 million refugees between 1936 and 1938. Nearly 8 million people were displaced in the eastern half of the continent, mostly through territorial losses, border shifts and ethnic 'adjustments' of emergent new states, during or immediately after the First World War. Up to a million Armenians were uprooted, and most of them subsequently died, in the horrific deportations by the Turks in 1915. Nearly a million Greeks and Turks were forcibly removed under the post-war population exchange of 1923. In Russia, devastated by the civil war that followed immediately upon world war and revolution, the numbers of dead and those forced to flee have been estimated at over 10 million. Millions more died or were displaced during the era of Stalinist collectivization and purges in the 1930s, then still further millions who fled eastwards from the path of the advancing German army in 1941. Stalin's wartime mass deportations of those deemed to pose a security threat brought yet further huge migrations, for example through the forced removal of 400,000 Volga Germans to the Soviet wastes of central Asia and Siberia in 1941 (and later the mass deportations of the Crimean Tartars together with the Kalmyks, Ingushi, Karachai, Balkars and Chechens – about a million in all – from the Caucasus).

By late 1941 the murder of the European Jews was rapidly escalating. Hundreds of thousands of refugees from Nazi Germany, most of them Jews, had sought succour in other countries before the war (though these had been reluctant to accept them). About half of them had found their way abroad, mainly to the USA and Palestine. But the war closed off these avenues of escape. Around five and a half million Jews perished in the subsequent German extermination policies. The border changes and expulsions after the end of the Second World War then led to further great population displacements. A third of the population of the new Federal Republic of Germany in 1950, for instance, had not been born within its territory. Its population influx would go on to make a vital contribution to West German post-war recovery.

The bald statistics of population displacement, like all macro-economic data, are wholly impersonal. They say nothing of the death, destruction, suffering and misery involved. Even so, they are import-ant in signifying change that in many ways altered the character of twentieth-century Europe. Equally impersonal are the data showing, on differing criteria, that living standards actually rose across Europe during the catastrophic first half of the century – at least for the majority of those whose lives were not lost or ruined by fighting, bombing, despoliation or deliberately murderous policies. Alongside rising life expectancy, income per head increased by over 25 per cent, there was greater purchasing power for the majority, average individ-ual height grew by 4 centimetres (an indicator of better diet as well as more income), and literacy was substantially extended. Although of course these trends conceal major variations caused by war and other privations, they were broadly general across the continent. The regions that had been least well developed before the First World War in southern and eastern Europe showed distinct signs of convergence with the more advanced western parts of the continent before the Second World War.

War and the Economy: Learning Lessons

Each of the world wars was a catastrophic, though relatively short-lived, interruption to long-term economic development. Average growth rates in most European states were lower over the disastrous era of 1914–45 than before the First or after the Second World War.

And it took the defeated countries in the First World War around a decade to recover. But they did recover; and growth, if slower than it had been before the war, continued. It has been estimated that, had pre-war growth before 1914 continued unabated, the level reached in world production by 1929 would have been attained in foodstuffs by 1923, in industrial goods by 1924 and in raw materials by 1927. Whatever caveats may be attached to such extrapolations – which are for world, not just European, production – they indicate a temporary brake on growth through the hostilities, not a long-term reversal.

The levels of globalization reached before 1914 were hampered and interrupted by war, then by protectionism and economic nationalism during the Great Depression of the 1930s. European economic output then fell again during the Second World War and much of what was produced had, of course, to be geared to military hardware. This time, however, the rebound was swift. Following the Second World War, growth was rapid, much stronger than in the aftermath of the First World War, and with more lasting impact. Lessons had been learnt. There was a readiness to embrace international cooperation, so badly lacking between the wars but now accepted as vital to recovery. New levels of state intervention were undertaken to restore stability and regulate the economy. The decisive factor was the complete economic dominance of the USA, and its crucial export of ideas, technology and capital. The basis for the unprecedented economic growth over the subsequent three decades was laid, however, within Europe itself, and in the continent's darkest years. For in strictly economic terms, war, even on the scale of the conflicts of 1914–18 and 1939–45, did not merely have a negative balance sheet of losses. It also had positive consequences of lasting importance.

The conditions of war provided a marked stimulus to economic growth and technological advance. Even democratic states, let alone dictatorships, were forced to intervene massively in the economy to direct enormously expanded production for the war effort. This necessitated state investment in construction, capital equipment and labour training as the conflict created new demand (which often proved lasting), for instance, for aluminium needed in aircraft production during the Second World War. Mass production of armaments required, already in the First World War, more efficient methods of factory organization and management and more intensive mechanization.

Agriculture benefited from increased mechanization to maximize production from the land at a time when farms were drained of labour. Around 3,000 new tractors were made available to farmers in Britain during the first year of the Second World War, for example, and production of all types of agricultural machinery was increased. In Germany, on the other hand, where the increasingly frantic demand for tanks, guns and planes left little productive capacity over for tractors, farmers had generally to make do with the efforts of family members, forced foreign labour and prisoners of war. Here, as in other parts of the continent where the modernization of farming methods made little headway during the war itself, the mechanization of agriculture and intensification of production largely had to await the era of post-war reconstruction – since there was no way of reversing the relentless long-term decline in availability of rural labour during the period of the conflict.

Technological and scientific innovation was striking in both wars, quite especially in the second, and with lasting effect. It was not necessarily the case that war produced entirely new discoveries. Yet even where a breakthrough had been made in peacetime, the urgency of wartime production often brought rapid advances. Aircraft technology had improved massively during the First World War, since aerial warfare was viewed as decisive in any future conflict, and the innovations fed into the expansion of passenger aviation during the 1920s and 1930s. The jet engine, simultaneously invented and developed in the 1930s by the British Royal Air Force engineer Frank Whittle and the German engineer Hans von Ohain, though first mass-produced in Germany in 1944 for the Me262 fighter, would revolutionize air travel after the Second World War. Later, space exploration would build upon the rocket technology that Wernher von Braun and other German scientists had developed to launch the V2 missile.

The abilities of Braun, a Nazi Party member and honorary SS officer, were swiftly recognized by the Americans and, transported to a new environment in the USA, he would play a major role in the development of the American space programme. The discovery of nuclear fission on the eve of the war, which led to the wartime programme in the USA to produce an atomic bomb, opened the way to the post-war peaceful usage of nuclear energy. Many more wartime innovations or rapid advances on existing technology – for example, radio transmission, radar, production of synthetic materials, electronic computers – were to have a massive impact on the post-war era. Without the war these advances, many of which built on pre-war pioneers, would doubtless have come about anyway. Most likely, however, their development would have been slower.

The Second World War was, to a far greater extent than the First, a 'total war', not just for societies under dictatorial rule. The leaders of states learned important lessons from the earlier conflict in running their wartime economies. They were far more effective than their predecessors had been, for instance, in controlling inflation, which was never allowed to gain destructive momentum as in some belligerent countries during the First World War. In Britain taxation was raised to far higher levels than it had been in the earlier conflict, reducing the need for short-term borrowing, and it enabled the government to continue to borrow long term at relatively low rates of interest. In Germany, where the paranoia about any new descent into hyper-inflation was never far from the surface, taxation could be kept much lower than in Britain because the soaring costs of war were paid in large measure by the occupied territories.

Germany and Britain were at opposite ends of the spectrum, too, in state control of the food supply to their populations. The unstoppable momentum of rising disaffection in Germany during the First World War, as living standards fell drastically and food shortages became acute, was deeply embedded in the political consciousness of Nazi leaders. Their ruthless exploitation of the continent's food and other resources prevented any recurrence during the Second World War. The first significant cuts in rations, made following the winter crisis of 1941–2, were highly unpopular, but drastic reductions did not occur until the final phase of the war. Occupied countries in much of Europe paid the price, with mounting severe food shortages reaching famine proportions in Ukraine and Greece, and near-famine in the 'hunger winter' of 1944–5 in Holland. Although food prices were officially controlled and allocations rationed, the black market was rampant everywhere. In Britain state subsidies and stringent rationing were used to ensure that food prices rose more slowly than farm incomes. The rationing of all staple foods except potatoes and bread inevitably gave rise to grumbling, but it was nevertheless widely accepted by the population and helped to sustain social harmony. It actually improved the health of many at the same time, though at the cost of dietary monotony.

During the Second World War leading figures from business and industry were brought in to help shape government policy even more than in the First World War. Industrialists were preoccupied not just with war production but with planning for the post-war world. Even in Germany, where the Nazi regime tightened its grip on the economy (as on everything else) and where Allied bombs wrought ever greater destruction on the country, industrialists married their intense war-time collaboration with secret plans for reconstruction. Anxious not to be dragged into the futile self-immolation of the Nazi regime in its death throes during the last months of the war, they worked alongside the Reich Minister for Armaments and Production, Albert Speer, to block the senseless destruction of industrial installations under Hitler's 'scorched-earth' orders of March 1945. In fact, in Germany the destruction of industry was nowhere near as great as the general level of devastation caused by the war, and industrialists were able to continue – in their own interest – their close involvement in measures to stimulate recovery. Much the same was true in other major economies. Mobilization for the war had unleashed enormous economic capacity, which was often badly damaged, but not destroyed, while huge labour resources were available to be used for peacetime reconstruction instead of armaments. The potential for reconstruction lay dormant among the ruins.

Recovery, like wartime economic mobilization, needed the state. The sheer level of material destruction in Europe made any retreat by the state from economic management impossible. Any belief that economies could repair themselves through market forces had been undermined by the economic nationalism of the interwar period. Only the state, French and British planners agreed, could provide the levels of investment necessary for the massive infrastructural projects to rebuild the economy. American leaders, though favouring the free market, could scarcely demur at this juncture, while rigid state control was of course long established in the Soviet Union. Huge house-building programmes had to be organized. Food scarcity also demanded continued state controls and allocation; in Britain rationing continued well into the 1950s.

In the immediate years after the Second World War the economy of Europe was, accordingly, shaped by levels of state expenditure and control in ways never contemplated in the 1920s and 1930s. Under American influence, however, western Germany would not come to follow the model of far greater *dirigisme* adopted in Britain and France (although in eastern Germany, under Soviet control, the development was of course entirely different). Experience of heavy state controls during the twelve years of Nazism would encourage the removal of constraints on the free market, the drastic reduction of bureaucratization and the abolition of industrial cartels. Indeed, the initially high level of state intervention and direction would soon start to be pared back in most countries, though by then recovery was well under way.

The Social Impact of Total War

By the time the Second World War was over, expectations that governments should do more to improve living conditions for their societies also compelled state intervention. Of course, expectations had been raised during the First World War, too, even if these had for the most part afterwards been sorely disappointed. In one crucial area, however, notable progress had been made. Under pressure from workers' parties, most of the economically more advanced countries in Europe had between the wars extended the limited social security provisions that some of them, notably Germany and Britain, had already introduced before 1914. There were still great variations in provision and coverage, while the systems themselves were far from uniform. But there was a common trend. Now, following a second great war, there could be no retreat from the building of a fully fledged welfare state. Expectations were even higher and states had no choice but to address them. Politicians of all colours, liberals and conservatives as well as leaders of labour movements, pressed, if with different agendas, for a wider welfare net. Even under the regimentation of fascist regimes, mass mobilization had increased expectations of a better future, including state welfare. Promises of improved living standards, new housing, comprehensive social insurance, extended leisure facilities and a car for every family – the 'people's car' or Volkswagen – were part of Nazism's appeal, and much the same was true of Fascism in Mussolini's Italy.

The promises remained largely unfulfilled before the descent into catastrophic war. But the expectation that the state would provide the framework for such material prosperity and improvements in welfare survived the demise of fascism and were taken up by post-war governments. In Britain the feeling was universal that the sacrifices made by the people in the 'total war' had this time to be honoured by the state in ensuring that the full employment that the conflict had brought would be sustained, that social welfare and medical care would be available for all, and that the poverty and deprivation of the 1930s could never return. In 1944 the British government committed itself to a programme of full employment, necessary for the success of the social insurance measures proposed by William Beveridge in his Report two years earlier. Social policy would obviously be high on the agenda of the post-war government.

It would be as well, however, not to exaggerate the extent of social change in Europe during the first half of the twentieth century. The position of women in society underlines the point. Before the First World War feminist movements had been relatively strong, especially in pressing for the vote for women, in Scandinavia and Britain (where the campaigns of the suffragettes had done much to draw the issue to wider public attention). But movements for women's rights had been far weaker in Catholic parts of Europe, notably in the east and south of the continent, where liberal forms of constitutional government were little developed. In German-speaking central Europe feminist movements had won support mainly among middle-class women. Their progress had been limited, however, since they were largely squeezed between the male domains of reactionary conservatism and socialism (which saw the quest for women's emancipation as a subordinate strand in the wider struggle for social and economic transformation).

The First World War had brought about the breakthrough, at least on the issue of women's votes, in many countries. The recognition of the vital contribution by women in the war effort had led to a change in the attitude towards women's suffrage, and after the war women had been given the vote in most of Europe. But France extended the franchise to women only in 1944, Italy in 1946, Romania and Yugoslavia the same year, Belgium in 1948. Greece followed even later, in 1952, after the country's civil war. In neutral Switzerland women gained the vote at the federal level only in 1971 (in individual cantons at various times from 1958) and in tiny Liechtenstein as late as 1984.

Beyond voting rights, women's status at home and in the workplace was little changed. Society was still completely male-dominated. In Britain the Beveridge Report left the wife dependent on her husband's social insurance contributions and benefits, while the French Constitution of 1946 still emphasized a woman's fulfilment of her role as mother. Women remained largely discriminated against in the labour market. This was particularly the case with married women, who continued to be regarded mainly as housewives and childbearers. The high ranks of the professions remained largely closed to them. Paid employment was for the most part still in what were seen as women's jobs – nursing, welfare, primary-school teaching, secretarial work or shop assistants.

In education, too, women continued to be grossly disadvantaged. Certainly, there was an upward trend across Europe between 1900 and 1940 in the numbers of women studying at universities. This was part of more than a doubling of (still small) student numbers over that period. But women played only a minor part in that growth. Before the Second World War the proportion of women among students was below a fifth across western Europe – at its highest with nearly a third in Finland, and more than a quarter in France, Britain and Ireland, but dropping to only 7–8 per cent in Spain and Greece. With so many young men called up to the armed services, the numbers of women in universities increased during the Second World War. But the big changes here, as in the position of women more generally, would only come about decades later.

The extent of social mobility was also far smaller than might be imagined. Certainly the immense destruction, the colossal disruption to the world economy and the political upheavals that stretched across the era of two world wars, interspersed with the Great Depression, inevitably made great inroads – especially into the wealth of the landed elite. Expropriation of property was, of course, a hallmark of the Bolshevik Revolution. Despite much resistance from landowners, a substantial redistribution of land also took place, for instance in Poland, Czechoslovakia, Romania and Bulgaria. The entire era that spanned the wars was a massive interruption to long-term trends of capital accumulation and growth of wealth. Nevertheless, those with wealth and social standing on the eve of the war tended still to retain them when the conflict was over, except those parts of eastern Europe that now fell under Soviet domination.

In Britain, which had not experienced enemy occupation, institutional and social continuities were more plainly evident than in most of Europe. Social elites indeed suffered significant inroads into their wealth through higher taxation, the requisitioning of their property for the armed services, or the loss of much of their estate to pay death duties. In particular, the wealth of the landed aristocracy, the country gentry and other private owners of large-scale capital was often drastically reduced. And, as they frequently bemoaned, domestic servants were hard to find; young women were no longer entering the long-term drudgery of domestic service in the homes of the upper classes. The patrician lifestyle of the pre-war years had largely vanished. But there was little loss of status, while in England and Wales a mere 1 per cent of the adult population still owned half of the total capital holdings in 1946–7.

In France there were some shifts in political and economic elites. New men – women, of course, only exceptionally – who had gained prestige from their role in the Resistance, replaced the pre-war, often discredited leaders of the Third Republic and the Vichy collaborators. At the local level, however, once the worst of the collaborators had been purged, there was much continuity. In Italy, too, when the immediate post-war purges of committed Fascists came to an end and the communists were forced out of the new government, the political class was left not radically altered. In the economy, once the dust started to settle, the families that had controlled Italy's business before the war and in the south owned the big *latifundia*, the great landed estates, were largely the same as before. As in France and elsewhere, however, a new, more technocratic and entrepreneurial class soon started to gain ground in Italian industry, while in big concerns such as Pirelli and Fiat powerful trade unions were the guarantors of a new climate in the workplace. It is easy, too, to underestimate the extent of the changes that took place in the state bureaucracy and judicial system, in the central government and in the provinces, after the fall of Fascism – especially where, as in much of the north, control of towns and cities was in the hands of the Left.

Members of the German upper class had been prominent in the plot to kill Hitler in July 1944. However, the upper class had also presided over some terrible atrocities. It had been over-represented in the army leadership, and also in the top ranks of the SS. Many business leaders were closely involved in expropriation of property, ruthless exploitation of the occupied countries, slave labour and the economics of genocide. Some of the worst cases would eventually be punished in post-war Allied trials. But levels of continuity in the elites in western Germany remained surprisingly high even across the devastation of 1945, except where they had lost their lands to war and occupation, as had estate-owners in the eastern provinces.

Overall, the political and economic elites had tended to reproduce themselves throughout the first half of the twentieth century. More significant changes would come during the second half. Upward mobility into the elites remained uncommon. A partial exception among the major belligerent powers was Germany, where the Nazi Party and its many affiliations had facilitated some social climbing. Something similar could be seen in Fascist Italy. But the extent of this is easy to exaggerate. A greater degree of change came later. Even the claim, sometimes made, that bombs knew no social differences and fell on rich and poor alike, was not true. The poorer parts of the population, huddled in the crowded tenements and slums of industrial towns and cities, were far more likely to experience the worst of the bombing. More salubrious middle-class suburbs and the stately homes on landed estates had much better chances of escaping unscathed.

What a later era would come to call the 'cycle of deprivation' still prevailed for the most part. Soldiers returning home from the Second World War generally went back to the sort of occupation that they had left when they joined up. Their social class was usually unchanged. So were the milieux that shaped their lives. The long-term trend from the countryside to the towns meant a bigger industrial working class, usually accommodated in poor-quality housing close to town centres, with little chance of upward mobility into the middle or professional classes. Possibilities of moving into less elevated white-collar clerical or administrative work were, however, widening as the service sector expanded throughout Europe, though at different rates of growth. Educational opportunities were still minimal for those born without social advantages. In rural areas the drop in population, the presence of fewer young people in the villages, and the diminution in available farm labourers were indicators of long-term change, intensified by the demands of the war economy. On farms in the more remote parts of Europe physically untouched by war, where mechanization and modern transport had hardly penetrated, the daily routines would have been familiar to a generation fifty years earlier. Much the same was true of the daily life of the factory worker – less grinding to be sure than it had been before the First World War, and with shorter hours, but still recognizable to an earlier generation of workers.

In the areas of Europe most devastated by the Second World War – mainly stretching from Germany across eastern and southern Europe to the western regions of the Soviet Union – there was little or no pre-war normality to return to. Huge tracts of Ukraine, Belarus and Poland had been laid waste, both during the ravages of the fighting and genocidal killing – worse here than anywhere else in Europe – and by 'scorched-earth' destruction as the Germans retreated. In Germany itself, where the refusal to capitulate inflicted colossal destruction on the country as defeat loomed, two-thirds of the population were displaced in one way or another as the war ended. Millions of soldiers were in captivity (most of those, almost 3 million, who had surrendered to the western Allies were gradually released by 1948 but the last of a further 3 million in Soviet hands only in 1955). The civilian population, swollen by the huge influx of refugees from the eastern provinces, shoehorned into overcrowded accommodation – 50 per cent of housing in the big cities had been destroyed – and cowed by total defeat, faced an uncertain future. They were glad, however, if they had managed to find their part of the country, as war ended, occupied by the western Allies and not by the feared and detested Soviets. For not just the immense loss of life and the devastation of the economy but the character of political power mattered more than anything else. The contours of their lives in the divided Germany in the immediate post-war years would be determined largely by the interests of the occupiers – in the west by the Americans, British and French, in the east by the Soviets.

For the Soviet population, the sense of triumph at the great victory and, no doubt, relief at having survived, was one side of the coin. The other was the mourning for millions of lost loved ones or the attempt to rebuild lives when their towns and villages had been obliterated by the enemy. The end of the war saw the continuation of a little-changed Stalinist system, now in fact strengthened and legitimized by wartime glory. It was still characterized by expropriations, heavy impositions of delivery or productivity quotas, exposure to the arbitrariness of the police state, and the inhumane treatment of millions of prisoners of war, those deemed 'unreliable', and conscripts deployed in the rebuilding of roads and railways. This system was now imposed on most of eastern Europe, which had comprised the poorest parts of the continent even before the First World War. Now, on top of the immense suffering and devastation suffered in the Second, those countries were to be sealed off from the economic impetus that would soon breathe new life into western Europe.

Prospects of Economic Recovery

In the international economy the Second World War accentuated the long-term trend that had already been marked following the First, of Europe's declining share of world production and trade. It also marked the definitive subordination of Britain to the USA as the dominant economic power in the world, again a development already pronounced since the First World War but now completely confirmed by the demands of war financing in the Second. As British debts soared to meet the war effort, economic dependency on America, which had emerged from the conflict as the world's industrial giant, became overwhelming. By the end of the war Britain was financially on its knees, the USA economically booming – the outright winner of the

Second World War. Industrial production there had been greater during the war than at any earlier period of its history. Output had increased by 15 per cent a year (compared with 7 per cent during the First World War), and the productive capacity of the economy is estimated to have grown by 50 per cent. By 1944 no less than 40 per cent of the world's armaments were produced in America. As British exports dwindled, American exports soared – two-thirds higher in 1944 than they had been in 1939.

The strength of its economy enabled the USA to go a long way towards financing the Allied war effort through the scheme of Lend-Lease, a brainwave of President Roosevelt that Congress agreed to back in the spring of 1941. This allowed the USA to supply its allies with 'loans' of equipment rather than demand payment from overstretched, grossly indebted countries. By the end of the war, the total value of American Lend-Lease exports had reached over $32 billion, of which nearly $14 billion went to Britain and an invaluable $9 billion to the Soviet Union (which was provided with foodstuffs, machine tools, lorries, tanks, aircraft, railway track and locomotives). America was the paymaster of the war. It would soon become the paymaster of the peace.

Its economic supremacy gave the USA the determining hand, before the war was over, in shaping the institutional arrangements for the post-war economy for the half of Europe that did not fall under Soviet rule after 1945, though the full impact of these decisions was only felt in later decades. During most of July 1944, a month after Allied troops had landed in Normandy, more than 700 delegates from the forty-four Allied countries that constituted the United Nations met for a conference in an American hotel in Bretton Woods, New Hampshire (somewhat uncomfortably, since the hotel was too small and in a poor state of repair). They tried to work out the principles of a global economic order for the post-war world that would permanently overcome the disasters which had given rise to economic nationalism, the Great Depression and the triumph of fascism during the 1930s. The most important delegations were the British and the American. But it was obvious which now ruled the roost. Some of the key ideas behind the agreement reached on the last day of the conference had been put forward by the head of the British delegation, John

Maynard Keynes, who had come to understand the dangers of the economic orthodoxy that had prevailed during the Depression and whose counter-cyclical theories advocating state intervention and deficit spending to overcome mass unemployment had gained significant influence during the war. But where the British and Americans diverged in their views, the interests of the United States, voiced by the head of the US delegation Harry Dexter White, prevailed.

The Bretton Woods Conference established a new monetary order (largely Keynes's inspiration) of freely convertible currencies, their exchange rates pegged to the US dollar, to replace the earlier discredited Gold Standard. (The first big test of 'convertibility' would, however, fail miserably in summer 1947 when Britain was forced to revoke the convertibility of sterling in the midst of financial crisis and heavy demands for exchange of sterling into dollars, seriously depleting dollar holdings.) Two proposals by White would eventually take shape as significant post-war institutions: an International Stabilization Fund (which became the International Monetary Fund), aimed at correcting budgetary problems of individual states while retaining stability within the system; and an International Bank for Reconstruction and Development (which turned into the World Bank) to provide necessary capital for post-war reconstruction, though its initial provisions were, in fact, small, relative to what was needed. Conference participants also recognized the need for a further institution to establish rules for liberalized global trade. This, however, never came to fruition, and international trade relations were eventually regulated under the General Agreement on Tariffs and Trade (GATT), reached in 1947 and initially signed by twenty-three nations.

Whatever the insurmountable political obstacles that prevented the initial success of Bretton Woods, the Conference marked a determination that there could be no return to the disasters of the interwar era. It was an indicator of the acceptance that the basis of the capitalist economy itself had to be reformed if a repeat of the breakdown of international trade and finance that had spawned the catastrophe were to be avoided. The US dollar, it was plain, had to take over from the weakened pound sterling as the pivot of international finance. The Americans were more than happy with that, as they were with the agreed liberalization of trade. Europeans, too, accepted this as a basic premise of the post-war economic order. But there was a difference of emphasis. For the British and the French, state intervention on a scale unimaginable before the war had become essential not simply for reconstruction, but to combat the vagaries of unconstrained capitalist economics and to prevent any return of mass unemployment. The resulting compromise – not applicable to the Soviet bloc, of course – was an emerging mixed economy of liberal free trade and state direction. Capitalism was everywhere reformed to some extent, though not radically changed or fundamentally challenged – apart from by the rapidly dwindling numbers of adherents of Communist parties (struggling to retain support as the Cold War took shape). Although it was hard to foresee in the devastation of 1945, the mixture of economic liberalism and social democracy – what the Germans came to call 'social market economy' (*soziale Marktwirtschaft*) – would come to provide untold prosperity and serve western Europe well politically for the next thirty years.

An important precondition for the success of this combination after 1945 had not existed following the First World War. No attempt was made by the western Allies to impose heavy reparation payments – in Germany's eastern zone it was a different matter – as had been done in 1919 with such baleful consequences for Germany and for other defeated nations. For a short time in 1944 the Morgenthau Plan, which proposed reducing post-war Germany to the status of a pre-industrial economy (thereby handing a propaganda gift to the Nazi regime), was given serious consideration. Although Roosevelt and Churchill agreed on notable restrictions to future levels of German industrial output, the futility of permanently impoverishing 70 million people and crippling the economic key to European recovery was swiftly recognized, all the more so once the Cold War set in.

The Iron Curtain would itself come to be an indirect advantage to the western half of the continent, while condemning the eastern part to an unenviable fate. This was a vast human tragedy for the peoples trapped behind it. No price can be placed on the deprivation of freedom that would last for more than four decades. But the loss, to the heavy hand of Soviet oppression, of those parts of Europe that after the First World War had been wracked by ethnic conflict, nationalist violence and border disputes, benefited the already wealthier parts of

Europe in the west. These countries, unlike those of the emerging Soviet bloc, were able to take advantage of American support in rebuilding their ruined economies.

The Europeans had seemed bent on destroying their own economic foundations between 1914 and 1945. That the next thirty years, in astonishing contrast, would bring for many in the west continued and unprecedented prosperity, was utterly unimaginable in the ruins of 1945. Sustained prosperity would transform living standards in western Europe. But even in the very different conditions of eastern Europe, too, living standards would rise and for the mass of the population far outstrip what they had been during the troubled interwar years. The European nations would have been incapable of bringing this transformation about themselves. In the separate halves of the continent they were heavily dependent upon the two new superpowers, the USA and USSR, for the reconstruction, in diametrically opposed ways, of their economic substance. Economically as well as politically, the two halves of Europe were set after 1945 to go their separate ways.

CHRISTIAN CHURCHES:
CHALLENGE AND CONTINUITY

How people framed their lives, beyond the precarious task of securing a livelihood, was still overwhelmingly influenced by the morality and values of the Christian Churches. Europe remained in the first half of the twentieth century a Christian continent, lying west of the officially atheistic Soviet Union and north-west of Turkey (a secular state with a Muslim population). The Churches still wielded enormous social and ideological power, especially among the peasantry and the middle classes. And they used it, as the Christian Churches were everywhere swept into the political convulsions that rocked Europe after the First World War.

Friedrich Nietzsche, the German philosopher, had famously announced already in 1882 that 'God is dead'. It was a premature obituary. During the first half of the twentieth century the Christian Churches certainly felt themselves to be on the defensive against the threat posed by modern society, above all 'atheistic Bolshevism'. Indeed, as people turned to the state, to political movements, or to other public institutions to answer their needs, the Churches in the eyes of increasing numbers had nothing to offer. 'Nationalism is the new religion. People don't go to church. They go to nationalist meetings,' said Count Chojnicki, one of the characters in Joseph Roth's gloomy view of modernity in his evocative 1932 novel, *The Radetzky March*. Max Weber's 'disenchantment of the world' meant that mystical beliefs in sacramental ritual, salvation, redemption and eternal happiness in an afterlife were losing their appeal. And as war and genocide ravaged Europe, Nietzsche's attack on belief in rationality and truth, his denial of morality rooted in religious belief, came to seem anything but misplaced. The Churches could not come out of this era untarnished. Yet neither the loss of belief nor fall in the numbers of followers of the main Christian denominations should be exaggerated or pre-dated. After two world wars that influence remained profound. For all their travails the Christian Churches survived the catastrophic first half of the twentieth century remarkably intact. Their main problems would come later.

The start of the First World War had given Christianity a boost. God was, it seemed, on everyone's side as war broke out. At any rate, the Christian Churches in every belligerent power claimed God's support for their cause. 'God with us' (*Gott mit uns*) said the Germans. 'God is on our side' (*Dieu est de notre côté*) claimed the French, as they declared a 'sacred union' (*union sacrée*) to defend their country. Other countries were equally quick to blend patriotism with Christianity. The clergy readily saw the war as a national crusade, a 'holy war' for civilization against barbarism, for good against evil. There were some pacifists, to be sure, but the majority of the clergy overwhelmingly backed their country's war. They blessed the troops going into battle and the arms with which they fought. They prayed for the success of imminent offensives. Nationalism everywhere swallowed the basic tenets of Christianity. For purported men of peace the belligerency of the clergy could be resounding. In an Advent sermon in 1915 the Anglican Bishop of London, Arthur Winnington-Ingram, exhorted British soldiers 'to kill the good as well as the bad, to kill the young men as well as the old' – though his Prime Minister, Herbert Asquith, thought this was the rant of a singularly stupid bishop. One Church leader at least consistently proclaimed his neutrality and exhorted the nations to conclude a just peace. In 1917 Pope Benedict XV (elected in September 1914) put forward a peace plan that advocated international arbitration, evacuation of occupied territories, renunciation of war indemnities and reduction in armaments. For his pains he was decried as a secret partisan, a hypocrite who would not admit his preferences. The French called him the 'Boche pope', the Germans the 'French pope'.

For the clergy the war brought the prospects of Christian revival, borne out by what observers labelled a 'return to the altars'. In England it is not clear that there was more than a fleeting growth in church attendance, which was in fact lower in 1916 than it had been before the war (not helped by so many men away at the front). However, belief in the efficacy of spiritualism – supposedly enabling the living to commune with the dead – sharply increased as the numbers of bereaved at home mounted. At a time of great anxiety it was unsurprising that people might turn to prayer. Soldiers often prayed before battle and those who survived gave thanks afterwards for coming through unscathed. Religion mingled with superstitition. Many carried religious symbols with them to the front. A cross, a set of rosary beads, or a pocket Bible served as a talisman. Should the worst happen, field chaplains were on hand to remind the dead soldier's comrades of the Christian symbolism of death as sacrifice, reinforced by the spread of temporary wooden crosses placed on the graves of the fallen.

There must have been those who asked how belief was still possible after the battles of Verdun and the Somme. How many soldiers lost their Christian belief amid the slaughter is impossible to know. One German pastoral report adjudged that 'the seeming lack of success of prayers, the long duration and the terrible brutality of the war have caused many soldiers to doubt God's justice and omniscience so that they do not bother about religion any more'. Most soldiers, however, like their families back home, retained at least a nominal allegiance to one or other form of Christianity when they returned to a changed world at the end of the war. Even where people did not attend church services, they generally still turned to the Church for baptism, marriage and burial. And there was little expression of militant or radical anti-religious feeling (though in some parts of southern Europe, especially, a good deal of vehement anti-clericalism). Where, however, religious ties had already weakened, most evidently in the urban population, they were not lastingly strengthened through the war. The long-term trend – more prominent among men than women – away from Christian belief and allegiance to the Churches continued.

Protestantism fared worse than Catholicism. In Switzerland, the Baltic countries, Scandinavia and the Netherlands there was a trend of decline in adherence to the Protestant Churches in the early decades of the twentieth century, though this was accompanied by continued vitality within the Churches themselves. The number of Easter communicants in the Church of England steadily dropped from the early 1920s to the 1950s. In Germany the numbers of those taking communion fell by 11 per cent between 1920 and 1930, and confirmations by as much as 45 per cent over the same period.

The Catholic Church showed itself more adept at holding on to its congregations. It continued the revitalization of Catholic faith that had begun in the mid-nineteenth century. It succeeded in broadening its popular appeal at the same time as it presented itself through doctrinal rigidity and organizational centralization, both embodied in the person of the Pope, as the bulwark against the threats posed by the modern world, particularly those of liberalism and socialism. The revived cult of the Virgin Mary, which followed Pope Pius IX's pronouncement in 1854 of her Immaculate Conception, had stirred popular piety. This was boosted by alleged Marian apparitions at Lourdes in the Pyrenees in 1858 (a site already attracting more than a million pilgrims a year before the First World War), Knock in western Ireland in 1879 and Fatima in Portugal in 1917. New levels of devotion to popular saints were encouraged. Less than two years after the end of the First World War, which had brought such immeasurable suffering to the people of France, the timing was deemed right to canonize the national heroine Joan of Arc, even though the Church had actually excommunicated her (on trumped-up charges from which she was later exonerated) and had her burnt for heresy five centuries earlier. The canonization sought to bolster the faith in a country whose state promoted secular values and where anticlericalism was strong. Further significant canonizations followed – of the young French Carmelite nun, Thérèse of Lisieux ('The Little Flower'), portrayed as a model of Catholic spiritual life, in 1925, and of Bernadette Soubirous, the cult figure of Lourdes, in 1933. A further boost to popular piety followed Pope Pius XI's proclamation in 1925 of the Feast of Christ the King, intended as a response to nationalism and secularism, which appealed to Catholics to place Christian morality at the centre of political and social life.

Social and charitable organizations that incorporated lay Catholics also helped to bind the population to the Church. 'Catholic Action', originally founded in the mid-nineteenth century, attempted with some success to galvanize lay involvement in Catholic life and to instil Christian values into worker and peasant movements. In some parts of Britanny priests ran popular local newspapers and organized farming cooperatives where peasants could buy fertilizers. In Lower Austria and rural areas of northern Spain, too, active involvement in credit banks and other ways of aiding peasants and tenant farmers helped to cement support for the Church and strengthen the hold of the clergy.

The Catholic Church prospered especially where it could blend allegiance into a strong sense of national identity or where it represented a disadvantaged minority. Both in Poland and in the Irish Free State, new states that emerged from the First World War, Catholicism became effectively an expression of national identity. As political and social tension grew in Poland during the 1930s, the Church associated itself closely with the conservative drive for national unity, and with a nationalism that emphasized the differences between Catholic Poles and the country's Ukrainian, Belorussian, German and, not least, Jewish minorities. In largely Protestant Northern Ireland, Catholics forged an identity out of discrimination – in housing, jobs, and practically all walks of social and political life – and a separate subculture bound up with nationalist aspirations for unity with the larger, Catholic, now independent southern part of Ireland.

In Britain, too, age-old prejudice encouraged a strong sense of Catholic identity and loyalty to the Church, not least among Irish immigrants who had moved to north-west Britain in great numbers following the famine of 1845. The close-knit Irish Catholic communities faced a great deal of animosity and discrimination from the Protestant majority, reflected even in sport. No Catholic was allowed to play for Glasgow Rangers football club, no Protestant for their neighbouring rivals, Celtic. In the Netherlands a minority subculture also provided a base for thriving Catholicism, while in the Basque lands the Church could become identified with sustaining a disadvantaged language community. In Germany, too, a strong subculture had arisen out of Bismarck's attacks on the Catholic Church (representing nearly a third of the Reich's population) in the 1870s. Catholic institutions and beliefs flourished until Hitler's takeover of power. At that point, like the Protestant Church in Germany, Catholics faced a radically new challenge.

Both the Protestant Church (in its varied forms) and the more unified Catholic Church saw the struggle against Bolshevism especially, but against the political Left more generally, as crucial to the defence of Christianity in the modern world. 'Modernity' in all its forms was viewed as a threat to be warded off. Both major denominations stood, therefore, axiomatically on the political Right, favouring conservative bastions of the state and the social power they wielded as a bulwark against the Left. Inevitably, therefore, the Churches and their followers became inextricably embroiled in the bitter conflicts of interwar Europe.

This did not necessarily make them anti-democratic. The Catholic Centre Party had been among the major political forces that had formed the Weimar Republic in Germany in 1919 and remained a mainstay of the new democracy in Germany during the 1920s. The Partito Popolari Italiano (People's Party), founded in 1919, gave a specifically Catholic political voice to its mainly rural clientele in the Italian pluralist political system before it was banned by Mussolini in 1926. In democratic Britain, where the political system was unthreatened, the Anglican Church was a pillar of the establishment – 'the Conservative Party at prayer', as it was often dubbed. By contrast, the various nonconformist Christian Churches, which retained significant support in Britain, tended to be more radical critics of the government, but not of democracy. Where a significant threat from the Left posed itself, however, the Churches of both major denominations invariably backed the authority of the state. And the more extreme they perceived the threat to be, the more extreme was the reaction they were prepared to support.

Nowhere was the reaction more extreme than in Germany. Here, the Protestant Church – actually divided doctrinally and regionally but in its various forms nominally embracing more than two-thirds of the German population – had since Martin Luther's time seen itself as closely aligned with state authority. The revolution of 1918, the removal of the Kaiser and the new democracy that replaced the monarchy brought widespread dismay in Church circles. The perceived 'crisis of faith' (*Glaubenskrise*) promoted hopes of a restoration of the monarchy or a new form of state leadership that would overcome Germany's moral as well as political and economic plight. A true leader was needed, in the eyes of many members of the Protestant clergy. He would be, in the words of one Protestant theologian writing in 1932, a 'true statesman' (as opposed to the mere 'politicians' of the Weimar Republic) who 'holds war and peace in his hand and communes with God'. In line with such thinking, Hitler's takeover of power in 1933 was widely seen by Protestant clergy as the start of a national reawakening that would inspire a revival of faith. There was even a nazified wing of the Protestant Church. The 'German Christians' rejected the Old Testament as Jewish and took pride in being 'the stormtroopers of Jesus Christ'. Such extremes, the preserve of a minority of the clergy (though with substantial support in some areas), were rejected, however, by most Protestants, whose ideas of a revival of faith were for the most part both doctrinally and organizationally conservative.

At first, the 'German Christians' looked as if they would triumph. But a reaction to their demands quickly formed. The initial Nazi aim of unifying the twenty-eight autonomous regional Churches into a single 'Reich Church' stirred enormous rancour and had eventually to be abandoned. Meeting at Barmen in 1934, a section of the clergy that outrightly rejected the 'heresy' of the 'German Christians' and the political interference aimed at forcing the centralization of the Church, publicly opposed any subordination of the Church to the state as 'false doctrine'. The Barmen Declaration restricted itself, however, to issues of doctrinal purity (under the influence of the Swiss theologian Karl Barth) and refrained from political opposition. In any case, the Confessing Church (as those behind the Declaration called themselves) represented only a minority of Protestant pastors. Most clergy continued to give Hitler's regime their backing. Some Protestant theologians provided what they saw as doctrinal reasons for antisemitism, racial ideals and Nazi rule. The Protestant Church raised no public protest at the treatment of Jews, the pogroms of November 1938, or the later deportation to the death-camps. And there were few Protestants who objected to a nationally assertive foreign policy, conquest in war, or the attempt to destroy the detested Bolshevik regime in Soviet Russia.

The political stance of the Catholic Church was largely determined by its rejection of socialism and the anathema of its most extreme variant, communism. In his encyclical 'Quadragesimo Anno' ('Fortieth Year') of 1931, Pope Pius XI criticized the inequities of capitalism and international finance, but his condemnation of communism was unequivocal and he decreed the materialist tenets of socialism to be incompatible with the teachings of the Catholic Church. The advocacy of a social order resting on solidarity, not conflict, and of industrial relations based upon the collaboration of industry, labour and government, lent itself without difficulty to adoption of the 'corporate state' by Italian Fascism, and by quasi-fascist regimes in Austria, Portugal and Spain. 'Solidarity' here was imposed by the state, favoured industry and was upheld by coercion.

The Catholic Church in Italy formed a somewhat uneasy truce with Mussolini, which was sealed in the Lateran Treaty of 1929. In return for the foundation of the Vatican State – the Papal States had earlier ceased to exist on completion of Italian unification in 1870 – and for recognition of Catholicism as Italy's only state religion, the Church committed itself in effect to political passivity and tolerance, at least, of Fascist rule in Italy. The Church kept quiet about the violence of fascist thugs, then later welcomed the triumph in Ethiopia and raised no objections to the introduction of racial laws. However awkward a bedfellow, Italian Fascism was, in the Church's eyes, in any case infinitely preferable to communism. In matters relating to the Church, however, the papacy put up sturdy and effective defence, vehemently resisting the 'total claim' of the state on all spheres of society. From the Church's point of view the policy was successful. There was a moderate revival of religious activity. There were increases in the numbers of clergy, of church marriages and of pupils attending Church schools. Pope Pius XI was especially protective of education and Catholic Action. He had to accept limitations on the latter's activities, but the state's attempt to abolish Catholic Action was abandoned.

In France the Catholic Church had long viewed the Third Republic with hostility. After all, it had fostered anticlericalism and promoted the secular values of a modern society, particularly in breaking the Church's hold over education. Between the wars the Church lent its considerable support to the reactionary (and sometimes extreme) Right, and later warmly welcomed Pétain's Vichy regime. In Spain the intense anti-socialism that underpinned the Church's enthusiastic support for Franco in the civil war had been long established. As early as 1916 the most widely read religious periodical in Spain had 'sounded the alarm against the audacities of socialism' and 'contagions of modernism'. Spain, the periodical repeatedly avowed, had been great when it was truly Catholic, and national decline had followed religious decline. It was soon calling for a 'crusade' to make Spain fully Catholic again. Unsurprisingly, given such views, the Catholic Church served on the Iberian peninsula as a bulwark against the 'ungodly' doctrine of Marxism, providing the ideological backbone after the civil war for Franco's rule in Spain, and for the Salazar regime in Portugal.

The German Catholic bishops, who had warned against the anti-Christian content of the Nazi Movement before 1933, performed a volte-face a few weeks after Hitler had become Chancellor and promised to uphold the rights and institutions of the Church, encouraging Catholics to support the new state. A Reich Concordat with the papacy (one of forty concordats that the Vatican concluded with various states during the interwar years) was ratified – despite indications from the very outset of the Nazi regime's hostility towards Catholic observances, organizations and institutions. From the beginning, the Concordat was a dead letter. It was a one-sided arrangement that was advantageous to the image of Hitler's regime as it established itself. But it did nothing in practice to protect the Catholic Church in Germany.

Attacks on the institutions of the Church began even before the Concordat was ratified. The Centre Party was swiftly dissolved. The large Catholic youth movement was soon banned. Church publications were suppressed. Priests were harassed and arrested. Restrictions were imposed on church processions. There was constant chicanery. The Vatican protested on more than seventy occasions between 1933 and 1937 over violations of the Concordat, though in vain. The key area of education became the centre of an attritional battle between Church and state, gradually won by the Nazi regime through heavy-handed pressure in the teeth of widespread resentment and some open protest. The Catholic hierarchy's stance towards Nazism was in principle hostile. It viewed the anti-Christian essence of the regime's ideology and total claim on its citizens as completely incompatible with Catholic belief. In practice, however, vigorous defence against attacks on the Church accompanied general compliance in other spheres of government policy to avoid even worse exposure to an all-out assault on the Church. The regime could be sure of the Church's support for its anti-Bolshevism and approval of its national assertiveness in foreign policy.

The Catholic Church in Germany offered no official condemnation of the mounting persecution of the Jews, even following the pogroms of 9–10 November 1938. As early as April 1933 the Archbishop of Munich-Freising, the redoubtable Cardinal Michael Faulhaber, had explained to the Papal Secretary of State and former nuncio in Germany, Cardinal Eugenio Pacelli (later to become Pope Pius XII), why the Catholic hierarchy 'does not step in on behalf of the Jews. This is not possible at the moment because the fight against the Jews would also become a fight against the Catholics,' he stated. It was an explanation that went to the heart of the Catholic Church's passivity towards the fate of the Jews in Nazi Germany.

Pius XI, it is true, in his 1937 encyclical 'Mit brennender Sorge' ('With Burning Concern') outrightly condemned racism. But the encyclical, initially drafted by Cardinal Faulhaber then refined by Pacelli, was less forthright than an earlier denunciation that the Vatican had prepared but then not issued, avoided explicit condemnation of Nazism, and did not directly refer to the persecution of the Jews. Moreover, it was late in coming, and, though it met with Nazi fury and increased harassment of Catholic clergy, had only muted impact within Germany. And when the Holy Office prepared a new statement during the summer and autumn of 1937 aimed at presenting 'concrete facts' to condemn Nazi theories, including antisemitism, Cardinal

Faulhaber advised against publication because of the danger to the Church in Germany.

The path was thereby laid for the continued inaction of the German hierarchy as the pressure on the Church intensified. During the war the deportation and extermination of the Jews prompted no public denunciation by Germany's Catholic bishops, in contrast to the courageous stance taken against the 'euthanasia action' by Bishop Galen of Münster in 1941. Meanwhile German Catholic soldiers, like their Protestant compatriots, had gone to war with the full backing of their Church, and in the belief, supported by the clergy, that in conducting a barbarous invasion of the Soviet Union they were fighting a crusade against atheistic Bolshevism for the defence of Christian values.

In Germany's satellite states the Christian Churches had at best a chequered record when it came to offering support for Jews and other victims of brutal racist policy. In Catholic Croatia the sickening sadism of the Ustaše towards Serbs and Roma as well as Jews met with no public condemnation by the Vatican. Ante Pavelić, the unspeakable head of state in Croatia, was even granted an audience with the Pope. Franciscan friars were involved in some of the worst Ustaše atrocities. While remaining loyal to the Croatian state the Primate of Croatia, Archbishop Alojzije Stepinac, did, however, intervene on thirty-four occasions on behalf of Jews or Serbs, unequivocally denounced racism, and appealed successfully to prevent the arrest and deportation of Jewish spouses and children of mixed marriages.

Nearly all the bishops in Slovakia, whose President, Monsignor Jozef Tiso, was himself a serving Catholic priest, backed the government's anti-Jewish policy, though there were some courageous exceptions. Remarkably, the Vatican chose not to remove Tiso's clerical status, probably because of his popularity in his own country, nor that of sixteen other priests who served in the State Council at Bratislava. Even Monsignor Domenico Tardini, assistant to the Vatican's Secretary of State, seemed puzzled, commenting in July 1942: 'Everyone knows that the Holy See cannot bring Hitler to heel. But who will understand that we cannot even control a priest?'

The Catholic hierarchy in Hungary was strongly supportive of Admiral Horthy's government and raised no objections to its anti-Jewish policy until 1944. Both the papal nuncio and the head of the Hungarian Church then intervened to try to prevent the deportation only of baptized Jews. The deportations, however, went ahead anyway. Only belatedly, after nearly half a million Jews had been sent to Auschwitz in 1944, did the bishops offer a weak protest at the deportations in a watered-down pastoral letter. The rabid antisemitism in Romania, which led to the deaths of hundreds of thousands of Jews under the country's leader, Marshal Antonescu, met at best with indifference, if not approval, on the part of the Orthodox hierarchy. Possibly an appeal by the papal nuncio in Bucharest contributed to the regime's growing resistance to German pressure in 1942 to deport a further 300,000 Jews. However, given the course the war had taken, Antonescu had already been dragging his feet for months over the deportations and, as the position of the Axis forces inexorably worsened, his reluctance to deport Romania's remaining Jews was by 1944 part of his attempt to leave the door open to negotiations with the Allies.

In Bulgaria, where the Jews were a fairly small minority of the population and antisemitism was relatively moderate, the stance of the Orthodox hierarchy differed notably from that in Romania. Here the Orthodox Church directly opposed the planned deportation of the Jews. The halting of the deportations from Bulgaria itself (though the deportation of Jews from recently acquired Macedonia and Thrace had gone ahead) had, however, nothing to do with any protest by the Church – towards which the King was unsympathetic. It was based on opportunism, not principle; it simply reflected the Bulgarian government's recognition of the lack of wisdom in ordering the deportations when Germany looked likely to lose the war.

In the German-occupied countries of Europe the position of the Churches and their reaction to the persecution of the Jews varied greatly. In the Baltic and the Ukraine the clergy mainly shared the extreme nationalism, antisemitism and anti-Soviet feelings of the population and remained silent, when not directly supportive of the murderous assault on the Jews. In Poland Catholic priests and members of religious orders provided help, at great personal risk, to thousands of Jews, though there were also overt expressions of antisemitism among clergy that matched the extensive hostility to Jews among the population. In the Netherlands both Protestant and Catholic Churches protested in July 1942 in favour of the Jews and demanded that they should not be deported. The Catholic hierarchy had received the prior sanction of the papacy. A strong telegram that had been sent to the Reich Commissar, Arthur Seyss-Inquart, protesting against the deportations, was read out in all churches on 26 July 1942. The protest was, however, to no avail. As retaliation for the public protest (unlike the private appeal by the Protestant Church leadership) and the uncompromising stance adopted by the Archbishop of Utrecht, Joachim de Jong, several hundred Jews who had been baptized into the Catholic Church were within a fortnight deported to their deaths in Auschwitz. Although the clergy in Holland, and in neighbouring Belgium, played their part in rescue networks for Jews, there was no further public denunciation of the deportations.

For the French Catholic episcopate, which had greeted Marshal Pétain so warmly as the restorer of religious values and herald of moral revival, the Jews were largely an irrelevance. French bishops accepted without demur the anti-Jewish legislation between 1940 and 1942. Their position changed with the commencement of deportations in the summer of 1942. There was some fear that a public protest might provoke retaliation against the Church. Some bishops nevertheless did speak out in strong and forthright terms against the deportations in public statements and pastoral letters. The Vichy government was worried by the protests. But they died down as quickly as they had arisen. The government played on the episcopate's loyalty to Pétain, sweetening this with tax concessions and other subsidies for religious associations. When the deportations recommenced in early 1943 there was no renewal of the protests of the previous year. Individual members of the clergy (and lay persons), Catholic and Protestant, as well as religious houses helped in hiding hundreds of Jews, many of them children (one of whom was the later renowned historian of the Holocaust, Saul Friedländer). The Catholic Church's leaders, however, resigned themselves largely to a fatalistic stance, accepting what they recognized they could not change.

Pope Pius XII had meanwhile made no open, public and unequivocal condemnation of the genocidal slaughter, the reality of which, if not its full dimensions or precise details, was plain to the Vatican by 1942 at the latest. The motives of this most enigmatic of pontiffs will probably never be plainly established, even if full access is granted to the closed Vatican archives of the period. Imputations that he was 'Hitler's Pope', heartless towards the fate of the Jews, or failed to act because of ingrained antisemitism, are, however, wide of the mark. Pius, who had secretly encouraged the German resistance to Hitler in 1939, leaked information to the western Allies on the date of the western offensive of the following year, arranged food supplies to the starving Greeks, and established a relief agency to aid refugees, was far from inactive with regard to the persecution of the Jews. But the paramount concern, in his eyes, was the protection of the Catholic Church. Seeing himself, like Pope Benedict XV in the First World War, as a peacemaker and defender of Catholicism, above all from atheistic communism, he tried to operate through quiet diplomacy behind the scenes.

Pius had a well-formed view that speaking out would make things worse – not just for the Catholic Church and Catholics, for whom he had a direct responsibility, but more widely for the victims of German atrocities. The German bishops had backed away from open confrontation with the Nazi regime already in the 1930s, fearing that this would make the position of the Church even worse. Polish bishops advised the Vatican in 1940 to refrain from outspoken denunciation of atrocities for fear of prompting horrific reprisals. 'The only reason we don't speak,' the Pope told the Italian ambassador, 'is the knowledge that it would make the lot of the Polish people still harder.' He appears to have taken the same view about the fate of the Jews.

By the autumn of 1942 the genocidal intent of Hitler's regime had become unmistakably clear. A public denunciation of German policy at this stage could hardly have made the plight of the Jews worse. Aware that he was helpless to deflect Hitler's regime from its unrelenting drive to destroy Europe's Jews, Pius was nevertheless unwilling to attempt a new strategy. His overriding concern remained to protect the Catholic Church. In September 1942 the American chargé d'affaires at the Vatican was told by Vatican officials that the Pope would not publicly condemn the extermination of the Jews because he wanted to avoid making the situation of Catholics worse in Germany and in the occupied territories.

In his Christmas message, broadcast to the world on 24 December

1942, the Pope did allude to the genocide, but only briefly and elliptically, speaking of 'hundreds of thousands who, without any fault of their own, sometimes only by reason of their nationality or race, are marked down for death or gradual extinction'. These twenty-seven words were in a text of twenty-six pages. He claimed the message was 'short, but it was well understood'. Whether or not that was the case, it amounted to his only public protest. In a letter to the Bishop of Berlin, Monsignor Konrad Graf von Preysing, in April the following year, Pius returned to the question of his reticence, remarking that 'the danger of reprisals and pressures ... counsel reserve'. He expressed his 'solicitude for all non-Aryan Catholics' – not mentioning 'non-Aryans' who were not Catholics – but added that 'unhappily in the present state of affairs, we can bring them no help other than our prayers'.

The Pope did intervene personally to protest to the Slovakian and Hungarian governments about the deportations, though once more he refrained from any public denunciation. In October 1943 he was confronted with the deportation of Jews before his very eyes. About a week before Rome's Jews were rounded up for deportation, the Vatican had been told about the imminent danger by the German ambassador to the Holy See, Ernst von Weizsäcker, but the Pope did not pass on the information to Jewish leaders. When the Jews were then seized, the Vatican protested officially to the German ambassador. Again there was no public protest, following a warning that this 'would only result in the deportations being carried out more vigorously'. Perhaps, too, so it has been speculated, the Pope feared the destruction of the Vatican City through bombing or military action if he incurred Berlin's displeasure – not an unlikely response. Whether or not this was a motive, the Church nonetheless did take practical steps to help Rome's Jews, hiding some 5,000 fugitives in convents and monasteries. No written order of the Pope to provide this life-saving measure has been found, but it is improbable that the simultaneous efforts to hide Jews in Church buildings arose spontaneously. One eyewitness, a Jesuit, Father Robert Leiber, later stated that Pius had personally ordered superiors of Church properties to open their doors to the Jews. Some 500 were given refuge in the Pope's own summer residence at Castel Gandolfo.

The public silence of Pius XII has irredeemably harmed his reputation. His Christmas message of 1942 was a missed opportunity, not least since only a week earlier the Allied powers had publicly condemned the 'bestial policy of cold-blooded extermination' of the Jews. Having decided to refer to the genocide, Pius ought to have followed this by condemnation that was loud, plain and unequivocal. As it was, the opaque language used ensured that his message had little impact. By this time, even so, however unequivocal, no public protest or condemnation by the Pope would, in all probability, have done anything to stop the German obsession with completing 'the final solution of the Jewish question'.

How much did this matter to ordinary churchgoers? The answer, probably, is: not much. Throughout most of Europe the Jews had been a small and usually disliked minority. The war had engulfed millions in a fight for their own survival, in which the fate of the Jews was most likely on relatively few minds. Where there was not hostility to them, there was widespread indifference. People had other concerns. The failings of both major denominations as the Jews of Europe were being destroyed had little effect on the behaviour of the churchgoing population, or their loyalty to the Churches, once the war ended.

In fact, even apart from their chequered response to the persecution of the Jews, the problems faced by the Churches in the interwar years and then during the Second World War itself did little to impair their standing, or greatly affect the behaviour of churchgoers, in the immediate post-war era. This, of course, did not apply to areas that fell under Soviet domination.

The Catholic Church even underwent something of a revival. Church attendance had grown in most countries during the war. It continued afterwards to remain strong, probably reflecting a sense of security that Catholicism seemed to offer believers after the violent traumas of the conflict. Political parties, some of them new, in west Germany, the Netherlands, Belgium, Italy, France and Austria, fostered Catholic principles. In Germany and Austria the Church successfully portrayed itself as the victim of Nazism, subjected to attack and persecution. In retrospectively turning the Church into a vehicle of resistance against Nazism, a veil was drawn over the pre-existing spheres of approval and collaboration.

The post-war Italian constitution confirmed Mussolini's Lateran Treaty of 1929 with the Church, which continued to shape education and determine public morality. In Salazar's Portugal and Franco's Spain national identity was closely bound up with the Church, which gave ideological legitimacy to the rooted anti-socialism of both dictatorships. In Spain the Church gained exemption from taxation, freedom from state interference and censorship rights in return for its unquestioning support for the regime and its stewardship of a one-sided memory of the civil war. In mainly Catholic Ireland the Church also flourished as never before, enjoying great popularity – it was the only country where the majority of the population were regular churchgoers – and huge political influence. In the Vatican, the pontificate of Pope Pius XII continued unchanged, its prestige even enhanced, a bastion of reaction against the perceived evils of the modern world, most prominent among them atheistic communism. The apogee of the papal monarchy was reached when the Pope used his *ex cathedra* authority to declare 'infallibly' in 1950 that the Virgin Mary had been bodily assumed into heaven. But in an increasingly secular, sceptical and democratic age, this form of absolutist monarchy was living on borrowed time.

The Protestant Church, divided doctrinally and organizationally and split nationally, could not draw on the international strength and solidity of Catholicism. In most of north-western Europe the long-term erosion of Protestantism continued. The population in Britain and the Scandinavian countries remained overwhelmingly Christian in a nominal sense, but the decline in church attendance was at best only marginally halted by the war. In neutral Sweden the decline was continuous, more marked as everywhere in the towns than in the villages. In Norway and Denmark the Churches' association with national resistance temporarily put the brakes on the earlier decline. In Holland, the Netherlands Reform Church was also able to build upon its record of opposition during the German occupation to reinvigorate Protestantism during the immediate post-war years. In Switzerland, too, home of Karl Barth, the most important theologian of his age, headquarters to a number of international Protestant organizations, and where the Protestant Church had played a part in refugee relief, there was continued vitality following the war, defying for some time the general trend toward secularism. British Protestantism also revived in the post-war years, reaching a peak of membership in the 1950s before entering a period of steep decline.

The Protestant Church in Germany had, of course, to confront its stance during the Third Reich. The continuity of the clergy from the Nazi era alone meant that this would remain for a generation or more incomplete and often apologetic in tone, as the role of the Church in resistance to the regime was emphasized and the high levels of support for Nazism were downplayed. At least, in contrast to their Catholic counterparts, Protestant Church leaders were prepared, in a general sense, publicly to admit to grave failings during the Nazi era. However, the Church's declaration of its guilt – though refraining from specifics – at Stuttgart in October 1945 proved more divisive than unifying. It went some way towards assuaging clerical consciences, though it was seen by many Germans as inadequate, while others rejected the implication of collective guilt for Nazi crimes.

Nevertheless, the Church did much soon after the war to reorganize and revitalize itself, and played an important role in the care of refugees. In line with the general pattern throughout north-western Europe, nominal adherence to the Church continued alongside declining attendance at services, particularly in towns and cities. In the eastern, almost wholly Protestant, Soviet zone of occupation the Church and its organizations were subjected to great pressure from the state. The Church continued to exist, but increasingly as a niche institution, while churchgoing declined to become the preserve of a small minority seeking to uphold belief within an officially godless society.

There was no Indian summer of Protestantism in Europe to match that of Catholicism. In both faiths, however, continuities prevailed in the immediate post-war world. Significant change would only come about in the 1960s. For the less committed and the more reflective, the horrors of the war and the revelations soon after its end of the magnitude of atrocities perpetrated during the great conflagration raised questions both about the Churches' behaviour and about a God who could let such evil prevail. Those doubts, too, would only grow, not diminish, as the Second World War receded further into history.

INTELLECTUALS AND EUROPE'S CRISIS

During almost the whole of the first half of the twentieth century Europe's intellectuals – its leading thinkers and writers in a variety of disciplines – were preoccupied with a society in crisis. The calamity of the First World War greatly intensified the sense of an irrational world, a notion already present in social thought since the 1890s. Society, it seemed, had descended into madness. Civilization was revealed as utterly fragile, to many morbid and diseased, on the knife-edge of further disaster. This feeling even helped to promote the cultural vibrancy of the 1920s. And for a brief few years during that decade it did appear that disaster might be avoided. But with the Depression, an unprecedentedly severe crisis of capitalism, ushering in the widening appeal of fascism, the perception among intellectuals of a cataclysmic crisis of civilization sharpened markedly.

The liberal bourgeois values that had produced this deformed civilization lay open to attack on all sides. Already in the 1920s intellectuals were coming to realize that lofty detachment in an ivory tower was no longer an option. Hitler's triumph in Germany confirmed it. The burning of the books in May 1933 of writers deemed unacceptable to Germany's new masters, forcing the emigration of many of the most outstanding figures in the German literary and artistic world, the majority of them Jewish, was a shock of the first order.

The sense of civilization in crisis was pervasive. Liberal democracy had ever fewer adherents among intellectuals. Most doubted that the fundamental change needed to resolve the crisis could come from a system that in their eyes had produced it. The immense disillusionment with bourgeois society and loss of faith in the political system that represented it polarized intellectual reaction. Most common was a move to the Left, towards some variant of Marxism. A minority, however, looked to the fascist Right. Common to both types of reaction, though in very different ways, was the feeling that the old must be swept away and replaced by a new society based on utopian ideals of social renewal.

Intellectuals seldom turned towards the social democratic Left, whose relative moderation appeared to be out of tune with the extremes that were confronting each other, and to have no real answer to the gravity of the crisis. (Britain, largely untouched by the political extremes that were besetting most of the European continent, and Scandinavia, where a consensus had emerged around social democratic reforms, remained relatively aloof from the general trend.) Many looked instead to communism for salvation, and frequently saw the Soviet Union as the one ray of light in the gathering darkness. Amid the deep gloom about the present, the promise of a communist world revolution offered great hope for the future. The Marxist tenets of classless equality, internationalism and abolition of the chains of capitalism were enormously appealing to intellectual idealists. Marxist political theorists – among them Antonio Gramsci (whose major writings were composed during his long imprisonment in Fascist Italy), the German August Thalheimer, the exiled Leon Trotsky, the Austrian Otto Bauer and the Hungarian Georg Lukacs – produced sophisticated analyses of the crisis of capitalism, outside the straitjacket of Stalinist orthodoxy.

Outside their ranks, however, intellectuals between the wars were generally motivated less by a close reading of Marxist theoretical writing than by an emotional commitment to Marxism (though not always to the political form the doctrine had taken in the Soviet Union) as the framework for a new social order based on freedom, justice and equality. Among many others were Henri Barbusse, Romain Rolland, André Gide and André Malraux from France; Bertold Brecht and Anna Seghers from Germany; Aleksander Wat from Poland; Manes Sperber, the French-domiciled exile from Poland; the Hungarian Arthur Koestler; and John Strachey, Stephen Spender, W. H. Auden and George Orwell from Britain.

Most important of all was anti-fascism: communism represented the complete rejection of the racism, hyper-nationalism and militarism of Nazism's blatantly brutal creed. Intellectuals were overwhelmingly repelled by Nazism's outright offensive against progressive values and cultural freedom. But what appalled them to the core was its assault on the very essence of humanistic beliefs. Its open advocacy of violence against those it saw as political and racial enemies, most obviously demonstrated in its merciless treatment of Jews, made it axiomatic for many intellectuals to make the only choice they felt was open to them: to support Soviet-backed communism, the most fervently committed force of anti-fascism.

As Eric Hobsbawm, long after the Second World War a world-famous historian and prominent intellectual of the Left, explained, the choice he made while still a teenager in Berlin, witnessing the death throes of the Weimar Republic, formed the basis of his lifelong commitment to communism, and to the Soviet Union. It was a commitment that survived in his case not only revelations about Stalinist crimes but also the invasions of Hungary in 1956 and Czechoslovakia in 1968 that would drive away many intellectuals. 'For someone like myself there was really only one choice,' Hobsbawm recalled. 'What was there left but the Communists, especially for a boy who arrived in Germany already emotionally drawn to the Left?'

Illusions about Soviet Communism held many intellectuals in thrall long after knowledge of the horrors of Stalinism became irrefutable. Some were simply uncritically blinded by Soviet propaganda about the glorious new society in the process of creation. Two of the leading lights of the British Labour Party, Sidney and Beatrice Webb, published an embarrassing paean of praise to Stalinism in 1935 entitled *Soviet Russia: A New Civilization?* They were so certain of their judgement that when the book was reprinted two years later, at the height of the purges, the question mark was left out of the title. Others, like the great German playwright Bertold Brecht, simply closed their eyes permanently to the inhumane reality of communist dictatorship while holding fast to the humane vision of the utopian communist society. Intellectuals were often simply in denial about the Soviet Union. They could not let the dream die. They were often psychologically incapable of abandoning their faith in communism as the one hope of mankind's ability to create a better world, even when there was plain evidence that Stalinism defied all parody of that belief.

Others held the enormity of the Stalinist bloodletting to be a regrettable side effect in the building of the utopia. If some innocents had to suffer as 'collateral damage', most of those killed, it was claimed, had been genuine enemies of the revolution. The extremity of the violence simply reflected the power of the revolution's internal enemies; it was an unfortunate necessity.

An alternative apologia was the frequently expressed conviction that Stalin marked not the continuation of the revolution, but its negation, a complete distortion of its ideals, a deviation from the 'true' path of Lenin, the founding father of the Soviet Union. The Polish poet Antoni Słonimski, for instance, consistently refused to blame Marxism or the revolution for the oppression of the Stalinist years. His compatriot Aleksander Wat, an avant-garde poet and editor of a Marxist newspaper who suffered grievously at the hands of the Soviet regime during the Second World War, later explained that he 'regarded Stalin as terrible, someone doing horrible things', but he would not criticize the Soviet Union, 'the homeland of the proletariat'.

The English philosopher Bertrand Russell was one of the few to visit Russia (which he did as early as 1920) full of enthusiasm for the revolution, only to come away repelled by the use of terror and the ruthless elimination of political opponents. He was well aware, however, that to say anything against Bolshevism at that time prompted accusations of supporting the reactionaries. The distinguished French writer André Gide was another who had sympathized with the aims of the revolution, only to change his mind after visiting the Soviet Union in the mid-1930s. The publication of his criticism of communism in 1936 brought him much personal abuse and the loss of former friends on the Left. Manes Sperber, a Polish-Jewish writer living in exile and working in Paris – a destination for numerous Jewish emigrés – once Hitler's takeover of power had forced him out of Germany, had growing doubts about Soviet Communism as early as 1931, following a visit to Moscow. But he 'shrank from knowledge that would cause me both political and emotional difficulties' and remained a party member, motivated primarily by the fight against fascism, until the absurdities of the Stalinist show trials forced him to make his exit in 1937.

Arthur Koestler, also Jewish, a Budapest-born prolific author and journalist, joined the German Communist Party in 1931 but began to be disillusioned with Soviet reality after he had witnessed forced collectivization and famine in Ukraine. The break did not, however, come abruptly or quickly. The Spanish Civil War shaped it. Like numerous other intellectuals on the Left, he had gone to Spain to fight fascism. But seeing communist policy there dictated solely by the interest of the Soviet Union and hearing of obviously faked charges in the show trials against loyal communists, he inwardly abandoned Stalinism while languishing in one of Franco's jails (for a while under a death sentence). Even then, for the sake of upholding anti-fascist unity he kept silent about it for months until he finally broke with communism in 1938. His brilliant novel, *Darkness at Noon* (1940), was a bleak reconstruction of the psychological pressure inflicted on those accused of any perceived deviation from orthodoxy in order to produce the absurd 'confessions' of former Soviet stalwarts in the Stalinist show trials. Koestler was directly confronting the crucial dilemma that faced many left-wing intellectuals in the 1930s: how to stay loyal to the only force capable of withstanding and defeating the menace of fascism while recognizing that the Soviet Union had become a grotesque caricature of the deeply held ideals that had motivated them.

For a sizeable minority among intellectuals, the ideals of the Left – let alone the levels of violence that had accompanied the Russian Revolution, the subsequent civil war and the Stalinist dictatorship – were anathema. These looked to the Right for salvation from Europe's crisis. Some became direct advocates of fascism. What they had in common was belief in the need for spiritual renewal to overcome the descent into barbarism and nihilism of degenerate mankind. Fascism in the 1920s and 1930s – its full expression of inhumanity in the genocidal horror of the Second World War still lay in the future – offered them an alternative utopia, one that blended a largely mythical elevation of past cultural values with a vision of a modern homogeneous and united nation that incorporated those values.

Fascism's appeal was not as such atavistic. The hopes, for instance, of Filippo Marinetti and the Futurists, who glorified the revolutionary violence of the modern machine age and lauded Mussolini, lay not in a resort to the past, but in the vision of a utopian modern society. An expressionist poet like Gottfried Benn could be drawn to Nazism as a revolutionary force that would create a new, modern aesthetics – though he was rapidly to become disillusioned. The influential modernist poet and critic Ezra Pound was born in the USA but based in London before the First World War. Disgusted by what he saw as the responsibility of international capitalism for the war and despising liberal democracy, he moved to Paris, then to Italy, where he lauded Mussolini and saw Italian Fascism as the harbinger of a new civilization. In contrast to Benn and others, Pound never became disillusioned. At any rate, he never recanted his belief in fascism.

Faith in the 'new man', in the renewal of 'true' culture and national rebirth, often resulted in mystical expression that defied intellectual rigour. For the French political writer and novelist, Pierre Drieu la Rochelle, obsessed as he was with national and cultural decadence, fascism (and the Nazi occupation of France) amounted to 'the great revolution of the twentieth century' – a 'revolution of the soul'. Another pro-fascist French writer, Robert Brasillach, saw fascism as 'the very poetry of the twentieth century', the spirit of 'national comradeship'.

The belief in spiritual renewal through national rebirth accounts in good measure for fascism's appeal to intellectuals. As many as 250 Italian intellectuals signed the Manifesto of Fascist Intellectuals in 1925, praising Fascism as 'the faith of all Italians who disdained the past and longed for renewal'. The Manifesto had been composed by Giovanni Gentile, a distinguished professor of philosophy at the University of Rome. Gentile looked to Italian Fascism to create an ethical state that would supersede the moral will of the individual and overcome the decadence of bourgeois liberalism. He spoke in the mid-1920s of 'the soul of the new Italy which slowly but surely will prevail over the old'. He was even ready to boast of Fascist barbarity 'as the expression of the healthy energies which shatter false and baleful idols, and restore the health of the nation within the power of a State conscious of its sovereign rights which are its duties'.

More remarkable still was the commitment to the Nazi Movement of Germany's leading philosopher, Martin Heidegger. The philosophy of this highly complex and sophisticated thinker, whose international renown had been established through his *Sein und Zeit* (*Being and Time*), published in 1927, predisposed him towards ideals that he saw represented by the Nazi Movement. Crucial was the belief in the 'spiritual decay' of his age, in the erosion of what Heidegger called 'authentic being', and his accompanying belief in the special destiny of the German people to bring about cultural renewal. Despite his brilliant mind, much of this came close to romantic mysticism. He saw Germany as centrally located between 'the great pincer-grip formed by Russia on the one hand and America on the other', which together produced 'the same desolate frenzy of unbounded technology and unlimited organization of the average human being'. Europe's 'road to annihilation', he wrote in 1935, could only be blocked by 'the unfolding of new historically spiritual forces from the centre'. By this time Heidegger had long since committed himself to Hitler's Nazi Movement, joining the party on 1 May 1933. Three weeks later he had delivered an encomium of praise to the new regime in his address as the newly appointed Rector of Freiburg University, had glorified Hitler (speaking of him as 'the German reality, present and future, and its law'), and had brought about the dismissal from the university of 'non-Aryan' colleagues (including his former teacher and mentor, Edmund Husserl).

Belief in the need for cultural or 'spiritual' revolution went hand in hand with a fundamental rejection of liberal democracy. Both tendencies were particularly strong in Germany, though they were far from confined to that country. The German cultural historian Arthur Moeller van den Bruck blamed 'the whole political misery of Germany' on political parties. His book *Das Dritte Reich* (*The Third Reich*), published in 1923, offered a chiliastic vision of German perfection that had to be striven after even though it could never be fulfilled. Bruck did not live to see his slogan adopted by the Nazi state and, like other German 'neo-conservative' radicals who advocated a 'conservative revolution', he might well have been disillusioned by experience of the reality of Hitler's regime. Another neo-conservative, Edgar Jung, who had foreseen the construction of an organic German nation as the way to national resurgence and spiritual renewal, swiftly became disenchanted with the reality of Nazi rule, leading to his murder by Hitler's henchmen during the infamous 'Night of the Long Knives' in June 1934.

The German theorist of constitutional law, Carl Schmitt, proved more easily capable of adjusting to the realities of the new order in Germany. Schmitt, who had already gained prominence during the 1920s, rejected parliamentary institutions as the true expression of democracy. He argued for a strong sovereign state and a leader who represented the unity of the rulers and the ruled and was capable of exercizing decisive power, if need be freed from any legal restraints, in order to serve the public interest. Law, in this sense, did not bind rulers and ruled. Rather, it derived from the 'decisionism' of the sovereign power whose responsibility it was to preserve order. Schmitt, who joined the Nazi Party in May 1933, later helped to legitimate the notion of the 'Leader State'. After Hitler had ordered the murder of his stormtrooper leadership in the 'Night of the Long Knives', it was no aberration that Schmitt published an article entitled 'The Führer Protects the Law'.

The complexity and variety of intellectual life in interwar Europe cannot, of course, simply be straitjacketed into the polarized opposites of Left and Right, of communism and fascism. Some intellectual trends were, in fact, as good as completely detached from politics. Logical Positivism, the branch of philosophy particularly associated with Ludwig Wittgenstein which argued that only propositions that could be empirically verified had any meaning at all, provides an example. Nor was economic and political thought inevitably drawn to the extremes. After all, among the most important intellectuals of the era was a British liberal, John Maynard Keynes, who loathed both communism and fascism. As Europe looked increasingly to models of society based on either Marxist state socialism or fascist authoritarianism, Keynes gave capitalist liberal democracy a lifeline by offering a way to a reformed capitalism in a reformed democracy. The most brilliant economist of his day, Keynes's work would make an indispensable contribution to the shaping of economic policy after the Second World War. His *General Theory of Employment, Interest and Money*, published in 1936, rejected classical economics orthodoxy, which looked to sound finance, balanced budgets and to the market to create its own equilibrium. Instead Keynes provided the theoretical basis for government intervention through increased state expenditure to stimulate the market and create full employment, and thus to provide the demand that would underpin economic growth. But Keynes was driven also by the sense of comprehensive crisis, even if his upper-class English background and the relative solidity of British political structures meant that he sought solutions through economic policy within the framework of liberal democracy.

Probably only in Britain, where the upper class continued to enjoy not just social status but also almost unique levels of political stability, was the sort of bizarre judgement articulated by the novelist

Evelyn Waugh possible. Waugh, a social snob, political reactionary and ardent convert to Tridentine Catholicism, who was entranced by the English aristocracy and contemptuous of the rest of society, was dismissive of politics altogether, absurdly stating that chances of happiness were 'not much affected by the political and economic conditions' in which people lived, and that no form of government was better than any other.

Such eccentric views were remote from the preoccupation with crisis of most European intellectuals. The later 1930s brought mounting despair for those on the Left. Many who went to Spain to join the fight against fascism returned disillusioned. Then came the profound dismay at the betrayal of Czechoslovakia in 1938. Franco's final victory the following year, and the Hitler-Stalin Pact – establishing friendship between the regime that they saw as the epitome of political evil and the country which so many had admired – were further extremely bitter pills to swallow. Meanwhile, the pluralism and openness on which intellectual life depends had been crushed in Germany, Italy, the Soviet Union and much of the rest of Europe. Soon afterwards, 'normal' intellectual life in Europe practically went into hibernation for the six long years of the war.

Many of the most powerful anti-fascist intellectual voices were now those of German exiles. Among them were members of the influential Frankfurt School (relocated to New York) of eminent Marxist (though not Leninist) philosophers and social scientists led by Max Horkheimer and Theodor Adorno, and writers of different political persuasion. These included Thomas Mann, his brother Heinrich, Alfred Döblin, Erich Maria Remarque, Lion Feuchtwanger and Anna Seghers. As Hitler's empire engulfed nearly all the European continent, Stefan Zweig, exiled in Brazil, despaired of Europe, its culture and the future of mankind itself. In February 1942 he and his wife took an overdose of sleeping tablets, held hands, and waited for death to come.

As vitality started to return to Europe's intellectual life after 1945, both pessimism and optimism about the future were evident. The very depths to which civilization had sunk evoked – especially within the Christian revival that was much influenced by the theology of Karl Barth – a sense of hope for the future if society could return to the values and beliefs of Christianity. There was also renewed hope, though it really gathered pace only in the 1950s, in liberal democracy, which had eventually triumphed over the Nazi menace. Raymond Aron, the distinguished French political philosopher (and ardent anti-Marxist), thought that 'we can close the age of hyperbolic wars without again falling beneath the yoke'. The lessons of the two wars had been learned. 'The unleashing of violence settles nothing.' The West's 'mission of liberty', he thought, had good chances of success.

For yet others, optimism rested precisely in the opposite direction, in their renewed hopes for the ultimate victory of communism. The Soviet Union had been victorious over Nazism. Communists had played a disproportionate role in resistance movements that had courageously fought Nazi occupation. However, in western Europe belief in the Soviet Union was dwindling. As the wartime alliance with the USSR dissolved into the early Cold War, as eastern Europe fell under the Soviet yoke, and as the horrors of Stalinism became more widely recognized, hope in the Soviet model of communism gave way to a new climate of hostility.

Probably no literary works were more important in the immediate post-war era in shaping the stance towards the Soviet Union in the emerging Cold War than the two dystopian novels of George Orwell, *Animal Farm* and *1984*. Orwell had been profoundly alienated by what he had seen in Spain during the civil war of Stalinist intolerance of any deviation from the rigid party line. His anti-communism had been intensified by the Hitler-Stalin Pact of 1939. And when Stalin became Britain's ally after the German invasion in 1941, Orwell was appalled that 'this disgusting murderer is temporarily on our side, and so the purges, etc., are suddenly forgotten'. Because of the wartime alliance with the USSR, publishers rejected his bitter satire of the emergence of Stalin's dictatorship, *Animal Farm*, on its completion in 1944. It finally appeared, to great acclaim, the following year, after the war in Europe had ended, both influencing and reflecting the new atmosphere of the Cold War. Even more influential was Orwell's frightening futuristic vision of what such a dictatorship would mean for individual freedom and political tolerance in his novel *1984* – the title was an inversion of the date of completion, 1948 – which was published in 1949 at a time when eastern Europe had fallen under the grip of Soviet domination.

A striking transition in the post-war intellectual climate was the new way in which the emerging criticism of Soviet Communism was linked to structural analysis of Nazism. The two systems were seen as separate manifestations of essentially the same phenomenon, and the evils of the dead Nazi regime were transposed to the perceived live threat from the Soviet Union. The concept of totalitarianism, though in existence since the 1920s, was now deployed in changed and devastating fashion to bracket together the gross inhumanity of both regimes. By the mid-1950s, in the climate of the Cold War, the publications of the American political scientist (of German origin), Carl Joachim Friedrich, would become central to this shift in usage.

But already before then the crucial work – highly influential throughout the western world – was that of Hannah Arendt, a German-Jewish exile to the USA, ironically a former lover of Hitler's philosopher-king, Martin Heidegger, meanwhile a distinguished political theorist herself. By 1949 she was completing her outstanding analysis, *The Origins of Totalitarianism*, which appeared two years later. The book was actually in the main an explanation of the rise to power of Nazism and focused in its first two sections on antisemitism and imperialism, themes with little relevance to the nature of Soviet power. The damning comparison with the Soviet Union came in the third part, 'Totalitarianism', much of which appeared only in a later, much revised edition. This comparative section painted the bleakest picture of a 'radical evil', an entirely new political phenomenon whose essence is 'total terror', which destroys all basis of law, 'breaks down all standards that we know', and produces a system resting on 'factories of annihilation' in which 'all men have become equally superfluous'.

It was a searing assessment of the collapse of civilization. In the eyes of many intellectuals, the path that Europe had taken since the Enlightenment of the eighteenth century, towards a civilized society based on principles of rationality and progress, lay in ruins. The very foundations of modern society itself had been undermined. The era of the Enlightenment, Horkheimer and Adorno had already concluded in 1944, had perversely culminated in the 'self-destruction of reason'.

But the critique of Horkheimer and Adorno was not confined to Nazism and Stalinism. It extended to capitalist modern mass culture.

And soon this 'culture industry', as they called it, would come to envelop the whole of western Europe.

'ON WITH THE SHOW': THE BUSINESS OF POPULAR ENTERTAINMENT

Few among Europe's mainly poorly educated masses were concerned with the tortured attempts of intellectuals to understand the crisis they were living through. And religion was losing its grip, slowly but surely. The more literate and educated the population, the higher the level of urbanization, the more advanced the industrial economy, the more the Catholic and Protestant Churches had to struggle to hold on to people's adherence. They had to compete not just with philosophies that rejected Christianity and offered alternative 'secular religions', but with the myriad everyday distractions of modern life in towns and cities (though less so in the countryside). The churches might be emptying; but bars, football grounds, dance halls and cinemas were bursting at the seams. Amid the hecatombs of the two wars, separated by the misery of the Depression, people still looked for what made life worth living. They wanted fun. However humdrum most people's lives were, they were shaped not only by economics or the moral strictures of the Churches, but by what made their existence more enjoyable – flashes of colour in the grey, diversions from the dreariness, relief from the unpalatable.

What people overwhelmingly wanted was entertainment, not priestly sermons, intellectual ruminations or the edification of 'high culture'. The spread of mass entertainment had already made enormous headway during the 1920s. But it was not yet the big business it was soon to become. Technological improvements were chiefly behind its stratospheric take-off during the following decade, even amid the deep pall of economic gloom. Where entertainment had once been dependent on live performance, which could reach at best only a few hundred people on each occasion, the mass production of affordable radios and gramophones (often combined in the 'radiogram') meant that millions at precisely the same moment, across an entire country and from the privacy of their own front rooms, could listen to their favourite entertainers.

Most of the impulses and innovations came from the United States. America represented all that was new, vibrant and exciting for millions – especially young people in western Europe. Popular music and film were the most dynamic forces. Britain, sharing the same language and with strong cultural ties to the USA, was more open than anywhere else to American influence (though barriers were erected in the 1930s to prevent British musicians being put out of work by imported American talent). Young people rushed to embrace it. The establishment was less enthusiastic. The founding Director General of the BBC, the austere and puritanical Sir John Reith, tried to stop what he saw as the cultural pollution of British radio through American influence. But his Canute-like efforts were doomed to failure. A burgeoning consumerism meant an insatiable demand for what the new cultural media had to offer – a demand avidly promoted by the rapidly growing entertainment business, and the armies of those who made money from it – show-business entrepreneurs, publishers of songs, artists' agents, record producers and many others.

The unstoppable advance of popular music went hand in hand with that of radio, which made overnight stars of its leading performers. The phonograph had been invented by Thomas Edison, along with the microphone, as long ago as the 1870s. But even in the 1920s sound recording remained fairly primitive. Hardly any of the popular songs of that era, or preceding decades, lasted to be heard by succeeding generations. That was soon to change. A decade or so later, microphones and recording techniques had improved massively. With better amplification, singers no longer needed powerful voices. They could 'hug' the microphone instead of having to project their voice into it from some distance and produced a far better sound than only a few years earlier. A new breed of 'crooners', who could ooze out smaltzy lyrics in more 'intimate' fashion, emerged to gain huge popularity. Bing Crosby was the first of the crooning 'superstars' whose massive popularity quickly crossed the Atlantic from the USA in the 1930s. Frank Sinatra did the same a few years later. Their records sold not in thousands, but in millions. Over 50 million records of Crosby's syrupy 'White Christmas', composed by Irving Berlin, have been sold since he first performed it in 1941. Even decades later the song is hard to avoid in the piped music of department stores and supermarkets as Christmas approaches.

European crooners also attained enormous popularity. This was often largely restricted to their own country, but some, like the British crooner Al Bowlly (actually born in Mozambique), whose 'The Very Thought of You' was a big hit, had a level of success in the USA. European female singers, too, became household names in their own countries, and sometimes beyond. Édith Piaf, 'the little sparrow', started out on her road to stardom in the mid-1930s, becoming within a few years France's most popular entertainer (and in later years an international celebrity). In England, Gracie Fields, a Lancashire mill-girl, whose singing and acting had already propelled her to national fame in the 1920s, reached the height of her popularity in the Depression era with a repertoire of comedy and sentimental songs. The war, and radio entertainment for the troops, produced its own female stars. Vera Lynn, already well known through radio and records by the later 1930s as a singer with some of the best-known British dance bands, was soon labelled the 'Forces Sweetheart'. There was hardly a British soldier who did not know her big hit, perfectly attuned to the times, 'We'll Meet Again'. Lale Andersen's 'Lili Marleen', though not liked by Nazi officialdom, became a favourite in the Wehrmacht and, remarkably, crossed the lines to become a hit also with Allied troops in its English version (sung by Marlene Dietrich).

The leading popular singers of the 1930s and 1940s were products of the transformation – and commercialization – of the music itself. The early small 'hot' jazz and blues bands of black musicians whose musical roots lay in African-American slave and country music, were by the later 1920s being supplanted by white-dominated big bands. Each was named after its leader, paraded its 'star' vocalist, and featured a smoother, more orchestrated sound and more sentimental appeal tailored to radio's broader audiences.

The new sound of the big bands had also begun in America, with the success of the Paul Whiteman Orchestra in the 1920s (giving Crosby his first major singing opportunity). There had, it is true, been some major big bands led by black musicians, such as Fletcher

Henderson. But black musicians still faced discrimination in the commercial music market. Some of the top jazz players, such as the great trumpeter Louis Armstrong, who had come to fame with his Hot Five and Hot Seven bands in the 1920s, acclimatized to the changing trend and became stars in the emerging big bands before going on to lead their own. In the 1930s, where his success in his own country, though notable, was still limited through racial prejudice that kept black performers out of the most lucrative contracts, Armstrong's greatest popular acclaim was achieved in Europe. When his band toured Europe in 1932, 'he found the most wildly enthusiastic acceptance that any American performer had ever experienced'. Duke Ellington, the most complex and innovative of all the early 'kings of jazz', experienced much the same when his band opened at the London Palladium in 1933 – 'the applause was so terrifying, it was applause beyond applause', as he put it. Six years later his second European tour reached a rapturous climax in Stockholm in April 1939, with huge celebrations from his Swedish fans for his fortieth birthday.

Even Armstrong and Ellington were losing ground, however, to the new trends of popular music in which 'Swing' became the new vogue. The chief exponent (and beneficiary) of the transition to Swing was Benny Goodman, whose father had fled to America from antisemitic terror in Russia. Goodman, dubbed the 'King of Swing', was a superb clarinettist whose band played an authentic version of jazz, profiting from the arrangements of Fletcher Henderson (who, like a number of other former leading black musicians, fell on hard times during the Depression). But Goodman had many imitators who were less innovatory and less gifted. They mainly converted Swing to popular dance music, which was directed at exploiting the 'dance craze' that crossed much of Europe during the 1930s.

Dance halls, even more than during the 1920s, were the thriving hub of live popular entertainment for young people, though the frantic rhythms of the Charleston gave way to the more sedate foxtrot, quickstep and waltz before American troops brought the jitterbug (or jive) to Europe during the war. The most popular dance-band leaders were major celebrities. Jack Hylton, the leader of Britain's most successful dance band, could command a weekly salary of £10,000, at a time when the pay for a week's grind in a factory was £2 to £3. In

1938 Hylton took his band (several of whose members were Jewish) to Berlin, where it played for a month to hugely enthusiastic dancers in a hall backed by an enormous swastika banner.

Swing music in Nazi Germany, like jazz generally, was, however, decried as 'negro music'. During the war, young people, deliberately aping British clothing styles and mannerisms, even turned their devotion to Swing into a form of youthful protest against the Nazi regime's regimentation, and were duly persecuted for their actions. But Hitler's Germany could not turn its back on the trend entirely, and, in fact, had its own 'official' Swing band, Charlie's Orchestra, which despite the war also had a radio following in Britain. Meanwhile, however 'politically incorrect', young SS officers in Paris continued to frequent jazz clubs. Even Nazism could not prevent the appeal of popular music.

What the Nazi regime could do, however, was to eliminate popular entertainers who did not fit its criteria for racial purity. Among them were the popular Jewish cabaret artist Fritz Grünbaum, who tried to flee from Austria immediately after the Anschluss in 1938 but was turned back at the Czech border. He was sent to Buchenwald then Dachau concentration camps and died in Dachau in 1941. Fritz Löhner-Beda, also Jewish, originally from Bohemia, a well-known lyricist who had worked on light musicals and operettas with Franz Lehár among others, was arrested in Vienna after the Anschluss, sent to Dachau, then Buchenwald, and finally deported in 1942 to Auschwitz. He was beaten to death in the attached industrial complex, Monowitz. And Ralf Erwin, born in Silesia, a Jewish songwriter particularly known for composing the hit song 'Ich küsse Ihre Hand, Madame' ('I kiss your hand, Madame') – made famous by the tenor Richard Tauber – fled Germany at the Nazi takeover in 1933. Erwin was captured during the German occupation of France and died in a French internment camp in 1943. In popular entertainment, as in other avenues of cultural life, the Nazis grotesquely impoverished Germany through their absurd, as well as evil, racial policies.

The heyday of Swing, and of big-band dance-hall music, was meanwhile passing. Dance halls obviously faced difficulties with so many young people away on military service. Bands were often forced to discontinue when their members were called up. Some carried on playing while in uniform. Others could no longer do so. Some were killed in action. Glenn Miller, the renowned leader of the forty-eight-strong American band of the Allied Expeditionary Force, went missing over the English Channel when the plane carrying him disappeared in December 1944, en route to entertain American troops in France. His death symbolically marked the beginning of the end for the big bands. They entered a lengthy period of terminal decline, replaced by smaller bands that were cheaper to run and to employ. However, the commercialization of music was at best interrupted by war, but never broken. It would expand dramatically in the post-war years.

Nowhere was the boom in the entertainment business more evident than in cinema. And in no sphere of entertainment was technological innovation more important than in film. A massive growth in cinema audiences had already taken place in the 1920s to watch silent films. But the breakthrough from silent film to sound movies saw the arrival of cinema's glory days. The first full-length feature film to include sound (actually no more than about ten minutes in an otherwise silent movie), *The Jazz Singer*, a sentimental musical featuring Al Jolson in blackface make-up, had been an instant triumph in the USA in 1927. Within two years most of Hollywood's films used sound. The rapid spread of 'talkies' (and increased production of feature films in colour, though these were expensive to make and still a small proportion of total output) was accompanied by the huge expansion of the film industry and Hollywood's enormous cultural influence.

A small number of vast corporations – MGM, Warner Brothers, Paramount, RKO Pictures and 20th Century Fox – soon effectively divided up production, cinema ownership and control of the market. By the mid-1940s, at their high point, Hollywood studios were turning out around 400 films a year, many of them comedies, musicals, westerns and Walt Disney's cartoons. Much of the vast outpouring quickly crossed the Atlantic. By the mid-1930s Mickey Mouse and Donald Duck were as well known in Europe as in the United States, while Disney's first full-length cartoon film, *Snow White and the Seven Dwarfs*, was a European as well as an American sensation following its release in 1937. Despite restrictions on the import of foreign films and an official aversion to what were viewed as the products of

Jewish-dominated American cultural debasement, even Hitler liked Disney's cartoons. He was delighted when his propaganda minister, Joseph Goebbels, gave him eighteen Mickey Mouse films as a Christmas present in 1937.

The once highly creative German film industry was by that time firmly in the grip of the Nazis. Among the products of the last, faltering years of democracy before Hitler came to power had been the first 'talkie' in German, *Der blaue Engel* (also made in an English-language version, *The Blue Angel*), released in 1930, a film that had catapulted Marlene Dietrich to overnight international stardom. But soon film producers, actors and directors were forced to emigrate, mainly to the USA. Thousands of 'non-Aryans' who remained in Germany were dismissed from their jobs. The creative talent left was now put to work for the regime. The young and glamorous Leni Riefenstahl displayed her artistic gifts as a film director in propaganda films, notably *Triumph des Willens* (*Triumph of the Will*; 1935) and *Olympia* (1938), which glorified Hitler and the regime.

But as Germans flocked to the cinema in unprecedented numbers – around a billion a year – entertainment, not propaganda, was what audiences wanted. Even Goebbels, the Nazis' master propagandist, recognized this. Most of the films produced in Nazi Germany were not – at least not explicitly – propaganda, but light entertainment. Romances and musicals – like *Wunschkonzert* (*Request Concert*; 1941) or *Die große Liebe* (*The Great Love*; 1942) – offered brief escapism from the grim reality of war. A sign of the importance Goebbels attached to escapist entertainment (and to sustaining morale through the medium) was the lavish funding he provided for the production of the colour film, *Münchhausen*, a comedy-fantasia about the adventures of Baron von Münchhausen, which in 1943 delighted and distracted German audiences as they reeled from the disaster at Stalingrad.

In Fascist Italy, too, the film industry suffered badly from regime control and censorship. As in Germany, the import of foreign films was restricted. Most Italian films were laced in some way with Fascist propaganda and glorification of war, though many were light comedies and romance dramas. Little or nothing has stood the test of time. Two legacies for the film industry did, however, endure. In 1937

Mussolini opened Italy's first film studio, endowed with technically advanced production facilities, at Cinecittà (Cine City) outside Rome. Five years earlier the Venice Film Festival had been established in 1932, at which 'Mussolini Cups' were awarded to the best Italian and best foreign film – nearly always German – each year.

Creativity was also almost completely stifled in the Soviet Union in the 1930s as Stalinist controls over all spheres of civilian life tightened immeasurably. Film production became heavily bureaucratized. Largely as a consequence of this and highly intrusive censorship, only half as many films were released each year as had been the case in the previous decade. The import of foreign films was halted more or less completely. And the experimentation of the avant-garde cinema that had been prominent in the 1920s was replaced by the dreary uniformity of 'socialist realism' – though, given the chance, Soviet film audiences were mainly attracted, as elsewhere, by comedies and light musicals (even if still heavily overlain with regime values).

Outside the constraints of authoritarian regimes, film production in Europe had greater chances to flourish. Nowhere, however, could compete with the financial muscle, glamour and ambition of Hollywood's giant corporations. This was a particular difficulty where language posed a barrier to penetration of the English-speaking market. In France, the birth-country of cinema and where film had been a prominent part of the artistic avant-garde during the 1920s, the advent of sound film not only turned the cinema from an intellectual art form into a major medium of mass entertainment, but caused problems in financing what was a heavily national market. The number of feature films produced grew sharply in the early 1930s, but a fragmented industry had trouble in funding production. Three-quarters of the films released in 1934 were foreign, leading to protests at the threat to French artistic production, expressions of disdain for the American 'invasion' of French cinema, and demands for protection. French filmmakers struggled to compete. There was no chance of funding through big private corporations, as in the USA. The state had to step in as it did when a report commissioned under the Popular Front recommended state financing, which was implemented shortly before the fall of the Third Republic and continued under the Vichy regime.

Finance, alongside competition from the USA, was also a problem for the British film industry. Attempts to boost British production and restrict foreign – that is, mainly American – imports simply led to a greater number of poor films. As elsewhere, the output of films was remarkable. In 1936 alone nearly 200 films were released – a high point for the British film industry. Meanwhile, however, production companies were struggling to survive. By 1937 there were only twenty survivors among film-production companies from over 600 that had existed over the previous decade. Even major producers with large budgets, such as the Hungarian emigré Alexander Korda, faced difficulties. Capital concentration was inevitable. By the later 1930s a small number of big organizations, prominent among them the Rank Organization (founded in 1937 by J. Arthur Rank), controlled much of the film production, cinema ownership and distribution business in Britain. Rank soon owned the big cinema chains, the Gaumonts and Odeons, that by now occupied prominent sites in nearly every British town centre.

These 'dream palaces' were often resplendent art deco buildings with lavish interiors, frequently able to seat audiences of over a thousand. The majority of cinemas, however, were less than 'palaces', sometimes in fact downright seedy 'flea-pits'. These were the smaller independents, reliant on the major distributors for their films and only able to show them after they had appeared in the main cinemas. By 1939 Britain had some 5,000 cinemas, most of them thriving as the popularity of the cinema reached new heights. A visit to the cinema was far cheaper than the theatre. The owners of many provincial theatres had, in fact, seen the way the wind was blowing and converted them into more profitable cinemas. Even in the Depression cinema seats had been affordable – and offered a couple of hours of warmth and escapism, out of the cold economic winds. Tickets at reduced prices in the 1930s enabled 80 per cent of the unemployed to visit the cinema regularly. In all, 23 million people went to 'the pictures' each week. Annual cinema ticket sales totalled by then close to a billion.

Cinemas were the new temples of worship, film stars the new deities. European countries produced their own stars, though their appeal for the most part did not cross national boundaries. One British actor who did establish an international reputation was the suave Robert

Donat, who became well known for his roles in *The Ghost Goes West* (1935), Alfred Hitchcock's *The 39 Steps* (also 1935) and *Goodbye, Mr. Chips* (1939). Outside the English-language sphere it was even more difficult for stars to gain an international following. Although a household name in Germany, Hans Albers found little recognition abroad. For that, it was necessary to go to America. Marlene Dietrich and Peter Lorre (of Austrian-Jewish descent) left for the USA and became international stars. Emil Jannings and the Swedish actress Zarah Leander, on the other hand, both turned their back on Hollywood and limited their celebrity largely to German-speaking countries. Given the near hegemonic influence of Hollywood, most international stars were inevitably American. As war descended on Europe, Clark Gable, in the biggest of contemporary Hollywood blockbusters, *Gone With The Wind* (1939), scaled new heights of international popularity, soon to be followed by John Wayne, Humphrey Bogart, Lauren Bacall, Orson Welles and others. The way was open for the continued American dominance of European popular culture – at least in the western half of the continent – once the war was over.

Beyond the continuities and silent transformations in the socio-economic framework, the patterns of belief and institutional position of the Christian Churches, the shifting intellectual currents and the pervasiveness of an increasingly US-dominated consumerist leisure industry, lay the inescapable reality: Europe had nearly torn itself apart in the catastrophic, almost suicidal first half of the century. In a war-ravaged continent the overwhelming question for the future was whether and how out of the ruins a new Europe, capable of overcoming the suicidal tendencies of the old, could begin to take shape.

Ideas of a united Europe were not new, but in the throes of Europe's catastrophe they were resurfacing as a way of transcending the nationalism that had taken the continent close to complete destruction. Already after the First World War, the Austrian aristocrat Richard von Coudenove-Kalergi (son of an Austro-Hungarian diplomat and a Japanese mother) had pleaded for a European customs and currency area stretching from Portugal to Poland to be constructed. He saw the overcoming of mutual hatred between the French and Germans as the essential basis of a new Europe. The French Foreign Minister, Aristide

Briand, had a few years later, in 1929, floated the idea of a federation of European nations, resting upon political and economic cooperation. Briand's fellow countryman, Jean Monnet, later the inspiration of what would emerge as the first moves towards European integration, declared while as part of the Free French government-in-waiting in Algiers in 1943 that there could be no peace in Europe until European states reconstituted themselves as part of a federation. Elsewhere, too, similar ideas were stirring, also in anti-Nazi circles in Germany.

Even in the darkest days of the war those who, with enormous courage, had joined the German resistance against Hitler and later often paid with their lives were contemplating a better Europe, built on cooperation, not conflict, between nations. The theologian Dietrich Bonhoeffer, when he met Bishop George Bell of Chichester in Stockholm in 1942, spoke of the readiness of a German government, once Hitler had been removed, to give active support to an interlocking economy of European nations and the construction of a European army. In elaborating their ideas for a new Europe after the war, members of the 'Kreisau Circle' resistance group were adamant in 1943 that 'the free and peaceful development of national culture can no longer be made consonant with the maintenance of an individual state's absolute sovereignty'. Another memorandum the same year, composed by the conservative Carl Goerdeler, spoke of the creation of a 'European federation' to safeguard Europe against any further war, with a permanent European economic council, removal of customs borders and common political organizations – European ministries of economics and foreign affairs, and European armed forces.

Such thoughts came to nothing – at the time. Those who mooted them in Germany were soon silenced for ever. But the idealism that they voiced, and even some of the concrete suggestions that they made, would, once the wreckage of the continent started to be cleared away, gain currency, their aims seem prescient. A new Europe, on entirely different principles, could then begin to rise from the ashes of the old.

10

Out of the Ashes

On this earth there are pestilences and there are victims – and as far as possible one must refuse to be on the side of the pestilence.

Albert Camus, The Plague *(1947)*

Europe in 1945 was a continent living under the shadow of death and devastation. 'Here is a burial ground. Here is Death' was how Warsaw, unrecognizable in its ruins, looked to the Polish writer Janina Broniewska, returning to the city immediately after its liberation. Arriving back in Germany after more than twelve years of enforced exile, Alfred Döblin, the celebrated author of *Berlin Alexanderplatz,* published in 1929, was shocked at seeing towns 'of which little more than the names exist'.

In continental Europe, railway networks, canals, bridges and roads had been wrecked by bombing, or destroyed by retreating troops. In many areas there was no gas, electricity or water. Food, medicine and, as 1945 drew on and winter approached, fuel for heating were in desperately short supply. Agricultural production had been nearly halved. Malnutrition was widespread. Everywhere there was piercing hunger, accompanied by the diseases it fostered. Housing was an overwhelming problem. Where people had a home at all, it often had to be shared with others, frequently strangers. But homelessness, in the wake of the vast destruction, was on a catastrophic scale. In the western parts of the Soviet Union, ravaged by German occupiers, 25 million people were without shelter. In Germany about 40 per cent of pre-war housing had gone, some 10 million dwellings in all.

Altogether, more than 50 million people were left without homes at the end of the war, desperate for food and shelter as they scratched around in the ruins of towns and cities.

Many more millions were in other ways without homes – 'displaced persons', former forced labourers, refugees, or prisoners of war. The Red Cross worked tirelessly to organize relief. The United Nations Relief and Rehabilitation Administration (UNRRA for short) had been established by the USA in 1943 (two years before the actual founding of the United Nations Organization). Backed by over forty countries, with its headquarters in Washington DC, it provided humanitarian workers who did what they could – and that was a great deal – to provide for and where possible repatriate 6.5 million displaced persons, many of them traumatized by their experiences. Most would eventually, though often after further harrowing travails, find their way back to their families. It was not always to the welcome they might have wished. Married couples had sometimes not seen each other for years and had meanwhile become estranged. Unsurprisingly, divorce rates shot up.

For many there would be no return. They would die far away from home, in displaced persons' camps or in captivity (especially in harsh conditions in the Soviet Union, where over a million prisoners of war died). Some did not want to return home; Russians and Ukrainians were among those rightfully fearful of what awaited them if they went back. Up to 2 million people, including tens of thousands of Cossacks who had fought on the Axis side, were 'repatriated' to the Soviet Union by the western Allies, in accordance with agreements made with Stalin towards the end of the war. Often their fate, where it was not immediate execution, was to be sent to the Gulag, or to distant exile, for many years. Few Jews, their relatives murdered, their communities destroyed, had any home to go back to at all. Still others – some political refugees, others war criminals – would be forced to look for new countries, sometimes to invent new identities.

The scale of physical devastation of the European continent far outstretched that of 1918. And human losses were at least four times higher than the military dead of the First World War. Yet that war had left a legacy of chronic political and economic turmoil, sowing the seeds of renewed conflict. An even worse catastrophe this time eventually led, in contrast, to a remarkable period of unpredicted stability and, certainly in the western half of the continent, unparalleled prosperity. How was that possible?

It certainly was not possible to imagine in the ruins of 1945. Nobody at that time could foresee the extraordinary changes that would come about in Europe within such a short time. Indeed, the immediate years after the war gave little inkling of the transformation to come. These were years of political uncertainty, economic disorder, social misery and further terrible inhumanity. Only by 1949 would the contours of a new Europe – by now a continent divided politically, ideologically and economically – have taken clear shape.

CATHARSIS (OF A SORT)

Before any beginnings of recovery from Europe's self-immolation could be made, there had to be a reckoning with those responsible for the horror of the immediate past. Europe was not just a devastated continent as the war ended. It was a wild continent. Chaos and disorder were widespread. Occupying forces were only gradually able to impose their rule. Local administration had frequently broken down. Conditions were often close to anarchic. Public authority, where it existed at all, was in no position to prevent, even where it did not outrightly encourage, the brutal settling of scores. Revenge offered some form of catharsis, however inadequate, for atrocities suffered, grotesque maltreatment, unbearable pain, and boundless misery that people had been forced to endure. For countless Europeans, the thirst for vengeance outweighed all else, even the joy of liberation, as soon as the war was over.

The violence of the once vanquished against their former tormentors was at first widespread and often unconstrained. Concentration-camp prisoners were sometimes encouraged to seek revenge, or at least not held back by troops of the western Allies shocked at what they had come across at Dachau, Buchenwald, Natzweiler-Struthof, Bergen-Belsen and other places of unimaginable horror. In some cases former prisoners turned on their guards in a murderous frenzy. Bands of displaced persons and former slave labourers looted shops, pounced on any alcohol they could find, and beat or killed German civilians. Within Germany itself, such wild atrocities were relatively quickly brought under control by the occupying forces. Elsewhere, Germans were far more exposed. In eastern Europe the ethnic German communities scattered across a swathe of countries reaped the whirlwind of the hatred their compatriots had sown.

In Yugoslavia the immediate post-war violence – on a scale probably unparalleled anywhere else in Europe – was actually not directed at Germans, who had left the country, fighting their way westwards during April 1945. Instead it was directed towards the hated Croat Ustaše and collaborationist Slovenes. And it was carried out not by rampant, uncontrolled mobs, but by organized bands of the victorious Partisan forces, mainly Serbian communists. Numerous massacres took place. There were mass shootings and horrific savagery. Much of the killing was ethnically driven revenge for earlier atrocities. The most reliable estimates suggest that the victims – civilians as well as collaborationist troops – numbered around 70,000. Relative to the size of the population, that was ten times worse than the scale of the vengeance killings in Italy, twenty times as bad as in France.

In western Europe, even so, there were wild reprisals for what the population had endured. The worst occurred in Italy, where those slaughtered during the final phase of the conflict are estimated to have been around 12,000, most of them former Fascists. For weeks at the end of the war partisans in some northern towns and cities carried out arbitrary executions of Fascist grandees, functionaries, collaborators and informers. Mobs broke into jails in some towns and lynched the Fascists who had been interned there. In France 9,000 or so former prominent supporters of the Vichy regime were killed, mainly around the time of the liberation in August 1944. But in neither Holland nor Belgium did the prophesied 'day of the axes', when the mob would take the law into their own hands, fully materialize; in the two countries taken together there were under 400 victims. Even so, there were brutal acts of revenge as around a hundred collaborators – mainly small fry – were summarily executed following Belgium's liberation in the autumn of 1944, with a second wave of executions in May 1945. Not all were singled out for political crimes. Among those arbitrarily executed were victims of personal enmities or business rivalry.

Women condemned as 'horizontal collaborators' – seen as guilty of sleeping with the enemy – often became scapegoats of the pent-up anger of entire communities in western Europe. In France, Italy, Denmark, Holland and the Channel Islands such women were turned into social outcasts and ritually humiliated in public by having their hair shorn, being stripped naked, and sometimes having their bodies daubed with excrement. In France alone about 20,000 women were subjected to degradation in front of large crowds – overwhelmingly male – from their local population.

Remarkable in retrospect is not that such violence took place, but how short-lived it was, even in one-time Vichy France or in the former German satellite states of Hungary, Slovakia, Romania and Croatia. Apart from Greece (where conditions conducive to civil war had been brewing during the war and would soon give way to a prolonged internecine conflict with great losses), occupying forces or newly installed civilian governments gained a good measure of control astonishingly quickly. The wild violence was increasingly held in check, except where the public authorities themselves continued to encourage retaliatory actions – as they did with the expulsions of ethnic Germans from many parts of formerly occupied central and eastern Europe.

The Allies had given their blessing when leaders of the exiled Polish and Czech governments had stated their intention of expelling all Germans from their countries at the end of the war. Expulsions – euphemistically called population transfers – were far from confined to ethnic Germans. Mass deportations of Poles and Ukrainians as well as Germans followed the border alterations agreed at Yalta and Potsdam – pushing the Soviet (Ukrainian) borders westwards to incorporate parts of former Poland and Polish borders westwards at the expense of former German territory. At least 1.2 million Poles and close to half a million Ukrainians were evicted from their homes, often amid great violence and brutality, and packed off to distant destinations. Another 50,000 Ukrainians left Czechoslovakia, while over 40,000 Czechs and Slovaks went in the opposite direction (many from Carpathian-Ruthenia, between the wars a province of Czechoslovakia but ceded to Ukraine in 1945). About 100,000 Hungarians were expelled from Romania, and nearly as many were deported from Slovakia to the Sudetenland, while 70,000 Slovaks entered Czechoslovakia from Hungary.

Astonishingly, the torment of the Jews who had survived the Nazi onslaught was not yet over. They too would form part of the flotsam and jetsam floating on post-war Europe's tide of inhumanity. About 220,000 Jews still existed in post-war Poland, perhaps a quarter of a million in Hungary. But outbursts of anti-Jewish violence in several Polish, Hungarian and Slovakian towns, the worst of them the pogroms in Kielce in Poland in July 1946 and, a few weeks later, in Miskolc in Hungary, left hundreds of Jews dead and forced many others to leave.

The Kielce violence erupted on 4 July after the father of a boy who had returned home after being missing for two days accused Jews of having kidnapped him. The rumour quickly spread that Jews had killed a Christian boy. Ritual murder allegations – the old calumny yet again revived – apparently found ready belief. The police and military authorities did nothing to dispel the crowds that gathered, baying for blood. In all, forty-one Jews were murdered in the pogrom. Although the worst incident, Kielce was part of a wider pattern of antisemitic violence that took the lives of 351 Jews in Poland. Lethal anti-Jewish prejudice had evidently persisted, despite the war, occupation and the Holocaust. The Nazi assault on Polish Jewry had, in fact, allowed many Poles to benefit from the despoliation of Jewish property. Implicit in the post-war violence was the sense that Jews still posed a threat to a social order which had partly been built on their exclusion and the expropriation of their possessions. Survivors from the death-camps could find on returning to their old homes – in other parts of eastern Europe as well as Poland – a hostile reception from those they had once taken to be friends, who were now far from glad to see those whose houses and possessions they had taken. Around 70,000 Polish Jews sought a new home in Palestine within three months of the riots in Kielce. Others followed in great numbers, from Poland, Hungary, Bulgaria, Romania and Czechoslovakia. They had finally concluded that they had no future in Europe.

For the peoples of eastern Europe, there could be no catharsis as long as Germans lived among them. Ethnic Germans, many in towns and villages where German communities had existed for centuries, were most exposed of all to immense brutality. The Allies had stipulated 'orderly and humane' transfers. The reality was far from that. No one had any interest in trying to protect those seen as responsible for the horror of the previous years. With the German defeat, the understandable hatred that had mounted during the years of war and occupation boiled over into unbounded, and at first uncontrolled, acts of revenge. By the end of July between half and three-quarters of a million Germans – robbed, raped, beaten, deprived of food or medical treatment – had been driven out of the new parts of Poland. Atrocities were commonplace. The Polish authorities did little or nothing to prevent them. Germans were effectively seen as wild beasts or vermin, to be hunted down or killed at will. Even the Soviets were shocked by the ferocity of Polish retribution for the suffering the Germans had inflicted. 'There are more and more frequent cases of unprovoked murders of German inhabitants, unfounded arrests, long prison confinements with purposeful humiliation', according to a Red Army report to Moscow on 30 August 1945.

In Czechoslovakia, Sudeten Germans, whether or not they had been Nazi sympathizers, were regarded as traitors. The Czechoslovak President, Edvard Beneš, spoke on the radio on 12 May 1945 of the need to 'liquidate the German problem definitively', immediately prompting the eviction at a moment's notice of more than 20,000 men, women and children from Brno, some of whom did not survive the forced march to the Austrian border. The Christian Commandment 'to love thy neighbour' did not apply to Germans, declared a Catholic priest. They were evil and the time had come to settle accounts with them.

Terrible violence predictably ensued from such expressions of hatred. Germans were driven from their homes and their property was plundered. They were brutally maltreated in internment camps, where living conditions were extremely harsh. Margarete Schell, born in Prague and once a well-known actress, kept a diary of her experiences in one such camp. She recounted how the men were assaulted with whips during the evening roll call and some of them forced to go around the parade ground on their haunches until they collapsed, before being whipped again. She herself, among other abuse and humiliation, suffered a thrashing by the camp commandant for sending out a letter without permission.

Outside the camps, Czech militia, communist action groups and other armed bands assaulted, humiliated and killed Germans at will. In one of the worst atrocities, at Usti nad Labem (Aussig) on 31 July 1945, hundreds of Germans were massacred. Many Germans took their own lives – 5,558 in 1946 alone, according to Czech statistics. About 3 million Germans were driven from Czechoslovakia by the autumn of 1947. A minimum of between 19,000 and 30,000 Sudeten Germans were killed. The overall figure is likely to have been much higher, however, if one includes the attendant disease, malnutrition and exposure that accompanied the brutal expulsions. After several weeks of wild ejections and atrocities, the deportations, though still brutally carried out, became more closely regulated, since not just the Czech government but also the Allies had an interest in halting the uncontrolled violence.

In all, at least 12 million Germans were deported from central and eastern Europe into the occupied zones of Germany which, in the dire situation after the war, were massively ill-equipped to receive them. The welcome within Germany itself for the German expellees was anything but warm. 'We are starving and greatly suffering. Lord God, send the rabble home. Send them back to Czechoslovakia, Lord God, free us from the rabble', some people prayed in rural Württemberg in 1946–7. In opinion surveys taken in 1949 around 60 per cent of the home population and 96 per cent of expellees described relations as bad. Resident Germans thought the new arrivals were arrogant, backward and unreliable; the incomers thought their hosts self-serving, unfeeling and mean. 'We know we are not wanted here and people don't want to see us', ran one plaintiff appeal to a local mayor in 1948, 'but we, too, you can believe us, would rather be in our homeland and a burden to nobody. We are not refugees. Contrary to all moral law we have been evicted from our houses, driven from our homeland, robbed of all we had, and brought here unwillingly and without being asked, at any rate not of our free will.'

The best estimates indicate that at least half a million Germans lost their lives in one way or another during the brutal expulsions; the fate of a further 1.5 million is unknown. Others, from long-standing German communities in Romania, Hungary and Yugoslavia, formed part of 'living reparations', deported to an unenviable fate in Soviet prison camps.

By 1950 there were far fewer minority populations of any size left in eastern Europe. Ethnic minorities had not altogether been eliminated. The Baltic states and Ukraine had sizeable Russian minorities, though they were not disadvantaged; the Soviet Union was after all dominated by ethnic Russians. And Yugoslavia, to be sure, was left with most of its pre-war patchwork quilt of ethnicities still in existence. But the population in eastern European countries had been left far more ethnically homogeneous than before the war. Old multi-ethnic eastern Europe was largely gone. The drastic expulsions and terrible ethnic cleansing had done their ghastly work.

After the explosion of elemental hatred that gave vent to such extreme and unconstrained violence in the early weeks after the German capitulation, the demands for justice were diverted more into state-controlled channels. This occurred more swiftly where there was some level of trust in the readiness of newly formed governments to bring about root-and-branch reforms, to purge the administration of earlier collaborators, to arrest and put these on trial, and to punish the guilty ones severely. The presence of respected former members of the national resistance in new governments helped to expedite the process. So did quick purges of the police, as occurred in Norway, Denmark and France, which contributed to some measure of restored confidence in the state. In much of Europe, too, the population – worn out by years of fighting, too anxious for a return to whatever could be called 'normality' to want to perpetuate the violence and conflict – was ready to comply with authority. Where trust in public authority had slowly to be re-established, however, as in much of southern and eastern Europe, the decline in unrestrained violence was more protracted. Often caches of arms remained in the hands of militias, vigilantes and former partisans who were reluctant to give them up. Amnesties for revenge killings persuaded some to surrender their weapons. But people had to believe that governments would take tough action against war criminals and collaborators before, gradually, the violence subsided or was suppressed by state authorities.

In countries now under the aegis of the Soviet Union the 'official'

purge of fascists and supporters of collaborationist regimes was drastic but soon became increasingly a fairly arbitrary vehicle for
determining loyalty towards the new rulers. Those seen as the worst
offenders were put on trial and executed, sometimes in public. A huge
crowd (though surely not the 100,000 some claimed) watched as
seven Germans were hanged in Riga in 1946. Obvious former collaborators were usually shot out of hand when the Soviets reoccupied
lost territory, such as the 1,700 executed in Lithuania in July and
August 1944. The most common form of punishment, however, was
deportation to exile in hard-labour camps in inhospitable parts of the
Soviet Union, from where there was usually no return. At least half a
million people are estimated to have been deported from Estonia, Latvia and Lithuania in the period from 1944 to 1949. Between
140,000 and 200,000 were arrested in Hungary and deported to the
Soviet Union, most of them to the Gulag. Large numbers of those
suspected of fascist sympathies or anti-communist activity – usually
seen as synonymous – were imprisoned. In Romania the number of
political prisoners rose to 250,000 by 1948 – as much as 2 per cent of
the entire population. By then the lines between actual collaboration
and actions deemed 'counter-revolutionary' by designated 'class
enemies' had long since become blurred.

In one Hungarian town during the autumn of 1945 Father Szaléz
Kiss, a Franciscan friar, and around sixty young men, many of them
members of a youth group that he ran, were arrested and accused of
belonging to a 'fascist conspiracy' that had carried out murders of
Soviet soldiers. Confessions were extracted by torture. Kiss and three
teenagers were executed; others were sent to jail or deported to the
Soviet Union. The fact that Marxist theory (and communist practice)
held fascism to be the most extreme form of reaction meant, however,
that judicial purging in eastern Europe faced difficulties in carrying
out systematic, targeted purges, since much of the non-communist
population was potentially implicated. Instead, purges became, as in
Romania, Bulgaria or Hungary, arbitrary ways of ensuring political
subservience. A completely innocent individual could, through personal malice, be denounced as a 'fascist' for betraying some minor
manifestation of political nonconformism.

The 'official' purges in western Europe were less draconian than in countries under Communist rule, and less, too, than the population generally wanted. Arch-collaborators – Vidkun Quisling in Norway, Anton Mussert in the Netherlands, Pierre Laval in France – were executed. (At eighty-seven years of age, Marshal Pétain had his sentence commuted to life imprisonment.) Purges were certainly taken seriously, especially immediately after the war. Across western Europe hundreds of thousands of individuals were arrested and faced trials for treason, war crimes or collaboration – 40,000 in Denmark, 93,000 in Norway, 120,000 in the Netherlands, as many as 405,000 in Belgium. But most of those convicted had been guilty of comparatively minor offences and were given light sentences. Many of them were released early or amnestied within a short time.

There were relatively few death sentences, or even very long prison sentences. More than 80 per cent of those arrested in Belgium, for instance, escaped prosecution altogether, 241 were executed, and most of the others convicted received short sentences. In the Netherlands there were 40 executions and 585 lengthy jail sentences out of 44,000 convictions (many for fairly trivial offences). Yet civil servants and the police, deeply involved in labour round-ups, Jewish deportations and reprisals for resistance, got off lightly. The purge in France was, on the other hand, relatively severe. Some 300,000 cases were pursued, resulting in 125,000 prosecutions. Nearly 7,000 death sentences were pronounced, though most *in absentia*. Even so, there were about 1,500 executions and 39,000 (mainly short) prison sentences. Most punishments were overturned by an amnesty in 1947. Only about 1,500 of the worst war criminals were still in prison by 1951.

About half a million Austrians, 14 per cent of the adult population, had been members of the Nazi Party, and Austria had produced some of the worst Nazi war criminals. However, the country was allowed to portray itself as the first victim of German aggression. Austria, it has been aptly deemed, was one of the safest places in Europe for collaborators. Only thirty death sentences for wartime crimes were carried out there. In the neighbouring Czech lands the equivalent figure was 686. Many in the Austrian police and legal profession were purged. Of the 270,000 Nazis employed in Austria in 1945, half were dismissed by mid-1946, though many were soon amnestied and re-employed. Courts meted out 13,600 prison sentences, mostly for short periods. In 1948 an amnesty reintegrated 90 per cent of the minor offenders. Amnesties for the more serious Nazis followed in the mid-1950s. Courts became generally more lenient as the immediacy of the war receded. Everywhere, rebuilding a functioning state took priority over punishment and retaliation for wartime behaviour, other than in the direst cases.

In all countries of occupied Europe there had been enthusiastic collaborators. But they had seldom, if ever, commanded the support of most of the population, and were by this time almost universally hated in their countries. In Germany, however, Hitler had for long enjoyed massive popularity, and his regime widespread support for the militaristic nationalism that had trampled on Europe's peace. Millions of Germans had been members of the Nazi Party and its affiliates. Many had backed the persecution of the Jews and other measures of dire inhumanity at home, while those in the forces of occupation – often with tacit support from people back in Germany – had often been complicit in actions of gross barbarity in occupied Europe. Alfred Döblin's early impressions on returning to his native land were that Germans themselves had 'a strangely distant relationship to the events of their own epoch', unable to comprehend the catastrophe that had befallen them, concentrating on nothing but daily routine. How and whether Germany could ever again play a positive role in Europe were questions that few could answer with confidence in 1945. Purging the country of its former Nazis was an obvious first step in the process of rebuilding Germany as a democracy, as the Allies had stipulated at the Potsdam Conference in the summer of 1945. But it was more easily said than done.

Some leading Nazis had escaped their fate by committing suicide, either as the Third Reich collapsed into ruins or shortly afterwards in Allied captivity. They included Joseph Goebbels, the Propaganda Minister, Martin Bormann, Hitler's right-hand man (whose remains were found decades later, not far from Hitler's Berlin bunker), Robert Ley, the fanatical boss of the Labour Front, and Heinrich Himmler, the feared head of the SS and German police. Some, like Rudolf Höss, the former commandant of Auschwitz, or Arthur Greiser, the cruel overlord of the 'Warthegau' in western Poland, were handed over to the Poles, whom they had so barbarically persecuted, and were executed. Still others, most notoriously Adolf Eichmann, the 'manager' of the 'Final Solution of the Jewish Question', were spirited away through Spain to South America, often – amazingly enough – through help from channels within the Vatican. But the Allies did capture twenty-one leading figures in the Nazi regime. Among them were Hermann Göring, once Hitler's designated successor, Joachim von Ribbentrop, the one-time Foreign Minister, Ernst Kaltenbrunner, Chief of the Security Police, Hans Frank, Governor General in Poland, and Rudolf Hess, deputy head of the Nazi Party until his bizarre flight to Scotland in 1941. Military leaders – Wilhelm Keitel (head of the High Command of the Wehrmacht), Alfred Jodl (Chief of Operations Staff), Erich Raeder (commander-in-chief of the navy until 1943) and Karl Dönitz (who succeeded him as head of the navy, and after Hitler's suicide was briefly Reich President) – were also included among the major war criminals soon to be put on trial.

Putting captured Nazi leaders on trial for their crimes was the straightforward part. This in itself was a legal minefield, however, since there was neither precedent nor established jurisdiction for the International Military Tribunal (with a judiciary and prosecutors from the four occupying powers) that sat at Nuremberg for a year in 1945–6. Churchill had proposed shooting major criminals as soon as they were caught. Stalin preferred them to be tried first and then shot. Popular opinion across Europe favoured summary justice. But American pressure to build a genuine legal case against those arraigned in order to demonstrate their guilt, not least to the German population, rather than simply presume it, carried the day. Twelve of those indicted, including Göring, Ribbentrop, Frank, Bormann (*in absentia*), Keitel and Jodl, were sentenced to death by hanging. (Göring committed suicide before his sentence could be carried out.) Most of the remainder, including Albert Speer who was particularly fortunate to avoid the hangman's rope, were given long jail sentences. The Nazi Party, the SS and the Gestapo were declared criminal organizations. Twelve further trials, carried out only by the Americans, followed at Nuremberg between 1946 and 1949. Leading figures, 185 in all, from government ministries, the military, industry, the medical and legal professions, and from the murderous *Einsatzgruppen* (task forces) of the Security Police, were indicted for complicity in heinous crimes during the war. The trials resulted in twenty-four death sentences, while twenty of the accused were sentenced to life imprisonment and ninety-eight to shorter prison terms.

There were many at the time, and there have been many since, who decried the Nuremberg Trials as 'victors' justice'. They claimed that the trials were little more than a farce since the Soviets had themselves perpetrated immense war crimes while the Allied bombing of Dresden, Hamburg and other cities was also a war crime. Certainly, by western judicial standards the trials were far from perfect. But not putting Nazi war criminals on trial would have been a grotesque omission in the eyes of the civilized world. In Germany itself opinion surveys conducted at the time, in fact, showed huge approval for the fairness of the trials and the verdicts. Big majorities favoured the indictment of whole organizations, such as the SA, SS and Gestapo. Some 70 per cent thought guilt for war crimes extended beyond those in the dock at Nuremberg. Other Nazi Party members and lesser leaders, it was widely felt, should also be charged. But there the problems began. Who were these people, how great was their guilt, how were they to be singled out? How were the occupying powers to distinguish not just between the guilty and the innocent, in their eyes, but between degrees of guilt, when over 8 million Germans – about 10 per cent of the population – had been Nazi Party members and tens of millions more had been members of one or other party affiliation?

The task of denazifying German society, it was soon recognized, was not just daunting; it was completely impracticable. In the three western zones, the Americans were, certainly in the early stages, the most determined to pursue it. The western Allies rapidly saw that it was administratively impossible for the small numbers of often untrained personnel from the occupying forces to cope with the millions of questionnaires that Germans had to fill in about their involvement with Nazi organizations during the Third Reich. The questionnaires were often scarcely worth the paper they were written on; remarkable to relate, not everyone told the truth in their entries. By the end of 1945 internment camps were bulging, thousands of state employees had been dismissed, but thorough denazification of German society was proving impossible. In the American zone alone only 1.6 million questionnaires had been processed while 3.5 million known Nazis still awaited classification – and the Americans were intending to withdraw from Germany in 1947.

The British and French were coping no better. The British had tried and executed some of those responsible for the horrific atrocities at Bergen-Belsen that had so shocked the public when the camp had been liberated by British troops in the spring of 1945. They also dismissed about 200,000 Germans – many from the civil service (including teachers), the police and leading posts in industry, though also people working on food production, on the railways and in the postal service. But the cost of the occupation was exorbitant for a bankrupt Britain. Denazification started to take a distant second place to the urgent need to rebuild Germany. And that had to be done by Germans. Many of these had extremely murky pasts. Nonetheless, the Germans would have to run their country themselves. The French, like the British, were rapidly compelled to turn to pragmatism. Early vengeful purging had to give way to practical needs. Three-quarters of the German teachers in the French zone were dismissed in the first weeks of the occupation. But when the schools reopened in September 1945 they were all re-employed. The French only managed to process in all around half a million questionnaires. And they were surprisingly lenient. Only 18,000 individuals incurred automatic penalties; 'major offenders' numbered 13 in the French zone, compared with 1,654 in the American zone.

In early 1946, acknowledging their failure, the western Allies made the Germans responsible for their own denazification. Hundreds of district tribunals were set up, staffed by Germans under overall Allied control. Questionnaires in a modified form continued. So did various categories of guilt, running from major offenders to those completely exonerated. Nearly every person brought before a tribunal seemed capable of finding someone of seemingly unimpeachable credentials to vouch for the accused's good behaviour during the Nazi era. Not for nothing were the testimonials dubbed 'Persil certificates' – 'washing whiter', as advertisements for the widely used cleansing detergent had it.

The entire denazification process gradually descended into little more than farce. More than 6 million cases were nominally heard; two-thirds were promptly amnestied. Of those who came before the tribunals, at least nine-tenths were judged to have been no more than minor offenders. Most were classed as mere 'fellow travellers' or exonerated altogether. The tribunals, aptly dubbed a 'fellow travellers' factory', had both lost credibility and become widely hated by the population long before they were finally brought to an end in 1951 by laws passed by the West German government that amnestied hundreds of thousands of all but the worst offenders. Meanwhile, most of the civil servants who had earlier been dismissed were reinstated. The failure of denazification reflected not only the growing unpopularity of the procedures, the widespread rejection of presumptions of collective guilt for Nazi crimes, and the pragmatic adjustments to administrative needs in a rapidly changing political situation. It also mirrored the popular feeling about National Socialism, registered in numerous opinion surveys, that it had been a good idea, badly carried out, and was, in any case, preferable to communism.

Denazification in the Soviet zone had followed a different, more draconian, path to that taken by the western Allies. Tens of thousands perished in camps (including former Nazi concentration camps) and prisons run by the Soviet secret police. Many more were dispatched to labour camps in the Soviet Union itself. Over half a million Germans in the eastern zone were dismissed from their posts by the end of 1945. Huge purges of judges and lawyers, public officials, university and school teachers were carried out. More than 40,000 new teachers were, in fact, already in post by the autumn of 1946. Between 1945 and 1950 two-thirds of judges and three-quarters of elementary-school teachers would be replaced. New teachers and bureaucrats were given minimal training, with predictable consequences for quality.

But even in the Soviet zone, practical considerations could not be ignored. Doctors, even with Nazi credentials, were for the most part left in place; they were less easily replaceable than teachers and bureaucrats. Ideology could also be overlooked when it served a purpose to do so. The Americans had spirited away hundreds of Nazi scientists for work on their rocket programmes. The Russians did much the same with former Nazis in the eastern zone. Moreover, the Soviet zone, too, could not simply be run into the ground – though the Soviets were doing their best to promote that end with the drastic dismantling of German industry. Eventually, lesser Nazis were encouraged to prove that they had recognized their errors, that they had been inwardly converted to the teachings of Marxism-Leninism, and that they recognized the way forward to a radically different society driven by the dictates of state socialism. Red was the new brown.

Could the purges have been differently implemented? Neither in eastern nor western Europe is it easy to see how alternative paths could have been taken. In the emerging Soviet bloc the purges were unquestionably ruthless, and a fairly blunt instrument for imposing political compliance. The swift, drastic purges aimed at eradicating 'reaction', 'subversive elements' and 'anti-Soviet tendencies', as well as genuine war criminals and collaborators, delivered their message. The majority of the population was not communist, let alone pro-Soviet, and unlikely to vote for Communists in free elections. But the purges gave plain intent of the ruthlessness of the new rulers. People were browbeaten into submission. Brutal though it was, the radical break with the past worked.

In western Europe the purges satisfied few. For many they were too lenient; for others too harsh. But rebuilding societies on a basis of consensus required integration, not the divisiveness of protracted recrimination and revenge. The understandable thirst for the punishment of those responsible had to be quenched, not left to poison the long-term efforts for social as well as political reconstruction. High passions had to be contained. Natural justice had to be subordinated to politics. Looking to the future had to take precedence over a more thorough cleansing of the past. Collective amnesia was the way forward.

Many with more than dubious pasts were able to live into old age and die in their beds, accorded a leniency they never showed their victims. The West's relative leniency towards former fascist sympathizers and the speed with which they were reintegrated into society played into the hands of Soviet propaganda. But the Soviet Union itself harboured many in the Red Army who had perpetrated grave atrocities, though there they were naturally seen to have acted in a just cause. As the Cold War set in, political considerations east and west determined that the time of purges was over, that a line be drawn under the past in favour of socialist unity in the east, increasingly strident anti-communism in the west.

In the eyes of victims of inhumanity, it was not remotely the case that due punishment had been meted out, that the poison had been fully drained. Nothing could possibly compensate for what they had suffered; no full catharsis was imaginable. Decades later, as an indication of the inevitably incomplete rendering of account, war criminals guilty of heinous crimes would still be pursued, uncovered and brought to trial. Europe, for the remainder of the twentieth century, would never be fully rid of the stench of the grotesque inhumanity of the war years.

POLITICS REAWAKENS: DIVISIONS AND UNCERTAINTIES

New forms of pluralist politics were remarkably quick to reassert themselves after the war. German conquest had broken continuity in all but a few countries. Politics had to take new shape. But the bases of political pluralism were still there. They had for long been suppressed, but could extraordinarily quickly be reactivated. Beneath the surface of prohibition and persecution the parties of the Left, especially, had not only held on to much of their earlier base of support but often extended it, buoyed by their record in resistance. For former liberal and conservative parties the discontinuities were greater. Even here, however, what is striking is how swiftly the former political bases, though behind parties with new names, could be reconstructed.

Nevertheless, the future political landscape had entirely uncertain contours. Fascism had been pulverized, at enormous cost, and a reversion to fascist-style authoritarianism could be ruled out (though worries about a Nazi revival in Germany were not immediately extinguished, while Spain and Portugal remained in a time warp). The prestige of Soviet Communism had, in contrast, risen with its military triumph. It enjoyed much support on a Left that had been revitalized and united in anti-fascism. Many still, or again, looked to Moscow for inspiration and hope. But most on the Left either expressly wanted a pluralist political system or at least accepted that pluralist democracy was for the time being necessary. And beyond the Left lay large sectors of society everywhere, particularly outside the big urban conurbations, that remained anti-socialist, conservative and often strongly under the influence of the Churches. In each country, the precise nature of the political system and the constellation of its popular base only gradually became resolved.

In the immediate aftermath of the war it looked as if the hour of the Left – demoralized, divided and defeated during the Depression, terrorized by fascists and driven into perilous opposition – had finally struck. The Popular Fronts of the 1930s, though short-lived, had gained their unity through common opposition to fascism. In 1945, flush with victory following the crushing of the mortal enemy, anti-fascism was again the cement that bonded the Left together. The communists, in particular, benefited from their record of resolute resistance. The Left – communist and socialist – looked to have the wind in its sails.

Pluralist Politics Reborn in Western Europe

In the first post-war elections in most countries Communist parties more than doubled their strength, compared with their pre-war levels of support. The highest Communist votes in 1945–6 were in France (over 26 per cent), Finland (23.5 per cent), Iceland (19.5 per cent) and Italy (almost 19 per cent). Support of between 10 and 13 per cent was gained in Belgium, Denmark, Luxembourg, the Netherlands, Norway and Sweden, and up to 14 per cent in some German regional elections – national elections in West Germany did not take place before 1949. There was only 5–6 per cent support for the Communists in Austria and Switzerland, however, and a paltry 0.4 per cent in Britain. Support for Socialist parties generally, however, outstripped that for the Communists, reaching over 40 per cent in the first post-war elections in Austria, Sweden, Norway and in some regional elections in West Germany, over 30 per cent in Belgium and Denmark, just below that level in the Netherlands. In France and Italy the total left-wing vote was sizeable – 47 per cent in France and 39 per cent in Italy – but fairly evenly split between Communists and Socialists.

Added to the essentially negative bond of anti-fascism and the deep-seated rejection of conservative establishments that had once consorted with the extreme Right was the desire for sweeping social and economic change of the kind, it was widely felt, that only the Left could bring about. In the Scandinavian countries, where the war had been less destructive (though Norway had lost 20 per cent of its economic infrastructure), the social democratic Left was able to consolidate the basis of power it had built before the conflict and introduce major, lasting changes in social welfare. Denmark's Social Democrats, initially somewhat damaged by their involvement in wartime collaborative government, soon regained the losses they had temporarily suffered at the hands of the Communists. Social democracy was strengthened in Norway, bolstered by its involvement in resistance, and remained strong in Sweden. In tiny Iceland, one of the few European countries to have prospered in the war and which had established its independence from Denmark in 1944, the Social Democrats continued to lag behind the Communist People's Unity Party. But both joined the conservative Independence Party in a coalition which, remarkably, had few fundamental disagreements in modernizing the country and improving living standards through support for the fishing fleet. In Scandinavia the war interrupted but did not break either the political structures or the policies of economic and social reform.

Social democracy also proved to be a major force in Finland, though this outcome did not look obvious in 1945. At that time, it looked more likely that Finland would end up as part of the Soviet bloc. In 1945 the Finnish Communists (calling themselves the 'People's Democrats') were able to contest elections for the first time since 1929. They won 23.5 per cent of votes, coming only marginally behind the Social Democrats' 25 per cent (far down from what they had won before the war). These two parties, together with the Agrarian Party (21 per cent), formed a coalition government whose left-wing programme included nationalization, tax and welfare reforms and extensive state control of the economy, treading a careful line to preserve independence while cultivating good relations with their Soviet neighbours. Communists were given the Ministry of the Interior and four other ministries. A communist, Mauno Pekkala, even became Prime Minister in 1946.

It looked as if greater communist infiltration of power networks, as was happening in the parts of eastern Europe under Soviet control, might also be Finland's fate. But Finnish Communists, themselves not united, faced fierce opposition from the Social Democrats and Agrarians, and lost ground to both in the 1948 elections. Anti-communism had been growing in the meantime, and the Communist takeover in Czechoslovakia in February 1948 concentrated minds. Finnish political leaders played their hand cleverly, not least in negotiations over a military alliance with the Soviet Union only a month later, which resulted in a less constraining agreement, a defensive 'Friendship, Co-operation and Mutual Assistance' treaty. But, most crucially, Stalin was ready, for his own pragmatic reasons – perhaps the negative international reaction to the Czech coup played a part – to leave Finland as an independent neighbour, and not force it into the satellite status of other countries in the Soviet sphere of influence. As it was the Social Democrats, though heavily attacked in Moscow, were able to play a substantial part in shaping Finland's politics and economy for some years after 1948.

The British Labour Party also triumphed at the end of the war. The party stood in essence for a version of social democracy, though its development had from its foundation differed markedly from that of continental social democratic parties. Most importantly, it had never faced any serious challenge from communism. So there was no split, no internecine strife, on the Left in Britain. And of course the Left had not had to face a fascist regime, persecution or Nazi occupation. The wartime National Government had seen conventional party politics suspended. But when they recommenced in 1945 the old structures were still there. The Conservative Party, which had only been out of government for a total of about three of the previous thirty years, was forced into opposition, and to a rethink of its political programme and its internal organization. But it was recognisably the same party, and in Churchill it had a leader of world renown.

Decisive in the election of 1945 were the memories of the Depression that had seared public consciousness in Britain. There could be no return to those dismal years. Demand for major social and economic reform to prevent a recurrence of such misery had unseated Winston Churchill and swept Labour to power in elections in July 1945 with over 60 per cent of parliamentary seats. The new government under Clement Attlee, the entirely uncharismatic but highly effective new Prime Minister, set out to build Jerusalem here and now 'in England's green and pleasant land' (as William Blake's early nineteenth-century poem had expressed it). Attlee was supported by a number of highly experienced and competent ministers. Among the most prominent was Ernest Bevin, who in the interwar years had been the dominant trade union leader in Britain. Bevin was a massive presence as Minister for Labour in the wartime government, and now, in one of Attlee's masterstrokes, he was made Foreign Secretary. Another key figure was his near-namesake Aneurin Bevan. A former miner and powerful orator, Bevan was deeply marked by the deprivation and hardship suffered by Welsh mining communities, and under Attlee he became Health Minister. The ascetic Sir Stafford Cripps, a former left-wing rebel in the party, whose earlier enthusiasm for Stalin had worn off during his wartime stay in Moscow as British ambassador and given way to a new liking for management, efficiency and New Deal-style planning within a mixed economy, was especially influential in directing Britain's post-war economy.

Nothing less than a social and economic revolution through democratic means was the aim of the new Labour government. Coal-mining, the railways, gas and electricity, and the Bank of England were nationalized. Under the Education Act introduced by the wartime coalition government in 1944, wider access to secondary schools became available. Workers' rights were improved. An extensive housing programme was undertaken. Above all, the 'welfare state', a term that has been aptly described as '*the* talisman of a better post-war Britain' and the crowning achievement of the Attlee government, was established. Family allowances, paid directly to mothers, were a universal provision, and a raft of welfare legislation (implementing much of Lord Beveridge's scheme for social security, laid out in 1942) started to reduce the worst of pre-war deprivation. The greatest achievement in most people's eyes, then and in later decades, was the foundation in 1948 of a National Health Service, chiefly the work of the inspirational Aneurin Bevan (and hotly opposed by the medical profession), which provided treatment without the patient having to pay directly (beyond, of course, the contribution through taxation). The result was a substantial improvement in health provision for the poorer sections of society and a reduction in deaths from pneumonia, diphtheria and tuberculosis. These were major and enduring advances.

For those who lived through the immediate post-war years in Britain, however, there was another side to the coin: austerity. Britain was victorious, but poor. It had huge debts to pay off. Its defence costs were still those of a big imperial power. And the much-needed and greatly welcomed social reforms meant higher state expenditure on welfare. For Britain to pay its way, exports had to be increased, imports drastically reduced. The result was a long continuation of wartime constraints on consumer spending.

Welfare reforms eliminated the worst deprivation. Even so, for the great mass of the population daily life was hard, drab and lacking in material comforts. Most staple foodstuffs were still rationed. The war had been fought and won without bread being rationed, but in 1946 bread rations were imposed and lasted for two years. 'I sometimes wonder who did win this war' – the comment of a housewife in northern England in 1946 – probably reflected a widespread sentiment. Many commodities were unavailable. Whenever and wherever supplies of some sort were said to have arrived, queues formed. Women especially had to find time to queue, sometimes for hours, and often without success.*

Food rationing only ended in 1954, long after rationing had been terminated in other parts of western Europe. Only then could children obtain sweets without ration coupons. And only once petrol rationing ended could those with cars find enough petrol to drive them any distance. Tolerance for the austerity, widely present at first, gradually wore thin. By 1950 some of its former voters were ready to desert Labour. The Conservatives were on the verge of regaining power.

Whatever the party-political divisions, however, the welfare reforms introduced by Labour were broadly supported by all parties (in contrast to economic changes, nationalization of industries, and other policies). The Conservatives recognized that there could be no return

---

* My Auntie Gladys joined a long queue in Oldham, hearing that nylon stockings were available. Finally nearing the front, she learnt that there were no nylons after all; people were queuing for tripe. 'Well, I'm not queuing so long for nothing. I'll have some tripe, then,' she said.

to the politics of the 1930s. They accepted the need for change and adapted well to it, thereby introducing a period of remarkable consensus on the essentials of social policy that would last for more than two decades. Labour's reforming momentum sagged after 1948, and its hold on power lasted only a total of five years. But it indelibly changed the country during that time. Britain's path had continued under Labour to diverge from that of continental Europe. The country's pronounced sense of separateness from a Europe that had twice within living memory drawn it into world war, and its identification of interest with the Commonwealth and its wartime ally, the United States of America, would continue to exert a powerful hold on British political culture for years to come.

In most of western Europe the hour of the Left quickly passed. One reason for this was that its own divisions were again soon laid bare. Anti-fascism alone was insufficient to hold the Left together. The old fissures inevitably opened up anew – between, on the one hand, Socialist parties committed to change within a pluralist democratic framework (and ready to work with a reformed and controlled capitalism) and, on the other, Communist parties wedded to Moscow, working for the destruction of capitalism altogether and an exclusive hold on power in the state.

A second reason was the emergence of the most important new political force after the war: Christian Democracy. This revitalized conservatism was wholly supportive of pluralist democracy. It proved able to widen the electoral base of the old confessional parties, integrating previously splintered social and political interests not just negatively, through anti-communism, but positively, through its backing for substantial social reforms. Conservative elites before the war had generally tried to block change and had often obstructed democracy, which they had seen as a threat to their interests. Following the war, a new political elite, untarnished by fascist associations, took a different approach. It saw the need to incorporate social change and to welcome parliamentary democracy, which it sought to bend to its own interests. As a consequence, large swathes of each country where socialism or communism had barely, if at all, penetrated, lay open to the appeal of conservative, but reformist, politics that embraced social change within the framework of Christian principles.

The third, and overriding, reason, underlying both the weakening of communism and growing division of the Left, as well as the emerging strength of Christian Democracy (and other forms of conservatism), was the deepening split between eastern and western Europe that soon hardened into the Cold War. This proved the most important factor of all. The more the unsavoury aspects of extended communist power in eastern Europe became apparent, the easier it was for west European Conservative parties to play upon long-standing antipathies towards the Soviet Union and fears of communism at home.

Political allegiance in much of western Europe in essence split rapidly in three ways, between socialism, communism and Christian Democracy. As antagonism between the western Allies and the Soviet Union deepened, divisions on the Left hardened, support for communism declined and the Christian Democrats gained ground. The Left found itself increasingly unable to shape the political agenda. This, with variations, was the trend in Belgium, Luxembourg, Austria, Italy, France and West Germany. In the Netherlands the Catholic People's Party retained a more narrow confessional basis than the new Christian Democrats in other countries. The distinctive political and cultural 'pillars' that had marked Dutch society before the war – socialist, Catholic and Protestant (with a looser liberal-conservative grouping) – largely reconstituted themselves in only slightly differing form. The political framework in Belgium, too, was a case of modified restoration. The dominant forces were conservative, as the middle class and rural population proved the main beneficiaries of a reformed capitalist economy, while the radical Left lost appeal among the industrial working class. In Austria – under four-power occupation but treated as a liberated country – the Communist Party was a negligible force from the outset, though it was allowed to join a grand coalition government, dominated by the new-style Christian Democratic Austrian People's Party and the Social Democrats. The outright priority was to establish national unity rather than renew pre-war divisions.

Italy's future seemed in 1945 likely to be determined by the revolutionary Left. But, amid continuing grave economic problems, before the end of the year the Christian Democrats, headed by Alcide de Gasperi, a former prominent member of the Catholic *Popolari*, were emerging as the most important new force in Italian politics. Italian

Christian Democracy blended a highly conservative wing with leftist sectors that included Catholic trade unionists. But de Gasperi proved a master of manipulating both wings of the party to retain control. He was helped in the early stages by the willingness of the Communist leader, Palmiro Togliatti, who had spent the war years in Moscow, to take the Communists into government. De Gasperi's government – a seemingly unlikely coalition of Christian Democrats, Communists and Socialists – effectively ended the purges, replaced many of the recently appointed police chiefs and regional Prefects with long-standing experienced officials, took big firms out of the hands of the 'commissars' who had been running them and put them back in private ownership, and began the restoration of public order. The coalition was confirmed in office in elections on 2 June 1946 at the same time that the electorate rejected the badly tarnished monarchy and turned Italy into a republic.

The three-way split in Italian politics was set to continue. Together, the Socialists and Communists formed the largest sector of popular support. But they were divided, in policy objectives as well as in their base of support. Moreover, the Left's support was heavily con-fined to the industrialized regions of northern Italy. The more rural parts of the country mostly backed the Christian Democrats, the clear winners with over a third of the total vote. In May 1947 the incipient Cold War led to tensions within the government that proved insuperable and led to the expulsion of the Communists. In the par-liamentary elections of April 1948, held under the shadow of a 'Red Threat', the combined vote of the Communists and Socialists fell from 40 per cent in 1946 to 31 per cent. Pope Pius XII had told Italians that anyone supporting an anti-Christian party was a traitor. Ameri-can anti-communist propaganda also proved highly effective. The Christian Democrats were able to increase their vote from 35 to 48.5 per cent, and with that attain a majority in the Chamber of Dep-uties. The transformation from the revolutionary violence of the partisans to a governmental majority of conservative Christian Dem-ocracy had been remarkable. The split on the Left meant that the Christian Democrats could manage, despite their own internal divi-sions, to retain control of an unstable political system for years to come.

France was the only country in western Europe where the Communists, with 26 per cent, attained a higher vote than the Socialists (24 per cent) at the first post-war elections. The new political force, however, was the *Mouvement Républicain Populaire* (Popular Republican Movement, or MRP), the French variant of Christian Democracy, which won 25 per cent at the legislative elections on 21 October 1945. Following the election the MRP, together with the Socialists and Communists (the main forces of the Resistance), formed part of a tripartite alliance, a Provisional Government with a mandate to devise a constitution for a Fourth Republic. Charles de Gaulle, who had already formed a Provisional Government at the liberation on 25 August 1944, continued as the head of this government. The MRP could profit from the part played in the Resistance by some of its leaders, such as Georges Bidault. Like other Christian Democratic parties, it managed to combine an appeal to a Left rooted in Catholic social thinking with a more traditional, conservative body of support. The MRP played a part in most governments throughout the Fourth Republic between 1946 and 1958. But unlike Christian Democracy in much of western Europe, within a few years its support withered rather than grew. The influence of the Catholic Church on politics was far smaller in France than, for example, in Italy or West Germany. But the gradual failure of the MRP was largely because, unlike other Christian Democratic parties, it faced a major challenge on the conservative Right – one that materialized in 1947 and was spearheaded by no less a figure than the outstanding French war hero, Charles de Gaulle.

The MRP had in fact been open at first to working together with the Socialists and Communists to bring about far-reaching social reform, and it supported the fostering of good relations with the Soviet Union. Each of the parties favoured greatly widened welfare provision and extensive nationalization – including banks, insurance companies, coal-mines, electricity and gas production, airlines, and the Renault car manufacturers. De Gaulle, despite his ingrained conservatism, accepted the move to state ownership and a planned economy (masterminded by Jean Monnet, an experienced economics expert empowered to oversee the measures needed to modernize the

French economy and restore production). The French 'New Deal' began to take shape, with massive political backing. Trade unions (often dominated by communists), the Communist Party itself, the Socialists and MRP played their part in ensuring high levels of industrial productivity, encouraging farmers to bring about rapid expansion in food supplies to the towns, and introducing better social security, pensions, maternity benefits, and other improvements to the lives of ordinary people. But the changes needed time to take effect. Living standards, undermined by high inflation and shortages of food and many basic commodities, remained low for at least two years following the liberation. Political conflict naturally grew. The impact on the government's popularity was predictable.

The continuing difficulties, mounting political disillusionment, and the return to the usual divisions and conflicts of party-politics in a pluralist system did not sit well with de Gaulle's lofty vision of himself at the pinnacle of a unified France. In January 1946 he suddenly resigned as head of the Provisional Government. He resurfaced in June to argue vehemently for an elected President with executive powers. There were no prizes for guessing who that should be. The electorate disagreed and voted instead – if in lukewarm fashion, with a third of voters not bothering to cast their ballot – for a Fourth Republic in which parliamentary powers outweighed those of the executive. The result was a system that would replicate many of the disadvantages of the pre-war Third Republic. By strengthening the powers of the legislature (elected through proportional representation) to dismiss the government, which invariably represented an uneasy coalition of conflicting political interests, the new constitution ensured continuing political instability.

De Gaulle, contemptuous of the new constitutional arrangements, announced in April 1947 that he intended to form and lead a new political movement, which he called the *Rassemblement du Peuple Français* (Rally of the French People, or RPF). Within a year his party, supposedly standing above conventional party politics and built on a platform of nationalist unity, anti-communism, and strong executive power vested in a President, was making inroads on the political Right. It gained half a million members (mostly from the middle class and peasantry) and up to 35 per cent of the vote in a number of municipal elections in northern France, though the breakthrough at the national level remained elusive.

The tripartite government coalition was, however, creaking. The Socialist Prime Minister, Paul Ramadier, took advantage of a wave of strikes by communist-dominated trade unions in April 1947, and Communist opposition to the government's use of force to uphold French imperialist rule in Madagascar and Indochina, to dismiss Communist ministers. Tripartite government was over. The Communists would not participate in government again for more than three decades. The MRP, the Socialists, Radicals and smaller parties were left to form a series of unstable governments, somewhat pretentiously depicted as a 'Third Force', but held together by little more than their hostility to both Communist and Gaullist opposition. By the early 1950s support for the MRP was crumbling as the French conservative Right failed to overcome its divisions. Weak governments were set to remain the pattern for the remainder of the Fourth Republic.

The western zones of occupied Germany were the pivotal arena of Europe's political reawakening. The reconstruction of the political landscape began remarkably quickly after German capitulation. Already in its foundation message in June 1945 the Christian Democratic Union (CDU) in Berlin appealed to Germans to unite all their efforts in rebuilding the homeland. The Social Democrats (SPD) and even the Communists, if in different ways, also made national unity the centre point of their immediate attempts to garner support for starting the recovery. Both Left and Right saw the need to widen their basis of support, and to overcome the crippling divisions that had poisoned politics during the Weimar Republic and paved the way for Hitler's triumph in 1933. The Nazi Party, on its way to power, had largely destroyed the old 'bourgeois' liberal and conservative parties, except for the Catholic Centre Party, while the Socialists and Communists had continued their disastrous internecine conflict that stretched back to the revolution of 1918 and its aftermath. Twelve long, bitter years of dictatorship and brutal persecution of opponents had then followed. What is striking about the immediate post-war years, however, is not just how quickly pluralistic politics recommenced, but how far the patterns of political support at first mirrored those of the Weimar years, and how far they were still determined not just by social class but by religious allegiance.

The Christian Democrats rapidly built a basis of support on the conservative Right that went far towards overcoming the debilitating divisions of the Weimar era. They saw themselves as a party that stood above class and confession, embodying the spirit of Christian renewal to overcome the criminality of the Nazi past and to combat the 'godless forces of the world' still in existence. They looked to a society that combined democracy with social justice in a fundamentally reformed capitalism, built on Christian principles. Already in 1946–7 the Christian Democrats frequently emerged as the largest party in regional and local elections in Germany's western zones, gaining over 50 per cent in parts of the south, usually more than 30 per cent further north.

The man who would become the party's first leader and the towering figure in German Christian Democracy for almost two decades was Konrad Adenauer, by this time already almost seventy years old. Before Hitler's takeover of power he had been Lord Mayor of Cologne and was subsequently imprisoned on two occasions during the Third Reich. He was strongly rooted in Rhineland Catholicism, fervently anti-communist and in favour of reconciliation with the West. As the Cold War became an inescapable reality from 1947 onwards, Adenauer moved the CDU away from its early leanings towards a substantial reform of capitalism in the direction of a liberal market economy. The party became more well disposed towards big business, promoted especially by its economics guru, Ludwig Erhard, though its programme continued to blunt the effects of the worst inequalities of free-market capitalism by social welfare measures. The move to the Right allowed the CDU to find a measure of common ground with the emerging, smaller Free Democratic Party (FDP), which was built on principles of economic as well as individual freedom, strongly pro-business, and opposed to all notions of nationalization. In the first national elections of 1949 the FDP gained 12 per cent of the vote, the SPD 29 per cent, with the CDU narrowly ahead on 31 per cent. The FDP's 12 per cent proved crucial in enabling the CDU (and its Bavarian sister-party, the more conservative Christian Social Union, heavily Catholic in its values) to provide the mainstay of a coalition government, under Adenauer as Federal Chancellor.

While the conservative Right was discovering new unity, the Left was returning to division. Social Democrats and Communists had joined together in the 'Antifas' – anti-fascist committees – that had sprung up in German industrial cities and big factories in 1945 in the common fight against the dying Nazi regime. But no sooner was the war over than the victorious western Allies disbanded the 'Antifas', seeing them less as constructive components in a new society than as a threat to order and an opening for communism. It was an early indication that the Allies were determined to block any radical alternative to a reversion to pluralistic liberal-conservative democracy. It seems unlikely, in fact, that the 'Antifas' could have provided a lasting basis for political reconstruction. But they were not given any opportunity. That accorded with the mood of the great majority of the German population, who wanted change but had little appetite for revolutionary experiments. The Communist Party was unable to break out of its earlier strongholds in the industrial working class. Even before the Cold War set in and almost completely undermined its support, the average vote for the Communists in the western zones was under 10 per cent, a third of the SPD's average level of support.

The SPD was itself committed to radical social and economic change. Its leader, Kurt Schumacher, whose moral authority derived from ten years in Nazi concentration camps, stood for the early restoration of German national unity, though one built firmly on democratic principles and a new economic order. He advocated the nationalization of major industries and the redistribution of farmland to be expropriated from big estates. But Schumacher was vehemently anti-communist. He blamed the communists as well as the Nazi-supporting middle classes for the disaster of 1933. And he increasingly feared that the Communist Party would open the door to Soviet dominance in Germany. However, his own rhetoric of class struggle predictably failed to win over the large tracts of conservative Germany.

The 1949 election to the Federal Parliament (*Bundestag*) was contested by a wide range of political parties. The political landscape was still taking shape. But its main contours – a threefold division between Christian, Free and Social Democrats – were already becoming clear.

In eastern Europe, including the eastern zone of Germany, the political landscape had taken a fundamentally different shape from the outset, long before the Cold War became set in stone. The western Allies certainly exerted their own controls over the rebuilding of politics in their zones – often favouring conservatives over social democrats, for example – but their level of intervention was in a minor key compared with that of the Soviets in areas of Europe under their domination.

Pluralist Politics Crushed in Eastern Europe

If at first the Soviets had been more uncertain than later seemed the case about the strategic development of the eastern zone of Germany, they increasingly paid only lip-service to pluralistic democracy. There was at first the appearance of pluralism. Liberal and conservative as well as Socialist and Communist parties were established. But the pressure in favour of the Communist Party was overt and relentless. Walter Ulbricht and other Communist leaders, who had spent the Nazi era exiled in Moscow, set out to ensure a firm base of Communist power, rapidly taking over crucial administrative positions. Nationalization of industry, redistribution of expropriated land, and purges of economic, administrative and professional elites proved predictably popular among those who possessed neither property nor wealth. But it became clear in local elections over the winter of 1945–6 that, despite their advantages, the Communists had far less support than the Social Democrats, and that they could not win a democratic majority through the polls.

By February 1946 the Communists were pressing to merge the two parties. Schumacher passionately led the SPD's opposition. Ruth Andreas-Friedrich, a former journalist, for long active in the resistance to Hitler's regime and now a fervent supporter of the SPD, was clear about the danger. 'For nine months,' she confided to her diary on 14 January, 'German Communism has been the recipient of orders from Moscow ... If we put our head in *this* noose, not only are we ourselves lost, Berlin and the whole of east Germany are lost too. Lost for democracy, won for the national-bolshevik claim to world power.' The Left split. 'People who a year ago had helped each other against the terror of the Gestapo, had risked their lives for the life of someone else, attack each other today like the bitterest enemies,' Andreas-Friedrich observed. In March a referendum was held in the western sectors of Berlin, though prohibited in the eastern sector, and over 80 per cent of SPD members rejected the merger. 'Against violence, threats and propaganda, the will to self-determination triumphed,' noted Andreas-Friedrich.

Nevertheless, in April 1946 a forced merger of both major parties of the Left took place in the Soviet zone to create the Socialist Unity Party of Germany (SED). The new party was from the start under Communist dominance, and it was seen as the main vehicle for imposing the Marxist-Leninist version of 'democratic centralism' on the eastern zone. Even now, with all the pressure it could exert, the SED failed to win an absolute majority of the votes in any of the regional elections in October 1946. But by this time the political arteries were hardening. The vestiges of genuine pluralism were gradually but systematically being eliminated. Those who opposed the transformation to a 'people's democracy' were dismissed from their positions and many of them imprisoned. The process of political (and social) separation from the western zones continued, by now irreversibly. By January 1949 the SED was formally proclaimed to be a Marxist-Leninist party, and a German variant of Stalinist dictatorship had been established.

What happened in the eastern zone of Germany ran parallel to the way Soviet domination was established over most of eastern Europe in the immediate post-war years. Soviet power was not the only factor that determined the political constellation; the discrediting of pre-war elites on account of their collaboration with the Nazis, the levels of support for native Communist parties, expectations of benefiting from a redistribution of wealth, and mounting distrust of the western Allies all played a part. But Soviet power was the constant in the equation, the common factor and single most important determinant. And, as in eastern Germany, the pattern was one of intensified pressure to ensure Communist dominance, once it was obvious that democratic pluralism would not yield the necessary support for Communist rule.

Hungary provided the clearest demonstration. A multi-party Provisional Government had won popularity by redistributing to the peasantry land sequestered from estate owners, leading to the mainly peasant Smallholder Party gaining as much as 57 per cent of the vote in elections in November 1945, whereas only 17 per cent of voters supported the Communists. This did not, however, prevent the gradual destruction of the Smallholder Party and other forms of political opposition through the Communists' brutal intimidatory tactics until, by 1949, the Communist Party, with Moscow behind it, had complete power in its hands.

In Poland the Moscow-backed 'Lublin Committee' had already by the end of 1944 been given official Soviet recognition as Poland's Provisional Government, and Communists took control of the police and security apparatus. The National Government, exiled in London since the beginning of the war, though still recognized as Poland's legitimate government by the western Allies, was powerless. But the Allies were keen to resolve the problem of Poland. In late June 1945 a few of the National Government's members, including Stanisław Mikołajczyk, who had served as its Prime Minister, were persuaded by western leaders to join a more broadly constituted Provisional Government of National Unity, with the prospect of elections to follow. With that, already before the Potsdam Conference the following month, the Allies bowed to the fait accompli in Poland in formally withdrawing their recognition of the government-in-exile in London.

At Yalta in February 1945, Stalin had promised democratic elections. But his version of democracy was not that of the western powers. When the elections finally took place in Poland, in January 1947, it was in the context of heavy Soviet repression and intimidation. Over a hundred opponents of the Communists were murdered, tens of thousands imprisoned, and many oppositional candidates disqualified. Officially, the Communist bloc won 80 per cent of the votes. What the true vote might have been in genuinely free elections is impossible to know. The western powers looked on impotently, unable to affect the deepening grip of Soviet control. Poles themselves asked, not unreasonably, what the war had been about. They had thought it had been to preserve Polish independence. A similar pattern of Communist infiltration of the governing apparatus, intimidation, arrest and imprisonment of political opponents, and rigging of elections, backed by Soviet military and security forces, characterized the pattern of the Communist takeover of power in Romania and Bulgaria.

Czechoslovakia was a different matter; and what happened there sent shock waves through the West (though some policy-makers in Washington claimed to have seen it coming). In unquestionably free elections in May 1946 – Soviet as well as American troops had withdrawn beforehand – the Communists won the largest proportion of votes, 38.6 per cent, giving them a degree of democratic legitimacy. Their success was not surprising. There was enormous social distress, huge levels of poverty, widespread homelessness, and vast economic disruption. The years of German occupation had, as elsewhere, also left much recrimination and resentment in their wake. Among the reasons why people turned to the Communists, there was undoubtedly, especially among the educated, much idealism – a fervent belief in communism as 'the eternal ideal of humanity', and a 'national road to socialism' that would subordinate individual interest 'to the good of all society'. This, at any rate, was how Heda Marolius Kovály later put it – a Jewish woman who had suffered grievously in German concentration camps and the wife of a Communist minister in the Czech government (who was to be executed in 1952 on trumped-up charges of 'anti-state conspiracy').

Nevertheless, though the largest party, the Communists still had only minority support (and even less backing in Slovakia than in the Czech lands). The new Prime Minister, Klement Gottwald, a long-standing Stalinist newly returned from wartime exile in Moscow, faced widespread opposition, even if from a range of parties divided among themselves. The popularity of the Communist-dominated government waned in 1947 as economic difficulties mounted, as the issue of relative autonomy for the Slovaks remained unresolved, and as the country was pressurized by Stalin to reject American economic aid, thereby being forced into the emergent Soviet bloc in eastern Europe. The Communists had reluctantly conceded new elections, to be held in May 1948. Their prospects of increasing their vote were poor. But when a number of non-Communist ministers foolishly resigned from the coalition government in February in protest at Communist measures to extend control over the police, it triggered a full-scale political crisis. The Communists organized mass demonstrations of support for their demands. The pressure on all waverers mounted. The Foreign Minister, Jan Masaryk, son of the first President of Czechoslovakia, was found dead on the pavement below his office window – a case of suicide, according to the official version, but most people thought he had been murdered by agents of the regime. Nothing less than a Communist coup was under way. The elections in May were controlled entirely by the Communists, who dominated the new parliament. The hapless President, Edvard Beneš, was compelled to appoint a new government, still under Gottwald as Prime Minister but now completely dominated by Communists.

In June 1948 Gottwald replaced the ailing Beneš as President. Early enthusiasm, where it genuinely existed, soon evaporated. Within months, as Heda Marolius Kovály saw it, 'the Soviet Union had become our model' and the rule of law was precarious. Huge repression of opponents followed as thousands disappeared into prisons and camps. A Soviet-style system was now in place in the only country in central Europe where pluralist democracy had survived before the war until it had been undermined by western appeasement policy and then devoured by Hitler. It was the definitive confirmation that Stalinism was incompatible with the establishment of western-style democracy anywhere in the Soviet sphere of influence.

Only in Yugoslavia did attempts to extend Soviet influence fail. But here quite special circumstances prevailed. Tito's partisans had already controlled most of Yugoslavia by the time the Red Army arrived in autumn 1944. Soviet troops withdrew again by the end of the war, leaving Tito to bask in the glory of being the liberator of Yugoslavia. Moreover, the Yugoslav Communists, led by Tito, had come to power unaided by Moscow – apart from Albania's the only Communist Party in Europe to have done so. Although he had earlier been a loyal agent of the Soviet Union, Tito's stature gave him a secure base of autonomous power that enabled him to defy Stalin's pressure to fall in line with Moscow's demands as the Cold War started to grip. The Soviet dictator's bullying cut no ice with Tito, secure in his Balkan stronghold and enjoying extensive popular support from across a country in which he personally symbolized a new unity that transcended the traditional ethnic divides. Short of invasion, which would have been a risky venture, there was nothing that Stalin could do. In

June 1948 the split between Moscow and Belgrade became official with the expulsion of the Yugoslavian Communist Party from the Cominform, the successor organization to the Comintern. Stalin's enmity was barely constrained. The Soviets and their satellites imposed an economic boycott to try to starve Yugoslavia into submission. It was to no avail. Tito, despite constant heavy vilification from Moscow, continued to steer an independent path.

In the Soviet Union itself people felt that the immense sacrifices could not be in vain. But the universal joy that had greeted the triumph in 1945 soon gave way to enormous disillusionment. Hopes that victory in 'the great patriotic war' would bring a more relaxed political climate were rapidly dispelled. Instead the Stalinist system tightened its hold, the repressive machinery cranked up once more. The leaders of the Soviet Union, Stalin more than any of them, saw great dangers ahead. There had been many Soviet collaborators with the Nazi occupiers; millions of new citizens had to be turned into communist believers; large expanses of newly won territory had to be incorporated; and the threat of capitalist imperialism still loomed large. Moreover, the country had to be rebuilt. Overcoming the colossal material losses meant renewed intensive programmes to produce rapid industrial growth.

Progress was impressive. By 1947 Soviet industry was, it was claimed, again matching pre-war output. The heavy price was a further decline in living standards, already woeful. Big strikes and demonstrations took place in defence factories in the Urals and Siberia in the autumn of 1945. The secret police registered over half a million letters of protest at living conditions. Poor harvests in 1945 and 1946 exacerbated the problems of agricultural production, which lagged far behind pre-war output for years to come. Famine, taking the lives of 2 million people, once more befell Ukraine and other regions of the Soviet Union. About 100 million Soviet citizens suffered from malnutrition. For Stalin and the Soviet leadership, the hardship had to be endured if the Soviet state were to survive, recover and rebuild its defences. All potential for unrest, every conceivable sign of opposition, had to be ruthlessly crushed. A new wave of arrests, purges and show trials, reminiscent of the terror of the 1930s, coursed through the Soviet Union and its satellites in eastern Europe.

Former prisoners of war, suspected dissidents, intellectuals and minority ethnic groups, not least Jews, were particular targets. Before long, Soviet camps and penal colonies once again held as many as 5 million prisoners. Far from creating a new society in the Soviet Union, the war had strengthened the old. The heavy hand of repression could not be even slightly lifted. Stalinism in all its horror continued unabated in the immediate post-war years.

By 1947 ice was forming on the Cold War. The divisions – a largely monolithic Soviet bloc confronted by an increasingly anxious but resolute American-dominated western bloc – were already by that time becoming firmly entrenched. By the following year they were rigidly fixed. Could they have been avoided? Could the revitalization of politics in western Europe, if not in the east, have taken a different course? In both cases it seems highly unlikely. Ultimately, the mutual distrust – fear of communist advance on the one hand, fear of aggressive capitalist imperialism on the other – was too deep to prevent Europe from splitting into two halves.

Stalinist policy in eastern Europe was, to be sure, less uniform and predetermined at the start than it often appears in retrospect. Even so, what was plain from the outset was that no alternative to communist dominance would be permitted. The vagaries of pluralist politics in the western style could not be risked. Once it was plain that Communist parties were not going to win power through genuinely open elections, intimidation, infiltration and pressure to ensure their domination by other means were inevitable. But that could only deepen the separation from the parts of the continent that had not fallen under Soviet influence.

Crucially, Communist parties were nowhere popular enough to come near to winning majority support in free elections in western Europe. And as Communist methods of gaining power in eastern Europe, looked on aghast by most people in western Europe, became easy targets for condemnation by anti-communist political parties and by the western Allies, support for communism in most of western Europe started to recede still further. The division, quickly widening, was unavoidable. It had been there from the beginning in 1945, caused in the first instance by the Soviet need for a protective buffer zone of satellites under Communist rule, and could only widen as the international antagonism between the major powers itself took on a defining form. It was cemented in 1947 when Stalin turned his back on the offer of American aid to rebuild Europe, insisting that eastern Europe went its own way – and under Soviet domination.

In western Europe the scope for radical economic policies became even more limited as the Cold War set in. The fear of communism extending a hold in the west was, not least in the pivotal country of Germany, a significant added ingredient in the backing of the occupying western Allies, especially the Americans, for conservative politics and for a liberalized economy. The chances of a different political course in western Europe to that which was in fact taken were, consequently, negligible from the outset. Europe's political reawakening after 1945 is unthinkable from the international context that shaped it. The search for blame in starting the Cold War is largely pointless. It could not have been avoided. The division of the continent was an ineluctable consequence of the Second World War and the conquest of Europe by the ideologically and politically antagonistic new superpowers, the USA and the Soviet Union.

THE IRON CURTAIN DESCENDS

Winston Churchill is usually credited with the graphic image of an 'iron curtain' dividing Europe, which he voiced in a famous speech at Westminster College in Fulton, Missouri, in March 1946. In fact, Hitler's Propaganda Minister, Joseph Goebbels, had already a year earlier referred publicly and privately to an 'iron curtain' in describing the Soviet occupation of Romania. Hitler and Goebbels had repeatedly, in the last months of the war, forecast the break-up of the Allied coalition of Anglo-American and Soviet forces. What they refused to see was that the aim of destroying Nazi Germany was precisely what held the wartime alliance together. Once that aim was accomplished, the dissolution of an alliance comprising such inherently antagonistic elements was as good as unstoppable. It did not take place immediately in one decisive rupture, but gradually, over a period of three years or so, and in a number of decisive, cumulative stages. But from the summer of 1945 onwards it went only in one direction – towards the division of Europe.

After the First World War the American President, Woodrow Wilson, had joined the leaders of Britain and France in determining the post-war order. Russia, convulsed by revolution and civil war and regarded with mounting horror by the western powers, had played no part. The USA had soon afterwards chosen not to join the League of Nations and withdrew from direct involvement in European affairs. The contrast with 1945 was stark. After the Second World War the once great European powers were too weak, militarily and economically, to shape a new order. France was beset by its own internal problems. Its economy was wracked by severe inflation, flight of capital and low levels of production. Britain's financial plight was only rescued by a sizeable American and Canadian loan in 1946. A sign of Britain's economic weakness was the beginning of its withdrawal from empire. India, the much-vaunted 'jewel in the crown' of the empire, was granted independence in 1947. In another move with huge far-reaching consequences, Britain withdrew from its troublesome Mandate in Palestine, leading to the foundation of the state of Israel in 1948. France, more reluctant to relinquish its overseas possessions, was meanwhile involved in an increasingly bitter colonial war in Indochina with Ho Chi Minh's forces in northern Vietnam, which already in 1945 had claimed to represent an independent 'Democratic Republic of Vietnam'. That, too, would later have momentous consequences. The First World War had preserved, and even extended, the colonial empires of the European great powers. The Second World War inaugurated their end. The age of imperial conquest was over.

The United States and the Soviet Union stepped into the vacuum left in Europe by the demise of the European great powers – Germany destroyed, France and Britain hugely enfeebled. The two remaining world powers were immensely strengthened in different ways by the war. The USA's economic might now massively outstripped that of any other country, and its military-industrial complex was formidable. The USSR had in contrast suffered immense economic losses in bearing the brunt of the continental war for four years, but had built a colossal military machine that gloried in the great victory it had attained and now bestrode practically the whole of eastern Europe. Soviet military strength far surpassed that of the western Allies. Even by 1947, after wartime military strength had been drastically reduced, the Soviet army still had around 2.8 million personnel at combat readiness; American forces in Europe had fallen to under 300,000 within a year of the war ending.

The wartime conferences of the 'Big Three' – Britain was still allowed the vanity of belonging to this exclusive 'club' – had revealed the dominance of the emerging superpowers. So had the foundation, in San Francisco on 24 October 1945, of the United Nations Organization. Foreseen as a more dynamic body than the defunct League of Nations had proved to be, it initially comprised the fifty member-states who had signed the Charter on 26 June (fewer than a third of them European). Five countries – the USA, the Soviet Union, Britain, France and China – formed the permanent members of the Security Council, the crucial body with powers of veto over any decision. But of these, Britain and France were greatly weakened by the war (and faced mounting problems in their colonial empires), while China was crippled after eight years of war with Japan and wracked by the continuing civil war between nationalists and communists. Plainly, the only dominant powers were the USA and USSR.

They demarcated the new Europe in their own image. And each interpreted its post-war role as part of a wider ideological mission. Liberalization and democratization as the outward extension of American political and economic philosophy encountered monopoly communist control of the state and direction of the economy. A clash of such polar opposites could not be long delayed. It would turn into a global, not just European, contest for power. But there was an imbalance. For the USA, Europe, though vitally important, was far from American shores. Communism was a geographically distant, though perceived as a growing, threat. For Stalin, Europe was on his doorstep, and had imperilled his country's existence twice within a generation. The forces of international capitalism were, moreover, undefeated – still a mighty enemy. Stalin's overriding concern was not the export of revolution but the safeguarding of Soviet security. Europe, therefore, would inevitably be the main battleground of the Cold

War. And within Europe, Germany, where the ideological antagonists stood cheek by jowl, would just as inevitably become the epicentre of the conflict.

The prospect of Soviet expansion in Europe was already before the end of the war concerning the British Foreign Office. The Americans were at that time more well disposed towards Stalin. But the spectre of Soviet power extending its grip in Europe and beyond started before long to preoccupy the American State Department as well. 'Containment' was soon the key concept, especially after George F. Kennan, a diplomat in the American Embassy in Moscow, had warned in dark tones in a famous 'long telegram' of February 1946 of the need to prevent Soviet expansion, which he envisaged as being pursued through infiltration and political pressure rather than direct military intervention.

However exaggerated in retrospect such anxieties proved to be, in 1946 they were palpable. The Soviet Union had that spring belatedly and reluctantly withdrawn from Iran (occupied by both Soviet and British forces since 1941). The Americans also saw serious grounds for concern in 1946 when the Soviets exerted pressure on Turkey to yield control over the Turkish Straits (the Dardanelles and Bosphorus), though Stalin eventually backed down in the autumn. More worrying still was the situation in Greece. Stalin had been content in 1944–5, as agreed with Churchill, to leave Greece in the British sphere of influence, and had given the communists no help in their insurgency. But when the insurrection began again in March 1946 – supported by Tito's Yugoslavia, though still with little help from Stalin – communist advances led to the first deployment of the 'containment' policy.

The danger of the Greek Civil War providing the opening for Soviet expansion seemed real to the Americans, all the more so when the British Foreign Secretary, Ernest Bevin, told them in February that a financially enfeebled Britain could no longer provide military or economic aid to Greece and Turkey. From March 1947 onwards the United States provided the Greek Right with military aid and training that proved decisive in defeating the Left – though the huge losses (around 45,000 killed and immense material damage) and subsequent repression inflicted lasting harm on Greece's prospects for genuine national unity. For the USA, however, 'containment' had proved a success. The President, Harry S. Truman, had even declared it a 'doctrine' – support for 'free peoples' against 'totalitarianism' to hold back the spread of communism. It became the mantra of the Cold War.

Germany, especially, was meanwhile coming to be seen as a decisive testing-ground. Friction between the occupying powers had grown during 1946 as the Soviets proved economically uncooperative, as the pressure built to give Communist parties outright dominance in the Soviet zone, and as the eastern zone of occupation went increasingly its own way. It had initially been envisaged that American troops would pull out of Europe in 1947. But in a major speech in September 1946 the American Secretary of State, James F. Byrne, announced that American troops would be staying. Byrne acknowledged the failure of unified administration of Germany through the Allied Control Council, as envisaged at Potsdam, and indicated that economic recovery for Germany, seen as vital to the whole of western Europe, would have to be undertaken on a zonal basis. He opened up the prospect of forming an economic unit between the American zone and the other western zones. By January 1947 this had become reality in the formation of the Bizone between the United States and Britain. With that, the formal division of Germany into separate states became only a matter of time.

The decisive moment in the division of Europe came in June 1947 with the announcement by the US Secretary of State, George C. Marshall, of a wide-ranging European Recovery Plan. The 'Marshall Plan', as it is usually called, was a step of great symbolic significance – profoundly political in aim, if economic in method – and of huge psychological importance in giving west Europeans new hope. It did not, as is often believed, create Europe's post-war prosperity, whatever the mythology that became attached to it. The Plan was simply too limited in scale to do that. It was highly important, nevertheless.

Economic growth pre-dated the Marshall Plan and reached back to 1945. All west European countries, apart from Germany, already registered higher capital formation in 1948 (the year that Marshall Aid started to flow) than in 1938. And only in Germany (massively) and Italy (marginally) did the gross national product remain lower than a decade earlier. But the Marshall Plan undoubtedly boosted the recovery. The index of gross national product in western Europe increased from 87 to 102 between 1948 and 1950 (taking 1938 to be 100), the beginning of a prolonged steep rise. The volume of exports also grew substantially and the revival of London capital markets helped trade within Europe and beyond. Not least, investment in rebuilding transport networks and the modernization of infrastructure benefited from Marshall Aid.

Defenders of the aid programme on both sides of the Atlantic claimed at the time that the Marshall Plan was about 'saving Europe' from economic collapse. This was also an exaggeration, though Europe was certainly still contending with drastic economic problems in 1947. Agricultural output was a third lower than before the war. Industrial production had by then still not recovered to its pre-war level. Housing and food shortages were acute. Not only were these particularly disastrous in Germany, where industrial production was still languishing. As was becoming ever plainer to the western Allies, without German economic recovery the rest of the continent would be held back. Prospects of recovery were greatly hindered by inflation as the supplies of money outstripped available goods to match the pent-up demand. In Hungary, Romania and Greece the currency collapsed. French prices were four times as high as they had been before the war. In Germany the amount of money in circulation was seven times higher, in Italy twenty times higher, than in 1938. Cigarettes and other commodities often replaced worthless currency in a barter-economy. Inflation was only gradually brought under control through austerity measures and currency reform through devaluation.

But the main problem hindering European economic recovery by 1947 was the 'dollar gap' – the shortage of dollars to pay for desperately needed imports of raw materials and capital goods for investment. This imbalance wrecked the arrangements carefully devised at the Bretton Woods Conference only three years earlier for the liberalization of trade based on currencies pegged to the dollar. Precisely this obstacle to sustained economic recovery was what the Marshall Plan set out to overcome. European countries were given over 12 billion dollars – 2 per cent of US gross national product – over a period of four years. Britain was the greatest beneficiary, receiving more than twice the amount provided for West Germany;

almost all of it went to repay British debts. But the impact of the Plan was greatest in West Germany, Italy and Austria, the former enemy countries. This was symbolic, as well as economic. These countries were now made to feel that they were no longer enemies, but part of an American-sponsored project that offered the prospects of long-term recovery and political stability.

The Marshall Plan was anything but altruistic. It helped American as well as European business, since most of the goods bought under the Plan were purchased from the USA. But beyond economic considerations, the Plan was overtly political. From its conception it was viewed as a weapon in the incipient Cold War. Helping to make Europe economically strong – and within Europe revitalizing the prostrate economic giant, Germany – would tie the western half of the continent to American interests, and provide the firmest barrier to Soviet expansionism.

All European countries, including the Soviet Union, were offered Marshall Aid. As Marshall himself had anticipated (and hoped), however, the Soviet Union rejected it, forcing the countries in their sphere of influence (including, with great reluctance, Poland and Czechoslovakia) to follow suit. Finland, anxious to avoid possible repercussions from the Soviet Union, also declined. Stalin's refusal of Marshall Aid was a decisive move. Was it a huge mistake? Rejection denied eastern Europe any possible benefits that the stimulus of the Marshall Plan could have provided. And in the eyes of millions of Europeans it handed the moral as well as the political high ground to the Americans. But from Stalin's perspective, worried that the security of the Soviet Union and its satellites was vulnerable to the superior economic power of the United States, refusing Marshall Aid determined that there could be no Western interference in the consolidation of Soviet power in eastern Europe. His fear, most likely justified, was that economic aid from the USA was a vehicle which would have undermined Soviet political dominance in its satellite states. Stalin's decision meant the definitive split of Europe into two halves.

The sixteen European countries (and representatives from the western zones of Germany) outside the Soviet bloc went ahead and by April 1948 had formed the Organization for European Economic Cooperation (OEEC) to coordinate the implementation of the Plan.

It presaged what would turn out to be a lasting division not just along the line of the Iron Curtain but among the west European states themselves. The Americans had envisaged the economic and also political integration of western Europe. The Marshall Plan was predicated upon steps in this direction, initially towards a European customs union, though involving a supranational organization. The Americans thought of constructing a new western Europe in the image of the USA. But the European countries were driven by their individual national interests. These would swiftly frustrate then defeat American notions of European integration. As the US diplomat George Kennan witheringly put it, Europeans had neither the political strength nor 'clarity of vision' to draft a new 'design' for Europe. Scandinavians were 'pathologically nervous about the Russians', the British were 'seriously sick', and the other nations suffered from a similar lack of resolve to that which afflicted the British.

France's leaders saw the country's national interests above all as providing security against the prospect of a rebuilt Germany and renewed military might that could again draw on the economic power of Ruhr heavy industry. This paramount interest would not be best served by the type of free-trade economic integration favoured by the United States. France's own post-war plans for reconstruction rested on the internationalization of the Ruhr to guarantee access to German coal and coke, weakening Germany permanently in the process. But when in June 1948 the western Allies decided to establish a unitary West German state, France was compelled to alter its policy into one of prospective cooperation on the allocation of German fuel resources and steel output. It was the genesis of the crucial Franco-German understanding that would form the basis of the later European Economic Community.

Britain had very different national interests. London policy-makers saw only disadvantages for Britain in the European customs union – an obvious starting point for future integration – envisaged in the Marshall Plan. Senior civil servants believed that 'There is no attraction for us in long-term economic cooperation with Europe.' They feared that such a step would subject Britain eventually to damaging economic competition, prevent the government taking independent steps towards recovery at home, aggravate the dollar drain, and thereby increase dependence upon US aid. Not least, British national interests were seen to lie in ties with the Commonwealth and a revival of world trade. The American diplomat William L. Clayton, one of the key figures behind the Marshall Plan, was close to the mark in his assessment: 'The trouble with the British is that they are hanging on by their eyelashes to the hope that somehow or other with our help they will be able to preserve the British Empire and their leadership of it.' As George Marshall himself summed up, Britain wanted to 'benefit fully from a European program[me] . . . while at the same time maintaining the position of not being wholly a European country'. Some of the smaller European states took a similar stance to that of Britain. The American aim of European economic integration was, therefore, a non-starter. European economic cooperation, when it gradually emerged, would not flow from the Marshall Plan but from the subsequent Franco-German rapprochement on Ruhr coal and steel. And Britain would have no part in it.

By the autumn of 1948, the economic divide of Europe was matching the political rift. The Soviet Union established the Cominform (Communist Information Bureau) – the successor to the Comintern – in October, with a designated aim to block what it called 'the American plan for the enslavement of Europe'. It spoke of the world breaking down into an imperialist (American-dominated) and a democratic (Soviet-influenced) bloc. By January 1949 the Soviet bloc had created its own economic framework, the Comecon (Council for Mutual Economic Assistance), as the counterpart to the American-sponsored Marshall Plan.

The Marshall Plan confirmed the division of Europe into two hostile blocs. The steps to create a West German state cemented the division. By June 1948 the western Allies had agreed to the establishment of a West German state. They introduced a currency reform that provided the financial basis for economic revival and which many Germans later came to view as the real end to the Second World War for their country. The introduction of the D-Mark (*Deutsche Mark*) and the lifting of price controls on many products shortly afterwards saw a rapid end to the black market and the beginning of economic normality. The Soviets responded with their own new currency in the eastern zone. Far more threateningly, they imposed a blockade on land connections between the western zones and the capital city, Berlin (itself under four-power control, but uneasily located about 150 kilometres inside the Soviet zone).

The Soviet aim was to force the western Allies out of Berlin. The Americans saw Berlin as a test-case. The Communist coup in Czechoslovakia was fresh in their minds. Retreat from Berlin would, they feared, be the prelude to the Soviets extending their stranglehold over western Europe. The blockade was broken by an improvised Allied airlift, beginning on 26 June, that delivered 2.3 million tons of supplies to the blockaded population in Berlin's western zones in 278,000 flights carried out over a period of 321 days, before Stalin finally conceded defeat by lifting the blockade on 12 May 1949. For the western powers the airlift naturally provided a propaganda triumph, and signalled the readiness and determination of the Americans to stay in Europe as a safeguard against the spread of Communist power.

Later in May, West German representatives drew up a 'Basic Law' – a constitution – for what was now foreseen as the Federal Republic of Germany ('West Germany'). The Federal Republic duly came into being on 20 September 1949. The Soviets were by this time reconciled to the creation of a separate state in their own zone. On 7 October the division of Germany for the indefinite future – many presumed for ever – was sealed with the foundation in the former eastern zone of the German Democratic Republic.

Over an extremely brief period Germany had been transformed in Western eyes from a threat to the future security of the continent to the bulwark against Soviet expansion. The French and British, meeting at Dunkirk in March 1947, had signed a defensive treaty still directed against the possibility of future German aggression. Within a year, this was extended in the Treaty of Brussels – to which the Netherlands, Belgium and Luxembourg added their signatures. But the Soviet Union, no longer Germany, was by now coming to be regarded as the main threat. The growing fear of Soviet power, together with the commitment of the United States to stay on the European continent indefinitely, meant that it was crucial to incorporate the USA formally in the security arrangements for the defence of western Europe. The Berlin crisis, which had fully revealed how exposed western

Europe would be without American military power to underpin it, was the spur to the creation of an Atlantic alliance as a barrier to any potential Soviet expansionism.

On 4 April 1949 the Brussels signatories together with the USA, Canada, Italy, Portugal, Denmark, Norway and Iceland signed the Treaty of Washington, establishing the North Atlantic Treaty Organization (NATO), committing themselves to mutual assistance in the event of an attack against any one of them. NATO offered western Europe a sense of security that its own threadbare defences could not provide. Its importance was to a large extent symbolic, as an expression of unified commitment to the defence of western Europe. In reality, it was a fig-leaf. Soviet ground forces outnumbered those of the western Allies by 12 to 1; and only two of the latter's fourteen divisions stationed in Europe were American.

Very soon European security had in any case to be rethought. On 29 August 1949 the Soviet Union exploded its first atomic bomb at a test site in modern-day Kazakhstan. It was a shock to the West. The Americans had imagined that their nuclear superiority would last for much longer. Instead, the two military superpowers glowered at each other across the Iron Curtain that now formed Europe's great divide. With a rapidly expanding nuclear arsenal on both sides, the Cold War now froze quickly into two great antagonistic power-blocs. It would remain that way for the next four decades.

By 1949 it was becoming clearer that – in very different ways – both eastern and western Europe were on the way to levels of stability and economic growth that had been impossible to foresee four troubled years earlier. The contrast with the protracted turmoil that had followed the First World War was stark. What explains it?

Five crucial elements interacted to provide the foundations for the unpredictable transformation that fully materialized only during the 1950s: the end of German great-power ambitions; the impact of the purging of war criminals and collaborators; the crystallization of Europe's division into lasting form; the economic growth that was beginning to take off by the end of the 1940s; and the new threat of atomic (and soon thermonuclear) warfare.

A crucial, and destructive, element of continuity running through and scarring European history from the period before the First World War to 1945 had been Germany's ambitions to become a world power – even the dominant world power. Those ambitions had formed part of the background to the explosion of 1914, they had subsided but not been extinguished under the ill-fated democracy after 1918, and they had returned, with greatly magnified aggression, after 1933, leading directly to the Second World War in 1939. But they had been smashed once and for all in the total defeat of 1945. The removal of this geopolitical turbulence of great force at the very heart of Europe gave the continent – even in the division of the Cold War – a new chance.

The purging of collaborators and those guilty of the worst war crimes, inadequate and unsatisfactory as they were, not only offered a degree of catharsis to the victims of Nazism and collaboration, but meant that the violent politics of the extreme Right had no opportunity to poison societies as they had done after 1918. A determining component of interwar political instability had all but disappeared. The border shifts and population transfers in eastern Europe, though carried out amid terrible bloodshed, produced far greater degrees of ethnic homogeneity than had existed in the interwar period. That, too, added to the pacification of the eastern half of the continent, even though this took place under the heavy hand of Soviet repression.

Perverse though it might seem, the Iron Curtain that divided Europe proved a basis for stability, though at a heavy cost to the peoples of eastern Europe, condemned to decades of Soviet domination. The more the Soviet Union asserted its monolithic control over eastern Europe, the more determined the Americans became to confront it by exerting their own influence over western Europe. Berlin, soon to become the one opening in the Iron Curtain through which millions of refugees poured in a one-way stream, turned into the symbol of American defence of the West following the Allied airlift of 1948. Without the US presence and the sense of protection it offered, it is hard to imagine anything approaching the extent of stability that the ideological blanket of anti-communism helped to create in the West.

It was not that there were any Soviet military plans to expand into western Europe (though such expansion was certainly feared at the time). But without American support for rebuilding western economies, underpinning fragile political systems, providing a defence umbrella, and leading a propaganda assault on the threat of communism, west European Communist parties might well have attracted greater support and lessened the chances of establishing stable pluralist democracy. Whether, if the Americans had indeed pulled out of Europe by 1947 as they had initially intended to do, the gravely weakened former European great powers, France and Britain, would have been capable of overseeing the successful reconstruction of western Europe is doubtful. The American presence in Europe guaranteed the triumph of capitalism there. That was certainly not universally welcomed. The Left, especially, hated it. Nor was the growing 'Americanization' of Europe, as many saw it, warmly greeted everywhere. As before the war, it was dismissed in some circles as a sign of Europe's cultural decline. Whatever disadvantages the lasting American presence brought, however, they were greatly outweighed by the advantages. Under the shield of the United States, western Europe had the opportunity to find its own forms of unity and start to put the nationalist dangers of the recent past behind it.

This might not have been possible anyway had not economic growth provided the basis for the unprecedented levels of prosperity that, despite the post-war austerity, soon started to become visible. The Marshall Plan, though not the cause of the growth, symbolized the new hopes for the future in western Europe. Instead of reparations, which had helped undermine economic stability in the 1920s, there was the impetus of American loans. Marshall Aid gave European economies important sustenance, and, as a report in 1951 put it, the 'strength to work their own recovery'. Huge amounts of spare labour and productive capacity, pent-up demand, and technical innovation lay behind the surge. Lessons learnt about reliance on market forces to restore pre-war conditions, as had prevailed after the First World War, and the application of Keynesian techniques of monetary policy to stimulate growth, also played a significant part. And western Europe became more economically interwoven with the technologically advanced and prosperous USA than ever before.

Eastern Europe, rejecting Marshall Aid, soon came to lag far behind the western half of the continent. But beneath the unremitting Soviet repression, economic growth there, too, accelerated sharply after the war and material progress was impressive. Where impoverished and underdeveloped societies had been torn apart by nationalist, ethnic and class conflicts in the interwar years, there was now a basis of relative prosperity and stability, however forced the process had been.

Finally, nuclear weapons concentrated minds on both sides of the Iron Curtain. The existence of such weapons of immense destruction, soon of far greater power than the atomic bombs that had destroyed Hiroshima and Nagasaki, offered such frightening prospects that they diminished the chances of hot, not just cold, war between the new superpowers. With the discovery of the hydrogen bomb, both the USA and the Soviet Union had acquired by 1953 the potential for 'mutually assured destruction' (aptly shortened to 'MAD'). The possession of nuclear weapons would soon come to be one of the most hugely contested strands of domestic politics in Europe, particularly once Britain and France – anxious to ensure their continuing place at the top table of great powers – had acquired them. But once discovered (and actually used, as they had been by the Americans, twice in 1945), they could not be wished away. Their very presence continues, unsurprisingly, to be viewed with fear, and the possibility that they might sometime be used regarded with outright horror. But it seems highly likely (even if it cannot actually be proved) that the possibility of a nuclear superpower confrontation, which could have brought about a calamitous third world war, was crucial to establishing a stability in the divided Europe after 1945 that had never been possible at the end of the first great European conflagration in 1918.

Europe's future in 1945, in so far as it appeared to have one, seemed to be that of a continent of independent nation states. And as Europe congealed into its two separate halves, it was still a continent of nation states. But this was starting to change. In eastern Europe the military power of the USSR meant the rapid subordination of national interests to those of the Soviet Union. The sovereignty of the nation state quickly ceased to exist. The countries of western Europe, though increasingly under American influence, were more sensitive to inroads into national sovereignty, none more so than Britain and France.

Few people in the first years after the war talked about supranational political entities, and when Winston Churchill did envisage a 'United States of Europe' in 1946, he neither included Britain in his proposed new political entity nor imagined a world that was not still dominated by the great powers (in which category he was determined to ensure Britain's presence). But the emerging Cold War and the need to ensure that the shoots of economic growth were not killed off by nationalist rivalries combined to create the beginnings of pressure for greater coordination and integration of both the economies and the security of western Europe. The formation of the Organization for European Economic Cooperation (OEEC) in 1948, and the following year of NATO and the Council of Europe (committed to European cooperation in matters relating to the rule of law and the upholding of fundamental human rights), marked a modest start. Combining idealism and pragmatism, these were still fairly small steps on the way towards reconciling national interests with greater levels of European integration.

The historic splits were too deep to allow national interests to be swiftly or comprehensively overcome – and Britain, especially, was allergic to any possible diminution of its status or sovereignty. When the French advanced a scheme – the Schuman Plan – in 1950 for joint control of Ruhr coal and steel production, questions of national security through controlling Germany's potential for rearmament, following the foundation of the Federal Republic of Germany, were more important than idealistic notions of European unity. But it turned out to be the decisive step – the beginning of the path that would lead to a 'common market' and the creation of a European Economic Community with its own governing institutions.

Out of the ashes, against all probabilities, a new Europe, divided within itself but with each part soon resting on more solid foundations than had ever seemed likely at the end of the war, had with remarkable speed taken distinct shape. The future lay open. But amid the lasting scars, physical and moral, of the most terrible war of all time, possibilities were emerging of a more stable and prosperous Europe than could ever have been imagined within living memory, in the decades when the continent had come close to self-destruction.

Select Bibliography

How long is a piece of string? A bibliography of Europe in the twentieth century is about the same length. So the following list, necessarily highly selective, is confined to works that I have found interesting and useful in writing this book. It includes only a few specialized research monographs and essays in learned journals, though both of these are the essential building blocks on which all historical scholarship is constructed. I have not included works of fiction, though some of these cast important light on the era. I have concentrated for the most part on general works, mainly in English. Many of these contain their own detailed bibliographies on specific countries or topics. Those works that I have drawn on to provide brief quotations from contemporaries are marked with an asterisk.

Abelshauser, Werner, Faust, Anselm and Petzina, Dietmar (eds), *Deutsche Sozialgeschichte 1914–1945*, Munich, 1985.

Adamthwaite, Anthony, *Grandeur and Misery: France's Bid for Power in Europe, 1914–1940*, London, 1995.

Addison, Paul, *The Road to 1945: British Politics and the Second World War*, London, 1975.

*Aldcroft, Derek H., *From Versailles to Wall Street 1919–1929*, Harmondsworth, 1987.

Aldcroft, Derek H., *The European Economy, 1914–1990*, London, 3rd edn, 1993.

Alexander, Martin (ed.), *French History since Napoleon*, London, 1999.

Alexander, Martin and Graham, Helen (eds), *The French and Spanish Popular Front: Comparative Perspectives*, Cambridge, 1989.

Aly, Götz, *'Final Solution': Nazi Population Policy and the Murder of the European Jews*, London, 1999.

Aly, Götz, *Hitler's Beneficiaries*, London and New York, 2007.

*Andreas-Friedrich, Ruth, *Schauplatz Berlin. Ein Deutsches Tagebuch*, Munich, 1962.

Angelow, Jürgen, *Der Weg in die Urkatastrophe*, Berlin, 2010.

*Annan, Noel, *Our Age: Portrait of a Generation*, London, 1990.

*Applebaum, Anne, *Iron Curtain: The Crushing of Eastern Europe 1944–1956*, London, 2012.

Arendt, Hannah, *The Origins of Totalitarianism*, Orlando, FL, 1966.

Aron, Raymond, *The Century of Total War*, London, 1954.

Ascherson, Neal, *The Struggles for Poland*, London, 1987.

Bach, Maurizio and Breuer, Stefan, *Faschismus als Bewegung und Regime. Italien und Deutschland im Vergleich*, Wiesbaden, 2010.

Bade, Klaus J. et al. (eds), *Migration in Europa. Vom 17. Jahrhundert bis zur Gegenwart*, Paderborn, 2008.

Balderston, Theo, *The Origins and Cause of the German Economic Crisis, November 1923 to May 1932*, Berlin, 1993.

Balderston, Theo, 'War Finance and Inflation in Britain and Germany, 1914–1918', *Economic History Review*, 42/2 (1989).

Balderston, Theo (ed.), *The World Economy and National Economies in the Interwar Slump*, Basingstoke, 2003.

Banac, Ivo, *The National Question in Yugoslavia: Origins, History, Politics*, Ithaca, NY, 1984.

Bankier, David (ed.), *Probing the Depths of German Antisemitism*, Jerusalem, 2000.

Barber, John, and Harrison, Mark, *The Soviet Home Front, 1941–1945: A Social and Economic History of the USSR in World War II*, London, 1991.

Bartov, Omer, *Hitler's Army*, New York, 1991.

Bartov, Omer, *Murder in our Midst: The Holocaust, Industrial Killing, and Representation*, New York, 1996.

Bartov, Omer, *Mirrors of Destruction: War, Genocide, and Modern History*, New York, 2000.

Barzun, Jacques, *From Dawn to Decadence, 1500 to the Present: 500 Years of Western Cultural Life*, London, 2001.

Bauer, Yehuda, *The Holocaust in Historical Perspective*, London, 1978.

Becker, Jean-Jacques, *The Great War and the French People*, Leamington Spa, 1980.

Beetham, David (ed.), *Marxists in Face of Fascism*, Manchester, 1983.

Beevor, Antony, *Stalingrad*, London, 1998.

Beevor, Antony, *Berlin: The Downfall, 1945*, London, 2003.

Beevor, Antony, *The Battle for Spain*, London, 2006.

Beevor, Antony, *D-Day: The Battle for Normandy*, London, 2009.

Beevor, Antony, *The Second World War*, London, 2012.

Beevor, Antony and Vinogradova, Luba (eds), *A Writer at War: Vasily Grossman with the Red Army 1941–1945*, London, 2006.

Bell, P. M. H., *The Origins of the Second World War in Europe*, London, 2007.

Bell, P. M. H., *Twelve Turning Points of the Second World War*, London, 2011.

Bellamy, Chris, *Absolute War: Soviet Russia in the Second World War – A Modern History*, London, 2008.

Benson, Leslie, *Yugoslavia: A Concise History*, London, 2001.

Berger, Heinrich, Dejnega, Melanie, Fritz, Regina and Prenninger, Alexander (eds), *Politische Gewalt und Machtausübung im 20. Jahrhundert*, Vienna, 2011.

*Berghahn, Volker, *Germany and the Approach of War in 1914*, London, 1973.

Berghahn, Volker, *Modern Germany: Society, Economy and Politics in the Twentieth Century*, Cambridge, 1982.

Berghahn, Volker, *The Americanisation of West German Industry, 1845–1973*, Leamington Spa, 1986.

Berghahn, Volker, *Sarajewo, 28. Juni 1914. Der Untergang des alten Europa*, Munich, 1997.

Berg-Schlosser, Dirk and Mitchell, Jeremy (eds), *Conditions of Democracy in Europe, 1919–39*, Basingstoke, 2000.

Berg-Schlosser, Dirk and Mitchell, Jeremy (eds), *Authoritarianism and Democracy in Europe, 1919–39: Comparative Analyses*, Basingstoke, 2002.

*Berkhoff, Karel C., *Harvest of Despair: Life and Death in Ukraine under Nazi Rule*, Cambridge, MA, and London, 2004.

Bessel, Richard, *Germany after the First World War*, Oxford, 1993.

Bessel, Richard, *Germany 1945: From War to Peace*, London, 2009.

Bessel, Richard (ed,), *Fascist Italy and Nazi Germany: Comparisons and Contrasts*, Cambridge, 1996.

Bessel, Richard and Schumann, Dirk (eds), *Life after Death: Approaches to a Cultural and Social History of Europe during the 1940s and 1950s*, Cambridge, 2003.

Blanning, T. C. W. (ed.), *The Oxford Illustrated History of Modern Europe*, Oxford, 1996.

Blatman, Daniel, *Les marches de la mort. La dernière étape du génocide nazi*, Paris, 2009.

Blinkhorn, Martin, *Carlism and Crisis in Spain, 1931–1939*, Cambridge, 1975.

Blinkhorn, Martin, *Democracy and Civil War in Spain, 1931–1939*, London, 1988.

Blinkhorn, Martin, *Fascism and the Right in Europe*, Harlow, 2000.

Blinkhorn, Martin (ed.), *Fascists and Conservatives: The Radical Right and the Establishment in Twentieth-Century Europe*, London, 1990.

Blom, Philipp, *The Vertigo Years: Change and Culture in the West, 1900–1914*, London, 2008.

Bloxham, Donald, *The Great Game of Genocide: Imperialism, Nationalism and the Destruction of the Ottoman Armenians*, Oxford, 2005.

Bloxham, Donald, 'The Armenian Genocide of 1915–1916: Cumulative Radicalization and the Development of a Destruction Policy', *Past and Present*, 181 (2003).

Bond, Brian, *War and Society in Europe, 1870–1970*, London, 1984.

Borodziej, Włodziemierz, *Geschichte Polens im 20. Jahrhundert*, Munich, 2010.

Bosworth, R. J. B., *The Italian Dictatorship*, London, 1998.

Bosworth, R. J. B., *Mussolini*, London, 2002.

Bosworth, R. J. B., *Mussolini's Italy: Life under the Dictatorship*, London, 2005.

Bosworth, R. J. B. (ed.), *The Oxford Handbook of Fascism*, Oxford, 2009.

Botz, Gerhard, *Krisenzonen einer Demokratie. Gewalt, Streik und Konfliktunterdrückung in Österreich seit 1918*, Frankfurt am Main, 1987.

Bourke, Joanna, *An Intimate History of Killing: Face-to-Face Killing in Twentieth-Century Warfare*, London, 1999.

Bracher, Karl Dietrich, *The Age of Ideologies: A History of Political Thought in the Twentieth Century*, London, 1985.

Brechenmacher, Thomas, 'Pope Pius XI, Eugenio Pacelli, and the Persecution of the Jews in Nazi Germany, 1933–1939: New Sources from the Vatican Archives', *Bulletin of the German Historical Institute London*, 27/2 (2005).

Brendon, Piers, *The Dark Valley: A Panorama of the 1930s*, London, 2001.

Breuilly, John, *Nationalism and the State*, Manchester, 1993.

*Brittain, Vera, *Testament of Youth* (1933), London, 1978.

Broadberry, Stephen and Harrison, Mark, (eds), *The Economics of World War I*, Cambridge, 2005.

Broadberry, Stephen and O'Rourke, Kevin H. (eds), *The Cambridge Economic History of Modern Europe. Vol. 2: 1870 to the Present*, Cambridge, 2010.

Broszat, Martin, *The Hitler State*, London, 1981.

Browning, Christopher, *Fateful Months: Essays on the Emergence of the Final Solution*, New York, 1985.

Browning, Christopher, *The Path to Genocide*, Cambridge, 1992.

Browning, Christopher, *The Origins of the Final Solution*, Lincoln, NB, and Jerusalem, 2004.

Brüggemeier, Franz-Josef, *Geschichte Grossbritanniens im 20. Jahrhundert*, Munich, 2010.

*Brussilov, A. A., *A Soldier's Notebook* (1930), Westport, CT, 1971.

Buber-Neumann, Margarete, *Under Two Dictators: Prisoner of Stalin and Hitler* (1949), London, 2008.

Buchanan, Tom, *Europe's Troubled Peace 1945–2000*, Oxford, 2006.

*Buckley, Henry, *The Life and Death of the Spanish Republic: A Witness to the Spanish Civil War* (1940), London, 2014.

Bulliet, Richard W. (ed.), *The Columbia History of the 20th Century*, New York, 1998.

Burgdorff, Stephan and Wiegrefe, Klaus (eds), *Der 2. Weltkrieg. Wendepunkt der deutschen Geschichte*, Munich, 2005.

Burleigh, Michael, *The Third Reich: A New History*, London, 2000.

*Burleigh, Michael, *Sacred Causes: Religion and Politics from the European Dictators to Al Qaeda*, London, 2006.

Burleigh, Michael and Wippermann, Wolfgang, *The Racial State: Germany 1933–1945*, London, 1991.

Burrin, Philippe, *La dérive fasciste*, Paris, 1986.

Burrin, Philippe, *Living with Defeat: France under the German Occupation, 1940–1944*, London, 1996.

Burrin, Philippe, *Fascisme, nazisme, autoritarisme*, Paris, 2000.

Buruma, Ian, *Year Zero: A History of 1945*, New York, 2013.

Calder, Angus, *The People's War: Britain 1939–1945*, London, 1971.

Calic, Marie-Janine, *Geschichte Jugoslawiens im 20. Jahrhundert*, Munich, 2010.

Cannadine, David, *The Decline and Fall of the British Aristocracy*, New Haven, CT, and London, 1990.

Cannadine, David, *Class in Britain*, London, 2000.

Caplan, Jane (ed.), *Nazi Germany*, Oxford, 2008.

Caplan, Jane and Wachsmann, Nikolaus (eds), *Concentration Camps in Nazi Germany: The New Histories*, London, 2010.

*Carey, John, *The Intellectuals and the Masses*, London, 1992.

Carley, Michael Jahara, *1939. The Alliance that Never Was and the Coming of World War II*, Chicago, IL, 1999.

Carr, Raymond, *Spain, 1808–1975*, Oxford, 1982.

Carsten, F. L., *The Rise of Fascism*, London, 1967.

Carsten, F. L., *Revolution in Central Europe 1918–19*, London, 1972.

Cecil, Hugh and Liddle, Peter (eds), *Facing Armageddon: The First World War Experienced*, London, 1996.

Cesarani, David, *Eichmann: His Life and Crimes*, London, 2004.

Cesarani, David (ed.), *The Final Solution: Origins and Implementation*, London, 1996.

*Charman, Terry (ed.), *Outbreak 1939: The World Goes to War*, London, 2009.

*Chickering, Roger and Förster, Stig (eds), *Great War, Total War: Combat and Mobilisation on the Western Front 1914–1918*, Cambridge, 2000.

Clark, Christopher, *Kaiser Wilhelm II*, Harlow, 2000.

Clark, Christopher, *The Sleepwalkers: How Europe Went to War in 1914*, London, 2012.

Clark, Martin, *Modern Italy 1871–1982*, London, 1984.

Clarke, Peter, *The Keynesian Revolution in the Making 1924–1936*, Oxford, 1988.

Clarke, Peter, *Hope and Glory: Britain 1900–1990*, London, 1996.

Clavin, Patricia, *The Great Depression in Europe, 1929–1939*, Basingstoke, 2000.

Clavin, Patricia, *Securing the World Economy: The Reinvention of the League of Nations, 1919–1946*, Oxford, 2013.

Clogg, Richard, *A Concise History of Greece*, 2nd edn, Cambridge, 2002.

*Clough, Shepard B., Moodie, Thomas and Moodie, Carol (eds), *Economic History of Europe: Twentieth Century*, London, 1965.

Conquest, Robert, *The Harvest of Sorrow: Soviet Collectivization and the Terror-Famine*, London, 1988.

Constantine, Stephen, *Unemployment in Britain between the Wars*, London, 1980.

Conway, Martin, *Catholic Politics in Europe 1918–1945*, London, 1997.

Conway, Martin, *The Sorrows of Belgium: Liberation and Political Reconstruction, 1944–1947*, Oxford, 2012.

Conway, Martin, 'Democracy in Postwar Europe: The Triumph of a Political Model', *European History Quarterly*, 32/1 (2002).

Corner, Paul, *The Fascist Party and Popular Opinion in Mussolini's Italy*, Oxford, 2012.

Corner, Paul (ed.), *Popular Opinion in Totalitarian Regimes*, Oxford, 2009.

Cornwall, M. (ed.), *The Last Years of Austria-Hungary*, Exeter, 1990.

Cornwell, John, *Hitler's Pope: The Secret History of Pius XII*, London, 1999.

Cornwell, John, *Hitler's Scientists: Science, War and the Devil's Pact*, London, 2003.

Costa-Pinto, António, *Salazar's Dictatorship and European Fascism – Problems of Interpretation*, New York, 1995.

Costa-Pinto, António, *The Blue Shirts: Portuguese Fascists and the New State*, New York, 2000.

Crampton, R. J., *Eastern Europe in the Twentieth Century*, 2nd edn, London, 1997.

*Cross, Tim (ed.), *The Lost Voices of World War I*, London, 1988.

Cull, Nicholas, Culbert, David and Welch, David (eds), *Propaganda and Mass Persuasion: A Historical Encyclopedia, 1500 to the Present*, Santa Barbara, CA, 2003.

*Dąbrowka, Maria, *Tagebücher 1914–1965*, Frankfurt am Main, 1989.

Dahrendorf, Ralf, *Society and Democracy in Germany*, London, 1968.

Davies, Norman, *God's Playground. Vol. 2: A History of Poland*, Oxford, 1981.

*Davies, Norman, *Europe: A History*, Oxford, 1996.

Davies, Norman, *Europe at War, 1939–1945: No Simple Victory*, London, 2006.

Davies, R. W. and Wheatcroft, S. G., *The Years of Hunger: Soviet Agriculture 1931–1933*, London, 2009.

Davies, Sarah, *Popular Opinion in Stalin's Russia: Terror, Propaganda and Dissent, 1934–1941*, Cambridge, 1997.

Dear, I. C. B. and Foot, M. R. D. (eds), *The Oxford Companion to the Second World War*, Oxford, 1995.

De Grazia, Victoria, *How Fascism Ruled Women: Italy, 1922–1945*, Berkeley, CA, 1992.

Diehl, James M., *Paramilitary Politics in Weimar Germany*, Bloomington, IN, 1977.

Dilks, David, *Churchill and Company: Allies and Rivals in War and Peace*, London, 2012.

*Dilks, David (ed.), *The Diaries of Sir Alexander Cadogan 1938–1945*, London, 1971.

*Döblin, Alfred, *Schicksalsreise. Bericht und Bekenntnis. Flucht und Exil 1940–1940*, Munich and Zurich, 1986.

*Duggan, Christopher, *The Force of Destiny: A History of Italy since 1796*, London, 2008.

*Duggan, Christopher, *Fascist Voices: An Intimate History of Mussolini's Italy*, London, 2012.

Eatwell, Roger, *Fascism: A History*, London, 1996.

Edgerton, David, *The Shock of the Old: Technology and Global History since 1900*, London, 2008.

Eichengreen, Barry, *Golden Fetters: The Gold Standard and the Great Depression, 1919–1939*, New York, 1995.

Ekman, Stig and Åmark, Klas (eds), *Sweden's Relations with Nazism, Nazi Germany and the Holocaust*, Stockholm, 2003.

Eksteins, Modris, *Rites of Spring: The Great War and the Birth of the Modern Age*, Boston, MA, 1989.

Eley, Geoff, *Forging Democracy: The History of the Left in Europe 1850–2000*, New York, 2002.

*Elger, Dietmar, *Expressionism: A Revolution in German Art*, Cologne, 1994.

*Englund, Peter, *The Beauty and the Sorrow: An Intimate History of the First World War*, London, 2011.

Erdmann, Karl Dietrich, *Das Ende des Reiches und die Neubildung deutscher Staaten*, Munich, 1980.

Evans, Richard J., *The Coming of the Third Reich*, London, 2003.

Evans, Richard J., *The Third Reich in Power*, London, 2005.

Evans, Richard J., *The Third Reich at War*, London, 2008.

*Evans, Richard J. and Geary, Dick (eds), *The German Unemployed*, London, 1987.

Faber, David, *Munich: The 1938 Appeasement Crisis*, London, 2008.

*Fainsod, Merle, *Smolensk under Soviet Rule*, (1958), Boston, MA, 1989.

Falter, Jürgen, *Hitlers Wähler*, Munich, 1991.

Feldmann, Gerald D., *Army, Industry and Labor in Germany 1914–18*, Princeton, NJ, 1966.

Feldmann, Gerald D., *The Great Disorder: Politics, Economics and Society in the German Inflation, 1914–1924*, New York, 1993.

Feldmann, Gerald D. (ed.), *Die Nachwirkungen der Inflation auf die deutsche Geschichte 1924–1933*, Munich, 1985.

*Ferguson, Niall, *The Pity of War*, London, 1998.

Ferguson, Niall, *The Cash Nexus: Money and Power in the Modern World 1700–2000*, London, 2002.

*Ferguson, Niall, *The War of the World: Twentieth-Century Conflict and the Descent of the West*, New York, 2006.

Ferro, Marc, *The Great War 1914–1918*, London, 1973.

Ferro, Marc (ed.), *Nazisme et Communisme. Deux régimes dans le siècle*, Paris, 1999.

*Figes, Orlando, *A People's Tragedy: The Russian Revolution 1891–1924*, London, 1996.

*Figes, Orlando, *The Whisperers: Private Life in Stalin's Russia*, London, 2008.

Figes, Orlando, *Revolutionary Russia 1891–1991*, London, 2014.

Finer, S. E., *Comparative Government*, Harmondsworth, 1970.

Fischer, Conan, *The Rise of the Nazis*, Manchester, 1995.

Fischer, Conan, *The Ruhr Crisis 1923–1924*, Oxford, 2003.

Fischer, Conan (ed.), *The Rise of National Socialism and the Working Classes in Weimar Germany*, Providence, RI, and Oxford, 1996.

Fischer, Fritz, *Germany's Aims in the First World War*, New York, 1967.

*Fischer, Fritz, *Krieg der Illusionen*, Düsseldorf, 1969.

Fischer, Fritz, *Juli 1914. Wir sind nicht hineingeschlittert*, Hamburg, 1983.

Fisk, Robert, *In Time of War: Ireland, Ulster, and the Price of Neutrality, 1939–45*, Philadelphia, PA, 1983.

Fitzpatrick, Sheila, *Everyday Stalinism: Ordinary Life in Extraordinary Times – Soviet Russia in the 1930s*, New York, 1999.

Flood, P. J., *France 1914–18: Public Opinion and the War Effort*, Basingstoke, 1990.

Flora, Peter et al. (eds), *Western Europe: A Data Handbook*, 2 vols, Frankfurt am Main, 1983.

Foot, M. R. D., *Resistance: European Resistance to Nazism 1940–45*, London, 1976.

Förster, Jürgen (ed.), *Stalingrad. Ereignis, Wirkung, Symbol*, Munich, 1992.

Foster, R. F., *Modern Ireland 1600–1972*, London, 1989.

Fox, Robert (ed.), *We Were There: An Eyewitness History of the Twentieth Century*, London, 2010.

Frei, Norbert, *National Socialist Rule in Germany: The Führer State*, Oxford, 1993.

Frei, Norbert, *Adenauer's Germany and the Nazi Past: The Politics of Amnesty and Integration*, New York, 2002.

Frei, Norbert, *1945 und wir. Das Dritte Reich im Bewusstsein der Deutschen*, Munich, 2005.

Frei, Norbert (ed.), *Was heißt und zu welchem Ende studiert man Geschichte des 20. Jahrhunderts?*, Göttingen, 2006.

Frevert, Ute, *Eurovisionen. Ansichten guter Europäer im 19. und 20. Jahrhundert*, Frankfurt am Main, 2003.

Friedländer, Saul, *Nazi Germany and the Jews: The Years of Persecution 1933–39*, London, 1997.

Friedländer, Saul, *The Years of Extermination: Nazi Germany and the Jews 1939–1945*, London, 2007.

Friedrich, Jörg, *Der Brand. Deutschland im Bombenkrieg 1940–1945*, Berlin, 2004.

Fröhlich, Elke, *Der Zweite Weltkrieg. Eine kurze Geschichte*, Stuttgart, 2013.

Fulbrook, Mary, *History of Germany: 1918–2000. The Divided Nation*, Oxford, 2002.

Fulbrook, Mary, *Dissonant Lives: Generations and Violence through the German Dictatorships*, Oxford, 2011.

Fulbrook, Mary (ed.), *20th Century Germany: Politics, Culture and Society 1918–1990*, London, 2001.

Fulbrook, Mary (ed.), *Europe since 1945*, Oxford, 2001.

Furet, François, *Le passé d'une illusion. Essai sur l'idée communiste au XXe siècle*, Paris, 1995.

Gaddis, John Lewis, *The Cold War*, London, 2005.

Garfield, Simon, *Our Hidden Lives: The Everyday Diaries of a Forgotten Britain 1945–1948*, London, 2004.

Gatrell, Peter, *A Whole Empire Walking: Refugees in Russia during World War I*, Bloomington, IN, 1999.

Gatrell, Peter, *Russia's First World War: A Social and Economic History*, Harlow, 2005.

Gay, Peter, *Weimar Culture*, London, 1974.

Geary, Dick, *European Labour Protest 1848–1939*, London, 1981.

Geary, Dick, *European Labour Politics from 1900 to the Depression*, Basingstoke, 1991.

Geary, Dick (ed.), *Labour and Socialist Movements in Europe before 1914*, Oxford, New York and Munich, 1989.

Gehler, Michael, *Europa. Ideen, Institutionen, Vereinigung*, Munich, 2005.

*Geiss, Imanuel (ed.), *July 1914: The Outbreak of the First World War – Selected Documents*, London, 1967.

Gellately, Robert, *Lenin, Stalin and Hitler: The Age of Social Catastrophe*, London, 2007.

Gentile, Emilio, *The Sacralization of Politics in Fascist Italy*, Cambridge, MA, and London, 1996.

Gerlach, Christian, *Extrem gewalttätige Gesellschaften. Massengewalt im 20. Jahrhundert*, Munich, 2010.

Gerlach, Christian and Aly, Götz, *Das letzte Kapitel. Der Mord an den ungarischen Juden 1944–1945*, Frankfurt am Main, 2004.

*Gerwarth, Robert, 'The Central European Counter-Revolution: Paramilitary Violence in Germany, Austria and Hungary after the Great War', *Past and Present*, 200 (2008).

Gerwarth, Robert, *Hitler's Hangman: The Life of Heydrich*, New Haven, CT, and London, 2011.

Gerwarth, Robert (ed.), *Twisted Paths: Europe 1914–1945*, Oxford, 2008.

*Gerwarth, Robert and Horne, John, 'Vectors of Violence: Paramilitarism in Europe after the Great War, 1917–1923', *The Journal of Modern History*, 83/3 (2011).

*Gerwarth, Robert and Horne, John (eds), *War in Peace: Paramilitary Violence in Europe after the Great War*, Oxford, 2012.

Gilbert, Felix, *The End of the European Era, 1890 to the Present*, 3rd edn, New York, 1984.

Gilbert, Martin, *Recent History Atlas 1860 to 1960*, London, 1966.

Gilbert, Martin, *First World War Atlas*, London, 1970.

Gilbert, Martin, *Atlas of the Holocaust*, London, 1982.

Gildea, Robert, *Marianne in Chains: Daily Life in the Heart of France during the German Occupation*, New York, 2002.

Gildea, Robert, Wieviorka, Olivier and Warring, Anette (eds), *Surviving Hitler and Mussolini: Daily Life in Occupied Europe*, Oxford and New York, 2006.

Glenny, Misha, *The Balkans 1804–1999: Nationalism, War and the Great Powers*, London, 1999.

Goltz, Anna von der and Gildea, Robert, 'Flawed Saviours: The Myths of Hindenburg and Pétain', *European History Quarterly*, 39 (2009).

Graham, Helen, *The Spanish Republic at War 1936–1939*, Cambridge, 2002.

Graml, Hermann, *Hitler und England. Ein Essay zur nationalsozialistischen Außenpolitik 1920 bis 1940*, Munich, 2010.

*Graml, Hermann, *Bernhard von Bülow und die deutsche Aussenpolitik*, Munich, 2012.

*Graves, Robert, *Goodbye to All That* (1929), London, 2000.

Gregory, Adrian, *The Last Great War: British Society and the First World War*, Cambridge, 2008.

Gregory, Adrian, 'British "War Enthusiasm" in 1914 – A Reassessment', in Gail Brayborn (ed.), *Evidence, History and the Great War: Historians and the Impact of 1914–18*, New York and Oxford, 2003.

Griffin, Roger, *The Nature of Fascism*, London, 1991.

Griffin, Roger, *Modernism and Fascism: The Sense of a Beginning under Mussolini and Hitler*, London, 2007.

*Griffin, Roger (ed.), *Fascism*, Oxford, 1995.

Griffin, Roger (ed.), *International Fascism: Theories, Causes and the New Consensus*, London, 1998.

Gross, Jan, *Fear: Anti-Semitism in Poland after Auschwitz*, Princeton, NJ, 2006.

Gruchmann, Lothar, *Der Zweite Weltkrieg*, Munich, 1975.

Gundle, Stephen, Duggan, Christopher and Pieri, Giuliana (eds), *The Cult of the Duce: Mussolini and the Italians*, Manchester, 2013.

*Hamann, Brigitte, *Der Erste Weltkrieg. Wahrheit und Lüge in Bildern und Texten*, Munich, 2004.

Hardach, Gerd, *The First World War 1914–1918*, Harmondsworth, 1987.

Harrison, Joseph, *An Economic History of Modern Spain*, Manchester, 1978.

Harrison, Joseph, *The Spanish Economy in the Twentieth Century*, London, 1985.

Hartwig, Wolfgang, *Utopie und politische Herrschaft im Europa der Zwischenkriegszeit*, Munich, 2003.

Hastings, Max, *Armageddon: The Battle for Germany 1944–45*, London, 2004.

Hastings, Max, *Finest Years: Churchill as Warlord 1940–45*, London, 2009.

*Hastings, Max, *All Hell Let Loose: The World at War 1939–1945*, London, 2011.

Hastings, Max, *Catastrophe: Europe goes to War 1914*, London, 2013.

Hayes, Paul (ed.), *Themes in Modern European History 1890–1945*, London, 1992.

Henke, Klaus-Dietmar and Woller, Hans (eds), *Politische Säuberung in Europa. Die Abrechnung mit Faschismus und Kollaboration nach dem Zweiten Weltkrieg*, Munich, 1991.

*Hennessy, Peter, *Never Again: Britain 1945–1951*, London, 1993.

Herbert, Ulrich, *Hitler's Foreign Workers*, Cambridge, 1997.

Herbert, Ulrich, *Geschichte Deutschlands im 20. Jahrhundert*, Munich, 2014.

Herbert, Ulrich, 'Europe in High Modernity: Reflections on a Theory of the 20th Century', *Journal of Modern European History*, 5/1 (2007).

Herf, Jeffrey, *The Jewish Enemy: Nazi Propaganda during World War II and the Holocaust*, Cambridge, MA and London, 2006.

Herwig, Holger H., *The Outbreak of World War I: Causes and Responsibilities*, Boston, MA, 1997.

Hewitson, Mark, *Germany and the Causes of the First World War*, London, 1983.

Hilberg, Raul, *The Destruction of the European Jews*, New York, 1973.

Hirschfeld, Gerhard, *Nazi Rule and Dutch Collaboration: The Netherlands under German Occupation, 1940–1945*, Oxford, 1988.

Hirschfeld, Gerhardt, Krumeich, Gerd and Renz, Irena (eds), *'Keiner fühlt sich hier mehr als Mensch …'. Erlebnis und Wirkung des Ersten Weltkriegs*, Frankfurt am Main, 1996.

Hirschfeld, Gerhardt, Krumeich, Gerd and Renz, Irena (eds), *Brill's Encyclopedia of the First World War*, 2 vols, Leiden, 2012.

Hobsbawm, Eric, *Age of Extremes. The Short Twentieth Century, 1914–1991*, London, 1994.

*Hobsbawm, Eric, *Interesting Times: A Twentieth-Century Life*, London, 2002.

Hobsbawm, Eric, *Fractured Times: Culture and Society in the Twentieth Century*, London, 2013.

Hoensch, Jörg K., *A History of Modern Hungary, 1867–1986*, Harlow, 1988.

Hoeres, Peter, *Die Kultur von Weimar. Durchbruch der Moderne*, Berlin, 2008.

Hoffmann, Peter, *The History of the German Resistance 1933–1945*, Cambridge, MA, and London, 1977.

Hogan, Michael, J., *The Marshall Plan: America, Britain, and the Reconstruction of Western Europe, 1947–1952*, Cambridge, 1987.

Horne, John and Kramer, Alan, *German Atrocities 1914: A History of Denial*, New Haven, CT, and London, 2001.

Horne, John (ed.), *State, Society and Mobilization in Europe during the First World War*, Cambridge, 1997.

Horne, John (ed.), *A Companion to World War I*, Oxford, 2012.

*Hosenfeld, Wilm, *'Ich versuche, jeden zu retten'. Das Leben eines deutschen Offiziers in Briefen und Tagebüchern*, Munich, 2004.

Hosking, Geoffrey, *A History of the Soviet Union*, London, 1985.

Hosking, Geoffrey, *Russia and the Russians*, London, 2001.

*Höss, Rudolf, *Kommandant in Auschwitz*, Munich, 1963.

Howard, Michael, *War in European History*, Oxford, 1976.

Howard, Michael and Louis, Wm. Roger (eds), *The Oxford History of the Twentieth Century*, Oxford, 1998.

*Hughes, S. Philip, *Consciousness and Society: The Reorientation of European Social Thought, 1890–1930*, New York, 1958.

Illies, Florian, *1913. Der Sommer des Jahrhunderts*, Frankfurt am Main, 2012.

Isaacs, Jeremy and Downing, Taylor, *Cold War*, London, 1998.

Jäckel, Eberhard, *Hitler in History*, Hanover and London, 1984.

Jäckel, Eberhard, *Hitlers Weltanschauung. Entwurf einer Herrschaft*, Stuttgart, 1991.

*Jäckel, Eberhard, *Das deutsche Jahrhundert. Eine historische Bilanz*, Stuttgart, 1996.

Jackson, Julian, *The Politics of Depression in France*, Cambridge, 1985.

Jackson, Julian, *The Popular Front in France: Defending Democracy, 1934–1938*, Cambridge, 1988.

Jackson, Julian, *France: The Dark Years*, Oxford, 2001.

Jackson, Julian, *The Fall of France: The Nazi Invasion of 1940*, Oxford, 2003.

*Jackson, Julian (ed.), *Europe 1900–1945*, Oxford, 2002.

*Jahoda, Marie, Lazarsfeld, Paul F. and Zeisel, Hans, *Marienthal: The Sociography of an Unemployed Community*, London, 1972.

James, Harold, *The German Slump: Politics and Economics 1924–1936*, Oxford, 1986.

James, Harold, *Europe Reborn: A History, 1914–2000*, London, 2003.

Jarausch, Konrad, *The Enigmatic Chancellor: Bethmann-Hollweg and the Hubris of Imperial Germany*, New Haven, CT, and London, 1973.

Jelavich, Barbara, *History of the Balkans. Vol. 2: Twentieth Century*, Cambridge, 1983.

Jenkins, Roy, *Churchill*, London, 2001.

Jesse, Eckhard (ed.), *Totalitarismus im 20. Jahrhundert. Eine Bilanz der internationalen Forschung*, Bonn, 1999.

Joll, James, *Europe since 1870: An International History*, London, 1973.

*Joll, James, *The Origins of the First World War*, London, 1984.

*Judt, Tony, *Postwar: A History of Europe since 1945*, London, 2005.

Judt, Tony, *Reappraisals: Reflections on the Forgotten Twentieth Century*, London, 2009.

Judt, Tony with Snyder, Timothy, *Thinking the Twentieth Century: Intellectuals and Politics in the Twentieth Century*, London, 2012.

*Jünger, Ernst, *Storm of Steel* (1920), London, 2003.

*Jünger, Ernst, *Kriegstagebuch 1914–1918*, ed. Helmuth Kiesel, Stuttgart, 2010.

Kaelble, Hartmut, *Historical Research on Social Mobility*, London, 1981.

Kaelble, Hartmut, *A Social History of Western Europe 1880–1980*, Dublin, 1989.

Kaelble, Hartmut, *Kalter Krieg und Wohlfahrtsstaat. Europa 1945–1989*, Munich, 2011.

Kann, R. A., Kraly, B. K. and Fichtner, P. S. (eds), *The Habsburg Empire in World War I*, New York, 1977.

Kater, Michael H., *The Nazi Party: A Social Profile of Members and Leaders, 1919–1945*, Oxford, 1983.

Kater, Michael H., *Different Drummers: Jazz in the Culture of Nazi Germany*, Oxford, 1992.

Kater, Michael H., *The Twisted Muse: Musicians and their Music in the Third Reich*, Oxford, 1997.

Kater, Michael H., *Weimar: From Enlightenment to the Present*, New Haven, CT, and London, 2014.

*Kedward, Rod, *La vie en bleu: France and the French since 1900*, London, 2006.

Keegan, John, *The First World War*, London, 1999.

Kershaw, Ian, *The 'Hitler Myth': Image and Reality in the Third Reich*, Oxford, 1987.

Kershaw, Ian, *Hitler*, 2 vols, London, 1998, 2000.

Kershaw, Ian, *Fateful Choices: Ten Decisions that Changed the World 1940–1941*, London, 2008.

Kershaw, Ian, *The End: Germany 1944–45*, London, 2012.

Kershaw, Ian and Lewin, Moshe (eds), *Stalinism and Nazism: Dictatorships in Comparison*, Cambridge, 1997.

Kertzer, David I., *The Pope and Mussolini: The Secret History of Pius XI and the Rise of Fascism in Europe*, Oxford, 2014.

*Keynes, John Maynard, *The Economic Consequences of the Peace*, London, 1919.

Kielinger, Thomas, *Winston Churchill. Der späte Held. Eine Biographie*, Munich, 2014.

Kiesel, Helmuth, *Geschichte der literarischen Moderne*, Munich, 2004.

Kindlberger, Charles P., *The World in Depression 1929–1939*, Harmondsworth, 1987.

Kirk, Tim and McElligott, Anthony (eds), *Opposing Fascism: Community, Authority and Resistance in Europe*, Cambridge, 1999.

Kitchen, Martin, *The Coming of Austrian Fascism*, London, 1980.

Kleine-Ahlbrandt, William Laird, *Twentieth-Century European History*, St. Paul, MN, 1993.

Knox, MacGregor, *Mussolini Unleashed 1939–1941*, Cambridge, 1986.

Knox, MacGregor, *Common Destiny: Dictatorship, Foreign Policy, and War in Fascist Italy and Nazi Germany*, Cambridge, 2000.

Knox, MacGregor, *To the Threshold of Power, 1922/33: Origins and Dynamics of the Fascist and National Socialist Dictatorships*, Vol. 1, Cambridge, 2007.

Koch, Stephen, *Double Lives: Stalin, Willi Münzenberg and the Seduction of the Intellectuals*, London, 1995.

Kochanski, Halik, *The Eagle Unbowed: Poland and the Poles in the Second World War*, London, 2012.

Kocka, Jürgen, *Facing Total War: German Society, 1914–1918*, Leamington Spa, 1984.

Kolb, Eberhard, *The Weimar Republic*, London, 1988

Kolko, Gabriel, *Century of War: Politics, Conflicts, and Society since 1914*, New York, 1994.

*Kovály, Heda Margolius, *Under a Cruel Star: A Life in Prague 1941–1968* (1986), London, 2012.

*Kossert, Andreas, *Kalte Heimat. Die Geschichte der deutschen Vertriebenen nach 1945*, Berlin, 2008.

Kramer, Alan, *Dynamic of Destruction: Culture and Mass Killing in the First World War*, Oxford, 2007.

Krumeich, Gerd (ed.), *Nationalsozialismus und Erster Weltkrieg*, Essen, 2010.

Kühlwein, Klaus, *Pius XII. und die Judenrazzia in Rom*, Berlin, 2013.

*Kulka, Otto Dov, *Landscapes of the Metropolis of Death*, London, 2013.

Kulka, Otto Dov, 'History and Historical Consciousness: Similarities and Dissimilarities in the History of the Jews in Germany and the Czech Lands 1918–1945', *Bohemia*, 46/1 (2005).

Kulka, Otto Dov and Jäckel, Eberhard (eds), *The Jews in the Secret Nazi Reports on Popular Opinion in Germany, 1933–1945*, New Haven, CT, and London, 2010.

Kulka, Otto Dov and Mendes-Flohr, Paul R. (eds), *Judaism and Christianity under the Impact of National Socialism*, Jerusalem, 1987.

Lamb, Richard, *The Ghosts of Peace 1935–1945*, Salisbury, 1987.

*Laqueur, Walter, *Europe since Hitler*, London, 1972.

Laqueur, Walter (ed.), *Fascism: A Reader's Guide*, Harmondsworth, 1976.

Larkin, Maurice, *France since the Popular Front*, Oxford, 1988.

Larsen, Stein Ugelvik, Hagvet, Bernt and Myklebust, Jan Peter (eds), *Who Were the Fascists?*, Bergen, 1980.

Larsen, Stein Ugelvik, with the assistance of Hagtvet, Bernt (ed.), *Modern Europe after Fascism 1943–1980s*, 2 vols, New York, 1998.

Latourette, Kenneth Scott, *Christianity in a Revolutionary Age. Vol. 4: The Twentieth Century in Europe*, Grand Rapids, MI, 1969.

Leitz, Christian, *Nazi Germany and Neutral Europe during the Second World War*, Manchester, 2000.

*Leonhardt, Jörn, *Die Buchse der Pandora. Geschichte des Ersten Weltkriegs*, Munich, 2014.

*Levine, Joshua (ed.), *Forgotten Voices of the Somme*, London, 2008.

*Levy, Primo, *If this is a Man*, London, 1960.

Lewin, Moshe, *The Making of the Soviet System*, London, 1985.

Lewin, Moshe, *The Soviet Century*, London, 2005.

Liddle, Peter (ed.), *Captured Memories 1900–1918: Across the Threshold of War*, Barnsley, 2010.

Liddle, Peter (ed.), *Captured Memories 1930–1945: Across the Threshold of War – The Thirties and the War*, Barnsley, 2011.

Lidegaard, B., *Countrymen: The Untold Story of How Denmark's Jews Escaped the Nazis*, London, 2014.

Lieven, D. C. B., *Russia and the Origins of the First World War*, London, 1983.

Linz, Juan J., *The Breakdown of Democratic Regimes: Crisis, Breakdown and Reequilibration*, Baltimore, MD, and London, 1978.

Linz, Juan J. and Stepan, Alfred, *The Breakdown of Democratic Regimes: Europe*, Baltimore. MD, and London, 1978.

Lipset, Seymour Martin, *Political Man*, London, 1960.

*Liulevicius, Vejas Gabriel, *War Land on the Eastern Front: Culture, National Identity and German Occupation in World War I*, Cambridge, 2000.

Longerich, Peter, *Holocaust: The Nazi Persecution and Murder of the Jews*, Oxford, 2010.

Longerich, Peter, *Himmler*, Oxford, 2012.

*Lounguina, Lila, *Les saisons de Moscou 1933–1990*, Paris, 1990.

Lowe, Keith, *Inferno: The Devastation of Hamburg, 1943*, London, 2007.

Lowe, Keith, *Savage Continent: Europe in the Aftermath of World War II*, London, 2012.

Lukacs, John, *At the End of an Age*, New Haven, CT, and London, 2002.

Lyttelton, Adrian, *The Seizure of Power: Fascism in Italy 1919–1929*, London, 1973.

Lyttelton, Adrian (ed.), *Liberal and Fascist Italy*, Oxford, 2002.

Macartney, C. A., *The Habsburg Empire, 1790–1918*, London, 1968.

*MacCulloch, Diarmaid, *A History of Christianity*, London, 2009.

Machtan, Lothar, *Die Abdankung. Wie Deutschlands gekrönte Häupter aus der Geschichte fielen*, Berlin, 2008.

Machtan, Lothar, *Prinz Max von Baden. Der letzte Kanzler des Kaisers*, Berlin, 2013.

Mack Smith, Denis, *Mussolini*, London, 1983.

MacMillan, Margaret, *Peacemakers: Six Months that Changed the World*, London, 2002.

MacMillan, Margaret, *The War that Ended Peace: How Europe Abandoned Peace for the First World War*, London, 2013.

Maier, Charles S., *Recasting Bourgeois Europe*, Princeton, NJ, 1975.

*Maier, Charles S. (ed.), *The Cold War in Europe: Era of a Divided Continent*, New York, 1991.

*Maier, Klaus A., 'Die Zerstörung Gernikas am 26. April 1937', *Militärgeschichte*, 1 (2007).

Maiolo, Joe, *Cry Havoc: The Arms Race and the Second World War 1931–1941*, London, 2010.

Mak, Geert, *In Europe: Travels through the Twentieth Century*, London, 2008.

Mamatey, Victor and Luža, Radomir, *A History of the Czechoslovak Republic, 1918–1948*, Princeton, NJ, 1973.

Mann, Michael, *Fascists*, Cambridge, 2004.

Mann, Michael, *The Dark Side of Democracy: Explaining Ethnic Cleansing*, Cambridge, 2005.

Mann, Michael, *The Sources of Social Power. Vol. 3: Global Empires and Revolution, 1890–1945*, Cambridge, 2012.

Marrus, Michael, R., *The Nuremberg War Crimes Trial 1945–46: A Documentary History*, Boston, MA, and New York, 1997.

Marwick, Arthur, *The Deluge: British Society and the First World War*, London, 1965.

Marwick, Arthur, *War and Social Change in the Twentieth Century: A Comparative Study of Britain, France, Germany, Russia, and the United States*, New York, 1975.

Marwick, Arthur (ed.), *Total War and Social Change*, London, 1988.

Mason, Timothy W., *Sozialpolitik im Dritten Reich. Arbeiterklasse und Volksgemeinschaft*, Opladen, 1977.

Mason, Timothy, W., *Nazism, Fascism and the Working Class: Essays by Tim Mason*, ed. Jane Caplan, Cambridge, 1995.

Mawdsley, Evan, *The Stalin Years: The Soviet Union, 1929–1953*, Manchester, 1998.

Mawdsley, Evan, *The Russian Civil War*, Edinburgh, 2000.

Mayer, Arno J., *The Persistence of the Old Regime: Europe to the Great War*, London, 1981.

Mayer, Arno J., *Why Did the Heavens not Darken? The 'Final Solution' in History*, New York, 1988.

Mazower, Mark, *Inside Hitler's Greece: The Experience of Occupation, 1941–44*, New Haven, CT, and London, 1993.

Mazower, Mark, *Dark Continent: Europe's Twentieth Century*, London, 1998.

Mazower, Mark, *The Balkans: From the End of Byzantium to the Present Day*, London, 2001.

Mazower, Mark, *Hitler's Empire: Nazi Rule in Occupied Europe*, London, 2008.

McCauley, Martin, *The Origins of the Cold War*, London, 1983.

McCauley, Martin, *The Soviet Union, 1917–1991*, 2nd edn, London, 1993.

McElligott, Anthony, *Rethinking the Weimar Republic*, London, 2014.

McElligott, Anthony (ed.), *Weimar Germany*, Oxford, 2009.

*McLeod, Hugh, *Religion and the People of Western Europe 1789–1970*, Oxford, 1981.

McMeekin, Sean, *The Russian Origins of the First World War*, Cambridge, MA, and London, 2011.

McMillan, Dan, *How Could This Happen? Explaining the Holocaust*, New York, 2014.

McMillan, James F., *Twentieth-Century France: Politics and Society 1898–1991*, London, 1992.

Meehan, Patricia, *The Unnecessary War: Whitehall and the German Resistance to Hitler*, London, 1992.

*Merridale, Catherine, *Night of Stone: Death and Memory in Russia*, London, 2000.

*Merridale, Catherine, *Ivan's War: The Red Army 1939–1945*, London, 2005.

Merriman, John, *A History of Modern Europe. Vol. 2: From the French Revolution to the Present*, 2nd edn, New York, 2004.

Michaelis, Meir, *Mussolini and the Jews*, Oxford, 1978.

Michalka, Wolfgang (ed.), *Die nationalsozialistische Machtergreifung*, Paderborn, 1984.

Michmann, Dan, *Angst vor den 'Ostjuden'. Die Entstehung der Ghettos während des Holocaust*, Frankfurt am Main, 2011.

Michmann, Dan (ed.), *Belgium and the Holocaust*, Jerusalem, 1998.

Milward, Alan S., *The Economic Effects of the World Wars on Britain*, London, 1970.

Milward, Alan S., *The Reconstruction of Western Europe 1945–51*, London, 1984.

Milward, Alan S., *War, Economy and Society 1939–1945*, Harmondsworth, 1987.

Mitchell, B. R. (ed.), *International Historical Statistics: Europe, 1750–2000*, Basingstoke, 2003.

Möller, Horst, *Europa zwischen den Weltkriegen*, Munich, 1998.

*Mombauer, Annika, *The Origins of the First World War: Diplomatic and Military Documents*, Manchester, 2013.

Mommsen, Hans, *From Weimar to Auschwitz: Essays in German History*, London, 1991.

Mommsen, Hans, *The Rise and Fall of Weimar Democracy*, Chapel Hill, NC, and London, 1996.

Mommsen, Hans, *Zur Geschichte Deutschlands im 20. Jahrhundert. Demokratie, Diktatur, Widerstand*, Munich, 2010.

Mommsen, Hans, *Das NS-Regime und die Auslöschung des Judentums in Europa*, Göttingen, 2014.

Mommsen, Wolfgang J., *Imperial Germany 1867–1918: Politics, Culture and Society in an Authoritarian State*, London, 1995.

Mommsen, Wolfgang and Kettenacker, Lothar (eds), *The Fascist Challenge and the Policy of Appeasement*, London, 1983.

Montefiore, Simon Sebag, *Stalin: The Court of the Red Tsar*, London, 2003.

Moore, Bob, *Refugees from Nazi Germany in the Netherlands 1933–1940*, Dordrecht, 1986.

Moore, Bob, *Victims and Survivors: The Nazi Persecution of the Jews in the Netherlands 1940–1945*, London, 1997.

Moore, Bob, *Survivors: Jewish Self-Help and Rescue in Nazi Occupied Western Europe*, Oxford, 2010.

Moore, Bob (ed.), *Resistance in Western Europe*, Oxford and New York, 2000.

Moorhouse, Roger, *Killing Hitler*, London, 2007.

Moorhouse, Roger, *The Devil's Alliance: Hitler's Pact with Stalin 1939–1941*, New York, 2014.

Morgan, Kenneth O., *Labour in Power 1945–1951*, Oxford, 1985.

Morgan, Philip, *Italian Fascism*, London, 2004.

Morris, Jeremy, *The Church in the Modern Age*, London, 2007.

Mosse, George L., *The Culture of Western Europe: The Nineteenth and Twentieth Centuries*, London, 1963.

Mosse, George L., *The Crisis of German Ideology*, London, 1966.

Mosse, George L., *The Nationalization of the Masses*, New York, 1975.

Mosse, George L., *Fallen Soldiers: Reshaping the Memory of the World Wars*, New York, 1990.

Mosse, George L. (ed.), *International Fascism*, London, 1979.

Mowatt, Charles Loch, *Britain between the Wars 1918–1940*, London, 1955.

Mowatt, C. L. (ed.), *The New Cambridge Modern History. Vol. XII : The Era of Violence 1898–1945*, Cambridge, 1968.

Mühlberger, Detlef, *The Social Bases of Nazism 1919–1933*, Cambridge, 2003.

*Münkler, *Der Grosse Krieg. Die Welt 1914–1918*, Berlin, 2013.

Naimark, Norman M., *The Russians in Germany: a History of the Soviet Zone of Occupation, 1945–1949*, Cambridge Mass., 1995.

*Naimark, Norman M., *Fires of Hatred: Ethnic Cleansing in Twentieth-Century Europe*, Cambridge, MA, and London, 2001.

Naimark, Norman M., *Stalin's Genocides*, Princeton, NJ, 2010.

Naimark, Norman M., 'Stalin and Europe in the Postwar Period, 1945–53: Issues and Problems', *Journal of Modern European History*, 2/1 (2004).

Neitzel, Sönke, *Weltkrieg und Revolution 1914–1918/19*, Berlin, 2008.

Newman, Karl J., *European Democracy between the Wars*, London, 1970.

*Nielsen, Frederick, *Ein Emigrant für Deutschland. Tagebuchaufzeichnungen, Aufrufe und Berichte aus den Jahren 1933–1943*, Darmstadt, 1977.

*Niethammer, Lutz, *Die Mitläuferfabrik. Die Entnazifizierung am Beispiel Bayerns*, Berlin, 1982.

*Noakes, Jeremy, 'Nazism and Eugenics', in Bullen, R. J., Strandmann, H. Pogge von and Polonsky, A. B. (eds), *Ideas into Politics: Aspects of European History 1880–1950*, London, 1984.

Noakes, Jeremy (ed.), *The Civilian in War*, Exeter, 1992.

*Noakes, Jeremy and Pridham, Geoffrey (eds), *Nazism 1919–1945: A Documentary Reader*, 4 vols, Exeter, 1983, 1984, 1988, 1998.

Nolte, Ernst, *Three Faces of Fascism*, London, 1965.

Nove, Alec, *Stalinism and After*, London, 1975.

Orth, Karin, *Das System der nationalsozialistischen Konzentrationslager. Eine politische Organisationsgeschichte*, Hamburg, 1999.

*Orwell, George, *Down and Out in Paris and London*, London, 1933.

*Orwell, George, *The Road to Wigan Pier*, London, 1937.

*Orwell, George, *Homage to Catalonia*, London, 1938.

Overy, Richard, *War and the Economy in the Third Reich*, Oxford, 1994.

Overy, Richard, *Why the Allies Won*, London, 1995.

Overy, Richard, *The Nazi Economic Recovery 1932–1938*, Cambridge, 1996.

Overy, Richard, *Russia's War 1941–1945*, London, 1999.

Overy, Richard, *The Dictators: Hitler's Germany and Stalin's Russia*, London, 2004.

*Overy, Richard, *The Morbid Age: Britain and the Crisis of Civilization, 1919–1939*, London, 2010.

Overy, Richard, *The Bombing War: Europe 1939–1945*, London, 2013.

Parker, R. A. C., *Struggle for Survival: The History of the Second World War*, Oxford, 1990.

Parker, R. A. C., *Chamberlain and Appeasement: British Policy and the Coming of the Second World War*, London, 1993.

Parker, R. A. C., *Churchill and Appeasement: Could Churchill have Prevented the Second World War?*, London, 2000.

Passmore, Kevin, *Fascism: A Very Short Introduction*, Oxford, 2002.

Paxton, Robert O., *Vichy France: Old Guard and New Order 1940–1944*, London, 1972.

Paxton, Robert O., *The Anatomy of Fascism*, London, 2004.

Payne, Stanley G., *Falange: A History of Spanish Fascism*, Stanford, CA, 1961.

Payne, Stanley G., *A History of Fascism 1914–1945*, London, 1995.

Petzina, Dietmar, Abelshauser, Werner and Faust, Anselm (eds), *Sozialgeschichtliches Arbeitsbuch III. Materialien zur Statistik des Deutschen Reiches 1914–1945*, Munich, 1978.

*Peukert, Detlev J. K., *The Weimar Republic: The Crisis of Classical Modernity*, London, 1991.

Phayer, Michael, *The Catholic Church and the Holocaust*, Bloomington, IN, 2000.

Piketty, Thomas, *Capital in the Twenty-First Century*, Cambridge, MA, and London, 2014.

*Pollard, Sidney and Holmes, Colin (eds), *Documents in European Economic History. Vol. 3: The End of the Old Europe 1914–1939*, London, 1973.

Polonsky, Antony, *The Little Dictators: The History of Eastern Europe since 1918*, London, 1975.

Pope, Stephen and Wheal, Elizabeth-Anne, *Macmillan Dictionary of the First World War*, London, 1995.

Pope, Stephen and Wheal, Elizabeth-Anne, *Macmillan Dictionary of the Second World War*, 2nd edn, London, 1995.

Preston, Paul, *Franco*, London, 1993.

Preston, Paul, *The Coming of the Spanish Civil War*, 2nd edn, London, 1994.

Preston, Paul, *The Politics of Revenge: Fascism and the Military in 20th Century Spain*, London, 1995.

Preston, Paul, *Comrades: Portraits from the Spanish Civil War*, London, 1999.

Preston, Paul, *The Spanish Civil War: Reaction, Revolution and Revenge*, London, 2006.

*Preston, Paul, *The Spanish Holocaust: Inquisition and Extermination in Twentieth-Century Spain*, London, 2012.

Preston, Paul and Mackenzie, Ann L. (eds), *The Republic Besieged: Civil War in Spain 1936–1939*, Edinburgh, 1996.

Priestland, David, *Merchant, Soldier, Sage: A New History of Power*, London, 2012.

Pritchard, Gareth, *The Making of the GDR, 1945–1953*, Manchester, 2000.

Pugh, Martin, *We Danced All Night: A Social History of Britain between the Wars*, Londn, 2009.

Raphael, Lutz, *Imperiale Gewalt und mobilisierte Nation. Europa 1914–1945*, Munich, 2011.

*Rees, Laurence, *The Nazis: A Warning from History*, London, 1997.

*Rees, Laurence, *War of the Century: When Hitler Fought Stalin*, London, 1999.

Rees, Laurence, *Auschwitz: The Nazis and the 'Final Solution'*, London, 2005.

Rees, Laurence, *Behind Closed Doors: Stalin, the Nazis and the West*, London, 2008.

Reich-Ranicki, Marcel, *Mein Leben*, Stuttgart, 1999.

Reynolds, David, *The Long Shadow: The Great War and the Twentieth Century*, London, 2013.

Reynolds, David, 'The Origins of the Two "World Wars": Historical Discourse and International Politics', *Journal of Contemporary History*, 38/1 (2003).

Reynolds, Michael A., *Shattering Empires: The Clash and Collapse of the Ottoman and Russian Empires, 1908–1918*, Cambridge, 2011.

Rhodes, Anthony, *The Vatican in the Age of the Dictators 1922–45*, London, 1973.

Richards, Michael, *A Time of Silence: Civil War and the Culture of Repression in Franco's Spain, 1936–1945*, Cambridge, 1998.

Roberts, Andrew, *Masters and Commanders: How Roosevelt, Churchill, Marshall and Alanbrooke won the War in the West*, London, 2008.

Roberts, Andrew, *The Storm of War: A New History of the Second World War*, London, 2009.

Roberts, J. M., *A History of Europe*, Oxford, 1996.

Roberts, J. M., *Twentieth Century: A History of the World, 1901 to the Present*, London, 1999.

Robertson, Ritchie, *Kafka: A Very Short Introduction*, Oxford, 2004.

Rodrigue, Aron, 'The Mass Destruction of Armenians and Jews in the 20th Century in Historical Perspective', in Kieser, Hans-Lukas and Schaller, Dominik J. (eds), *Der Völkermord an den Armeniern und die Shoah*, Zurich, 2002.

Rogger, Hans and Weber, Eugen (eds), *The European Right*, London, 1965.

Röhl, John C. G, *Wilhelm II. Der Weg in den Abgrund 1900–1941*, Munich, 2008.

Rose, Richard, *What is Europe?*, New York, 1996.

Roseman, Mark, 'National Socialism and the End of Modernity', *American Historical Review*, 116/3 (2011).

Rosenberg, Emily S. (ed.), *Geschichte der Welt 1870–1945. Weltmärkte und Weltkriege*, Munich, 2012.

Rothschild, Joseph, *East Central Europe between the Two World Wars*, Seattle, 1977.

Rousso, Henry, *Le syndrome de Vichy de 1944 à nos jours*, Paris, 1990.

Rousso, Henry, *Les années noires: vivre sous l'occupation*, Paris, 1992.

Rousso, Henry, *Vichy, L'événement, la mémoire, l'histoire*, Paris, 2001.

Rousso, Henry (ed.), *Stalinisme et nazisme. Histoire et mémoire comparées*, Paris, 1999.

Sartori, Roland (ed.), *The Ax Within: Italian Fascism in Action*, New York, 1974.

Sassoon, Donald, *The Culture of the Europeans: From 1800 to the Present*, London, 2006.

*Schell, Margarete, *Ein Tagebuch aus Prag 1945–46*, Kassel, 1957.

Schoenbaum, David, *Hitler's Social Revolution: Class and Status in Nazi Germany 1933–1939*, New York, 1967.

Schweitzer, Arthur, *The Age of Charisma*, Chicago, IL, 1984.

Sebestyen, Victor, *1946: The Making of the Modern World*, London, 2014.

Service, Robert, *The Bolshevik Party in Revolution: A Study in Organisational Change 1917–1923*, London, 1979.

Service, Robert, *The Russian Revolution 1900–1927*, London, 1986.

Service, Robert, *A History of Twentieth-Century Russia*, London, 1998.

Service, Robert, *Lenin: A Biography*, London, 2000.

Service, Robert, *Stalin: A Biography*, London, 2004.

Sharp, Alan, *The Versailles Settlement: Peacemaking in Paris, 1919*, Basingstoke, 1991.

Sheehan, James, *The Monopoly of Violence: Why Europeans Hate Going to War*, London, 2010.

Sheffield, Gary, *Forgotten Victory: The First World War – Myths and Realities*, London, 2002.

Shephard, Ben, *The Long Road Home: The Aftermath of the Second World War*, London, 2010.

Sherratt, Yvonne, *Hitler's Philosophers*, New Haven, CT, and London, 2013.

*Shirer, William L., *Berlin Diary 1934–1941*, London, 1941.

*Shore, Marci, *Caviar and Ashes: A Warsaw Generation's Life and Death in Marxism, 1918–1968*, New Haven, CT, and London, 2006.

Simms, Brendan, *Europe: The Struggle for Supremacy, 1453 to the Present*, London, 2013.

Sirinelli, Jean-François (ed.), *Histoire des droites en France. Vol. 1: Politique*, Paris, 1992.

Skidelsky, Robert, *J. M. Keynes: Economist, Philosopher, Statesman*, London, 2003.

*Słomka, Jan, *From Serfdom to Self-Government: Memoirs of a Polish Village Mayor*, 1842–1927, London, 1941.

Smith, L. V., Audoin-Rouzeau, Stephane and Becker, Annette, *France and the Great War, 1914–18*, Cambridge, 2003.

Smith, S. A., *Red Petrograd: Revolution in the Factories 1917–1918*, Cambridge, 1983.

*Snowden, Ethel ['Mrs. Philip'], *A Political Pilgrim in Europe*, London, 1921.

*Snyder, Timothy, *Bloodlands: Europe between Hitler and Stalin*, New York, 2010.

Soucy, Robert, *French Fascism: The First Wave, 1924–1933*, New Haven, CT, and London, 1986.

Soucy, Robert, *French Fascism: The Second Wave, 1933–1939*, New Haven, CT, and London, 1995.

*Sperber, Manès, *Bis man mir Scherben auf die Augen legt. All' das Vergangene . . .*, Vienna, 1977.

Stachura, Peter D., *Poland in the Twentieth Century*, London, 1999.

Stachura, Peter D., *Poland, 1918–1945*, London, 2004.

Stachura, Peter (ed.), *Unemployment and the Great Depression in Weimar Germany*, Basingstoke, 1986.

*Stachura, Peter D. (ed.), *Poland between the Wars, 1918–1939*, London, 1998.

Stargardt, Nicholas, *The German Idea of Militarism: Radical and Socialist Critics 1866–1914*, Cambridge, 1994.

Stargardt, Nicholas, *Witnesses of War: Children's Lives under the Nazis*, London, 2005.

*Stargardt, Nicholas, *The German War: A Nation under Arms, 1939–45*, London, 2015.

Stargardt, Nicholas, 'Wartime Occupation by Germany: Food and Sex', in Richard Bosworth and Joseph Maiolo (eds), *Cambridge History of the Second World War. Vol. 2: Politics and Ideology*, Cambridge, 2015.

Staritz, Dietrich, *Die Gründung der DDR*, Munich, 1984.

Steinberg, Jonathan, *All or Nothing: The Axis and the Holocaust 1941–43*, London, 1991.

*Steiner, Zara, *The Lights that Failed: European International History 1919–1933*, Oxford, 2005.

*Steiner, Zara, *The Triumph of the Dark: European International History 1933–1939*, Oxford, 2011.

Steinert, Marlis, *Hitlers Krieg und die Deutschen*, Düsseldorf and Vienna, 1970.

Stern, Fritz, *Einstein's German World*, London, 2000.

Stern, Fritz, *Five Germanys I Have Known*, New York, 2006.

Stern, Fritz, *Der Westen im 20. Jahrhundert. Selbstzerstörung, Wiederaufbau, Gefährdungen der Gegenwart*, Göttingen, 2008.

Sternhell, Zeev, *Ni Droite, ni Gauche. L'idéologie fasciste en France*, Paris, 1987.

Stevenson, David, *Armaments and the Coming of War: Europe 1904–14*, Oxford, 1996.

Stevenson, David, *Cataclysm: The First World War as Political Tragedy*, New York, 2004.

Stevenson, John and Cook, Chris, *The Slump: Society and Politics during the Depression*, London, 1977.

Stone, Dan, *Histories of the Holocaust*, Oxford, 2010.

Stone, Norman, *The Eastern Front 1914–1917*, London, 1975.

Stone, Norman, *World War One: A Short History*, London, 2007.

Strachan, Hew, *The First World War. Vol. 1: To Arms*, Oxford, 2001.

Strachan, Hew, *The First World War*, London, 2006.

Sugar, Peter F. (ed.), *Fascism in the Successor States 1918–1945*, Santa Barbara, CA, 1971.

Suny, Ronald Grigor, *The Soviet Experiment: Russia, the USSR, and the Successor States*, New York, 1998.

*Taylor, A. J. P., *English History 1914–1945*, London, 1970.

Taylor, A. J. P., *From Sarajevo to Potsdam: The Years 1914–1945*, London, 1974.

Taylor, Frederick, *Exorcising Hitler: The Occupation and Denazification of Germany*, London, 2011.

Taylor, Frederick, *The Downfall of Money: Germany's Hyperinflation and the Destruction of the Middle Class*, London, 2013.

Thamer, Hans-Ulrich, *Verführung und Gewalt. Deutschland 1933–1945*, Berlin, 1986.

Thomas, Hugh, *The Spanish Civil War*, London, 1961.

Thränhardt, Dietrich, *Geschichte der Bundesrepublik Deutschland*, Frankfurt am Main, 1986.

Thurlow, Richard, *Fascism in Britain: A History, 1918–1985*, London, 1987.

Todorov, Tzvetan, *The Fragility of Goodness: Why Bulgaria's Jews Survived the Holocaust*, London, 2001.

Todorov, Tzvetan, *Hope and Memory: Reflections on the Twentieth Century*, Princeton, NJ, 2003.

Tomka, Béla, *A Social History of Twentieth-Century Europe*, London, 2013.

Tooze, Adam, *The Wages of Destruction: The Making and Breaking of the Nazi Economy*, London, 2006.

Tooze, Adam, *The Deluge: The Great War and the Remaking of Global Order 1916–1931*, London, 2014.

Traverso, Enzo, *The Origins of Nazi Violence*, New York, 2003.

Traverso, Enzo, 'Intellectuals and Anti-Fascism: For a Critical Historization', *New Politics*, 9/4 (2004).

Traverso, Enzo (ed.), *Le Totalitarisme. Le XXe siècle en débat*, Paris, 2001.

Trentmann, Frank and Flemming, Just (eds), *Food and Conflict in Europe in the Age of the Two World Wars*, Basingstoke, 2006.

Tucker, Robert C., *Stalin in Power: The Revolution from Above, 1928–1941*, New York, 1990.

*Ulrich, Bernd and Ziemann, Benjamin (eds), *German Soldiers in the Great War: Letters and Eyewitness Accounts*, Barnsley, 2010.

Unger, Aryeh L., *The Totalitarian Party: Party and People in Nazi Germany and Soviet Russia*, Cambridge, 1974.

Verhey, Jeffrey, *The Spirit of 1914: Militarism, Myth and Mobilisation in Germany*, Cambridge, 2000.

Vickers, Miranda, *The Albanians: A Modern History*, London, 1995.

Vincent, Mary, *Spain 1833–2002: People and State*, Oxford, 2007.

Vinen, Richard, *A History in Fragments: Europe in the Twentieth Century*, London, 2000.

Volkogonov, Dmitri, *Stalin: Triumph and Tragedy*, London, 1991.

Wachsmann, Nikolaus, *KL : A History of the Nazi Concentration Camps*, New York, 2015.

Waddington, Lorna, *Hitler's Crusade: Bolshevism and the Myth of the International Jewish Conspiracy*, London, 2007.

Walker, Mark, *Nazi Science: Myth, Truth, and the German Atomic Bomb*, New York, 1995.

Waller, Philip and Rowell, John (eds), *Chronology of the 20th Century*, Oxford, 1995.

Wasserstein, Bernard, *Barbarism and Civilisation: A History of Europe in Our Time*, Oxford, 2007.

Wasserstein, Bernard, *On the Eve: The Jews of Europe before the Second World War*, London, 2012.

Watson, Alexander, *Ring of Steel: Germany and Austria-Hungary at War, 1914–1918*, London, 2014.

Watt, Donald Cameron, *How War Came: The Immediate Origins of the Second World War, 1938–1939*, London, 1990.

*Weber, Eugen, *Varieties of Fascism*, New York, 1964.

*Weber, Eugen, *The Hollow Years: France in the 1930s*, New York, 1996.

Wee, Herman van der, *Prosperity and Upheaval: The World Economy 1945–1980*, Harmondsworth, 1987.

Wehler, Hans-Ulrich, *Deutsche Gesellschaftsgeschichte. Vol. 4: 1914–1949*, Munich, 2003.

Weinberg, Gerhard, *The Foreign Policy of Hitler's Germany*, 2 vols, Chicago, IL, and London, 1970, 1980.

Weinberg, Gerhard, *A World at Arms*, Cambridge, 1994.

Weindling, Paul, *Health, Race and German Politics between National Unification and Nazism*, Cambridge, 1989.

Weiss-Wendt, Anton, *Murder without Hatred: Estonians and the Holocaust*, Syracuse, NY, 2009.

Welch, David, *Germany, Propaganda and Total War 1914–18*, London, 2000.

Werth, Alexander, *Russia at War 1941–1945*, New York, 1984.

Winkler, Heinrich August, *Geschichte des Westens. Die Zeit der Weltkriege 1914–1945*, Munich, 2011.

Winkler, Heinrich August, *Geschichte des Westens. Vom Kalten Krieg zum Mauerfall*, Munich, 2014.

Winstone, Martin, *The Dark Heart of Hitler's Europe: Nazi Rule in Poland under the General Government*, London, 2015.

Winter, Jay, *Sites of Memory, Sites of Mourning: The Great War in European Cultural History*, Cambridge, 1995.

Winter, Jay, *Dreams of Peace and Freedom: Utopian Moments in the 20th Century*, New Haven, CT, and London, 2006.

Winter, Jay and Prost, Antoine, *The Great War in History: Debates and Controversies 1914 to the Present*, Cambridge, 2005.

Winter, Jay, Parker, Geoffrey and Habeck, Mary R. (eds), *The Great War and the Twentieth Century*, New Haven, CT, and London, 2000.

Wirsching, Andreas, 'Political Violence in France and Italy after 1918', *Journal of Modern European History*, 1/1 (2003).

Woller, Hans, *Die Abrechnung mit dem Faschismus in Italien 1943 bis 1948*, Munich, 1996.

Woller, Hans, *Geschichte Italiens im 20. Jahrhundert*, Munich, 2010.

Woolf, S. J. (ed.), *The Nature of Fascism*, London, 1968.

Woolf, S. J. (ed.), *Fascism in Europe*, London, 1981.

*Woodruff, William, *The Road to Nab End: A Lancashire Childhood*, London, 2000.

*Woodruff, William, *Beyond Nab End*, London, 2003.

*Wright, Jonathan, *Gustav Stresemann: Weimar's Greatest Statesman*, Oxford, 2002.

Wrigley, Chris (ed.), *Challenges of Labour: Central and Western Europe 1917–1920*, London, 1993.

Wróbel, Piotr, 'The Seeds of Violence: The Brutalization of an East European Region, 1917–1921', *Journal of Modern European History*, 1/1 (2003).

Ziemann, Benjamin, *Contested Commemorations: Republican War Veterans and Weimar Political Culture*, Cambridge, 2013.

Ziemann, Benjamin, *Gewalt im Ersten Weltkrieg*, Essen, 2013.

Ziemann, Benjamin, 'Germany after the First World War – A Violent Society?', *Journal of Modern European History*, 1/1 (2003).

Zimmermann, Moshe (ed.), *On Germans and Jews under the Nazi Regime*, Jerusalem, 2006.

Zürcher, Erik J., *Turkey: A Modern History*, London, 2004.

Zuckmayer, Carl, *Geheimbericht*, ed. Gunther Nickel and Johanna Schrön, Göttingen, 2002.

Zuckmayer, Carl, *Deutschlandbericht für das Kriegsministeriuim der Vereinigten Staaten von Amerika*, ed. Gunther Nickel, Johanna Schrön and Hans Wagener, Göttingen, 2004.

*Zweig, Stefan, *The World of Yesterday*, 3rd edn, London, 1944.

*Zweig, Stefan, *Tagebücher*, Frankfurt, 1984.

Index